W9-BVD-556

READINGS in INDUSTRIAL SOCIOLOGY

Sociology Series

John F. Cuber, Editor
Alfred C. Clarke, Associate Editor

HD6971
301.5
F3
F

READINGS in INDUSTRIAL SOCIOLOGY

WILLIAM A. FAUNCE, Editor

Michigan State University

New York

APPLETON-CENTURY-CROFTS

Division of Meredith Publishing Company

123995

JUL 22 1968

Copyright © 1967 by
MEREDITH PUBLISHING COMPANY
All rights reserved.

This book, or parts
thereof, must not be used or reproduced
in any manner without written permission.
For information address the publisher,
Appleton-Century-Crofts, Division of
Meredith Publishing Company, 440 Park
Avenue South, New York, N. Y. 10016.

677-1

Library of Congress Card Number: 67-21992

Printed in the United States of America
E 30390

Contents

INTRODUCTION

The concerns of industrial sociologists have been rapidly changing during the past decade. Some would maintain that the field has suffered the "ultimate transformation" and no longer exists as a viable subdiscipline within sociology. This view is rooted in the assumption that some of the traditional subject matter of industrial sociology is no longer relevant to the changing character of mature industrial societies, and that much of what is relevant is best incorporated into other subdisciplines, such as the sociology of organizations.

One of the purposes of this reader is to suggest (paraphrasing Mark Twain) that reports of the death of the field have been greatly exaggerated. There is a common thread of interest in some central features of industrialism as a way of life that runs through industrial sociology. Industrialism is still the most widespread single set of cultural patterns. It has not yet been superseded by the developing postindustrial epoch in societies like the United States, and it represents the direction of change in economically underdeveloped areas throughout the world. In addition, there is still widespread interest in the study of industrialism. There is a considerable amount of research in progress and an increasing number of courses in industrial sociology are being taught to classes that become larger each year.

The Nature of Industrial Sociology

Concern with the proper scope of industrial sociology, and even with whether it represents an appropriate speciality among the substantive concerns of sociology, is not new. Sociological journals have probably contained more articles dealing with the status and prospects of industrial sociology than with any other subdiscipline in the field.[1] Almost twenty years ago

[1] Cf. Wilbert E. Moore, "Industrial Sociology: Status and Prospects," *American Sociological Review*, 13 (August, 1948), 382-391; Delbert C. Miller, "Industrial Sociology," *American Sociological Review*, 16 (February, 1951), 75-77; William F. Whyte, "Problems of Industrial Sociology," *Social Problems*, 4 (October, 1956), 148-160; Everett C. Hughes, "The Relation of Industrial to General Sociology," *Sociology and Social Research*, 41 (March-April, 1957), 251-256; Edward Gross, "Some Suggestions for the Legitimation of Industrial Studies in Sociology," *Social Forces*, 33 (March, 1955), 233-239; Amitai Etzioni, "Industrial Sociology: The Study of Economic Organizations," *Social Research*, 25 (Autumn, 1958), 303-324.

Delbert C. Miller wrote, "If we were to single out one statement that stamps the progress of industrial sociology up to and through 1947, we should probably record the fact that sociologists were still struggling to define the field."[2] The issue is still not resolved but, in spite of lack of consensus regarding the appropriate boundaries of the field, there is a common set of core concerns, and considerable progress has been made since 1947 in the development of theory and methods for the analysis of these concerns.

Definitions of industrial sociology suggest both the basic focus and the variable limits of the field. Miller and Form describe the field as being "concerned broadly with the study of industrial society [and] also . . . with the analysis of the social organization of work."[3] They suggest that because it deals with all types of work organizations, industrial sociology might be more accurately labelled, "the sociology of the economy." Moore defines the field as follows: "Industrial sociology then is concerned with the application or development of principles of sociology relevant to the industrial mode of production and the industrial way of life."[4] Schneider describes his text, *Industrial Sociology*, as dealing with the industrial institutions of the United States with a focus on the social structure of large-scale manufacturing organizations.[5] Etzioni suggests that industrial sociology is most fruitfully considered as an applied field and as a branch of organizational sociology involving the study of economic organizations; that is, those organizations having the "primary aim of producing goods and services, exchanging them, or organizing and manipulating monetary processes."[6]

While industrial sociologists differ in their definitions of the field, there is remarkable consistency in the kinds of material included in industrial sociology texts. All these texts include sections on the work group, on the structure of industrial bureaucracy, and on union-management relations. Almost all contain some discussion of the industrialization process, of major work roles in industry, and of the internal organization of trade unions. Because these six areas represent traditional core concerns of industrial sociology, they have been selected as the major sections for this reader. Some other related topics—for example, the sociology of occupations or of industry-community relations—have been excluded. Although these areas were once regarded as part of the field, the rapid growth of knowledge has made it impossible to do justice to all of them in a single college course.

Yet accepting the notion that the six topics listed above represent the core of industrial sociology does not resolve the issue of the proper scope of

---

[2] Delbert C. Miller, "Discussion of Industrial Sociology: Status and Prospects," *American Sociological Review*, 13 (August, 1948), 394.

[3] Delbert C. Miller and William H. Form, *Industrial Sociology* (New York: Harper & Row, 1964), p. 5.

[4] Moore, *op. cit.*, p. 383.

[5] Eugene V. Schneider, *Industrial Sociology* (New York: McGraw-Hill, 1957), p. 1.

[6] Etzioni, *op. cit.*, pp. 305-309.

the field. How much stress should be placed, for example, upon the industrialization process and related broad concerns with industrialism as a way of life? Should we be concerned with all types of work organization, with economic organizations only, as Etzioni proposes, or should we narrowly focus on manufacturing plants? Should the field include the study of all types of occupational associations including, for example, the National Education Association and the American Medical Association, or should it be limited, as it has been in the past, to a particular type of association—the trade union?

There are no sound theoretical bases for answering questions of this kind. There is, in fact, no sound *theoretical* justification for any of the "special" sociologies like medical sociology, sociology of the family, sociology of education, political sociology, sociology of leisure, or industrial sociology. The institutional context of social interaction, which is the primary basis for differentiating these fields, does not provide the most appropriate boundaries for circumscribing theories of social behavior. Fundamental social processes are the same irrespective of whether the occasion for social interaction is familial, economic, political, or educational.

Ultimately the concerns of each of the special sociologies may be incorporated into a theoretical system composed of *general* laws of human behavior. In the meantime, however, what have been called "theories of the middle range" would appear to be best constructed at a level of abstraction that cuts across particular institutions and focusses upon basic types or fundamental attributes of interactional systems. The boundaries of these middle range theories are not coterminous with boundaries of any of the special sociologies as they have been traditionally defined.

The point here is that industrial sociology does not exist as a separate field by virtue of a central theoretical focus. It draws its theory and methods from a variety of subdisciplines within sociology. The analysis of industrialization draws heavily upon general theoretical and methodological approaches to the study of social change; the study of work groups and industrial bureaucracy are simply special cases in the analysis of the small group and formal organization; and the analysis of union-management relations relies mainly on concepts drawn from broader theories dealing with collective behavior, power, and social conflict. Ideally, the application of these various perspectives to the study of industry not only enhances our understanding of social behavior in this setting but contributes to the development of the sociological theories from which they are derived. As Wilbert Moore has noted, "If the study [industrial sociology] has any significance for the general body of sociological principles, it will be sociology before it is 'industrial'."[7]

While industrial sociology lacks a single, unifying theoretical framework, it is organized around a set of interrelated substantive areas, and is

[7] Moore, *op. cit.*, p. 383.

characterized by a number of general themes that give it some integrity as a separate field of study. An academic division of labor based upon substantive rather than theoretical grounds can be justified at the present level of development of general sociological theory. What sociology has to offer to the student of industrial social organization today is not a body of laws of social behavior, but rather a particular perspective or a special way of looking at the world of work. Great progress has been made in the past few decades in the development of this frame of reference, and important new insights have been gained through its application. The use of a frame of reference, however, is quite a different process from invoking a set of invariant scientific laws. The sociologist not only needs to have facility with the "tools of his trade," sociological concepts, and methods, but he also needs considerable, general familiarity with the material to which these tools are applied. The more knowledgeable one is about the field of application of the sociological perspective, the more productive this process will be of new ways of ordering the field. There is, of course, the danger of becoming overspecialized, of attending to idiosyncratic rather than general features of social structure in a particular area, and of failing to relate research findings to generalizations that cut across the specific contexts in which studies are conducted. While noting these dangers, Everett Hughes nevertheless maintains that sociologists must remain close to facts and ongoing events, and states that it is "doubtful whether we will ever have fruitful contributors to general sociology—meaning to theories of broad application—who have not at some point in their careers been deeply involved in some one of the 'special sociologies'."[8] As a consequence of concerns of this sort, most sociologists have selected fairly narrow fields of specialization. For most industrial sociologists, the area of specialization has been the sociology of large-scale manufacturing industries.

The proliferation of narrowly defined "sociologies of" has been generally deplored. The objection is based primarily on the grounds noted above —that they do not provide meaningful boundaries for the development of sociological theory. Perhaps for this reason, industrial sociologists have generally defined their field more broadly than is warranted by the actual range of subject matter studied within it. The majority of industrial sociological studies undertaken have been conducted in manufacturing plants and even the offices selected for study have generally been in manufacturing industries.

The justification for focussing primarily upon manufacturing does not rest solely on the grounds that this industry is the one that industrial sociologists know best and consequently can study most effectively. Manufacturing industries occupy a critical position in industrial societies. The introduction of large-scale manufacturing operations has been, historically, one of the important occurrences in the sequence of events leading to the industrial

[8] Hughes, *op. cit.*, p. 252.

way of life. The word "industrialization" is, in fact, most often used to refer to the shift from an agriculturally based economy to one based upon manufacturing. Miller and Form, for example, note that industrializing societies follow a particular pattern in which the largest proportion of the labor force is employed initially in agriculture, then in manufacturing, and eventually in service industries.[9]

Even in nations like the United States that have reached the third or "service stage" in terms of industrial composition of the labor force, manufacturing industries exert a disproportionately large influence on the economy and on the society generally. The enormous impact of industries, such as steel and automobile manufacturing, on the economy need not be documented here. There are, however, more subtle ways in which industries of this kind shape the character of industrial societies. Discussion of this topic will form a major part of Chapter I which is concerned with the industrialization process and its effects.

The view of industrial sociology suggested in the discussion above is the one that will be used in this book. To summarize, the field is treated as a loosely related set of substantive areas, the core of which is composed of the study of industrialization, industrial bureaucracy, major industrial work roles, the work group, trade union structure, and union-management relations. No attempt will be made to develop a theory encompassing all of these areas—social theories, even those of the middle range, are regarded as most fruitful when oriented around basic social processes rather than around the institutional contexts of social interaction. The major focus of the book is on the sociology of large-scale manufacturing industries because most industrial sociological research has been conducted in industries of this type and, as a field of study, the sociology of manufacturing is narrow enough to be manageable and still important enough to be worthwhile.

The History of Industrial Sociology

As is true of all of the special sociologies, industrial sociology has its roots in nineteenth- and early twentieth-century European social theory. The work of Max Weber, Karl Marx, Emile Durkheim, Vilfredo Pareto, and George Simmel is particularly important for the study of industrial organization and industrial society. The influence of some of this work, most notably that of Max Weber, is still very evident in contemporary industrial studies. There is, in fact, a substantial tradition in industrial sociology that developed prior to its formal appearance as a recognized field. American sociologists and institutional economists had a very early interest in issues related to unemployment and poverty, problems accompanying the rapid growth of cities, the alienation of industrial workers, and labor protest movements. In addition, the long history of sociological and anthropological concern with the

[9] Miller and Form, op. cit., p. 4.

contrast between folk and urban societies focussed attention upon the nature of industrial social organization. Although the kinds of issues that would be regarded as central in industrial sociology today were often only peripherally relevant to this early work, we should recognize that there is a direct and continuous line of development from some of the earlier to some of the more recent sociological concerns with industry and industrial societies, and that a considerable amount of knowledge relevant to the area had accumulated before the label "industrial sociology" was applied to it.

There is virtually complete agreement that industrial sociology as a separate field dates from the extensive studies conducted by Elton Mayo and his associates at the Hawthorne Plant of the Western Electric Company between 1924 and 1932. It has even been suggested that the field dates from a particular phase of a single experiment in this study—the point at which it became apparent to the investigators that their findings could only be accounted for in social psychological terms.[10]

It is ironic that Elton Mayo, who was not a sociologist, is identified as the father of industrial sociology and that the Hawthorne studies did not, in fact, have a single sociologist among the people who were primarily responsible for the research. In the early phases of the Hawthorne studies, Mayo and his chief collaborators, F. J. Roethlisberger and W. J. Dickson, were not at all concerned with industrial social structure but with the effects of physical and physiological factors, such as amount of light and fatigue and their relation to productivity. It was only in the latter phases of the research that the importance of social structural factors was discovered. The elements of social structure with which the Hawthorne researchers became concerned were for the most part the patterns of interpersonal relations that develop in specific social situations—as contrasted with the more broadly defined or established elements of social structure, such as social roles, social class, authority levels, or prescribed communication channels. This distinction between a primary concern with interpersonal relations and a primary concern with patterns of interaction prescribed in institutionalized role definitions is an important one, and we shall return to it in Chapter V which deals with the industrial work group. A more detailed discussion of the findings of the Hawthorne studies will also be deferred until this section of the book since they consist primarily of generalizations regarding intragroup behavior.

Our primary concern with these studies at this point is with their impact upon the subsequent development of industrial sociology. The Hawthorne research initiated, or at least gave added impetus to, two sets of activities both labelled "human relations in industry." One of the things to which this phrase refers is what is by now a very large number of studies

[10] William F. Whyte and Frank B. Miller, "Industrial Sociology," in Joseph B. Gittler, ed., *Review of Sociology: Analysis of a Decade* (New York: Wiley, 1957), p. 289. This chapter contains a history of the development of industrial sociology. For another discussion of this topic, see S. M. Miller, "The Rise of Industrial Sociology," *Sociology and Social Research*, 36 (November, 1951), 90-96.

of interpersonal relations in industry. These studies were initially focussed upon relations among industrial workers in the factory, but they have subsequently been concerned with a wider variety of relationships including, notably, social interaction between first level supervisors and employees. Among the representative contributors to this type of research have been Elton Mayo, T. N. Whitehead, F. J. Roethlisberger, Burleigh Gardner, William Foote Whyte, and George Homans. A considerable amount of knowledge regarding interpersonal relationships in industry has been accumulated by these men and others with similar interests.

Human relations in industry is also the label applied to a social movement in industrial management. The Hawthorne studies and others like them provided evidence that improving human relations resulted in increased productivity. Today there is scarcely a major industry without some sort of human relations training program for its supervisors. This emphasis upon the role of the supervisor as an expert in human relations is entirely consistent with Mayo's approach to the resolution of the problems of industrial society. Mayo was influenced by the work of the Italian sociologist, Vilfredo Pareto. Pareto was impressed with the extent to which human behavior was nonlogically based, and he emphasized the necessity of logical behavior as a methodological principle for social science. Mayo shifted the concern with logical behavior from a methodological issue to an operating principle for industrial management.[11] It was Mayo's hope that the application of this principle in dealings with nonlogical workers would make it possible to rebuild satisfying interpersonal relations that had been eroded by the impersonal nature of urban industrial society.[12]

The distinction that has been made here between relations in industry as a label for industrial sociological research dealing with interpersonal relations as opposed to a social movement in industrial management has not always, in practice, been particularly clear. The results of sociological studies used by management to increase worker productivity, particularly where this application of research findings made the invidious distinction between logical managers and nonlogical workers, generated a major controversy in industrial sociology. There was a period during which the number of published criticisms of the human relations in industry approach probably exceeded the number of published accounts of studies using this approach.[13]

---

[11] Cf. Andrew Hacker, "The Use and Abuse of Pareto in Industrial Sociology," *American Journal of Economics and Sociology*, 14 (July, 1955), 321-333.

[12] Elton Mayo, *The Social Problems of an Industrial Civilization* (Boston: Harvard University Graduate School of Business Administration, Division of Research, 1945).

[13] See, for example, Harold Sheppard, "Managerial Sociology" (unpublished Ph.D. dissertation, University of Wisconsin, 1948) and "Approaches to Conflict in American Industrial Sociology," *British Journal of Sociology*, 5 (December, 1954), 324-341; Daniel Bell, "Adjusting Men to Machines," *Commentary*, 3 (January-June, 1947), 79-88; Herbert Blumer, "Sociological Theory in Industrial Relations," *American Sociological Review*, 12 (June, 1947), 271-278; R. Bendix and L. H. Fisher, "The Perspectives of Elton Mayo," *Review of Economics and Statistics*, 31 (November, 1949), 317; Moore, *op. cit.*

The amount of concern stimulated by this issue is suggested by the title of one critical article—"Deep Therapy on the Assembly Line: Moo, moo, moo, say the cow sociologists, but they don't even give skimmed milk."[14]

In order to understand the history of industrial sociology, it is important to take this controversy into account. First of all, occurring as it did early in the development of the field, it produced an initial burst of interest that was eventually translated into a considerable body of research. Much of the work of the critics of the human relations approach appears to be, in some measure, a response to what they considered the deficiencies in this approach. Noting the almost total disregard of trade unions by Mayo and his early followers, some sociologists turned to the study of the structure and functioning of unions. Others, rejecting the value placed by Mayo on cooperation, studied union-management relations and the functions of social conflict. Still others proceeded to demonstrate that cohesive work groups are potentially as effective in *subverting* as they are in achieving management goals. Some industrial sociologists, rejecting the preoccupation of the human relations researchers with inplant, interpersonal relations, became concerned with developing more general sociological frameworks which would deal with the broader context of work relationships. While it would obviously be overstating the case to suggest that these studies were motivated solely by a reaction against the human relations perspective, many were, in fact, couched specifically in these terms.

Both the Hawthorne studies and the controversy surrounding and growing out of them served to focus industrial sociological research upon manufacturing industries. The studies by Mayo, his followers, and his critics established a pattern of research concerns that has been followed until very recently in industrial sociology.

The human relations in industry approach has often been mistakenly viewed as characteristic of all research in industrial sociology. Even among sociologists whose primary research interest is the work group, a large number have not been influenced directly by the Mayo tradition. There are, in particular, a number whose work is more closely related to group dynamics and the research of Kurt Lewin. At least since the establishment of its Institute for Social Research in 1946, the University of Michigan has been a major center for this kind of research dealing with the work group and supervisory relations. Examples of people who have made contributions in this type of research are Daniel Katz, R. L. Kahn, Stanley Seashore, Lester Coch, J. R. P. French, Jr., George Strauss, Leonard R. Sayles, and Rensis Likert.

Another early development in the field was the emergence of interest in industrial research among social anthropologists. W. Lloyd Warner, who

[14] Lewis Carliner, "Deep Therapy on the Assembly Line: Moo, moo, moo say the cow sociologists, but they don't even give skim milk," *Ammunition*, 7 (April, 1949), 47-51.

had served as a consultant on the Hawthorne studies in their later phases, conducted a pioneering study of a shoe factory and the organization of a union within it.[15] Conrad Arensberg also became interested in industrial social organization and industry-community relations.[16] Among other social anthropologists interested in industrial research were Eliot Chapple, F. L. W. Richardson, Jr., and Burleigh Gardner, mentioned earlier as a contributor to the development of the human relations approach.

The work of Max Weber on bureaucracy has influenced directly or indirectly a number of other major contributors to the field of industrial sociology. Not all of these people would call themselves industrial sociologists. Their concerns have been more broadly sociological and the conceptual frameworks they have used are more general in the sense of their applicability to a wider variety of contexts of social behavior. One of the classic studies of industrial social organization is Alvin Gouldner's *Patterns of Industrial Bureaucracy*.[17] A selection based upon this study is included in Chapter III of this reader. Other classic studies of bureaucracy have been conducted by Peter Blau; Philip Selznick; and S. M. Lipset, Martin Trow, and James Coleman.[18] The Weberian tradition influenced a number of other sociologists who made major, early contributions to the development of industrial sociology. Among others that might be cited here are Wilbert Moore, Robert Dubin, C. Wright Mills, Reinhardt Bendix, William H. Form, Delbert C. Miller, and Herbert Blumer. Some of these sociologists have been concerned with power and union-management relations and have also, to some extent, been influenced by the work of George Simmel and Karl Marx on social conflict.

While the Hawthorne studies were completed by 1933, the major reports of the research, F. Roethlisberger and W. J. Dickson's *Management and the Worker* and Elton Mayo's *The Social Problems of an Industrial Civilization*, did not appear until 1939 and 1945, respectively. The initial burst of interest referred to above occurred, for the most part, during the 1940's and early 1950's. Some institutional support for the field began to develop during this period. The Department of Industrial Research of the Graduate School of Business Administration of Harvard University, with which Mayo was associated, was established earlier, in 1926. A number of other major centers of industrial research were established in the 1940's: the Committee on Human Relations in Industry was organized at the Univer-

15 W. Lloyd Warner, *The Social System of the Modern Factory* (New Haven: Yale University Press, 1947).
16 Conrad M. Arensberg, "Industry and the Community," *American Journal of Sociology*, 48 (July, 1942), 1-12.
17 Alvin W. Gouldner, *Patterns of Industrial Bureaucracy* (New York: Free Press, 1954).
18 Peter M. Blau, *The Dynamics of Bureaucracy* (Chicago: University of Chicago Press, 1955); Philip Selznick, *T.V.A. and the Grass Roots* (Berkeley: University of California Press, 1949); S. M. Lipset, Martin Trow, and James Coleman, *Union Democracy* (New York: Free Press, 1956).

sity of Chicago in 1943; the Labor Management Center at Yale in 1944; the New York State School of Labor and Industrial Relations at Cornell in 1945; the Institute of Industrial Relations at the University of California in 1945; the Institute for Social Research at the University of Michigan in 1946; and the Institute of Labor and Industrial Relations at the University of Illinois, also in 1946. Since this period, a large number of universities have established institutes or centers supporting industrial sociological research.

Additional early support for the field came with the establishment of the journal of the Society of Applied Anthropology; originally named *Applied Anthropology* but now called *Human Organization*. This journal published many reports of industrial sociological reesarch. *The American Journal of Sociology* also published a large number of industrial studies during this period.

By the middle of the 1950's, industrial sociology had become firmly established as a part of the curriculum in most universities. Probably the highest *proportion* of doctoral degrees with a specialization in this field were granted between 1945 and 1955. Textbooks in industrial sociology began to be published during the latter half of this period. *Industrial Relations and the Social Order* by Wilbert Moore was published in 1946.[19] The first text to use the title industrial sociology was by Delbert C. Miller and William H. Form, published in 1951.[20] At least seven other textbooks used in courses in this field were published in the following decade.[21]

Industrial sociology has existed as a distinct field for only slightly more than thirty years, and has been an established area of teaching and research for only about half of that time. The field is still evolving and the major issues of today are quite different from those of the 1940's. The controversy between the Mayo "school" and its critics, so influential in shaping the early character of the field, has subsided and is rarely mentioned in current publications. As with so many issues of this kind it has largely disappeared, not because it was resolved, but because it is no longer relevant. While the general outlines of the field have not changed radically, as evidenced by the similarity in content of earlier and more recent textbooks, there has been a substantial shift in the focus of interest within these broad limits. Some general trends in the development of the field will be discussed in the next

---

[19] Wilbert E. Moore, *Industrial Relations and the Social Order* (New York: The Macmillan Company, 1946).

[20] Miller and Form, *op. cit.*

[21] John B. Knox, *The Sociology of Industrial Relations* (New York: Random House, 1955); Schneider, *op. cit.*; Edward Gross, *Work and Society* (New York: Crowell, 1958); Robert Dubin, *The World of Work* (Englewood Cliffs, N.J.: Prentice-Hall, 1958) and *Working Union Management Relations* (Englewood Cliffs, N.J.: Prentice-Hall, 1958); Melvin J. Vincent and Jackson Mayers, *New Foundations for Industrial Sociology* (New York: Van Nostrand, 1959); Charles Spaulding, *An Introduction to Industrial Sociology* (San Francisco: Chandler Publishing Co., 1961); William F. Whyte, *Men at Work* (Homewood, Ill.: Irwin, 1961).

section of this chapter, and subsequent chapters will contain more detailed analyses of specific directions of change.

Current Trends in Industrial Sociology

Industrial sociology began primarily as an applied field. The concerns of the early researchers were, for the most part, ameliorative or oriented toward establishing policies. The question of how to improve the morale of industrial workers, in particular, was the implicit or explicit issue of a substantial proportion of the studies conducted. Since the end of World War II, there has been a general shift in American sociology away from a social philosophical, and social problems orientation and toward a more social scientific perspective.[22] The rapid advances that occurred during this period in the development of systematic research methods has been an important factor in this change. The use of high-speed digital computers, developed during World War II, also permitted more elaborate data analysis designs and stimulated some of the recent methodological advances in sociology. In addition, the development of more adequate, systematic theory has encouraged the change from limited, practical research objectives to a concern with building a science of social behavior.

This change, while proceeding at an accelerated rate in the past twenty years, has actually been going on over a much longer period in the history of sociology. In industrial sociology the change has been more abrupt. There are, of course, industrial sociologists whose research is still directed toward the solution of specific problems. For the most part, however, the work that is currently being done on issues related to the traditional concerns of industrial sociology is not of this sort. The field has increasingly become "sociology before it is industrial" as Wilbert Moore suggested that it should. Current studies are directed toward the development of more broadly applicable generalizations, and there is greater concern with the relationship of theory and research. Industrial sociology has become more and more integrated into the mainstream of sociological concern with the discovery of laws of social behavior.

Another general trend in sociology has been toward a greater specialization and narrowing of substantive interests. At one time the training and research interests of industrial sociologists tended to span the range of topics included in the field. Today it is much more likely that sociologists working in this area will define themselves as specialists in, for example, formal organizations, small group interaction, or comparative institutions and industrialization. Studies by people with these specialities are being conducted in a variety of organizational settings. To the extent that they deal with the structure, functioning, or effects of large scale manufacturing, however, they

[22] Seymour Martin Lipset and Neil J. Smelser, "Change and Controversy in Recent American Sociology," *British Journal of Sociology*, 12 (March, 1961), 41-51.

represent contributions to industrial sociology as the field has been defined here.

One of the effects of this trend is that there are relatively fewer sociologists whose research is focussed *primarily* upon manufacturing and relatively fewer who define themselves as industrial sociologists. There has been an *increase*, however, in the amount of research relevant to industrial social organization. The decline in use of the label is one explanation for the view that industrial sociology is no longer a viable subdiscipline. The increasing number of studies being done in the field is the major reason for the optimistic view of the future of industrial sociology expressed at the beginning of this chapter.

The growth in the number of industrial sociological studies has not been evenly distributed among the six areas constituting the core of the field. Interest in two of these areas has been declining while there has been a dramatic increase in interest in two others. There have been relatively few studies recently of trade union structure or of union-management relations. During the late 1930's and the 1940's, when industrial sociology was in the process of emerging as a separate field, a number of major industrial unions were just being organized. A union organizational drive provides a particularly good research setting for sociologists interested in protest movements and social conflict. Today trade unions are a generally accepted institution in American society, and standard procedures for the accommodation of union-management conflict have been instituted. Sociologists whose professional interests led them into studies of trade unions twenty years ago are more likely today to be studying events like the civil rights movement. Other sociologists whose concern with unions stemmed primarily from an interest in their potential effect upon income distribution, social stratification, and lower class standards of living are more likely to be engaged in studying governmental programs for dealing with poverty. There is also in sociology, as in other fields, an ebb and flow in what are defined as important research topics, and the study of trade unions is apparently no longer in fashion.

There has been, on the other hand, a burgeoning interest in the study of complex, formal organizations. Until fairly recently the focus of sociological concern with such organizations had been upon either case studies of particular organizations or upon abstractions regarding general characteristics of bureaucracy. The increasing awareness in American sociology of the need for comparative organizational studies of different *types* of formal organizations is partly responsible for the rapid growth of this area of study. Etzioni, for example, has pointed out the need for middle range theory that would allow the formulation of statements concerning subcategories of organizations. According to Etzioni, theories of this kind should make it possible to avoid the overgeneralization resulting from attempts to relate case study findings to abstract organizational theory, and the undergeneralization that often results when no attempt is made to apply research findings beyond the specific organization in which the case study was conducted.[23]

While earlier studies of formal organizations were done most often in manufacturing industries, studies today include hospitals, schools, government agencies, military units, and others that differ in important ways from economic organizations. This trend toward comparative organizational analysis has been beneficial to industrial sociology because it has stimulated interest in research dealing with formal organizations, and has encouraged the attempt to validate propositions from general organizational theory that could not be tested using a case study approach. There is the danger (noted above), however, that contemporary students of formal organizations will not become sufficiently familiar with any one type of organization to develop an understanding in depth of the results of their research.

Another important development in the analysis of complex organizations that has contributed to the growing interest in this area is the application of formal logical and mathematical models to the study of organizational processes. Some promising beginnings have been made in the use of game theory, computer simulation, information theory, operations research, and communications theory. These developments, along with comparative research design and other current directions of change in the sociology of organizations, will be discussed later in the introduction to the section on industrial bureaucracy.

The study of the industrialization process is the other area within industrial sociology in which a major increase in research activity has taken place. The increasing interest in studies of this kind is, like the growth in the sociology of organizations, partly a response to the recognition of the need for comparative research. Until fairly recently, American sociology has been exceptionally parochial in its concerns, focussing almost exclusively upon the United States. It has become apparent, however, that we need to test propositions about social structure in a variety of cultural contexts. The rapid industrialization occurring in many economically underdeveloped areas of the world provides a unique opportunity for the study of social change generally and, specifically, of the effects of the shift from an agricultural to an industrial economic base.

Hundreds of books have been written about the industrial revolution of the eighteenth and nineteenth centuries in the United States and Western Europe. These studies do not tell us, however, which characteristics of Western civilization result from the industrialization process and which result from unique aspects of the historical, geographical, and cultural context in which this process occurred. The introduction of large-scale manufacturing operations into widely divergent cultural settings in Africa, Asia, and Latin America makes possible studies designed to isolate those changes

[23] Amatai Etzioni, A Comparative Analysis of Complex Organizations (New York: Free Press, 1961), pp. xi-xiv.

directly attributable to industrialism. The discovery of the common attributes of this cultural system will permit more accurate predictions of the consequences of economic development.

The obvious utility in being able to make predictions regarding directions of change in developing nations is reflected in the large sums of money available from the federal government and private foundations for studies of industrialization. The availability of research funds has undoubtedly contributed to the growth of interest in this area. This is probably particularly so in this instance since there is some correspondence between the needs of social science and the more immediate "practical" objectives of the agencies granting research funds.

Industrialism, Differentiation, and Rationalization

The search in industrial sociology for common or defining attributes of industrialism as a way of life provides the major theme of this book. The kind of theme required to link together such diverse areas as the study of the work group, union-management relations, and the development of industrial society is necessarily at a relatively high level of abstraction. Moreover, because we have only recently begun to engage in systematic, empirical studies of the concomitants of industrialization, we have to deal with this issue in general rather than in specific terms.

Briefly stated, this book will show how the shift in the economic base of a society from agriculture to manufacturing induces, at some point in the process, an accelerated rate of social change and an increasingly high level of differentiation of social structure. Social change and social differentiation result in pervasive problems of social integration for industrializing societies. The response to these problems, under the conditions in which they occur, is an increase in the rationalization of organizational structure. Increased rationalization, in turn, stimulates further social change and structural differentiation. The cyclical nature of this process tends to propel societies at an increasing rate toward an industrial way of life. The relationships involved in this sequence of events are presented in graphic form in the figure below.

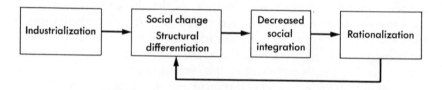

The relationship between industrialization and social change should not require any extensive explanation or documentation. Traditional preindustrial societies tend to be highly integrated in the sense that a change in any part of the society ramifies throughout the whole system. Changes in the economy are likely to have especially pervasive effects since the economic institution is an important determinant of patterns of social stratification, the structure of the family, the nature of government, the type of educational system required, and even (to some extent) the nature of religious values and observances. As the traditional ways of doing things become less appropriate as guides to social action, an important barrier to social change is removed, and the rate of innovation throughout the society is increased.

The relationship between industrialization and social structural differentiation is also well documented. The shift to an economic system based upon manufacturing increases the degree of differentiation in two directions, horizontally and vertically. The extensive division of labor characteristic of industrial societies, an example of horizontal differentiation, is linked directly to the nature of production technology and the form of economic organizations found in these societies. As the division of labor increases, other forms of horizontal differentiation also appear. A high level of functional specialization generates special interests and organizations such as trade unions, management associations, professional societies, political parties, and producers' or consumers' cooperatives emerge as a device for pursuing these interests. The pattern of representation of special interests through formal organizations spreads to nonoccupationally based interest groups as well. Looking through any urban telephone directory, one can find large numbers of "societies for the prevention of" or "societies for the preservation of"; an almost endless variety of aspects of industrial culture.

There are many other types of structural differentiation that accompany industrialization. Most of the older universities in the United States were, for example, at one time church-related. Their emergence as autonomous units reflects both the segmental character and the secularism of industrial societies. These societies are also vertically differentiated to a greater extent than are traditional societies. The class, status, and power structures of tribal, peasant, feudal, or other types of preindustrial social systems are generally not complex and involve relatively few strata or levels. There are, of course, exceptions, as in the Indian caste system, and it is clear that processes other than industrialization can give rise to complexity in the hierarchical ordering of a society. The fact remains, however, that most nonindustrial societies are not characterized by a complex stratification system whereas *all* industrial societies are. The explanation for this rests primarily upon the form of division of labor typical of an industrially based economic system. A complex division of labor produces occupational roles that are not only functionally specialized but also widely divergent in the amount of social honor and power that accompany role performance, and in the economic life chances of the role incumbent. The division of labor is the form of structural differentiation that is most directly related to industrialization and the one that has the most pervasive effect upon the nature of industrialism as a way of life. We will return to this topic again in the next chapter.

A rapidly changing and increasingly segmentalized society is almost inevitably characterized by a decreasing level of social integration. Social integration is defined here positively as "the degree of interconnectedness of the social units comprising a social system," and negatively as "the absence of institutionalized conflict in the system." The relatively smaller number of units differentiated from each other in preindustrial societies, whether they are extended families, formal organizations, or broad social strata, tend to be linked together in such a manner that there is little isolation of one unit from another. There also appears to be little conflict that is institutionalized or built into the system. This does not mean that nonindustrial societies are free from social conflict. Some recent anthropological studies have suggested, for example, that a high level of conflict is common in certain types of peasant communities. This conflict occurs for the most part, however, at an interpersonal level and is not a product of the mutually exclusive objectives of social units in the same sense that, for example, union-management conflict is generated by the fact that wages represent a cost to management and income to workers.

With the proliferation of social units accompanying industrialization, many segments of the society become virtually isolated from each other. The boundaries of social units become barriers in the sense that more social interaction occurs within them than across them. Isolation fosters the development of unique sets of norms and values that may add to the amount of conflict growing out of the special interests that provide the original basis for differentiation.

Many social units, such as the National Association of Manufacturers and the Society for the Preservation and Encouragement of Barber Shop Quartet Singing in America, are neither linked together in any meaningful way, nor necessarily in conflict with each other. Both intersegmental linkages and social conflict occur only within particular spheres of common interest. The differing self interests of upper and lower social classes are channelled through a variety of interrelated organizations and come into conflict primarily in the political arena. Various coalitions of civil rights organizations have instituted court cases in which they were opposed, in effect, by the Ku Klux Klan, White Citizen's Councils, and similar organizations. The National Collegiate Athletic Association and the Amateur Athletics Union have been engaged, in the past few years, in a bitter jurisdictional struggle for control of participation by U.S. athletes in international competition. Presidents of the United States have intervened in this dispute on two different occasions. At an entirely different level, the parents of a high school student in a large metropolitan school system recently complained because their daughter's lunch hour had been scheduled by a computer for 9:30 A.M.

These examples suggest the difficulty in achieving coordination within a highly segmentalized social system as well as the conflicting interests generated by such a system. They also suggest a particular pattern of response to lowered levels of social integration in industrial societies. This response is what Max Weber has termed "rationalization." The process of rationalization is at the core of Weber's philosophy of history. He sees the major direction of change in Western civilization over the past several centuries as a shift from traditionalism to rationalism. This process involves a very broad spectrum of types of change. Weber speaks of the disenchantment of the world and the decline in magical elements of thought. Rationalism also refers to a kind of "writing down" process including everything from bureaucratic record-keeping to the development of more concise musical notation. It also meant, for Weber, systematic thought processes resulting in an "increasing theoretical mastery of reality by means of increasingly precise and abstract concepts," and is related in this sense to the development of science.

The meaning of rationalism that is most relevant to our purposes here is the following: "Rationalism means . . . the methodical attainment of a definitely given and practical end by means of an increasingly precise calculation of adequate means."[24] In this sense rationalism refers to a habit of thought involving a persistent questioning of the adequacy of means to ends and a constant search for more adequate means. It also is used to refer to the social organizational forms that serve to instill and sustain these habits of thought. The large-scale support of formal education and of science and technology that follows industrialization is an example of the rationalization process. But so also is the development of bureaucratic administrative procedures, collective bargaining, and legislative and judicial processes designed to achieve a more "precise calculation of adequate means" for coordinating functionally specialized social units and accommodating social conflict.

It is important to recognize that the distinction here is not between irrational, economically underdeveloped societies and rational, industrial ones. The patterns of behavior in a tribal society in the jungles of Bolivia may be eminently rational in the sense of their perceived adequacy as means to culturally defined ends. The contrast is rather between a type of society in which the traditional ways are infrequently questioned and social structural patterns are dedicated to the maintenance of tradition, and societies in which questioning of the usual ways is a common mode of approach and is, in fact, institutionalized as the *prescribed* mode in many social roles.

It is easy to see how rationalization in this sense gives added impetus to social change. It has also, historically, given added impetus to the process

24 H. H. Gerth and C. Wright Mills, *From Max Weber: Essays in Sociology* (New York: Oxford University Press, 1958), p. 293.

of social structural differentiation. Functional specialization of roles, administrative units, and entire social organizations has been a major device in industrial societies for achieving greater efficiency in the attainment of objectives. Change and segmentation result in important and often unanticipated problems in social integration which induce further rationalization and the total process continues at a constantly accelerating rate.

For convenience of expression we have been contrasting industrial and nonindustrial societies throughout this chapter. It would be more accurate, however, to say more and less industrialized. The industrial revolution is still in progress virtually everywhere in the world in the sense that the sequence of processes that has been described, while it has only just begun in most parts of the world, is a continuing and important attribute of even the most advanced industrial nations. There is some evidence, however, of a developing postindustrial epoch involving a culmination of the differentiation-rationalization process. This topic will be one of the major issues discussed in the concluding chapter of this book.

Plan of the Book

It might appear from the general theme of this book that its major focus would be upon economically underdeveloped areas. As was just noted, however, this theme is as applicable to the United States as it is to Tasmania. In fact, most of the readings in the book deal with mature industrial societies. Industrial sociology has been a peculiarly American discipline, and most of the research in this field has been done in this country.

The major criterion used in selecting the readings included here was to bring together in one place the original reports of classic studies in industrial sociology. Most of these research reports originally appeared in professional journals. At least some part of almost all of the works that are most frequently referred to in industrial sociology texts have also been included.

Three other types of readings have been selected to supplement these basic studies. One of these deals with some recent developments in more industrialized societies including, particularly, the effects of automation and the effects of the increasing employment of professionals in industry. Most of the sections of the book contain at least one reading dealing with one or the other of these issues. An attempt has also been made to balance the older, classic studies with reports of research using more recently developed theoretical and methodological approaches. A brief statement summarizing contemporary approaches has also been included in the introduction to each section. Finally, the relevance of the material to the general theme of the book was used as a criterion for inclusion. Because of the level of generality of this theme, almost any work in industrial sociology is in some measure relevant to it. A few readings were selected, however, primarily because they dealt in a more direct way with the processes serving as the theme for this book.

With the exception of the introductory and concluding chapters, the various sections of the book can be read in any order. The first set of readings, those dealing with industrialization, was placed at the beginning, however, because it sets forth in somewhat more detail the differentiation-rationalization framework and provides at least some historical and cross-cultural comparative base for the other readings. The remaining sections follow the order in which these topics are discussed in most industrial sociology texts, moving from analysis of the formal organization of industry and major roles within it to work groups and the relationship between formal and informal patterns of organization. Next is a discussion of trade union administration focussing upon the problem of maintaining a control structure in unions that embodies both democratic participation and bureaucratic efficiency. The next to the last chapter, dealing with union-management relations, proceeds from a view of these relations as occurring between powerful contending interest groups; it is primarily concerned with the exercise of power and the accommodation of conflict.

The introduction to each chapter contains a brief resume of major points made in the readings, a review of recent developments in the field, and a discussion of the relationship of the readings to the theme of the book. In the concluding chapter an attempt will be made to predict, on the basis of this theme and the general directions of change suggested by the previous readings, some aspects of the future of industrial societies. The range of possibilities is suggested by the two readings in this section, one of which presents a relatively sanguine view and the other a very gloomy view of the prospects of industrialism as a way of life.

Bibliography

Anderson, N., *Work and Leisure* (New York: Free Press, 1961).

Arensberg, C., and Geoffrey, T., "Plant Sociology: Real Discoveries and New Problems," in Mirra Komarovsky, ed., *Common Frontiers of the Social Sciences* (New York: Free Press, 1957), pp. 310-337.

Baritz, L., *The Servants of Power: A History of the Use of Social Science in American Industry* (Middletown, Conn.: Wesleyan University Press, 1960).

Bell, D., *Work and Its Discontents* (Boston: Beacon Press, 1956).

Blumer, H., "Sociological Theory in Industrial Relations," *American Sociological Review*, 12 (June, 1947), 271-278.

Braunde, L., "Work: A Theoretical Clarification," *The Sociological Quarterly*, 4 (Autumn, 1963), 343-348.

Caplow, T., *The Sociology of Work* (Minneapolis: University of Minnesota Press, 1954).

Dubin, R., *The World of Work* (Englewood Cliffs, N.J.: Prentice-Hall, 1958).

Durkheim, E., *The Division of Labor in Society* (New York: Macmillan, 1933).

Etzioni, A., "Industrial Sociology: The Study of Economic Organizations," *Social Research*, 25 (Autumn, 1958), 303-324.

Form, W., and Miller, D. C., *Industry, Labor, and Community* (New York: Harper & Row, 1960).

Friedmann, G., *The Anatomy of Work: Labor, Leisure and the Implications of Automation* (New York: Free Press, 1961).

Friedmann, G., *Industrial Society* (New York: Free Press, 1956).

Friedmann, G., and Naville, P., *Traite de Sociologie du Travail*, 2 volumes (Paris: Armand Colin, 1962).

de Grazia, S., *Of Time, Work, and Leisure* (New York: Twentieth Century Fund, 1962).

Gross, E., *Industry and Social Life* (Minneapolis: Industrial Relations Center, University of Minnesota, 1965).

Gross, E., *Work and Society* (New York: Crowell, 1958).

Gross, E., "Some Suggestions for the Legitimation of Industrial Studies in Sociology," *Social Forces*, 33 (March, 1955), 233-239.

Hacker, A., "The Use and Abuse of Pareto in Industrial Sociology," *American Journal of Economics and Sociology*, 14 (July, 1955), 321-333.

Hart, C. W. M., "Industrial Relations Research and Social Theory," *The Canadian Journal of Economics and Political Science*, 15 (February, 1949), 53-73.

Homans, G. C., "The Strategy of Industrial Sociology," *The American Journal of Sociology*, 54 (January, 1949), 330-337.

Hughes, E. C., *Men and Their Work* (New York: Free Press, 1958).

Hughes, E. C., "The Relation of Industrial to General Sociology," *Sociology and Social Research*, 41 (March-April, 1957), 251-256.

Hughes, J. E., "Recent Trends in Industrial Sociology," *American Catholic Sociological Review*, **19** (October, 1958), 194-209.

Kerr, C., and Fisher, L., "Plant Sociology: The Elite and the Aborigines," in Mirra Komarovsky, ed., *Common Frontiers of the Social Sciences* (New York: Free Press, 1957), pp. 281-304.

Knox, J., "Sociological Theory and Industrial Sociology," *Social Forces*, **33** (March, 1955), 240-244.

Knox, J., *The Sociology of Industrial Relations: An Introduction to Industrial Sociology* (New York: Random House, 1956).

Koivisto, W. A., "Value, Theory, and Fact in Industrial Sociology," *The American Journal of Sociology*, **58** (May, 1953), 564-572.

Kriesberg, L., "Industrial Sociology," in Hans Zetterberg, ed., *Sociology in the United States of America: A Trend Report* (Paris: UNESCO, 1956), pp. 71-77.

Massarik, F., and Brown, P., "Social Research Faces Industry," *Personnel*, **30** (May, 1954), 454-462.

Meadows, P., *The Culture of Industrial Man* (Lincoln: University of Nebraska Press, 1950).

Miller, D., and Form, W., *Industrial Sociology* (New York: Harper & Row, 1964).

Mills, C. W., "The Contributions of Sociology to Studies of Industrial Relations," *Proceedings of the First Annual Meeting, Industrial Relations Research Association, Cleveland, Ohio, December 29-30, 1948*, pp. 199-222.

Moore, W. E., "Current Issues in Industrial Sociology," *American Sociological Review*, **12** (December, 1947), 651-657.

Moore, W. E., *Industrial Relations and the Social Order* (New York: Macmillan, 1951).

Moore, W. E., with discussion by Robert Dubin, Delbert C. Miller, Paul Meadows, and Alvin W. Gouldner, "Industrial Sociology: Status and Prospects," *American Sociological Review*, **13** (August, 1948), 382-400.

Noland, E. W., "Industrial Sociology and the Businessman," *Social Forces*, **39** (October, 1960), 5-18.

Parsons, T., and Smelser, N. J., *Economy and Society* (New York: Free Press, 1956).

Pestridge, V., and Wray, D. E., *Industrial Sociology: An Annotated Bibliography* (Urbana: Institute of Labor and Industrial Relations, University of Illinois, 1953).

Powell, F. D., "Recent Trends in Industrial Sociology," *American Catholic Sociological Review*, **18** (October, 1957), 194-204.

Presthus, R., *The Organizational Society: An Analysis and Theory* (New York: Knopf, 1962).

Princeton University, Industrial Relations Section, *Outstanding Books on Industrial Relations: Selected References* (1949-1955), (Princeton: Industrial Relations Section, Princeton University, 1955).

Rosen, N., and McCoy, R. E., *Doctoral Dissertations in Labor and Industrial Relations* (Champaign: Institute of Labor and Industrial Relations, University of Illinois, 1955).

Schneider, E. V., "Areas of Research in Industrial Sociology," *Sociology and Social Research*, 42 (July-August, 1958), 451-455.

Schneider, E. V., *Industrial Sociology: The Social Relations of Industry and the Community* (New York: McGraw-Hill, 1957).

Schneider, E. V., "Limitations on Observation in Industrial Sociology," *Social Forces*, 28 (March, 1950), 279-284.

Shepard, H. A., "Nine Dilemmas in Industrial Research," *Administrative Science Quarterly*, 1 (December, 1956), 259-309.

Sheppard, H. L., "Approaches to Conflict in American Industrial Sociology," *British Journal of Sociology*, 5 (December, 1954), 324-341.

Smelser, N., *The Sociology of Economic Life* (Englewood Cliffs, N.J.: Prentice-Hall, 1963).

Smigel, E. O., *Work and Leisure: A Contemporary Social Problem* (New Haven, Conn.: College and University Press Services, 1963).

Spaulding, C. B., *An Introduction to Industrial Sociology* (San Francisco: Chandler Publishing Co., 1961).

Van Kleeck, M., "Towards an Industrial Sociology," *American Sociological Review*, 11 (October, 1946), 501-505.

Vincent, M. J., and Mayers, J., *New Foundations for Industrial Sociology* (Princeton: Van Nostrand, 1959).

Wallenstein, L. B., "Sociology as an Area of Industrial Relations Research," *Sociology and Social Research*, 39 (September-October, 1954), 22-23.

Warner, W. L., and Martin, N. H., eds., *Industrial Man* (New York: Harper & Row, 1959).

Webbink, P., "Methods and Objectives of Industrial Relations Research," in Reed Tripp, ed., *Proceedings of the Seventh Annual Meeting of the Industrial Relations Research Association, December 1954* (Champaign: Industrial Relations Research Association, 1955), pp. 102-106.

Whyte, W. F., *Men At Work* (Homewood, Ill.: Irwin, 1961).

Whyte, W. F., "Problems of Industrial Sociology," *Social Problems*, 4 (October, 1956), 148-160.

Whyte, W. F., and Miller, F. B., "Industrial Sociology," in Joseph Gittler, ed., *Review of Sociology: Analysis of a Decade* (New York: Wiley, 1957), pp. 289-345.

Wilensky, H. L., *Syllabus of Industrial Relations: A Guide to Reading and Research* (Chicago: University of Chicago Press, 1954).

THE INDUSTRIALIZATION PROCESS

Introduction

Industrialization has been variously defined by sociologists. Central to all of the definitions, however, is the idea of a shift in the economic base of a community or society from agriculture to manufacturing. The customary index of this shift is a decline in the proportion of the labor force employed in agriculture and an increase in the proportion employed in manufacturing and service industries.

Conceived in this way, industrialization serves as the label for a wide variety of changes. The immediate effects of introducing a steel mill in an economically underdeveloped area are quite different from the effects of introducing a petroleum refinery. Similarly, the effects of industrialization differ depending upon whether the agricultural system it supplants consists predominantly of large farms with paid farm laborers or of subsistence level farming in isolated peasant communities.

In spite of this diversity, there are some common features of the industrialization process no matter where it occurs. These common features lie, for the most part, in what Paul Meadows has called the inner structure of industrialism, i.e., "specialized machines and tools; a body of knowledge about machine processes, properties and tasks; and human beings disciplined for machine work."[1] There are, in other words, some intrinsic elements of industrial technology that appear irrespective of the point in time at which industrialization occurs and irrespective of the particular cultural heritage upon which it is superimposed. One of these elements and the one which seems to have the most far-reaching effects, is a complex form of division of labor. Increasing complexity in the division of labor as a result of industrialization is one of the major themes in several of the selections included in this chapter and is referred to again below.

The major question to which this chapter is addressed is, What are the social effects of industrialization? Answering this question may, at first

[1] Paul Meadows, *The Culture of Industrial Man* (Lincoln: University of Nebraska Press, 1950), p. 13.

glance, appear to be a simple matter. It would seem that we would need only to compare the industrial areas of the world with the nonindustrial areas and catalogue the differences we observe. It is not at all clear, however, that a process that has gone on for almost two hundred years in England and over one hundred years in the United States will have the same effects when it occurs over a much shorter period in Costa Rica, Tanzania, or Indonesia. It is also not clear whether the similarities among the more highly industrialized nations of the world are a product of industrialization or of a common cultural base in Western civilization. There are other questions that would also need to be answered. Are the instances of common features in industrial societies and those in the process of industrializing a result of simple imitation of forms established earlier in the United States and Western Europe or are they an inevitable consequence of the industrialization process itself? How can we separate the effects of industrialization from the effects of urbanization and other processes occurring at the same time?

One of the major themes (and one of the important unanswered questions) in the recent literature on industrialization centers around the issue of whether the widespread initiation of the process is moving in the direction of a common world culture or a diversity of forms of industrialism.[2] This is another way of posing what was identified above as the central question of this chapter: Are there effects of industrialization that can be predicted without regard to considerations of time or place?

There is a wide range of opinion among sociologists regarding the answer to this question. Also the collection of data necessary for an adequate answer has only recently begun and, consequently, any answers proposed in this chapter must be regarded as tentative. One extreme position on the effects of industrialization is that of Herbert Blumer who maintains that ". . . industrialization, by its very make-up, can have no definite social effect."[3] Although few sociologists would agree with this statement, there is less than complete consensus regarding what social effects may be attributed to the introduction of manufacturing industries. Particularly in analyses of the "outer structure of industrialism," i.e., the patterns of social organization of firms, communities, and various social institutions,[4] it has become clear that a variety of organizational forms may serve the same needs. Wilbert Moore has used the phrase "principle of structural substitutability" to refer to the fact that the "general functional requirements for the persistence of any society set only very wide limits on the appropriate structural ways of accomplishing those requirements."[5] While it would be difficult to

---

[2] Cf. Wilbert E. Moore, *The Impact of Industry* (Englewood Cliffs, N.J.: Prentice-Hall, 1965), pp. 9-20.

[3] Herbert Blumer, "Early Industrialization and the Laboring Class," *Sociological Quarterly*, 1 (January, 1960), 9.

[4] Meadows, *op. cit.*, pp. 15-21.

[5] Moore, *op. cit.*, p. 83.

demonstrate at this time that they are *necessary* consequences of industrialization, there are clearly some *common* attributes of the outer structure of industrialism in all economically developed countries. Joseph Kahl, in the first selection in this chapter, summarizes some of the evidence regarding these common attributes.

Within the inner structure of industrialism it is easier to demonstrate the causal relationships between industrial technology and particular social structural forms. We will single out only one of these relationships for further comment. Industrial technology inevitably results in a more complex division of labor than that found in traditional agricultural societies. The nature of jobs involving specialized machinery, differentiation in the managerial function, and the development of a variety of necessary service industries each contributes to the increasing specialization of a developing industrial occupational structure.[6] Data regarding the changes in the labor force composition of the United States over the period from 1860 to 1950 are presented in Tables 1-1 and 1-2 in the first selection in this chapter. Each of the major changes shown in these tables represents a shift from a less occupationally differentiated to a more occupationally differentiated industry or from a less specialized to a more specialized occupational type.

The effect of industrialization upon the degree of division of labor has been given special attention here not only because any change in the form of division of labor has far-reaching consequences, as was noted earlier, but also because of its special relevance to the major theme of this book. Increasing occupational specialization is, in itself, an important form of structural differentiation and in addition tends to produce more differentiated stratification patterns, increases the number and variety of special interest organizations, and in various other ways contributes to the segmentalized character of industrial societies. Complexity in the division of labor also tends to give rise to some particular problems for the integration of industrial societies that are customarily resolved through an increasing rationalization of work relations. Several examples of this process are presented in the readings included in this chapter.

Apart from the general issue of isolating the specific effects of industrialization, it is difficult to see any dominant emerging themes in the recent sociological work in this area. This work consists, for the most part, either of broad conceptual analyses or case studies of specific instances of change. There is a growing recognition of the necessity for cross-cultural comparative studies in which hypotheses regarding effects of industrialization can be tested in various cultural contexts as well as for comparative studies of developing societies over time. Research of this kind is very expensive and most of the genuinely comparative studies have been limited to demographic analyses using census data. There have been, however, some com-

---

[6] William A. Faunce, "Automation and the Division of Labor," *Social Problems*, 13 (Fall, 1965), 149-160.

parative sociological studies employing a wider range of variables and many others are now in progress.

Findings from some of these studies have been summarized in the first reading in this chapter, Joseph Kahl's, "Some Social Concomitants of Industrialization and Urbanization." He indicates that current studies leave some important unanswered questions, including whether the findings he reports are generalizable to all industrial societies and whether they are results of urbanization or of industrialization. And he suggests that one of the primary tasks for future sociological analysis of industrialization is to find out how much variation is possible in the nature of industrial societies. The significance of Kahl's article for the general theme of this book lies in the following points of emphasis: the breakdown of traditional culture under the impact of industrialization; the increase in division of labor and resulting complexity in patterns of social stratification; and the emergence of rational forms of integration which can be noted, among other places, in his discussion of "organic solidarity."

The selection by Neil Smelser, "Social Change in the Industrial Revolution," has been included because it specifies a sequence of stages in the process of structural differentiation. In the book from which this reading was extracted, Smelser presents extensive evidence that this particular sequence can be seen in the differentiation of jobs within the cotton textile industry and within the family structure of the working class during the industrial revolution in England. While some of this evidence is summarized in the portion of the book presented here, the important point in this selection is its analysis of the *process* of differentiation as it occurs during the early stages of industrialization. Most sociological comparative studies have not involved any real processual analysis but have analyzed, at a single point in time, societies that are presumably at different stages of industrialization. They have then *assumed* that the observed differences are accounted for by the operation of various sets of processes.

The third selection, "The Early Impact of Industrialization on Society," by Harold Wilensky, describes some of the problems accompanying the early stages of industrialization in the United States. Its emphasis is upon the changing nature of work occasioned, in part, by increasing occupational specialization. The problems of adjustment of rural migrants to industrial employment and the effects of the changing nature and conditions of employment upon early labor protest are discussed. In these discussions, and in the analysis of the widening gap between the working and entrepreneurial classes, the impact of increasing division of labor is stressed. It should be noted that this selection has been taken out of the context of a broader discussion of both early and later effects of industrialization. In the later stages of industrialization, the pattern of effects appear to be different and includes a blurring rather than a sharpening of class lines as Kahl (and Wilensky elsewhere) points out.

The selection by Rudolf Heberle, "Social Consequences of the Industrialization of Southern Cities," is a discussion of industrialization in an area within the United States that is still economically underdeveloped—the South. The major emphasis is upon the relationship between industrialization and urbanization including a discussion of the factors affecting the location of factories in rural or urban areas and of the differences among industries in the extent to which they contribute to population growth in an area. Heberle also notes an increasing differentiation and isolation of socioeconomic and racial groups and points out that both employer-employee and interracial relations are developing a more rationalized and contractual form.

The concluding selection in this chapter, "Problems of Management and Authority in a Transitional Society: A Case Study of a Javanese Factory," by Ann Willner, describes the pattern of traditional work relationships in East Java and contrasts them with the relationships in a textile plant in the same area. She notes that status and authority structures in the factory are more differentiated than those in other areas of the Javanese workers' experience and describes the problems occasioned by the conflict between the needs of the factory and the traditional patterns of social relations. The role conflicts confronting the foremen in this plant appear to be similar to those of foremen in contemporary plants in the United States (described by Wray in Chapter III of this book), which suggests that these problems are not resolved by further bureaucratization of the organizational structure of the factory. There is also an interesting comparison between this East Javanese factory and a factory in the United States studied by Gouldner (reported in Chapter II of this book). Many of the problems resulting from lack of integration and from conflict between traditional and rational organizational forms in the Javanese plant are the same problems that forced an increased bureaucratization of the American plant. The ascendance of rationalized patterns of work relationships also represents the probable direction of change in the plant described by Willner.

1. Some Social Concomitants of Industrialization and Urbanization

Joseph A. Kahl

The transformation of society by industrialization and urbanization is currently of great concern to men of affairs and to men of science.[1] Since the second World War the rate of industrialization has increased as people in previously isolated or tradition-bound societies have entered the main stream of world history to demand the material benefits of modern technology. They often seek those material benefits while hoping to retain their traditional cultures, yet, since England pointed the way in the eighteenth century, experience indicates that their hopes are utopian, for a radical change in the mode of production has profound repercussions on the rest of culture. This generalization is as sure as any in all of social science, but it is so abstract as to offer little guide to one who wants to know what the specific consequences of industrialization are likely to be. Some recent research helps us to do better.

The process of "development" involves a series of inter-twined economic changes: (1) the integration of previously isolated, self-sufficient rural economies into a single national economy with strong ties to the international economy; (2) the dominance of production for sale over production for barter or for use, thus the increasing emphasis upon money; (3) the introduction of new technological devices in farming and in manufacture which are based on world-wide science and involve large capital expenditures; (4) a tremendous growth of the means of communication and transport; (5) a steady growth of towns and cities (through internal migration from the farms) as bases of manufacturing, trade, and political control which become consumers of surplus food produced on the modernized farms; (6) a steady development of specialization in the division of labor between occupations, between farm and city, and between regions.[2]

Although economic development, industrialization and urbanization

Reprinted from Joseph A. Kahl, Society for Applied Anthropology, *Human Organization*, 18 (Summer, 1959), 53-71.

[1] The author takes pleasure in recording his indebtedness to students in two seminars who have given bibliographic assistance, and to several of his colleagues from Washington University and beyond it who read the first draft of this paper and offered useful critical comments.

[2] For background in economics the author relied principally upon Norman S. Buchanan and Howard S. Ellis, *Approaches to Economic Development* (New York: Twentieth Century Fund, 1955).

can be conceived of as separate variables, in most real instances the three unfold as an over-all complex. The changes listed in the preceding paragraph occur together, and no country can go far along the road to development unless they occur in a fairly harmonious pattern. Consequently, the sociologist can take the entire complex as a given, and seek its repercussions upon social organization in the growing cities. For present purposes, I shall concentrate upon changes in family, career, education, and stratification, and shall pay little attention to changes in politics and religion or to the modernization of the countryside.

The question raised here are old ones: they have been at the center of social theory since Karl Marx. Consequently, many of the ideas discussed in this paper have a long and worthy tradition. But in the postwar years there has been a florescence of research data that carry us considerably beyond the traditional formulations, which were mostly based upon historical studies. The new data can be grouped into two classes: direct field studies carried out in rapidly-growing cities, and national statistics from censuses or from series of vital statistics. My purpose is to organize the new data into a meaningful pattern, relying upon those of the older theoretical ideas which are most congruent with the empirical results. No attempt at a complete survey of the new literature is implied; I shall discuss only the major monographs, and at times will sample from among them.

I am going to stress the general, the universal—those social effects of the development process which tend to occur regardless of the traditions of the particular culture under consideration. Obviously, local traditions make a difference, and the final outcome will show a compromise between the ecumenical social forms of modern, industrial society and the local forms of a given culture. We do not yet know how much "leeway" exists, how much variation around the central theme of industrial society is possible. It is one of the prime tasks of current comparative research to find out.

Population Growth

A traditional society composed of isolated, self-sufficient villages has a very slow rate of population growth: it takes at least a century for the population to double, and ordinarily the counteracting forces of plague and famine decimate the growth almost as fast as it occurs. Economic development changes that picture: better means of transport make it possible to move food from areas of plenty to areas of scarcity; economic resources become available which permit the basic devices of sanitation, namely, fresh water and adequate sewage disposal; and contact with the outside world permits the rapid importation of cheap devices, such as DDT and penicillin, for the control of contagious disease. When economic development goes a bit further, and the general standard of living rises and provides better nutrition and medical care, the reduction in the death rate is dramatic.

Population growth is obviously the result of an excess of births over deaths. Economic development affects both the birth rate and the death rate, but at different periods in the development process. During the early industrialization of Europe, improvements in transport, urban sanitation, and general nutrition reduced the death rate slowly over a long period of time; when the great discoveries of modern medicine appeared in the 19th century and further cut the death rate, the birth rate had *already* begun to decline as a result of those gradual changes in family life which generally led urban people to prefer fewer children than do rural people. But nowadays the rate of change is faster and the sequence of steps is different: during the earliest stages of modernization, a country simultaneously improves its transport and communication, increases its food supply, cleans up its cities, and introduces scientific medicine by importing it from advanced countries. All of these changes can occur *before* any important alteration in the average size of family takes place as a result of urbanization. The consequence is a rapid reduction of the death rate, the maintenance of a high birth rate, and a population explosion.[3]

Recent data from Mexico, the one developing country with which I have firsthand experience, illustrate this process of sudden growth.[4] The pre-conquest population of Mexico is estimated at around nine million. The conquest in the early 16th century and its immediate aftermaths reduced the population by about one-half; thereafter, a stable though stagnant social system emerged and a very slow growth in population resulted. There were some six million by 1800, and twelve and a half million by 1895. Industrialization began under the Diaz dictatorship; just before the overthrow of his regime in 1910, the population reached 15 million. The severity of the civil war during the decade of the 1910's reduced it by almost one million people. Thus, 400 years after the conquest the population had only grown by about 60 percent.

In the 1920's peace was restored and a new surge of economic and social development began. The result was an unprecedented spurt in population: 16,553,000 in 1930; 19,654,000 in 1940; 25,791,000 in 1950; 33,-000,000 in 1958.

The birth rate has probably been between 40 and 46 per thousand per year since the end of the revolution, but the death rate has steadily declined: it was over 30 before the revolution, about 25 during the 1920's and 1930's, about 20 in the 1940's, and is about 12 now.[5]

[3] Bert F. Hoselitz, ed., "Agrarian Societies in Transition," *Annals of American Academy of Political and Social Science,* 305 (May, 1956), 1-12.
[4] For statistical details, see Jose E. Iturriaga, *La Estructura Social y Cultural de México* (Fondo de Cultura Económica, México, 1951); Manuel Germán Parra, *La Industrialización de México* (Imprenta Universitaria, México, 1954); and Julio Duran Ochoa, *Población, México* (Fondo de Cultura Económica, 1955).
[5] Much of the decline in the death rate is due, of course, to diminishing infant mortality. The latter rate (deaths in the first year of life per thousand live births) has fallen from 317 in 1895 to 95 in 1953.

The disparity between the birth and death rates produces the annual rate of natural increase, and note its trend: from about 14 per thousand before the revolution, to about 19 in the 1930's, about 25 in the 1940's, and between 31 and 34 now (that is, a compounded growth of between 3.1 and 3.4 percent per year).[6] The current rate of natural increase is sufficient to double the population *in less than 24 years* instead of in 400 years as was previously the case. But Mexico, although close to the top of the list of the countries of the world in current rate of increase, is by no means a special case. Other countries in Latin America, the Near East, and Asia are experiencing roughly the same phenomenon.

If a country is to progress in the economic sense—to raise the standard of living of its people and to have a surplus available for capital investment —it must increase its agricultural and industrial production faster than it increases its population. For the years since the second World War, Mexico has been able to expand production about twice as fast as the growth of population; as a result, she currently has a tremendous "boom." But it is of recent origin; from the revolution to the war, population growth appears to have outstripped production increase.

Those countries which are industrializing now, and as a result are having a population explosion, face a problem that is much greater than the one faced by Europe or the United States during their periods of rapid development. For example, Great Britain's population increased at an annual rate of about 1.4 percent during the first half of the 19th century, and 1.1 percent during the second half. The United States had an annual rate of increase of about 2.4 percent during the second half of the 19th century (including immigration), and its present rate of growth, despite the continuing postwar "baby boom," is about half that of Mexico's. The current rates for such countries as India and Russia are similar to that of the United States.

General industrial development and deliberate government action in sanitation and medicine can reduce a death rate from forty per thousand to close to ten per thousand in a generation's time. Birth rates usually go down much more slowly. The availability of mechanical devices for birth control, plus the forces of urban living which caused a desire for smaller families (which will be detailed below), had, by World War II, slowly cut the birth rates in countries in Western Europe and in the United States until a stable population was reached or expected. Since then, there has been a slight increase in birth rates but the resulting population growth is slow compared to what is happening in the newly developing countries. The data available so far indicate that Latin American and Asian cities do show reductions in birth rates over their surrounding rural districts, but there is as yet no as-

[6] All statistics in Mexico are suspect, and that is particularly true of vital statistics until recent years. Consequently, the estimates of natural increase given in the text have been adjusted somewhat to reflect growth as measured by the census, which is more accurate than growth measured by vital statistics. See Manuel Germán Parra, *op. cit.*, Table 23. Immigration has been negligible since the 17th century.

surance that the family size will ever go down as low as it has in countries of northwestern European culture.[7] And we cannot yet predict the course of population in Negro African cities.

Time is a crucial factor. For the development process to occur, a surplus must be available for capital investment. Factories must be built, mines sunk, farm machinery and fertilizers bought. Cities must be created as centers of industry and as sources of jobs to absorb the excess population from rural areas. Also, highways, railroads, schools, and hospitals have to be constructed. And to make matters more tense, the people, once aroused from a traditional way of life which assumes a fixed standard of living, start demanding new consumption goods; they institute a "revolution of expectations." Consequently, a country that once initiates the changes that lead it toward modernization must, to maintain self-sustained growth, increase its production considerably faster than its population; merely keeping even is impossible without chaos and revolution. There exists a critical period of rapid population growth which must be met by rapid industrialization before the gradual effects of urbanization can produce a decline in the birth rate and thus initiate a later period of slower growth.

From Rural to Urban

The traditional world is a rural world; seventy percent or more of the people live on farms, and the surplus of food which they grow with their crude techniques of production can support but a few urbanites. Each village is self-sufficient in most of its needs, and engages in only a small amount of trade with the outside world.

But the modern world is an urban world. Less than ten percent of the population (given good farmland and scientific techniques of production) can feed ninety percent living in towns and cities. Even if the urban proportion is smaller than ninety percent, urban control in science, commerce, manufacturing, mass media, and politics comes to dominate. Modern culture originates in cities and spreads outward to farms.

During the period of rapid development, there is an enormous flow of young people from farm to city. If a farmer has eight children who reach maturity, only two may remain on the farm, if a stable rural population is to be maintained. Actually, in the early stages of development, there is usually a slow growth in the rural population as new lands are opened for exploitation and as old ones become more crowded (in the later stages of development, the absolute size of the rural population is likely to shrink, for farms become larger and are worked by machinery instead of by hand). But a slow growth in the rural population is not enough to absorb all of the

[7] T. Lynn Smith, "The Reproduction Rate in Latin America: Levels, Differentials and Trends," *Population Studies*, XII (July, 1958), 4-17.

farmers' children; many of them must move cityward when they are young adults to seek urban jobs.

Once again, Mexico can serve as an illustration: 22 percent of its population lived in urban places in 1910, but 43 percent did so by 1950.[8] In those forty years the rural population grew from 10,812,000 to 14,808,000, an increase of 37 percent. But the urban population expanded from 4,348,000 to 10,983,000, or an increase of 153 percent. The growth rate of the nation's capital, Mexico City, has been phenomenal: from 721,000 in 1910 to 3,050,000 in 1950. In 1958, its population was estimated at 5,000,000, and its current growth rate at 7 percent per year, or a doubling in less than 12 years. Almost half of its inhabitants are migrants from farms and from smaller towns and cities.

Cities are large and heterogeneous.[9] The contacts between men tend to be contacts in specialized roles rather than as total personalities. Workplace is different from home and both are different from worship-place. At each, a man has different associates. Salesman and customer, teacher and student, fellow members of the Society for the Preservation of Ancient Choral Music, even "neighbors," interact for particular purposes and do not allow themselves to become totally involved with one another: there is not enough time, and it would interfere with the efficiency of the specialized interaction (for example, a teacher is not supposed to consider "family background" in awarding grades to students—or, to use an overworked phrase, "business is business"). The immediate family and very few "close friends" are the limits of social relationships based on long contact, personal rather than business attitudes, emotional rather than rational purpose, total rather than specialized and thus superficial involvement.

The link between men in the city is mediated by money: urbanites buy and sell goods and services, and they play in ways which cost money so that only those with similar incomes can play the same games and join the same clubs. Even one's neighbors are determined by money, for the economic competition for space sorts out neighborhoods according to "quality" or cost. The cash nexus tends to replace kinship and local community as the main determinant of social position and consequently of social relationships.

It is often said that life in the city is "individualistic." This term is to me one of the vaguest and least useful in the social science lexicon. It is true that many people in the city are lonesome; it is true that the clan is non-existent, the extended family is weak, and the neighborhood is amorphous,

[8] In 1910, an urban place was classified as one with 2,000 or more inhabitants; in 1950, the more standard definition of 2,500 was used.
[9] Louis Wirth, "Urbanism as a Way of Life," American Journal of Sociology, 44 (July, 1938); reprinted in Hatt and Reiss, eds., Cities and Society, (New York: Free Press, 1957), pp. 46-63.

thus the individual has a range of free choice in his decisions which goes beyond that of the peasant or tribal member. But it is not true that the individual is lacking in group ties. The key to city life is the multiplicity of group ties: each may have strong influence on the individual, but each is limited to a specific area of behavior and is balanced by others. In the folk society, the family group generally controls property, marriage, work, and much of religion. The individual is a member of a *single* small group whose activities cover all the important aspects of his life. In the city, the individual interacts with many groups: he has his own personal career and he meets on the job a team of workmates; at home, he sorts the claims of parents, extended kin, wife, and children into different compartments; he may belong to a church which tells him that the goals of business are not the only important ends of life, etc. He has a great range of choice, and can use one group to offset the other. He must manipulate their various claims by means of rational decision, and thus may at times seem like an extreme individualist organizing his life to suit himself. But the fact is that his own goals are taken over from various of these groups; he follows group codes, gets emotional satisfaction from group memberships, thinks in terms of maximizing group performance. Work groups, recreational cliques, nuclear families—these are "tight" groups which bind the individual to them, shape him in their image. The typical urbanite is not an isolate; he is a group member whose total involvement in collective life is very great but whose involvement in any one group is limited.[10]

As long as the rapidly growing cities contain so many citizens who are migrants from rural areas, we must distinguish between their transitional way of life—combining rural and urban traits—and the more adapted pattern which eventually develops among those born and reared in city environments. Persons in transition may cling to many rural characteristics, such as devotion to the extended-family system, which give them security in their new situation. Indeed, many new city workers are temporary workers, leaving families behind in the villages. On the other hand, some transitional individuals throw over the rural patterns before they have time to learn functionally adapted urban ways, and their lives show the "disorganization" noticed in many urban studies. But neither rural survivals nor temporary disorganization last through time; if we are to predict the future, we must concentrate on the city-bred persons who have turned their back on the farms and are committed to an urban style of life.

[10] Perhaps some of the overemphasis upon individualism, even on isolation, in urban society stems from the attempts of Park's students in Chicago to find and portray "extreme" types of urbanites, like taxi dance hall girls and rooming house inhabitants. But such extremes cannot be used to construct an "ideal-type" of life in the city. Durkheim, in discussing his model of modern society, emphasized *both* the loosening of the old social controls of rigid tradition in small communities *and* the emergence of new social controls in terms of segmental groups functionally adapted to the urban milieu.

From Localism to Nationalism

The creation of a modern economy demands a large market. There must be a division of labor and an exchange of produce from one region to another. Modern means of communication and transport are constructed to facilitate this exchange.

The social effects of these new means of communication are enormous —I think it was Ralph Beals who remarked that one road is worth twenty schools as a stimulus to social change. The harmony of tribal and even of peasant society is based on small communities which are at least partially isolated, for isolation produces inbreeding of genes and ideas and leads to the stability of a fixed tradition.[11]

The new economy breaks down local isolation. Not only goods but men and ideas move freely from one region (and one country) to another. The powers of local landlords, local chieftains, local clans, and most important, local traditions, are weakened. This sets men free to experiment, but it also isolates them from their previous bases of personal security.[12] If you do not belong to a village, where your family has lived since time began, who are you?

The answer is: you are a member of a nation. The national state must exert its supremacy over local districts if a large market is to exist in security and order. Those countries which developed an effective national government and sense of national identity before they industrialized, such as England and Japan, had an enormous advantage over those countries which are trying simultaneously to create national unity and modernize their economies, such as Indonesia and Ghana. The fact of national economic and political dominion goes hand in hand with the spirit of national belongingness. Perhaps the test question is this: for whom will you fight unto death? Your family, in the spirit of the blood feud? Your tribe? Your region? Your country? An alliance of like-minded countries?

The spirit of nationalism which sweeps new countries thus stems from a combination of a rational impetus toward the building of a new society, and an emotional need to replace the broken sense of local identification with new symbols of group membership (often reinforced by the desires for freedom from colonial overlords). These are powerful forces of mind and heart, and, until they are spent, we should not expect a new identification with the world community, despite the obvious fact that both economic and political realities are now pushing us toward international rather than national bonds of organization.

[11] Robert Redfield, "The Folk Society," *American Journal of Sociology*, **52** (1947), 293-308.
[12] Erich Fromm, *Escape from Freedom*, (New York: Holt, Rinehart and Winston, 1941).

The breakdown of a sense of local identity and its replacement by a national (and occasionally international) view results from a double process: the actual movement of men from the village to the city, and the spread of the mass media throughout the cities and eventually into the villages. This latter process has been studied through sample surveys of some 300 respondents in each of six countries in the Middle East by the Columbia University Bureau of Applied Social Research. The surveys they did in 1950 have recently been synthesized by Daniel Lerner in *The Passing of Traditional Society*, 1958. This book is worth our special attention, for it reports a pioneer effort to study the transition from a situation focused on the murmurings of old men, who recite from memory the ancient traditions of the local folk, and deduce therefrom permanent rules of conduct, to a situation focused on the voices of young men who are excited about the national happenings of today and tomorrow, and seek new rules of conduct for a new world they hope to build. In this new world, the mass media are crucial, and with the arrival of radio and movies, no longer depend completely upon literacy; Nasser has shown us the power of the electronic voice. And let it be remembered that the mass media originate in the cities, from the centers of power; they represent the national, the urban, the sophisticated points of view, and they give people something to think about that carries their minds beyond the implications of the immediate locality.

Lerner maintains that modernization in communication involves a single package of interrelated phenomena, and he demonstrates, for over fifty countries, high correlations among the following variables: urbanism, literacy, participation in elections and media participation (newspaper circulation; cinema attendance; radio ownership). The effects of this package upon individual mentality, upon a man's sense of identity, are described as follows (pp. 50-51):

Traditional society is nonparticipant—it deploys people by kinship into communities isolated from each other and from a center; without an urban-rural division of labor, it develops few needs requiring economic interdependence; lacking the bonds of interdependence, people's horizons are limited by locale and their decisions involve only other *known* people in *known* situations. Hence, there is no need for a transpersonal common doctrine formulated in terms of shared secondary symbols—a national "ideology" which enables persons unknown to each other to engage in political controversy or achieve "consensus" by comparing their opinions. Modern society is participant in that it functions by "consensus"—individuals making personal decisions on public issues must concur often enough with other individuals they do not know to make possible a stable common governance. Among the marks of this historic achievement, which we call Participant Society, are that most people go through school, read newspapers, receive cash payments in jobs they are legally free to change, buy goods for cash in an open market, vote in elections which actually decide among competing candidates, and express opinions on many matters which are not their personal business.

Especially important, for the Participant Style, is the enormous proportion of people who are expected to "have opinions" on public matters—and the corollary expectation of these people that their opinions will matter.

Lerner calls the ability to have opinions about many things beyond one's immediate personal business the capacity for *empathy*, and he measures it by the simple device of the number of questions answered with an opinion instead of a "don't know" in a battery of semi-projective questions that ask people to take the roles of others, such as:

If you were made editor of a newspaper, what kind of a paper would you run?
Suppose that you were made head of the government. What are some of the things you would do?
If for some reason, you could not live in our country, what other country would you choose to live in?

On the basis of the index of empathy, in combination with certain other key characteristics, Lerner sorts the respondents into five basic types:

Modern: literate, urban, high media participation, high empathy
Transitional:
A. Non-literate, urban, high media participation, high empathy
B. Non-literate, rural, high media participation, high empathy
C. Non-literate, low media participation, high empathy
Traditional: non-literate, rural, low media participation, low empathy

Note that the transitional individuals are persons who are beginning to leave the complete mental isolation of the village but only by partial steps: they may still live in the village, but they show an interest in the outside world and develop opinions about it. Once this interest is aroused, they tend to pay attention to the mass-media, particularly the radio and the cinema. The next step is for them (or their children) to learn to read and perhaps eventually to migrate to the city. There are not many cases of Type B in most villages, but they are of very great importance for they are carriers of the new viewpoints and have much influence on their neighbors.

The contrasting viewpoints of dwellers in the old society and participants in the new are vividly shown by some quotations from the interviews (pp. 319-345):

Bedouins believe that having to travel far from one's country and relatives and friends is a curse that descends from the forefathers to the child. . . . We Bedouins don't need the cinema. Those who go are not real men. They are useless and have lost all value of morals. . . . Those who read are politicians and trouble seekers. If you don't read you are far away from trouble and the government. . . . The U. S.? What is it? Where is it? . . . We don't like to hear about war in far away countries. When Bedouins start a fight among themselves, they never bother other people about it. So why should we bother about what other countries have to go through whether in war or peace. . . . I am interested in news about my household and my camel because these are my life and my link with this world. I don't care for anything else because what is outside my concern I am not supposed to care for.

Radio is a very good friend at home who is very loyal and useful. I consider it my best friend. . . . Movies are the best means of communicating a people's culture and civilization to the other parts of the world. It is a mirror of a country's advance in life. Movies are one of the modern means of entertainment which is quite indispensable as a part of our daily life. I couldn't imagine how flat life would be without the movies. It has become very essential that everybody should go to movies and learn many things about the secrets of life.

Lerner suggests that much of the instability in the Near East can be linked to a development process which is out of phase and has not achieved harmonious rates of progress among its interrelated elements. For example, in some areas the authority of the village elders has been weakened but no new elite has arisen which is tied to the national scene but keeps roots in the local villages and offers an alternative to the traditional elders as a source of guidance and support. In other places, an urban elite of university graduates has emerged before there are places for them in the new division of labor— lacking jobs and a future, they are a source of revolutionary agitation. In some countries, urbanization has moved too fast, for the rural excess population flocks to cities which have no industries and therefore no jobs.

Lerner's book is a rich collection of data, insights, and theories. Unfortunately, they are not well put together, for the surveys in the various countries were originally analyzed separately by different interpreters, and Lerner does not succeed in completely unifying the results. Furthermore, Lerner tries to present between two covers a general theory of development, a series of case studies of six countries in flux, and a report of a specific sample survey. Nobody could have synthesized all of this into a neat monograph. But nobody else raises such pointed questions about the role of communications and of self-image in the transition from village identity to national consciousness.

New Division of Labor

An urban population supported by industrial and commercial activity develops a division of labor markedly different from that of a rural population. The latter contains farmers plus a very few specialists (artisans, merchants, priests, soldiers, governors). The former contains thousands of different specialists (the United States Government catalogues over 20,000 in the Dictionary of Occupational Titles) whose existence is dependent upon an intricate system of exchange which integrates the labor of bricklayer, machine-tool maker, automobile assembly worker, and clerk, so that all end up with complete houses and automobiles. The occupational division of labor is the economically determined skeleton on which the flesh of modern social organization develops; it is somewhat analogous in function to the kinship system which is the base of much of primitive society. Therefore we can use the division of labor as a convenient index of the degree of industrialization-urbanization reached by any given society—it is probably the most meaningful index for sociological purposes.

The division of labor is conventionally portrayed by two distributions: that among branches of activity (industry, agriculture, and services, including commerce), and that among socioeconomic levels (professionals, clerks, laborers, etc.). Let us examine both measures. If we use the historical experience of the United States as a model (and it appears that other countries tend to follow the same general trends), we find that economic development involves a steady shift from an early period in which agricultural labor predominates, with a secondary emphasis upon industry and services, to an intermediate period in which there is a shift from agriculture into both industry and services in equal proportions, to a later period of maturity when industry stops growing and the remaining shift is from agriculture into services. In other words, there appears to be a limit upon the need for industrial labor, for as the system matures the machines get more efficient and increases in production can be obtained without increases in manpower.[13] However, services cannot so easily be mechanized, and they continue to absorb excess agricultural workers. The data for the United States since 1860 are given in Table 1-1.

Table 1-1.
American Labor Force, by Type of Activity, 1860-1950

| | PERCENT OF LABOR FORCE | | |
	1860	1900	1950
Agriculture, fishing, and forestry	59	38	12
Industry, construction, and mining	20	30	33
Services (professional, administrative, transport, and commerce)	20	31	53
Other	1	1	2
Total	100%	100%	100%
Number in labor force	10,530,000	29,070,000	56,239,000

Sources: *Historical Statistics of U. S. 1789-1945*, p. 64; *Statistical Abstract of U. S.* (1954), p. 208.

If we turn our attention to the distribution by socioeconomic levels, we get a complementary picture (see Table 1-2). Here we notice that as the industrial system matures, there is a greater need for professional and tech-

[13] Colin Clark, *The Conditions of Economic Progress* (London: Macmillan, 1957).

nical people (they almost tripled in proportion from 1870 to 1950), and for clerks and salesmen (they increased fivefold). There is a smaller need for more workers at the semi-skilled level (they doubled). The skilled workers increased by a still smaller amount (about fifty percent), and the unskilled workers not at all. Thus there is a constant up-grading of the labor force as the system matures: from blue-collar to white-collar work, from lower levels to higher levels of technical competence.

Table 1-2.

American Labor Force, by Socio-Economic Level, 1870-1950

| | PERCENT OF LABOR FORCE | |
	1870	1950
Professional persons	3	9
Proprietors, managers, and officials		
farmers	24	7
others	6	9
Clerks, salespeople, and kindred	4	19
Skilled workers and foremen	9	14
Semiskilled workers	10	22
Unskilled workers		
farm laborers	29	4
laborers, except farm	9	8
servant classes	6	6
Not reported	—	2
Total	100%	100%
Number in labor force	12,924,000	56,239,000
Percent of labor force, female	15%	30%
Total population	39,818,000	150,697,000

Source: Joseph A. Kahl, *The American Class Structure* (New York, Holt, Rinehart and Winston, 1957), p. 67; based on the U.S. Census.

The implications of these shifts in the labor force are far-reaching. For instance, it becomes less likely that a boy will become a farmer like his father and learn his occupation within the family context; instead, he follows a personal career and prepares for it by going to school, and that takes him out of the home (and often away from the community) and thus weakens the family while it strengthens the system of formal education. Furthermore, since many urban occupations are open to women, they are no longer thought of solely as daughters, wives and mothers, but become individuals who can pursue careers.

Finally, the interactions of city life become, as was suggested above, contacts between specialists acting in their occupational roles rather than human beings as total personalities. If the trading of the marketplace is the framework for the interaction, cold-blooded rationality and pursuit of personal gain will come to the fore. If entrepreneurship in long range enterprises based on substantial capital is the focus, then attitudes of planning, of husbanding of resources, of efficiency in the use of expensive time and equipment will predominate. If bureaucratic organization is emphasized, the relationships between people will take on the coloration of attention to the rules, limitation of authority to the specifics of the job, a conservative and cautious approach toward life.[14] If the interaction is between professional and client, then the traditions of intellectual mastery, of pride, of devotion to the traditions of the professional group and its ethics will largely govern behavior.[15] If assembly-line workers are observed, a routinization of behavior and a psychological alienation from work will be noted. In general, the more specialized the job is, the more bureaucratized the organizational context in which it occurs, and the bigger the price tag on the product or service, the more narrowly is the interaction likely to be confined to the business at hand.

We can explore some of the implications of a changing division of labor through recent research reports on areas that are currently industrializing.

The best survey of new industrial workers that we have was produced by faculty and students of the University of Dacca (East Pakistan). The fact that it was executed by unpaid volunteers in a short space of time shows what can be done with limited resources under powerful leadership. The study was directed in 1953-54 by A. F. A. Husain and reported in his two volumes entitled: *Human and Social Impact of Technological Change in Pakistan*, 1956. The first volume tells of the statistical survey; the second contains sixty-eight case studies, averaging some four pages in length, which summarize the results of open-ended interviews with workers representing various types of adjustment to industrial impact: those who have moved from farm to factory, those whose traditional crafts were displaced by factory production and who may or may not have themselves taken up factory labor, those who continue to work the farms but in areas where factories have entered, etc. The cases are often referred to as illustrations of statistical findings, an innovation in method worthy of emulation.

East Pakistan is just starting its industrialization: of its forty-two million people, over eighty percent are agriculturalists. The dominant pattern of life is village life, often on lands that have been tilled by ancestors for many generations. But population is increasing rapidly, and many families

---

[14] Robert K. Merton, "Bureaucratic Structure and Personality" in his *Social Theory and Social Structure* (New York: Free Press, 1949), pp. 195-206.

[15] Talcott Parsons, "The Professions and Social Structure," *Social Forces*, 17 (May, 1939); reprinted in his *Essays in Sociological Theory* (New York: Free Press, 1949), pp. 185-199.

who are landless, or whose fields are inadequate to support them, are sending sons to seek paid employment. The most progressive and educated of these are the ones who end up in factories.

Husain surveyed the workers in nineteen factories of various types, some located in cities and others in rural areas. For the most part, these factories were large establishments which processed agricultural products: cotton, jute, rubber, etc. About half were newly established since the partition of India and Pakistan in 1947, the rest having a longer history. In each factory, 3.5 percent of the workers were chosen on a random basis and were interviewed from a fixed schedule. In addition, the bicycle-rickshaw drivers of Dacca were sampled (by a less formal method). In all, the sample included 471 workers and 90 drivers.

Only a quarter of the workers came from villages close to the factory where they worked; the rest travelled great distances to find work. Less than ten percent of these men had fathers who were industrial workers. Most of the workers were young men under thirty-five, four-fifths were Muslims, and slightly more than one-half were literate (compared to 20 percent of the total population). Most workers were assisted in getting jobs by a relative or fellow-villager who already worked in the factory. They were trained in a haphazard manner, often just by standing next to their relatives and watching.

Slightly over one-half of the workers were living away from their families (despite the fact that seventy percent of those living away from their families were married). Those who lived with their families were mostly those who worked in factories within commuting distance of their native villages. Thus the predominant pattern of this labor force is one of young men, mostly married, who leave their homes in order to earn money. Their wives and children are taken care of under the joint-family system, for eighty percent of the workers belonged to such joint families made up of brothers and often the father, together with their respective wives and small children, all living in a single household. The workers sent remittances of about one-third of their pay home to help support their families. Only in the relatively rare instances where a worker took his wife and small children away from the village and to the factory site did the joint-family system disintegrate.

A recurring theme in Husain's report is the ease with which this new industrial labor force was recruited (essentially as a result of overpopulation on the land, for those with enough land preferred to remain farmers) and the small amount of change in social life that followed the switch to factory employment. The joint-family system, deep belief in religion and execution of its responsibilities in prayer and in daily life, a conservative, peasant outlook on life permeated with fatalism—all of these continued for the majority of workers. Yet the seeds of more radical change were planted. There were some workers, particularly those who took their spouses with them to the city, who began to change their outlook. They weakened in religious belief (at least they modernized their religious views and ceased to follow the detailed instructions of reactionary religious leaders). They reported that contact with many other workers had stimulated their minds and showed them the "stupidity" of merely following tradition. They believed in the practicality of the nuclear as against the joint family, and a few began to practice birth control. They learned new methods of cooperation through union activity. They began to plan and to agitate for a better future rather than accept what fate might bring.

And even in the villages where the conservative social structures continued to operate without much alteration, some changes were beginning. People saw that educated men got better factory jobs, and a general belief in the value of education (even for women) was growing. Literacy brought contact with the outside world and with modern medicine and science, weakening the belief in some aspects of tradition.

Husain's report on East Pakistan is convincing evidence of the degree to which early industrialization is compatible with much of family-centered and village-centered traditionalism.[16] But it also suggests that when people move permanently to the city more radical changes begin, for without a close tie to the land and the total village community, the older social structures weaken.

Some thirty-three studies of the effects of wage-labor on social life in Africa have recently been summarized by Merran McCulloch.[17] He indicates that there are important variations from one region to another, especially with respect to the policies of the various colonial powers and to the proportion of white men in the different populations. Nevertheless, there are striking similarities stemming from the universal problems arising from the imposition of colonial rule upon native peoples. The colonial powers at first were interested in the profits from mines and from plantation agriculture. They needed abundant supplies of cheap native labor. The workers were recruited at times by force but more frequently by the establishment of head and hut taxes which had to be paid in cash. Young men left the villages to work for a period of a few years in the mines and on the plantations to earn enough money to pay the taxes for their families. They worked, therefore, *as representatives of the group*, and they went home as soon as possible. They lived on the job in male barracks, and were either unmarried or would leave their wives in the villages, for the fields had to be tilled at home and there was no work for women in the mines. This system has been in operation for two or three generations, and is wide-

---

[16] For a detailed study of how a single factory can enter a well-organized village community and find ways of accommodating to its culture with few disrupting effects, see Manning Nash, *Machine Age Maya, The Industrialization of a Guatemalan Community* (New York: Free Press, 1958).

[17] International African Institute, London, *Social Implications of Industrialization and Urbanization in Africa South of the Sahara* (Paris: UNESCO, 1956).

spread throughout Negro Africa; indeed, the migration is often across colonial frontiers.

In recent years, however, the system has started to change. The natives have learned new tastes which depend upon money and they thus demand cash beyond the needs of taxes—cash for clothing, cigarettes, beer, bicycles, sewing machines, phonographs. In many areas, the traditional "bride-wealth" paid by the groom to his father-in-law has been changed from cattle (contributed by the relatives of the groom) to cash (usually earned primarily by the young man himself). In some areas, increasing population is creating a pressure on the land that "pushes" people out. Furthermore, increasing proportions of the natives are going to work in the towns and cities rather than on the mines and plantations, and some of them want to stay once they have tasted the joys of city life. The trade and service industries of the cities, the political staffs centered in them, and the emerging light consumer-goods industries which they stimulate, all demand a different type of labor. They need workers who are more educated, more skilled, and more stable. A three-year hitch by an ignorant boy from the bush may be a suitable system for hiring a miner or possibly an unskilled factory hand, but it does not work for an automobile mechanic, a teacher, or a clerk.

The United Nations estimates that about six percent of the Africans south of the Sahara currently live in large cities of over 20,000, though many more live in them from time to time. In 1953, some five million workers (out of a population of some 160 million) were dependent upon wages for their livelihoods.[18] About 38 percent of these were in the Union of South Africa and another 17 percent in the Belgian Congo. Moreover, some 50 percent of the men in most areas were thought to be dependent upon wages during some period of their lives.

The cities are growing so fast that it is not unusual to find that three-quarters of the inhabitants were born elsewhere (in smaller towns or villages). Furthermore, these are usually male cities, with a very high disproportion of men over women, and they are young cities, with the bulk of the population being young men between 15 and 45. There are few children, few women, few old people. McCulloch writes:[19]

Some children are brought up in the country and then come to town; others know no other environment except the town; numbers of young men and women live between two worlds; others are settled in towns; old people remain in the country and become increasingly estranged from their children. Perhaps one of the most fundamental results of this situation is that it hinders the emergence of an urban public opinion—which would set norms of behavior between the sexes, within the family, and within the community.

[18] United Nations, *Report on the World Social Situation* (New York, 1957).
[19] International African Institute, *op. cit.*, p. 210.

Some details on life in one of these new towns can be had from a survey made in Jinja, Uganda, by Cyril and Rhona Sofer, 1955. Jinja grew from 8,400 to 20,800 persons in the few years from 1948 to 1951. It had a high proportion of males to females, and most of the men did not anticipate permanent settlement. There were almost 15,000 Africans (some 5,000 Asians, and about 800 Europeans. The latter dominated the administrative positions in government and business, and also included some skilled workers (especially those brought in to aid in the construction of a new dam which was to supply cheap electric power). The Asians dominated trade and many of the skilled and clerical occupations. The Africans occupied the lower-level jobs. This racial division tended (despite protestations that only skill mattered) to create job ceilings which limited the advancement, and consequently the motivation, of most of the Africans and some of the Asians.

The Sofers conducted a sample survey which included 15 percent of the African households, 33 percent of the Asian, and all of the European. They found that four percent of the Africans were professional and clerical workers, six percent traders, thirty percent artisans, forty-five percent unskilled, six percent military or police, and nine percent held other types of jobs. Regarding age and sex, three-quarters of the Africans were between 16 and 45; two-thirds were men. About half of the men were married, but 40 percent of the wives were still living in the villages. The men came to town to earn tax and bride money, plus cash for a few simple objects useful on the farm, but, once there, they found that food alone took more than 70 percent of their earnings, leaving little for saving. Furthermore:[20]

In the town horizons shift and standards are raised. The African who enters the town does so largely because of his need for an increased supply of cash to supplement the subsistence economy of his rural home, but he develops many new wants in the town for more or better Western-type goods and urban facilities. Many Western consumption items, such as soap, sugar, salt, have already become conventional necessities even in the countryside. To these are gradually added others such as lamps, paraffin, cycles, watches, cameras, brick houses and European-style clothing. Desires to possess these articles increase incentives to participate in the urban economy.

The single man who comes to town lives in a barracks with several men to a room, usually assigned according to the convenience of the landlord rather than the preferences of the tenants. Thus men from various regions and tribes become mixed. Later on, if he marries and brings a wife to town, he has difficulty in finding adequate quarters, and usually continues to think of himself as a temporary resident even though he may be in town

[20] Cyril and Rhona Sofer, *Jinja Transformed: A Social Survey of a Multi-Racial Township* (Kampala, Uganda: East African Institute of Social Research, 1955).

for many years. The result is poor care of housing and a lack of interest in local politics or community affairs. Even voluntary associations are lacking. Indeed, other than the immediate family which exists for a small portion of the men, the only social groupings of significance are informal networks of friends, clansmen and tribesmen who provide sociability and mutual assistance:[21]

Extending to aid in times of unemployment and illness, this informal system of help constitutes, in the absence of formal community agencies and of tightly integrated kinship groups, the basic form of "social security" locally available to the urban African.

The theme of the works thus far reported is that changes in the division of labor draw people from farming to urban jobs, and that wage-work has repercussions on the rest of life. Three areas of special importance will be noted below: education, social class, and family.

Education

A complex division of labor demands a system of formal education to prepare men for their jobs—apprenticeship is too conservative, too slow, too clumsy. Consequently, instead of walking beside his father at the plow, a young man prepares for life by going to school.

A modern school system, like modern industry, tends to emphasize norms of impersonal efficiency: promotion is based upon demonstrated performance. As industrialization proceeds and men begin to recognize the extent to which formal education is the key to their careers, the demand for schooling grows, as well as the feeling that it ought to be available to everybody regardless of his position in society. Thus the state is led to establish free public schools, and progressively to adapt their curricula from the old-fashioned subjects which were designed to perpetuate the traditional lore of the local culture among the upper classes (i.e., to prepare the elite for a life of leisure, or of governance or theology) to the new-fashioned subjects designed to prepare men for industrial and commercial careers.

Modern schools tend to separate young men from their fathers (in ideas and skills, if not in space); they lead the minds of the young outward from the locality to the nation; they teach a *personal* skill which can be sold anywhere. Such schools unfreeze the social class order by permitting, even encouraging, geographical and social mobility. They make inherited capital and inherited family status less important as the determinants of a man's career, and make intelligence, personality, and will-power more important.

[21] For additional details on factory labor in Jinja and in the near-by town of Kampala, see W. Elkan, *An African Labour Force* (Kampala, Uganda: East African Institute of Social Research, 1956). Probably the most detailed—and least synthesized—study of work in a new African city is the report on Stanleyville by Clement, Pons, and Xydias, International African Institute, *op. cit.*

Each level of education is designed to prepare students for an appropriate level in the occupational hierarchy. Thus, university education leads toward professional, technical and executive positions, secondary education toward skilled and clerical jobs, primary education toward semi- and unskilled jobs.

Mexican statistics show the extent of the transformation in education brought about by industrialization. In the old society before the revolution, the upper class sought literary education in Europe. Only a small number of professionals, mainly in the law, received university training in Mexico. Secondary schools were mostly private institutions which prepared a tiny segment of society for university education at home or abroad. The mass of the people were illiterate, for peasants needed no schooling.

In recent years, the entire school system has been changed. University training at home has gained in prestige, and the emphasis has shifted from literary toward technical and business subjects. Iturriaga[22] indicates that as many *titulos* (diplomas showing completion of a specialized university course often at the level of an American M.A. degree) were granted from 1938 to 1948 as in the whole period from 1901 to 1937. And notice these changes in subjects: 60 percent of the lawyers got their degrees in the earlier period, but over 80 percent of the chemical engineers and 95 percent of the economists graduated after 1937. In 1930, there was a medical doctor for every 3,451 persons in the nation; in 1950 there was a doctor for every 2,274 persons. In 1930, there were four small universities in the country; in 1948, there were twelve universities with a total enrollment of over 30,000 students. And, by 1954, the National University in Mexico City alone had 22,000 students, while the Instituto Politecnico in that city had an additional 5,000.[23]

Similarly, public secondary education has enormously expanded. Before the revolution, it was almost non-existent; in recent years, terminal secondary education has become the route to jobs at the level of skilled manual work and clerical positions. By 1950 there were 1,091 schools above the primary level with 176,000 students.[24]

Primary education is changing the character of lower-class life. The proportion of the population classified by the census as "alphabetized," or able to read and write, rose from 26 percent in 1900 to 57 percent in 1950. In 1930, there were 11,349 primary schools; in 1950, there were 24,075 of them, serving three million students (who constituted about one-half of the children in the country between the ages of 6 and 14; most children now start school, but the drop-out rate in the first few years is very high[25]).

The educational levels of the Mexican and the American people are

22 Jose E. Iturriaga, *op. cit.*, p. 178.
23 *Annuario Estadistico*, Mexico, 1954, pp. 282-287.
24 *Annuario Estadistico*, Mexico, 1951-52, pp. 228-308.
25 *Ibid.*

compared in Table 1-3, which shows the number of years of schooling completed by the population over 25 years of age in 1950. A little over one percent of the Mexicans had some college training, versus eleven percent of the Americans; an additional five percent of the Mexicans had gone to secondary school, versus twenty-nine percent of the Americans. Mexico is making educational progress, but the demands of an industrial society will force her to go much further.

Table 1-3.
Years of School Completed, Persons 25 Years of Age or More
(Mexico, Mexican Federal District [Mexico City] and United States, 1950)

Years Completed	All Mexico	Federal District	Years Completed	United States
0	43%	16%	0-5	14%
1-6	45	60	5-6	11
7-9	3	9	7-8	35
10-12	2	6	9-11	15
13 or more	1	5	12	14
Unknown	6	4	13-15	6
			16 or more	5
Total 100%		100%		100%

Note: Mexican primary education extends from grades 1 through 6; secondary, through grade 9; college preparatory, through grade 11; university training in specialized careers begins with grade 12. U.S. primary education extends from grades 1 through 8; secondary, through grade 12; university "general education," through grade 14; university training in specialized careers usually begins with grade 15.

Sources: *Censo General* (1950), *Resumen General*, p. 56; *Statistical Abstract of United States* (1953), p. 115.

In Africa, education for Negroes is just beginning, but the passion to obtain it is already intense. One pupil in the Belgian Congo said:[26]

I should be happiest of all if I could continue my studies. I think of this every night as I lie in bed counting the leaves in the roof of the room, I think of it all the time . . . for I see that I am slowly moving toward civilization.

The available education in the French and Belgian Congo regions is mostly limited to primary school (the first university is now being organized), and the teaching is usually under the control of Catholic missionaries. They still emphasize the older literary tradition in both content and method. The limitation on higher education leads many Africans to suspect that the whites do not wish to "reveal all their secrets" to the natives. But

[26] International African Institute, *op. cit.*, p. 333.

once schools are established, the natives are quick to respond, for they wish to learn the secrets, to move toward civilization, and to obtain better jobs. Miss Xydias, in her report on Stanleyville, writes:[27]

School attendance is gradually taking its place among the customs of the Congo. Whereas formerly the children came forward at 9, 10 or 12 years of age, a marked change has been recorded during the last few years. In Stanleyville they are now brought to school at the age of six or seven, and on enrollment day the parents queue up at dawn outside the director's office to make sure of a place for their children. All teachers in the town testify to the regular attendance of their pupils; those absenting themselves without due cause are rare. *To a far higher degree than in Europe*, the young folk of all ages are fired with a keen desire to learn [italics added].

Social Classes

A truly "primitive" society has no class system: all families live at about the same socioeconomic level. As agricultural production grows, and the society transforms itself into a settled, peasant-type of structure, a surplus of food is produced which is used to support landlords, priests, and rulers. Ordinarily, there exist only two classes: those who work with their hands, and those who engage in administrative or ritual activities and enjoy leisure. There may exist the germs of an in-between group of clerks and merchants who are aids to the leisure class, but they are relatively insignificant.

The development of a commercial civilization enormously expands the role of trade and thus the in-between group grows into an independent middle class. Industrialization speeds this process for it increases the flow of goods which are traded, it up-grades many hand-workers into skilled machine-tenders who have middle-class educations and incomes, and it produces enough surplus wealth to support many people in service activities which enrich the leisure hours of the majority of the people rather than just the upper class.

The new industrial class order is divided into a series of groupings which overlap with one another; there are no sharp divisions, and the terms we use such as "upper class," "middle class," and "working class" are but convenient rubrics, rather than precisely denotative classifications. There are gradations of occupation, education, and life-style within each broad class, and there is considerable mobility from one level to another. Instead of the great gap between landlord and peasant, we get the series of small gaps between the factory worker, skilled laborer, foreman, engineer, plant manager, and company president, with young workers aspiring to be foremen and young engineers dreaming of the presidency. This series of small gradations means that communication from one level to another is easier

[27] *Ibid.*

and class-consciousness is weaker. Marx was wrong: industrial capitalism does not simplify the class order into two antagonistic groups, but rather makes it much more complex.

Stable city life is dependent upon a social class system. Public opinion in cities—that substitute for firm tradition maintained by the social controls of an homogeneous village—is never a single entity, but rather a series of opinions, each adapted to the needs of a given class level, and supported by networks of overlapping cliques which articulate basic values and teach them to new members. Ideals of family life (including the size of family desired), patterns of expected education for children, attitudes toward work and career, modes of consumption in matters of dress, food, house furnishings, and to some extent religious and political beliefs, all these emerge within the framework of relatively homogeneous strata of society which share a given level of education and a given type of job and income. The conversations of men on the job, and women and children in the area of residence (which is segregated by ecological competition according to income), create an appropriate style of life or class subculture.

The changing class pattern in Mexico has been analyzed through the use of occupational and income statistics by Iturriaga. Unfortunately, his data (shown in Table 1-4) go only to 1940, and it is likely that there has been as much change in the 19 years since as in the 45 years preceding that date.

Table 1-4.
Mexican Social Class Distribution, 1895 and 1940

	1895	1940
Upper Class		
urban	0.4%	0.6%
rural	1.0	0.5
total	(1.4)	(1.1)
Middle Class		
urban	6.1	12.0
rural	1.7	3.8
total	(7.8)	(15.8)
Lower Class		
urban	14.2	22.4
rural	76.6	60.7
total	(90.8)	(83.1)
Total	100.0%	100.0%

Source: Jose E. Iturriaga, *La Estructura Social y Cultural de México*, Fondo de Cultura Economica, México, 1951, p. 28.

As a result of the revolution, the power of the rural upper class—a small number of families who owned great plantations or *haciendas*—was broken; many fled to the city and some succeeded in reinvesting a portion of their capital in new commercial enterprises. In recent years, a new upper class of big businessmen has grown, but their point of view looks forward to further industrial growth rather than backward toward the maintenance of a life of leisure based on rent.

The middle class in Mexico doubled from 1895 to 1940, according to Iturriaga's calculations. This means that there were far more people with secondary and university educations, with steady incomes derived from profits, salaries, and professional fees, and with standards of consumption which offered a regular market for industrial goods and for sophisticated services.

The lower class decreased in size and shifted toward urban concentration. Generally, the urban proletariat are a bit better educated and have a slightly higher level of consumption than their peasant cousins.

Shifts in the distribution of the population among the class levels are of considerable importance. For one thing, it is misleading to calculate the consumption gains from industrialization and to ignore this factor. One cannot compare the lot of peasants in 1905 with peasants in 1940, or of clerks in 1895 with clerks in 1940, and get the full picture of the change that has occurred (indeed, when inflation is considered, some groups are not a great deal better off now than they were then). One must realize that there are, relatively speaking, a lot more clerks and a lot fewer peasants than there used to be. Furthermore, shifts in class distributions open up new markets for industrial goods (e.g., peasants drink native brews, city people drink bottled beer and Coca-Cola), they shift the balance of political power,[28] they change the "tone" of a culture by altering education, taste, even the style of interpersonal relations.

So far, there has been a very slow emergence of class differences among Negro, urban Africans. The cities are new, the populations include many transients, the old people tend to remain in the villages. The net result is what McCulloch called the lack of an "urban public opinion."

An additional reason for the amorphousness of social class differences in Africa is the widespread backwardness of women. Education is primarily for men, and is thought of as preparing them for jobs. Women are usually illiterate and are more likely to engage in petty trade than to work for wages. Consequently, an educated man who becomes a skilled clerk finds it hard to secure a wife who can be a good companion, who can intelligently budget the use of money, who can entertain his friends, who can

---

[28] For an account of the effects of class changes on politics in Latin America, see Merle Kling, "Towards a Theory of Power and Political Instability in Latin America," *Western Political Science Quarterly*, **9** (March, 1956), 21-35.

create the kind of home that the husband thinks is appropriate to his new status (one that is modeled after European middle-class patterns).

Of course, the continuing attempts in many areas by the European masters to limit Negro workers to low-level tasks in order to preserve European superiority is a basic fact which prevents the emergence of a fully differentiated class structure. In South Africa, even the skilled trades are reserved, where possible, for white men, and until recently higher education and professional careers in French and Belgian Africa were closed to Negroes.

The struggles in Africa for a class culture and a personal sense of identity—and the two are closely linked—are well portrayed by Georges Balandier in *Sociologie des Brazzavilles Noires*, 1955. This book, like most of those reported here, is a general survey of a new city, and contains demographic statistics, a sampling of public opinion, a comparison of aspects of town culture with surrounding village culture, a history of the city, etc. But Balandier adds something more: considerable attention to detailed case studies with attention to the changing attitudes of citizens who are becoming urbanized—what he calls the "psychological" approach. Balandier focusses upon the *évolués*, the evolved natives who seek an entirely urban way of life. He writes (p. 235):

The *évolué* can be defined as an individual projected outside of his customary milieu by reason of a system of education in which he finds himself or by reason of his participation in economic and administrative processes established by the colonizer, conscious of the fundamental changes taking place in his milieu, and becoming suspect by the elders of his own society, and by European society, as a result of his modernist spirit.

The *évolué* is a man in search of a self-image. He looks up to European culture as being "advanced"; he looks down upon village culture as being "backward, uncivilized, outmoded." But he learns of European culture through a language, studied in school, which never becomes fully comfortable. He has as his models Europeans who are playing the special role of "colonizer" and thus do not behave as they would at home. Furthermore, those Europeans do not accept him as an equal regardless of his degree of acculturation. For instance, every new group activity is scrutinized by the colonial officials for possible "subversive" political tendencies. And many of the European modes of behavior are not functional in a tropical town that lacks a firm economic base. Thus the *évolué* is constantly seeking and never fully finding; he has turned his back on one culture and is unable— in fact, not allowed—to create an adequate new one by imitation or by invention.

Balandier sketches the plight of the advanced native with warm insight; unfortunately, he does not give a systematic account of the new culture which is being created (weak though it may be) because he concentrates upon the difficulties more than the successes, and he emphasizes the disintegration of the old more than the reintegration of the new. I say this despite his many pages on new urban associations—occupational, religious, political—for what he fails to do is to show how these combine to create a social system for the urbanized individual which has a sense of pattern comparable to the pattern of kinship in the village.

The problem of the *évolué* is ordinarily the problem of a nascent middle class. The working-class individual is less likely to move so far from the native culture, for he has less education, and his job is precarious and provides little income beyond the needs of barest subsistence according to the native pattern. It is only when some individuals gain more education and have an economic stake in the new order which really promises something substantial that they begin to turn their backs upon the old ways and seek to identify with the new ones.

Once class culture begins to appear, it is passed on from one generation to the next. Thus sons born of urban fathers, and especially of urban middle-class fathers, have a great advantage in the occupational world over sons born in the rural villages. The report on Stanleyville, previously cited, gives us a rare statistic on African occupational inheritance:[29] 43 percent of the white-collar men, 26 percent of the skilled and semiskilled men, but only 16 percent of the unskilled men had fathers who were wage earners rather than subsistence cultivators. The white-collar men, incidentally, earned three times as much as the unskilled men; and 83 percent of the former, but only 14 percent of the latter, had achieved four or more years of schooling.

Expectations of an Increasing Standard of Living

Partly because of the new wealth produced by industrial techniques, partly because of the greater fluidity in the class system which encourages people to try to move up in the hierarchy and thereby redistribute existing wealth, there grows among men in modern societies an expectation of a constantly increasing standard of living. This is a radical shift: in the old society, the consumption standards were fixed for each segment of the hierarchy, and men did not expect to move from bottom to top. Good times were times when the customary standard could be reached; bad times were times when a man was unable to live the way he and his parents had always lived. A fixed expectation induced a man to work hard until the customary level of income was achieved; after that, he rested, and he was likely to be satisfied whatever the actual income happened to be.

Modern man is constantly expecting more. New gadgets are invented, and advertising turns them from novelties into necessities. If a man has a "lower-middle" income, he begins to reach for an "upper-middle" income.

[29] International African Institute, *op. cit.*, p. 267.

To be satisfied implies a lack of ambition, an acceptance of failure. Much of the emotional restlessness of modern society stems from this new notion of a constant increase in consumption goods, as well as much of the drive that makes man work hard and produce much. Under the new conditions, political and social unrest cannot be thought of as results of "poverty," for there is no fixed line between "poverty" and "plenty." Dissatisfaction, rather, stems from a discrepancy between what people have and what they want and feel they are entitled to, and the impact of industrialization raises standards of expectation at a very rapid pace—often faster than production itself goes up. Thus, we see the paradox: the more people get, the more they demand.[30]

The Family[31]

In general, urban-industrial society is conducive to the nuclear rather than the extended-family system; it tends to equalize the power of the sexes and the generations; it reduces the economic functions performed by the nuclear family to a minimum, and instead centers it upon sex, companionship, and the socialization of the very young. Let us examine these trends and their causes in some detail, and also note certain exceptions and countertrends.

In African rural life, the domestic unit frequently consists of more than one nuclear family. The members of the extended family cooperate in herding or agriculture, in the raising and distribution of the dowry or bride-wealth that permits young people to marry (thereby uniting not just individuals but family lines), in religious ceremonies (including ancestor worship), in the education of adolescents and its symbolization in *rites-de-passage*, in social control which keeps individuals from straying from the path of customary virtue, in political organization. All of these activities are based on the assumption that the crucial family members (the lineage, howsoever it be defined, and the spouses of its members) live and work in the same area; through the structure of kinship is organized the life of a homogeneous community. There results a strong sense of kin obligation and dependence: one shares with his relatives, one grows strong and safe through having many family ties that are actively functioning. One submits to family discipline because it pays off (and because there is no alternative).

At first, the urban migrant clings to the old family values. Indeed, he often goes to the city as a young man to raise money for his parents and expects to send cash home at regular intervals. But he quickly finds that the cost of housing and food absorbs most of his income, leaving little for remittance home. If he stays in the town and learns a skill which brings a

[30] The early stages of adaptation to modern habits of consumption are discussed by Elizabeth E. Hoyt, "The Impact of a Money Economy on Consumption Patterns," *Annals of American Academy of Political and Social Science*, **305** (May, 1956), 12-22.

[31] This section has greatly benefited from my conversations with my colleague Irving Kaplan.

higher income, he may be able to get a wife and settle down as an urbanite. Then he finds that rural relatives expect him to house them without pay when they come to town for a visit or a job; sometimes they send their children to him for schooling, or he sends his young children to the village to keep them from being "spoiled" by the undisciplined ways of city youth.

As long as it manages to stay alive during the period of transition from rural to urban life, this system of kinship obligations has several effects: it slows down the emergence of class differences, for wealthier men are called upon to give more to their relatives than are poorer ones; it blurs the distinctions between town life and village life, for it stimulates interchange between them; it serves as a system of social security providing benefits during times of illness or unemployment. *Particularly during the period of transition*, while individuals brought up in the villages are trying to adjust to the demands of the city, are they likely to lean upon the family for help. Jean Comhaire stresses this theme in "Economic Change and the Extended Family"[32] and shows the continuing strength of certain family ties. Indeed, he suspects that these will continue beyond the period of transition, but the evidence he cites mainly concerns behavior which shows a way of life which is partly rural, partly urban. He says that often the bride-wealth continues to be expressed in cattle, and the urban dweller is dependent upon his rural relatives for care of the beasts. He indicates that often the young man expects his kinsmen to help him raise the necessary price for a bride (but note that Mair, below, stresses the increasing tendency for the groom to raise the price himself and pay it entirely in cash). Cohaire continues:[33]

In Leopoldville, the capital of the Belgian Congo, the growth of the nuclear family and of a native middle class is impeded by low wages as well as by the absence of private property for African residents. The extended family thus remains a necessary institution for security and for educational and religious purposes. The newcomer in town and the unemployed both expect from their cousins some help, which they will be prepared to return when fortune changes. Children born in town are often sent to relatives in the rural home who can more easily take care of them and who educate them in customs which include the recognition of kinship ties up to the level of ancestor worship. On the other hand, prosperous native farmers send their children to Leopoldville, where they receive school education while staying with relatives. Urban social life centers around *matanga*, week-long funeral proceedings which include both rites and entertainment, and to whose considerable cost distant relatives must contribute.

As time passes, kinship obligations are put under more and more strain. They grew out of a village way of life which integrated all the institutions into a functioning equilibrium. That integration weakens in the city *because the wage job is an individualistic affair, and because the members of the kin-group no longer live close together*. A man eventually comes to feel

[32] *Annals of American Academy of Political and Social Science*, **305** (May, 1956).
[33] *Ibid.*, p. 47.

that his wage income belongs to him and his wife and children, and he resists the claims of relatives. This process is described by L. P. Mair in "African Marriage and Social Change," a summary of many field studies:[34]

On the basis of the existing evidence it is possible to discern certain general trends. Many of these can be correlated with the general increase in freedom from control by personal authority which can be seen in every sphere of African life. This arises directly from the fact that the African village is no longer an almost isolated, self-contained world, within which each member is dependent on the good-will of the rest and must secure it by conformity with accepted rules, and which he cannot leave without considerable danger. The African of today depends for his material needs at least as much on sources of income outside the village as on the cooperation of his family and kinsmen, and colonial rule has established law and order which make it safe for him to leave his village, and means of communication which make it easy.

One consequence of this situation is that marriage is becoming increasingly a matter of personal choice rather than an arrangement between groups in which the elders have a dominant say. . . .

Where the marriage is made legal by a payment, the husband is coming more and more to be expected to provide for this from his own resources. . . . The substitution of cash for some or all of the gifts or services included in the marriage formalities has often had the consequence of introducing a mercenary element that was not present in the old days. . . .

The family found in the towns is usually the elementary family. Circumstances rarely make it possible for a wider group of kinsfolk to live in close contact. As a result, the influence of the "family council" in maintaining the stability of the marriage is weakened or even removed. There is no longer any organization outside the family for inculcating accepted rules and values in the next generation, and it is difficult for the family to meet this need when mothers as well as fathers have to earn money. . . .

Balandier, in the book previously cited, also stresses the weakening of kinship ties under the impact of urban individualism, and adds the further point that this tends to undermine the entire traditional social structure, for it was closely tied to kinship. Once resident in the city, the young man is offered many choices between a variety of alternatives which did not exist before. He can choose his work, his place of residence, his friends, his wife; the authority of the elders to control his life is broken. Balandier writes:[35]

We think that the determining fact, in the urban milieu, is the destruction (or alteration) of the framework of the family in which the individual is placed—even when he keeps some contact with his original kinship group. For kinship structures remain, in central Africa, above all after the reduction in number

[34] Arthur Phillips, ed., *Survey of African Marriage and Family Life* (London: Oxford University Press, 1953), pp. 152-155.
[35] Georges Balandier, *Cahiers de la fondation nationale des sciences politiques,* "Sociologie des Brazzavilles Noires," no. 67 (Paris: Armand Colin, 1955).

and efficacy of specialized associations, the social framework that defines and regulates traditional groups and behavior. In dislocating the family, urban society alters, then ruins, the last support of the traditional cultures. We have shown . . . how extended family groups only have a provisional existence and tend to create isolated, nuclear families. It is a movement that is part of the general "process of individualization" that the city creates and makes predominant. The fact of having to hire out one's capacity to work for money . . . plus the fact of the shortage of women . . . turn marriage and the relations between the sexes into individual more than group affairs. . . . Finally, the shrinking of social bonds—the solitude of the city—leaves to the individual a large range of choice with regard to new groupings that he may join which lack any element of constraint. . . . This double movement of weakening family and of general individualization is transforming the ancient cultures.

A recent monograph probably offers more detail than any other on the changing family pattern in urban Africa: Georges Forthomme, *Mariage et Industrialisation*, 1957. It is a study of railroad workers in Elisabethville, Belgian Congo, conducted in 1952. Forthomme gives minute descriptions of the various customs connected with birth, adolescence, courtship, marriage, divorce, and death as they were practiced in traditional village environments among the surrounding Baluba tribal peoples, and then offers point-by-point contrasts from the current trends in the city. Unfortunately, his data appear to be based on a limited number of informants who describe how things are "usually" done—there is insufficient information on the range of variation; furthermore, a list of traits does not always produce a picture of the urban family as a functioning institution.

Forthomme points out that the patrilineal clan structure and patrilocal extended-family ties begin to weaken the moment an individual moves out of the ancestral village to go to work in the city. Nevertheless, such individuals continue to follow many of the practices they had learned as children; the fundamental changes come among those who are born and reared in the urban environment (p. 17):

In the city, children grow up in groups that are not based on tribe or clan membership. Friendships are founded not only in the neighborhood but also in school. A friend is chosen according to certain common interests, and becomes a person in whom one can confide, from whom one expects aid in times of difficulty. With him, a helping hand is not so much an obligation but rather a sign of affection. When one can surround himself with such true friends, why sacrifice for a group that uses the tie of blood to put one at their mercy? It is not just a question of an exchange of services with clan members, but the fact that the aid they usually demand is in the form of money, that thing so hard to obtain, which is lost once it is loaned to a relative.

Besides, the elders use the blood tie in order to impose their authority. But that right can be asserted only in the age-group that recognizes it. That authority was justified formerly by all knowledge resulting from experience, but currently the occupational opportunities permit a young man to have a social role almost as important as that of an elder.

Such are the changing conceptions of those who are currently forming families. Although not excluding his parents, the modern young man primarily considers his family to be made up of his wife and children. Without doubt, he still hears the mystical voice of the clan: exogamy remains a vigorous principle, and one dares not break certain tabus, but the rules that were the base of the old social order appear old-fashioned and are progressively abandoned.

The native of the city, regardless of his tribe, is proud of his young independence which was won by work outside of the clan context. He no longer counts on the clan and if, in important decisions, he consults his father, it is mainly a gesture of protocol for he expects his father's views to differ from his and he will follow his own inclinations. The cases of young people marrying against the wish of their parents are not rare.

Forthomme agrees with other observers of African life that the urban woman demands and receives much more independence from the authority of her husband (and before marriage, her parents) than does the rural woman. There is usually a shortage of women in the city, which gives them increased bargaining power; their ready contacts with other men during the day while their husbands are away at work offer them easy alternatives to spouses who may not satisfy; the possibilities of earning a living as a trader, a prostitute, or occasionally a factory worker or domestic servant free women from the economic necessity of having husbands. All of this means that women assert a greater degree of independence, including the right to easy divorce.

The mixture of young people of different tribal groups in the city leads to intermarriage. Forthomme reports that 17 percent of a sample of almost 2,000 married persons had crossed tribal lines; the percentage is higher in some other cities reported in the literature. Insofar as tribal customs vary, it is obvious that mixed marriages will show individualistic adaptation to current needs.

The most acculturated African sample discussed in the literature are the Zulu inhabitants of a government housing project in Durban, Natal, Union of South Africa. Almost all of the 118 households in the "Baumanville" project were interviewed in 1954 by a group from the Institute for Social Research of the University of Natal under the acting directorship of H. P. Pollack; the report was edited by Hallenbeck, 1955.[36]

Despite the fact that the people of Baumanville are an old, settled and highly urbanized group with weak ties to rural culture, they continue to live in large households. I do not think it is appropriate to conclude that they

---

[36] Wilbur C. Hallenbeck, ed. (for Pietermaritzburg University of Natal), *The Baumanville Community: A Study of the Family Life of Urban Africans*, Institute for Social Research (Durban: University of Natal, 1955).

have an extended-family system, though the statistics may so suggest: three-quarters of the "core" families (the nuclear family that rents the house) have relatives living with them. The latter are about equally divided between single persons and married couples (often with their children). The modal house has six to eight inhabitants, despite the fact that it contains but two rooms and often a makeshift porch added to the rear.

The authors suggest that the great overcrowding in Durban puts pressure on people to absorb relatives, and that there has emerged a cultural norm which assumes that a "normal" house will contain three or four persons per room. This pressure for space, plus the old traditions of family hospitality, lead to large households. However, these households are created for practical reasons, reflecting the space shortage, and are not functioning systems of extended families based on the norm that certain classes of relatives *should* live together and *should* cooperate on economic tasks. Indeed, in the city, there is a wide variety of arrangements for sharing in the rent and the household tasks, showing the lack of clear cultural patterning. It seems to me that we have a situation in Baumanville that is similar to that in the Negro ghettos in American cities: great overcrowding and a flexible adaptation thereto, but not an institutional form of the extended-family, for when a particular nuclear family can afford separate accommodations, they are likely to seek it.

The practice of bride-wealth continues in Baumanville (along with Christian marriage) although it has been converted into a cash transaction. This has the effect of delaying the age of marriage for the boys, as they cannot easily raise the necessary money. The modal time for men to marry is from 26 to 30 years of age, for women, five years earlier. The delayed age of marriage is leading to a large increase in illegitimacy which the people find distressing but do not know how to control.

The various reports on African cities uniformly speak of weak control of adolescents by their parents and the community. Especially among the first-generation urban families, young people feel that their parents' norms are poor guides to the future. Adolescent gangs wander the streets and perplex the older generation by their disregard for authority. But *none* of the reports tells us what happens to these adolescents as they grow older and take up regular occupations; *none* of the studies contrasts rebellious youths with those who obey and respect their parents. Do the latter come from those families in which the parents have made a more successful adjustment to city life and therefore can serve as realistic role models for their children? A careful analysis of the years of late adolescence and early maturity, based on a study of an urban group as they pass through the various stages of growth, with sub-samples representing families of different degrees of urbanization, and different levels of the class hierarchy, would add immensely to our understanding of the emerging urban culture.

In contrast to the foregoing studies, Oscar Lewis in "Urbanization

Without Breakdown: A Case Study," 1952, offers an analysis of new urbanites in Mexico City which seems to contradict many of the trends thus far
discussed. He reports his data against a background of findings from the
United States which indicate that farmers who move to the city often experience family disorganization leading to divorce and desertion, adolescent
rebellion against parental authority leading to delinquency, and personal
disorganization leading to neurosis and psychosis. Lewis interviewed 69
families who had moved from the village of Tepoztlan (which he had previously studied in great detail) to the capital city. They included families
who had moved before the revolution of 1910 and others who had come
more recently; in occupation, they ranged from professionals to domestic
servants. He summarized his findings as follows (pp. 40-41):

From our study of Tepoztecans living in Mexico City, we find that peasants in
Mexico adapt to city life with far greater ease than do American farm families.
There is little evidence of disorganization and breakdown, of culture conflict,
or of irreconcilable differences between generations. . . . Family life remains
strong in Mexico City. Family cohesiveness and extended family ties increase
in the city, fewer cases of separation and divorce occur, no cases of abandoned
mothers and children, no cases of persons living alone or of unrelated families
living together.

How can these findings be reconciled with the usual picture of disorganization among new urbanites? Lewis himself suggests several ways, and
I shall add a few more:

1. Lewis' sample is a special one. Tepoztlan is only two hours' bus ride
from Mexico City, and the cohesive social structure of the village is reflected by the continuing ties of the urbanites to village life: over half of
the city dwellers still own houses in the village, and visits back and forth
are common.

2. The Mexican rural family system is better adapted to urban needs
than is the African, and thus less change is produced when people move
cityward. The Mexican rural family is essentially a nuclear family; there
are patterns of aid among extended kin and ritual kin (compadres) based
on mutual exchange, but these are flexible and much choice according to
personal taste is permitted. The basic economic functions of farming and
trading are carried on by nuclear families who have a strong sense of independence and a long acquaintance with money markets and personal gain.
Residence is nuclear whenever economic conditions permit: 70 percent of
the village families in Tepoztlan (and 67 percent of the Tepoztecans in
Mexico City) lived in nuclear households. Furthermore, Lewis does not tell
us of adaptations to urban needs that many parents probably made which
allowed them to retain solidary ties with their children.

3. Catholic religious traditions in Mexico reinforce its family pattern.
The homogeneity of Mexico City, which draws most of its immigrants from

Mexican rural districts which have basically similar traditions of family and religion is in great contrast to the American cities with their many foreign immigrants and their many competing religious creeds, and it is in great contrast to the African cities where the strictly urban culture patterns are in large part imitations of European modes of behavior.

4. The statistics on disorganization—whether they be African, American, or Mexican—exaggerate the differences between the city and the country. Recordkeeping is much better in the city, so more cases of divorce, delinquency, and psychological illness are reported. The same differentials between urban and rural statistics exist in Mexico as in the United States; we cannot draw conclusions from a comparison of a small sample of solidary families in Mexico City with American national statistics on family disorganization.

5. Case studies of American urban families are rare, and are often interpreted through middle-class eyes. Consequently, certain patterns of adolescent sexual behavior, of "rebellion," of adult behavior that appears odd to middle-class observers, may represent differences in culture pattern and not necessarily "disorganization."

In summary, I think it clear that the evidence so far does suggest a general pattern, but we must specify in detail the circumstances in which the pattern holds. The pattern is an abstraction of tendencies noted in many cultures; in concrete fact, each situation will show a combination of the general trends and the local traditions—the very nature of abstraction involves the overlooking of some aspects of reality in order to emphasize others.

The urban family tends to be nuclear; women have considerable independence and there is a trend toward sexual "equality"; young people have considerable freedom to move about the city, make friends, seek their own careers and wives. Now, where the rural family patterns are at variance with these urban forms, there will be culture shock and strain when people first move to the city and until they have had time not only to break loose from the old forms but *to institutionalize the new ones.* These new forms grow out of the economic life of the city (just as the old ones grew out of the economic life of the country), and only when persons achieve stabilized careers will they be able to develop new patterns of stabilized family life. As Mair said in her report on African families previously cited (p. 155):

In the towns . . . most observers have found that an ideal of marriage and home life exists, and that great efforts are often made to attain it. If irregular unions are regarded with tolerance, yet legal marriage is still regarded as the ideal; homes are kept clean in the midst of slums, and children cared for as well as may be. Where higher standards of living are attainable, marriage is more stable, women stay at home and look after their children, and children go regularly to school. The answer here lies surely as much in the attack on African poverty as in moral exhortation.

Young people will respect their elders when the elders deserve respect. In rural cultures, the old people are wise in the ways of farming and in most matters of life, secular and sacred; furthermore, they control the land which is vital to the fate of their children. In the city, lower-class migrants from the farms tend to be ignorant people who know less about city life than do their children. But when parents adjust to the city environment, when they have good jobs with steady incomes, when they themselves have had city schooling, then they can serve as potent role models for their children. Eventually, working-class and middle-class cultures emerge which produce new stability within the nuclear family in the urban milieu.

Indeed, the noneconomic functions of the nuclear family are likely to be strengthened in the city. For example, it is this group that gives basic emotional warmth and support in an environment which tends to be impersonal and calculating; it is the agent of socialization, which becomes more conscious and deliberate as modern theories of personality-formation diffuse; it is a major center of consumption activities, and they grow in significance as the length of the work day diminishes; and for many members of the middle and upper classes, it is a group which shares career responsibility by aiding the father in his duties of entertainment of customers, clients, or fellow-executives.

The urban family tends to be smaller than the rural family. On the farm, children cost less to rear, for space is cheap, food is home-grown, and formal education unnecessary. From a young age, farm children contribute labor which is worth more than their upkeep. But, in the city, children are more expensive to rear and they do not start earning until a much later age. Especially in the middle classes, where economic wants (including the symbols of consumption necessary for upward mobility) tend to outrun income, children become a burden and parents gladly turn to methods of birth control.

I have stressed that individualistic jobs and geographic separation are the keys to the breakdown of close kinship solidarity beyond the nuclear family. But these two forces do not operate equally throughout city life. The urban proletariat (once stabilized) tends to be less geographically mobile than the middle class; working-class siblings may grow up in the same area and, when married, may exchange services such as baby-care or aid in housebuilding which tend to keep solidarity alive. These mutual exchanges can function well so long as social mobility is not present: if one of a pair of siblings climbs into the middle class, opportunity for equal reciprocity is lost, the less successful sibling feels awkward in the presence of the more successful one, and interaction declines. Thus, social mobility has effects similar to geographical mobility.

Family businesses often serve as ties between siblings and between generations. Especially where great property is present, as in the upper class, kinship solidarity is likely to remain strong.

In other words, it is only an approximation to use the shorthand phrase "urban life affects the family." One must specify the particular urban processes which are at work, and recognize that they operate with differential force among different groups. All urbanites are not alike.

Organic Solidarity

In *The Division of Labor in Society*, 1893,[37] Durkheim developed a distinction between two forms of social solidarity. The simple rural or folk society is held together by similarity: there is very little specialization of function; there is a single, coherent, homogeneous, and sacred cultural tradition which tells everybody how to behave; there is a strong public opinion based on face-to-face interaction (perhaps the word should be "gossip") which brings deviants back into line. This type of social cohesion Durkheim labeled "mechanical solidarity." Based upon custom and the similarity of one man's life to that of another in a small community, it created a strong but static society which continually reproduces itself without much variation.

Modern societies cannot be held together by such means. There is an elaborate division of labor which makes one man unlike another; men engage in systems of production and exchange which promote attitudes of rationality and calculation; there is constant economic and social change which weakens sacred custom. But Durkheim pointed out that the very elaborateness of the division of labor makes each man more dependent upon his neighbor than in the past: no one can be self-sufficient when he is a specialist in some one, minute task. This interdependence creates the conditions for a new form of social cohesion which Durkheim called "organic solidarity." Let us examine its components.

In part, organic solidarity is based on the sheer fact of interdependence in the market place. I am connected with the Brazilians who grew my morning coffee, with the assembly-line workers in Detroit who made my automobile, with the members of the world-wide organization of the Standard Oil Company which supplies my gasoline. Under ordinary circumstances, my dealings with these people are impersonal: I am interested in their goods and not their lives. I may, in objective fact, share with them a common destiny, but I do not subjectively feel a common identity. Our attitudes towards each other are attitudes of rational calculation of personal gain; our dealings are controlled by price competition.

However, market ties may become personalized through continued face-to-face contact. I begin to know my local gas station proprietor and become concerned about his health. I work not as an isolate but as a member of a team, and my teammates and I become mutually involved as individuals as well as participants in a common career.

[37] Emile Durkheim, *The Division of Labor in Society*, George Simpson, trans. (New York: Free Press, 1947).

And I have links to people not based on market relationships. My family is of central importance; I live in a local community and become conscious of the fact that my life is intertwined with the lives of my neighbors; I have interests in music, literature, the free life, and stand together with those who share such interests. I learn to have a concern for the maintenance of the type of society which permits me to live the kind of life I cherish. I may enlarge my sense of community beyond the immediate locality to my nation, my nation's allies, all the free world, humanity.

Organic solidarity is thus a complex thing of many parts. There is a dearth of research on how the parts fit together to make a whole, but some of the more important components can be listed in outline form:

1. Market interdependence.
2. "Rules of the game" or norms that regulate market dealings, such as honesty, fulfillment of contract, efficiency.
3. "Rules of the game" that regulate internal behavior within firms which operate in the market; that is, the norms of bureaucracy such as devotion to the benefit of the organization, limitation of authority to the proper confines of the job, elimination of private interests which conflict with those of the organization.
4. Occupational codes which create a subculture appropriate to each group, such as the professional ethics of the physician or the teacher, or the craftsmanlike creed of the skilled machinist.
5. Functioning face-to-face groups at work and in the residential community.
6. Organized interest groups which represent the concerns of occupational or regional segments of the society.
7. Legitimate structures of government which articulate and control the competing interests. There must evolve an emotional conviction in the supremacy of legal procedure, regardless of the content of particular decisions, to subdue the potential war of each against all. If a decision is reached legally, we must feel constrained to accept it even if it threatens our personal interests.
8. Ultimate values about the ends of life in society which are shared by all within it.
9. Rational awareness of common destiny and thus rational willingness to share for common good.
10. Organized public opinion based on a combination of long-term values, personal or group interests, and knowledge of current events. The mass media are the agents of opinion formation.

A smoothly functioning society based upon organic solidarity must somehow combine all of these elements into a totality. Obviously, it is a totality which is quite different from the mechanical solidarity of a rural village. This qualitative difference is of such magnitude that we ought to avoid analyses of urban society based upon rural models. Those who look toward urban society wearing glasses shaped in the villages see it as impersonal to the point of being inhuman, disorganized[38] to the point of imminent collapse, so distorting to innate human nature as to produce mass psychosis. I do not believe it. If one wishes to reverse the perspective and view village society with the glasses of an urbanite, one can call it stultifying to the personality because it shapes everybody into the same mold, repressive of creativity and innovation, exploitative of the labor of the many for the benefit of the few, so tightly organized and conservative that life lacks zest. One stereotype is as bad as the other.[39]

Research Methods

There remains space for only a few comments on research procedures. Many of the books discussed above are "social surveys" of new cities. As such, they attempt to describe the situation as it exists at a given moment: How many people are there, what is the age and sex distribution, how many of them are married, where were they born, how long do they expect to stay in the city, do they send money home to villages, etc.? Only indirectly do these studies focus on the processes of change which are of central concern to the construction of general theory. For the latter purpose, the important data do not concern the proportion who appear to be committed to the new urban life at a given moment, but the processes which commit them and the changes which they undergo as a result of commitment. For an understanding of such processes of change, we need a number of detailed case studies selected according to a sampling scheme which draws upon all the crucial types of persons, defined according to combinations of the following variables: length of residence in the city, rural-born versus city-born, ties with rural life, education, occupation. The case studies must be cast in the form of life-histories, and must gather considerable data on behavior, on norms, and on feelings.

Simple transfer of traditional methods of anthropology or sociology

[38] The concept of "disorganization" is risky, for rarely is the comparative base of "organization" clearly specified. Particularly when we are studying social change must we be wary. Does the concept refer to a lack of close relationship between various segments of a culture, as Redfield defines it? Then what is the standard of proper integration?—a complex urban culture will, when well organized, show more variation, more alternatives, than a simple rural culture. Does the concept refer to social control over individual behavior? Then what is a proper standard of homogeneity within a given type of society and its various segments? American urban life is called disorganized by some observers, overconformist by others.

[39] For the sake of simplicity, I speak of the village versus the city. Obviously, the urbanization of a society is a matter of degree. Early urbanization, a limited division of labor, a partially developed class hierarchy—such as in many African cities—will produce a social system quite different from the more advanced Mexican society. But I leave it to the reader to fill in the shades of gray.

will not serve adequately. For instance, the anthropologist usually seeks a "community." If he goes to the city, he may well concentrate on one small residential district under the impression that he is studying something analogous to the village community. However, he will be mistaken, for a residential area of a city—even in a slum where there appears to be much interaction among the neighbors—is but a pale imitation of a village community. The men (and many of the women) leave the area to go to work; the children leave to go to school; economic and much of social and religious life is not centered on the residential district. For the working-class, the factory is as much a community as the residential district, and for the middle classes, the network of clique ties which is rarely based on a single geographical district serves many community functions. *It is of the essence of urban life that interpersonal relations are based on several functions and groups and these do not all overlap in a single small geographic center.*

The currently fashionable methods in sociology are equally limited for the problem at hand. They interrelate a small number of variables, statistically measured, for a large sample. In most instances these variables all refer to a single moment of time. A great deal of previous knowledge about the culture is assumed in such research; e.g., the American researcher has an enormous body of accumulated data that he takes for granted in constructing his sample controls. When the culture being studied is not well known, and when change through time under certain defined circumstances is the focus of the research, the modern survey methods are of limited use.

It seems to me that the appropriate procedure is to recognize that the structure of urban life is based upon the division of labor. We must sample systematically among various levels of the hierarchy and then collect cases with full life-history data. We cannot rely upon a few informants to tell us what the traditions are, for the traditions are changing and informants have knowledge that is limited to their own immediate social type. We must observe behavior and get detailed verbal accounts of behavior in a large number of specific situations for a large number of different types of persons. Then the scientific observer can construct a picture of the general forms of behavior in such a way that central tendencies and significant variations from them can be described and analyzed and even explained. When he recognizes that there is integration in urban society, albeit not based on the local community, he will be able to relate the life-histories of the different types of informants into a picture of the functioning totality. Of what use is a knowledge of servants without an understanding of employers? Of tradesmen without customers? Of political bosses without followers? The division of labor integrates as much as it divides men from one another. Durkheim was not using a meaningless phrase when he spoke of "organic solidarity," and we must devise research procedures appropriate to its nature.

One World, All Alike?

I have been stressing in this paper what seem to me to be the processes of change which tend to create a universal way of life in modern industrial cities. No doubt some features that appear to me to belong to this universal culture are only special aspects of Western European or American life, and my own ethnocentrism has led me to generalize them. I invite colleagues from other cultures to correct my biases.

I think the major research task in the years ahead is the design of comparative studies which will help us determine in a systematic way how the universal aspects of industrial civilization combine with local cultural traditions to create living societies. In other words, to what degree will all nations of the future be alike under the dictates of industrial life, and to what degree can they retain features of uniqueness? It is perfectly obvious that pre-industrial cultures must undergo drastic reorganization under the impact of industrialization and urbanization; it is impossible to adopt a new economy and retain an old society. But perhaps intellectual understanding of the minimum social prerequisites of an efficient industrial order will permit a planned readjustment which can keep strong those aspects of the various traditional orders which are compatible with the realities of the new one. To state a personal value of my own: I hope the intellectuals will join in leading such a readjustment, for I would not enjoy a world without diversity. Unfortunately, too many intellectuals, especially in the humanities, fight the new order blindly and without understanding, and thus lose the power to influence constructively the evolution of the emerging society.

2. Social Change in the Industrial Revolution

Neil J. Smelser

When comparing a society with its past or with another society, we often employ a dichotomy such as "advanced vs. backward," "developed vs. underdeveloped," "civilized vs. uncivilized," or "complex vs. simple." Sometimes these words yield too little information because they claim simply that one society is superior to another. Sometimes they yield too much, for terms like "advanced" shroud a galaxy of vague connotations. Hence to use such words may generate conflicts of pride and conflicts of meaning, both of which subvert intelligent discourse.

The dichotomies are, however, not completely useless. Common to all are the dimensions of *complexity* and *differentiation*. In other words, an "advanced" or "developed" society possesses a complex organization of differentiated social and cultural components. To illustrate, a religion becomes a religious tradition only after it shakes off its undifferentiated tribal elements and develops a complex, independent organization. A military machine is more developed than spontaneous warfare because it operates under specific, explicit, and sometimes autonomous rules. Bureaucratic administration is more advanced than a household staff not only because it is more complex but also because it is less mingled with personal loyalties.[1] A highly developed economy has a complexity of organization and a differentiation of units which do not characterize underdeveloped forms.[2] Political behavior "advances" when it is carried on with political institutions free from nepotism, tribal loyalties, and bald economic interests. In short, one element in "growth," "advancement," and "civilization" is that the social structures in question become *more differentiated* from each other.

This implicit concept underlies much of our discourse about social development. We seldom ask, however, whether the *very process* of passing from a less differentiated to a more differentiated social structure possesses

Reprinted from Neil J. Smelser, *Social Change in the Industrial Revolution* (Chicago: University of Chicago Press, 1959), pp. 1-2; 402; 404-408.

[1] M. Weber, "Bureaucracy," in *From Max Weber: Essays in Sociology* (London: Oxford University Press, 1947), pp. 198-199.

[2] These elements are implied in Adam Smith's view of an economy. Book I of *The Wealth of Nations* (New York, 1937) is entitled: "Of the Causes of Improvement in the Productive Powers of Labor . . . ," or we might say, "of the causes of economic growth." Chapter I, "Of the Division of Labor," and Chapter III, "That the Division of Labor Is Limited by the Extent of the Market," contain the twin ideas of complexity and differentiation from the market.

definite regularities, and whether the sequence itself produces phenomena which can be analyzed systematically. It is my assertion that such regularities do exist, and can be extracted from societies in flux.

In the following [discussion] I shall analyse several sequences of differentiation. Above all I shall be attempting to apply social theory to history. Such an analysis naturally calls for two components: (1) a segment of social theory; and (2) an empirical instance of change. For the first I have selected a model of social change from a developing "general theory of action"; for the second I have chosen the British industrial revolution between 1770 and 1840. From this large revolution I have isolated the growth of the cotton industry and the transformation of the family structure of its working classes. Let us sketch the model and the historical processes in turn.

The model of structural differentiation is an abstract theory of change. When *one* social role or organization becomes archaic under changing historical circumstances, it differentiates by a *definite and specific sequence of events into two or more* roles or organizations which function more effectively in the new historical circumstances. The new social units are structurally distinct from each other, but taken together are functionally equivalent to the original unit. The differentiation of an economy's distribution system into "retail" and "wholesale" is an example. These branches of distribution differ, of course, but together they fulfill the same function as a more primitive distribution system. Another example is the differentiation of courtship from kinship. In a system of classificatory marriage (e.g., cross-cousin), the basis for marriage is simply extended kinship. When, on the other hand, the basis for marriage is personal acquaintance outside the family circle, courtship has become *differentiated* from the structure of kinship. Any sequence of differentiation is set in motion by specific disequilibrating conditions. Initially this disequilibrium gives rise to symptoms of social disturbance which must be brought into line later by mechanisms of social control. Only then do specific ideas, suggestions, and attempts emerge to produce the more differentiated social units.

. . . Our basic problem in this research was to characterize and explain the growth or development of social systems. To this end we attempted to apply in two separate structural contexts—the industry and the family—a model of differentiation which posits a typical sequence of events which occurs when the system increases in complexity. The sequence begins when members of the system in question (or some larger system) express *dissatisfaction* with some aspect of the system's functioning (Step 1). This dissatisfaction may concern role-performance in the system, the utilization of its resources, or both. In either case the dominant values governing the system legitimize the expression of the initial dissatisfaction. Accompanying the dissatisfaction, furthermore, is the prospect of facilities to overcome the source of dissatisfaction. The immediate responses to the dissatisfactions

(Step 2) are undirected or misdirected symptoms of disturbance—phantasy, aggression and anxiety. Even though non-specific with regard to concrete methods of overcoming the dissatisfactions, these symptoms are related symbolically to the original foci of dissatisfaction. Gradually these disturbances are brought into line by mechanisms of social control (Step 3), and their energy turned to the generation of more specific solutions for the original problems giving rise to the dissatisfactions. In this way future lines of action are encouraged (Step 4), specified (Step 5), and tried (Step 6). The social units which emerge, if the sequence is successful, constitute a structure *more differentiated* than the old. The new units, being more specialized, function more effectively than the old. Finally, after a period of extraordinary progress, the new units are consolidated into the social system and thereby routinized (Step 7). . . . The starting-point for a sequence of structural differentiation of roles [in industry] (and reorganization of resources) is the historical appearance of dissatisfactions with industrial production (Step 1). This dissatisfaction may be directed at classes of economic agents, or may be phrased in terms of the misallocation or misuse of the resources of labor, capital, and organization. Whatever the specific foci of dissatisfaction, however, it is justified and legitimized in terms of the current values relating to production. Before any specific action is taken to overcome the sources of dissatisfaction, diverse symptoms of disturbance appear (Step 2). Next a number of agencies of social control engage in a series of holding operations against these disturbances to prevent them from reaching disruptive proportions (Step 3). Simultaneously there is a reaffirmation of the basic values governing production and an encouragement of ideas designed to implement these values in new, more effective ways (Step 4). Inventions and experiments in rearranging the division of labor carry these ideas to a still greater degree of specification (Step 5). Finally, entrepreneurs translate these suggestions into concrete attempts to reorganize the basis of production (Step 6). If successful, the entrepreneurial attempts lead to an explosive growth of production, capitalization, profits, and reorganization, which return gradually to routine levels as the new methods become consolidated in the industrial structure (Step 7). . . .

We applied this formal statement to the cotton industry of Great Britain during the industrial revolution of the late eighteenth and early nineteenth centuries. Our structural starting-point was the putting-out and domestic system of manufacture—treated as a social system—of the mid-eighteenth century. We first observed the fusions between this system of manufacture and the family-community structure of the time. The initial signs of dissatisfaction with these methods of production appeared in various complaints concerning productive bottlenecks, imbalances between spinning and weaving, and the master's inability to control the work-people under the putting-out system (Step 1). The expanding foreign and domestic markets for cotton textiles in the middle and late eighteenth century aggravated such dissatisfaction. The complaints were legitimized, furthermore, by the values invigorated by the recent burst of Wesleyan Methodism, particularly in the manufacturing districts. Initially the complex of growing demand, complaints, and favorable legitimizing values gave rise to a period of scapegoating the working classes and dreams of immediate fortunes (Step 2).

After this initial period of confusion, inventors and entrepreneurs turned to the more practical business of overhauling the productive apparatus. Over the next several decades the factory system conquered the cotton industry gradually and irregularly with the successive introduction of the spinning jenny, the water-frame, the mule, the power-loom, the steam-engine, and the organizational changes accompanying each. To each of these innovations we applied the model of differentiation. By its logic we traced the structural modifications of production, the behavior of economic indices such as production, capitalization, and innovation, and the occurrence of "regressive" symptoms of disturbance such as movements for protectionism and favoritism among various classes of manufacturers.* We qualified each sequence of differentiation, furthermore, by reference to the influence of "external" factors such as the Revolutionary and Napoleonic war period.

For our second major field of empirical application of the model of differentiation, we turned to the family of the working classes. The *principles* of applying the model to a family economy are identical with those of applying it to an industry, even though a family is in no sense an industry except in so far as both are social systems. First we refilled the abstract concepts of a social system with categories appropriate to the family economy. In this operation we identified the major functions of the family economy as the generation of motivation appropriate to occupational performance (goal-attainment), the utilization of family income to this end (adaptation), the organization of family roles (integration), and the processes of socialization and tension-management (latency). In addition, we classified the several resources which the family economy utilizes in fulfilling these functions.

As for the dynamics of family reorganization, a sequence of structural differentiation begins when dissatisfaction is expressed over the performance of familial roles or the utilization of familial resources (Step 1). Frequently industrial pressures on the family generate such dissatisfactions. As in the industrial case, the expression of these dissatisfactions is given the weight of legitimization by reference to the dominant family values of the time. When these conditions, plus a sense of opportunity, are present, the stage is set for the differentiation of the family economy. The first reaction to the dissatisfactions is the appearance of symptoms of disturbance, which are

---

* Editors note: In the book from which this section is abstracted, a large amount of data is presented in support of the view that each of these innovations followed the sequence of steps in the model of differentiation described here.

classifiable into phantasy, aggression, and anxiety, and which are traceable to the original foci of dissatisfaction with the family (Step 2). At first these disturbances are handled by mechanisms of social control (Step 3). Only after these more explosive elements are brought into line is it possible to take the more positive steps of encouraging ideas (Step 4), specifying lines of social action (Step 5), and translating these ideas into definite social experiments (Step 6). If these latter steps are successful, one or more new social units takes its place in the social structure (Step 7). In the family economy, as in the industry, the salient directions of the final differentiation correspond to the salient foci of dissatisfaction with the older units.

We applied this model of differentiation to two subsectors of the family economy: (a) the family division of labor; (b) the structure of family consumption.

(a) In the early nineteenth century the technological changes in the cotton industry created the conditions of urbanization, industrial centralization, and depersonalization of the factory community. More specifically, the enlargement of mules and the introduction of power-looms threatened to separate the labor of children from that of adults (often parents). These technological pressures, while long in the making, reached a critical point in the mid-1820's. For the family economy of the factory operatives, the pressures represented a serious dissatisfaction (Step 1). The worker and his family could no longer work on the basis which fused the family economy with other, more general family functions. If the worker refused to accept the new conditions of employment, he could no longer support his family satisfactorily; if he accepted labor on the new basis, certain non-economic relations in his family—particularly the rearing of children—might suffer. These pressures, magnified by an appeal to independence and personal responsibility as a family value, pressed for a thoroughgoing reorganization of family relationships.

The factory operatives, especially the adult male spinners, reacted immediately and fiercely to this pressure in a number of disturbed social movements (Step 2)—a series of vigorous but unsuccessful strikes to resist the improved machinery; a commitment to the ten-hour agitation of the 1830's, one effect of which would have been to preserve the old work structure; a prolonged attempt to subvert the Factory Act of 1833, which threatened to separate the labor of adult and child even further; and a brief though intensive flirtation with the Utopian co-operative movement.

To outline how these disturbances eventually led to new and more differentiated family units, we analysed first the course of factory legislation in the 1830's and the 1840's. Parliamentary investigation of the factory question represented a process of "handling and channeling" the disturbed elements of factory agitation (Step 3). Factory legislation between 1833 and 1847, in its turn, gradually eased the family structure into more differentiated directions (Steps 4-6). The working-class family which emerged about the time that the ten-hour day became normal was more specialized than the factory family of a quarter-century earlier; the economic performance of adults and children was segregated definitively, and certain minimum educational responsibilities had slipped from the family to an embryonic school system under the Factory Acts.

Meantime, the domestic hand-loom weavers were slowly differentiated "out" of the industry by the more productive hand-loom and power-loom factories. Until the hand-loom weavers were absorbed into other trades—a process which took many decades—their history was a story of one symptom of disturbance after another (Step 2)—pleas for assistance; schemes for artificial perpetuation of hand-loom weaving by means of permanent legislative support; violence; heavy emigration; withdrawal from community functions; and attraction to a sequence of Utopian schemes.

We also traced the history of trade-unionism in the early nineteenth century as a simultaneous though distinct line of differentiation in the family economy. Thrown into disorganization by the technological changes of the 1820's and 1830's (Step 1), the unions displayed several symptoms of disturbance in these years (Step 2). Gradually, however, through police activity, governmental investigations, public debate, and journalistic controversy, these disturbances were brought into line (Step 3). Later, by a sequence of exploration, debate, speculation, and social experimentation (Steps 4-6), the unions rose to a point of greater specialization in the 1840's than, for instance, as friendly societies in the eighteenth century or as the embryonic unions of the Napoleonic war period. In the important respects, therefore, this evolution of unions conformed to the model of structural differentiation.

(b) The signs of dissatisfaction with the structure of consumption in the late eighteenth century (Step 1) dealt with the inability of the poor-laws and the friendly society to safeguard the economic welfare of the working classes. The resulting symptoms of disturbance (Step 2) took the form primarily of attacks upon the friendly society, though occasionally food riots broke out, e.g., in the lean years of the 1790's and the remainder of the war period. The earliest social responses to these troubles was to encourage the working classes in the art of frugality; to prevent outright starvation by subsidizing families through the poor-laws; and to encourage the further development of the friendly societies. Dissatisfactions continued, however, and in the end gave rise to several social units geared to stabilizing the economic welfare of the family in its new social environment. The most important of these were the savings banks, which developed most rapidly in the first thirty years of the nineteenth century, and the co-operative stores which—after a period of experimentation in the 1820's and 1830's—became solidly established among the working classes in the 1840's and thereafter. We applied the model of differentiation to the rise of both, tracing in each case the parade of dissatisfactions, disturbances, new ideas, suggestions for implementation, social experimentation, and finally, successful incorporation.

To apply this model to the cotton industry and to the family economy of its working classes by no means exhausts the social changes of the industrial revolution. In fact, it would be instructive to follow other instances of structural differentiation—the segregation of education from religion through a process of secularizing the schools; the segregation of political parties from the system of aristocratic family cliques; the segregation of the military and civil service from the earlier system of political and class patronage, and so on. It seems possible, by examining a series of closely-linked processes of differentiation, to contrast the *relative* stability and institutional calm of the era preceding the industrial revolution with the storm and confusion of the period of the industrial revolution itself, and again with the *relative* stability of the prosperous and optimistic Victorian period, say after 1850. The eighteenth century was a period of growing pressure on the rural-aristocratic society—pressure generated by the train of domestic and international events and by the strength of the Nonconformist ideology, which seemed conducive to the initiation of social change on so many fronts. Some time after the middle of the century the pressure broke unevenly into a number of violent disturbances which signalled the early stages of structural differentiation—the debates, the uncertainty, the anxiety and gloom, the uneasy theorizing, and the grand projects. After this period of disturbed transition, new social forms began to find a solid place in the social structure—the new industrial organization, the reformed parliament, the beginnings of a formal educational system, modern political parties, and a new family and community life. The whole society thereby levelled into the relatively quiescent state of optimistic Victorianism, dominated by urbanism and the new middle classes.

3. The Early Impact of Industrialization on Society

Harold L. Wilensky

Many of the problems that underdeveloped areas are facing today are the problems America faced in the decades following the Civil War. These were the years of mushroom growth in population—31 million in 1860 to 92 million in 1910; of the development of a vast railroad system and a national market; of mass immigration, old and new. With the settlement of the national domain went the transformation of rural peoples into urban. On the day of Lincoln's first election four in five of the population lived on farms; by the end of the century the proportion was less than two in five. The population of New York City jumped from 814,000 in 1860 to 3,437,-000 in 1900; that of Chicago from 109,000 to 1,700,000.

More people, more urbanites, many of them new types of men: the landless proletarian; the "captain of industry," a wealthy owner-manager; and in between a middle order of small entrepreneurs—merchants and independent professionals. It was the time, too, of violent business fluctuations; the great depressions of the seventies and nineties and the crisis of the mid-eighties brought poverty and insecurity to many. Darwinian biology and Spencerian philosophy combined to tell Americans that life is a fierce competitive struggle which only the fittest survive. Industrial strife, poverty, insecurity could thus be seen as signs of the working of immutable laws of evolution, and evolution could be seen as progress. The century closed with Andrew Carnegie declaring, "The millionaires who are in active control started as poor boys and were trained in the sternest but most efficient of all schools—poverty."[1] And: "There is not one shred of privilege to be met with anywhere in all the laws. One man's right is every other man's right. The flag is the guarantor and symbol of equality."[2] About the same time and with equal enthusiasm a million voters put their stamp of approval on a Populist platform which declared that America was ruled by a plutocracy, that the press was a tool of wealth, that labor was impoverished, "that the fruits of the toil of millions are boldly stolen to build up colossal fortunes

Reprinted from Harold L. Wilensky and Charles N. Lebeaux, *Industrial Society and Social Welfare* (New York: Russell Sage Foundation, 1958), pp. 49-50; 56-67; 83-89.

[1] Richard Hofstadter, *The American Political Tradition* (New York: Vintage Books, 1954), p. 166.
[2] Charles A. Beard and Mary R. Beard, *The Rise of American Civilization*, Vol. II (New York: Macmillan, 1933), p. 209.

for a few unprecedented in the history of mankind; and possessors of these in turn despise the republic and endanger liberty."[3]

There is no other period in American history when the need and demands of industry so dominated the nation's political and social life. If the industrial entrepreneur ever had free reign it was then. This era—roughly from the Civil War to World War I—is therefore a good one for highlighting the needs of industry as they shape its initial social impact. . . .

The Factory System: Discipline, Insecurity, Specialization, and Mobility

"Scarcely any evil associated with the factory system was entirely a new evil in kind."[4] This concession comes from the Hammonds, in their classic indictment of the industrial revolution. In many home industries preceding the factory system the hours were long, the pay was poor, children were sweated, and both home and workshop were overcrowded and unattractive by virtue of their combination under a single roof. The same can be said of the agriculturalist of peasant villages, whose long hours of backbreaking labor and low levels of living were matched by his dependence on the labor of his women and children.

It is not that the American worker of 1870 was still on an eleven-hour day and sometimes a seven-day week, nor that his women and children often worked that accounts for his grievances. Nor is the evidence good that the peasants who were transformed into industrial workers—in America or in Britain—experienced any drastic decline in a material standard-of-living (even initially). When we think of the transition from European peasant to American industrial worker we are often comparing a run-down rural economy with an expanding industrial economy. It is surprising that life in the urban-industrial setting did not seem wonderful by contrast.

The charge that the machine has enslaved man seems to be based on four major changes that the factory system brought about: (1) Work in modern industry must be regular, workers punctual. (2) The modern worker is dependent for his livelihood on a corporation or an employer who owns the machines and controls the conditions of work (the peasant or the homeworkers often owned his own tools and usually set his own conditions of work). (3) The machine often is in direct competition with the worker: mechanization means continual change in jobs; both the number of workmen and the skills needed in the workplace are in constant flux. (4) The modern worker must often move his residence in response to the demands of changing technology and opportunity (accelerating technological changes affect the competitive position of companies and even whole industries, which in turn makes for shifts in demand for numbers and kinds of work-

---

[3] *Ibid.*, p. 210.
[4] John L. Hammond and Barbara Hammond, *The Town Labourer*, 1760-1832, Vol. II (London: Longmans, 1949), p. 31.

ers). The following sections consider these effects of the factory system one at a time.

The new discipline

Specialized machine processes must be coordinated with flawless timing; for the worker this means subjection to schedule and disciplined routine. The time clock, the plant roles, the presence of a host of supervisors and other control specialists, the close attention to quantity and quality of output—these add up to a demand for discipline on the job, and acceptance of individual responsibility for performance of the job.

We half forget the sustained regularity insisted upon in office, store, and factory—we are so used to it. But the difficulties of adapting to industrial routines are experienced afresh in each area invaded by modern industry and by each new recruit. It may be a Bemba tribesman who has come to work in a North Rhodesia mine or a Mississippi sharecropper newly arrived at the plant gates of a Chicago steel mill; it may be a Soviet farm youth drafted into a factory training center in Leningrad or an American farm girl now employed in a large typing pool in Hartford. Newcomers to industry everywhere resist a full commitment to industrial ways of life. This is clear in all underdeveloped countries, where absenteeism is the major labor problem of the managers of mines, factories, and plantations. (Many Indian factories have had to hire a group of substitutes who take the place of workers who have run away without giving notice.) It is clear, too, in the more developed countries—including both the Soviet Union and the U.S.A.—where absenteeism and labor turnover are also high among the rural newcomers.[5]

Dependence on employers and the labor market

The peasant newcomer may have worked long hours in the Old Country, but they were his own hours. His wife and children may have worked, but they worked beside him and they were not confined to jobs considered degrading (as maid, laundress, shoeshine boy). The weather and war made life seem full of risks in the Old Country; but the high rate of industrial accidents in the New World seemed to be within the employer's control, a sign of his callousness. The peasant may have been a slave of tradition

[5] Alexander S. Vucinich, *Soviet Economic Institutions* (Stanford, Calif.: Stanford University Press, 1952), p. 33; Bert F. Hoselitz, ed., *The Progress of Underdeveloped Areas* (Chicago: University of Chicago Press, 1952), p. 91; Lewis M. Killian, "The Effects of Southern White Workers on Race Relations in Northern Plants," *American Sociological Review*, 17 (June, 1952), 327-331; William F. Whyte, ed., *Industry and Society* (New York: McGraw-Hill, 1946); Wilbert E. Moore, *Industrialization and Labor* (Ithaca, N.Y.: Cornell University Press, 1951), pp. 38-39, 114 ff.; Julius H. Boeke, *The Structure of Netherlands Indian Economy* (New York: Institute of Pacific Relations, 1942), p. 95.

and the daily round a fixed and monotonous one requiring considerable self-control; but the disciplines of factory life did not permit even the illusion of independence, for the supervisor was always there, personal embodiment of an impersonal system of control. The peasant or the homeworker may have experienced crop failure or unemployment—but in the Old Country a man was his own boss or was hired for the year or the season; and in time of crisis, he had some comforting (if not very effective) insurance policies to fall back on—land ownership or personal ties with landlords, or moral ties with kinsmen. In industry he had nothing to sell but his labor and the employer bought it by the hour or the day. Should the workings of an impersonal market cast him in the role of unemployed, he had to hunt out another job (if there was one), which often meant another neighborhood or community. Should illness cut off his income, the family and community supports were no longer as strong.

In short, the risks of an agricultural existence (even on a narrow margin above starvation) were spread widely among the extended family or whole village; they seemed more like "acts of God." The risks of an industrial existence were his: they were not so easily shared; and they seemed unreasonable, inflicted on him by evil men. It takes even the willing peasant a while to get used to the idea that responsibility for adversity lies with the law of supply and demand. It takes him even longer to realize that security may be had if he shifts from job to job, community to community; acquires some skill; forms a union; becomes active in a political party—if, in short, he adopts the ways by which experienced industrial workers in the early years of industrialization achieve some stability of income and some improvement of conditions.

Early changes in specialization

It is commonplace to say that industrialization brings increased complexity in the division of labor, more specialized jobs. The extent, the kinds, and the trends in specialization and their precise impact on social life are not so obvious.

It has been estimated that there are 30,000 different occupations in the United States today;[6] the *Dictionary of Occupational Titles* gives definitions of more than 22,000.[7] These lists show astonishing specialization. In the baking industry one can make a living as a cracker breaker, meringue spreader, a pie stripper, or pan dumper. In the slaughter and meat-packing industry one can specialize as: a large stock scalper, belly shaver, crotch buster, gut snatcher, gut sorter, snout puller, ear cutter, eyelid remover,

[6] Carroll L. Shartle, *Occupational Information* (Englewood Cliffs, N.J.: Prentice-Hall, 1952), p. 24.
[7] U.S. Employment Service, Division of Occupational Analysis, *Dictionary of Occupational Titles* (Washington, D.C.: U.S. Government Printing Office, 1949).

stomach washer (sometimes called belly pumper), hindlegs toenail puller, frontlegs toenail puller, and oxtail washer.

The kind of specialization suggested by these bizarre titles is typical of manufacturing in the early phases of industrialization; it is the specialization that results from the subdivision and simplification of tasks. The writers who complained that the industrial revolution would make automatons of men, turn them into machine slaves, and dehumanize them were preoccupied with this type of specialization. What they had in mind was an old phenomenon first described in Adam Smith's story of the pinmakers: one drew out the wire, another straightened it, a third cut it, a fourth pointed it, a fifth ground it at the top, two or three others did the necessary operations to make the head. All of this resulted in marvelous economies, but, as Adam Smith saw at that early date, work simplification could also result in a kind of mental stupor for the worker.[8]

The dilution of skills, then, is one effect of this type of specialization. By this we mean that complex operations are broken down into easily learned components.[9] Processes formerly handled by one person are torn apart. The separate components or tasks are then mechanized and/or assigned to unskilled workers. The results: Workers suffer a "loss of workmanship" or "pride of craft." They lose socially recognized skills (even the wives of many machine-tenders have only the vaguest notion of what their semi-skilled husbands do). They also lose independence and individual self-reliance. When we hear protests about these things, it is typically the dilution of skills due to work simplification that is at issue.

The auto-assembly plant—featuring a conveyor system that grips the worker bodily to the line—has been since 1914 the epitome of this type of specialization, though by no means its first example.[10] Mechanically controlled workpace, repetitiveness, minimum skill, predetermination of tools and techniques, minute subdivision of product, surface mental attention—these characteristics of production-line jobs in auto-assembly have, indeed, taken the joy out of work. A careful study by Walker and Guest of one auto plant, where few of the workers had previously been exposed to an assembly line, reports that: (1) the worker's feelings about their work were over-

---

[8] Some modern occupational analysis also points toward this conclusion. Shartle reports data on 7,955 occupations in 87 industries as compiled by the USES, 1935-1941. They were grouped by work performed and materials used. Almost all required working under supervision; about half required the worker to adjust to a machine (over half the machine occupations had an on-the-job training period of one week or less, less than half required previous experience); about a third of all occupations were repetitive in nature; more than half had no special educational requirements as stated by the employer and a "high degree of intelligence" was estimated to be necessary only in about one in ten. (See Shartle, *op. cit.*, pp. 185 ff.) Note, however, that occupations in the administrative and professional areas were underrepresented in this study.

[9] Wilbert E. Moore, "Occupational Structure and Industrial Conflict," in Arthur Kornhauser, *et al.*, *Industrial Conflict* (New York: McGraw-Hill, 1954), pp. 221-231.

[10] Long before, Chicago meatpackers had applied the principle of a continuous "disassembly line" to cut up carcasses.

whelmingly negative; (2) the technology of the line kept workgroups weak; (3) worse than either the boredom or the tension that arose from repetitive and machine-pace work was the sense of becoming depersonalized, of becoming anonymous as against remaining oneself; (4) simplified and standardized jobs had reduced wage spreads and all but wiped out job progression—thereby striking at the heart of America's free mobility ideology.[11] This case study is given broader significance by the fact that in 1953, at a time when jobs were plentiful, the automobile industry had the fifth highest quit rate for 52 durable goods manufacturing industries for which data are reported. The average voluntary quits per month per 100 employees for auto was 3.0; the average rate for the 52 industries was 2.3.[12]

While there is little evidence on this point, it seems possible that the frustrations of the work routine on the assembly line place a heavy hand on the worker's off-the-job thought and feeling, that the deadening rhythms of the factory tend to be repeated in his leisure time. Lacking satisfaction on the job, he may seek synthetic substitutes in passive comsumption of the standardized products of "mass culture" off the job. If this passive exposure to TV, film, comics, and sports arena itself offers insufficient release of tension, it may help to explain the explosiveness of life in a factory city like Detroit—the race riots and bar brawls, the passionate hostility to management shown in workplace and union meeting.[13] In what circumstances frustrating job routines and disciplines lead to explosive activity off work, when they lead to dull passivity, when they produce other patterns of leisure use, and when they have little or no effect, are questions only now beginning to interest social researchers. Observations about the links between occupational roles and nonoccupational roles are therefore more speculative than our analysis of the impact of technological change on job satisfaction.

The dilution of skills for those who had experienced the craft life before meant a drastic decline of job satisfaction and self-esteem. For those fresh from the farm it meant an intensification of the industrial disciplines which in any case were hard for them to take. In so far as industrialization

[11] Charles R. Walker and Robert H. Guest, The Man on the Assembly Line (Cambridge: Harvard University Press, 1952), pp. 116-117; Ely Chinoy, Automobile Workers and the American Dream (New York: Doubleday, 1955).

[12] Low job satisfaction and high labor turnover seem to have characterized mass production plants from the first: In the early years of the century, for example, "Ford's radical technology was in a constant state of flux. . . . To give the new machine processes a tryout, men had to be commandeered, uprooted, shunted from job to job at a moment's notice. As early as 1910 the man on the bottom at Ford's had come to feel . . . he had no work he could call his own from one day to the next. . . . A certain factory process at Highland Park which had once required the skills of a craftsman . . . by 1914 had been split up into thirty-four separate operations. . . ." Ford later wrote that turnover of his working force had run to 380 percent by the year 1913 alone: see Keith T. Sward, The Legend of Henry Ford (New York: Holt, Rinehart and Winston, 1948), pp. 47, 49.

[13] Irving Howe and B. J. Widick, The UAW and Walter Reuther (New York: Random House, 1949), pp. 42-43.

brings increased specialization involving work simplification, the evidence suggests a large class of "de-humanized" workers, men who are alienated from their work and from the industrial way of life.[14]

While work simplification spells dilution of skills for some, it spells *obsolescence* of skills for others. By this we mean a decline or disappearance of demand for certain skills.[15] This may be due to falling demand for certain products (when horse-drawn vehicles were replaced by cars, skilled carriage makers were no longer needed); or it may be due to changes in production methods (as in the mechanization of shoe production just after the Civil War).[16] In 1910, to cite a case of mechanization recent enough to furnish accurate data, about half the workers in the tobacco industry were craftsmen, foremen, and other skilled workers—mainly hand cigarmakers. By 1930, after new mass production methods had been introduced, only one in ten was a skilled worker. Some students of labor took the trouble to find out what happened to the displaced skilled workers. Very few of the cigarmakers were converted to machine operators (the latter were usually recruited directly from the ranks of the unskilled).[17] A study of one group of skilled cigarmakers in the Manchester, New Hampshire area (mechanized around 1931) showed that the average length of unemployment was about one year; one in five remained unemployed more than five years. During the seven-year period studied, over half the workers had experienced a minimum of three years of joblessness. Only about half of those who got jobs between 1931 and 1937 stayed in the cigar-manufacturing industry. The skilled older workers were especially hard hit.[18] A study of displaced textile workers in New England in 1953-1954 suggests that lack of information, opportunity, and motive spells much difficulty even where new industries and other areas offer the displaced worker alternative possibilities.[19]

Technological unemployment, then, is the most dramatic effect of this sort of specialization; and the problems of adjustment are greatest for the oldest and most skilled. Even in years of prosperity men who have invested their time, their money, their very selves in their work are reluctant to accept downgrading or begin new occupational ventures.

In sum: specialization based on mechanization in the early years of industrial development can mean robotization for some workers, technologi-

[14] At any given time, the extent of such subservience to the machine depends on what proportion of jobs is organized on these lines. Recent technological changes suggest that these jobs may be the model of the past, not for the future.

[15] Moore, *op. cit.*

[16] W. Lloyd Warner and Joseph O. Low, *The Social System of the Modern Factory* (New Haven: Yale University Press, 1947), p. 60.

[17] Abram J. Jaffee and Charles D. Stewart, *Manpower Resources and Utilization* (New York: Wiley, 1951), pp. 265-266.

[18] Daniel B. Creamer and Gladys V. Swackhamer, *Cigar Makers, After the Lay-off* (Philadelphia: Works Progress Administration, National Research Project L-1, 1937), pp. 36-38.

[19] William H. Miernyk, *Inter-Industry Labor Mobility* (Boston: Northeastern University, Bureau of Business and Economic Research, 1955).

cal unemployment for others. Both have a drastic impact on life in the family and community.[20]

Who you are to what you can do: changes in the basis of specialization[21]

Work in the primitive tribe or peasant village is traditional; the division of labor is simple. This means several things. Work does not change much from generation to generation; the son can do what his father did. There are only a few special roles to fill (for example, hunting, fishing, gardening, fighting, and religious ceremony); practically anyone can learn all of them. Work can be assigned on the basis of traditional criteria, criteria often irrelevant to the performance of the role—age, sex, and perhaps, as in the Indian caste system, family origin. The elders of the tribe or village may occasionally look for promising young men and in some kinship systems, as among the Manus and the Chukchi "adopt" them, and sponsor their progress. But generally, even in these cases, little competition need accompany the "placement" of the individual in the economic order.

Contrast the industrial society. Work changes with changing technology and the pace of change accelerates; the division of labor is complex; and work is assigned more often on the basis of ability. Industrialization makes the shift away from traditional criteria of work assignment inevitable. Large portions of the population cannot do what their fathers did, cannot inherit occupations because the occupations change too rapidly. (If occupations were assigned by family origin, we would have too many of one thing and not enough of another.) There are not enough age and sex differences to represent the vast number of specialized roles that need to be filled. For example, we cannot expect all American males to learn to be carpenters, barbers, doctors, lawyers, research chemists, labor leaders, corporation executives, and so on. Some of these roles are so complex that they cannot be left to the accidents of inheritance. Despite the great plasticity of human nature, some individuals are born without the capacity to fill some roles; and modern society cannot afford an idiot as President. In fact, industrialization, by creating complex and important occupational roles, accents the importance of even *small* differences in ability. For these small differences may mean enormous differences in output. Compare, for example, the difference in amounts that can be accomplished by two machine-shovel operators of different degrees of skill. Or think of the amount

[20] Howe and Widick, *op. cit.*; Edward W. Bakke, *The Unemployed Man* (New York: Dutton, 1934); Robert C. Angell, *The Family Encounters the Depression* (New York: Scribner, 1936); Mirra Komarovsky, *The Unemployed Man and His Family* (New York: Holt, Rinehart and Winston, 1940).

[21] The following discussion draws upon Ralph Linton, *The Study of Man* (New York: Appleton-Century-Crofts, 1922); Talcott Parsons, *Essays in Sociological Theory, Pure and Applied* (New York: Free Press, 1949), 189 ff.; Moore, *Industrialization and Labor, op. cit.*; Marion J. Levy, Jr., *The Family Revolution in Modern China* (Cambridge: Harvard University Press, 1949); and Hoselitz, *op. cit.*

of damage that can be done by a relatively less able (that is, responsible) stillman in an oil refinery. This is an operator who has heavy responsibility for expensive processes and equipment. If he goes to sleep on the job he can ruin thousands of dollars in machinery and material, as can many semi-skilled machine operators.

In short, the number, complexity, importance, and frequency of change of occupational roles in industrial society have meant a shift in the basis of role assignment. "Who you are" becomes less important; "what you can do or learn to do" becomes more important.

The fact that work roles in modern society tend to be achieved, assigned on the basis of ability, intensifies competition for these roles. If no one is excluded from consideration, then everyone is potentially a competitor. This is why there is less chance for the development of a hereditary elite. This is, moreover, why modern industry everywhere is such a sifter, sorter, and above all *mixer* of diverse racial and ethnic groups.[22] It is a major reason, too, for the increased proportion of women who work. Everywhere, industrialization, by challenging traditional criteria of work assignment, by accenting ability instead of sex, invites women to participate as occupational equals. Although there are limits in the extent to which this goes, there is no doubt that industrial societies offer marked contrast to nonindustrial societies in the degree to which women are released from the home. Underscoring this shift is the fact that industrialization has everywhere been accompanied by agitation for the emancipation of women both within the family and within the society—often taking the form of feminist movements.[23]

More competition, more mixing of minority groups, more women at work—these are three of the main consequences of the shift in the basis of specialization, the new accent on ability.

[22] Cf. Everett C. Hughes, "The Knitting of Racial Groups in Industry," *American Sociological Review*, 11 (October, 1946), 512-519 and "Queries Concerning Industry and Society Growing Out of Study of Ethnic Relations in Industry," *American Sociological Review*, 14 (April, 1949), 211-220. Discrimination in American industry, of course, still exists; and in the underdeveloped areas it is one of the great blocks to rapid economic development. For instance, where persons of west European origin are in control and treat the natives as inferior, the possibilities of developing aspirations, motives, and work habits appropriate to industry are reduced; and caste exclusiveness in India still survives as a block to industrialization. Even after the rigor of caste law had decayed, attempts to introduce factory organization in the jute industry in the nineteenth century encountered the difficulty that every caste had a different ritual and different rest pauses and demanded different holidays: see Max Weber, *General Economic History* (New York: Free Press, 1950), p. 176. What is argued here is that advancing industrialization inevitably brings a decline in racial discrimination, and the American experience seems to bear this out: see Robert Carr, *et al.*, "Civil Rights in America," *Annals of the American Academy of Political and Social Science*, 275 (May, 1951), 1-238; Morroe Berger, *Equality by Statute* (New York: Columbia University Press, 1952), and "To Secure These Rights: Report of the President's Committee on Civil Rights" (Washington, D.C.: U.S. Government Printing Office, 1947).

[23] Levy, *op. cit.*, p. 12.

Status to contract: the shift from diffuse to specific obligations

Along with the new emphasis on ability as the main criterion for role assignment has gone a shift in the quality of work relations.

In the primitive tribe or peasant village work is hardly distinguished from the rest of life, from one's duties and rights as husband, son, father, clansman. A man's work obligations, which come to him by virtue of his age, sex, and birth, are, like his kinship obligations, broad and diffuse. Both output and consumption are traditionally confined to needs appropriate to his age, sex, and membership in clan or family. When a crisis or dispute arises in the allocation of goods and services, traditional patterns of mutual aid come into play. Help is not likely to be refused on the grounds that the asker has not proved his right to "something extra"; rights and obligations covered by clan and family relations are not so clearly defined and delimited. Loosely put, the formula for preindustrial living is this: the family equals the community equals the insurance against disaster—and none of the rights and duties need be specified in advance.

Contrast the situation in industrial society. Work relations tend to be functionally specific. That means that the rights and obligations and activities covered by economic relationships are clearly defined and delimited —as in a business contract. In the case of dispute over what is due, the burden of proof lies with the one who asks for "something extra." Moreover, work tends to be sharply separated from home and family. Physically, place of work is located some distance from place of residence; socially, family relations remain personal and diffuse, work relations (and increasingly other nonfamilial relations) tend to become impersonal and contractual.

There are good reasons for expecting this to happen in all industrial societies. If there is an inevitable emphasis on ability to perform the role as a basis for role assignment, the rights and duties that make up the role must be spelled out. Otherwise, how could the individual's ability to fill the role be judged? The change in the basis of specialization discussed above, then, means that relationships must become increasingly contractual.

A second reason for the decline in the number and range of diffuse (family-type) relationships is the problem of employing people and disposing of goods in a complex economy with complex specialization. Personalized, familial relations between employer and employee in a large steel mill are obviously impossible. And the auto manufacturer can hardly dispose of goods through personal friends; he does it through dealers, people with whom he has specific and delimited relations. If the steelworker should break a leg, or the car dealer should receive damaged cars, neither can invoke any tradition of mutual aid. The employee might appeal to the

Workmen's Compensation Claims Board, the dealer might go to the insurance company; both would have to prove a claim.

Industrialization and mobility

Much of what we have said adds up to this: industrialization represents a multi-front attack on tradition, an attack symbolized by the words "change" and "movement." In the early decades of America's industrial development, and this is matched in the economic growth of other countries, families by the millions were uprooted and pushed into industry. Everywhere advancing industrialization makes the worker dependent on the employer and the labor market (whose changing demands necessitate frequent job shifts), and the nature of his work changes with changing technology (which brings the dilution and obsolescence of skills). The basis of assignment of individuals to work roles changes. In competition with others, the individual can thus move from one job to another with changes in his own ability or the abilities demanded by jobs. Place of work is separated from place of residence; the industrial way of life includes a journey to work. In other words, all of these changes that accompany industrialization make for a *vastly increased mobility* of the population— movement within a single career from job to job, company to company, neighborhood to neighborhood, community to community; movement between generations from father's occupation down, up or across to a new occupation. In addition to these moves to which all are exposed, industrialism has also established a seasonal flow which carries a portion of the population from winter tasks to summer and back again. . . .[24]

The Factory System and Stratification

Part of the early indictment of the industrial revolution was that it made the rich richer and the poor poorer; that it gave interesting and varied

[24] Since the work of Turner, many have argued that America in the years before 1890 was uniquely shaped by its expanding frontier, which permitted the underpriviledged industrial worker and the unsuccessful small trader to pick up stakes and move West. We hear much about the sense of expanding opportunity; the self-reliant willingness to move. As Hacker points out, however, "The free farmers of the American West, beginning with the 1820's, were not recruited from the industrial workers of the East, for these simply could not afford the . . . long journey [and] a family farm:" see Louis M. Hacker, *The Triumph of American Capitalism* (New York: Simon and Schuster, 1940), p. 9. Moreover, while the expanding frontier may have intensified the mobility of Americans in the period under discussion, it is not at all clear that this mobility lessened when the frontier closed. It is not just America's empty spaces that give its social life its fluid character (contrast Manchuria, Siberia, Canada), it is also industrialization. The frontier and the impetus to change and mobility it symbolizes, exist not only in land but in industry; and the high degree of geographical and social mobility is rooted in the demands industry makes wherever it develops rapidly and far.

work to the few, and boring, repetitive and physically exhausting work to the many; that "democratic rights" for the great laboring masses meant the right to sleep on park benches, to be out of a job or feel insecure in one. In general, it was said, the industrial revolution brought a polarization of social classes and intensified class conflict. An American quotation spells out the theme:[25]

We find the wealth and luxury of our cities mingled with poverty and wretchedness and unremunerative toil. A crowded and constantly increasing urban population suggests the impoverishment of rural sections, and discontent with agricultural pursuits . . . .

We discover that the fortunes realized by our manufacturers are no longer solely the reward of sturdy industry and enlightened foresight, but that they result from the discriminating favor of the government, and are largely built upon undue exactions from the masses of our people. The gulf between employers and the employed is constantly widening, and classes are rapidly forming, one comprising the very rich and powerful, while in another are found the toiling poor.

. . . We discover the existence of trusts, combinations, and monopolies, while the citizen is struggling far in the rear, or is trampled to death beneath an iron heel. Corporations . . . are fast becoming the people's masters.

This was no Populist soapboxer, no Marxist agitator speaking. This was President Grover Cleveland, hardly a radical fellow, in an annual message to Congress, written in December, 1888. Increasing inequality of income, declining opportunity to rise to fortune, the concentration of power in the hands of a few corporations—Cleveland was articulating charges widespread in that decade, when industrialism was making its most rapid strides. There was much in the decades following the Civil War to give such complaints plausibility. A brief look at the evidence on distribution of income and the facts of labor protest may give us a hint of what was going on.

Initial Polarization of Social Classes

The decade of the 1880's was a period in which our national income (adjusted to 1950 prices) increased by 73 per cent—its biggest jump upward in all the decades between 1850 and 1950.[26] But did the rich and the poor share equally in the gains? Usable data on income distribution in the United States before 1900 are scarce. S. Kuznets, the leading expert on the matter, suggests, however, that there is an early phase of industrialization

---

[25] Quoted in Hofstadter, *op. cit.*, p. 183.
[26] Based on J. Frederic Dewhurst, *et al.*, *America's Needs and Resources* (New York: Twentieth Century Fund, 1955), p. 40.

in which income inequality may widen. He places this phase in the United States from about 1840 to 1890, especially after 1870, but warns that this is "conjecture."[27] One early study suggests that of the 12½ million families in the country in 1890, 11 million had an income of under $1,200 with an average annual income from labor of $380.[28] Industrial employment tended to be irregular.[29] Whatever the precise figures, it seems very probable that large numbers of American workers in the late nineteenth century lived below the poverty line even by the standards of that day.

Whatever picture of economic misery one can draw for the working class of the 1880's, it cannot explain the bitter militancy of labor protest in that decade, or the willingness of conservative Presidents to speak on behalf of the underdog. Wages rose in the period.[30] Many of the workers described as living in poverty had experienced worse poverty on the farms they fled from (where a series of bad harvests could create suffering to match that caused by urban unemployment). Others had experienced worse poverty in industrial jobs the previous decade. There is no evidence that it was more difficult to rise out of the working class than it had been in earlier decades; and what data we have indicate that the men who in the 1880's were at the top of the heap—the business elite—were in larger proportion from the "lower" or "lower middle" classes than were their counterparts in any generation in history. Forty-three per cent of business leaders born in the period 1820-1849 and listed in the *Dictionary of American Biography* had fathers in these categories.[31]

What pained the working class was the perception that the wealth around them was increasing rapidly (on the farm, poverty had been traditional); that it was visibly powerful (this was the age of the "spoilsmen," when many businessmen in politics took their cues from businessmen in

[27] Cf. Simon Kuznets, "Economic Growth and Income Inequality," *American Economic Review*, **45** (March, 1955), 1-28. The evidence for the initial decades of industrialization in Britain is similarly inconclusive. Economic historian T. S. Ashton, considering "The Standard of Life of the Worker in England, 1790-1830," concludes: "A greater proportion of the people came to benefit from [the factory system] both as producers and as consumers. . . . There were, however, masses of unskilled or poorly skilled workers—seasonally employed agricultural workers and hand-loom weavers in particular—whose incomes were almost wholly absorbed in paying for the bare necessities of life. . . ." While he concedes that the relative position of the worker in the decade 1810-1820 "almost certainly worsened" he implies that a reversal took place after 1821: see Friedrich A. Hayek, ed., *Capitalism and the Historians* (Chicago: University of Chicago Press, 1954), pp. 133-136, 158-159. Kuznets, on the other hand, ventures the guess that "in England during the first half of the 19th century . . . income inequality may have widened" (Kuznets, *op. cit.*, p. 27).

[28] Charles B. Spahr, *An Essay on the Present Distribution of Wealth in the United States* (New York: Crowell, 1896), p. 128.

[29] Henry David, *The History of the Haymarket Affair* (New York: Holt, Rinehart and Winston, 1936), p. 19.

[30] U.S. Department of Labor, "Wages in the United States and Europe, 1870-1898." *Bulletin of the Department of Labor*, **3** (September, 1898), 665-693.

[31] C. Wright Mills, "The American Business Elite," *The Tasks of Economic History, Journal of Economic History*, Supplement 5 (December, 1945), 20-44.

industry without shame); and that the worker's lot did not seem to improve at so great a pace. The insecurities of industrial life described above —the new dependence on the employer, the obsolescence and dilution of skills, the difficult adaptation to factory disciplines, the new insecurity of old age—these added to the unrest. At the same time, the very increase of wealth that had been achieved raised the people's hopes and aspirations. Even if the poor were not getting poorer, even if they had shared equally in the great gains of the decade, economic suffering might have seemed more conspicuous and less justified.

Early labor protest

The creation of an industrial labor force everywhere brings forth labor protest. Such protest takes many forms: absenteeism, loafing, passive or active insubordination, sabotage, strikes, political protest movements. As industrialization proceeds, various people contend for control over this labor protest, for the right to channel it and direct it: employers, union leaders, politicians, government administrators, religious leaders, military cliques.[32] The protest is channeled in varied directions: a combination of trade unions and labor parties in Great Britain and the Scandinavian countries; revolutionary syndicalist, Catholic, or Communist organizations in France and Italy; state-managed "labor fronts" in Nazi Germany and the Soviet Union; "business unions" in the U.S.; paternalistic "company unions" or government "captives" in Nehru's India.[33]

Labor protest in the early phases of economic development seems typically to be sporadic and loosely organized (labor movements come and go, showing wild fluctuations in membership). Such protest encounters tenacious employer opposition, which generally involves use of the police power. It is often treated as illegal, and sometimes goes underground in the form of the secret society. It is easily shaped to political ends by outside intellectuals who assume early labor leadership.[34] (In nonwestern underdeveloped areas labor movements have generally been meshed with nationalist movements and antiimperialist agitation.)

America is no exception to these generalizations. Until just before the turn of the century, labor protest was intermittently tame and violent, economic and political; labor organizations were unsteady, easily diverted to elaborate political programs (from greenbackism to the Single Tax, from

[32] Clark Kerr, et al., "The Labour Problem in Economic Development: A Framework for a Reappraisal," International Labour Review, 71 (March, 1955), 223-235.

[33] Walter Galenson, ed., Comparative Labor Movements (Englewood Cliffs, N.J.: Prentice-Hall, 1952); Franz L. Neumann, Behemoth (New York: Oxford University Press, 1942); S. D. Punekar, Trade Unionism in India, C. N. Vakil, ed. (Bombay: New Book Co., 1948).

[34] Selig Perlman, A Theory of the Labor Movement (New York: Macmillan, 1928); Harold L. Wilensky, Intellectuals in Labor Unions (New York: Free Press, 1956).

revolutionary anarchism to Marxian socialism, from Owen's "state guardianship" to producers' and consumers' cooperation). Obstinate employers used private armies, the courts declared unions to be criminal conspiracies (even after the Civil War until use of the injunction gave them a better weapon), and the government broke strikes by use of local, state, and federal troops.

The decade of the 1880's is worth special attention both as an instance typifying labor protest in a free society in the early years of rapid industrialization, and as the turning point which led to the emergence of the contemporary American labor movement and the dominance of collective bargaining as the main form of industrial conflict today. That decade produced a near-revolutionary upheaval.

The 1870's had seen a long and devastating panic. The accelerated tempo of industrialization, depression unemployment, and wage cuts had precipitated a nationwide railway strike accompanied by pitched battles of workers against vigilante committees and militia. Conditions peculiar to the coalfields (after the defeat of the strong anthracite miners' union in 1869) had produced a secret organization known as the Molly Maguires which disposed of its opposition by terrorism and assassination. But it was in the 1880's, especially during and just after the depression of 1884-1885, that labor protest began to sweep the land. Skilled and unskilled, women and men, native and foreign-born—never before (and not again until the 1930's) had American labor displayed such a rush to organize. The peak of immigration was reached that decade, and streams of newcomers captured the enthusiasm. "Labor organizations assumed the nature of a real class movement. . . . General strikes, sympathetic strikes . . . nationwide political movements became the order of the day."[35] Employer associations quickly counteracted with lockouts, blacklists, armed guards, and detectives. When the wave of strikes failed, a consumer boycott movement of epidemic proportions got under way. This was the time of the great upheaval of the Knights of Labor, an inclusive labor organization espousing the ideal of producers' cooperation. The Knights spearheaded a mid-eighties mass movement culminating in an unsuccessful nationwide strike for the eight-hour day. It was the time, too, of the famous bomb explosion of Haymarket Square, which touched off a period of hysteria and police terror in Chicago, and resulted in the unjust conviction and execution of some innocent men.[36] The strength of employer opposition and the unwieldiness of the Knight's own organization threw the labor movement into decline. The defeat of Henry George in a spirited campaign for mayor of New York City marked the end of its political reverberations. As the movement broke up, the American Federation of Labor (AFL) was established to organize workers on straight trade union lines, for better wages,

[35] Perlman, *op. cit.*, p. 84.
[36] *Ibid.*, pp. 68-105; Beard and Beard, *op. cit.*, Vol. II, pp. 220 ff.; David, *op. cit.*

hours, and working conditions through collective bargaining—foreshadow-
ing the form in which labor protest was to be cast during the next century.
The last gasp of working class militancy came in the form of the Home-
stead strike of 1892 (which involved a violent battle between an army of
300 Pinkerton detectives hired by Carnegie and armed strikers, including
women and boys, who were finally overcome by the militia), and the great
Pullman strike of 1894 which was broken with the aid of federal troops, a
federal injunction, and the imprisonment of its leaders.

This period represents an enormous thrust upward from the people
of poverty and low status—not again repeated until the early days of the
New Deal and provoking much the same militant fear on the part of the
wealthy and well-born. The mass movement of the 1880's and the big
strikes of the early 1890's were the fruit of the sweeping industrialization
that followed the Civil War. They had their historical counterpart in the
Luddite movement of 1811-1817 in England (in which workers rioted and
smashed the new machines that confronted them), and their contemporary
counterpart in the social movements of underdeveloped lands today. The
ferment of labor and radical movements of this period provided impetus
to parallel movements for social reform and social welfare. The enactment
by World War I of factory codes requiring proper ventilation and sanitary
appliances, workmen's compensation laws, bars on contract labor, child
labor laws, the regulation of prison labor, the creation of a Department of
Labor and many state labor bureaus, the achievement of first the ten, then
the eight-hour day (railroad workers in 1916, nationwide in 1938)—these
reforms must be seen in the context of late nineteenth century agitation,
epitomized by the great upheaval of the 1880's.

4. Social Consequences of the Industrialization of Southern Cities

Rudolf Heberle

The subject to be discussed in this paper is the effect of the growth of manufacturing industries upon cities and towns in the South or, more precisely, upon urban society. Although we have a wealth of good studies of urbanization and of industrialization in this region, very little actual research seems to have been done on our particular subject. The following observations are largely a fruit of my travels in the region and, to some extent, a by-product of my forthcoming study of the *Labor Force in Louisiana.** I am also indebted to several of my former students for information, particularly on small cities and towns.

I. Industrialization Versus Urbanization

Industrialization and urbanization should not be considered as identical processes, as we might be tempted to do because of the decisive influence which modern industry has had upon the development of cities in the last century and a half. But cities have been in existence before industrialization began, and not all cities are highly industrialized. This certainly holds for many cities in the South. Furthermore, much of the industrial development has been a consequence rather than a cause of city growth. We shall therefore have to consider first, the economic origins of southern cities, and second, the role of industries in the development of cities in the region, before we can discuss the effect of industrialization upon urban society. The latter discussion will be limited to the immediate effects upon the ecology and social structure of urban communities, while the indirect consequences and the changes in the occupational composition of the labor force and other economic consequences of industrialization will not be considered.

II. Origin and Development of Southern Cities

1. With few exceptions, southern cities did not originate as industrial communities. This is particularly true of the larger cities, with Birmingham as

Reprinted from Rudolf Heberle, "Social Consequences of the Industrialization of Southern Cities," *Social Forces,* **28** (October, 1948), pp. 29-37, published by the University of North Carolina Press.

* Louisiana State University Press, 1948.

the most notable exception. The South being a rural region with a colonial type of agriculture, most of its older cities developed as ports, railway and commercial centers, or as local trading and marketing towns[1] and as temporary residences of wealthy planter families. The oldest industries in the South, those engaged in processing the products of the farm and the forest, were largely located in rural communities and small towns. The cities had to depend almost entirely on commerce and trade. Purely commercial cities, however, seldom attain very large size. Those old cities of the South whose commercial function faded away through changes in the transportation system were doomed to stagnation unless they offered also factors of attraction for manufacturing industries. Like some of the old cities of Europe that ceased to grow when trade routes changed, many of the older cities in the South stagnated when the transatlantic and inland trade shifted to northern cities; and just as some of the old commercial towns of Europe experienced another spell of growth when, for some reason or other, manufacturing industries began to locate in them, thus New Orleans, Mobile, and other southern cities experienced an economic rejuvenation when manufacturing industries began to develop, while Savannah, Georgia (population, 1940—118,000), and Charleston, South Carolina (population 1940—99,000), illustrate the other type.[2]

Contrary to the most important European commercial cities which were also old centers of handicraft, producing many commodities for long distance trade, the older southern cities lacked such a broad basis of industrial production. Until late in the nineteenth century they were places of export and import trade, exporting mainly products of primary industries and importing the products of European handicraft and manufacturers. Apparently, the wealth of planters and merchants did not support a broad layer of local artisans and craftsmen. This fact has been of great significance for the social changes that took place when industrialization began.

2. We shall now turn to our second question: The role of industrialization in the development of southern cities. By industrialization we mean the development and growth of "secondary" industries: the extraction of coal, oil, natural gas, and other minerals, the construction industry and, most important of all, the manufacturing and mechanical industries. The role of an industry in urbanization depends in the first line on the factors that determine its location. Some of these industries are *consumer-ori-*

[1] Walter J. Matherly, "The Emergence of the Metropolitan Community in the South," *Social Forces,* 14 (March, 1936), 323. The cities of the Old South were exclusively commercial; they were centers of surrounding agricultural territories; they were largely the product of agrarianism. But with the rise of industrialism, new types of cities appeared. Since the turn of the century the industrial cities emerged. . . . The growth of trade has likewise contributed, more greatly than any other factor, to the rise of metropolitan centers in the South. . . ." See also Francis Butler Simkins, *The South, Old and New* (New York: Knopf, 1947), pp. 68-69.

[2] See Simkins, *op. cit.,* p. 375.

ented,[3] like bakeries, printing shops, gas, power plants, and to some extent the construction industry. Their location tends to correspond to the distribution of population; they are to be found in all larger communities and in fairly fixed ratios to the population of the community and its trade area. In the case of these industries it is hardly meaningful to speak of a contribution to urbanization or an "effect" upon urban society. They develop as urban society develops and they are part and parcel of it. A great deal of the earlier growth of secondary industries in the South has been in this class and a great deal of recent development also belongs to it.[4]

Other industries are either *raw-material-oriented*, like steel mills and sugar refineries, or *labor-oriented* like most of the southern textile industry. Among these two groups are the truly city-building industries, those that draw people into cities and whose growth tends to speed up the growth of an urban population. Consequently, our analysis should be primarily concerned with them.

Now it so happens that in the South, a large proportion of the important secondary industries are raw-material oriented. This is not merely due to the presence of resources, but is also a consequence of the well-known freight rate structure. Whether these industries will be located in cities or in rural areas, whether they tend to develop large industrially diverse urban communities or tend to create only small or medium-sized industrially specialized towns, depends on the nature of their main raw materials and the location of resources, together with the industry's dependence upon cheap transportation facilities and other factors.[5]

[3] The terminology with regard to location of industries is that of Alfred Weber's, on whose theory this section is based. See Alfred Weber, "Industrielle Standortslehre," *Grundriß der Sozialökonomie*, VI (Tubingen, 1923).

[4] It should be noted, however, that with the increasing dependence of the rural population upon urban industry and commercial services, the development of these consumer-oriented industries tends to be increasingly influenced by the demands of rural customers in the metropolitan region of the city. Bakeries, for instance, sell increasing proportions of their production in rural territory. But a large-scale bakery is not likely to be established except in a city of considerable size.

[5] Harriet L. Herring, *Southern Industry and Regional Development* (Chapel Hill: University of North Carolina Press, 1940), p. 72, shows the share of the South in 55 industries in 1937. Among the twenty industry groups of whose total wage earners the Southeast had 25 percent or more, only about ten may be considered as definitely city-building industries. Of the entire list the same proportion is probably in this class. See also Rupert B. Vance, *All These People* (Chapel Hill: University of North Carolina Press, 1945), p. 276.

In Louisiana we found that of all workers in manufacturing industries in 1940, 57.6 percent were living in urban communities, 33.7 percent were rural-nonfarm, and 8.7 percent rural farm. In the lumber industry, however, only 29 percent of the workers were living in urban communities, whereas in the paper industry 51.5 percent were classified as urban residents. In the crude petroleum and gas production only 41.0 percent were living in urban communities, 49.6 were classified as rural-nonfarm residents, and 9.4 percent lived on rural farms, while in the group petroleum products and chemical industries, 51.0 percent were urban, 42.8 percent rural nonfarm, and 6.2 percent rural farm. Although these data need considerable refinement, they do give an idea of the differences in the urbanizing effect between various industry groups.

One of the oldest industries in the South and one of the most important industries in regard to employment is the lumber industry. It is definitely raw-material oriented. The rapid exhaustion of timber resources made it a temporary industry in many localities. The sawmills were rarely located in large cities, but rather spread and scattered over the country side. Consequently, this industry created a large number of small mono-industrial communities, but contributed little directly to the growth of larger cities. However, in many cases it laid the foundation for a larger community, as some of the sawmill towns developed beyond the mono-industrial stage and became cities of more diversified industrial structure. In some cases this was due to the establishment of additional wood-using industries. The furniture industry, the production of paper and cardboard containers, and the rayon industry belong in this group. The wood-using industries are, as a rule, more concentrated locally than the lumber industry. Consequently, the workers in these industries tend to be living in cities, while the sawmill workers tend to be living largely in rural areas and small towns. A striking example of city development due to the sequence of saw mills and paper mills is the town of Bogalousa in Louisiana, an urban community of very recent origin. Another example is Monroe in north Louisiana.

In other cases the continued growth of lumber towns was due to the agglomeration of new industries oriented towards different raw materials at the locations of the lumber industry. This happened in several cities of the deep South and coastal Southwest with the coming of the petroleum industry. Refineries and chemical plants using the products and by-products of oil refineries—as well as natural gas—were in several cases established in old lumber industry towns.

Reasons for this "agglomeration" of two entirely different industries were probably the dependence of both upon water transportation,[6] the location of their respective raw materials in the same general areas, and the advantage, for the most recent industries, of finding already a local nucleus of industrial labor. Baton Rouge or even better Lake Charles and the area of Beaumont-Port Arthur in the southeastern corner of Texas are good examples of this sequence.

However, the job-creating capacity of the petroleum and basic chemical industries is low[7] and the direct effect of these industries upon urban

[6] Oil refineries are not necessarily located near the origin of petroleum, which can be transported economically over long distances by pipeline or water transportation. The Baton Rouge refinery receives petroleum in both ways, from oil fields in the region and from Venezuela. Coastal lumber mills also receive part of their raw material (valuable tropical timber) from overseas. The shipment of bulky products like saw timber and gasoline by water way is of course also advantageous.

[7] See Herring, op. cit. Some recent expansions at the Esso Standard Oil Co. refinery at Baton Rouge indicate a range of investment per job created from about 10,000 to about 90,000 dollars per job: State Times, Baton Rouge (April 13, 1948), p. 1.

growth is not very strong. On the other hand, these are high wage industries which exert a considerable stimulus upon the development of trade and services, and they also attract a variety of auxiliary industries. Among the raw-material oriented branches of the food industry, which are very important with regard to employment in the deep South, none can be considered as city-building industries if taken by themselves. The canning and drying of seafood and of fruits and vegetables are typically rural industries, scattered over many small towns and villages. Cane sugar refineries, too, tend to be located in rural communities.

The greatest city-building industry, the iron and steel industry, is so far almost entirely concentrated in the Birmingham metropolitan area. Here, of course, was an ideal location for this industry because iron, coal, and limestone—the three basic materials in steel production—occur in this same locality. Birmingham, which incidentally was founded in the same year of 1871, when the German steel magnate, Friedrich Krupp, had already reaped great profits from his armament factory in Essen, is an outstanding example of the urbanizing force of the iron and steel industry. It is probably the most outstanding example in the South of purely industrial origin of a *large* city. However, Birmingham has for a long time been lagging behind the chief northern centers of iron and steel production as far as diversification is concerned. This has been explained by the relatively restricted size of the southern market for steel products.[8]

Another and most striking example of industrial origin of a city is Oak Ridge, Tennessee, child of World War II and product of the most recent industry in the region. While its population in 1946 was estimated at 48,-000, it may grow into a considerably larger center, provided that other industries will locate at the same place.

If we turn now to the *labor-oriented* industries in the South, we have to consider in the first line the South's most notorious problem child: the cotton textile industry. One of the main city builders in nineteenth century Europe and in New England, this industry had its main period of growth in the South at a time when electrification in connection with a relatively ample labor supply in rural areas made concentration in large cities unnecessary and decentralization in small urban communities possible. Thus, the growth of the textile industry in the Piedmont, while certainly contributing to urbanization, did not result in the development of an American Manchester or Chemnitz. With few exceptions, the southern textile communities are small.[9] However, in some cases textile mills have been located in

8 Andreas Predoehl, "Die oertliche Verteilung der amerikanischen Eisenund Stahlindustrie," *Weltwirtschaftliches Archiv,* 27 (Jena, 1928), 240, 246, 270, 276, 289. See also, Temporary National Economic Committee, Investigation of Concentration of Economic Power, Monograph No. 42, *The Basing Point Problem* (Washington, D.C.: 1941), pp. 17, 18 *passim.*
9 According to R. B. Vance, *op. cit.,* p. 307, Table 84 (Percent of Manufacturing Establishments by Size of City and Type of Manufacture, North Carolina Catawba Val-

cities where an already established but more or less exclusively men-employing industry left a sufficient supply of female labor unutilized. The agglomeration of the hosiery industry at a furniture manufacturing center like High Point, North Carolina, illustrates this case. The fuller utilization of the labor force will, of course, result in larger aggregate payrolls and thereby stimulate the growth of trade and services.

The concentration of the cigarette and tobacco industry in two larger North Carolina urban areas, Winston-Salem and Durham, is most likely the result of a combination of labor- and raw-material orientation, and without the additional factor of an extraordinary concentration of capital, this industry as such would scarcely have created any important urban centers.[10]

So much for the urbanizing effect of southern industries. A more refined and comprehensive analysis would have to take into consideration the importance of secondary factors of location, such as water transportation, water supply, and the availability of electric power and natural gas.

The indirect effects of industrialization upon city development were demonstrated in a highly dramatic fashion during the Second World War when increases in manufacturing employment in cities like New Orleans were accompanied by very strong increases in employment in trade, transportation, and services.[11]

Before we proceed to discuss the consequences of industrialization for urban society, let us briefly consider the pattern of geographic distribution of cities in the South as it results from the factors determining the location of raw-material-oriented and labor-oriented industries.[12]

We saw that the South has relatively few large cities which owe their existence to the agglomeration of raw-material-oriented industries, like the big manufacturing cities of the North. In the labor-oriented industries, two contradictory tendencies can be observed in a society where labor is free to move: the workers tend to concentrate at the large labor markets, where employment opportunities are most numerous and diverse, while employ-

---

ley, 1938), the furniture and chemical industries were more concentrated in larger cities than the textile industry. Among the latter, plants making wearing apparel, silk rayon, and dyeing and finishing plants were more concentrated in cities of 10,000 or over than plants making cotton yarns and cotton fabrics. Only 35 percent of all establishments in the area were in cities of 25,000 and over (65.1 percent in cities 10,000 or over).

[10] Simkins, op. cit., p. 377: "Concentration of the (tobacco) industry into fewer cities in larger factories . . . (was) part of the Duke strategy."

[11] Rudolf Heberle, "Survey of the War-time Labor Force of Louisiana" (U.S. Employment Service, Louisiana, 1945) p. 22 f. passim. In New Orleans these increases were concentrated in the central business district rather than in the "neighborhood" shopping centers; in other words, they occurred in establishments serving the war-industry workers (and soldiers).

[12] The important work of the late August Losch, Die räumliche Ordnung der Wirtschaft, 2nd ed. (Jena: Fischer, 1944), came to my attention too late to find consideration in this article. If translated it should prove to be of great value in all studies dealing with the location of cities and industries.

ers, unless the nature of their enterprise ties them also definitely to the large labor markets, tend to move away from the big cities in order to evade high land prices and high wage levels. This latter tendency has been strong in the South. One recalls the typical advertising of entrepreneurs who want to establish a plant in a small community with an ample supply of labor and without competing enterprises, in order to attain a virtual monopoly over the local labor market. This tendency has been favored on the workers' part by lack of knowledge of employment opportunities in distant large cities and probably in many cases by the desire to be able to fall back on farming in old age or depression,[13] all of which factors have contributed to hold labor in small cities and in the surrounding country. The result has been a wide dispersion of manufacturing industries in many but relatively small cities and a relative sparsity of large cities.

Distances between large cities are much greater than in the older manufacturing regions of the North, and there are in the South no very large clusters of smaller cities. While we find in some highly industrialized subregions, like the Piedmont, strings of cities lined up along the highways, there are no large compactly urbanized areas; even in the more densely industrialized parts of North Carolina, which have been studied by Howard W. Odum, Rupert B. Vance, Harriet L. Herring and their associates, there appears to be evolving a new constellation pattern of urban communities, consisting of small central cities with still smaller satellite communities and considerable dispersion of workers in the open country.[14] Similar patterns can be observed along the Gulf Coast from Pensacola to Galveston and Houston.

However, in order to see this pattern in its true significance, one ought to realize that the war-time industrial boom did not result in much further decentralization of industry in the region; on the contrary, most of the gains in population and increases in industrial employment were concentrated in already established centers of manufacturing.[15] Oak Ridge is an exception rather than a typical case.

These statements concerning the pattern of city location are, of course, more or less hypothetical. To analyse the economic factors which have contributed to the development of the present geographic distribution of cities in the South would be very interesting. One would probably find: (1) a system of major export- and import-trade cities, (2) a much more numerous system of smaller local trading centers, and (3) a system of industrial cities, partly new, partly evolved out of cities of type (1) or (2).

[13] Therel R. Black, *Part-time Farming among Industrial Workers in East Baton Rouge Parish* (M.A. thesis in Sociology, L.S.U., 1941) finds that this was one of the most frequent reasons given for acquisition of a farm by petroleum refinery workers.

[14] Vance, *op. cit.*, Chaps. 19 and 20, especially pp. 306, 317.

[15] Rudolf Heberle, "The Impact of the War on Population Redistribution in the South," *Papers of the Institute of Research and Training in the Social Sciences*, no. 7 (Nashville, Tenn.: Vanderbilt University Press, 1945), pp. 24-30.

III. The Effects on Urban Society

1. The most obvious, most easily observable effects of industrialization are changes in the social ecology or human geography of the cities. These changes have been far from uniform.

In the older cities of the South, where industrialization began in the age of the steam engine and the street car, the pattern of ecology and the process of its evolution has been quite similar to that of American cities in general. This led authors like E. W. Parks to the conclusion that *all* southern cities would become more like the northern and eastern cities.[16] But in the majority of cities, especially the smaller ones, where industrialization occurred mainly in the age of electrification and the automobile, the ecological pattern seems to deviate from the older one. The more recent the industry, the greater seems to be the deviation.

In many cases the industrial plants were from the beginning located far outside the city, where unobstructed sites were available at low cost. If there had not yet been developed any large working class areas, the workers tended to live near the plants, even where the employer did not, as in the case of textile mill villages, provide dwellings for the employees. This tendency towards peripheral location of factories and plants is particularly pronounced in the case of the more recent basic industries, which, like the petroleum refineries and chemical plants, require ample space and cannot be located in densely populated areas, for reasons of health and security. The location of the major industrial plants at Baton Rouge and the development of adjoining suburban areas inhabited by the employees is an outstanding example. The same pattern exists in an even more extreme form in Lake Charles, Louisiana, where the plants which were established during the second world war are located far out in the country, and where entirely separate workers' communities have sprung up at considerable distance from the old town. A more or less typical "ribbon" development along the main highways leading out of town is a characteristic element in this pattern.

This scattered growth may agree with the prevailing inclinations or preferences and particularly with the likings of workers of rural origin; it may make their accommodation to urban life easier; and it has definite military advantages as it reduces the vulnerability of a city from air attacks. But it certainly increases the overhead cost of road maintenance, sewerage,

[16] The statement by E. W. Parks that "Every possible forecast implies that the continued growth of the city, with the concomitant advance of industrialism, will tend to standardize our cities and make them completely like all other American cities," appears exaggerated in the light of more recent developments. See, E. W. Parks, "Towns and Cities," in W. T. Couch, ed., *Culture in the South* (Chapel Hill: University of North Carolina Press, 1933), p. 518. I owe this quotation to Ira de A. Reid's stimulating paper "Methodological Notes for Studying the Southern City," *Social Forces*, **19** (December, 1940), 228-235.

and utilities if it results in a population density below the minimum at which, according to the experience of city planners, those services cannot be provided at reasonable rates.[17]

The general extent of suburban expansion can be inferred from the high rate of population increase in the outlying parts of metropolitan districts[18] and also from the high rates of increase of "rural nonfarm" population in counties containing large urban centers, an increase which is largely concentrated in suburban areas.

Another significant development can be observed with regard to the location of wealthy people's homes. It seems to be characteristic for the older, smaller cities in the South that the homes of the socially prominent families were to be found just outside the central—and only—business district. A few streets with not too pretentious homes under magnificent old trees in luxuriant gardens usually made up the areas of highest social status. As the city grew and as wealth increased, the "old" families tended to move towards the periphery—following the general fashion of our age. The more industrialized the area, the better are (most likely) the roads and the greater the inducement to move into the cooler country side. The old homes are then converted into rooming houses and "tourist homes." This in itself is nothing peculiar to the South. However, it so happens that in the kind of city under consideration, the poorer people usually lived at the edge of the town. This was particularly the case with Negroes. It happens, therefore, quite frequently that white people infiltrate into suburban areas occupied by Negroes, buying their property or cancelling their leases. This process, which has been observed by Woofter and others, has been studied in Baton Rouge by my former colleague, Edgar A. Schuler; here the same process of displacement of Negroes by whites has also occurred in the more desirable parts of the old town.[19] As a result, the Negroes now tend to congregate in poorly drained and otherwise disadvantageous areas.[20]

---

[17] Bartholomew and Associates, "The 25-Year City-Parish Plan for Metropolitan Baton Rouge, Louisiana Preliminary Reports," Chap. 3, *Population* (1945), p. 13 f. See also T. R. Ford, *Maplewood: A Planned Community in the Industrial South* (M.A. thesis in Sociology, L.S.U., 1948).

[18] During the period of 1930 to 1940 the population growth in southern metropolitan districts conformed to the national pattern: higher rates of growth in outside areas than in the central city. The rates were very high in some cases. There seems to exist a fair correlation between rates of population increase of the total metropolitan district and rates of growth in outside areas. See U.S. Bureau of the Census Release P-3, no. 26.

[19] See Reid, *op. cit.*, quoting Woofter. Schuler's study is not published. See also Bartholomew and Associates, *op. cit.*, Chap. 3 *passim.* The same phenomenon has been observed in Jackson, Mississippi, by Dorothy Melvin (unpublished paper in urban sociology).

[20] A similar change in racial ecology was observed in New Orleans by Harlan W. Gilmore, "The Old New Orleans and the New," *American Sociological Review,* 9 (August, 1944), 385-394. Here the Negroes, formerly in close symbiosis with the whites moved into the low lying areas as these were drained and public transit systems developed—Industrialization invariably leads to the growth of radically segregated suburban working class areas.

The close ecological symbiosis of whites and Negroes which seems to have been characteristic at least of the older cities in the coastal plantation zone,[21] gives way to spatial segregation. Neighborly contacts become rare, and estrangement between the two races tends to increase. At the same time, industrialization is likely to reduce the frequency of interracial contacts through domestic and other personal service (because larger proportions of Negroes find other employment, and because the proportion of whites not wealthy enough to keep servants increases), while on the other hand, contacts in the industrial plants tend to be more formalized and restricted. The same tendency is, of course, observable in the relations between various social strata of the white population: greater isolation and exclusivity of "upper class" residential areas on the one hand, and the growth of exclusively working class areas on the other hand tend to widen the social distance between the top and the bottom of the social pyramid. At the same time, the concentration of large masses of factory workers, their living together in relatively crowded and less desirable urban areas is likely to contribute to the strengthening of their class consciousness.

2. Thus, the effects of industrialization in the South upon the social stratification of urban society are in principle the same as everywhere. The main differences in the South are due to the late beginning of industrialization and to the presence of the Negroes. In the old cities, the former social pyramid tends to be broadened at the base and perhaps to become more pointed at the top. The old "independent middle class" consisting of cotton merchants, bankers, small manufacturers and other small businessmen as well as lawyers and other professional people is gradually being superseded by a smaller but economically more powerful group composed of larger manufacturers and of the executives of big corporations. It is essentially the same process which has been described by Lynd in *Middletown in Transition* and by C. Wright Mills in *Small Business and Civic Welfare*.[22] Whether these changes in the local élite are always detrimental to the civic spirit in the community, as Mills thinks, remains to be seen. From personal observation it would seem to me that the executives and higher professional personnel of big corporations are sometimes more farsighted and progressive in civic affairs, such as public health work or city planning, than the old local ruling class. It is undeniable, however, that the latter tends to lose in power and prestige.

At the same time, there occur changes in the stratification of the middle and lower classes of white people. On the one hand, industrialization opens a greater variety of job opportunities to these people, especially to the women, who formerly were very limited in their employment op-

[21] Concerning differences in Negro concentration in southern cities, see Reid, *op. cit.*, p. 232.

[22] *Small Business and Civic Welfare*, Report of the Smaller War Plants Corporation to the Special Committee to Study Problems of American Small Business, United States Senate (Washington, 1946).

portunities because the large traditional field of domestic service was closed to them in the South. Thus a broad layer of clerical, technical and supervisory personnel develops, mostly recruited from the "lower middle class" of white people.

On the other hand, there is now developing a permanent, more or less hereditary class of white factory workers. The older southern cities did not have a large class of white manual workers. The Negroes did most of the menial work, and the relatively few white craftsmen and artisans were not widely separated in status from the middle classes. Now, with the increase in white wage earners employed in capitalistic manufacturing enterprises, there develops a new class of city-born and industry-bred factory workers, whose socio-economic position tends to be passed on from one generation to the other. This process is even more evident in the textile mill towns. While the large proportion of the older workers in these communities is still farm born, the great majority of the younger generation are now natives of industrial communities.[23] Like the mill workers who are set apart ecologically and in status as a separate class, the masses of white factory workers in the cities are becoming more separated by widening social distances, emphasized by ecological segregation, as indicated before, from the middle and upper strata. The craftsman in the smaller cities came into frequent personal and business contacts with the socially more prominent people in the community; the factory worker of today tends to live in a separate world. This change has occurred in all American and European cities under the impact of industrialization. In the South, however, it is taking place at a late hour when the industrially more advanced sections of the country have already found new patterns and new institutions in employer-employee relationships. The diffusion of these new patterns into a region where until now the white upper strata have adhered to a paternalistic pattern of labor relations is bound to result in frictions and conflicts of a somewhat different sociological quality than those familiar to us from other regions where these changes began earlier and extended over a longer period of time. Here lies an important field for empirical research.

Further complications arise from the transformation of an increasing proportion of the Negro population from an agricultural and domestic labor group into an industrial working class. The modern industrial system requires a maximum of interchangeability of workers, particularly in the semiskilled jobs. Any factors that impede the free movement of workers from job to job will interfere with the rational allocation of the labor force and therefore appear objectionable to the entrepreneurs. Everywhere in the world industrialization has tended to break down barriers of nationality, caste and status in industrial employment. This at least has been the long run trend. In the short run it may be advantageous for the employer to exploit status differentials among the workers in order to strengthen his

[23] Vance, op. cit., pp. 285-287.

bargaining power and his authority. Contrary to the long run trend the recruitment of supervisory personnel from those classes of white people who have traditionally looked upon the Negro primarily as a potential competitor rather than as a servant or employee also operates. These are the people who now have most of the direct personal relations with the Negro industrial worker. They have none of the elements of an aristocratic code of social conduct which was the basis of the relations between master and slave, or landlord and tenant, where they were at their best. Consequently, the old paternalistic pattern cannot endure. What will follow in its place depends on a variety of factors which cannot be discussed in this paper.[24]

In many of the smaller industrial cities and towns of the South, employers have been able to establish and maintain an unusual degree of control over the entire social existence of "their" workers. The devices used —such as the unincorporated company town or mill village—and the conditions which made such policies possible are too well known to need further elaboration. But it is quite inconceivable and would be contrary to all experience in older industrialized sections of the country that such practices should continue in the long run. Some are, in fact, already disappearing. The main reason for our forecast is, of course, the increasing significance of the labor vote in southern urban areas. We indicated before how the growth of a city is usually accompanied by an increasing diversification of industries. This is bound to result in greater economic independence of workers from employers and to reduce the control of employers over the workers' vote.

Conclusion

In summary we may say that manufacturing in the South began chiefly in rural locations and in smaller urban communities; the older larger cities owe their growth primarily to commerce and transportation and only in the second line to manufacturing industries. Very few major cities of the South were from the beginning primarily manufacturing cities.

The relatively late beginning of industrialization has significant consequences for the ecological development of southern cities as well as for the changes in social stratification. The impact of technically most advanced, recently developed branches of manufacturing upon ecology and the rather immediate transition from traditionalistic patterns of labor and race relations to more contractual forms represent some of the significant aspects of the social consequences of industrialization for urban society in the South.

---

[24] While the caste or status system becomes more and more annoying to the employer, and while labor's objective interest lies in the abolition of discriminations, noneconomic motivations may prevail and prevent the evolution of a new harmony in race relations.

5. Problems of Management and Authority in a Transitional Society: A Case Study of a Javanese Factory

Ann Ruth Willner

The problems of managerial leadership in a transitional society can be examined in many contexts of organizational activity. The one employed in this article is that of an industrial organization in a primarily preindustrial setting in East Java, Indonesia. For the industrial context brings into sharp focus the dilemmas that confront those who attempt to impose unfamiliar organizational forms and norms on a society reluctant or only partially prepared to accept the behavioral innovations demanded by the new organization.

The leaders of most new nations are ideologically committed to industrialization and to the development of concomitant industrial structures modelled on prototypes in advanced industrial societies. Yet the introduction of new and complex forms of organization, such as a modern factory, in a traditional agrarian environment frequently sets up tensions between operational requirements of the organization and the cultural norms and expectations of those members of the local community recruited to fill the organizational roles. Where such organizations were introduced under conditions of colonial domination, their operational goals received first priority. These could be attained, in the last resort, through the application of various forms of coercive control by largely foreign management whose authority could not easily be brought into question.

Political and social changes in nations that have undergone successful revolutions have altered the staffing patterns of organizations and the sociocultural determinants of organizational behavior. Most intermediate and many top managerial posts are filled by indigenous personnel. However desirous they may be of securing rank-and-file compliance with organizational needs, their problems are more complex than those of their foreign predecessors. For, unlike the latter, they cannot resort to arbitrary measures in maintaining discipline without arousing strong opposition among their subordinates to tactics now labelled "colonial." They must therefore obtain some degree of consensus.

Reprinted from Ann Ruth Willner, Society for Applied Anthropology, *Human Organization*, 22 (Summer, 1963), 133-141.

Successful political nationalism, however, tends to produce dissensus in the sphere of authority. On the one hand, it strengthens the claims of those who have learned to advocate and accept rational and utilitarian bases for decision and action. On the other hand, it is generally accompanied by a cultural nationalism that reinvigorates prescriptions traditionally governing social interaction. Thus there may be little agreement on such questions as who has the right to be assigned roles of authority or what are the means by which authority can properly be exercised. Every such issue complicates the possibility of reconciling the impersonal requirements of organizational efficiency with the expectations of those who are part of the organization.

These dichotomies are elaborated in the following description[1] of patterns of authority in a Javanese textile factory during two periods of its history. The first period is that immediately preceding the Second World War when the factory, which I here call Pabrika, was owned and largely managed by Europeans. In 1954-55, when I observed its operations, it was Indonesian-owned but managed by a Dutchman. With the exception of three other members of the managerial staff of Chinese ethnic origin, the rest of the managerial and supervisory posts were held by Indonesians.

The factory at this time employed a labor force of 1000, about half of whom were drawn from predominantly agrarian villages outside the small town in which it is located. A seven-hour work day and rotating shifts enabled many to retain some ties with agriculture. One-fifth of the workers were women and one-fifth were migrants from other areas, some of urban provenience.

Traditional Patterns and the Early Factory System

Of the many aspects of the factory routine, those relating to supervision and the enforcement of regulations and discipline appeared to have undergone the most significant changes between the early period of Pabrika's operations and when I observed them. The picture I derived from the reminiscences of older workers and supervisors suggested that this was the area which had formerly provoked the strongest resentment among the workers. For the new recruit, entry into the factory meant not only the necessity to adapt to a new type and schedule of activities. It also meant exposure to an unfamiliar pattern of interaction with rather alien kinds of people. In the first place, he found himself at the lowest level of a hierarchic order in

[1] This is part of an unpublished study, *From Rice-Field to Factory: the Industrialization of a Rural Labor Force in Java*, based on my field investigations. For support of the study I am indebted to Professor Bert F. Hoselitz and the Research Center in Economic Development and Cultural Change of the University of Chicago. What little knowledge I have of the disciplines of Social Anthropology and Sociology I owe to my sister, Professor Dorothy Willner, who cannot be held responsible for its shortcomings.

which all authority emanated from above and unquestioned and prompt obedience was expected from below.

Neither hierarchy as a mode of organization nor obedience as a duty to status superiors seems strange in itself to the Javanese reared in the traditional social environment. For as a young child he becomes aware of a ranking system within the family and within the larger kinship group. He soon learns the different terms[2] by which he must denote and address his immediate and more distant kin and the behavior appropriate to each with respect to degree of relationship, line of descent, and age. He realizes that within the nuclear family paternal position is paramount and unquestioned and that he also owes a measure of respect and obedience to elder siblings and is owed the same by younger ones. Later he discovers the ranking system in the village that distinguishes its families on the basis of hereditary rights to land. And he learns to recognize the primacy of the village head and to accede to his instructions. While his encounters with members of the *prijaji* or gentry may be rare, he is nonetheless aware of the deference due them from him by virtue of their superior place in the wider society.[3]

Although stratification is a familiar element in almost every group in which a Javanese participates, the particular hierarchy of the factory differs in several respects from the hierarchal structures he knows. In the first place, the factory hierarchy is organized for a specific goal, that of production, and status within it is primarily determined by appointment theoretically based on abilities relative to this purpose. Traditional social groups may serve a multitide of functions. Status within them, as suggested by the above, is allocated by birth, age, and other ascriptive criteria that do not necessarily relate to the achievement of a particular goal. Leadership roles in the factory are specific to factory activity and may not overlap with the exercise of leadership elsewhere. Those with higher ascribed status in traditional groups appear to exert generalized leadership for a number of activities. Power conferred by leadership positions in the factory tends to be channeled downward and responsibility upward. In traditional structures those who hold power through status have concomitant responsibility toward those over whom they exercise it.

Supervision—The New Role

Moreover, the factory as a work organization introduces a set of intermediary roles generally unknown in groups organized for work in the traditional

---

[2] These terms indicate not merely degrees of kinship but differentiate between junior and senior kin of the same degree. There are separate terms for elder brother and younger brother, elder sister and younger sister, and similarly for elder and younger brother of parents.

[3] It could well be said that every encounter between two Javanese involves a mutual recognition in gesture, language, and attitude of relative place in a stratified order.

village. These roles are those of foreman, supervisor and other positions intervening between the employer and the man who performs the visible physical tasks of labor. The wage worker in the village deals directly with the man who wants work done and pays for it. The farmer hires field workers himself and he or a member of his family exercises whatever supervision may be necessary. Even when farming takes place on a tenant or sharecropping basis in which several parties profit from the proceeds, neither serves as a "go-between" between the other and the wage workers. Whoever is the cultivator has full discretion over the employment of laborers and the terms of work and payment until the harvest. When the plot is divided at harvest time, each party to the agreement then hires his own harvesters. Similarly, in small industrial establishments in villages and towns, the proprietor is both the direct employer and serves as his own supervisor. And in most organized work activities, the employer works together with his laborers so that supervision as a discrete function is indistinct.[4]

The direct and face-to-face contact between employer and worker in these situations results in a work relationship in which the personal element is rarely absent. It allows for the continual possibility of negotiation and adjustment between the parties concerned. It makes possible loans and advances to workers in times of need. Thus there is no analogue[5] in village work structures for the figure who is just a link in a chain of command, directive but not responsive. He who is neither an owner nor visibly engaged in production but merely passes on orders with no power to negotiate the terms of their execution is an anomaly.

Nevertheless, however obscure the functions of those directly above him may have appeared to the new worker in Pabrika's early period, he might not have found it difficult to reconcile himself to taking orders from them. For these superiors were mainly Dutch and Chinese. And in the larger colonial society outside the village, a society in which stratification was partly based on ethnic origin, these people held high status. In the eyes of the villager they stood in the same relationship to him as his own gentry, government officials, and similar figures of prestige and authority.

However, while the fact of ethnic dissimilarity might have legitimized these unfamiliar roles, this ethnic difference was accompanied by cultural differences affecting their interpretation. The behavior of those who occupied these positions, behavior offensive to the workers, rendered both

---

[4] Even when he does not share the work, his right in the land or his ownership of the enterprise might be seen as the factor authorizing him to direct it.

[5] Perhaps the nearest analogue to the "Intermediate" role is that of the village head in his capacity as recipient of orders from higher governmental levels to which he is expected to obtain village compliance. In the eyes of the villagers, however, he is the only visible authority besides being the symbol of the community and its intactness. Directives are not given to him in the village but at meetings with sub-district officials at their offices.

them and their roles objectionable. The workers were faced with a group of superiors whose demands could not easily be anticipated, whose responses were startling, and whose very language could often not be understood. Even the most submissively anxious worker might not understand instructions barked at him in a mixture of Dutch and Malay or the most crude Javanese. His bewilderment or hesitation, taken for stupidity or obstinancy, was likely to produce impatience, annoyance, and vituperation in these "bosses." Action resulting in errors called down upon him loud-voiced anger and humiliating curses. A worker who stopped to rest or fell asleep from the fatigue induced by a long work day might be cuffed on the head[6] or beaten.

Work and Traditional Values

Such conduct offered a great contrast to that displayed by superiors in the customary environment. Perhaps because the Javanese is conditioned from childhood to respect and obey properly constituted authority figures and can anticipate and understand the content of their directives, these figures rarely find it necessary to exert visible effort or force[7] to obtain compliance. Indeed the very act of doing so might itself be taken as an implicit admission of their uncertainty of their right to make demands. If those to whom orders are given appear to hesitate in following them or in some other way subtly indicate some degree of resistance, similarly subtle and indirect means of persuasion are applied.

Resistance itself is rarely overt but takes the form of polite evasion. Prolonged non-compliance, which may often be accompanied by outward assent,[8] generally results in the issue being shelved or temporarily deferred until a more favorable occasion arises for obtaining acquiescence. For to bring an issue to the point of open conflict might disturb the harmony of the social order whose maintenance is deemed indispensable in the traditional Javanese view of society.

Such circumspection in avoiding overt discord is not only characteristic of encounters between social unequals but permeates nearly all face-to-face interchange. Thus the treatment workers in the factory received from their

---

[6] A whack on the head is more than an affront, for the head of an individual is sacred and not to be touched by another.

[7] On the rare occasions when force is resorted to, it is not directly applied by the authority figure himself. Thus, a former district head, recalling that repeated efforts to persuade farmers to plant paddy at the time suggested by the agricultural advisors were of no avail, stated: "I was finally obliged to order two farmers to be beaten as an example to the rest."

[8] It is customary to assent to requests of orders whether or not one has the intention of fulfilling them. Either the tone of voice or the rhetoric of the assent may convey whether it is merely a polite affirmative or substantive and, in any case, time will tell.

foreign[9] overseers, in addition to affording sharp contrast with that accorded them by traditional group leaders, also violated their notions of appropriate behavior between human beings irrespective of status. No matter how incensed a Javanese may feel toward another, he refrains from expressing irritation, anger, or vituperation directly toward that other or in his presence. Incipient or active hostility toward another finds an outlet in making him the butt of humor or in deriding him to others behind his back. But he who expresses an aggressive impulse overtly is regarded as immature, improperly socialized, and deplorably crude. And he who lifts his hand against another,[10] except under the most extreme provocation,[11] is considered no longer a true Javanese, certainly not civilized.

Just as bewildering to the factory recruit, if not as directly humiliating as the supervisory procedures, was his subjection to a strange system of penalities that seemed arbitrarily enforced. For failing to meet a standard of workmanship he might only dimly comprehend, he could lose part of his wages. For infractions of regulations of whose existence he might not have been aware, or of whose purport he could not understand, he could be fined, suspended, or otherwise penalized. Damage to equipment or theft might result in immediate dismissal. What is recalled as having seemed most unjust was the occasional instance, generally involving theft, of the punishment or dismissal of a whole group because none of its members would admit to being the culprit or accuse any of the others. And what seemed least comprehensible was that these penalities were impersonally administered with reference to the offense itself and often without—what to the worker seemed most relevant—concern with intention, cause, or extenuating circumstances.

My observations of work relationships in the traditional settings[12] produced little evidence of an analogous system of sanctions. Neither in the field nor in the handicrafts enterprise does there seem to be a precise standard against which the quality of work is measured. In the first place, since time and speed are not emphasized, there is more opportunity for a task

---

[9] Occasionally such treatment was also meted out by Javanese foremen as well but, if my informants are to be believed, generally upon direct orders and in the presence of those above them. What was more typical of the exploitation of workers under them by Javanese foremen, although perhaps not necessarily regarded as such, was the "commission" taken from the wages of those workers whom they brought into the factory.

[10] Even disobedient children are not as a rule spanked or slapped but nipped or pinched.

[11] An example I was given of extreme provocation provoking violence was adultery. Even here, according to informants, retaliation is often indirect, such as by poison or soliciting the aid of a "black *dukun*." Outright violence is much more likely to be perpetrated by a group rather than an individual and usually after the group has been harangued or has whipped itself up to an emotional frenzy. The most noted type of individual violence—of which I have had no personal experience—is *amok*.

[12] Here I am speaking of labor in agriculture and small enterprises in this area and not domestic services. Where I observed the latter in the homes of Javanese aristocrats, especially in the principalities of Central Java, it was not unusual for domestic servants to be sharply reprimanded for unsatisfactory performance and even occasionally physically chastised.

to be performed meticulously and mistakes avoided. In the second place, approximation is acceptable and exactness of product is not demanded. *Pentjars*, or bundles, of paddy may vary somewhat in size but are paid for at the same rate. Some bricks or tiles or copper kettles are not as well made as others, but only the most obviously unfit are discarded and not paid for at the piece-work rate. Sometimes a differential rate is paid to workers according to relative skill (most generally there is only a distinction between apprentices and experienced workers) on the assumption that each sustains over the average the quality of which he is capable and there are no deductions for pieces that later may be discarded.

In accordance with the prescribed decorum for interpersonal behavior described above, discontent with the performance of an individual is rarely expressed in direct or scolding fashion. A dissatisfied employer is likely to dispense with the services of an unsatisfactory worker with a face-saving pretext, such as telling him that he has not enough work in the near future or that some relative has suddenly turned up whom he is obliged to hire. Or he might, without being in any way sharply critical, convey sufficient lack of appreciation for the worker's efforts to induce the latter to decide to seek a living elsewhere. Similarly, a discontented worker does not complain of conditions of work or payment or announce that he can do better elsewhere but finds that some urgent situation in the family forces him to sever the connection temporarily.[13]

Direct dismissal as a punitive measure appears to be difficult, in any case, for several reasons. Work associations are rarely a mere exchange of labor for payment. They are often within the context of kin, neighborhood, and village ties involving a number of reciprocal obligations in which skill or performance may play a minor role. Beyond this and related to it is the tradition in agrarian communities that those with land rights or in other respects in superior economic circumstances should provide as many as possible opportunities for work for the landless and those in a needy position. This results in the apportionment of available work among as many hands as possible rather than the recruitment of labor on the basis of efficiency. The converse of this is the implicit recognition of the individual's "right to work" as a concomitant of community membership apart from considerations of skill or level of performance.[14]

If despite all precautions a disagreement should arise in a situation in

---

[13] These pretexts do not, of course, deceive anyone as to the underlying reasons but are appreciated and, indeed, expected as a face-saving ritual.

[14] I asked a farmer who was complaining of the high cost of labor why he did not select a few of the faster and more skilled field workers and employ them over a longer period of time, thus cutting his costs. The reply was that he couldn't risk the resultant disapproval of the community and the possible accusations of being penny-pinching and unconcerned with the welfare of his poorer neighbors. A small entrepreneur who was maintaining two extra hands during the off-season when he had little work for them in the shop but tried to keep them occupied with odd jobs around his compound said: "After all, they cannot easily find other work and they must eat. What else should I do, let them starve?"

which custom has not created a precedent,[15] its resolution would appear[16] to be based on a consideration of more factors than those directly pertinent to the issue itself. Perhaps the most important of these is that tension should be diminished and any sustained bitterness averted. Friends and neighbors often serve as mediators, attempting to press mutual concessions on the contestants rather than trying to assess guilt or support the claims of one to the exclusion of those of the other. Should the issue be taken to the village head or some other prestige figure, the ultimate decision generally favors neither one nor the other completely but is a compromise in which each party obtains some satisfaction.

The problems of supervision and authority can thus be understood in terms of the contrast between the structuring of work relationships in traditional Javanese society and in the factory system. In the early period of Pabrika's operations, this antithesis found little expression within the factory itself. The workers faced the full burden of making the transition and their problems of adaptation were further complicated by language and cultural barriers. Some managed to overcome the strains of adjustment; many, following the traditional way of withdrawal from stress, quietly retreated to the familiar environment.

The Current Search for Accommodation

Today the contradictions between these systems are being acted out within the walls of Pabrika. And they are no longer exclusively personified by the workers on the one hand and the supervisory and managerial personnel on the other. Instead there exists an uneasy interplay of elements of both systems in the behavior of each of these groups toward the others. In circumstances that can best be characterized as a search for a pattern of accommodation permitting an integrated order, the workers tend to exercise a strong measure of control over the means by which they are controlled. This has come about as a result of the following factors:

1. The replacement of foreign supervisory and managerial staff by those of an ethnic background identical with or similar to that of the workers;
2. the entry of workers who have been exposed to both urban and revolutionary influences and are not reticent in making known their views;
3. the formation of unions through which these views can be channeled;
4. the appointment of a general manager familiar with Javanese values and behavior and capable of employing them himself.

[15] For the disposition of shares of harvest and for the provision of a certain minimum of food to workers, custom is sufficiently strong to preclude the possibility of disagreement.

[16] I have not directly observed the course of a disagreement between wage worker and employer in a village work situation but am drawing an analogy from disputes observed over debts and work contracted with artisans.

The formal organization of the factory with its hierarchic structure has not changed. But the present recruit from the village finds that those in roles above his interpret them in ways that are not disconcerting. His foreman and supervisor[17] are likely to share with him a common language and a common understanding of how people treat each other. They issue instructions in calm quiet voices or in gestures that are meaningful to him. They are patient with his initial fumbling, recognizing that he needs time to accustom himself to this new world. Subsequent errors are more likely to arouse not anger but good-natured ridicule that will shame him into avoidance of mistakes that are likely to provoke it.

In fact in the present scene it is the middle group of foremen and supervisors who are taxed with the burden of reconciling the formal requirements of the factory with the expectations generated by the culture. Discussion with them makes it clear that they do understand the requirements of their roles. They know that their major task is to pass on to those under their jurisdiction the directions they have received from their superiors and to see that these are carried out. They recognize that with respect to the workers this involves more or less the following tasks: (1) to make explicit and clear the instructions for the job at hand, (2) to exert continued surveillance over the pace and quality of worker performance, (3) to issue reprimands when called for, and (4) to impose the prescribed sanctions within their competence when necessary.

According to management criteria, only the first of the above functions is consistently and satisfactorily performed by all the supervisory personnel. Although most keep a fairly steady eye on the workers, some appear to observe only sporadically the operations under their control, mainly when their own bosses are present. Fewer reprimand their subordinates with any conviction. And practically none dares to impose penalties without resort to higher authority. In principle, there is delegation of responsibility and allocation of concomitant power down the line. In practice, responsibility is often evaded and the exercise of authority shoved upward. In the words of one department head:

Only the foremen are supposed to watch and direct the workers; my supervisor is supposed to control the foremen; my assistant should check only on the supervisor and serve as liaison between him and me; and I should spend most of my time in planning and conferences. What really happens is that the supervisor has to keep an eye directly on the workers as well as upon the foremen; my assistant must control the supervisor, foremen and workers; and I have to be in the shop most of the day to be sure everything goes smoothly.

This department head did not mean that he necessarily substitutes for his subordinates in any specific function, although that takes place also, but

[17] Almost three-fourths of the present supervisory personnel are Javanese and many have been recruited from the ranks of former workers.

that his physical presence is necessary to insure their adequate performance. In his absence, a foreman might turn his back on a group of workers
who are not following instructions, pretending not to notice them; the supervisor might somehow neglect to scold the foreman for his inattention;
and the assistant might hesitate to inform the head that production is not
proceeding smoothly. To affix responsibility for the resulting snarl-up would
not be easy. For the foreman would explain that he had been so busy
watching another group of workers at a crucial task that he had not had
time to notice the first group. The supervisor would have been occupied
in explaining the requirements of a new work order to the other foreman.
The assistant might admit to an inkling that something was wrong, but
since it was not his place to address the workers directly and there was
nothing he could do about it at the time, he had not wanted to disturb his
so busy superior.[18]

External Status and Factory Authority

Many of the foremen with whom I talked confessed to a sense of being
almost constantly caught between conflicting currents. And although this
can be said of the position of foremen in almost any factory, placed as it
is at the point where demands from above and pressures from below tend
to converge, it is doubly true at Pabrika. For if on the one hand managerial
staff expects the foremen to obtain compliance from the workers, they also
expect this to be done without coercion of the type that would arouse
worker hostility and union protest. If the foreman is to gain acquiescence
without resort to pressure, it is necessary for the workers to recognize the
role of the foreman and to accept the individual assigned to that role.
Many of the foremen cannot always depend on such acceptance. When

---

[18] An example of this, which was observed in some detail, occurred during the installation of some new looms. On a Thursday morning, under the direction of its foreman, a work crew began on the first loom. A technical advisor stood by checking the
directions on the blueprint. The factory manager came in frequently to survey the
progress and the general manager stopped by several times. By early afternoon, the first
loom had been installed. The work on the second loom went faster and was finished by
the end of the afternoon. This time the technical advisor looked in several times, the
factory manager twice, and the general manager once to assure themselves that the complexities of installation had been mastered. On Friday morning, work began on the
third loom. The general manager left in the middle of the morning for the city, the
factory manager spent most of the morning in conferences and the afternoon at home
and the technical assistant also did not appear after lunch. The foreman seemed to be
giving the same instructions but somehow the work was proceeding more slowly. Two
of the members of the crew did not report back after the usual Friday break for mosque
attendance. By 4 P.M., when the general manager returned from the city, the third
loom had not yet been completely installed. Called to account, the foreman explained
that he had not been any less explicit or assiduous in giving orders than the previous
day but the workers had responded more slowly and lackadaisically. Slightly stronger
pressure on his part had not produced visibly better response. He had not dared to
become really rough with the workers. Besides, there had been nobody there to back
him up.

uncertain they hesitate, in Javanese style, to put their authority to a crucial test.

I have earlier indicated that in the traditional system, he who directs the work of others, with the exception of work performed as a reciprocal obligation, generally has higher status than those who work for him. Obviously the landholder ranks higher in the village stratification system than the workers he employs. The small entrepreneur is often a *hadji* with the prestige acquired from his trip to Mecca. Work on community projects is organized and often directed by the village head not because of superior organizational skill on his part but in his capacity as village head. Thus conversely the right to direct labor may be seen as flowing from status derived from other criteria than the work situation itself.

Some of the foremen in the factory hold such status in the environment beyond the factory. Two of them are leading landholders in nearby villages and one of these is also well educated by town as well as village standards. It is significant that these two seem to find little difficulty in maintaining discipline among their workers. Another supervisory official who has no feeling that his authority is challenged is a Eurasian who in the earlier period was slightly assimilated to the European element in the town and was regarded as such by the Javanese.

It is conceivable that some of the others might have little difficulty in gaining acceptance as authority figures in the eyes of workers recently recruited from the rural area. For even though they themselves may have originally come from low-status groups of the population, by this time they have acquired some of the attributes of higher status. To the villager, their style of living and mode of behavior may seem more comparable to that of the town officials than to his own. And he is likely to regard them, at least initially, with similar respect and a shade of deference.

Non-Traditional Workers' Challenge to Authority

Many of the workers, however, are not from the traditional village background. Those with prior residence and work experience in larger centers than Namakota have themselves acquired some of the attributes of urban sophistication whose possession gives their holders higher status in the eyes of agrarian villagers. Many of them have had equivalent if not more education than their foremen, have become accustomed to similar material possessions and ascribe to themselves the traditionally associated symbolic significance these carry. Those who hold superordinate status in the factory are more likely to be regarded by them outside of the factory as their equals rather than their superiors. This attitude often carries into the factory where they can be seen retorting freely to admonitions of their foremen and not hesitating to tease and joke with them.

It is not easy to determine what constitutes legitimation of authority for this group. Some of its members appear to consider seniority as the sole criterion for the elevation of others to a position of direction over them. They do not question the right of men who have been in the factory for ten or twelve years to supervise their work.[19] Others seem somewhat amenable to authority exercised by someone whose skill is manifestly superior to theirs as long as this skill is amply demonstrated. One foreman told me that he constantly hopes for situations to arise in which workers need his direct assistance. Then his stock rises and his crew appear to respect him; in between these occasions they seem to regard his presence as superfluous.

Those workers with a background of revolutionary activity and ideology, most influenced by the new emphasis on democracy and egalitarianism, tend implicity and often explicitly to challenge the notion of any authority imposed from above. In their minds such authority carries about it the aura of colonialism and should similarly be abolished. Valid authority over a group, according to their interpretation of democracy, is that derived through selection by and voluntary agreement of the members of the group. This attitude is frequently encountered in other contexts than the political one in which it originated. Within the factory it finds expression in the intimations that workers should have some voice in the selection of those who supervise them, if not directly at least through right of rejection.

During the period of my residence, the general manager received a petition signed by over forty workers requesting the removal of a recently appointed supervisor. The major charge levelled against him was that he was "unproductive." When asked to explain what they meant by this term, the leader of the delegation replied that this supervisor seemed to spend most of his time observing and studying[20] and had not been seen working with his hands. Further investigation revealed that there was resentment at what the workers felt to be an aloofness and a sense of superiority on the part of this man toward them. There was also some grumbling at the fact that he was not Javanese, but from another Indonesian ethnic group.

This was but one of a number of instances in which workers have communicated objections by means of organized protest rather than individual withdrawal. Previously there had been overt resistance by workers in one section to taking orders from a foreman brought in from outside. They declared that they would prefer to have someone from their own

[19] When questioning workers concerning their opposition to a new foreman in circumstances related below, I received numbers of replies to the effect that only a man who has done a certain sort of work for years would know enough to be able to tell others how to do it.

[20] Since this was in the dyeing department which engaged in experiments with different dyes, the new supervisor was also being trained in the technical aspects of dyestuffs.

ranks. This approach had been initially tried and then discarded when those so promoted had proved in management's eyes to be even more than normally reluctant to assume effective authority over former colleagues and the latter even less than normally disposed to accept it from them. This was succeeded by an experiment of transferring workers who seemed to be promising supervisory material to other departments for a few months before returning them with higher status to their original ones.[21] The first retransfer on this basis also encountered worker resistance, from some on the grounds that the individual in question was "too young," from others because he was now "an outsider" from "another department." Ultimately, the worker opposition in these cases was overcome by rather skillful rhetoric from top management.[22] But a formula has not yet been found for locating new supervisory personnel who are both effective and acceptable.

The Ambiguities of the Managerial Role

Given such attitudes on the part of even a small number of workers, it is not surprising that few of those in middle-level positions have the confidence to assert authority to the point where it may be challenged. Although none would admit to desiring a return to the "hard old days," it is clear that a situation in which a worker may dare to ignore one of them, turn his back on him, or complain over his head counteracts whatever sense of security is derived from their selection to their posts by management. For many of them share the background of the workers and to some degree are similarly influenced by the attitudes that affect worker recognition of them. Although they have therefore formally mastered the roles assigned to them, they have not yet sufficiently internalized them to implement them adequately.

Traditional Javanese values and modern egalitarian notions also appear to affect the way in which supervisory personnel fulfill the task of transmitting information upward. Yearly wage raises for workers are based upon the three criteria of work efficiency, quality of work, and regularity of attendance. The foremen are expected periodically to give objective

[21] The underlying rationale was that time and distance might lessen the familiarity which was considered to be the major deterrent on both sides to the assumption of the new relationship, while the added experience might be accepted by the workers as justification for the new status of their former equal.

[22] For example, in the first instance mentioned above, the general manager addressed the delegation, taking as a starting point the comments that the foreman was from another *bangsa* or ethnic subgroup. He stated that he was shocked to hear that his workers could speak so in this period of national unity. "After all, hasn't Bung Karno (affectionate diminutive for President Sukarno) said that now all Indonesians are one *bangsa?*" Then the delegation was urged by him and other management officials to show by their acceptance of the foreman that they were good supporters of national unity.

evaluation of individual worker performance. It is not at all unusual for a foreman to grade all workers under him as satisfactory on all counts. For, apart from the group solidarity developed through working together, the foreman often lives in the same neighborhood as some of his workers and may have formed a number of other ties resulting from this propinquity.[23] The obligations resulting from such ties make it difficult for him to risk offending them by adverse judgments. They may go so far as to enable workers to induce foremen to record stoppage periods to their advantage. Possibly also bearing on the uniformly favorable grading is the attitude that an advantage should be indiscriminately apportioned, an attitude that may have its origins in the village tradition of sharing benefits and hardships or perhaps it is derived from the post-revolutionary emphasis on equality.

Management's scepticism of the reliability of such blanket approval has resulted in a technique that combines checking of record and attendance books[24] with a sort of bargaining process. The supervisor checks the records with the foremen and generally succeeds in working out with them some downward revisions; the department head engages in the same process with the supervisors and so on up the line. This is done on the assumption that with each step further removed from the worker there is less likelihood that personal considerations influence judgment. At the same time, those closest to the workers can avert recriminations from them by attributing unfavorable judgments to pressure from those above.

Many of the criticisms levelled against foremen and supervisors by most of the managerial staff are also applied to the managerial staff by the European general manager. In several respects he has attempted to follow a different course than that of his predecessor. Whereas the latter made most of the policy decisions unilaterally, he holds daily meetings with his staff for joint discussion and decisions. His predecessor reportedly spent much of his day observing the execution of his instructions and often directly supervising operations. He attempts to delegate as many functions as possible to his subordinates, appearing only briefly out of his office. He tells them that the department heads are more technically qualified than he, that they have wide latitude in the execution of decisions and should

[23] I have observed workers and supervisory personnel in joint recreation, such as playing cards and gambling together. One supervisor is engaged in financing credit purchasing of bicycles by workers, i.e., he makes the initial payment to the dealers and collects from the workers on an installment basis. On the one hand, this is regarded by the workers as a form of assistance, despite his profit on interest; on the other hand, since collection of debts of this sort reportedly can no longer be legally enforced, he is somewhat subtly intimidated to stay in the good graces of these workers to ensure that they retain their sense of obligation to repay him.

[24] There is a daily book for each section of the factory in which is recorded the production of each loom or other machine, stoppages, problems, etc. If a worker complains that errors recorded against him or lower production is the fault of the loom rather than of his efforts, this book is used to compare his production rate with that of other workers on the same loom in different shifts.

only resort to him when major problems arise. He defines his task to them as primarily that of planning, coordination, and liaison with the owners.

Thus far this "loose reins" strategy has been more successful in retaining the goodwill of his subordinates than in achieving its objective of forcing them to function as executives. Perhaps two have risen to the challenge and perform satisfactorily at the level required of managerial staff by the factory model without stimulus and pressure from him. The others seem to require at least his presence, if not his occasional prodding, to sustain them and they tend to relax their efforts in his absence.[25] Like the foremen and supervisors, they are only too eager to pass up to him the responsibility for the enforcement of discipline. The usual reason given in such instances[26] is the desire to avert possible difficulties with the communist-dominated union.

Implicit in statements of this type is a more basic motive—the disinclination to make embarrassingly obvious the latent ambiguities of their position. For all of the foremen and supervisors and many of the managerial staff are also members of the same unions as the majority of the workers. Several are even members of the governing body of this union. The development of unions has facilitated the crystallization of worker sentiment and the participation of managerial personnel in union affairs is an additional factor conditioning their responsiveness to this sentiment. Although such participation could serve as a means of channeling union policy in a direction most advantageous to management aims and sometimes does, this is limited by the existence of a rival union and competition between the two for membership.

Those in the dual roles of middle-level or higher-managerial officials and active union members or officials profess to feel no real conflict between them. They see themselves in a median or conciliatory position, carrying out the traditional Javanese ideal of maintaining harmony by reconciling divergent interests. It is clear, however, that this inhibits their full identification as members of a distinct "management team." And it may be adduced as another of the factors[27] explaining their inclination

25 Although the general manager spends much of this time outside the factory premises, conducting many of its affairs from his home across the street, it is as if his "being on call" serves as a catalyst for the normal conduct of affairs. During a period when he was on home leave, production declined steadily and he was cabled by the owners to cut short his vacation and return.

26 One instance I observed when an electrician, careless a second time after a warning, caused a small fire. The regulations provided for immediate dismissal in such a case and either the foreman of the crew or the supervisor of maintenance, both present, was empowered to discharge him. Instead, they called the factory manager and suggested that he do so; he, in turn, went to the general manager. The latter firmly told the factory manager that it was his affair and he, in turn, prevailed upon the supervisor with the statement that the "big boss" expected him to do it.

27 It is not easy to attribute relative weights to the various factors that have here been advanced to explain the behavior of this group. For example, in the neighboring British-managed textile factory, there is a separate union for Indonesians above the rank

to leave any drastic disciplinary action to the very top managerial officials.

In the last analysis this throws the major burden of decision in the sphere of authority on the general manager.[28] Unable to depend upon unequivocal support from his subordinates and aware of the psychological complexities of their position, he does not try to compel their strict adherence to the formal mechanisms of control as apparently did his predecessor. Instead, he assumes the paternalistic but non-authoritarian role they seem to demand of him and works with them in trying to evolve techniques which outwardly satisfy cultural expectations while achieving the goal of maintaining the factory in relatively efficient operation. And he is not above employing the circuitous Javanese modes of behavior himself in attaining his objectives.

Flexibility and the System of Sanctions

This is seen most clearly in the ways in which the system of sanctions is enforced. The formal outline of this system has not been greatly altered since the period when it constituted a major source of worker grievance. Workers are still subject to wage deductions for errors, suspension and dismissal for infringement of regulations. However, the regulations themselves are now the outcome of union-management negotiation. Most of the workers I encountered are fairly familiar with them, having been generally informed of them at the time of entry or shortly afterwards. Should one feel himself unfairly disciplined, he has the right of appeal. The very reluctance of his immediate superiors to administer punitive measures means that a worker has a good chance of carrying his case to the highest authorities with the opportunity to defend himself personally.

I received the impression that workers now venture evasion or transgression of regulations in the spirit of a game of chance in which the player is willing to risk the consequences of losing. In fact, the risk is not so great, for in practice the major penalties are rarely administered without investigation of the particular circumstances by higher management officials and often in consultation with the union heads. For example, a worker who has been recorded as dismissed for prolonged absence should not, according to the rules, be reinstated upon reappearance. In actuality, a good weaver stands an excellent chance of being taken back if he can

---

of worker. Nevertheless, the British department heads and supervisors complain that the Javanese supervisors and foremen under them never translate literally their reprimands to the workers but always "soften" them and are generally "too easy" with the workers. The union membership of managerial personnel at Pabrika may be a less important factor than the others.

[28] The three other management officials who are not affiliated with a union are of Chinese ethnic origin. And, although they are not subject to the same inhibitions as their Indonesian colleagues, they also tend to be circumspect and a bit wary because of the peculiar position of even those Chinese who are Indonesian citizens in the present nationalistic period.

justify his absence with a plausible explanation or even with an original and entertaining—if somewhat implausible—excuse. Occasionally, a worker trades shifts by private agreement with a worker on an alternate shift in the same department. As long as the machine is not left unattended, such arrangements are not objected to by management.

A worker who proves to be repeatedly inept, careless, or lazy is no longer dismissed on these grounds. Instead he is exposed to a technique that embodies the utmost Javanese finesse. He is progressively transferred to less demanding tasks which carry with them lower prestige. An ex-weaver assigned to a job that requires him to carry loads through the mill under the eyes of his former colleagues is likely to feel himself so degraded that he leaves voluntarily after several days. As a result workers who fall below the standard of skill of which they are known to be capable are sometimes brought to rapid recovery by the mere suggestion that they might be happier with a transfer to another part of the factory.

The most drastic penalty of dismissal is generally applied only in cases of theft and action leading to damage or danger to safety. Even here a concession may be made in extraordinary circumstances. For example, one of the men in the storeroom had worked out an elaborate system of checking and recording supplies which had enabled him to withdraw and somehow take out of the factory a sizeable stock of cloth for three months before he was caught. The offender pleaded at his hearing that his original intention had been to make only a single haul to fill one pressing family need for money,[29] but that the system he had evolved forced him to continue his depredations to avoid detection. The staff listened to this explanation and examined the system. They were so impressed with its ingenuity and the intelligence it implied on the part of the worker that instead of being dismissed, he was assigned a job that would utilize his initiative.

There is no doubt that such pliancy on the part of present management has contributed to the improved morale of the workers and to the growth of a more stable work force. On the other hand, continued divergence of practice from principle may well obstruct the development of integrated and self-sustaining procedures of supervision and authority needed by a factory system. The present ways of reconciling various worker pressures with the requirements of efficient production rely rather heavily on the father-figure of the general manager and on a sort of stop-gap improvisation. But perhaps improvisation is the only mode of dealing with an unstable situation that offers many variables and few constants. The situation in Pabrika is not unique. It merely mirrors in microcosm the

[29] Many of the workers, especially those from the rural environment, cannot understand why they cannot borrow money from the factory in case of personal need and repay in gradual stages through wage deductions. This arrangement, as has been earlier mentioned, is not uncommon in village work arrangements, especially in small-scale enterprises.

confusion prevalent throughout organizational life in Indonesia as old norms of authority have been wholly or partially repudiated and generally accepted new ones have not yet emerged.

Bibliography

Alder, J., "Some Policy Problems in Economic Development," *Economic Development and Cultural Change*, 9 (January, 1961), 111-119.

Alexander, R. J., *A Primer of Economic Development* (New York: Macmillan, 1962).

Anderson, C. A., "The Impact of the Educational System on Technological Change and Modernization," in Bert F. Hoselitz and Wilbert E. Moore, eds., *Industrialization and Society* (Paris: UNESCO and Mouton, 1963), pp. 259-278.

Aronsen, R. L., and Windmiller, J. P., *Labor and Management and Economic Growth: Proceedings of a Conference on Human Resources and Labor Relations in Underdeveloped Countries* (Ithaca: New York State School of Industrial and Labor Relations, Cornell University, 1954).

Ayres, C. E., *The Theory of Economic Progress: A Study of the Fundamentals of Economic Development and Cultural Change* (New York: Schocken Books, 1962).

Baldwin, G., *Industrial Growth in South India* (New York: Free Press, 1959).

Barngrover, C., "The Service Industries in Economic Development: A Note," *The American Journal of Economics and Sociology*, 22 (April, 1963), 331-334.

Bendix, R., "Industrialization, Ideologies, and Social Structure," *American Sociological Review*, 24 (October, 1959), 613-623.

Bendix, R., "A Study of Managerial Ideologies," *Economic Development and Cultural Change*, 5 (January, 1957), 118-128.

Bendix, R., *Work and Authority in Industry* (New York: Wiley, 1956).

Berle, A. A., Jr., *The Twentieth Century Capitalist Revolution* (New York: Harcourt, Brace & World, 1954).

Berry, B., "City Size Distributions and Economic Development," *Economic Development and Cultural Change*, 9 (July, 1961), 573-588.

Bertrand, A., and Osborne, H., "Rural Industrialization: A Situational Analysis," *Rural Sociology*, 25 (December, 1960), 387-393.

Blumer, H., "Early Industrialization and the Laboring Class," *Sociological Quarterly*, 1 (January, 1960), 5-14.

Blumer, H., "Industrialization and the Traditional Order," *Sociology and Social Research*, 48 (January, 1964), 129-138.

Bottomley, A., "Economic Growth in a Semi-Nomadic Herding Community," *Economic Development and Cultural Change*, 11 (July, 1963), 407-419.

Boulding, K. E., "Toward a General Theory of Growth," *Canadian Journal of Economic and Political Science*, 19 (August, 1953), 326-340.

Braibanti, R., and Spengler, J., *Tradition, Values, and Socio-Economic Development* (Durham, N.C.: Duke University Press, 1961).

Bressler, M., and Westoff, C. E., "Leadership and Social Change: The Reactions of a Special Group to Industrialization and Population Influx," *Social Forces*, **32** (March, 1954), 235-243.

Cameron, R. E., *France and the Economic Development of Europe, 1800-1914: Conquests of Peace and Seeds of War* (Princeton, N.J.: Princeton University Press, 1961).

Cottrell, W. F., *Energy and Society* (New York: McGraw-Hill, 1955).

Daniel, G. I., "Labor and Nationalism in the British Caribbean," *Annals of the American Academy of Political and Social Sciences*, **310** (March, 1957), 162-171.

Dasgupta, A., "India's Cultural Values and Economic Development: A Comment," *Economic Development and Cultural Change*, **13** (October, 1964), 100-102.

Datta, A., *A Century of Economic Development of Russia and Japan* (Calcutta: World Press Private, 1963).

Davis, K., "The Demographic Consequences of Changes in Productive Technology," in International Social Science Council, *Social, Economic and Technological Change: A Theoretical Approach* (Paris, 1958), 193-227.

Deyrup, F., "Backward Economies: The Problem of Partial Development," *Social Research*, **22** (Winter, 1955), 399-416.

Dinkel, R., "Population Growth and Economic Development: Recent U.S. History and Computer Models of Analysis," *Social Forces*, **43** (May, 1965), 461-470.

Dyer, W., and Affleck, M., "Labor Mobility and Industrialization in a Utah County," *Social Forces*, **36** (March, 1958), 214-217.

Eisenstadt, S. N., "Breakdowns of Modernization," *Economic Development and Cultural Change*, **12** (July, 1964), 345-367.

Eisenstadt, S. N., "Institutionalization and Change," *American Sociological Review*, **29** (April, 1964), 235-247.

Eisenstadt, S. N., "Social Change, Differentiation and Evolution," *American Sociological Review*, **29** (June, 1964), 375-385.

Ellis, H., and Wallich, H., *Economic Development for Latin America* (New York: St. Martin's, 1961).

Epstein, T. S., *Economic Development and Social Change in South India* (New York: The Humanities Press, 1962).

Epstein, T. S., "European Contact and Tolai Economic Development: A Schema of Economic Growth," *Economic Development and Cultural Change*, **11** (April, 1963), 289-307.

Faunce, W. A., and Smucker, M. J., "Industrialization and Community Status Structure," *American Sociological Review*, **31** (June, 1966), 390-399.

Fillol, T., *Social Factors in Economic Development: The Argentine Case* (Cambridge, Mass.: The Massachusetts Institute of Technology Press, 1961).

Florence, S., *Economics and Sociology of Industry: A Realistic Analysis of Development* (London: Watts, 1964).

Galbraith, J., *Economic Development in Perspective* (Cambridge, Mass.: Harvard University Press, 1962).

Galenson, W., *Labor in Developing Economies* (Berkeley: University of California Press, 1962).

Gibbs, J. P., "A Note on Industry Changes and Migration," *American Sociological Review*, **29** (April, 1964), 266-269.

Gibbs, J. P., and Martin, W., "Urbanization, Technology, and the Division of Labor: International Patterns," *American Sociological Review*, **27** (October, 1962), 667-677.

Goldsmith, R., "The Economic Growth of Tsarist Russia 1860-1913," *Economic Development and Cultural Change*, **9** (April, 1961), 441-475.

Gussman, B., "Industrial Efficiency and the Urban African," *Africa*, **23** (April, 1953), 135-144.

Harbison, F., and Myers, C., *Education, Manpower, and Economic Growth: Strategies of Human Resource Development* (New York: McGraw-Hill, 1964).

Hartshorne, R., "Geography and Economic Growth," in Norton Ginsburg, ed., *Essays on Geography and Economic Development* (Chicago: Department of Geography, University of Chicago, 1960), Ch. 1.

Hawkins, E., Palmier, L., and Guthrie H., *Entrepreneurship and Labor Skills in Indonesian Economic Development: A Symposium* (New Haven, Conn.: Yale University, Southeast Asia Studies, Monograph Series 1, 1961).

Hecksher, A., "Goals of the Have-Not Nations," *The American Journal of Economics and Sociology*, **20** (October, 1960), 45-46.

Horowitz, I., "Sociological and Ideological Conceptions of Industrial Development," *The American Journal of Economics and Sociology*, **23** (October, 1964), 351-374.

Hoselitz, B., "Patterns of Economic Growth," *Canadian Journal of Economics and Political Science*, **21** (November, 1955), 416-431.

Hoselitz, B., *Sociological Aspects of Economic Growth* (New York: Free Press, 1960).

Hoselitz, B., "Some Problems in the Quantitative Study of Industrialization," *Economic Development and Cultural Change*, **9** (April, 1961), 537-549.

Hoselitz, B., and Moore, W., *Industrialization and Society* (Paris: UNESCO and Mouton, 1963).

Hou, C., "External Trade, Foreign Investment, and Domestic Development: The Chinese Experience, 1840-1937," *Economic Development and Cultural Change*, **10** (October, 1961), 21-41.

Husain, A., *Human and Social Impact of Technological Change in Pakistan* (Dacca, Pakistan: G. Cumberlege, Oxford University Press, 1956), 2 volumes.

Jaffe, A. J., *People, Jobs, and Economic Development: A Case History of Puerto Rico, Supplemented by Recent Mexican Experiences* (New York: Free Press, 1959).

Kahan, A., "Entrepreneurship in the Early Development of Iron Manufacturing in Russia," *Economic Development and Cultural Change*, **10** (July, 1962), 395-422.

Kerr, C., "The Labour Problem in Economic Development: A Framework for a Reappraisal," *International Labour Review*, **71** (March, 1955), 223-235.

Kerr, C., Dunlop, J., Harbison, F., and Myers, C., *Industrialism and Industrial Man* (Cambridge, Mass.: Harvard University Press, 1960).

Kunkel, J. H., "Economic Autonomy and Social Change in Mexican Villages," *Economic Development and Cultural Change*, 10 (October, 1961), 51-63.

Lagos, G., *International Stratification and Underdeveloped Countries* (Chapel Hill: The University of North Carolina Press, 1963).

Langley, K., *The Industrialization of Iraq* (Cambridge, Mass.: Harvard University Press, 1961).

Lefebure, G., "A Historian's Remarks on the Transition from Feudalism to Capitalism," *Science and Society*, 20 (Summer, 1956), 241-246.

Levy, M., "Some Aspects of Individualism and the Problem of Modernization in China and Japan," *Economic Development and Cultural Change*, 10 (April, 1962), 225-240.

Lopreato, J., "Economic Development and Social Change," *Human Organization*, 21 (Fall, 1962), 182-186.

Marczewski, J., "Some Aspects of Economic Growth of France, 1660-1958," *Economic Development and Cultural Change*, 9 (April, 1961), 369-386.

McClelland, D. C., *The Achieving Society* (Princeton, N.J.: Van Nostrand, 1961).

McGranahan, D., "Some Remarks on the Human Implications of Technological Change in the Underdeveloped Areas," *Social Problems*, 1 (June, 1953), 13-16.

Metha, A., "The Mediating Role of the Trade Union in Underdeveloped Countries," *Economic Development and Social Change*, 6 (October, 1957), 16-23.

Moore, W. E., *The Impact of Industry* (Englewood Cliffs, N.J.: Prentice-Hall, 1965).

Moore, W. E., *Industrialization and Labor* (Ithaca, N.Y.: Cornell University Press, 1951).

Moore, W. E., "Urbanization and Industrialization of the Labor Force in a Developing Economy. Labor Attitudes Toward Industrialization in Underdeveloped Countries," *American Economic Review*, 45 (May, 1955), 156-165.

Moore, W. E., "The Exportability of the 'Labor Force' Concept," *American Sociological Review*, 18 (February, 1953), 68-72.

Moore, W. E., "Social Aspects of Economic Development," in Robert E. L. Faris, ed., *Handbook of Modern Sociology* (Chicago: Rand McNally, 1964), Ch. 23.

Moore, W. E., "The Adaptation of African Labor Systems to Social Change," in Melville J. Herskovits and Mitchell Harwitz, eds., *Economic Transition in Africa* (Evanston, Ill.: Northwestern University Press, 1964), Ch. 13.

Moore, W. E., "Measurement of Organizational and Institutional Implications of Changes in Productive Technology," in International Social Science Council, *Social, Economic, and Technological Change: A Theoretical Approach* (Paris, 1958), 229-259.

Moore, W. E., and Feldman, A. S., *Labor Commitment and Social Change in Developing Areas* (New York: Social Science Research Council, 1960).

Mumford, L., *Technics and Civilization* (New York: Harcourt, Brace & World, 1934).

Nash, M., *Machine Age Maya* (New York: Free Press, 1958).

Nash, M., "Social Prerequisites to Economic Growth in Latin America and Southeast Asia," *Economic Development and Cultural Change*, 12 (April, 1964), 225-242.

Nash, M., "Some Notes on Village Industrialization in South and East Asia," *Economic Development and Cultural Change*, 3 (April, 1953), 271-277.

Parker, W. N., "Economic Development in Historical Perspective," *Economic Development and Cultural Change*, 10 (October, 1961), 1-7.

Pesek, B. P., "Economic Growth and Its Measurement," *Economic Development and Cultural Change*, 9 (April, 1961), 295-315.

Phillips, W., "Technological Levels and Labor Resistance to Change in the Course of Industrialization," *Economic Development and Cultural Change*, 11 (April, 1963), 257-266.

Rice, A. K., "The Experimental Reorganization of Non-Automatic Weaving in an Indian Mill," *Human Relations*, 8 (August, 1955), 199-249.

Rice, A. K., "Productivity and Social Organization in an Indian Weaving Shed," *Human Relations*, 6 (November, 1953), 297-330.

Rice, A. K., "Productivity and Social Organization in an Indian Weaving Mill, II," *Human Relations*, 8 (November, 1955), 399-428.

Rice, A. K., *Productivity and Social Organization: The Ahmedabad Experiment* (London: Tavistock Publications, 1958).

Ridker, R., "Discontent and Economic Growth," *Economic Development and Cultural Change*, 11 (October, 1962), 1-15.

Rosen, B. C., "The Achievement Syndrome and Economic Growth in Brazil," *Social Forces*, 42 (March, 1964), 341-353.

Rostow, W. W., *The Stages of Economic Growth* (New York: Cambridge University Press, 1960).

Ruttan, V. W., "Industrial Progress and Rural Stagnation in The New South," *Social Forces*, 34 (December, 1955), 114-118.

Salisbury, R. F., *From Stone to Steel: Economic Consequences of a Technological Change in New Guinea* (New York: Cambridge University Press, 1963).

Schramm, W., *Mass Media and National Development: The Role of Information in the Developing Countries* (Stanford, Calif.: Stanford University Press, and Paris: UNESCO, 1964).

de Schweinitz, K., Jr., *Industrialization and Democracy: Economic Necessities and Political Possibilities* (New York: Free Press, 1964).

Shetty, M. C., *Small-Scale and Household Industries in a Developing Economy* (New York: Asia Publishing House, 1963).

Silvert, K. H., *Expectant Peoples: Nationalism and Development* (New York: Random House, 1963).

Singer, H., "Problems of Industrialization of Underdeveloped Countries," *International Social Science Bulletin*, 6 (1954), 217-227.

Sivertsen, D., *When Caste Barriers Fall: A Study of Social and Economic Change in a South Indian Village* (New York: The Humanities Press, 1963).

Sjoberg, G., *The Preindustrial City: Past and Present* (New York: Free Press, 1960).

Smelser, N. J., Social Change in the Industrial Revolution: An Application of Theory to the British Cotton Industry, 1770-1840 (Chicago: University of Chicago Press, 1959).

Somers, J. C., "The Process of Technology in Industrial Development," The American Journal of Economics and Sociology, 22 (July, 1963), 393-396.

Stockwell, E. G., "Fertility of Underdeveloped Areas," Social Forces, 41 (May, 1963), 390-394.

Suranyi-Unger, T., "The Role of Knowledge in Invention and Economic Development," The American Journal of Economics and Sociology, 22 (October, 1963), 463-471.

Theodorson, G. A., "Acceptance of Industrialization and Its Attendant Consequences for the Social Patterns of Non-Western Societies," American Sociological Review, 18 (October, 1953), 477-484.

Thomas, B., International Migration and Economic Development: A Trend Report and Bibliography (Paris: UNESCO, 1961).

Udy, S. H., Organization of Work: A Comparative Analysis of Production Among Nonindustrial Peoples (New Haven, Conn.: HRAF Press, 1959).

Udy, S. H., "The Structure of Authority in Non-Industrial Production Organizations," American Journal of Sociology, 14 (May, 1959), 582-584.

Udy, S. H., "Technical and Institutional Factors in Production Organization: A Preliminary Model," American Journal of Sociology, 67 (November, 1961), 247-254.

Warren, R. I., "The Common Land in South-West Germany: The Behavior of a Prefeudal Institution Under the Strains of Industrialization," Rural Sociology, 22 (September, 1957), 271-273.

White, L., Medieval Technology and Social Change (New York: Oxford University Press, 1962).

Wilensky, H. L., and Lebeaux, C. N., Industrial Society and Social Welfare (New York: Russell Sage, 1958).

Wilkinson, T. O., "Family Structure and Industrialization in Japan," American Sociological Review, 27 (October, 1962), 678-682.

Wilkinson, T. O., "Urban Structure and Industrialization," American Sociological Review, 25 (June, 1960), 356-363.

Willner, A. R., "A Case Study of a Javanese Factory," Human Organization, 22 (Summer, 1963), 133-141.

Wipper, A., "A Comparative Study of Nascent Unionism in French West Africa and the Philippines," Economic Development and Cultural Change, 13 (October, 1964), 20-55.

Wrigley, E. A., Industrial Growth and Population Change: A Regional Study of the Coalfield Areas of North-West Europe in the Latter Nineteenth Century (New York: Cambridge University Press, 1961).

Zelinsky, W., "Rural Population Dynamics as an Index to Social and Economic Development: A Geographic Overview," The Sociological Quarterly, 4 (Spring, 1963), 99-121.

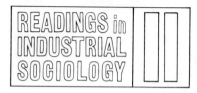

INDUSTRIAL BUREAUCRACY

Introduction

Social scientific interest in the study of complex, formal organizations has grown at an extraordinary rate in the past decade. Important developments in the field have occurred not only in sociology but in psychology, political science, economics, and business management as well. The study of organizations appears, in fact, to be on the way toward becoming a separate multidisciplinary field with its own distinctive body of theory and research methods. James G. March, in his introduction to the recently published *Handbook of Organizations*, describes the history of organizational studies as follows:

The field as a more or less identifiable cluster of research interests within a number of social sciences dates for most purposes from a group of books written between 1937 and 1942—Barnard, Roethlisberger and Dickson, and Simon. As the field has become defined, it has coopted groups with traditions extending beyond this primary trinity (most conspicuously the Weberians in sociology and the natural heirs of the Commons traditions in economics).[1]

The volume of published literature in the field, its multidisciplinary character, and the rate at which new developments are occurring in recent years combine to make it virtually impossible to cover the field of organizational studies in this chapter, and no attempt has been made to do so.[2] The selection of readings was instead limited in two ways. First, since the primary concern of this book is with the sociology of manufacturing industries, the selections included deal, for the most part, with industrial bureaucratic organizations. Secondly, most of the authors whose work is

---

[1] James G. March, ed., *Handbook of Organizations* (Chicago: Rand McNally, 1965), p. xiii. The three books referred to are C. I. Barnard, *The Functions of the Executive* (Cambridge: Harvard University Press, 1938), F. J. Roethlisberger and W. J. Dickson, *Management and the Worker* (Cambridge: Harvard University Press, 1939), and H. A. Simon, *Administrative Behavior* (New York: Macmillan, 1947).
[2] For a book which does survey the field of organizational studies, see March, *op. cit.*

included could be characterized as "Weberians" in the sense that March uses the term in the passage quoted previously. The work of Max Weber contains the seminal principles from which the sociology of formal organizations has developed.[3] Many sociologists, including several of the authors of selections included in this chapter, have been critical of various aspects of Weber's analysis of bureaucratic organizations. They uniformly acknowledge their indebtedness, however, to the contributions Weber made to this field.

Weber's interest in bureaucracy was part of a broader concern with authority or legitimate control structures. The subsequent contributions of sociology to the field of organizational studies have been primarily, though not exclusively, in the area of organizational control, and it is this area that forms the central focus of this chapter. Another area of concern to sociologists has been the informal patterns of social relationships that develop within the formal structure of large, complex organizations. Some of this concern is reflected in the readings in this chapter and we will return to it again in Chapter IV which deals with the work group. There has also been a growing interest in studies of organizational change and two of the readings in this chapter are concerned directly with this process.

The two areas in which most of the major, recent developments in the field have occurred are in the analysis of the processes of communication and decision-making. For several reasons little attention has been given to these developments in this chapter. Many of the recent advances in these areas have been primarily methodological rather than substantive—that is, advances in the techniques for acquiring knowledge rather than in the amount that is known. The application of formal logical, or mathematical models to the analysis of communication and decision-making represents the major development of this sort. Game theory, statistical decision theory, graph theory, information theory, linear programming, and computer simulation are examples of these new techniques. The use of these models has been, for the present at least, more often normative than descriptive—more concerned with the solution of problems than with understanding human behavior. For example, decision-making models based upon game theory have been designed more often to determine the optimal choice among alternatives in decision situations than to predict the behavior of individuals in these situations. Similarly, the work done with computers in the area of "artificial intelligence," where the attempt is made to find the best possible solution to problems, is exclusively normative and even in the area of computer simulation, where the attempt is to simulate human problem-solving processes, the concern is primarily

[3] Cf. Max Weber, *The Theory of Social and Economic Organization* (New York: Free Press, 1957); H. H. Gerth and C. Wright Mills, *From Max Weber: Essays in Sociology* (New York: Oxford University Press, 1958); Reinhardt Bendix, *Max Weber: An Intellectual Portrait* (Garden City, N.Y.: Doubleday, 1960).

normative and there has been very little attention given, for example, to the understanding of individual differences.

So far the applications of these models have not been able to capture more than a minor portion of the empirical richness of organizational life. They have also, with a few exceptions, been more concerned with psychological than with sociological processes in the sense that they have focused upon the individual rather than upon social structure. They are potentially, however, very powerful tools for the analysis of formal organizations and the student who is interested in the general field of organizational studies would be well advised to become familiar with these techniques.[4]

As noted above, this chapter is concerned mainly with the authority structure of industrial organizations. The reason for this focus of attention is not only because it represents both historically and at present the main interest of industrial sociologists in formal organization, but also because of its relevance to the theme of this book. In complex organizations in which the work to be done has been divided into highly specialized jobs, a differentiated, hierarchically ordered authority structure is required to coordinate these jobs and to ensure that they are done properly. Routine, specialized tasks require, to a much greater degree than tasks involving more skill and responsibility, rationalized patterns of supervision, rational procedures for rewarding performance, and also formal, contractual agreements regarding the conditions of employment. The organizational form of industrial bureaucracy is a good example of the rationalized social structure necessitated by the problem of achieving integration in highly differentiated social systems.

It should be noted, however, that even where there is not a hierarchically ordered authority structure, other elements of structural rationality may be present. Udy, in a cross-cultural comparative study of work organizations,[5] and Stinchcombe, in a study of the construction industry,[6] have both demonstrated that this is the case. These studies illustrate the value of another recent methodological development in the sociology of organizations—an increasing emphasis upon studies involving systematic comparisons of different types of organizations (as distinct from case studies of single organizations). These two studies are discussed briefly in the selection by Blau in this chapter.

There is a dilemma inherent in the differentiation-rationalization process that is the major theme of several of the readings in this chapter: it is

[4] One of the important early books in this area was John von Neumann and Oskar Morgenstern, *Theory of Games and Economic Behavior* (Princeton: Princeton University Press, 1944). For an overview of recent developments see March, *op. cit.*, pp. 48-86, 305-386, 534-573, 614-649, 1171-1211.

[5] Stanley H. Udy, " 'Bureaucracy' and 'Rationality' in Weber's Theory," *American Sociological Review*, 24 (1959), 791-795.

[6] Arthur L. Stinchcombe, "Bureaucratic and Craft Administration of Production," *Administrative Science Quarterly*, 4 (1959), 168-187.

impossible to maximize both organizational control and individual freedom. Industrial bureaucracies contain not only functionally specialized tasks requiring close supervision, but highly skilled and professional tasks in which individual freedom of action is important for successful performance. Organizational constraints under bureaucratic systems of authority pose particular problems for skilled workers and professionals but are generally resented by semiskilled blue-collar and clerical workers as well.

One of the criticisms of Weber's theory of bureaucracy is that he apparently assumed that the decisions of administrators would necessarily be more expert in the area of their jurisdiction than would the decisions of their subordinates. The problems discussed by Dalton and by Marcson in this chapter clearly illustrate the point that this is not always so. This criticism is related to a general lack of attention in Weber's work to the problems created by (or the dysfunctions of) features of bureaucratic organization, such as minute division of labor and differentiated authority structures. Because of his preoccupation with the formal, rationalized attributes of bureaucracy, Weber also gave little attention to informal interaction networks or, in other words, to the recurring patterns of social relationships that emerge irrespective of or, in some instances, in spite of the patterns prescribed in formal job descriptions and organization charts. Nevertheless, Weber's work remains the starting point for most sociological studies of organizations and a brief selection from one of his books is included here as the first reading in this chapter.

This selection originally appeared in Weber's, *Wirtschaft und Gesellschaft*, Part III, Chapter 6, which was written before World War I but published posthumously in 1922. The discussion of bureaucracy appears in the context of a much longer analysis of three types of authority: traditional, charismatic, and rational.[7] Weber's contention that authority structures in industrialized nations have become increasingly rational is clearly related to the major theme of this book. The selection from Weber included here presents in abbreviated form the essential elements of bureaucracy with the emphasis being upon clear-cut division of labor and specialization, hierarchical authority, formal rules and regulations, impersonal orientation of officials, and employment as a career for officials.

"On the Nature of Industrial Bureaucracy" by Wilbert Moore, which follows the reading by Weber, discusses in more detail some of the elements identified by Weber as characteristic of bureaucratic organization. It includes a discussion of job specialization, resulting problems in coordination, and rational principles of organization such as routinization and formalization, hierarchical authority, professionalization, and indirect lines of communication. Moore also discusses some dysfunctions of bureaucracy including overconformity to rules and regulations, resistance to

[7] A brief discussion of these types of authority can be found in the selection by Gouldner in this chapter.

change, and information bottlenecks, and stresses the importance of informal or "noncharted" social relationships.

The third selection is based upon one of the classic studies of bureaucracy, reported in full in Alvin Gouldner's, *Patterns of Industrial Bureaucracy* published in 1954. This study traces the development of bureaucratic forms in a factory following the replacement of the plant manager. Most of the attributes of bureaucracy discussed in the preceding two selections can be seen as they evolved in this factory. The emphasis in this reading is on the effects of succession of leadership upon the emergence of rational, bureaucratic authority. Gouldner also emphasizes, however, the relationship between informal and formal patterns of organization and the importance of reinforcement of formal rules by a framework of nonrational values.

The next reading, Melville Dalton's frequently cited study of staff-line conflict, illustrates the weakness noted above in Weber's assumption of correspondence between authority and technical expertise. At some level of the organization, professional staff officials are customarily subordinate to line officials. Conflicting values, age differences, and a limited mobility potential for staff members within the staff hierarchy also produce problems in the relationship between the staff and the line in industrial organizations. Dalton emphasizes the necessity of understanding the actual as contrasted with the formally prescribed relations in industry and concludes with some suggestions for the resolution of staff-line conflict.

The selection from Blau and Scott's *Formal Organizations* describes three dilemmas in organizations of this kind. The first of these is the fact that a free flow of communication improves problem-solving but makes it difficult to achieve coordination of activities while a hierarchical authority structure improves coordination but restricts communication. The second dilemma stems from the differences in the authority patterns appropriate in bureaucratic and professional organizations in conjunction with the increasing employment of professionals in industrial and governmental bureaucracies. The third dilemma is that both centralized planning and exercise of individual initiative are necessary although procedures which maximize one necessarily restrict the other.

All three of these dilemmas are special cases of the general dilemma of freedom versus control that was referred to above. Blau and Scott indicate that this dilemma is particularly noticeable in "mutual benefit" organizations like trade unions. This issue is the major theme in Chapter V of this book which deals with the internal structure of unions.

The next reading, that by Simon Marcson, focuses specifically upon the conflict between bureaucratic or "executive" authority and professional or "colleague" authority. He illustrates this problem in the study of a large, industrial research laboratory. The issue considered here is similar to that described by Dalton but exists in a more pronounced form in this setting. There has been a dramatic increase in recent years in the number of professionals employed in industry. Studies, like Marcson's, of the problems occasioned by this development represent a major recent trend in the sociology of industrial organization.

Another recent development, as was noted above, is an increased attention by sociologists to the process of organizational change. The final selection in this chapter is Mann and Williams' study of the introduction of an electronic data processing system in a large industrial office. This study indicates that there is a difference in the managerial skills called for at different stages in the introduction of a technological change. It also analyzes some of the consequences of organizational change generally, for example, the fact that managerial philosophies are called into question by this process, and details some of the specific effects of the particular change studied. One of the effects of office automation appears to be increased centralization of authority which is of interest in terms of the central theme of this chapter.

6. Characteristics of Bureaucracy

Max Weber

Modern officialdom functions in the following specific manner:

I. There is the principle of fixed and official jurisdictional areas, which are generally ordered by rules, that is, by laws or administrative regulations.

1. The regular activities required for the purposes of the bureaucratically governed structure are distributed in a fixed way as official duties.
2. The authority to give the commands required for the discharge of these duties is distributed in a stable way and is strictly delimited by rules concerning the coercive means, physical, sacerdotal, or otherwise, which may be placed at the disposal of officials.
3. Methodical provision is made for the regular and continuous fulfilment of these duties and for the execution of the corresponding rights; only persons who have the generally regulated qualifications to serve are employed.

In public and lawful government these three elements constitute "bureaucratic authority." In private economic domination, they constitute bureaucratic "management." Bureaucracy, thus understood, is fully developed in political and ecclesiastical communities only in the modern state, and, in the private economy, only in the most advanced institutions of capitalism. Permanent and public office authority, with fixed jurisdiction, is not the historical rule but rather the exception. This is so even in large political structures such as those of the ancient Orient, the Germanic and Mongolian empires of conquest, or of many feudal structures of state. In all these cases, the ruler executes the most important measures through personal trustees, table-companions, or court-servants. Their commissions and authority are not precisely delimited and are temporarily called into being for each case.

II. The principles of office hierarchy and of levels of graded authority mean a firmly ordered system of super- and subordination in which there is a supervision of the lower offices by the higher ones. Such a system offers the governed the possibility of appealing the decision of a lower office to its higher authority, in a definitely regulated manner. With the full development of the bureaucratic type, the office hierarchy is monocratically organized. The principle of hierarchical office authority is found in all bu-

From *Max Weber: Essays in Sociology* edited and translated by H. H. Gerth and C. Wright Mills. Copyright 1946 by Oxford University Press, Inc. Reprinted by permission.

reaucratic structures: in state and ecclesiastical structures as well as in large party organizations and private enterprises. It does not matter for the character of bureaucracy whether its authority is called "private" or "public."

When the principle of jurisdictional "competency" is fully carried through, hierarchical subordination—at least in public office—does not mean that the "higher" authority is simply authorized to take over the business of the "lower." Indeed, the opposite is the rule. Once established and having fulfilled its task, an office tends to continue in existence and be held by another incumbent.

III. The management of the modern office is based upon written documents (the files), which are preserved in their original or draught form. There is, therefore, a staff of subaltern officials and scribes of all sorts. The body of officials actively engaged in a "public" office, along with the respective apparatus of material implements and the files, make up a "bureau." In private enterprise, "the bureau" is often called "the office."

In principle, the modern organization of the civil service separates the bureau from the private domicile of the official, and, in general, bureaucracy segregates official activity as something distinct from the sphere of private life. Public monies and equipment are divorced from the private property of the official. This condition is everywhere the product of a long development. Nowadays, it is found in public as well as in private enterprises; in the latter, the principle extends even to the leading entrepreneur. In principle, the executive office is separated from the household, business from private correspondence, and business assets from private fortunes. The more consistently the modern type of business management has been carried through the more are these separations the case. The beginnings of this process are to be found as early as the Middle Ages.

It is the peculiarity of the modern entrepreneur that he conducts himself as the "first official" of his enterprise, in the very same way in which the ruler of a specifically modern bureaucratic state spoke of himself as "the first servant" of the state.[1] The idea that the bureau activities of the state are intrinsically different in character from the management of private economic offices is a continental European notion and, by the way of contrast, is totally foreign to the American way.

IV. Office management, at least all specialized office management—and such management is distinctly modern—usually presupposes thorough and expert training. This increasingly holds for the modern executive and employee of private enterprises, in the same manner as it holds for the state official.

V. When the office is fully developed, official activity demands the full working capacity of the official, irrespective of the fact that his obligatory time in the bureau may be firmly delimited. In the normal case, this is only the product of a long development, in the public as well as in the

[1] Frederick II of Prussia.

private office. Formerly, in all cases, the normal state of affairs was reversed: official business was discharged as a secondary activity.

VI. The management of the office follows general rules, which are more or less stable, more or less exhaustive, and which can be learned. Knowledge of these rules represents a special technical learning which the officials possess. It involves jurisprudence, or administrative or business management.

The reduction of modern office management to rules is deeply embedded in its very nature. The theory of modern public administration, for instance, assumes that the authority to order certain matters by decree —which has been legally granted to public authorities—does not entitle the bureau to regulate the matter by commands given for each case, but only to regulate the matter abstractly. This stands in extreme contrast to the regulation of all relationships through individual privileges and bestowals of favor, which is absolutely dominant in patrimonialism, at least in so far as such relationships are not fixed by sacred tradition.

7. On the Nature of Industrial Bureaucracy

Wilbert E. Moore

The old-time boss is a member of a diminishing species. Because of both the separation of ownership and management and the tremendous increase in the size of managerial personnel (both closely related to the introduction of corporate enterprise and the various advantages of bigness), the paternalistic or exploitative employer has been largely replaced by the professional officeholder. In a period characterized by the multiplication of governmental bureaus and their functionaries—often viewed bitterly by industrial representatives—industry has also moved in a similar direction, namely, full-blown bureaucracy. Lest this should be understood as simply a name-calling characterization, it may be well to examine the features of bureaucratic organization and to see if the term is indeed aptly applied to contemporary big business.

Specialization

An outstanding feature of the type of organization that may be properly called bureaucratic is specialization. More than any other variety of organization, bureaucracy rests upon a selection and distribution of personnel according to specialized abilities and particular duties.[1] It is thus in marked contrast to social units like the family or community which recruit their members chiefly by natural reproduction, and must therefore limit the division of labor in accordance with the quality of the human resources available.

Bureaucratic specialization depends not only upon an adequate re-

Reprinted with permission of The Macmillan Company from *Industrial Relations and the Social Order* by Wilbert E. Moore. Copyright 1950 by The Macmillan Company.

[1] The classic analysis of bureaucratic organization is that of Max Weber, *Wirtschart and Gesellschaft* (Tubingen: J. C. B. Mohr, 1922), pp. 650-678. See also the following: Marshall E. Dimock and Howard K. Hyde, *Bureaucracy and Trusteeship in Large Corporations*, United States Congress, Temporary National Economic Committee, Investigation of Concentration of Economic Power, Monograph No. 11 (Washington, D.C.: U.S. Government Printing Office, 1940), Part II, "Causes and Manifestations of Bureaucracy"; Carl Joachim Friedrich and Taylor Cole, *op. cit.*, pp. 1-28; Otto Heinrich von der Gablentz, "Industriebureaukratie," *Schmollers Jahrbuch*, **50**, 539-572, 1926; Robert K. Merton, "Bureaucratic Structure and Personality," *Social Forces*, **18** (May, 1940), 560-568.

cruitment process, but upon an effective classification and coordination process as well. Specifically, the high degree of division of labor character-istic of modern industrial organization rests upon three types of differences in the personnel available for productive labor. (1) It assumes and utilizes differences in native ability. One important distinction between bureau-cratic principles of organization and those operating in other types of cooperative social systems is that the former frankly take into account both qualitative and quantitative differences in ability. These differences are not only taken into account negatively, as a limitation to possible occupational diversification, but positively as available human resources for particular positions. (2) The differences in native ability, however, are in general meaningless or useless without specific training along the lines of existent or possible future occupational demands. In fact, bureaucratic specializa-tion goes so far beyond any "natural" (untrained) differences in ability that it calls for high degrees of skill often requiring long preliminary train-ing or apprenticeship. (3) Since, as will be noted, position in a bureaucratic organization demands a good deal of loyalty to the system as a whole (sometimes called esprit de corps) and to the duties required by the indi-vidual's particular place in that system, it may be said to depend upon differences in occupational interests. This expectation sometimes poses some neat problems, for the individual in our society is in general supposed to be dissatisfied with his particular place in society, yet proud of his im-portance to his occupation, business organization, industrial plant, or inde-pendent profession. It is precisely in the bureaucratic organization that this pull-hauling upon the individual's occupational sentiments is reduced to a minimum by various devices which will be discussed in subsequent para-graphs.

Ideally, the three types of differences in the available personnel are expected to operate together. That is, the methods of selection and training are expected to provide a general sifting process on the basis of ability (as defined by the particular standards of selection considered important), and to induce the appropriate sentiments in regard to the specialized task and the system as a whole. In American society, where choice of occupational interests exists to an unusually high degree, the recruitment of the neces-sary qualified personnel for specialized industrial positions depends to a marked extent upon the advantages which such positions seem to offer to the individual. It is thus not simply necessary that the quantity and quality of the laboring population should have the necessary native ability, but that ability must be translated into usable skills through training, mediated by interest.

A shortcoming in any one of the three prerequisites to bureaucratic specialization may reduce the possible diversification of activities. The cur-rent shortage in skilled laborers of almost all kinds is a case in point. Given a reasonably satisfactory solution to the general problem of personnel supply, however, the organizational problems resulting from specialization are not all taken care of.

Coordination

Whether in society as a whole, or in a smaller social system like a branch plant of a large steel corporation, the higher the degree of specialization, the greater the necessity of coordination. The integration of almost count-less activities toward the achievement of the goals of the organization as a whole is one of the most persistent sources of difficulty in industrial man-agement.[2] This would be true even if labor were simply divided. It is all the more true since the division takes place in the form of functional specialization.

The industrial executive, technical specialist, junior manager, line su-pervisor, and to some degree the productive laborer have special spheres of competence based upon particular abilities of functional importance to the organization as a whole. Within these broad or narrow spheres of compe-tence the individual specialist reigns supreme. Thus a given riveter or welder may know considerably more about his job than does the foreman who supervises his work. The equivalent situation is most certainly true in the relation of the research chemist to the president or general manager. This is the reason that a "pure line" organization will not ordinarily work in a contemporary manufacturing plant. Authority is divided as well as delegated. Of this we shall have more to say presently, but it should be observed at once that this does not settle the issue of coordination: it sim-ply documents its importance.

A good deal of the coordination of diversified activities is ensured by the character of the formal organization itself. Thus every person's (or at least every "manager's") status in the organization is, formally considered, a well-defined position or office. This means that the rights and duties of the person occupying the office are largely determined by the relation of the position to others (and only incidentally, or even accidentally, by the rela-tion between concrete persons). Under the triple assumption that the sys-tem is already established, that it is perfectly integrated, and that the occupants of the various positions will in fact fulfill precisely those official expectations demanded by the positions (no more, no less), the coordina-tion might properly be viewed as automatic. That this result is rarely if ever achieved implies that ordinarily one or more of these assumptions is not in fact borne out. Nevertheless, the organizational advantages of the typical bureaucratic formalization merit some further consideration.

---

[2] The recognition of the importance of coordination of diversified activities is im-plicit in most of the treatises on industrial management, but is perhaps most clearly stated in that field by E. H. Anderson and G. T. Schwenning, *The Science of Produc-tion Organization* (New York: Wiley, 1938), pp. 203-210.

Routine and formalization

One of the most consistent criticisms of bureaucratic organization, and one that usually makes of the term bureaucracy an epithet, is its emphasis upon routine and form. From certain points of view (that is, with certain ends in mind) the criticism is undoubtedly justified. But from the point of view of maintaining a smoothly operating social system with a complex structure and diversified personnel, the criticism loses some of its merit. The elaborate ritual associated with interpersonal relations in a bureaucratic structure is well designed to maintain the division of spheres of competence, and to a certain degree the coordination of these. To the layman, or the person seeking help or information, the characteristic "passing the buck" is a sign of inefficiency. To the bureaucratic officeholder in government or industry, this is simply a process of referring a problem to the person or department within whose sphere its solution lies. Failure to follow this pattern would destroy the efficacy of the organizational specialization and cause general confusion of well-defined roles in the total system.

A major function of "rules and regulations" in any social organization is that of ensuring predictability of behavior within the organization. Thus the formal pattern of relations fixes responsibility for various decisions and standard activities. In this way it prevents overlapping authority, gaps in responsibility for important duties, and the arbitrary exercise of authority. To the extent that the rules are formal and the expected activities attached to the office and not to the particular occupant, the organization can maintain a high degree of stability with a changing personnel. (This principle is most strikingly illustrated, of course, in the organization of the army, where the most general rule is that a subordinate reacts to the uniform, and not to its wearer.)

A further corollary of the function of rules in ensuring predictability is their function in reducing or eliminating friction. The importance of this function is directly related to the highly diversified personnel making up the organization. The abilities, training, and interests represented are ordinarily such as to make impossible a friendly informal cooperation throughout the organization. Formal rules make it possible even for potential enemies, and especially for those who would under informal conditions remain indifferent toward one another, to maintain cooperative relations. To the extent that the person's significance for the system is determined by his position, and his relations with others follow predetermined routines, the significance of the total personality is minimized. What is of primary importance in a highly formal structure is rather the "organizational personality." Again this principle is of much more general application than its usefulness in a governmental bureau or a business main office. The elaboration of rules of etiquette in "polite society," for example, allows strangers who are familiar with the rule book to act properly toward one another, and minimizes the necessity of making personal adjustments. Its relevance to operation of an extended bureaucratic organization is enhanced, however, by the diversity of the personnel, the specialization of activity, and the necessary coordination if the goals of the entire organization are to be achieved. It is in bureaucracy that a social system most closely approximates the coordinated complexity of the modern machine.

Hierarchical organization

The distinctions among personnel in any social organization are not all representable on a "horizontal" plane, for authority is never distributed evenly throughout a social system. Even if the source of the authority is a "popular mandate" expressed through some democratic procedure, the importance of responsibility and unified direction are such as to require a demarcation of persons on a "vertical" plane. The wide extension of functional specialization does not remove the necessity for centralized administration and control, but rather increases it. Thus bureaucratic organization, wherever its field of operation, is typically characterized by definite gradations in relative rank.

Part of the necessity of a rather elaborate hierarchy is to be found simply in the size of industrial organizations, since convenience and effective organization require that the number of persons directly supervised by a single administrator not be large. This means that general policies or goals are passed down from one rank to the next, becoming more definite at each step, until they become explicit directions for the performance of those activities which will produce the general results desired.

The importance of "functional authority," that is, authority within special spheres of competence, has led some observers to minimize the importance of "final authority."[3] They argue, quite reasonably, that this specialization reduces the area of explicit authority of the executive. But they also argue that there is no final authority, but only the functional coordination of specialists. This is a sufficiently important issue in determining the general character of industrial organization, as well as the specific roles of members of the managerial personnel, to merit close examination.

One striking result of functional division of authority is that the executive ceases thereby to be the most skilled workman, or even the most competent "authority" in the organization. But this does not mean that the necessity for hierarchical organization is removed. On the contrary, the reduction of the area of the explicit authority of the executive increases the importance of the coordinating function of the "line" official. Besides

[3] See especially M. P. Follett, "The Meaning of Responsibility in Business Management," in Henry C. Metcalf, ed., *Business Management as a Profession* (New York: McGraw-Hill, 1927), pp. 319-338.

coordination, which might conceivably be maintained by the formal structure of the organization, a "final authority" is further necessary for two reasons: (1) the over-all policies of the organization must proceed from the responsible center of control of that organization, and (2) this is more particularly true since the organization must be prepared to adapt itself to changed conditions.

The function of coordinating specialized activities is, in practice, not adequately guaranteed by the formal relationships between specialists. There are a number of reasons for this but one of the outstanding ones is precisely the problem of organizational elasticity to allow for major or minor changes in the goals of the organization. In an elaborate social system, part of the units may be viewed as "structural," that is, as integrating the actions of various distinct units.

The addition of the problem of coordination to the general necessity of subdelegation of authority in a large organization increases, rather than decreases, the necessity of hierarchical arrangement of ranks and corresponding authority and responsibility. In fact, the wider the horizontal extension of functional specialization, the greater the necessity for vertical subdelegation of authority. This, in the absence of a better term, may be called the pyramidal principle of bureaucratic organization.

Professionalization

The growth of professional management is further evidence of the bureaucratic character of industrial organization. The amount of technical training required for specialized offices in a modern business or manufacturing establishment goes a long way toward ensuring that the individual officeholder will think of a career in terms of the organization. This does not necessarily mean that he expects to end his working life in the position he held when he first became part of the system. On the contrary, he will ordinarily expect considerable advancement through various ranks during the course of his active career. How well these expectations are satisfied, or their failure justified and accepted, may well determine the extent of effective esprit de corps throughout the organization, and the presence or absence of an attachment to the organization as a whole.

Perhaps governmental bureaucracy, particularly as exemplified in the British and American "permanent civil service," has achieved this professionalization and regularized advancement through clear-cut ranks more completely than has industrial bureaucracy. This is probably due partly to the longer period of development of complex governmental administration and partly to the more rapid changes in industrial organization demanded by the constant orientation to an expanding technology.

In political administration and, to a lesser extent, in industrial administration, the attachment of the individual to the organization as a whole has been ensured by a number of interrelated devices. (1) No matter what major department or section of an organization the individual enters, the steps to the top of the organization are sufficiently well defined to leave little doubt as to the usual line or direction of promotion. (2) The absolute and relative importance of any particular position is recognized not only by salaries proportional to rank, but by honorific titles ("coordinator," "director," "specialist," "executive secretary," and so on almost indefinitely), glass doors, large desks, letterheads, and the like. (3) The intrusion of a too highly competitive spirit in a cooperative organization is largely made unnecessary by the elaborate formal definition of rights and duties attaching to the particular office, and the likelihood of its appearance is often further reduced by basing advancement upon the relatively nonrational seniority principle rather than on technical qualification as determined on other grounds. It has been only within the comparatively recent past that industrial managers have given much consideration to the character of the promotional system, both as a part of the general problem of adequate selection of personnel and as a method of maintaining "morale" within the organization.

If the career bureaucrat understands his position in the organization and complies with the organizational expectations in fulfilling his various duties, he must of course accept the rules and routines which presumably lead to the ultimate goals of the organization. This raises a series of problems, however, in a complex and partially elastic organization. Devotion to duty, that is, strict compliance with all the technical regulations, may persist in the face of their obvious inefficacy in attaining the officially prescribed end. A widespread characteristic of bureaucratic organizations of all kinds is this tendency of the officeholder to treat the rules as ends in themselves. Since in an extremely complex system the relation of any particular activity to the general goals of the organization may be difficult or impossible for the functionary to see, and since he is likely to feel that his only security in the organization is in a religious devotion to duty (narrowly defined), it is understandable that he should attach high significance to strict conformity with the rule book. To an outsider, who is much more likely to have his attention fixed upon the general goals and fail to appreciate the problems of technical specialization, this lays the functionary or the entire organization open to charges of becoming enmeshed in "red tape."

In a very real sense, the "career man" who occupies a particular position in an elaborate organization has a "vested interest" in the preservation not only of the entire organization, but of the various formal activities and relationships that characterize his role in it. This vested interest is often more sentimental than rational, but is nevertheless real. Subjectively considered, preservation of the formal relations is necessary for his security.

The characteristic routine and professionalization of bureaucracy make it a system which operates more effectively in a stable social order than in a changing one. External changes as reflected in modifications or transformations in general policies may also require changes in the social machinery. Within the organization, however, there is a profound resistance to change. Since manufacturing companies must be oriented both to changes in the market and to changes in technology (as well as to possible social controls through legislation), this becomes a critical problem in industrial management.

Indirect lines of communication

The essence of social interaction, and a primary condition for the existence of any social group, is to be found in communication. It is impossible to talk about a social relationship, or social organization, without implying the existence of communication among the several units (persons) said to be related or organized. But unlike animal societies, the human capacity for abstract and symbolic communication through various forms of language makes it possible for those not actually in one another's presence to maintain a social system. All large organizations are likely to maintain at least some indirect communication among the membership through the sheer necessities created by size. A large organization which is also formally organized and functionally specialized will rely on indirect communication to an even higher degree. Thus we arrive at an outstanding, although little recognized attribute of industrial bureaucracy.[4]

Individuals who initiate action of the highest importance for a given workman, or foreman, may exist for that person simply by name and reputation. Even within the direct line organization, the executive may be separated by several or many stages from those expected to carry out the activities to implement an executive order. With functional specialization the lines of communication become even more indirect, for specialists are chiefly bound together in formal organization through the line officer or executive charged with coordinating their activities and, if necessary, putting their recommendations into effect.

Well-established bureaucracies have definite arrangements for routeing various types of communications. Ordinarily these will emphasize vertical channels rather than contact among equals in rank. This is, as previously implied, due to the coordinating functions of the executive, and to the necessity for orders to go "down" through the staff through regular patterns of superiors and subordinates. A consequence of the indirect lines of communication which is always a potential threat to effective operation is the tendency for the intermediate functionary or the executive to be

---

[4] An outstanding work which emphasizes indirect communication and the role of the executive in maintaining the lines of communication is that of Chester I. Barnard, *The Functions of the Executive* (Cambridge: Harvard University Press, 1938), especially pp. 82-91, 106-111, 217-226.

overloaded with masses of routine business and thus act as a bottleneck to the free passage of directions and information. A deluge of interoffice communications, which may or may not have to proceed by way of a common superior officer, will tend to hold up essential information or provide work for endless secretaries and filing clerks without necessarily contributing to the effective operation of the entire system.

On the other hand, the executive who wants to cut out the "red tape" by reducing the volume of routine correspondence is faced with possible human forgetfulness, errors in interpretation, conscious or unconscious errors in passing along verbal directions.

Indirect lines of communication cannot avoid increasing the formality of an organization already formally established. By reducing personal contact to a minimum and eliminating it almost entirely among persons widely separated in rank and function, the operation of the whole system by reference to the rule book is made easier. That is, the difficulty of distinguishing the concrete person from his specialized position and roles is not great if one's relation to that person is not only formally prescribed, but indirect. Thus in so far as the existing structure and the formal rules adequately provide for the activities and social relationships necessary for effective operation of the organization, indirect lines of communication may actually enhance the strength of that organization. To the extent that personal contact and informal relationships are essential, or are thought to be, the very formality of the established structure may be a barrier to cooperative action. The latter possibility has been inadequately recognized by industrial managers, who understandably are inclined to view the formal organization as a mechanical contrivance ensuring "efficiency" (whatever that may be).

Peculiarities of organizational charts

The use of charts is widespread among industrial managers as a method of graphic summary of the delegation and division of authority, functional division of responsibility, and lines of communication.[5] This general practice is further evidence of the bureaucratic structure of modern industrial organization, and gives basis for the reference to "blueprint organization."

The pyramidal principle of bureaucratic organization is well illustrated by most organizational charts, and this has further significance in the actual attitudes and policies of industrial management. Although pyramidal in form, an organization chart is rarely consulted by a person whose position is at the bottom of the pyramid. In other words, the arrangement of the chart assumes that one is looking at the organization from the top down.

[5] For discussion and illustration of the use of organizational charts see Arthur G. Anderson, *Industrial Engineering and Factory Management* (New York: Ronald, 1928), Chap. IV, "Organization for Management," and Chap. V, "Modern Industrial Organizations"; Anderson and Schwenning, *op. cit.*, pp. 117-123; Mitchell, *op. cit.*, p. 238.

This is symbolic of the tendency for precision of lines of communication, specialization of roles, and so on to "blur out" as one approaches the bottom of the pyramid. It is symbolic precisely because the organizational chart is consulted and relied upon by those at or near the top, and the tendency for these persons to be in touch with those at the bottom by extremely indirect lines of communication poses a general problem of complex formal organization—the relation of the worker at the bottom with the policy-forming executives at the top. This peculiarity of the organizational chart has been aptly summarized by Roethlisberger:

We . . . find the observer in the office of the general manager of a large industrial enterprise. The latter is poring over something which is to be a never-ending source of astonishment and mystery to the observer—an organization chart. The general manager's desk, which the observer had noticed when he entered the room was free of all objects except a telephone and a calendar pad, is now littered with blue charts which show the formal relations each person in the company is supposed to have to those people who work for him as well as to those people for whom he works. He is being initiated by the general manager into such mysteries as "staff and line," "centralization and decentralization of authority," "straight-line production," "functional as opposed to product-shop organization."

Although our observer's mind is in a whirl over all these new terms, he is still capable of making two simple observations: (1) The people at the top of the organization, including the person to whom he is talking, appear to be separated by many steps from the people at the bottom of the organization. (2) Although every place on the organization chart has a label attached to it, the labels at the top and middle of the chart refer to single persons, whereas the labels at the bottom, such as "workers," "clerks," etc., refer to groups of persons.

These observations raise three questions in the observer's mind, so he asks the general manager: (1) Do the people at the bottom of the organization have any difficulty in understanding the economic and logical objectives of the people at the top? (2) Do the people at the top have difficulty in understanding the way the people at the bottom feel? (3) Although this chart shows how management is organized, how are all the people labeled "workers" (who, he understands, constitute two-thirds of the population) organized?[6]

Professor Roethlisberger's observer received no satisfactory answer to these questions from the general manager, and indeed, the basis for a satisfactory answer is often lacking in managerial circles in contemporary industry. Yet the questions raised may well have an important bearing on the activities and functions of management (and thereby on the general adequacy of the organization as a whole).

[6] From F. J. Roethlisberger, *Management and Morale* (Cambridge: Harvard University Press, 1941), Chap. V, "A Disinterested Observer Looks at Industry," pp. 73-74. Reprinted by permission of Harvard University Press.

8. The Problem of Succession and Bureaucracy [1]

Alvin W. Gouldner

Introduction

Classical political scientists, attuned to the vicissitudes of crowns and courts, have, in their concept of succession, left a residue of observation and analysis that bears reexamination by modern social scientists. Limiting their attention to the *highest* authorities of government, they have noted that replacement of a new for an old ruler was often attended by intense public crises. "Such periods have frequently been characterized by bitter conflicts occasionally developing into full-fledged wars, of which the Spanish, Polish and Austrian wars of succession are outstanding examples."[2] Political scientists have conceived of the method of succession as "one of the principal factors determining the stability of any given form of government" and have therefore used it as an attribute for the classification of types of governments.

It is interesting, however, that modern sociologists, far from being influenced by these judgments, have almost entirely ignored the phenomenon of succession. It is possible that the political scientists' association of the concept of succession with problems of the most supreme authorities may partially account for this, for modern sociology is largely secular in outlook and, carrying the stamp of disenchantment common to our age, looks to "pedestrian" things for enlightenment.

While reserving fuller treatment of this question for later discussion, it may be observed that the sociologists' neglect of the concept of succession becomes acutely problematical if account is taken of the pivotal role it acquired in the work of Max Weber. Insofar as Weber had a theory of historical change, his major analytical categories posited an alternation of charismatic and bureaucratic or traditional modes of authority. These rotations were conceived of as cyclical fluctuations within a trend which moved toward increasing rationalization of social action.[3]

Reprinted from Alvin W. Gouldner, ed., *Studies in Leadership: Leadership and Democratic Action* (New York: Harper & Row, 1950), pp. 644-659.

[1] This paper was unpublished prior to its appearance in *Studies in Leadership*.
[2] Frederick M. Watkins, "Political Succession," *Encyclopedia of the Social Sciences*.
[3] Cf. Introduction by H. H. Gerth and C. Wright Mills, eds., *From Max Weber: Essays in Sociology* (New York: Oxford University Press, 1947), for a similar interpretation. My colleague, Jeremiah Wolpert, has suggested that *continuing* rationalization increasingly delimits the possibility of traditionalistic authority and, also, radically modifies

Charismatic authority, involving the acceptance of a ruler because of his singular personal attributes, was held to disrupt the process of rationalization when existent routines proved inadequate to growing problems. Hostile to workaday procedures, a charismatic movement is alienated from economic and familial institutions and supports itself irregularly. Charismatic authority is, then, ephemeral to the extreme. Ordinarily, its instability provokes insecurity among the charismatic leader's staff and followers—who seek to safeguard their material and ideal interests. Their anxiety, Weber states, is brought to a climax by the problem of succession.

Weber proposes that the methods used to secure a successor result in routinizations which, depending mainly on the economic context, move in either a traditionalistic or bureaucratic direction. *To Weber, then, the problem of succession is the umbilical cord which connects charisma to its heir.* Succession is the key concept which in his analysis bridges the polarized modes of authority. Yet despite this concept's analytically strategic role, Weber fails to give a coherent picture of its content and its function in his system of theory. Exactly how succession leads in the one case to bureaucratic, and in the other to traditionalistic authority is unclear.

More recently, some of the problems attendant upon succession in a bureaucracy have received comment from Arnold Brecht[4] and Marshall Dimock.[5] Both Brecht and Dimock have focused, in particular, on the problem of "bureaucratic sabotage," the resistance of the "permanent" staff of a bureaucracy to the policies of their superior, especially when he is new to office. Dimock attributes this soundproofed conflict to a short circuit in communication between the successor and the old staff, who over the years of their association have developed subtly expressed understandings of which the successor is ignorant. Why the communication failure occurs, and in particular what its institutional conditions are, is not considered in any detail. While noting that the successor makes his entrance primed for change, Dimock gives no explanation of the circumstances which engender this attitude.

In actuality, empirical studies of the process of succession and its concomitant problems are practically nonexistent. In the following discussion observations will be drawn from a study of an absentee-owned factory near Buffalo, New York. This factory, which combines both mining and surface processing operations, is located in a rural community into which urban characteristics are only slowly seeping. These observations are offered with the following intentions:

---

the nature of charismatic authority, so that the latter's traits may be deliberately manipulated. This type is, perhaps, more meaningfully characterized as pseudocharismatic, suggests Wolpert.

[4] Arnold Brecht, "Bureaucratic Sabotage," *Annals of the American Academy of Political and Social Science*, (June, 1937).

[5] Marshall E. Dimock, "Bureaucracy Self-Examined," *Public Administration Review* (Summer, 1944).

1. To suggest and provide a warrant for certain hypotheses concerning the interrelations between succession and the development of bureaucracy.
2. To outline a theoretical context in which one commonly noted industrial phenomenon, "strategic replacements," may be usefully fitted.
3. To illustrate the potential utility of employing a "secularized" concept of succession in the study of organization. By a "secularized" concept of succession is meant the replacement (for any reason) of an individual in a strategic position in any formal or informal group, without prejudice as to whether this group is large or small, autocephalous or heterocephalous, of broad or narrow jurisdiction and composition. Such a concept of succession would, it seems, escape the Carlylean implications of that employed by political scientists.

Case History of a Succession[6]

At the time we began our study two things were at the center of the plant personnel's attention: first, an accelerating degree of bureaucratization and, second, a series of replacements among foremen and supervisors.

Among many evidences of growing bureaucratization[7] was an increasing separation between the company's and workers' property; the company having begun a stricter control over its machinery, raw material, and finished product, making these less accessible to workers for personal use than formerly. The old personnel manager, an informal, community-conscious man with little formal education and a "dislike of paperwork," was replaced by a rule-sensitive, company-conscious man with some college education.

The number of paper reports required from supervisors was being increased; a formal, printed "warning" notice used for disciplinary purposes was introduced. The no-absenteeism rule was being strictly enforced; new modes of punching in and out were promulgated; the supervisory staff was being extended and divided into two groups—"know-how" and "do-how" foremen. The characteristic impersonalized "atmosphere" of bureaucratic structures began to pervade the plant.

These innovations, it is crucial to observe, began shortly after the arrival of a new plant manager, Vincent Peele.[8] The correlation between succession and crystallization of bureaucratic trends was, in this instance, striking.

Shortly after his arrival, Peele began to remove some of the old supervisors and foremen and to bring in new ones. Four replacements were made

[6] I should like to record my deep appreciation to Maurice Stein, Paul Mahany, Joseph Davis, John Sommers, Cornelius Vodicka, Gunnar Hanson, George Amos, and Jo Ann Setel, students who assisted in the field work.

[7] Max Weber's ideal-type bureaucracy has been used as a heuristic guide and most of the variables mentioned below are stressed in his concept of bureaucracy.

[8] This name, like all others used, is fictitious in order that anonymity of the company, plant, and personnel will be preserved.

with men in the plant. The new personnel manager was brought in from the plant at which Peele had formerly been manager. (It had been a smaller and less important factory.) Several new foremen's positions were opened up and promotions made to these. This rapid change of supervisory personnel following a succession is so familiar in an industrial situation that it deserves a distinctive name and, in this paper, has been called "strategic replacement."

What is there about the role of a successor that conduces to *increased* bureaucratization and strategic replacement? The problem may be separated into two parts: (1) the frame of reference of the successor and the definitions of his situation to which it disposes, and (2) the objective attributes of the factory situation.

The successor's frame of reference

In this case, succession involved advancement for Peele, the new plant manager. The main office personnel, who determined his promotion, reminded Peele of his predecessor's inadequacies and expressed the feeling that things had been slipping at the plant for some while. They suggested that the old plant manager, Godfrey, was perhaps getting overindulgent in his old age and that he, Peele, would be expected to improve production quotas. As Peele put it, "Godfrey didn't force the machine. I had to watch it. Godfrey was satisfied with a certain production. But the company gave me orders to get production up." With the pressure of renewed postwar competition things would have to start humming; traditionalized production quotas were to be rationalized.[9]

Peele, grateful for his opportunity to ascend in the company hierarchy, of course heeded the main office counsels. It may be emphasized that a "briefing" does more than impart technical data; it also functions to structure attitudes toward an assignment. *Peele, therefore, came to his new plant keenly sensitive to the impersonal, universalistic criteria which his superiors would use to judge his performance.* He knew his progress would be watched; he desires also to express his gratitude and is, consequently, anxious to "make good." As a member of the main office administrative staff commented: "Peele is trying hard to arrive. He is paying more attention to the plant. But he lacks Godfrey's [the old plant manager's] personal touch. Peele will follow along organizational lines, while Godfrey handled things on the personal basis."

[9] Roethlisberger and Dickson have emphasized the tendency of informal cliques of *workers* to limit in a traditionalistic way their output, by their beliefs concerning a "fair day's work." Our comment indicates that restriction of output, or "sabotage" as Veblen referred to it, is not manifested solely by operatives but is found among *managerial* personnel as well. Veblen has, of course, long since noted this; he tended, however, to focus on the rational motives for "sabotage" among managers, neglecting the traditionalistic component.

There is, however, a second and apparently conflicting element in the new plant manager's frame of reference. On his way up, he may have made friends whose loyalty and help expedited his ascent. Since the time of succession is often a time of promotion and enhanced power, it may be the moment of reckoning awaited by the friends when their past favors to the successor can be reciprocated. There seems little question, however, that this particularistic element in the new plant manager's frame of reference is a minor one.

For if worse comes to worst, he may evade the old obligations since he is now no longer among those to whom he owes them. Or, more likely perhaps, he may interpret fulfillment of old particularistic obligations as a *means of securing personnel* which would enable him to guarantee successful accomplishment of his new mission and of the abstract, impersonal goals to which he is mainly oriented. This need evoke no conflict of values within the successor, for one's friends are most often viewed as "competent" people, and in the case of a highly placed individual there are reasons why this is very probable.

Thus, even before setting foot into the plant, Peele had a notion of the kinds of things which needed "correction," and was tentatively shaping policies to bring about the requisite *changes*. He defined the situation as one calling for certain *changes*, changes oriented to the abstract, rational standards of efficiency. *Because* he is a *successor*, new to the plant, a stranger among strangers, as yet untied by bonds of friendship and informal solidarity with the people in his new plant, both his perceptive and executive capacities may be relatively devoid of nonrational considerations.

The factory situation

Oriented toward efficiency and the minimization of nonrational aspects of the factory organization which would impede it, the new plant manager entered the factory. He found that to which his frame of reference has been sensitized. Inevitably a factory, like any other social organization, reflects a compromise between formal and informal organization, between rational and nonrational norms. Peele found that workers "borrowed" tools from the plant for their own personal use, that they have *customarily* helped themselves to raw materials and even finished products for use about their homes, workshops, and farms. He found that some workers preferred to "punch in" early and accumulate a little overtime, or "punch out" early on special occasions. The miners, far from eager to conform with Protestant norms of regular work, believed that a certain amount of absenteeism was one of their traditional prerogatives and a normative way of manifesting that "down here, we are our own bosses." The new plant manager's expectations were confirmed: the plant was in "evident" need of specific changes to heighten its efficiency.

Whom could Peele hold responsible for this "lax" state of affairs? Oriented to formal and individualistic diagnoses, he tended to place responsibility on the old supervisory staff, and indicated that he considered it their duty to remedy the situation along lines he suggested. At this point he encountered his first sharp resistance. "Every foreman had set ways," explained Peele.

When I wanted to make some changes the supervisors told me, Godfrey used to do this and that. . . . I didn't make many changes and I'm satisfied with the changes I've made. The foremen are getting smoothed off now. [You had some difficulty with the supervisors . . . ?—interviewer] Yes, I had some trouble in straightening out shirkers. Some of them thought they were going to get fired. I could work on *these* guys. But others, who didn't expect to get fired, were. Each foreman is just a little bit on edge now. They don't know whether they're doing right. . . . A new plant manager is going to make some changes —to suit my own way. *I had to watch them.* I made those changes.

Thus among the things the new plant manager resolves to change, when he encounters their resistance, are the old supervisory personnel. But why is it that the old supervisory staff resists the new manager's plans?

A new manager is faced with a heritage of promises and obligations that his predecessor has not had an opportunity to fulfill. These old obligations are most important when made to the old supervisory staff, or to others constituting the old plant manager's informal social circle. For placed as they often are in powerful positions, they may be able to mobilize sentiment against him, or use dilatory tactics to impede his efforts, unless he fulfills his "inherited" obligations.

An interesting illustration of this at the plant involves the present union president, Ralph Byta. Byta was a neighbor of Godfrey and had been induced by him to come to work at the plant. Godfrey had made Byta some promises which he was unable to meet, due to his sudden death.

Some four months after Peele's arrival, Byta ran for and was elected president of the local union. Byta's new position was now much more invulnerable than those of the other "old lieutenants" who held supervisory positions. He could not be replaced or fired and had to be "dealt with." As Byta put it: "The good men know that a union's the best way to get ahead. You can't walk into the company and ask them for a raise for yourself. It's different though if you represent 150 men. *Then, too, if the company sees you're a leader (and the company sees it!) well, maybe you can get yourself a raise.*"

Nor was Byta's expectation a fanciful one; it had solid justification in the company's previous actions. As a member of the main office administrative staff told an interviewer: "Some of our foremen are ex-union presidents. . . . The union can pick out a good man for president. If you want a good man pick the president of the union. If you have good morale, the men elect responsible people to the union leadership."

At first Byta played the role of a "militant" and was characterized by management as "bitter." Months after his election, the new plant manager had a "man to man" talk with him, and Byta is now viewed by management as much more "reasonable" than when newly elected. Byta's case is an example of the problems with which a new manager is confronted through the old lieutenants and members of the old informal group.

Resistance to a new plant manager by the old group of lieutenants may be provoked for reasons other than the former's reluctance to acknowledge the old manager's obligations. The new manager, for example, may not be viewed as a *legitimate* successor by the old lieutenants; they may consider one of their own group as the legitimate heir. In this company, the supervisor of ——— building is *customarily* viewed as "next in line" for promotion to manager. It seems significant, then, that Peele was most hostile to the supervisor of ——— building, considering him to be the "least strict" of all the supervisors.

On one occasion Peele had to be hospitalized during a siege of heated wage negotiations. The supervisor of ——— building became acting plant manager. From *management's point of view*, he played an extremely ineffectual role in the negotiations, not attempting to "handle" or "control" the situation when it headed toward a strike.

In general, the annoyance of the old lieutenants is sharpened when they find their once-favored status incompletely understood or deferred to and perhaps ignored by the successor. The old lieutenants' resistance to the new manager finds its counterpart among the rank-and-file operatives when measures planned to foster efficiency are initiated. The operatives resist because they resent the infringements that these make on their established prerogatives. That an increase in efficiency often means greater work effort on their part, without compensatory rewards, is viewed as unjust.

They may also, like the supervisors, question the legitimacy of the new manager. Whether or not this occurs depends, in part, on the specific yardsticks used by a particular group of workers to evaluate a manager's "right" to hold his job. The point to be underscored is that *succession provides an occasion when questions about the legitimacy of a manager will be elicited and considered most permissible.*

The *manner* in which a manager *gets* his position may be one of the criteria of legitimacy. For example, "coming up from the ranks" may be a criterion of legitimate authority among workers in present-day industry. The way in which the manager *exercises* his authority may be another measure of his legitimacy. If, for example, he recognizes workers' traditional rights and "does not act superior," the workers in this plant are likely to consider his authority legitimate. These workers, also, think a manager should "stand on his own feet" and not be meticulous about clearing problems through the company's main office.

Sensitized, however, as the manager has been by his main office briefing, the successor is quick to define some of the workers' customary rights as impediments to efficiency. He will, too, again influenced by his status as a successor, tend to await main office dispositions of problems, thus irking operatives who still think of a manager very much as an independent entrepreneur. As a main office staff member recognized, "A new plant manager is more prone to lean on the top administration than is a more experienced one."

An index of the degree of rank-and-file resistance to a new manager is the prevalence of what may be called the "Rebecca Myth."[10] Some while ago, Daphne DuMaurier wrote a book about a young woman who married a widower, only to be plagued by the memory of his first wife, Rebecca, whose virtues were widely extolled. The idealization of the absent is a well-known phenomenon. One may suspect that almost every former plant manager is, to some extent, idealized by the workers, even though he may have been disliked while present.

It was precisely such a situation that confronted Peele. In fact, workers' reminiscences about the regime of "Old Godfrey" are scarcely less than a modern version of "Paradise Lost." The workers' comments spontaneously contrast and compare, playing the old manager off against the new. The social function of the Rebecca Myth seems plain enough. By attaching themselves to Godfrey's memory, the workers can, in his name, *legitimate* their resistance to changes planned or implemented by Peele.

The new manager was, therefore, faced with two interrelated problems. First, how to implement the efficiency goals he had set himself. Second, how, as a necessary condition for solution of the first problem, to eliminate the resistance to his plans by workers and supervisors. In addition, Peele was enmeshed in a problem on a totally different, a psychological, level. This is the problem of coping with his own mounting anxiety which, situationally aroused by the definition of his promotion as a "test," is further accentuated by the resistance he meets. He has, broadly, two major tactics of solution available to him: (a) the technique of informal solidarity and/or (b) the technique of impersonal routinization or other changes in the formal organization.

Bureaucratization and Strategic Replacement as Problem Solutions

The successor can attempt to arouse informal solidarity and group sentiment, harnessing them to his goals. Such an approach might be exemplified by the appeal: "Let's all pitch in and do a job!" The use of gemeinschaft

---

[10] In another connection, the Lynds have commented on this phenomena. "Middletown is wont to invoke old leaders against new leaders who threaten to leave the 'safe and tried middle of the road.'" Robert S. Lynd and Helen Merrell Lynd, *Middletown in Transition* (New York: Harcourt, Brace and World, Inc., 1937), p. 413. Cf. also Chap. VIII, "Managers and Owners, Then and Now," in W. Lloyd Warner and J. O. Low, *The Social System of the Modern Factory* (New Haven, Conn.: Yale University Press, 1947), for a pithy account of the functioning of the Rebecca Myth during a strike.

or, more properly, pseudo-gemeinschaft[11] as a tactic for promoting his ends is employed by Peele, within the limits permitted by his personality. He has, for example, taken pains to get to know the men. "I talk with them," he says, "I congratulate them about births and things like that, *if I can only get an inkling of it.* Personal touches here and there help." But pseudo-gemeinschaft is an inadequate means to the manager's ends because it premises two things not always available.

1. It requires, firstly, a greater consensus of ends and sentiments between management and workers than exists. As an obvious example, Peele (like most managers) was primarily concerned about meeting his production quota and keeping costs down. The workers are, however, much less interested in these. It is difficult to maintain, to say nothing of creating, informal solidarity in pursuit of ends which are differentially valued by group members.

2. Secondly, the successor wise to the ways of pseudo-gemeinschaft would require *knowledge* of the informal networks and the private sentiments they transmit, if he were to manipulate them successfully. But *because he is a successor,* and has little "inkling" of the subtle arrangements and understandings comprising the informal structure, these are inaccessible for his purposes. As already indicated, he even has difficulty with the informal group nearest his own level, the old lieutenants.

The successor is, therefore, impelled by these circumstances to respond to his problems by resort to tactics more congruent with his role: impersonal techniques or formalized controls and the use of strategic replacements.

The problem of disposing of the old lieutenants is one which takes *time.* A new manager cannot, and often will not, act too hastily for fear of precipitating a conflict for which he is not yet prepared. He does not wish to be accused of failing to give the old lieutenants a "chance," nor of seeking to install his favorites with indecent haste. He spends some time "sizing up" the situation, looking for possible allies and lining up replacements.

In the meanwhile, however, the manager has no social "connective tissue," that is, no informal group structure, between himself and the lower echelons. Relatively isolated at this point, he receives mainly formal and technical communications. His anxiety is channeled into suspicion of what is happening below. One worker sized up the situation as follows: "When Godfrey was here, it was like one big happy family. Peele is all business. Why, Godfrey could get on that phone, call up the foreman and have the situation well in hand. *Peele has to come around and make sure things are all right.* Maybe that's why he's bringing in his own men."

---

[11] Cf. Robert K. Merton with the assistance of Marjorie Fiske and Alberta Curtis, *Mass Persuasion* (New York: Harper & Row, Publishers, 1946), pp. 142-144, for a general discussion of the concept of pseudo-gemeinschaft.

One of the familiar ways Peele used to relieve his anxiety was by being omnipresent. His practice of always being in the plant and walking all around drew universal comment, always hostile. This is not enough, however, because the manager is well aware that the men modify their behavior on seeing him approach.

In the absence of a position in a well-developed system of informal relations within the plant, and because he cannot be everywhere at once, personally checking up, the new manager begins to introduce and emphasize adherence to the rules. He elaborates a system of "paper reports" which enable him to "keep his finger on things." Observing informal gatherings of workers chatting, he is somewhat upset not merely because of what they are *not* doing, but also by what they *may be saying and doing* and is attracted to a "make work" policy. He seeks to keep the men busy, perhaps acting on the Protestant precept that the "devil finds work for idle hands."

When he considers the moment judicious he begins to make the strategic replacements, spinning out a new informal group that will conform to his needs, support his status, and through whose network he can guarantee that the meaning or "spirit" of his orders will be communicated. This last point deserves emphasis, for no matter how model a bureaucratic structure he may mold, its formal rules will be enmeshed in and in need of reinforcement by a framework of nonrational values.[12]

The technique of strategic replacements obligates the new lieutenants to the successor, establishing extra-formal ties between the two, which the manager may draw upon to implement his goals. The degree to which this technique does obligate the new lieutenant to the successor was observed in an interview with a newly appointed foreman. Unlike his references to the preceding managers, this foreman called the new manager by his first name, was very reluctant to give voice to near-universal references to Peele's strictness, and fantasies that Peele is better liked than Godfrey. Thus strategic replacement—changing the occupants of certain formal statuses—is, by way of its consequences upon informal organization, functional to the status security of a successor.

To summarize this discussion of the interplay of succession, bureaucratization and strategic replacements: It should be clear that, as this was a plant with a history of some twenty-five years, and part of a large expanding company, it was far from innocent of bureaucratic procedures. Nor was Peele devoid of bureaucratic intentions prior to his arrival. There was no such pure case available for study. On the contrary, the plant had experienced a degree of bureaucratization, and the new manager was oriented to values which might have led him in a bureaucratic direction, regardless of the circumstances of succession.

[12] Cf. Reinhard Bendix, "Bureaucracy: The Problem and Its Setting," *American Sociological Review* (October, 1947), for a discussion of this problem.

The point here, however, is that the role of a successor apparently involves the occupant with certain problems which, from his viewpoint, are *conditions* of his action. *These conditions conduce to the same process of bureaucratization as do the new manager's company-structured values.* The existence of the conditions concurrent with succession makes bureaucratization *functional* to the successor. Put in another way, it is the emergence of the problems of succession which require that the successor *learn* and use bureaucratic methods. The presence of these conditions exerts pressure on the successor to organize bureaucratically. He organizes bureaucratically, not only because he wants to or because he *values* these above other methods, but because he is compelled to by the conditions of succession—if he wishes to maintain his status.

In this plant there were about six managers from the time of its inception: an average of about one for every five years of its existence. This suggests that it is necessary to consider another specific dimension of succession, the *rate* of succession. When contrasted with comparable institutions of societies antecedent to our own, the rate of succession in the modern factory seems "high." The modern corporation, one of whose manifest functions is to enable business organizations to persist beyond the life of their founders, is an institutional condition for this high rate. Another institutional condition for the high rate of succession is, in one of its facets, absentee ownership or, more fundamentally, private ownership of large-scale means of production.

In such a situation authority becomes something of a commodity handed back and forth under certain general conditions. Like a commodity, it can then be only rarely custom-tailored, fitted to size, and tends to be standardized to facilitate its transference. Where authority may have to be transferred frequently, personalized loyalty to those who wield it may impede its mobility. It is therefore functional to the mobility of authority to attach workers' loyalty to the rules, not the plant manager. Thus bureaucratization is functional to an institutionally conditioned high rate of succession while, in turn, a high rate of succession operates as a selecting mechanism sifting out a bureaucratic mode of organization.

Reference to authority as a "commodity," while somewhat inexact in the above paragraph, nevertheless serves to call attention to some distinctive dynamics of certain modern forms of social control. In modern business-industrial societies, as in all their Western European predecessors back to the epoch of tribal disintegration, property is a basis for the acquisition of authority, prestige, influence, and power. In itself, "property" connotes the *superiority* of those who have specific rights in a valuable object as against those who do not—at least, insofar as these valuable objects are concerned. Thus the factory owner, by virtue of his ownership of a specific property form, is simultaneously endowed with *authority* over his employees. In current business societies, authority is a customary con-comitant of ownership of means of production.

Insofar, then, as production property is involved in a market, and can be bought and sold for cash and credit, so, too, is the correlate authority. If modern property forms are distinguished by the extent of their involvement in a market so, also, are modern means of social control, including author-ity.[13] The high rate of succession in the economy has, therefore, as a further institutional condition, a *market* for production property. If the problem of succession is translated into the economist's terms, "labor turnover" among strategic personnel, another of the institutional conditions of a high rate of succession emerges: a *free labor* market. There seems reason to believe that a high labor turnover, on any level, would disrupt informal group systems, deteriorate nonrational consensus, and impede integration of worker and job. The careful specification and delimitation of functions, an emphasis on rule-oriented behavior, crucial aspects of bureaucratic organization, may serve as functional equivalents for disorganized informal patterns.

Informal organization and consensus is not, of course, disrupted solely by succession or labor turnover. Other crucial sources of their disorganiza-tion, which cannot be developed here, would include cleavage along status lines. Moreover, it seems uncertain whether the conclusions tentatively presented here would apply, *on the same level of abstraction*, to other insti-tutional spheres such as political parties and governmental organization. It may, however, prove fruitful to examine the differential degrees of bureauc-ratization manifested by the Democratic and Republican parties on the one hand and small radical parties on the other. Despite the greater size of the former (and this should seem crucial to those who account size a com-pelling determinant of bureaucratization), they have only recently begun to develop in a decidedly bureaucratic way.[14]

The tiny groups of the left, however, are far more advanced in this respect. Whether the persevering traditionalistic loyalties to the larger parties, creating a low degree of succession and turnover, and the much-remarked-upon high turnover among radical groups, is a mechanism re-lated to their differential degree of bureaucratization is a hypothesis worth investigation. In a similar area, the history of the Russian Bolshevik party is rich with data suggestive of the role played by rapid succession in foster-

---

[13] Nor, of course, is authority the only means of social control involved in market transactions in modern society. A recent New York Court decision awarded J. Moffett $1,150,000 from the Arabian-American Oil Co. for using his Washington "influence" to obtain Saudi Arabian concessions for the company. "Influence isn't illegal; it's a salable commodity. . . ." T. R. B., *The New Republic* (March 7, 1949). Similarly, the La-follette Committee on "Education and Labor" revealed, by its study of labor spies, that violence was purchasable for use by established institutions. As the availability of the modern public-relations counselors or "press agents" indicates, prestige is also pur-chasable.

[14] Cf. Edward J. Flynn, *You're the Boss* (New York, 1947).

ing bureaucratization. Lenin's definitive defense of his bureaucratic conception of party organization (*What Is To Be Done?*) is largely oriented to the problem of maintaining "continuity of organization," and the need to cope with repeated police arrests of "leading comrades." The history of the development of civil service in the United States (or elsewhere) would, on the face of it, also appear to contain data for evaluating the hypothesis presented here. Two aspects of succession in this area apparently deserve close study: (1) the high rate of succession among elected or appointed departmental heads, which is institutionally conditioned by periodical elections; (2) the "spoils system" with its rapid "rotation in office," as the historical antecedent of American civil service.

It may be well to close this section with a caution: *No systematic theory of bureaucracy is here intended.* All that has been suggested is that a *high rate of succession is one mechanism,* among others, apparently functional to the development of bureaucratic organization.

Deserving of more positive emphasis, however, is this: Since groups possess forms of stratification, it cannot be tacitly assumed that all individuals, or all positions, in the system of stratification exert equal influence on those decisions from which bureaucratization emerges as planned, or unanticipated consequence. Pedestrian as this point is, Weber's analysis of bureaucracy largely ignores it. Bureaucratic behavior in a factory must be either initiated by the manager, or in any event finally ratified by him or his superiors. What has here been essayed is an analysis of some institutionally derived pressures convergent on certain strategic positions compelling their occupants to behave in ways which make them accept or initiate bureaucratic patterns.

9. Conflicts Between Staff and Line Managerial Officers

Melville Dalton

In its concentration on union-management relations, industrial sociology has tended to neglect the study of processes inside the ranks of industrial management. Obviously the doors to this research area are more closely guarded than the entry to industrial processes through the avenue of production workers, but an industrial sociology worthy of the name must sooner or later extend its inquiries to include the activities of all industrial personnel.

The present paper is the result of an attempt to study processes among industrial managers. It is specifically a report on the functioning interaction between the two major vertical groupings of industrial management: (1) the *staff* organization, the functions of which are research and advisory; and (2) the *line* organization, which has exclusive authority over production processes.

Industrial staff organizations are relatively new. Their appearance is a response to many complex interrelated forces, such as economic competition, scientific advance, industrial expansion, growth of the labor movement, and so on. During the last four or five decades these rapid changes and resulting unstable conditions have caused top industrial officials more and more to call in "specialists" to aid them toward the goal of greater production and efficiency. These specialists are of many kinds including chemists, statisticians, public and industrial relations officers, personnel officers, accountants, and a great variety of engineers, such as mechanical, draughting, electrical, chemical, fuel, lubricating, and industrial engineers. In industry these individuals are usually known as "staff people." Their functions, again, for the most part are to increase and apply their specialized knowledge in problem areas, and to advise those officers who make up the "line" organization and have authority[1] over production processes.

This theoretically satisfying industrial structure of specialized experts advising busy administrators has in a number of significant cases failed to function as expected. The assumptions that (a) the staff specialists would

Reprinted from *American Sociological Review*, 15 (June, 1950), 342-351.

[1] *Inside* their particular staff organizations, staff officers also may have authority over their subordinates, but not over production personnel.

be reasonably content to function without a measure of formal authority[2] over production, and that (b) their suggestions regarding improvement of processes and techniques for control over personnel and production would be welcomed by line officers and be applied, require closer examination. In practice there is often much conflict between industrial staff and line organizations and in varying degrees the members of these organizations oppose each other.[3]

The aim of this paper is, therefore, to present and analyze data dealing with staff-line tensions.

Data were drawn from three industrial plants[4] in which the writer had been either a participating member of one or both of the groups or was intimate with reliable informants among the officers who were.

Approached sociologically, relations among members of management in the plants could be viewed as a general conflict system caused and perpetuated chiefly by (1) power struggles in the organization stemming in the main from competition among departments to maintain low operating costs; (2) drives by numerous members to increase their status in the hierarchy; (3) conflict between union and management; and (4) the staff-line friction which is the subject of this paper.[5] This milieu of tensions was not only unaccounted for by the blue-print organizations of the plants, but was often contradictory to, and even destructive of, the organizations' formal aims. All members of management, especially in the middle and lower ranks,[6] were caught up in this conflict system. Even though they

[2] To the extent that staff officers influence line policy they do, of course, have a certain *informal* authority.

[3] Some social scientists have noted the possibility of staff-line friction, and industrial executives themselves have expressed strong feelings on the matter. See Burleigh B. Gardner, *Human Relations in Industry* (Chicago: Irwin, 1945) and H. E. Dimock, *The Executive in Action* (New York: Harper & Row, 1945). Dimock believes that we are too "staff-minded" and that we should become more "executive-minded" (p. 241). A high line officer in a large corporation denounced staff organizations to the writer on the ground of their "costing more than they're worth," and that "They stir up too much trouble and are too theoretical." He felt that their function (excepting that of accountants, chemists, and "a few mechanical engineers") could be better carried out by replacing them with "highly-select front-line foremen [the lowest placed line officers] who are really the backbone of management, and pay them ten or twelve thousand dollars a year."

[4] These plants were in related industries and ranged in size from 4,500 to 20,000 employees, with the managerial groups numbering from 200 to nearly 1,000. Details concerning the plants and their location are confidential. Methodological details concerning an intensive study embracing staff-line relations and several other areas of behavior in one of the plants are given in the writer's unpublished doctoral thesis, "A Study of Informal Organization Among the Managers of an Industrial Plant" (Department of Sociology, University of Chicago, 1949).

[5] Because these conflict areas were interrelated and continually shifting and reorganizing, discussion of any one of them separately—as in the case of staff-line relations—will, of course, be unrealistic to some extent.

[6] From bottom to top, the line hierarchy consisted of the following strata of officers: (1) first-line foremen, who were directly in charge of production workmen; (2) general foremen; (3) departmental superintendents; (4) divisional superintendents; (5)

might wish to escape, the obligation of at least appearing to carry out formal functions compelled individuals to take sides in order to protect themselves against the aggressions of others. And the intensity of the conflict was aggravated by the fact that it was formally unacceptable and had to be hidden.

For analytical convenience, staff-line friction may be examined apart from the reciprocal effects of the general conflict system. Regarded in this way, the data indicated that three conditions were basic to staff-line struggles: (1) the conspicuous ambition and "individualistic" behavior among staff officers; (2) the complication arising from staff efforts to justify its existence and get acceptance of its contributions; and, related to point two, (3) the fact that incumbency of the higher staff offices was dependent on line approval. The significance of these conditions will be discussed in order.

Mobile Behavior of Staff Personnel

As a group, staff personnel in the three plants were markedly ambitious, restless, and individualistic. There was much concern to win rapid promotion, to make the "right impressions," and to receive individual recognition. Data showed that the desire among staff members for personal distinctions often over-rode their sentiments of group consciousness and caused intra-staff tensions.[7]

---

assistant plant manager; (6) plant manager. In the preceding strata there were often "assistants" such as "assistant general foreman," "assistant superintendent," etc., in which case the total strata of the line hierarchy could be almost double that indicated here.

In the staff organizations the order from bottom to top was: (1) supervisor (equivalent to the first-line foreman); (2) general supervisor (equivalent to the general foreman); (3) staff head—sometimes "superintendent" (equivalent to departmental superintendent in the line organization). Occasionally there were strata of assistant supervisors and assistant staff heads.

The term "upper line" will refer to all strata above the departmental superintendent. "Middle line" will include the departmental superintendent and assistants. "Lower line" will refer to general and first-line foremen and their assistants.

"Lower," "middle," and "upper" staff will refer respectively to the supervisor, general supervisor and staff head.

"Top management" will refer to the upper line and the few staff heads with whom upper line officers were especially intimate on matters of policy.

[7] In a typical case in one of the plants, a young staff officer developed a plan for increasing the life of certain equipment in the plant. He carried the plan directly to the superintendent of the department in which he hoped to introduce it, but was rebuffed by the superintendent who privately acknowledged the merit of the scheme but resented the staff officer's "trying to lord it over" him. The staff organization condemned the behavior of its member and felt that he should have allowed the plan to appear as a contribution of the staff group rather than as one of its members. The officer himself declared that "By G— it's my idea and I want credit. There's not a damn one of you guys [the staff group] that wouldn't make the same squawk if you were in my place!"

The relatively high turnover of staff personnel[8] quite possibly reflected the dissatisfactions and frustrations of members over inability to achieve the distinction and status they hoped for. Several factors appeared to be of importance in this restlessness of staff personnel. Among these were age and social differences between line and staff officers, structural differences in the hierarchy of the two groups, and the staff group's lack of authority over production.

With respect to age, the staff officers were significantly younger than line officers.[9] This would account to some extent for their restlessness. Being presumably less well-established in life in terms of material accumulations, occupational status, and security, while having greater expectations (see below), and more energy, as well as more life ahead in which to make new starts elsewhere if necessary, the staff groups were understandably more dynamic and driving.[10]

Age-conflict[11] was also significant in staff-line antagonisms. The incident just noted of the young staff officer seeking to get direct acceptance by the line of his contribution failed in part—judging from the strong sentiments later expressed by the line superintendent—because of an age antipathy. The older line officers disliked receiving what they regarded as instruction from men so much younger than themselves, and staff personnel clearly were conscious of this attitude among line officers.[12] In staff-line

[8] During the period between 1944 and 1950 turn-over of staff personnel in these plants was between two and four times as great as that of line personnel. This grouping included all the non-managerial members of staff and line and all the hourly-paid (non-salaried) members of management (about 60 assistant first-line foremen). Turnover was determined by dividing the average number of employees for a given year (in line or staff) into the accessions or separations, whichever was the smaller.

[9] Complete age data were available in one of the larger plants. Here the 36 staff heads, staff specialists, and assistants had a mean age of 42.9 years. This value would have been less than 40 years, except for the inclusion of several older former line officers, but even a mean of 42.9 years was significantly less (C.R. 2.8) than that of the 35 line superintendents in the plant who had a mean age of 48.7 years. The age difference was even more significant when the staff heads were compared with the 61 general foremen who had a mean age of 50.0 years. And between the 93 salaried first-line foremen (mean age of 48.5 years) and the 270 salaried nonsupervisory staff personnel (mean age of 31.0 years) the difference was still greater.

[10] One might also hypothesize that the drive of staff officers was reflected in the fact that the staff heads and specialists gained their positions (those held when the data were collected) in less time than did members of the line groups. E.g., the 36 staff officers discussed above had spent a median of 10 years attaining their positions, as against a median of 11 years for the first-line foremen, 17 years for the general foremen, and 19 years for the superintendents. But one must consider that some of the staff groups were relatively new (13-15 years old) and had grown rapidly, which probably accelerated their rate of promotion as compared with that of the older line organization.

[11] E. A. Ross in *Principles of Sociology* (New York: Appleton-Century-Crofts, 1938), pp. 238-248, has some pertinent comments on age conflict.

[12] Explaining the relatively few cases in which his staff had succeeded in "selling ideas" to the line, an assistant staff head remarked: "We're always in hot water with these old guys on the line. You can't tell them a damn thing. They're bull-headed as

meetings, staff officers frequently had their ideas slighted or even treated with amusement by line incumbents. Whether such treatment was warranted or not, the effects were disillusioning to the younger, less experienced staff officers. Often selected by the organization because of their outstanding academic records, they had entered industry with the belief that they had much to contribute, and that their efforts would win early recognition and rapid advancement. Certainly they had no thought that their contributions would be in any degree unwelcome. This naivete[13] was apparently due to lack of earlier first-hand experience in industry (or acquaintance with those who had such experience), and to omission of realistic instruction in the social sciences from their academic training. The unsophisticated staff officer's initial contacts with the shifting, covert, expedient arrangements between members of staff and line usually gave him a severe shock. He had entered industry prepared to engage in logical, well-formulated relations with members of the managerial hierarchy, and to carry out precise, methodical functions for which his training had equipped him. Now he learned that (1) his freedom to function was snared in a web of informal commitments; (2) his academic specialty (on which he leaned for support in his new position) was often not relevant[14] for carrying out his formal assignments; and that (3) the important thing to do was to learn who the informally powerful line officers were and what ideas they would welcome which at the same time would be acceptable to his superiors.

Usually the staff officer's reaction to these conditions is to look elsewhere for a job or make an accommodation in the direction of protecting himself and finding a niche where he can make his existence in the plant tolerable and safe. If he chooses the latter course, he is likely to be less concerned with creative effort for his employer than with attempts to de-

---

hell! Most of the time we offer a suggestion it's either laughed at or not considered at all. The same idea in the mouth of some old codger on the line'd get a round of applause. They treat us like kids."

Line officers in these plants often referred to staff personnel (especially members of the auditing, production planning, industrial engineering, and industrial relations staffs) as "college punks," "slide-rules," "crackpots," "pretty boys," and "chair-warmers."

13 John Mills, a research engineer retired from the telephone industry, has noted the worldly naivete of research engineers in that field in his The Engineer in Society (New York: Van Nostrand, 1946).

14 Among the staff heads and assistants referred to earlier, only 50 percent of those with college training (32 of the 36 officers) were occupied with duties related to their specialized training. E.g., the head of the industrial relations staff had a B.S. degree in aeronautical engineering; his assistant had a similar degree in chemical engineering. Considering that staff officers are assumed to be specialists trained to aid and advise management in a particular function, the condition presented here raises a question as to what the criteria of selection were. (As will be shown in a separate paper, the answer appeared to be that personal—as well as impersonal—criteria were used.) Among the college-trained of 190 line officers in the same plant, the gap between training and function was still greater, with 61 percent in positions not related to the specialized part of their college work.

velop reliable social relations that will aid his personal advancement. The staff officer's recourse to this behavior and his use of other status-increasing devices will be discussed below in another connection.

The formal structure, or hierarchy of statuses, of the two larger plants from which data were drawn, offered a frustration to the ambitious staff officer. That is, in these plants the strata, or levels of authority, in the staff organizations ranged from three to five as against from five to ten in the line organization. Consequently there were fewer possible positions for exercise of authority into which staff personnel could move. This condition may have been an irritant to expansion among the staff groups. Unable to move vertically to the degree possible in the line organization, the ambitious staff officer could enlarge his area of authority in a given position only by lateral expansion—by increasing his personnel. Whether or not aspiring staff incumbents revolted against the relatively low hierarchy through which they could move, the fact remains that (1) they appeared eager to increase the number of personnel under their authority,[15] (2) the personnel of staff groups *did* increase disproportionately to those of the line,[16] and (3) there was a trend of personnel movement from staff to

[15] This was suggested by unnecessary references among some staff officers to "the number of men under me," and by their somewhat fanciful excuses for increase of personnel. These excuses included statements of needing more personnel to (1) carry on research, (2) control new processes, (3) keep records and reports up-to-date. These statements often did not square with (1) the excessive concern among staff people about their "privileges" (such as arriving on the job late, leaving early, leaving the plant for long periods during working hours, having a radio in the office during the World Series, etc.); (2) the great amount of time (relative to that of line officers) spent by lower staff personnel in social activities on the job, and (3) the constantly recurring (but not always provoked) claims among staff personnel of their functional importance for production. The duties of middle and lower staff personnel allowed them sufficient time to argue a great deal over their respective functions (as well as many irrelevant topics) and to challenge the relative merit of one another's contributions or "ideas." In some of the staffs these discussions could go on intermittently for hours and develop into highly theoretical jousts and wit battles. Where staff people regarded such behavior as a privilege of their status, line officers considered it as a threat to themselves. This lax control (in terms of line discipline) was in part a tacit reward from staff heads to their subordinates. The reward was expected because staff superiors (especially in the industrial relations, industrial engineering, and planning staffs) often overlooked and/or perverted the work of subordinates (which was resented) in response to pressures from the line. This behavior will be noted later.

[16] In one of the larger plants, where exact data were available, the total staff personnel had by 1945 exceeded that of the line. At that time the staff included 400 members as against 317 line personnel composed of managerial officers and their clerical workers, but not production workers. By 1948 the staff had increased to 517 as compared with 387 for the line (during this period *total* plant personnel declined over 400). The staff had grown from 20.8 percent larger than the line in 1945 to 33.6 percent larger in 1948, and had itself increased by 29.3 percent during the three years as against a growth in the line of 22.1 percent. Assuming the conditions essential for use of probability theory, the increase in staff personnel could have resulted from chance about 1.5 times in a hundred. Possibly post-war and other factors of social change were also at work but, if so, their force was not readily assessable.

line,[17] rather than the reverse, presumably (reflecting the drive and ambition of staff members) because there were more positions of authority, as well as more authority to be exercised, more prestige, and usually more income in the line.

Behavior in the plants indicated that line and staff personnel belonged to different social status groups and that line and staff antipathies were at least in part related to these social distinctions. For example, with respect to the item of formal education, the staff group stood on a higher level than members of the line. In the plant from which the age data were taken, the 36 staff officers had a mean of 14.6 years of schooling as compared with 13.1 years for 35 line superintendents, 11.2 years for 60 general foremen, and 10.5 years for 93 first-line foremen. The difference between the mean education of the staff group and that of the highest line group (14.6-13.1) was statistically significant at better than the one per cent level. The 270 non-supervisory staff personnel had a mean of 13.1 years—the same as that of the line superintendents. Consciousness of this difference probably contributed to a feeling of superiority among staff members, while the sentiment of line officers toward staff personnel was reflected in the name-calling noted earlier.

Staff members were also much concerned about their dress, a daily shave, and a weekly hair-cut. On the other hand line officers, especially below the level of departmental superintendent, were relatively indifferent to such matters. Usually they were in such intimate contact with production processes that dirt and grime prevented the concern with meticulous dress shown by staff members. The latter also used better English in speaking and in writing reports, and were more suave and poised in social intercourse. These factors, and the recreational preferences of staff officers for night clubs and "hot parties," assisted in raising a barrier between them and most line officers.

The social antipathies of the two groups and the status concern of staff officers were indicated by the behavior of each toward the established practice of dining together in the cafeterias reserved for management in the two larger plants. Theoretically, all managerial officers upward from the level of general foremen in the line, and general supervisors in the staff, were eligible to eat in these cafeterias. However, in practice the mere taking of one of these offices did not automatically assure the incumbent the privilege of eating in the cafeteria. One had first to be invited to "join the association." Staff officers were very eager to "get in" and did considerable

---

[17] This movement from staff to line can disorganize the formal managerial structure, especially when (1) the transferring staff personnel have had little or no supervisory experience in the staff but have an academic background which causes them to regard human beings as mechanisms that will respond as expected; (2) older, experienced line officers have hoped—for years in some cases—to occupy the newly vacated (or created) positions.

fantasying on the impressions, with respect to dress and behavior, that were believed essential for an invitation. One such staff officer, a cost supervisor, dropped the following remarks:

There seems to be a committee that passes on you. I've had my application in for three years, but no soap. Harry [his superior] had his in for over three years before he made it. You have to have something, because if a man who's in moves up to another position the man who replaces him doesn't get it because of the position—and he might not get it at all. I think I'm about due.

Many line officers who were officially members of the association avoided the cafeteria, however, and had to be ordered by the assistant plant manager to attend. One of these officers made the following statement, which expressed more pointedly the many similar spontaneous utterances of resentment and dislike made by other line officers:

There's a lot of good discussion in the cafeteria. I'd like to get in on more of it but I don't like to go there—sometimes I have to go. Most of the white-collar people [staff officers] that eat there are stuck-up. I've been introduced three times to Svendsen [engineer], yet when I meet him he pretends to not even know me. When he meets me on the street he always manages to be looking someplace else. G— d— such people as that! They don't go in the cafeteria to eat and relax while they talk over their problems. They go in there to look around and see how somebody is dressed or to talk over the hot party they had last night. Well, that kind of damn stuff don't go with me. I haven't any time to put on airs and make out I'm something that I'm not.

Complications of Staff Need to Prove Its Worth

To the thinking of many line officers, the staff functioned as an agent on trial rather than as a managerial division that might be of equal importance with the line organization in achieving production goals. Staff members were very conscious of this sentiment toward them and of their need to prove themselves. They strained to develop new techniques and to get them accepted by the line. But in doing this they frequently became impatient, and gave already suspicious line officers the impression of reaching for authority over production.

Since the line officer regards his authority over production as something sacred, and resents the implication that after many years in the line he needs the guidance of a newcomer who lacks such experience, an obstacle to staff-line cooperation develops the moment this sore spot is touched. On the other hand, the staff officer's ideology of his function leads him to precipitate a power struggle with the line organization. By and large he considers himself as an agent of top management. He feels bound to contribute something significant in the form of research or ideas helpful to management. By virtue of his greater education and intimacy with the latest theories of production, he regards himself as a managerial consultant and an expert, and feels that he must be, or appear to be, almost infallible once he has committed himself to top management on some point. With this orientation, he is usually disposed to approach middle and lower line with an attitude of condescension that often reveals itself in the heat of discussion. Consequently, many staff officers involve themselves in trouble and report their failures as due to "ignorance" and "bull-headedness" among these line officers.

On this point, relations between staff and line in all three of the plants were further irritated by a rift inside the line organization. First-line foremen were inclined to feel that top management had brought in the production planning, industrial relations, and industrial engineering staffs as clubs with which to control the lower line. Hence they frequently regarded the projects of staff personnel as manipulative devices, and reacted by cooperating with production workers and/or general foremen (whichever course was the more expedient) in order to defeat insistent and uncompromising members of the staff. Also, on occasion (see below), the lower line could cooperate evasively with lower staff personnel who were in trouble with staff superiors.

Effect of Line Authority over Staff Promotion

The fact that entry to the higher staff offices in the three plants was dependent on approval of top line officers had a profound effect on the behavior of staff personnel. Every member of the staff knew that if he aspired to higher office he must make a record for himself, a good part of which would be a reputation among upper line officers of ability to "understand" their informal problems without being told. This knowledge worked in varying degrees to pervert the theory of staff-line relations. Ideally the two organizations cooperate to improve existing methods of output, to introduce new methods, to plan the work, and to solve problems of production and the scheduling of orders that might arise. But when the line offers resistance to the findings and recommendations of the staff, the latter is reduced to evasive practices of getting some degree of acceptance of its programs, and at the same time of convincing top management that "good relations" exist with officers down the line. This necessity becomes even more acute when the staff officer aspires (for some of the reasons given above) to move over to the line organization, for then he must convince powerful line officers that he is worthy. In building a convincing record, however, he may compromise with line demands and bring charges from his staff colleagues that he is "selling out," so that after moving into the line organization he will then have to live with enemies he made in the staff. In any case, the need among staff incumbents for pleasing line officers in order to perfect their careers called for accommodation in three major areas:[18] (1) the observance of staff rules, (2) the introduction of new techniques, and (3) the use of appropriations for staff research and experiment.

With respect to point one, staff personnel, particularly in the middle and lower levels, carried on expedient relations with the line that daily evaded formal rules. Even those officers most devoted to rules found that, in order not to arouse enmity in the line on a scale sufficient to be communicated *up* the line, compromising devices were frequently helpful and sometimes almost unavoidable both for organizational and career aims. The usual practice was to tolerate minor breaking of staff rules by line personnel, or even to cooperate with the line in evading rules,[19] and in exchange lay a claim on the line for cooperation on critical issues. In some cases line aid was enlisted to conceal lower staff blunders from the upper staff and the upper line.[20]

Concerning point two, while the staff organizations gave much time to developing new techniques, they were simultaneously thinking about how their plans would be received by the line. They knew from experience that middle and lower line officers could always give a "black eye" to staff contributions by deliberate mal-practices. Repeatedly top management had approved, and incorporated, staff proposals that had been verbally accepted down the line. Often the latter officers had privately opposed the changes, but had feared that saying so would incur the resentment of powerful superiors who could informally hurt them. Later they would seek to discredit the change by deliberate mal-practice and hope to bring a return to the

---

[18] The relative importance of one or more of these areas would vary with the function of a given staff.

[19] In a processing department in one of the plants the chemical solution in a series of vats was supposed to have a specific strength and temperature, and a fixed rate of inflow and outflow. Chemists (members of the chemical staff) twice daily checked these properties of the solution and submitted reports showing that all points met the laboratory ideal. Actually, the solution was nearly triple the standard strength, the temperature was about ten degrees Centigrade higher than standard, and the rate of flow was in excess of double the standard. There are, of course, varying discrepancies between laboratory theory and plant practice, but the condition described here resulted from production pressures that forced line foremen into behavior upsetting the conditions expected by chemical theory. The chemists were sympathetic with the hard-pressed foremen, who compensated by (1) notifying the chemists (rather than their superior, the chief chemist) if anything "went wrong" for which the laboratory was responsible and thus sparing them criticism; and by (2) cooperating with the chemists to reduce the number of analyses which the chemists would ordinarily have to make.

[20] Failure of middle and lower staff personnel to "cooperate" with line officers might cause the latter to "stand pat" in observance of line rules at a time when the pressures of a dynamic situation would make the former eager to welcome line cooperation in rule-breaking. For example, a staff officer was confronted with the combined effect of (1) a delay in production on the line that was due to an indefensible staff error; (2) pressure on the line superintendent—with whom he was working—to hurry a special order; and (3) the presence in his force of new inexperienced staff personnel who were (a) irritating to line officers, and (b) by their inexperience constituted an invitation to line aggression. Without aid from the line superintendent (which could have been withheld by observance of formal rules) in covering up the staff error and in controlling line personnel, the staff officer might have put himself in permanent disfavor with all his superiors.

former arrangement. For this reason there was a tendency for staff members to withhold improved production schemes or other plans when they knew that an attempt to introduce them might fail or even bring personal disrepute.

Line officers fear staff innovations for a number of reasons. In view of their longer experience, presumably intimate knowledge of the work, and their greater remuneration, they fear[21] being "shown up" before their line superiors for not having thought of the processual refinements themselves. They fear that changes in methods may bring personnel changes which will threaten the break up of cliques and existing informal arrangements and quite possibly reduce their area of authority. Finally, changes in techniques may expose forbidden practices and departmental inefficiency. In some cases these fears have stimulated line officers to compromise staff men to the point where the latter will agree to postpone the initiation of new practices for specific periods.

In one such case an assistant staff head agreed with a line superintendent to delay the application of a bonus plan for nearly three months so that the superintendent could live up to the expedient agreement he had made earlier with his grievance committeeman to avoid a "wildcat" strike by a group of production workmen.[22] The lower engineers who had devised the plan were suspicious of the formal reasons given to them for withholding it, so the assistant staff head prevented them (by means of "busy work") from attending staff-line meetings lest they inadvertently reveal to top management that the plan was ready.

The third area of staff-line accommodations growing out of authority relations revolved around staff use of funds granted it by top management. Middle and lower line charged that staff research and experimentation was little more than "money wasted on blunders," and that various departments of the line could have "accomplished much more with less money." According to staff officers, those of their plans that failed usually did so because line personnel "sabotaged" them and refused to "cooperate." Specific costs of "crack-pot experimentation" in certain staff groups were pointed to by line officers. Whatever the truth of the charges and counter-charges, evidence indicated (confidants in both groups supported this) that pressures from the line organization (below the top level) forced some of the staff groups to "kick over" parts of the funds appropriated for staff use[23] by top management. These compromises were of course hidden from top manage-

[21] Though there was little evidence that top management expected line officers to refine production techniques, the fear of such an expectation existed nevertheless. As noted earlier, however, some of the top executives *were* thinking that the development of a "higher type" of first-line foreman might enable most of the staff groups to be eliminated.

[22] This case indicates the over-lapping of conflict areas referred to earlier. A later paper will deal with the area of informal union-management relations.

[23] In two of the plants a somewhat similar relation, rising from different causes, existed *inside* the line organization with the *operating* branch of the line successfully applying pressures for a share in funds assigned to the *maintenance* division of the line.

ment, but the relations described were carried on to such an extent that by means of them—and line pressures for manipulation of accounts in the presumably impersonal auditing departments—certain line officers were able to show impressively low operating costs and thus win favor[24] with top management that would relieve pressures and be useful in personal advancement. In their turn the staff officers involved would receive more "cooperation" from the line and/or recommendation for transfer to the line. The data indicated that in a few such cases men from accounting and auditing staffs were given general foremanships (without previous line experience) as a reward for their understanding behavior.

Summary

Research in three industrial plants showed conflict between the managerial staff and line groups that hindered the attainment of organizational goals. Privately expressed attitudes among some of the higher line executives revealed their hope that greater control of staff groups could be achieved, or that the groups might be eliminated and their functions taken over in great part by carefully selected and highly remunerated lower-line officers. On their side, staff members wanted more recognition and a greater voice in control of the plants.

All of the various functioning groups of the plants were caught up in a general conflict system; but apart from the effects of involvement in this complex, the struggles between line and staff organizations were attributable mainly to (1) functional differences between the two groups; (2) differentials in the ages, formal education, potential occupational ceilings, and status group affiliations of members of the two groups (the staff officers being younger, having more education but lower occupational potential, and forming a prestige-oriented group with distinctive dress and recreational tastes); (3) need of the staff groups to justify their existence; (4) fear in the line that staff bodies by their expansion, and well-financed research activities, would undermine line authority; and (5) the fact that aspirants to higher staff offices could gain promotion only through approval of influential line executives.

If further research should prove that staff-line behavior of the character presented here is widespread in industry, and if top management should realize how such behavior affects its cost and production goals—and be concerned to improve the condition—then remedial measures could be considered. For example, a corrective approach might move in the direction of (1) creating a separate body[25] whose sole function would be the coordi-

---

[24] The reader must appreciate the fact that constant demands are made by top management to maintain low operating costs.

[25] This body, or "Board of Coordination," would be empowered to enforce its decisions. Membership would consist of staff and line men who had had wide experience in the plant over a period of years. The Board would (a) serve as an arbiter between staff

nation of staff and line efforts; (2) increasing the gradations of awards and promotions in staff organizations (without increase of staff personnel); (3) granting of more nearly equal pay to staff officers, but with increased responsibility (without authority over line processes or personnel) for the practical working of their projects; (4) requiring that staff personnel have a minimum supervisory experience and have shared repeatedly in successful collaborative staff-line projects before transferring to the line; (5) steps by top management to remove the fear of veiled personal reprisal felt by officers in most levels of both staff and line hierarchies (this fear—rising from a disbelief in the possibility of bureaucratic impersonality—is probably the greatest obstacle to communication inside the ranks of management); (6) more emphasis in colleges and universities on realistic instruction in the social sciences for students preparing for industrial careers.

---

and line; (b) review, screen, and approve individual recommendations submitted; and (c) evaluate contributions after a trial period. Such a body would incidentally be another high status goal for seasoned, capable, and ambitious officers who too often are trapped by the converging walls of the pyramidal hierarchy.

10. Dilemmas of Formal Organization

Peter M. Blau and W. Richard Scott

We shall review three dilemmas of formal organization: (1) coordination and communication; (2) bureaucratic discipline and professional expertness; (3) managerial planning and initiative.

Coordination and communication

The experiments and field studies on communication and performance we have reviewed lead to the conclusion that the free flow of communication contributes to problem-solving. There are three ways in which decisions are improved by the unrestricted exchange of ideas, criticisms, and advice. First, social support relieves the anxieties engendered by decision-making. In the discussion of problems with others, their social approval of the first step taken toward a solution mitigates the anxieties that might otherwise create a blocking of associations, and it thus facilitates reaching a solution. Once consultation patterns have become established, moreover, the very knowledge that advice is readily accessible makes it less disturbing to encounter a difficult problem, and the experience of being consulted by others strengthens self-confidence; both factors lessen anxieties that impede decision-making.

Second, communication processes provide an error-correction mechanism. Different persons are guided by different frameworks in their approach to a given problem, and the differences make it easier for them to detect the mistakes and blind spots in the suggestions of one another. Although social support and error correction are in some respects opposite processes, both of them are, nevertheless, important for problem-solving, as indicated by Pelz's finding that optimum research performance is associated with consulting some colleagues whose orientation differs from one's own (who challenge one's ideas) and some who share one's orientation (who support one's ideas).[1]

Third, the competition for respect that occurs in the course of discussing problems furnishes incentives for making good suggestions and for criticizing the apparently poor suggestions of others.

From *Formal Organizations* by Peter M. Blau and W. Richard Scott, published by Chandler Publishing Company, San Francisco. Copyright 1962 by Chandler Publishing Company, San Francisco. Reprinted by permission.

[1] Donald C. Pelz, "Some Social Factors Related to Performance in a Research Organization," *Administrative Science Quarterly*, 1 (1956), 310-325.

While the free flow of communication improves problem-solving, it impedes coordination. Unrestricted communication creates a battleground of ideas; the battle helps in selecting the only correct or best among several alternative suggestions, but makes it difficult to come to an agreement; and coordination always requires agreeing on one master plan, even though different plans might do equally well. Processes of social communication, consequently, make the performance of groups superior to that of individuals when the task is finding the best solution to a problem but inferior when the task is one of coordination.

Hierarchical differentiation is dysfunctional for decision-making because it interferes with the free flow of communication. Studies of experimental and work groups have shown that status differences restrict the participation of low-status members, channel a disproportionate amount of communication to high-status members, discourage criticism of the suggestions of the highs, encourage rejecting correct suggestions of the lows, and reduce the work satisfaction of the lows and their motivation to make contributions. All these factors are detrimental to effective problem-solving. If hierarchical differentiation does not block but frees the flow of communication, however, it improves decision-making; this observation indicates that the adverse effects that hierarchical differentiation typically has for problem-solving are specifically due to the obstacles to free communication it usually creates. But the very restriction of communication that makes hierarchical differentiation dysfunctional for problem-solving improves performance when the task is essentially one of coordination. Experiments with various communication networks show that differentiation, centralized direction, and restricted communication are necessary for efficient coordination. However, the achievement of such a differentiated organization—itself a problem-solving task—seems to have been easier for groups in which communication flowed than for those where it was experimentally restricted.

These conclusions point to a fundamental dilemma in formal organizations. Organizations require, of course, both effective coordination and effective problem-solving to discharge their functions. But the very mechanism through which hierarchical differentiation improves coordination—restricting and directing the flow of communications—is what impedes problem solving. In peer groups, moreover, the free flow of communication that contributes to problem-solving also creates an informal differentiation of status as some members earn the respect and deference of others, and this differentiation, once established, creates obstacles to communication. This dilemma appears to be inherent in the conflicting requirements of coordination and problem-solving. To be sure, some types of centralized direction are more compatible with work on complex problems than others, but the fundamental dilemma posed by the need for unrestricted and for restricted communication cannot be resolved—it must be endured.

Bureaucratic discipline and professional expertness

Weber's approach to the study of administration fails to distinguish the principles that govern bureaucratic organizations from professional principles, as both Parsons and Gouldner have emphasized.[2] To be sure, these two sets of principles have much in common. Both require that decisions be governed by universalistic standards independent of any personal considerations in the particular cases handled. The orientations of both professionals and bureaucrats are expected to be impersonal and detached, a principle designed to facilitate rational judgment. Both bureaucracy and professionalism are marked by specialized competence based on technical training and limit the official's or professional's authority to a specialized area of jurisdiction. Both professionals and bureaucrats occupy an achieved rather than ascribed status, with the selection of personnel governed by such performance criteria as competence and training. These are important similarities, but they should not be allowed to obscure the equally important differences between the two.

The first difference between the organizing principles of a profession and those of a bureaucracy is that the professional is bound by a norm of service and a code of ethics to represent the welfare and interests of his clients, whereas the bureaucrat's foremost responsibility is to represent and promote the interests of his organization. Only in the case of service organizations do the ultimate objectives of serving clients and serving the organization coincide, and even here the specific immediate objectives often conflict. For a service organization is oriented to serving the collective interests of its entire clientele, which demands that the interests of some clients may have to be sacrificed to further those of the majority or of future clients, while the distinctive feature of the professional orientation is that each client's interests reign supreme and must not be sacrificed for the sake of the welfare of other clients.

A second basic difference concerns the source of authority. The bureaucratic official's authority rests on a legal contract backed by formal sanctions, but the professional's authority is rooted in his acknowledged technical expertness. Although some technical competence may be required for performing the duties of a customs official, it is not this skill but his legal status that authorizes the customs inspector to decide whether goods can be imported duty-free or not. An individual is legally obligated to submit to the authority of the policeman, whatever he thinks of his decision, but the same person submits to the authority of his doctor because, and

---

[2] Talcott Parsons, "Introduction" to Max Weber, *The Theory of Social and Economic Organization*, A. M. Henderson and Talcott Parsons, trans., and Talcott Parsons, ed. (New York: Free Press and Falcon's Wing Press, 1947), pp. 58-60; and Alvin W. Gouldner, *Patterns of Industrial Bureaucracy* (New York: Free Press, 1954), pp. 22-24.

only if, he acknowledges that the doctor has the technical knowledge to determine whether he should have surgery, medicine, or neither.

A third difference, related to the foregoing, is that the bureaucrat's decisions are expected to be governed by disciplined compliance with directives from superiors, whereas the professional's are to be governed by internalized professional standards. To be sure, superiors may be more highly qualified in a field than their subordinates. The crucial problem, however, is that bureaucratic management must base its decisions in part on administrative considerations, which often conflict with purely professional considerations.

Finally, the differences between the two systems are reflected in the locus of the last court of appeal in case of disagreement. When a decision of a bureaucrat is questioned, the final judgment of whether he is right or not is a prerogative of management, but when a decision of a professional is questioned, the right of reviewing its correctness is reserved to his professional colleague group. The actions of the professional expert, therefore, are under the ultimate control of his peers who have the same specialized skills as he, whereas control over the bureaucrat's action is exercised by superiors in the organization whose technical skills tend to differ from his. One complains to the medical society or to the bar association about a physician's or a lawyer's actions, and there his professional colleagues will judge whether or not the complaint is justified; but one complains to a mechanic's boss about a mechanic's actions, and the boss who judges the mechanic is typically not an expert mechanic himself.

With increasing numbers of professionals being employed in bureaucratic settings, much attention has been directed toward examining conflicts between the demands of the administrative organization and those of professional standards. These conflicts usually find expression in contrasting orientations of employees; some adopt management as their major reference group, and others, their professional colleagues. The significance of this difference is indicated by the fact that studies of professionals or semiprofessionals in formal organizations have consistently found that the conflict between bureaucratic and professional orientation is a fundamental issue. Hughes reports conflicts between itinerants and the homeguard in numerous working settings;[3] Francis and Stone emphasize the distinction between a service and a procedure orientation in their study of a public employment agency;[4] and Gouldner focusses on the contrast between cosmopolitan and local orientations in his study of a college faculty.[5] Our research, too, found that semiprofessional workers in a public assistance

[3] Everett C. Hughes, *Men and Their Work* (New York: Free Press, 1958), pp. 31, 129-130, 136.
[4] Roy G. Francis and Robert C. Stone, *Service and Procedure in Bureaucracy* (Minneapolis: University of Minnesota Press, 1956).
[5] Alvin W. Gouldner, "Cosmopolitans and Locals," *Administrative Science Quarterly*, 2 (1957), 281-306.

agency could be differentiated on the basis of whether their orientation was confined to the organization or extended to the profession of social work. Those oriented to their profession tended to be less attached to the welfare agency, more critical of its operations—particularly of service to clients—and less confined by administrative procedure. Although a professional orientation motivates a person to do better work in terms of professional standards, it also gives him a basis for ignoring administrative considerations and thus may lead to poorer performance in terms of the standards of the organization. Thus, professionally oriented caseworkers were more apt than others to fail to visit their clients on schedule.

Research on production organizations in widely different social contexts indicates that a rational organization for the collective pursuit of formally established goals may exist whether or not the specific mechanism employed for this purpose is a bureaucratic structure. Stinchcombe presents a comparative analysis of construction and mass-production industries in our highly complex and industrialized society.[6] Udy reports a quantitative investigation of rudimentary production organizations in a large number of simple, non-Western societies.[7] Despite the great difference in source materials, the two studies arrive at essentially the same conclusion. The findings of both indicate that a rational formal organization may be but is not necessarily bureaucratic. Specifically, the fact that an organization is governed by such rational principles as specialization, rewards for performance, and contractual agreements is independent of the existence of a bureaucratic structure, that is, a hierarchy of authority and an administrative apparatus. Stinchcombe concludes that the professionalized labor force in the construction industry serves as an alternative to bureaucratization for assuring rational production, because seasonal fluctuations in this industry make it impractical to maintain continuous bureaucratic organizations. Seasonal variations, however, is not the only condition that encourages employment of a professional labor force; another is the complexity of the services to be performed. When the overall responsibility of the organization cannot be broken down into fairly routine specialized tasks—as exemplified by organizations responsible for research, the care of the ill, and casework service—expert judgments of professionals rather than disciplined compliance with commands of superiors must govern operations in the interest of efficiency.

Professional expertness and bureaucratic discipline may be viewed as alternative methods of coping with areas of uncertainty. Discipline does so by reducing the scope of uncertainty; expertness, by providing the knowledge and social support that enable individuals to cope with uncertainty

[6] Arthur L. Stinchcombe, "Bureaucratic and Craft Administration of Production," *Administrative Science Quarterly*, 4 (1959), 168-187.

[7] Stanley H. Udy, Jr., " 'Bureaucracy' and 'Rationality' in Weber's Theory," *American Sociological Review*, 24 (1959), 791-795.

and thus to assume more responsibility. The dilemma, however, remains and, indeed, affects wider and wider circles as the number of people subject to both these conflicting control mechanisms grows, since the work of professionals is increasingly carried out in bureaucratic organizations, and since operations in bureaucracies seem to become increasingly professionalized, modern warfare being a conspicuous example.

Managerial planning and initiative

The need for centralized planning and individual initiative poses a third dilemma for formal organizations—or, perhaps more correctly, a third manifestation of the basic dilemma between order and freedom.[8] Notwithstanding the importance of free communication, freedom to follow one's best professional judgment, and conditions permitting the exercise of initiative, effective coordination in a large organization requires some centralized direction. But the assumption that managerial coordination necessitates control through a hierarchy of authority is questionable, since it can be and is often achieved by other methods, notably through various types of impersonal mechanisms of control designed by management.

The assembly line is such an impersonal mechanism through which managerial planning effects coordination of the production processes without the uses of directives that are passed down the hierarchy. As a matter of fact, the impersonal constraints exerted on operators tend to reserve the flow of demand in the hierarchy. Since the moving line makes most of the demands on workers, the role of the foreman is changed from one who primarily makes demands on workers to one who responds to their demands for help and assistance, and similar changes occur on higher levels. There is centralized direction, but it is not attained through commands transmitted down the hierarchy.

Performance records are another impersonal mechanism of control, one suitable for controlling nonmanual as well as manual tasks. The regular evaluation of employee performance on the basis of quantitative records of accomplished results exerts constraints that obviate the need for routine supervisory checking. Performance records, like the assembly line, reverse the flow of demand in the organization and cast the supervisor in the role of adviser and helper to workers rather than in the role of a person who makes continual demands on them. This evaluation system also facilitates coordination, since it centralizes the direction of operations in the hands of the higher managers who design the records.

Both performance records and assembly lines minimize reliance on hierarchical authority and discipline to control operations, and therefore improve relations between supervisors and subordinates. However, there is

---

[8] See the discussion of the dilemma between bureaucracy and enterprise, as he calls it, by Marshall Dimock, *Administrative Vitality* (New York: Harper & Row, 1959).

an important difference between these two mechanisms. Assembly-line production reduces the discretion workers can exercise and hence lowers their work satisfaction. In contrast, evaluation of performance on the basis of a quantitative record of results achieved increases the discretion employees are allowed to exercise and thus raises their work satisfaction.

We had expected that automation would be an impersonal control mechanism more similar in its consequences to performance records than to the assembly line. We further anticipated that most workers in automated plants, where routine tasks are performed by machines, would be technical experts engaged in maintenance and trouble-shooting, and they, consequently, would enjoy more discretion and have higher work satisfaction. The surprising findings of studies conducted in automated organizations by Walker, Faunce, and Mann and Williams is that the average level of skill and responsibility of workers was not superior to the level that had existed prior to automation.[9] The discretion permitted workers had not been increased. Indeed, in the automated factory studied by Faunce, supervision was closer than on the assembly line, because foremen were concerned with preventing costly machine breakdowns. Since automation removed some of the higher positions in the organization as well as some lower ones, it reduced chances for advancement, a situation which was a source of considerable dissatisfaction. It appears that automated plants have not yet reorganized their work processes to take full advantage of the technological innovations. This reorganization would require, in our opinion, the training or recruitment of expert mechanics and the redesigning of the division of labor to include minor machine maintenance in the duties of operators. Under these conditions, machine breakdowns, or the impending danger of them, would not lead to closer supervision as it did in the plants studied, and the highly technical operations would permit the exercise of considerable discretion.

It is conceivable that union pressure to increase wage rates on automated jobs will force management to institute such a reorganization. Higher labor costs constrain management to attempt to improve productivity, and one means for accomplishing this improvement is through further automation that eliminates routine jobs. The remaining highly paid workers could be held responsible for acquiring the skills needed for the maintenance functions now discharged by foremen or specialists. Such changes would give them more discretion, lessen the need for close supervision, and thus probably raise work satisfaction. These predictions are in line with Melman's conclusion that union pressures and high wages have induced management to introduce technological innovations more rapidly

    [9] William A. Faunce, "Automation in the Automobile Industry," *American Sociological Review*, **23** (1958), 401-407; and Floyd C. Mann and Lawrence K. Williams, "Observations of the Dynamics of a Change to Electronic Data-Processing Equipment," *Administrative Science Quarterly*, **5** (1960), 217-256. Charles R. Walker, *Toward the Automatic Factory* (New Haven: Yale University Press, 1957).

than would otherwise have been the case.[10] Such a professionalization of the labor force might also require a reorganization of the reward system, since piece rates do not furnish incentives suited for professionalized tasks. Even in the semiautomated department studied by Walker, where tasks were far from professionalized, and where workers were quite satisfied with their rate of pay, there was much dissatisfaction with the piece-rate system for failing to take mental work and judgment into account. A reward system that emphasizes advancement chances rather than immediate earnings and evaluation of results rather than sheer productivity would seem to furnish more effective incentives for professionalized tasks.

Managerial planning of the production process and a professionalized labor force that can exercise initiative and is motivated to do so by opportunities for advancement would sharply reduce the need for hierarchical supervision and control through directives passed down the pyramid of authority. Indeed, coordination appears to be achieved frequently through centralized planning and by means of direct communication between responsible managers rather than through the cumbersome process of passing messages up and down the hierarchy. But our suggestion that managerial planning interferes less with the exercise of initiative than hierarchical authority is not meant to imply that the dilemma between managerial control and initiative is resolved. The best that can be hoped for, as Bendix has suggested, is that

. . . the employee of all ranks in industry and government strike a balance between compliance and initiative, that they temper their adherence to rules by a judicious exercise of independent judgment and that they fit their initiative into the framework of the formal regulation.[11]

But even this best is too much to expect. For this balance is continually disrupted by the need for more order on the one hand and the need for more freedom on the other.

Dialectical Processes of Change

The conception of dilemma directs attention to the inevitability of conflict and change in organizations. Mary Parker Follett, an astute observer of administrative practice, has noted: "When we think that we have *solved* a problem, well, by the very process of solving, new elements or forces come into the situation and you have a new problem on your hands to be solved."[12] The innovations instituted to solve one problem often create

[10] See Seymour Melman, *Decision-Making and Productivity* (Oxford, England: Blackwell, 1958), pp. 105-106, 141-143.

[11] Reinhart Bendix, "Bureaucracy," *American Sociological Review*, 12 (1947), 503.

[12] Mary Parker Follett, *The Process of Control*, Luther Gulick and L. Urwick, eds., *Papers on the Science of Administration* (New York: Institute of Public Administration, 1937), p. 166 (italics in original).

others because effectiveness in an organization depends on many different factors, some of which are incompatible with others; hence, the dilemma. The very improvements in some conditions that further the achievement of the organization's objectives often interfere with other conditions equally important for this purpose. A by now familiar example is that hierarchical differentiation promotes coordination but simultaneously restricts the communication processes that benefit decision-making.

New problems are internally generated in organizations in the process of solving old ones. However, the experience gained in solving earlier problems is not lost but contributes to the search for solutions to later problems. These facts suggest that the process of organizational development is dialectical—problems appear, and while the process of solving them tends to give rise to new problems, learning has occurred which influences how the new challenges are met.[13] Consequently, effectiveness in an organization improves as a result of accumulated experience. These dialectical processes are illustrated by the introduction of assembly-line production. This new production method raised productivity and effected centralized control and coordination without the need for hierarchical directives. However, by routinizing tasks and lowering work satisfaction, the assembly line created problems of absenteeism and turnover—problems that were particularly serious given the interdependence of operations on the assembly line. Management had succeeded in solving one set of problems, but the mechanism by which they were solved produced new problems which were quite different from those that existed in earlier stages of mechanization. Contrary to our expectations, the introduction of automation has not yet met the problems created by monotonous tasks and low work satisfaction. But should these problems be solved through a reorganization of the work force that requires operators to assume more responsibility as we have suggested, management would no doubt again be faced with new difficulties. For example, increased responsibility and discretion in performing complex, interdependent tasks might engender anxieties over decision-making which would impede effective performance, and these new problems would require management to devote attention to developing mechanisms that reduce such anxieties.

Conflicts of interest between various groups or persons in the organization are another source of dialectical change. What constitutes satisfactory adjustment for one group may be the opposite for another, since different interests serve as the criteria of adjustment. Thus, when the efforts of managers are judged by the results they achieve and they are given freedom to exercise responsibility and initiative in achieving them, conflicts between them are likely to ensue. For each manager will seek to promote the in-

---

[13] If we classify problems into dichotomies or other very broad categories, it inevitably seems as if the same one recurs, simply because all new ones are put into one of the few existing categories.

terests and expand the jurisdiction of his department, and his endeavors will bring him into conflict with others who have staked out the same claims. Compromises will be reached and coalitions will be formed, but since the responsibilities and interests of the managers continue to differ, new conflicts are apt to arise as changing conditions produce new challenges. Moreover, as various occupational subgroups in the organization try to improve their economic position, their interests may come into conflict, particularly if the success of one group upsets the existing status hierarchy and motivates the others it has displaced to recoup their advantage. Conflicts of interest are most conspicuous in the relation between union and management. The union is interested in obtaining higher wages and better working conditions, while management is interested in lowering costs and improving productivity. Collective bargaining furnishes mechanisms for resolving issues, but the conflicting interests generate new ones. Thus, management introduces new machines in an attempt to improve efficiency, disturbing the existing adjustment and producing a variety of difficulties with which the union has to deal. Similarly, once workers have attained the right to collective bargaining, they use it to fight for pensions and other fringe benefits, thereby creating new problems for management.

Another source of disruption and change is turnover in personnel. Valuable experience is lost as older workers are replaced by new trainees, and social ties are disrupted by transfers and loss of personnel. As we have seen, the methods available to a new manager in discharging his responsibilities are dependent in part on those of his predecessor. If the latter commanded the loyalty of subordinates, the successor will find it difficult to do so and be constrained to resort to bureaucratic methods, whereas the successor to an authoritarian bureaucrat will find it advantageous to use more informal managerial practices. Again we see that organizational developments alternate in direction in a dialectical pattern. The succession of goals leads to such an alternating pattern of change in the relations between organizations. Once earlier objectives are achieved, management seeks new objectives and by doing so disturbs the existing equilibrium in the network of organizations. The dominance of one organization in a sector restores order as former competitors become exchange partners, but further power struggles are stimulated by a further succession of goals as groups of sellers start to compete with groups of buyers for dominant power over a set of related markets.

In mutual-benefit associations, there is still another source of dialectical change. These organizations are subject to conflicts that arise from the dilemma posed by their twofold formal purpose. One purpose, just as in the case of other organizations, is the effective accomplishment of the specific objectives of the organization—for example, improving employment conditions in the case of unions. But another distinctive purpose of these associations is to provide their members with a mechanism for arriving at agreements on their common objectives. For to serve the interests of its members a mutual-benefit association must furnish mechanisms for ascertaining what their collective objectives are as well as mechanisms for implementing them, and the ascertaining of objectives requires democratic self-government and freedom of dissent. Endeavors to attain one of these purposes frequently impede the attainment of the other. In the interests of effective accomplishment of union objectives, as Michels has pointed out, democratic processes are often set aside. Conversely, preoccupation with democratic self-government and freedom of dissent may interfere with efforts to implement the common objectives. But the study by Lipset and his colleagues shows that a strong union which has accomplished some of its specific objectives can and sometimes does turn its attention and energy to maintaining internal democracy.

Democratic societies are in this respect organized like mutual-benefit associations. They have the double purpose of remaining strong enough to survive and yet maintaining the freedoms that permit the democratic establishment of common objectives. Under current conditions in the world, the issue of promoting national security and strength versus preserving civil liberties and freedom of dissent poses the dilemma most sharply. No final solution is possible for this dilemma. Indeed, attempts finally to resolve it tend to sacrifice one purpose for the other and thus endanger the very nature of democratic societies. For we surely need to survive in order to preserve our democratic institutions, but we just as surely do not want to survive at the cost of losing our freedom.

11. Organization and Authority in Industrial Research

Simon Marcson

All organizations have a system of authority that governs the determination of policy, establishes criteria for selection and advancement of individuals, and gives expression to organizational goals. An understanding of these facets of authority in the industrial laboratory is vital to the adequacy of its administration. This article is concerned with the problems of control and administration as they relate to research work in the industrial laboratory. Implementing organizational control in the industrial laboratory hinges on the balance achieved between the scientist's sense of participation in the direction of his work and the exercise of adequate administrative controls by management. The solution to this problem is inherent in the manner in which the laboratory organizes its authority system.[1]

The industrial laboratory as a research organization seems to require that its objectives be adequately expressed through its authority system. The major objective of the Pacific Electronics Corporation (P.E.C.)[2] laboratories is contributing new findings in the electronics field that will in turn advance the objectives of the corporation.[3] These new findings are a product of the work of the scientist in his professional role. The values of this role[4] are so deeply imbedded in the scientist's professional self-conception as to impel him to seek a system of organizing authority[5] that will permit their expression.

Reprinted from Simon Marcson, "Organization and Authority in Industrial Research," *Social Forces*, **40** (October, 1961), pp. 72-80, published by the University of North Carolina Press.

[1] See the analysis of authority as a system which "can operate 'upward' and 'sidewise' as well as 'downward' in the organization" in Herbert A. Simon, *Administrative Behavior* (New York: Macmillan, 1951), p. 12.

[2] The Pacific Electronics Corporation is a fictitious name for a large electronic and engineering corporation. Its research is centralized in a laboratory employing about 300 scientists. A detailed methodological statement is contained in my recent monograph *The Scientist in American Industry* (New York: Harper & Row, 1960). Frederick Harbison and J. W. Riley, Jr. made many helpful comments on an earlier draft of this paper.

[3] The main authority in the P.E.C. laboratories, as will be seen, is directly related to this primary objective.

[4] The concept of authority is not a central issue in the ideology of the professions. The member of a profession expects to defer only to superior professional knowledge and competence. In governmental and industrial bureaucracies there is a structured expectancy about authority and it is viewed as legitimate. For example, see: Talcott Parsons, "Suggestions for a Sociological Approach to the Theory of Organizations," II, *Administrative Science Quarterly*, **1** (1956), 237.

[5] R. K. Merton, *Social Theory and Social Structure* (New York: Free Press, 1949), p. 315.

The scientist needs an authority system that recognizes the characteristics of his professional role. He needs an authority system which allows him to search, discover, analyze, and publish his findings subject only to the "pre-established impersonal criteria"[6] of science. He needs an authority system which permits autonomy and protects his self-esteem. In the face of these organizational requisites what type of authority system prevails in the industrial laboratory?

Executive Authority and Colleague Authority[7]

Authority, as a system of controls prevailing in an organization, may be viewed as a continuum: at one end of the continuum is a type of organizational authority which may be described as executive or nonprofessional authority;[8] at the other end of the continuum is a colleague or professional type of authority. Executive authority has reference to a system of controls in which a superior in a hierarchical organization exercises ultimate control over his subordinates. It is an authority according to Merton which accrues to the executive based on his incumbency in a position and "occurs within the framework of pre-existing rules of the organization."[9] It is not based on either devotion or respect for him as a person, "but on an adaptation necessitated by his rating power."[10] Industrial organizations are frequently examples of this type of authority system. Colleague authority refers to a system of control in which authority is shared by all the members of the working group. Authority is deemed to rest in the group rather than in an individual, as in executive authority. It is true that in colleague authority systems there is delegation of decision-making authority to individuals, but the members view such authority as originating in the colleague membership.

Executive authority

The traditional industrial organization,[11] notwithstanding the rise of the professional management movement,[12] is tied to a system of authority based

[6] *Ibid.*, p. 309.

[7] In this connection it is interesting to examine A. W. Gouldner's two types of bureaucracy in R. K. Merton, *et al.*, eds., *Sociology Today* (New York: Basic Books, 1959), p. 403.

[8] Frederick Harbison and Charles A. Myers' analysis of "Management as a System of Authority" in *Management in the Industrial World* (New York: McGraw-Hill, 1959), pp. 40-67.

[9] Merton, *op. cit.*, p. 151.

[10] P. M. Blau, *The Dynamics of Bureaucracy* (Chicago: The University of Chicago Press, 1955), p. 172.

[11] H. A. Shepard points out that, "industry respects certain kinds of orderliness in productive organization, and takes them as evidence of efficiency." "Nine Dilemmas in Industrial Research," *Administrative Science Quarterly*, 1 (June, 1956), 300.

[12] A. M. Carr-Saunders and P. A. Wilson state that the reason business management is difficult to regard as a profession is because its "technique is generalized rather

on incumbency in office. Here, in the ideal type organization, the individual with decision-making responsibility functions without significant consideration of the views of subordinates. Within prescribed limits he engages in issuing directives and orders. He is viewed by his subordinates as the "boss."[13] The organization does not expect him to defer to the competencies of those in lower ranking positions, and he does not create any organizational means for drawing on the participation of his subordinates.

The traditional industrial organization, being tied to an ideological position of executive authority, tends to resist the emergence of a colleague authority system for professional employees.[14] It is hostile to an authority system for professionals based on persuasion and indirect control. Insofar as it does move toward such a system, however, it sees itself as diluting its own authority and decision-making ability.

To some extent the industrial laboratory reflects the values of the traditional industrial organization. At the P.E.C. laboratories the executive is selected for expertness; however, his expertness is in science and not in management. It is true that such an individual has frequently had experience as a group leader and section leader, but these leadership positions are in no way comparable to those of laboratory director, director of research, or general manager of the laboratories which are full-time management positions occupied by scientists but requiring expertness in managerial decision making. Nonetheless, it is assumed that since the research executive occupies a managerial position and performs this function, he is now expert in this area also. The executive is now dominant both in the field of science and in the field of management. His authority is now partly a result of his being an incumbent of a particular position, and is only partly based on his scientific expertise.

The emergence of large complex organizations employing scientists, such as the P.E.C. laboratories, has increased the necessity for a shift to less arbitrary, less direct, and less dominating practices of authority. Arbitrary

---

than specialized. Where a technique is specialized, the rise of a profession is unescapable; where it is generalized, its coming must wait upon the growth of a sense of a common responsibility in order that the loose bond, created by the possession of a common but ill-defined technique, may be drawn more tightly." *The Professions* (Oxford, England: Oxford University Press, 1933), p. 491.

13 See James C. Worthy, *Big Business and Free Men* (New York: Harper & Row, 1959), p. 56. "Certain businesses today resemble the authoritarian state. All direction, all thinking, all authority tends to flow from the top down. While the top administrator may delegate certain parts of his responsibility to those at lower levels, he is merely authorizing them to implement and effectuate policies and directives he has set up." On the other hand see H. A. Shepard, *op. cit.*, "The scientific and professional organizational traditions are based on assumptions that are different from those of industry in some respects. . . . The idea of a boss is an anathema, as are the other external controls imposed by industrial methods of organization—in fact they are held to be inconsistent with the basic tenets of professionalism."

14 Shepard states that "most laboratory managements make certain gestures in recognition of the scientists' 'rights' as a professional." *Op. cit.*, p. 301.

authority is possible in industrial organizations that emphasize formal titular status, but as scientists and engineers are introduced into a work organization, the dependence on such devices as title and rank become less effective, and positive mechanisms of incentives and participation become necessary. The technical staff member at the P.E.C. laboratories is not impressed by titles. He recognizes that titles alone do not fill the void of unacknowledged status. He has a vague feeling that his relationship to the organization should be different, but he cannot specifically explain how. As a scientist pointed out: "Recognition is absent . . . Recognition is necessary. . . . I am not sure what kind."

The occurrence of executive authority is explained by a technical staff member:

Parts of the laboratories, especially in applied research with paternalistic leadership, actually designated problems for the individual scientist. I find this completely unacceptable and would not be able to work under such circumstances.

The occurrence of arbitrary, direct, and paternalistic authority not only evokes the scientist's resentment but also causes him to resist such working conditions.[15] He is implicitly expressing the need for an authority system based on persuasion.[16] It is of interest to note that this arbitrary direct type of control is most common in the more applied research areas of the laboratories.

The research organization has not entirely escaped the effect of a long history of industrial management, which has resulted in the direction of professional employees by nonprofessionals; so that while research and development in industrial organizations is usually managed by professionals, these professionals are in turn subordinate to nonprofessionals. The executive hierarchy of industrial organizations, even though their origins are in a physical science professional field, come to be identified with nonprofessional business management.[17] Their central executive positions in the organization give them decision-making power in all parts of the organization, including nonprofessional as well as professional workers such as scientists and engineers. The professional executives who manage these professional employees are frequently subject to arbitrary decision by nonprofessional superiors. A member of research management pointed out:

[15] Traditionally, to the intellectual worker any type of administrative control is suspect. See D. R. Willson, "Budgets and Administrative Controls," *The Direction of Research Establishments* (London: H. M. Stationery Office, 1957), p. 3.
[16] Simon Marcson, "Role Concept of Engineering Managers," *Trans. Inst. Radio Eng.*, EM-7 (March, 1960), p. 33.
[17] See Norman Kaplan who, in discussing the research administrator, states, "the research administrator is oriented toward management and administration, toward the internal organization and in general toward groups not concerned with science as such." *Administrative Science Quarterly*, 4 (1959).

In research what has always come first has been the critical objectives of P.E.C., such as the development of computers. When these objectives have been gotten out of the way, then more latitude for research has occurred.

The implicit demand of the professional worker for self-rule is readily observable in industry. He resents authority that originates outside the professional unit.[18] These are nonprofessional people and there is, therefore, a question about their legitimacy. He views and accepts his professional superior as his supervisor with some reservations,[19] but he actually resents the executive authority of the nonprofessional superior.

While the scientist grudgingly accepts the supervision of professionals, he views them as essentially powerless.[20] He knows from frequent experience that vital decisions finally have to be taken by some nonprofessional executive. The dominant control of the budget for research, the scientist knows well, rests in the hands of nonprofessional executives. He learns, for instance, that decisions pertaining to travel, sick leaves, and holidays are all decided by an executive in the general administration of the research organization rather than by a scientist. The scientist learns in time that the power wielders in the organization are often nonprofessional executives.

Colleague authority

The term "colleague" has its origins in professional working groups. It emphasizes a relationship of association, alliance, and working together, while at the same time accepting whatever inequality in status that may be present. These inequalities are subordinated to the association of colleagues for work purposes, but at the same time the controls of authority and the decision-making mechanisms remain in force. In colleague authority, therefore, authority in the final analysis rests in the group rather than in the individual. Colleague authority exists, then, within a framework of "representative bureaucracy"[21] based on rules established by agreement, and to which the individual voluntarily consents.

In its ideal type, colleague authority would be expected in the university.[22] In the university organization, tradition and myth have precluded an

[18] The resentment of the professional is towards lay authority. As Kaplan points out: "The greater the number of nonscientists in higher authority, the more likely that there will be a greater demand for controls and information about the nonscientific aspects of the research operation." *Op. cit.*, pp. 31-32. See also B. E. Noltingk's discussion of the relations of scientists and lay management, *The Human Element in Research Management* (Amsterdam: Elsevier, 1959), p. 35.

[19] See H. A. Shepard, "Superiors and Subordinates in Research," *Journal of Business*, **29** (1956), 266.

[20] Powerless is used here as a lack of organizational power. See Parsons' discussion of power as "the generalized capacity to mobilize resources in the interest of attainment of a system goal. The generation and utilization of power constitutes one of the fundamental functional imperatives of any social system." *Op. cit.*, p. 225.

[21] Gouldner, *op. cit.*, p. 403.

[22] C. V. Kidd states that "the long struggle for academic freedom has provided our

executive authority system.[23] Faculty self-rule within a parliamentary framework has emphasized the expected value system of a democracy and modified (although not necessarily eliminated) the occurrence of arbitrary despotic behavior. The prevailing system of faculty organization has emphasized the mechanisms of persuasion and indirect control. Faculty self-rule has tended, too, to emphasize the notion that the source of authority is within the faculty, notwithstanding the fact that it functions within the framework of administrative controls.

In the university organization the professional imperative is expressed by the acceptance of the principle (albeit at times in theory only), that the faculty member is to be chosen for his scholarly skills alone and not for his amenability to supervision.[24] Although in an industrial organization, the traditional authority system demands a manageable individual, this is not entirely true of research organizations. The P.E.C. laboratories in their recruitment and selection practices reduce such considerations to a minimum. The shortage of highly trained scientific workers has pressed research laboratories into a continuing search for talent. Under these pressures even traditional discriminatory bars to Negroes in industry have been eliminated. Talent is an overriding consideration, even when the recruit has a reputation for being temperamental.

Authority in a Research Organization

Not all universities are characterized by colleague authority systems nor all industries by executive authority systems. As a matter of fact, one would expect to find that all organizations employing professional workers would fall somewhere along a continuum between these two polar types. The P.E.C. laboratory, as an organization exhibiting elements of both executive authority and colleague authority, tends to fall towards the center of the continuum. Elements of both executive authority and colleague authority are found in these laboratories. A scientist explained this in the following manner:

It is a fact that the industrial laboratory is different from the university and different from the corporation. The industrial laboratory necessarily functions

---

universities with the means of protecting the scientist from many of the immediate pressures of convention or prejudice." *American Universities and Federal Research* (Cambridge, Mass.: Belknap Press, 1959), p. 29.

[23] Talcott Parsons in "Sociological Approach to the Theory of Organization," *Administrative Science Quarterly*, 1 (1956), p. 236, states: "A university cannot be organized mainly on a 'line' principle, with the president issuing orders through his deans to the members of the faculty. The faculty tends, rather, to be a collegial 'company of equals' who bear a good deal of corporate responsibility. The 'administration' is more a facilitating agency responsible for financial resources, physical facilities, and largely for public relations."

[24] This constitutes perhaps the most sensitive area in the relations between faculty and administration. Parsons points out that "the results is usually a balance of responsibility, with the initiative mainly in faculty hands, and a veto power, effectively if not formally, on both sides." *Ibid.*, p. 236.

within narrower limits than the university. This is a fact of life. What causes difficulties is the dicta that come from higher levels.

P.E.C., as a research organization, has not settled into a particular organizational pattern. It is doubtful that it can simply adopt an organizational model from some other area of activity. What seems to be emerging is a convergence of the industrial, organizational, and university models into a new type of organizational model.

Authority is not always organized on a hierarchical basis in a research organization. The skills of the scientist demand recognition in addition to whatever informal lines of power may be present in the organization. "Thus a superior must often defer where technical considerations are decisive."[25] In the P.E.C. laboratories members of top research management are aware as are scientists of the needs of a colleague system of relationships. As a member of research management pointed out:

It is the job of the research supervisor to communicate to the individual that he is essentially working on what he is interested in. This places an important reliance and burden on the research supervisor. The research supervisor is expected to be astute in the management of research personnel.

While, on the one hand, realizing that the research supervisor has to depend on persuasion as a method of supervision, administrative management expresses the expectation of its occurrence in an executive fashion. What is more, administrative management conceives of adequateness of supervision as largely astuteness. Colleague relationships are not established by astuteness alone but by the recognition that the professional worker has a right to participate in decisions affecting him in his capacity as a professional worker. The executive system thus fails to take into account and to implement the fundamental characteristics of colleague authority relationships.

Research management tries to avoid overt assignment of research at the P.E.C. laboratories, and acts as if the scientist were autonomous in his work. Research management is aware, however, of the organizational controls that are present in the work situation and assists it in guiding the scientist's work.

When the laboratory has a particular need, it does not ask a staff man to carry it out. It runs down the appropriate individual and puts it up to him. Sometimes the individual turns it down, not being interested. He is perfectly free to do so. I think, however, a staff man has to recognize our needs. I feel that when a man turns down an organizational need, then he most likely experiences a pang of conscience. This is good, and if he continues to do this, then he establishes the reputation of being nonco-operative.

The "nonco-operative" designation is a controlling mechanism which directs the scientist into the acceptance of the more desirable assignments that he is given. He is autonomous within limits, i.e., he is a participant in colleague authority relationships within the limits of the controls exercised by executive authority.

The strains and conflicts in the authority system within which professional employees function in this industrial research organization lead it to adapt elements of the university system of colleague authority to its own needs. This is clearly observable in one research area of the P.E.C. laboratories headed by a section leader. He explained his approach to supervision in the following terms:

In supervising research it is most important to maintain the enthusiasm of the individuals involved. This is a delicate problem when it involves shifting an individual from one type of research to another. It has to be done at length with a great deal of diplomacy. In the case of some individuals, I would not dare to shift them, or direct them, or supervise them. These are people who are very good. They know what they are doing. They know how to do it. I leave them completely on their own. They budget their own time, and are continually publishing. I read their monthly reports.

In this part of the laboratories the supervisor is adapting the university system of colleague authority to the needs of the scientist.[26] While attempting to help the professional worker accommodate to industry's traditional authority system, the supervisor is not relying on limited doses of pseudo-human-relations techniques.

Colleague authority permits the exercise of initiative and creativity within the hierarchical organization. A discerning scientist pointed this out as follows:

Invariably in the research units of the laboratory where members accept passively autocratic leaders, such individuals are not of the highest levels of competence. This reflects itself in the fact that their creative productivity when measured against that of other groups is not as high and not as good.

The colleague is not constrained by a concern for rituals that circumscribe individual initiative in a bureaucratic organization. Colleague authority, therefore, limits the emergence of organizational rigidity and enables the member to exercise greater autonomy. The preference that the professional worker has for this type of organization and authority system is to be seen in the preference which he shows for supervision which depends upon colleague authority. According to management in industrial research, the scientist, as a professional employee, shows a marked preference for universities as employing organizations rather than industrial research laboratories. The scientist tends to view the university as a more adequate employ-

---

[26] Kidd points out that, "A major function of universities is to serve as the place where individuals can conduct free inquiries into all aspects of the physical universe and of man as an individual and social animal. By free inquiry is meant a search for knowledge not limited by institutional objectives or external forces." Op. cit., p. 30.

ing organization for the creative individual than any other employing organization.

The leaders of some of the foremost industrial research organizations, in describing the basic principle in which their laboratories operate, have been at pains to point out that for several centuries the best research results have come from the centers of learning—the universities. They have concluded that the closer organizations can approach the atmosphere and methods of working of a university, the better will be its results.[27]

As a result industrial research organizations having a high degree of rigidity find it difficult to retain creative individuals.

Mechanisms of Authority

Both executive and colleague authority rely on a variety of mechanisms for implementing the control they exercise over their members. In the executive authority system, major reliance is placed in control by domination, while in the colleague authority system the members are subject to control through manipulation. Traditionally, the industrial organization has relied on controlling its members through the imposition of edicts and orders. This restriction of the individual's autonomy and freedom has been supported by a system of negative sanctions and by the acknowledged status of the superior.[28] In the university organization members are in a position to choose a variety of means to achieve the university's broad goals. Individual members are guided to these goals more by internalizing such goals and values rather than by edict and order. There is a dependence in the university organization on persuasion and indirect manipulation rather than domination and direction.

As an occupational group scientists require more education, talent, and skills than, for instance, a railroad engineer. They also require an entirely different compliance system for the individual than occupations of low levels of education, talent, and skill. The compliance of the individual is obtained through the manipulation of sanctions and the administration of rewards in terms of informal symbolic status, rather than economic needs.

Compliance in professional areas of work is especially based on interlinking systems of anxiety, conformity, and approval. The scientist's motivations are affected by his need to gain approval and recognition for his accomplishments, which in turn induce both anxiety and conformity on his part. The university organization wittingly or unwittingly depends upon these factors of anxiety, conformity, and approval to motivate its members.

27 Willson, *op. cit.*, p. 5.

28 P. M. Blau points out that among "civil service servants the group's insistence that the supervisor discharge his duty issuing directives—'that's what he gets paid for'— serves to emphasize that their obedience to him does not constitute submission to his will but adherence, on his part as well as theirs, to abstract principles which they have socially accepted." *Op. cit.*, pp. 172-173.

The industrial research laboratory, as an organization utilizing professionals, also depends upon this interlinkage of anxiety, conformity, and approval. In this sense, the industrial research laboratory approximates the university organization insofar as similar mechanisms are at work in the motivation of members of both organizations.

Manipulation[29] has a popular connotation of a Machiavellian character. Here it is used without such evaluative content, but has reference to the overt or implicit recognition of organizational goals, and the selection of appropriate indirect means for their achievement by the individual. Manipulation depends upon persuasion and participation: that is, the individual's finding his own way to a decision which colleague authority has defined, rather than a decision being forced on him by executive authority. The professional in the course of his training internalizes the norms of colleague relations and becomes responsive to manipulation and the acceptance of colleague authority. He has taken over the informal norms of the group which emphasize an equalitarian climate. Failure to conform does not even carry such sanctions as the displeasure of the boss since no stated expectation is involved with a specific individual.

At the same time, the professional develops resistance to domination and executive authority especially if their source is nonprofessional.[30] The likelihood of executive authority especially by nonprofessionals is markedly increased when the professional becomes an employee in a large industrial research organization. In the P.E.C. laboratories the number of direct contacts with nonprofessional executives is limited. However, when they do occur, as with personnel or accounting, for instance, they are a source of irritation and strain. This is expressed very frequently in statements disparaging the competence and abilities of the nonscientific executive leadership of these programs.

There is often trouble with the heads of administrative services. These fellows are always trying to run your life when they can't even run their own departments. Look who they get in these positions!

As an occupational group increases in skill and in the complexity of its work, and requires increasing education and talent, it ceases to be adequately administered within the framework of domination and depends increasingly on administration through indirect manipulation. The scientist, as a professional employee, cannot be readily managed through domination expressed by negative sanctions, since this does not increase his

---

[29] See Morris Janowitz's discussion of manipulation. "Manipulation involves influencing an individual's behavior less by giving explicit instructions and more by indirect techniques of group persuasion and by an emphasis on group goals." *Sociology and the Military Establishment* (New York: Russell Sage Foundation, 1959), p. 39.

[30] See the Public Opinion Index for Industry study, "The Scientific Mind and The Management Mind" (Princeton: Opinion Research Corp., 1959), p. 12. "Because management lacks readily recognized symbols of professionalism, it's easy for the scientist and engineer to doubt his competence."

involvement and motivation. The scientist, as the university faculty member, responds to an emphasis on participation and positive group goals. Traditional industrial organizations have resisted the acceptance of the concept of indirect manipulation based on positive group cohesion. Industrial research organizations have often failed to understand that indirect manipulative control is essential in maintaining the initiative of individuals in semiautonomous work situations. Appealing to professional pride, encouraging the scientists to publish scientific papers and to attend scientific meetings are instances of effective use of indirect means of control.

The management of scientists by indirect control is difficult and complicated. It cannot be done by assuming an exaggerated permissiveness when the relationship to the scientist remains a hierarchical one, and it cannot be successful as long as the scientist is aware that his superior is attempting to camouflage his executive authority. It requires extensive training and expertise in the development of indirect techniques of control. When it is carried out inadequately, as in some of the attempts of industrial personnel departments, it arouses the resentment of the scientist and contributes to conflict. The P.E.C. laboratories have at times conducted management training discussions. When these have remained on an informal level about the organization, there has been grudging acceptance; when they have touched on managerial skills involving the camouflaging of executive authority, they have been criticized.

Bureaucratic organizations have an inherent resistance to colleague authority. As an organization grows in size it adopts an increasing number of rules, regulations, and routines. The large organization makes a conscious effort to increase its predictability and internal discipline through such an emphasis. There emerges a resistance to the dependence upon positive group cohesion as a means of manipulating its professional members and instead an increasing reliance on the impersonal rules for the control of the organization's membership is developed. At the P.E.C. laboratories, rules regulate such activities as the following: starting and stopping times of work, lunch hour, coffee break, store room hours, filling in of the weekly time card, vacations, sick leaves, attendance at professional meetings, ordering equipment, keeping a notebook, writing brief reports on research ideas and reports on completion of a project, salary increases, and evaluation ratings, among others. They do, however, try to shelter their scientists from such annoyances as punching time clocks. That the consequences of rules and regulations are at times realized by the industrial laboratory is pointed out by Boehm[31] in discussing General Motors:

Vice President Lawrence R. Hafstad lets his men come and go pretty much as they please. The result, he suspects, separates the men from the boys. The good people work better, and the weak ones get worse.

[31] G. A. W. Boehm, "Research Management: The New Executive Job," *Fortune* (October, 1957), p. 222.

The professional worker in the industrial organization is expected to accommodate himself to these rules and regulations but resists and resents them. Scientists in industrial laboratories frequently rebel against the attempts to place them within the stated routines of the large organization. A supervisory staff member at the P.E.C. laboratories pointed out:

Strain arises between the research man and the laboratories about budgetary rules regarding research supplies, evaluation ratings, obtaining research credit, and salary increases.

A member of research management stated the problem as follows:

I think there is a constant conflict between the individual and the organization. The organization has its own needs and demands.

The impersonal rules are resisted while at the same time compliance is obtained because of the scientists' striving for approval and recognition from the research organization. Some anxiety is never absent from the scientist's research work, for approval is greatly desired.

Consequences for Prestige and Power

Both executive and colleague types of authority systems affect the power and prestige of both the holders of authority and those subject to that authority. In executive authority the office holder has high prestige since he has control[32] over others. The authority structure explicitly recognizes his superordinate status.[33] In the colleague authority system, prestige depends upon achievement as judged by the scientists' colleagues. Recognition of achievement does not, however, carry the power of command, although it does contribute to the prestige and influence of the individual.

The traditional industrial organization assumes a correlation between rank, ability, and power. The introduction of larger numbers of highly talented scientists disturbs this assumed relationship. The numerous scientists in any one corporation do not have high corporate rank and power conferred upon them. The traditional industrial organization has developed on the assumption that ability is invariably rewarded with appropriate promotions in rank. The implied corollary assumption is that individuals of lower rank have lesser abilities. Differentials in rank brought requisite degrees of power to the occupant of the designated level. In the creation of research divisions, industry has introduced large numbers of talented scientific personnel into their organizations. This has been done without modifying the previous system of assumptions about the relationships of rank, ability, and power; that is, they were injected into the organization just as if

[32] Merton, *op. cit.*, p. 151.
[33] See C. A. Gibb's statement, "Leadership," in G. Lindzey, ed., *Handbook of Social Psychology* (Reading, Mass.: Addison-Wesley, 1954), pp. 887-920.

they were another group of employees without concern for the inherent relationship between ability and rank.

The significance of the fact that the scientist is not only an individual of high ability but is professionally trained has frequently not been appreciated by industry. As a large group in simply another employee category, their rank and power within the corporation as a whole, therefore, tends to be low. At the P.E.C. laboratories research management has had to develop a special niche in the corporation for its scientific staff. It has had to develop and protect the special professional privileges it has created for the laboratories, such as a library and merit award trips to European laboratories.

The number of scientists employed by corporations has increased so much that no unique status accrues to them as an unusual and scarce type of employee. As a matter of fact, in the P.E.C. so little uniqueness is attached to scientists that they are lumped together in one general occupational category with some 7,000 engineers as one large engineering category of employees. They are viewed by the corporation as a relatively low-ranking group, and are certainly not given the rank and power commensurate with their abilities. This, in turn, inevitably affects the manner in which the corporation as a whole tends to view their abilities, for it seems obvious that since they can be employed in large numbers and their abilities purchased at relatively low rates as compared to executive salaries, their talent is not of a high order. It should be noted that at the P.E.C. laboratories such views are not held by research management, but can be found among corporate management, and nonresearch administrators in the laboratories.

In the traditional corporate organization, the executive has conferred upon him both power and prestige. This power is tremendous as seen from the vantage point of the professional employee. The professional employee in the industrial organization is a powerless individual without seeming protection from the arbitrariness of limitless executive power. This is somewhat modified for the scientist in the industrial laboratory. In the P.E.C. laboratories research management serves as a buffer in any direct attempt by corporate nonprofessionals to exercise executive authority.

12. Organizational Impact of White Collar Automation

Floyd C. Mann

Lawrence K. Williams

The working vocabulary of the office worker is slowly changing to include such words as programming, write-outs, bits, core memory, and drum storage. This new vocabulary has come to the office with the introduction of high-speed computers and accessory equipment. These complexes are not coming to be known in the literature as electronic data processing (EDP) systems. Computer systems like the IBM 705 or Rand's "Univac" are being introduced into the office to compute and prepare customer bills, inventories, cost statements, premium notices, payrolls, and a host of other both simple and complicated tasks which have long provided the work base for the white collar worker.

In this paper we shall present some of the organizational and social psychological problems associated with these advanced automatic data processing systems. We will touch on both the problems of managing the change-over to such systems and on the effect of these new systems on the organization and its personnel. Our focus here[1] will be on changes relevant to industrial relations—changes in management philosophy, organizational structure, job content, and transitional problems. We will draw primarily on our own observations from an on-going, longitudinal study in a single firm over a period of years and on the research findings or observations of other investigators studying the impact of this new technology on the office. Our knowledge in this field is restricted in that our research has concentrated on the *intra-organizational* effects of these changes in a single firm. We have not examined certain broad economic and social consequences such as the effects of this white collar automation on the composition of

Reprinted from *Annual Proceedings Industrial Relations Research Association,* 1958, pp. 59-68, by permission of the authors and the IRRA.

[1] A more complete description of our findings at this stage of our research is given in Floyd C. Mann and Lawrence K. Williams, "Observations Concerning a Change-Over to Electronic Accounting Equipment: A Case Study," unpublished paper presented at the 13th Congress, International Association of Applied Psychology, Rome, 1958. These observations have resulted from informal on-the-job interviews. Since 1954 we have been interviewing personnel at all levels involved in this change-over. This is one of a series of studies being conducted in the Organizational Behavior & Organizational Change Programs of the Survey Research Center, University of Michigan.

the labor force, the "unhired employee," leisure time activities, and other equally significant issues.

A number of empirical studies now provide us with a better basis for understanding the shape of things to come in this area. These include studies of large computer installations in insurance companies,[2] a study of an automatic airline ticket reservation system,[3] the use of EDP for maintaining inventory control in a shoe company,[4] and several studies of the introduction of IBM 650's in large and small insurance companies.[5] It is important to stress that the general impact on the organization is greatly dependent upon the degree of mechanization prior to change. This undoubtedly accounts for some of the marked differences in organizational change noted in these studies even where identical equipment is installed.

Technological changes which have been occurring in the past few years in the factory and the office are increasingly labeled "automation." While this general label is useful to connote simply "more automatic,"[6] most descriptions of these new automated processes have stressed the following basic characteristics: greater mechanization with more frequent use of automatic equipment and multiple, closed-loop feedback systems as controls. These technical and engineering characteristics in combination result in greater integration and centralization of control in systems of production and data processing.

Brief Description of a Change-Over

A change-over to an electronic data processing system is different than a model conversion in an automobile plant, a turnaround in an oil refinery, or the starting up of a new plant. There can be no stock-piling in advance of suspending operations; there is little or no opportunity to make trial runs of new systems without the continual maintenance of the older system. Because continuity of office activities must be maintained and because the data of the old system can seldom be transferred directly to the new system, a change-over usually extends over a long period of time—from six months

[2] *Studies of Automatic Technology: The Introduction of an Electronic Computer in a Large Insurance Company*, Bureau of Labor Statistics, 1955; R. G. Canning, *Installing Electronic Data Processing Systems* (New York: Wiley, 1957).

[3] *Studies of Automatic Technology: A Case Study of an Automatic Airline System*, Bureau of Labor Statistics, Report No. 137, 1958.

[4] E. Wallace, *Management Decisions and Automatic Data Processing*, unpublished doctoral dissertation, University of Chicago, 1956.

[5] N. F. Craig, *Administering a Conversion to Electronic Accounting* (Cambridge, Mass.: Riverside Press, 1955); E. Jacobson, "Employee Attitudes Toward the Installation of an Electronic Computer in a Medium Sized Insurance Co.," unpublished paper presented at the 13th Congress, International Association of Applied Psychology, Rome, 1958.

[6] James Bright, in his new book *Automation and Management* (Boston: Division of Research, Harvard Business School, 1958), feels that the "common usage of automation to mean a significant advance in automaticity is a literal and appropriate application to the phenomena" with which he was concerned (p. 55).

to three or four years. A period of transition of this duration results in the organization having to establish and manage three work forces: (a) a group which continues to maintain operations under the old system, (b) a group responsible for converting records and procedures from the old to the new system, and (c) a group responsible for beginning and maintaining operations under the new system.

A successful change-over to a complex EDP system necessitates a major reorganization of existing operations as well as the establishment of entirely new operations. There is a compounding of changes as the new equipment and its processes require large-scale structural and functional realignments in the organization. An organizational level may be added during the change-over, and functions are transferred across divisional lines as well as among sections and departments within the division at the vortex of the change.

The change-over is accompanied by a dramatic shift in the activity level of the organization. The equilibrium and relative stability of the organization before the change gets underway is slowly replaced as increasing demands are focused successively on each segment and level involved in the change. Pressures mount as the physical installation of the equipment nears completion, new programs which have been in the process of preparation for months are readied for testing, and the conversion itself gets underway. There is no quick return to normalcy as the change-over nears completion. The organization, slowly adjusting to the new system, settles down to the level of activity required by it.

A change-over to EDP is thus a multiple-phase operation in which there is frequently a compounding of technological and organizational changes in an ongoing system over an extended period of time.

Problems Relevant to Industrial Relations

Management's conception of the change-over

Management's conception of the principal problems involved in a change-over determines the extent to which attention is focused solely on the equipment or on the entire system of which the equipment will become a part. When attention is focused on the equipment—"the hardware approach"—management is primarily concerned with the selection of the correct machine or machines for a given operation. The problem is conceived to be one of substitution of machines for existing operations. The potential to be realized by rethinking the division of labor and the resultant organizational structure in a broad way is ignored.

In the system approach, on the other hand, the introduction of electronic equipment is seen as an opportunity for reevaluating organizational objectives and procedures and redesigning relevant sub-systems within the organization. This approach may result in not only a more efficient alignment and consolidation of functions in the immediate area of the change-over, but may also furnish the impetus for reconsideration of activities and procedures in other distant parts of the organization. Changes which could have been brought about without the introduction of an EDP system, but had been postponed for one reason or another, are incorporated into this broader conceptualization of the task. Thus, the change-over is seen as a complex parcel of organizational, administrative, human, *and* technical problems—not simply a technical problem of selection and installation of equipment within old organizational lines. The management which fails to realize that more than hardware is being changed also probably fails to understand the implications of such a change for its personnel policies and its people.

Elaboration of management philosophy

A change-over brings a number of revisions in management philosophy and its implementation. Existing policies must be reexamined, made explicit, occasionally changed; new policies must be developed; both old and new policies are given a thorough test as they are translated into action.

As functions, employees, and their supervisors are transferred from one major division to another, the extent to which common philosophies and policies exist is revealed. Contradictions and inconsistencies in the sharing of information, the joint planning of work, and the delegation of responsibility are the basis of some of the problems in this period for both supervisors and employees. The greater interdependence of divisions and their departments necessitates the consideration and resolution of these differences before the new operating system can be established.

A change-over forces further development and elaboration of management's personnel philosophy. That which was implicit becomes explicit; that which was ill-defined and ambiguous is clarified through discussions regarding operating problems; untested assumptions are evaluated against the hard criteria of employee support and rate of progress toward the conversion goal. In particular, the implications of the company's philosophy for the management of change are elaborated.

One of the principal long-range objectives of the introduction of EDP systems is the reduction of white collar clerical and supervisory personnel. This eventual reduction in the number of jobs coupled with the gross redistribution of personnel accompanying the reorganization sets the stage for serious morale problems and resistance to change. To ensure the continued cooperation of the work force throughout the long change period, policies regarding employment security—policies of not laying off or down-grading permanent and long service employees—are commonly developed. All accounts of the problems faced in this period stress the imperativeness of formulating and communicating company policy regarding security of employment in advance of initiating change.[7]

These policies typically provide employment security, but not the assurance of a particular job. Regular employees whose jobs are discontinued are transferred to other equivalent assignments at the same rates of pay. Management assumes the responsibility of placing and retraining employees and supervisors in jobs for which they can be qualified.

There are a number of forces which lead management to this formalization of its obligation to its permanent work force. These include: (a) the maintenance of the morale of employees directly and indirectly affected by the change; (b) the utilization of the skill potential of existing personnel; (c) the demonstration of the organization's concern for the welfare of its employees; and (d) the meeting or anticipating of union demands where the group is organized or in reducing the likelihood of unionization. These forces in combination have resulted in organizations installing electronic equipment and developing policies which cushion the effects of such technological changes for white collar employees. Thus, the "social shock absorbers" which Baldwin and Schultz implied would have to be developed at the societal level have been accepted by many companies as a part of the cost of the change-over.[8]

Capacity of the organization for change

Organizations vary markedly in their capacity for change. Resources—such as previous experience with change, managerial talents, work force skills, values and attitudes—are important conditioning variables. For example, organizations having serious morale problems are obviously ill prepared for such a period of change. Previous failures to manage change effectively, irrespective of the causes, create a pessimistic and apprehensive climate that impedes the transition. Managerial talent barely adequate to maintain existing operations places the success of such a change in even greater jeopardy.

Personnel who have gone through successful periods of change are more willing to accept another round of instability; those whose experiences have been particularly trying have less tolerance for another change. The periodicity with which changes occur in the system is also important. It is probable that organizations having changes every year or two have learned to accommodate to such changes better than those in which major changes occur only once every five or ten years.

The white collar work forces of many companies are probably less pre-

---

[7] Craig, *op. cit.*; Bureau of Labor Statistics, *op. cit.*, 1955; Bureau of Labor Statistics, *op. cit.*, 1958.

[8] G. B. Baldwin and G. P. Schultz, "Automation: A New Dimension to Old Problems," *IRRA Proceedings* (1954).

pared for the prolonged instability involved in a change-over than their blue collar counterparts in the automated factory. The value-orientations of the white collar worker in the large utility, insurance company, and government office are apparently different from the unskilled worker in the plant. The stability of these organizations has been an important factor for these security-minded employees; the instability of the change-over probably finds them, by personality and experience, less ready to meet the demands for adjustments.

The managerial and supervisory capability for administering the change is equally important to an effective transition. Conceptually, we have found it useful to think of the effective supervisor as having three classes of skills: technical, administrative, and human relations skills. Our observations indicate that during a change period different combinations of these supervisory skills are required at different levels in the organization at the same time, and of the same supervisors at different times. There appears to be a shift in emphasis from human relations to technical and administrative and back again to human relations skills.

In the early stages of the change-over when the upper levels of supervisory personnel—managers and department heads—are confronted with the job of planning for broad organizational changes consistent with the specific functions of their responsibilities to the organization as a whole, administrative and technical skills become very important for them. Human relations problems are not unimportant, but technical problems of laying down broad outlines of the change-over from old procedures to new procedures demand more time. Simultaneously first-line supervisors are primarily concerned with the human relations problems raised by announcements of impending major changes. Technical skills of the first-line supervisors are not tested until the broad outlines of the change are spelled out and the job of implementing these changes is delegated to lower levels of supervision.

Toward the end of the change-over human relations skills become more important again as employees manning the old and transitional systems have to be fitted into permanent jobs in the new system. By this time the basic technical and organizational problems have been solved, what remain are principally human relations problems: (a) the selection of the personnel for the permanent work force, (b) the elimination of the large transitional work force, and (c) the difficult task of finding appropriate jobs for permanent, long service employees consistent with the organization's policy of employment security.

Deficiencies in managerial and supervisory capacity become obvious at different phases of the change as different levels are exposed to the pressure by carrying the brunt of the change. These marked shifts in the mix of the three skill components provide a rigorous test for the organization's criteria for promotion. The organization whose supervisory personnel do not have adequate resources in this respect finds the going extremely difficult in the change-over to new EDP systems.

Organizational structure

Transfer of functions, centralization of control, and greater interdependency of units are some of the inter-related structural modifications that accompany such a large-scale change.

The transfer of functions between major divisions and among departments within a division creates problems for both employees and supervisory personnel. In some cases the work force moves when functions are reassigned, in others only the functions are transferred. These kinds of changes result in the employees being faced with new supervision, new jobs, or both. Strains created by the usual reluctance of managers to relinquish responsibilities are also felt by the employees.

Centralization of control and decision-making follows greater integration in the system. Autonomy and flexibility are reduced. As supervisory tasks cease to exist, the supervisory level of work leader may be eliminated. The first line supervisor's area of freedom is also further restricted. Variations in work rate and work process within a work unit are reduced; most decisions must be made with the larger organizational system in mind. Many of these changes point toward a further loss of self-direction and the motivation which stems from this.

Increased integration also places a greater premium on the rapid transmission of information; communication cannot be left to chance but must be highly formalized. There is a need for a nerve center with complete understanding of the integrated system where normal operations can be coordinated and where breakdowns in some part of the system can be interpreted for all other parts.

Job content and structure

There are a number of similarities between the technological changes in the factory and the office as they affect the content and structure of jobs. The most routine jobs are eliminated, work pace is tied more closely to machines, promotional opportunities are reduced, and some shift work is introduced.

A few statistics from our research site provide some insight into the changing structure of the jobs and their content. Prior to the change, there were 140 jobs and approximately 450 positions in the central accounting area. It is estimated that 80 per cent of the jobs were either substantially changed or eliminated, and that this affected 90 per cent of the positions. Moreover, there was about 50 per cent reduction in the number of jobs.

While EDP installation eliminates the routine and more menial clerical jobs, a general up-grading of jobs is not a necessary consequence.[9] The net effect on the organization we studied was a change in average job grade from 8.0 to between 8.1 and 8.2, where the range is from 3 to 13. Tasks previously done by employees holding high job grades and by lower level supervisors, and which involved known criterion decisions also have been programmed.[10]

New jobs that are created tend to require either new skills or new combinations of skills previously used. While these jobs may be less routine and therefore more socially desirable, within the single organization there is considerable problem that dislocated individuals may not be able to fill these new jobs. Retraining personnel having a restricted range of talent is not an adequate solution.

Job enlargement does not necessarily accompany a change-over. It did however in the situation we were studying. The work of the non-mechanized accounting groups responsible for the steps preparatory to machine processing was consolidated into a station arrangement with each member trained to handle five operations previously performed separately. The removal of many middle level decision-making jobs also means that there is even less opportunity for progression in the organization. This has long been true for the assembly line worker. The effect that such a promotion limit will have on the white collar worker is unknown as yet, but it will probably disturb his illusion of mobility.

The white collar worker has often thought of his regular, eight hour, daylight working schedule as one of the rewards of his job. Now that management finds it economically desirable to run EDP systems on a two shift basis, it becomes necessary for some white collar workers to accept shift work. The recruitment of these white collar shift workers presents new problems. One organization has now changed its hiring policy and employs married women almost exclusively on the evening shift.

Another characteristic of the new work conditions is the low tolerance for error. The highly rationalized system provides less opportunity for multiple checking than previously, and errors may not be caught until they reach either the central processing equipment or in some cases the customer. Specific allocations of work to a single position means that errors are almost always traceable to an individual. For the white collar worker, accustomed to the somewhat anonymous conditions of the typical office organization, this accountability is a new experience.

The specific allocation of work within a rationalized system also means that each job is of greater significance in the continuity of the process. Ab-

---

[9] Bright has compiled data from several *factory* sites which corroborate this point. See J. Bright, "Does Automation Raise Skill Requirements?" *Harvard Business Review*, 36 (1958), 85-98.

[10] The removal of such jobs has also been cited by Rush. See C. H. Rush, "Implications of Electronic Data Processing for Industrial Relations Research," *IRRA Proceedings*, 1957.

sences, tardiness, and a high turnover rate take on added importance, and relevant policies are more rigorously enforced.

The new white collar worker also has problems of machine pacing. Operating on a fixed schedule, the system imposes very specific deadlines. While the office worker still has more freedom to leave his work place or to vary his production level than does the blue collar worker, very specific work quotas have been imposed. Feelings of loss of autonomy are reported by both the worker and his supervisor.

Transitional problems

Problems concerning temporary help, overtime, training, and allocation of the work force are encountered during the transition period. The change-over is a period of increasing work load for the organization. Paradoxically, the very system which is installed to eliminate jobs often necessitates a greater number of workers during the transition period. Added duties and the need for constant retraining result in a significant increase in required working hours. Both overtime and a temporary work force are needed. The recruitment of this temporary work force and its introduction into the organization presents important issues, especially where the workers are organized.

In our study as well as in Craig's,[11] supervisors complained persistently about training and overtime. The problem of overtime was heightened because of the large number of women employees who were restricted in the total amount of allowable overtime as well as the amount permissible in any one day. Excess in overtime appeared to result in lower productivity, and certainly in complaints about home life and leisure activities.

Training is a burden for all personnel during the change-over. In the two major divisions affected by the change-over in our study, there were 800 individuals who had to be retrained to some degree. Training for new jobs is often relatively abstract. The trainer can only describe what the new jobs will probably be like. Initially there is no opportunity for on-the-job training. In addition, many have to be trained for jobs that are not to be permanent assignments but instead are transition jobs, and some of the motivation for learning is thus lessened.

Because of the simultaneous operation of the new, transitional, and old systems, the efficient assignment and reassignment of the work force becomes an important problem. Care must be exercised that those assigned to the old or the transition jobs are not overlooked for eventual assignment to new jobs. Another problem exists if one has to replace an individual who has been operating at a new job for a year or more with a more qualified candidate who was essential to the maintenance of the old or transitional systems.

[11] Craig, *op. cit.*

While these are problems of transition in terms of their origin, their effects will be felt in the organization for an extended time unless properly managed.

The six major problem areas we have selected for presentation in this paper are not exhaustive of the problems confronting the organization or its personnel during a change-over to electronic data processing. The topics considered here have been included because they have received less attention.

It has of course been possible to indicate only the broad dimensions of these problems. These findings do indicate however something of what we have learned about the effects of these technological changes on the work world of the white collar worker. This is clearly an area where quantitative, longitudinal, multidisciplinary research in a number of organizations is needed.

Bibliography

Abegglen, J. C., *The Japanese Factory: Aspects of its Social Organization* (New York: Free Press, 1958).

Abegglen, J. C., "Subordination and Autonomy Attitudes of Japanese Workers," *American Journal of Sociology*, 63 (September, 1957), 181-189.

Argyris, C., *Human Behavior in Organization* (New York: Harper & Row, 1957).

Argyris, C., "The Individual and Organization: Some Problems of Mutual Adjustment," *Administrative Science Quarterly*, 2 (June, 1957), 1-24.

Argyris, C., *Personality and Organization* (New York: Harper & Row, 1957).

Argyris, C., *Understanding Organizational Behavior* (Homewood, Ill.: The Dorsey Press, 1960).

Baker, A. W., and Davis, R. C., *Ratios of Staff to Line Employees and Stages of Differentiation of Staff Functions: A Study of Ohio Manufacturing Co.* (Columbus: Bureau of Business Research, College of Commerce and Administration, Ohio State University, 1954).

Bakke, E. W., and Argyris, C., *Organizational Structure and Dynamics: A Framework for Theory* (New Haven, Conn.: Yale University Labor and Management Center, 1954).

Bass, B. M., "Experimenting with Simulated Manufacturing Organizations," in S. B. Sells, ed., *Stimulus Determinants of Behavior* (New York: Ronald 1963), 117-196.

Bendix, R., "Bureaucratization in Industry," in Arthur Kornhouser, *et al.*, eds., *Industrial Conflict* (New York: McGraw-Hill, 1954), 164-175.

Bendix, R., *Work and Authority in Industry* (New York: Wiley, 1956).

Berger, M., "Bureaucracy East and West," *Administrative Science Quarterly*, 1 (March, 1957), 518-529.

Bidwell, C. E., and Vreeland, R. S., "Authority and Control in Client-Serving Organizations," *The Sociological Quarterly*, 4 (Summer, 1963), 231-242.

Blau, P. M., *Bureaucracy in Modern Society* (New York: Random House, 1956).

Blau, P. M., "Cooperation and Competition in a Bureaucracy," *American Journal of Sociology*, 59 (May, 1954), 530-535.

Blau, P. M., *The Dynamics of Bureaucracy* (Chicago: University of Chicago Press, 1955).

Blau, P. M., "Formal Organization: Dimensions of Analysis," *American Journal of Sociology*, 63 (July, 1957), 58-69.

Blau, P. M., and Scott, W. R., *Formal Organizations: A Comparative Approach* (San Francisco: Chandler Publishing Co., 1962).

Boulding, K. E., *The Organizational Revolution: A Study of the Ethics of Economic Organization* (New York: Harper & Row, 1957).

Boulding, K. E., *et al.*, *Conflict Management in Organizations* (Ann Arbor: Foundation on Human Behavior, 1961).

Bowers, D. G., "Organizational Control in an Insurance Company," *Sociometry*, **27** (June, 1964), 230-244.

Brecht, A., "How Bureaucracies Develop and Function," *The Annals of the American Academy of Political and Social Science*, **292** (March, 1954), 1-10.

Brown, P., "Bureaucracy in a Government Laboratory," *Social Forces*, **32** (March, 1954), 259-268.

Burns, T., and Stalker, G. M., *The Management of Innovation* (London: Tavistock, 1961).

Cadwalladen, M. L., "The Cybernetic Analysis of Change in Complex Social Organizations," *American Journal of Sociology*, **65** (September, 1959), 154-157.

Caplow, T., "The Criteria of Organizational Success," *Social Forces*, **32** (October, 1953), 1-9.

Caplow, T., "Organizational Size," *Administrative Science Quarterly*, **1** (March, 1957), 484-505.

Cartwright, D., ed., *Studies in Social Power* (Ann Arbor: University of Michigan, Institute for Social Research, 1959).

Chandler, M. K., and Sayles, L. R., *Contracting Out: A Study of Management Decision Making* (New York: Graduate School of Business, Columbia University, 1959).

Chapple, E. D., "Quantitative Analysis of Complex Organizational Systems," *Human Organization*, **21** (Summer, 1962), 67-87.

Christensen, C. R., *Management Succession in Small and Growing Enterprises* (Boston: Harvard Graduate School of Business Administration, Division of Research, 1953).

Churchman, C. W., *Prediction and Optimal Decision* (Englewood Cliffs, N.J.: Prentice-Hall, 1961).

Crozier, M., *The Bureaucratic Phenomenon: An Examination of Bureaucracy in Modern Organizations and Its Cultural Setting in France* (Chicago: The University of Chicago Press, 1964).

Cyert, R. M., and March, J. G., "Organizational Factors in the Theory of Oligopoly," *Quarterly Journal of Economics*, **70** (February, 1956), 44-64.

Cyert, R. M., and March, J. G., "A Behavioral Theory of Organizational Objectives," in M. Haire, ed., *Modern Organization Theory* (New York: Wiley, 1959), pp. 76-90.

Cyert, R. M., Simon, H. A., and Trow, D. B., "Observation of a Business Decision," *Journal of Business*, **29** (October, 1956), 237-248.

Dakin, R. E., "Variations in Power Structures and Organizing Efficiency: A Comparative Study of Four Areas," *The Sociological Quarterly*, **3** (July, 1962), 228-250.

Dale, E., "New Perspectives in Managerial Decision-making," *Journal of Business of the University of Chicago*, **26** (January, 1953), 1-8.

Dill, W. R., "Environment as an Influence on Managerial Autonomy," *Administrative Science Quarterly*, **2** (March, 1958), 409-443.

Draper, J. E., and Strother, G. B., "Testing a Model for Organizational Growth," *Human Organization*, 22 (Fall, 1963), 180-194.

Drucker, P. F., *The Concept of the Corporation* (New York: John Day, 1958).

Eby, K., "Organization, Bureaucracy, Loyalty," *Antioch Review*, 15 (Summer, 1955), 195-203.

Eells, R., *The Government of Corporations* (New York: Free Press, 1962).

Eisenstadt, S. N., "Bureaucracy and Bureaucratization: A Trend Report and Bibliography," *Current Sociology*, 7 (August, 1958), 99-163.

Eisenstadt, S. N., "Bureaucracy, Bureaucratization, and Debureaucratization," *Administrative Science Quarterly*, 4 (December, 1959), 302-320.

Ellsworth, J. S., *Factory Folkways: A Study of Institutional Structure* (New Haven, Conn.: Yale University Press, 1953).

Entwisie, D. R., and Walton, J., "Observations on the Span of Control," *Administrative Science Quarterly*, 5 (March, 1961), 522-533.

Etzioni, A., "Authority Structures and Organizational Effectiveness," *Administrative Science Quarterly*, 4 (June, 1959), 43-67.

Etzioni, A., *A Comparative Analysis of Complex Organizations* (New York: Free Press, 1961).

Etzioni, A., *Complex Organizations: A Sociological Reader* (New York: Holt, Rinehart and Winston, 1961).

Etzioni, A., "Two Approaches to Organizational Analysis: A Critique and a Suggestion," *Administrative Science Quarterly*, 5 (September, 1960), 257-278.

Etzioni, A., and Taber, W. R., "Scope, Pervasiveness, and Tension Management in Complex Organizations," *Social Research*, 30 (Summer, 1963), 220-238.

Firth, R., *Essays on Social Organization and Values* (London: Athlone Press, 1964).

Frank, A. G., "Goal Ambiguity and Conflicting Standards: An Approach to the Study of Organization," *Human Organization*, 17 (Winter, 1958-1959), 8-13.

Golembiewski, R. T., *Behavior and Organization* (Chicago: Rand McNally, 1962).

Georgopoulos, B. S., and Tannenbaum, A. S., "A Study of Organizational Effectiveness," *American Sociological Review*, 22 (October, 1957), 534-540.

Gould, N., and Melbin, M., "Formal Structure and Rational Organization Theory," *Human Organization*, 24 (Winter, 1964), 305-311.

Gouldner, A. W., "Metaphysical Pathos and the Theory of Bureaucracy," *The American Political Science Review*, 49 (June, 1955), 496-507.

Gouldner, A. W., "Organization Analysis," in Robert K. Merton *et al.*, eds., *Sociology Today* (New York: Basic Books, Inc., Publishers, 1959), 400-428.

Gouldner, A. W., *Patterns of Industrial Bureaucracy* (New York: Free Press, 1954).

Green, E. J., and Redmond, G. H., "Comments on a General Theory of Administration," *Administrative Science Quarterly*, 2 (September, 1957), 235-243.

Grusky, O., "Administrative Succession in Formal Organizations," *Social Forces*, **39** (December, 1960), 105-115.

Grusky, O., "Corporate Size, Bureaucratization, and Managerial Succession," *American Journal of Sociology*, **67** (November, 1961), 261-269.

Grusky, O., "Managerial Succession and Organizational Effectiveness," *American Journal of Sociology*, **69** (July, 1963), 21-31.

Guest, R. H., "Managerial Succession in Complex Organizations," *American Journal of Sociology*, **68** (July, 1962), 47-54.

Guest, R. H., *Organization Change: The Effect of Successful Leadership* (Homewood, Ill.: Irwin, 1961).

Guetzkow, H., and Bowes, A. E., "The Development of Organizations in a Laboratory," *Management Science*, **3** (July, 1957), 380-402.

Haas, E., Hall, R. H., and Johnson, N. J., "The Size of the Supportive Component in Organizations: A Multi-Organizational Analysis," *Social Forces*, **42** (October, 1963), 9-16.

Haire, M., ed., *Modern Organization Theory* (New York: Wiley, 1959).

Haire, M., ed., *Organization Theory in Industrial Practice: A Symposium of the Foundation for Research on Human Behavior* (New York: Wiley, 1962).

Haire, M., "Size, Shape, and Function in Industrial Organizations," *Human Organization*, **14** (Spring, 1955), 17-22.

Hall, R. H., "The Concept of Bureaucracy: An Empirical Assessment," *American Journal of Sociology*, **69** (July, 1963), 32-40.

Hamilton, D., "The Ceremonial Aspect of Corporate Organization," *American Journal of Economics and Sociology*, **16** (October, 1956), 11-23.

Harbison, F. H., and Burgess, E. W., "Modern Management in Western Europe," *American Journal of Sociology*, **60** (July, 1954), 15-23.

Hartmann, H., *Authority and Organization in German Management* (Princeton: Princeton University Press, 1959).

Heady, F., "Bureaucratic Theory and Comparative Administration," *Administrative Science Qaurterly*, **3** (March, 1959), 509-525.

Heflebower, R. B., "Observations on Decentralizations in Large Enterprises," *Journal of Industrial Economics*, **9** (November, 1960), 7-22.

Hickman, C. A., "Managerial Motivation and the Theory of the Firm," *American Economic Review*, **45** (May, 1955), 544-554.

Howton, W. F., "The Moral Crisis of Corporations," *Social Research*, **30** (Summer, 1963), 253-260.

Inkeles, A., and Levinson, D. J., "The Personal System and the Sociocultural System in Large-scale Organizations," *Sociometry*, **26** (June, 1963), 217-229.

Jackson, J. M., "Reference Group Processes in a Formal Organization," *Sociometry*, **22** (December, 1959), 307-327.

Jacobson, E., Kahn, R., Mann, F. C., and Morse, N., "Research in Functioning Organizations," *Journal of Sociological Issues*, **7** (March, 1951), 64-71.

Janowitz, M. and Delany, W., "The Bureaucrat and the Public," *Administrative Science Quarterly*, **2** (September, 1957), 141-162.

Jacques, E., *The Changing Culture of a Factory* (London: Tavistock, 1951).

Jacques, E., "The Measurement of Responsibility," (Cambridge, Mass.: Harvard University Press, 1956).

Klein, M. W., Berkowitz, N. H., and Malone, M. F., "Judgments on Organizational Performance," *Sociology and Social Research*, **46** (October, 1961), 26-35.

Knauth, O. W., "Group Interests and Managerial Enterprise," *Journal of Industrial Economics*, **1** (April, 1953), 88-98.

Kriesberg, L., "Careers, Organization Size, and Succession," *American Journal of Sociology*, **68** (November, 1962), 355-360.

Krupp, S., *Pattern in Organization Analysis: A Critical Examination* (Philadelphia: Chilton, 1961).

Kuethe, J. L., and Levenson, B., "Conceptions of Organizational Worth," *American Journal of Sociology*, **70** (November, 1964), 342-348.

Landsberger, H. A., "The Horizontal Dimension in Bureaucracy," *Administrative Science Quarterly*, **6** (December, 1961), 299-332.

Lane, R. E., "Businessmen and Bureaucrats," *Social Forces*, **32** (December, 1953), 145-152.

Lawrence, P. R., *The Changing of Organizational Behavior Patterns: A Case Study of Decentralization* (Boston: Graduate School of Business Administration, Harvard University, 1958).

Lazarsfeld, P. F., "Reflections on Business," *American Journal of Sociology*, **65** (July, 1959), 1-31.

Leavitt, H. J., ed., *The Social Science of Organizations* (Englewood Cliffs, N.J.: Prentice-Hall, 1963).

Lieberson, S., "The Division of Labor in Banking," *American Journal of Sociology*, **66** (March, 1961), 491-496.

Likert, R., "Measuring Organizational Performance," *Harvard Business Review*, **36** (March-April, 1958), 41-50.

Likert, R., *New Patterns of Management* (New York: McGraw-Hill, 1961).

Litchfield, E. H., "Notes on a General Theory of Administration," *Administrative Science Quarterly*, **1** (June, 1956), 3-29.

Litterer, J. A., ed., *Organizations: Structure and Behavior* (New York: Wiley, 1963).

Litwak, E., "Models of Bureaucracy which Permit Conflict," *American Journal of Sociology*, **67** (September, 1961), 177-184.

Mann, F. C., and Neff, F. W., *Managing Major Change in Organizations: An Undeveloped Area of Administration and Social Research* (Ann Arbor, Mich.: The Foundation of Research on Human Behavior, 1961).

March, J. G., ed., *Handbook of Organizations* (Chicago: Rand McNally, 1965).

March, J. G., and Simon, H. A., *Organizations* (New York: Wiley, 1958).

Marcson, S., "Organization and Authority in Industrial Research," *Social Forces*, **40** (October, 1961), 72-80.

Martin, N. H., "Differential Decisions in the Management of an Industrial Plant," *Journal of Business*, **29** (October, 1956), 249-260.

Martin, N. H., and Strauss, A. L., "Patterns of Mobility within Industrial Organizations," *Journal of Business*, **29** (April, 1956), 101-110.

Marvick, D., *Career Perspectives in a Bureaucratic Setting* (Ann Arbor: Institute of Public Administration, University of Michigan, 1954).

Mechanic, D., "Some Considerations in the Methodology of Organizational Studies," in H. Leavitt, ed., *The Social Science of Organizations* (Englewood Cliffs, N.J.: Prentice-Hall, 1963), pp. 139-182.

Meltzer, L. and Salter, J., "Organizational Structure and Performance and Job Satisfaction," *American Sociological Review*, 27 (June, 1962), 351-362.

Merton, R. K., *Social Theory and Social Structure* (New York: Free Press, 1957).

Moore, W. E., *The Conduct of the Corporation* (New York: Random House, 1962).

Morse, N. C., and Reimer, E., "The Experimental Change of a Major Organizational Variable," *Journal of Abnormal and Social Psychology*, 52 (February, 1956), 120-129.

O'Leary, P. M., "The Problem of the Large Corporation Twenty-five Years Later," *The American Journal of Economics and Sociology*, 20 (October, 1960), 39-44.

Page, C. H., "Bureaucracy's Other Face," *Social Forces*, 25 (October, 1946), 88-94.

Parsons, T., "Suggestions for a Sociological Approach to the Theory of Organizations—I," *Administrative Science Quarterly*, 1 (June, 1956), 63-85.

Parsons, T., "Suggestions for a Sociological Approach to the Theory of Organizations—II," *Administrative Science Quarterly*, 1 (September, 1956), 225-239.

Patchen, M., "Alternative Questionnaire Approaches to the Measurement of Influences in Organizations," *American Journal of Sociology*, 69 (July, 1963), 41-52.

Payne, R., "An Approach to the Study of Relative Prestige of Formal Organizations," *Social Forces*, 32 (March, 1954), 244-247.

Perrow, C., "The Analysis of Goals in Complex Organizations," *American Sociological Review*, 26 (December, 1961), 854-866.

Perrow, C., "Organizational Prestige: Some Functions and Dysfunctions," *American Journal of Sociology*, 66 (January, 1961), 335-341.

Pfiffner, J. M., and Sherwood, F. P., *Administrative Organization* (Englewood Cliffs, N.J.: Prentice-Hall, 1960).

Presthus, R. V., "Authority in Organizations," *Public Administration Review*, 20 (Spring, 1960), 86-91.

Presthus, R. V., *The Organizational Society* (New York: Knopf, 1962).

Presthus, R. V., "Social Bases on Bureaucratic Organization," *Social Forces*, 38 (December, 1959), 103-109.

Presthus, R. V., "Toward a Theory of Organizational Behavior," *Administrative Science Quarterly*, 3 (June, 1958), 48-72.

Price, J., "Use of New Knowledge in Organizations," *Human Organization*, 23 (Fall, 1964), 224-234.

Record, W., "The Sociological Study of Municipal Bureaucracies," *Social Problems*, 11 (Winter, 1964), 301-305.

Reissman, L., "A Study of Role Conceptions in Bureaucracy," *Social Forces*, 27 (March, 1949), 305-310.

Richmond, A. H., "Conflict and Authority in Industry," *Occupational Psychology*, **28** (January, 1954), 24-33.

Riley, J. W., ed., *The Corporation and Its Publics: Essays on the Corporate Image* (New York: Wiley, 1963).

Sayles, L. R., *Managerial Behavior: Administration in Complex Organizations* (New York: McGraw-Hill, 1964).

Sayles, L. R., "The Change Process in Organizations," *Human Organization*, **21** (Summer, 1962), 62-66.

Schein, E. H., and Ott, J. S., "The Legitimacy of Organizational Influence," *American Journal of Sociology*, **67** (May, 1962), 682-689.

Scott, W. R., "Field Work in a Formal Organization," *Human Organization*, **22** (Summer, 1963), 162-168.

Seashore, S., "Field Experiments with Formal Organizations," *Human Organization*, **23** (Summer, 1964), 164-170.

Seashore, S., and Bowers, D. G., *Changing the Structure and Functioning of an Organization: Report of a Field Experiment*, Survey Research Center Monograph No. 53, Ann Arbor: Institute for Social Research, University of Michigan, 1963.

Seeman, M., "Social Mobility and Administrative Behavior," *American Sociological Review*, **23** (December, 1958), 633-642.

Selznick, P., "An Approach to a Theory of Bureaucracy," *American Sociological Review*, **8** (February, 1943), 47-54.

Selznick, P., *Leadership in Administration* (New York: Harper & Row, 1957).

Shubik, M., "Games, Decisions and Industrial Organization," *Management Science*, **6** (July, 1960), 455-474.

Shuster, J., "Bureaucratic Transition in Morocco," *Human Organization*, **24** (Spring, 1965), 53-58.

Simon, H. A., *Administrative Behavior*, 2nd ed. (New York: Macmillan, 1957).

Simon, H. A., "Authority," in C. M. Arensberg, *et al.*, eds., *Research in Industrial Human Relations* (New York: Harper & Row, 1957), pp. 103-115.

Simon, H. A., *The New Science of Management Decision* (New York: Harper & Row, 1960).

Simon, H. A., "Staff and Management Controls," *Annals of the American Academy of Political and Social Science*, **292** (1954), 95-103.

Simon, H. A., Guetzkow, H., Kozmetsky, G., and Tyndall, G., *Centralization vs. Decentralization in Organizing the Controller's Department* (New York: Controllership Foundation, 1954).

Simpson, R. L., "Vertical and Horizontal Communication in Formal Organizations," *Administrative Science Quarterly*, **4** (September, 1959), 188-196.

Smith, C. G., and Tannenbaum, A. S., "Organizational Control Structure: A Comparative Analysis," *Human Relations*, **16** (November, 1963), 299-316.

Soemardjan, S., "Bureaucratic Organization in a Time of Revolution," *Administrative Science Quarterly*, **2** (September, 1957), 182-199.

Stinchcombe, A. L., "Bureaucratic and Craft Administration of Production: A Comparative Study," *Administrative Science Quarterly*, **4** (September, 1959), 168-187.

Stinchcombe, A. L., "On the Use of Matrix Algebra in the Analysis of Formal Organization," in A. Etzioni, ed., *Complex Organizations* (New York: Holt, Rinehart and Winston, 1961), pp. 478-484.

Stinchcombe, A. L., "The Sociology of Organization and the Theory of the Firm," *Pacific Sociological Review*, 3 (Fall, 1960), 75-82.

Stogdill, R. M., and Shartle, C. L., *Patterns of Administrative Performance* (Columbus: Bureau of Business Research, College of Commerce and Administration, Ohio State University, 1956).

Stogdill, R. M., Shartle, C. L., Wherry, R. J., and Jaynes, W. E., "A Factorial Study of Administrative Behavior," *Personnel Psychology*, 8 (Summer, 1955), 165-180.

Stogdill R. M., and staff associates, *Aspects of Leadership and Organization* (Columbus: Ohio State University Research Foundation, 1953).

Stone, R. C., "Factory Organization and Vertical Mobility," *American Sociological Review*, 18 (February, 1953), 28-35.

Strauss, E., *Bureaucracy in Russia, France—and Britain? The Ruling Servants* (London: Allen & Unwin, 1961).

Sykes, G. M., "The Structure of Authority," *Public Opinion Quarterly*, 17 (Spring, 1953), 146-150.

Talacchi, S., "Organization Size, Individual Attitudes and Behavior: An Empirical Study," *Administrative Science Quarterly*, 5 (December, 1960), 398-420.

Tannenbaum, A. S., and Kahn, R. L., "Organizational Control Structure," *Human Relations*, 10 (May, 1957), 127-140.

Terrien, F. W., and Mills, D. L., "The Effect of Changing Size upon the Internal Structure of Organizations," *American Sociological Review*, 20 (February, 1955), 11-13.

Thompson, J. D., "Authority and Power in 'Identical' Organizations," *American Journal of Sociology*, 62 (November, 1956), 290-301.

Thompson, J. D., "Organizations and Output Transactions," *American Journal of Sociology*, 68 (November, 1962), 309-324.

Thompson, J. D., and Bates, F. L., "Technology, Organization and Administration," *Administrative Science Quarterly*, 2 (December, 1957), 325-345.

Thompson, V. A., "Hierarchy, Specialization, and Organizational Conflict," *Administrative Science Quarterly*, 5 (March, 1961), 485-521.

Thompson, V. A., *Modern Organization* (New York: Knopf, 1961).

Udy, S. H., "Bureaucracy and Rationality in Weber's Organization Theory: An Empirical Study," *American Sociological Review*, 24 (December, 1959), 791-798.

Udy, S. H., "Bureaucratic Elements in Organizations: Some Research Findings," *American Sociological Review*, 23 (August, 1958), 415-418.

Udy, S. H., "Technical and Institutional Factors in Production Organization," *American Sociological Review*, 23 (August, 1958), 415-418.

Udy, S. H., *The Organization of Work* (New Haven, Conn.: Human Relations Area Files, 1959).

Udy, S. H., "Technical and Institutional Factors in Production Organization," *American Journal of Sociology*, 67 (November, 1961), 247-260.

Urwick, L. F., "The Managers' Span of Control," *Harvard Business Review*, **34** (May-June, 1956), 39-47.

Wager, L. W., and Palola, E. G., "The Miniature Replica Model and Its Use in Laboratory Experiments of Complex Organizations," *Social Forces*, **42** (May, 1964), 418-428.

Warner, W. L., *The Corporation in the Emergent American Society* (New York: Harper & Row, 1962).

Weber, M., *General Economic History* (New York: Greenberg, 1927).

Weber, M., *The Theory of Social and Economic Organization* (New York: Oxford University Press, 1947).

Weiss, R. S., and Jacobson, E., "A Method for the Analysis of the Structure of Complex Organizations," *American Sociological Review*, **20** (December, 1955), 661-668.

Whyte, W. F., *Man and Organization* (Homewood, Ill.: Irwin, 1959).

Whyte, W. F., "Small Groups and Large Organizations," in J. H. Rohrer and M. Sherif, eds., *Social Psychology at the Crossroads* (New York: Harper & Row, 1951), pp. 297-312.

Whyte, W. H., Jr., *The Organization Man* (New York: Simon and Shuster, 1956).

Williams, V., "Bureaucratic Proliferation: A Theoretical Approach," *The American Journal of Economics and Sociology*, **22** (July, 1963), 337-345.

Worthy, J. C., "Organizational Structure and Employee Morale," *American Sociological Review*, **15** (April, 1950), 169-179.

Zelditch, M., and Evan, W. M., "Simulated Bureaucracies: A Methodological Analysis," in H. Guetzkow, ed., *Simulation in Social Science: Readings* (Englewood Cliffs, N.J.: Prentice-Hall, 1962), pp. 48-60.

Zelditch, M., and Hopkins, T. K., "Laboratory Experiments with Organizations," in A. Etzioni, ed., *Complex Organizations* (New York: Holt, Rinehart and Winston, 1961), pp. 464-478.

MAJOR INDUSTRIAL WORK ROLES

Introduction

In most respects this chapter is simply a continuation of the preceding one. It is concerned primarily with the formal organizational and technological determinants of behavior in some of the common and more frequently studied roles in industry. As in the previous chapter, each of the selections contains some discussion of the authority structure of industrial bureaucracy. Most of the papers also consider the relationship between formally prescribed patterns of behavior and spontaneously generated or informal patterns. Several of the readings focus specifically upon occupational specialization and its consequences. This chapter differs from Chapter II in that it is concerned to a greater degree with the reactions of people or their satisfactions and dissatisfactions with the kinds of jobs that are created by the social structure and technology of modern industry.

There has been a gradual shift in the kinds of positions in industry that have received most attention from industrial and occupational sociologists. One of the early concerns in industrial sociology was with the alienated industrial worker. A large number of studies documented the deadening effects of work on repetitive, routinized, and machine-paced tasks. Because the focus of these studies was upon the *alienated* worker, however, the kinds of industries that were selected for study were ones having the highest proportion of jobs with attributes likely to produce alienation. The result was a somewhat distorted picture of industrial work. Robert Blauner, in a recent study, has demonstrated that there are important differences among industries in the potential of factory jobs to alienate.[1] He found, for example, that the automobile assembly line is most likely to produce alienation while jobs in highly automated industries, such as chemical processing, may have little or none of this effect. Although comparative studies like Blauner's, which indicate that our understanding of the role of the factory worker is far

[1] Robert Blauner, *Alienation and Freedom: The Factory Worker and His Industry* (Chicago: University of Chicago Press, 1964).

from complete, may stimulate some renewed interest in this area, there has been a relative decline in the number of sociological studies of the industrial worker in recent years.

Another area that received more attention earlier than at the present is the study of lower level clerical workers. The increasing mechanization of office operations, which tended to make jobs in the office more like those in the factory, generated a number of studies of this process. Some recent research dealing with the introduction of computers in offices suggests that this change produces an even larger number of repetitive, machine operator jobs than did the earlier changes.[2] One reason for the lack of sustained interest by sociologists in lower level white collar work may be that many of the people in these jobs are females who are only marginally attached to the labor force.

Two industrial work roles in which there has been an increase in sociological interest recently are the executive and the professional. The growing number of studies of these two roles may be seen as a part of the generally increasing interest of sociologists in the analysis of formal organizations. Study of the professional in industry involves important theoretical and practical problems stemming from the differences between professional and bureaucratic authority structures, the possibility for alternative, conflicting commitments of the professional to his discipline or his work organization, and the rapid growth in the number of professionals employed in industry. Recent developments in the analysis of the decision-making process along with a continuing high level of concern with organizational control have contributed to an expanding interest in the role of the executive. There has also been a large number of studies of the career patterns and social background of executives where the primary concern, however, is with the process of upward social mobility rather than with the nature of formal organization.

The classic study of the role of the executive is that by C. I. Barnard. The first reading in this chapter is taken from his *The Functions of the Executive* which, as was noted in the preceding chapter, is one of the most frequently cited, early studies in the field of organizational sociology. Barnard, who had personal experience as an executive in both government and private industry, does not deal exclusively with the industrial executive in this reading but does make frequent reference to this role. His concern here is not with the day-to-day activities of the executive but rather with the broad functions performed by persons at this organizational level. The functions discussed in this selection are the maintenance of organizational communication, securing of essential services from individuals, and formulation of purposes and objectives.

In the next reading we move from the top level of supervision to the

---

[2] See, for example, Ida R. Hoos, *Automation in the Office* (Washington, D.C.: Public Affairs Press, 1961).

bottom level—the foreman. The foreman has been called "the man in the middle" because of the conflicting pressures and demands put upon him by management on the one side and the workers he supervises on the other. Donald Wray describes some of the problems in performing this role and points out that foremen are only peripherally members of management since they have no real decision-making function. He shows that this is the case in both a large bureaucratized plant and a smaller one in which most of the authority is vested in a single owner-manager. Wray questions the common assumption that the foreman is an important link between management and the worker but indicates that the role of the foreman may be more important where workers are not represented by a union.

The selection by C. Wright Mills is one of the studies mentioned above that describe the increasing similarity between the jobs of lower level clerical workers and machine operators in the factory. Mechanization and rationalization of office procedures have resulted in more functionally specialized and routine jobs. These processes have also had the effect of reducing the prestige of previously skilled office workers such as the bookkeeper and, to some extent, the secretary and have created a highly differentiated but often artificial status hierarchy in the office. Also of interest in regard to the general theme of this book is Mills' discussion of the necessity for closer and more differentiated supervision resulting from the low incentive to achieve in narrowly specialized jobs.

The Man on the Assembly Line by Walker and Guest contains a good description of the jobs found in an automobile assembly plant and an analysis of the reactions of workers to these jobs.[3] The authors note that there are differences among assembly line jobs but emphasize that repetitiveness and mechanical pacing, both of which are sources of dissatisfaction with work, are characteristic of most jobs in this plant. The inability to control the pace of work, the difficulty in forming cohesive work groups, the fact that each job involves no more than a minute part of the production of an automobile and other similar factors contributing to the alienation of the worker from his job are all characteristic of assembly line work. It would be well when reading this selection, however, to keep in mind the point made by Blauner, in the study mentioned above, that these attributes are not characteristic of all industrial work and that assembly line jobs are an extreme rather than a typical case in terms of the alienation they produce. Walker and Guest conclude with the suggestion that techniques like job enlargement, job rotation, and the fostering of teamwork on the job may help to alleviate some of these problems.

In the final reading in this chapter we return once more to the role of the professional in industry. In this selection Kornhauser discusses the

[3] The complete report of this study can be found in Charles R. Walker and Robert H. Guest, *The Man on the Assembly Line* (Cambridge, Mass.: Harvard University Press, 1952).

alternative possibilities for a primary commitment of the professional: commitment to the profession, to the work organization, to neither, or to both. He notes that there are a variety of functions to be performed by the professional in most industrial settings and suggests, as his major proposition, that those who are professionally oriented or committed will be most concerned with research, those who are organizationally oriented will be most involved in the administration of research departments, and that the "mixed types" will be most interested in the application or communication of research results. Kornhauser then presents the findings from a large number of recent studies that support this proposition.

13. The Functions of the Executive

Chester I. Barnard

I. The Maintenance of Organization Communication

When a complex of more than one unit is in question, centers of communication and corresponding executives are necessary. The need of a definite system of communication creates the first task of the organizer and is the immediate origin of executive organization. If the purpose of an organization is conceived initially in the mind of one person, he is likely very early to find necessary the selection of lieutenants; and if the organization is spontaneous its very first task is likely to be the selection of a leader. Since communication will be accomplished only through the agency of persons, the selection of persons for executive functions is the concrete method of establishing the *means* of communication, though it must be immediately followed by the creation of positions, that is, a *system* of communication; and, especially in established organizations, the positions will exist to be filled in the event of vacancies.

In other words, communication positions and the "locating" of the services of a person are complementary phases of the same thing. The center of communication is the organization service of a person at a place. Persons without positions cannot function as executives, they mean nothing but potentiality. Conversely, positions vacant are as defunct as dead nerve centers. This is why executives, when functioning strictly as executives, are unable to appraise men in the abstract, in an organization vacuum, as it were. Men are neither good nor bad, but only good or bad in this or that position. This is why they not infrequently "change the organization," the arrangement of positions, if men suitable to fill them are not available. In fact, "executive organization" in practice cannot be divorced from "executive personnel"; and "executive personnel" is without important meaning except in conjunction with a specific arrangement of positions.

Therefore, the problem of the establishment and maintenance of the system of communication, that is, the primary task of the executive organization, is perpetually that of obtaining the coalescence of the two phases, executive personnel and executive positions. Each phase in turn is the strategic factor of the executive problem—first one, then the other phase, must be adjusted. This is the central problem of the executive functions. Its

Reprinted by permission of the publishers from Chester I. Barnard, *The Functions of the Executive*, Cambridge, Mass.: Harvard University Press, Copyright, 1938, by the President and Fellows of Harvard College.

solution is not in itself sufficient to accomplish the work of all these functions; but no others can be accomplished without it, and none will unless it is well done.

Although this communication function has two phases, it is usually necessary in practice to deal with one phase at a time, and the problems of each phase are of quite different kinds. The problems of positions are those of location and the geographical, temporal, social, and functional specializations of unit and group organizations. The personnel problems are a special case of general personnel problems—the recruiting of contributors who have appropriate qualifications, and the development of the inducements; incentives, persuasion, and objective authority that can make those qualifications effective executive services in the organization.

A. The scheme of organization

Let us call the first phase of the function—the definition of organization positions—the "scheme of organization." This is the aspect of organization which receives relatively excessive formal attention because it can apparently be reduced to organization charts, specifications of duties, and descriptions of divisions of labor, etc. It rests upon or represents a coordination chiefly of the work to be done by the organization, that is, its purposes broken up into subsidiary purposes, specializations, tasks, etc.; the kind and quantity of *services* of personnel that can be obtained; the kind and quantity of *persons* that must be included in the cooperative system for this purpose; the inducements that are required; and the places at which and the times when these factors can be combined, which will not be specifically discussed here.

It is evident that these are mutually dependent factors, and that they all involve other executive functions which we shall discuss later. So far as the *scheme* of the organization is separately attacked, it is always on the assumption that it is then the strategic factor, the other factors of organization remaining fixed for the time being; but since the underlying purpose of any change in a scheme of organization is to affect these other factors as a whole favorably, any scheme of organization at any given time represents necessarily a result of previous successive approximations through a period of time. It has always necessarily been attacked on the basis of the present situation.

B. Personnel

The scheme of organization is dependent not only upon the general factors of the organization as a whole, but likewise, as we have indicated, on the availability of various kinds of services for the executive positions. This becomes in its turn the strategic factor. In general, the principles of the economy of incentives apply here as well as to other more general personnel problems. The balance of factors and the technical problems of this special class, however, are not only different from those generally to be found in other spheres of organization economy but are highly special in different types of organizations.

The most important single contribution required of the executive, certainly the most universal qualification, is loyalty, domination by the organization personality. This is the first necessity because the lines of communication cannot function at all unless the personal contributions of executives will be present at the required positions, at the times necessary, without default for ordinary personal reasons. This, as a personal qualification, is known in secular organizations as the quality of "responsibility"; in political organization as "regularity"; in governmental organizations as fealty or loyalty; in religious organizations as "complete submission" to the faith and to the hierarchy of objective religious authority.

The contribution of personal loyalty and submission is least susceptible to tangible inducements. It cannot be bought either by material inducements or by other positive incentives, except all other things be equal. This is as true of industrial organizations, I believe, as of any others. It is rather generally understood that although money or other material inducements must usually be paid to responsible persons, responsibility itself does not arise from such inducements.

However, love of prestige is, in general, a much more important inducement in the case of executives than with the rest of the personnel. Interest in work and pride in organization are other incentives that usually must be present. These facts are much obscured as respects commercial organizations, where material inducements appear to be the effective factors partly because such inducements are more readily offered in such organizations and partly because, since the other incentives are often equal as between such organizations, material inducements are the only available differential factor. It also becomes an important secondary factor to individuals in many cases, because prestige and official responsibilities impose heavy material burdens on them. Hence neither churches nor socialistic states have been able to escape the necessity of direct or indirect material inducements for high dignitaries or officials. But this is probably incidental and superficial in all organizations. It appears to be true that in all of them adequate incentives to executive services are difficult to offer. Those most available in the present age are tangible, materialistic; but on the whole they are both insufficient and often abortive.[1]

Following loyalty, responsibility, and capacity to be dominated by or-

[1] After much experience, I am convinced that the most ineffective services in a continuing effort are in one sense those of volunteers, or of semi-volunteers; for example, half-pay workers. What appears to be inexpensive is in fact very expensive, because non-material incentives—such as prestige, toleration of too great personal interest in the work with its accompanying fads and "pet" projects, the yielding to exaggerated conceptions of individual importance—are causes of internal friction and many other undesirable consequences. Yet in many emergency situations, and in a large part of political, charitable, civic, educational, and religious organization work, often indispensable services cannot be obtained by material incentives.

ganization personality, come the more specific personal abilities. They are roughly divided into two classes: relative general abilities, involving general alertness, comprehensiveness of interest, flexibility, faculty of adjustment, poise, courage, etc.; and specialized abilities based on particular aptitudes and acquired techniques. The first kind is relatively difficult to appraise because it depends upon innate characteristics developed through general experience. It is not greatly susceptible of immediate inculcation. The second kind may be less rare because the division of labor, that is, organization itself, fosters it automatically, and because it is susceptible to development (at a cost) by training and education. We deliberately and more and more turn out specialists; but we do not develop general executives well by specific efforts, and we know very little about how to do it.

The higher the positions in the line of authority, the more general the abilities required. The scarcity of such abilities, together with the necessity for keeping the lines of authority as short as feasible, controls the organization of executive work. It leads to the reduction of the number of formally executive positions to the minimum, a measure made possible by creating about the executives in many cases staffs of specialists who supplement them in time, energy, and technical capacities. This is made feasible by elaborate and often delicate arrangements to correct error resulting from the faults of over-specialization and the paucity of line executives.

The operation of such systems of complex executive organization requires the highest development of the executive arts. Its various forms and techniques are most definitely exemplified in the armies and navies of the major powers, the Postal Administrations of several European countries, the Bell Telephone System, some of the great railway systems, and the Catholic Church; and perhaps in the political organization of the British Empire.[2] One of the first limitations of world-wide or even a much more restricted international organization is the necessity for the development of these forms and techniques far beyond their present status.

Thus, jointly with the development of the scheme of organization, the selection, promotion, demotion, and dismissal of men becomes the essence of maintaining the system of communication without which no organization can exist. The selection in part, but especially the promotion, demotion, and dismissal of men, depend upon the exercise of supervision or what is often called "control."

Control relates directly, and in conscious application chiefly, to the work of the organization as a whole rather than to the work of executives as such. But so heavily dependent is the success of cooperation upon the

[2] From a structural point of view the organization of the United States of America is especially noteworthy, but from the viewpoint of the executive functions it is intended to be defective; that is, the system of States Rights or dual sovereignty and the separation of legislative, judicial, and executive departments precludes a common center of authoritative communication in American government as a formal organization. It is intended or expected that the requirements will be met by informal organization.

functioning of the executive organization that practically the control is over executives for the most part. If the work of an organization is not successful, if it is inefficient, if it cannot maintain the services of its personnel, the conclusion is that its "management" is wrong; that is, that the scheme of communication or the associated personnel or both, that is, the executive department directly related, are at fault. This is, sometimes at least, not true, but often it is. Moreover, for the correction of such faults the first reliance is upon executive organization. The methods by which control is exercised are, of course, numerous and largely technical to each organization, and need not be further discussed here.

C. Informal executive organizations

So far we have considered the first executive function only as it relates to the formal communication system. It has been emphasized several times in this treatise that informal organization is essential to formal organizations, particularly with reference to communication. This is true not only of the organization as a whole, or of its ultimate subordinate units, but also of that special part which we call the executive organization. The communication function of executives includes the maintenance of informal executive organization as an essential means of communication.

Although I have never heard it stated that this is an executive function or that such a thing as an informal executive organization exists, in all the good organizations I have observed the most careful attention is paid to it. In all of them informal organizations operate. This is usually not apparent except to those directly concerned.

The general method of maintaining an informal executive organization is so to operate and to select and promote executives that a general condition of compatibility of personnel is maintained. Perhaps often and certainly occasionally men cannot be promoted or selected, or even must be relieved, because they cannot function, because they "do not fit," where there is no question of formal competence. This question of "fitness" involves such matters as education, experience, age, sex, personal distinctions, prestige, race, nationality, faith, politics, sectional antecedents; and such very specific personal traits as manners, speech, personal appearance, etc. It goes by few if any rules, except those based at least nominally on other, formal considerations. It represents in its best sense the political aspects of personal relationship in formal organization. I suspect it to be most highly developed in political, labor, church, and university organizations, for the very reason that the intangible types of personal services are relatively more important in them than in most other, especially industrial, organizations. But it is certainly of major importance in all organizations.

This compatibility is promoted by educational requirements (armies, navies, churches, schools); by requirement of certain background (European armies, navies, labor unions, Soviet and Fascist governments, political parties); by conferences and conventions; by specifically social activities; by class distinctions connected with privileges and "authority" (in armies, navies, churches, universities). A certain conformity is required by unwritten understanding that can sometimes be formally enforced, expressed for its negative aspect by the phrase "conduct unbecoming a gentleman and an officer." There are, however, innumerable other processes, many of which are not consciously employed for this purpose.

It must not be understood that the desired degree of compatibility is always the same or is the maximum possible. On the contrary it seems to me to be often the case that excessive compatibility or harmony is deleterious, resulting in "single track minds" and excessively crystallized attitudes and in the destruction of personal responsibility; but I know from experience in operating with new emergency organizations, in which there was no time and little immediate basis for the growth of an informal organization properly coordinated with formal organization that it is almost impossible to secure effective and efficient cooperation without it.

The functions of informal executive organizations are the communication of intangible facts, opinions, suggestions, suspicions, that cannot pass through formal channels without raising issues calling for decisions, without dissipating dignity and objective authority, and without overloading executive positions; also to minimize excessive cliques of political types arising from too great divergence of interests and views; to promote self-discipline of the group; and to make possible the development of important personal influences in the organization. There are probably other functions.

I shall comment on only two functions of informal executive organization. The necessity for avoiding formal issues, that is, for avoiding the issuance of numerous formal orders except on routine matters and except in emergencies, is important.[3] I know of major executives who issue an order or judgment settling an important issue rather seldom, although they are functioning all the time. The obvious desire of politicians to avoid important issues (and to impose them on their opponents) is based upon a thorough sense of organization. Neither authority nor cooperative disposition (largely the same things) will stand much overt division on formal issues in the present stage of human development. Hence most laws, executive orders, decisions, etc., are in effect formal notice that all is well—there is agreement, authority is not questioned.

The question of personal influence is very subtle. Probably most good

[3] When writing these lines I tried to recall an important general decision made by me on my initiative as a telephone executive within two years. I could recall none, although on reviewing the record I found several. On the other hand, I can still recall without any record many major decisions made by me "out of hand" when I was a Relief Administrator. I probably averaged at least five a day for eighteen months. In the latter case I worked with a very noble group but a very poor informal organization under emergency conditions.

organizations have somewhere a Colonel House; and many men not only exercise beneficent influence far beyond that implied by their formal status, but most of them, at the time, would lose their influence if they had corresponding formal status. The reason may be that many men have personal qualifications of high order that will not operate under the stress of commensurate official responsibility. By analogy I may mention the golfers of first class skill who cannot "stand up" in public tournaments.

To summarize: the first executive function is to develop and maintain a system of communication. This involves jointly a scheme of organization and an executive personnel. The processes by which the latter is accomplished include chiefly the selection of men and the offering of incentives; techniques of control permitting effectiveness in promoting, demoting, and dismissing men; and finally the securing of an informal organization in which the essential property is compatibility of personnel. The chief functions of this informal organization are expansion of the means of communication with reduction in the necessity for formal decisions, the minimizing of undesirable influences, and the promotion of desirable influences concordant with the scheme of formal responsibilities.

II. The Securing of Essential Services from Individuals

The second function of the executive organization is to promote the securing of the personal services that constitute the material of organizations.

The work divides into two main divisions: (a) the bringing of persons into cooperative relationship with the organization; (b) the eliciting of the services after such persons have been brought into that relationship.

A. The characteristic fact of the first division is that the organization is acting upon persons who are in every sense outside it. Such action is necessary not merely to secure the personnel of new organizations, or to supply the material for the growth of existing organizations, but also to replace the losses that continually take place by reason of death, resignation, "backsliding," emigration, discharge, excommunication, ostracism. These factors of growth or replacement of contributors require bringing persons by organization effort within range of the consideration of the incentives available in order to induce some of these persons to attach themselves to the organization. Accordingly the task involves two parts: (a) bringing persons within reach of specific effort to secure services, and (b) the application of that effort when they have been brought near enough. Often both parts of the task occupy the efforts of the same persons or parts of an organization; but they are clearly distinct elements and considerable specialization is found with respect to them.

(a) Bringing persons within reach of recruiting or proselyting influence is a task which differs in practical emphasis among organizations in respect both to scope and to method. Some religious organizations—especially the Catholic Church, several Protestant Churches, the Mormon Church, for example—have as ideal goals the attachment of all persons to their organizations, and the wide world is the field of proselyting propaganda. During many decades the United States of America invited all who could reach its shores to become American citizens. Other organizations, having limits on the volume of their activities, restrict the field of propaganda. Thus many nations in effect now restrict substantial growth to those who acquire a national status by birth; the American Legion restricts its membership to those who have acquired a status by a certain type of previous service, etc. Others restrict their fields practically on the basis of proportions. Thus universities "in principle" are open to all or to all with educational and character qualifications but may restrict their appeals to geographical, racial, and class proportions, so as to preserve the cosmopolitan character of their bodies, or to preserve predominance of nationals, etc. Industrial and commercial organizations are theoretically limited usually by considerations of social compatibility and additionally by the costs of propaganda. They usually attempt no appeal when the geographic remoteness makes it ineffective.

Although the scope of the field of propaganda is for most organizations not clearly conceived or stated and as a problem only requires active consideration at intervals usually long, the question is nevertheless fundamental. This is best indicated by the methods practically employed in connection with it. In churches the organization of mission work and its territorial scope are the best indications of its importance. In most governments, at present, the accretion of members takes the form of stimulating reproduction by active promotional efforts, as in France and Italy, for example, or by the ease of acquiring citizenship and free land, as until recently in the United States. In many industrial organizations foreign recruiting was once an important aspect of their work, and directly or indirectly the appeal for contributors of capital or credit has been fundamentally international in scope until recent exchange restrictions. In fact, the most universal aspect of industrial organization appeal has been in respect to this type of contributor—for many practical purposes he is not usually regarded as the material of organization, though in the present study he is.

(b) The effort to induce specific persons who by the general appeal are brought into contact with an organization actually to become identified with it constitutes the more regular and routine work of securing contributors. This involves in its general aspects the method of persuasion which has already been described, the establishment of inducements and incentives, and direct negotiation. The methods required are indefinitely large in number and of very wide variety.[4] Fundamentally, most persons

---

[4] I must repeat that although the emphasis is on the employee group of contributors, so far as industrial organizations are concerned, nevertheless, "customers" are equally included. The principles broadly discussed here relate to salesmanship as well as employing persons.

potentially available are not susceptible at any given time of being induced to give service to any particular organization, large or small.

B. Although the work of recruiting is important in most organizations, and especially so in those which are new or rapidly expanding or which have high "turnover," nevertheless in established and enduring organizations the eliciting of the quantity and quality of efforts from their adherents is usually more important and occupies the greater part of personnel effort. Because of the more tangible character of "membership," being an "employee" etc., recruiting is apt to receive more attention as a field of personnel work than the business of promoting the actual output of efforts and influences, which are the real material of organization.[5] Membership, nominal adherence, is merely the starting point; and the minimum contributions which can be conceived as enabling retention of such connection would generally be insufficient for the survival of active or productive organization. Hence every church, every government, every other important organization, has to intensify or multiply the contributions which its members will make above the level or volume which would occur if no such effort were made. Thus churches must strengthen the faith, secure compliance by public and private acknowledgments of faith or devotion, and secure material contributions from their members. Governments are concerned with increasing the quality of the citizenry—promoting national solidarity, loyalty, patriotism, discipline, and competence. Other organizations are similarly occupied in securing loyalty, reliability, responsibility, enthusiasm, quality of efforts, output. In short, every organization to survive must deliberately attend to the maintenance and growth of its authority to do the things necessary for coordination, effectiveness, and efficiency. This, as we have seen, depends upon its appeal to persons who are already related to the organization.

The methods, the inducements and incentives, by which this is done have already been in general indicated in our discussion of incentives and authority. As executive functions they may be distinguished as the maintenance of morale, the maintenance of the scheme of inducements, the maintenance of schemes of deterrents, supervision and control, inspection, education and training.

III. The Formulation of Purpose and Objectives

The third executive function is to formulate and define the purposes, objectives, ends of the organization. It has already been made clear that, strictly speaking, purpose is defined more nearly by the aggregate of action taken than by any formulation in words; but that the aggregate of action is a residuum of the decisions relative to purpose and the environment, re-

---

[5] As an instance, note the great attention in civil service regulations, and also in political appointments, to obtaining and retaining employment, and the relatively small attention to services.

sulting in closer and closer approximations to the concrete acts. It has also been emphasized that purpose is something that must be accepted by all the contributors to the system of efforts. Again, it has been stated that purpose must be broken into fragments, specific objectives, not only ordered in time so that detailed purpose and detailed action follow in the series of progressive cooperation, but also ordered contemporaneously into the specializations—geographical, social, and functional—that each unit organization implies. It is more apparent here than with other executive functions that it is an entire executive organization that formulates, redefines, breaks into details, and decides on the innumerable simultaneous and progressive actions that are the stream of syntheses constituting purpose or action. No single executive can under any conditions accomplish this function alone, but only that part of it which relates to his position in the executive organization.

Hence the critical aspect of this function is the assignment of responsibility—the delegation of objective authority. Thus in one sense this function is that of the scheme of positions, the system of communication, already discussed. That is its potential aspect. Its other aspect is the actual decisions and conduct which make the scheme a working system. Accordingly, the general executive states that "this is the purpose, this the objective, this the direction, in general terms, in which we wish to move before next year." His department heads, or the heads of his main territorial divisions say to their departments or suborganizations: "This means for us these things now, then others next month, then others later, to be better defined after experience." Their subdepartment or division heads say: "This means for us such and such operations now at these places, such others at those places, something today here, others tomorrow there." Then district or bureau chiefs in turn become more and more specific, their sub-chiefs still more so as to place, group, time, until finally purpose is merely jobs, specific groups, definite men, definite times, accomplished results. But meanwhile, back and forth, up and down, the communications pass, reporting obstacles, difficulties, impossibilities, accomplishments; redefining, modifying purposes level after level.

Thus the organization for the definition of purpose is the organization for the specification of work to do; and the specifications are made in their final stage when and where the work is being done. I suspect that at least nine-tenths of all organization activity is on the responsibility, the authority, and the specifications of those who make the last contributions, who apply personal energies to the final concrete objectives. There is no meaning to personal specialization, personal experience, personal training, personal location, personal ability, eyes and ears, arms and legs, brains and emotions, if this is not so. What must be added to the indispensable authority, responsibility, and capability of each contributor is the indispensible coordination. This requires a pyramiding of the formulation of purpose that becomes more and more general as the number of units of basic organization becomes larger, and more and more remote in future time. Responsibility for abstract, generalizing, prospective, long-run decision is delegated up the line; responsibility for definition, action remains always at the base where the authority for effort resides.

The formulation and definition of purpose is then a widely distributed function, only the more general part of which is executive. In this fact lies the most important inherent difficulty in the operation of cooperative systems—the necessity for indoctrinating those at the lower levels with general purposes, the major decisions, so that they remain cohesive and able to make the ultimate detailed decisions coherent; and the necessity, for those at the higher levels, of constantly understanding the concrete conditions and the specific decisions of the "ultimate" contributors from which and from whom executives are often insulated. Without that up-and-down-the-line coordination of purposeful decisions, general decisions and general purposes are mere intellectual processes in an organization vacuum, insulated from realities by layers of misunderstanding. The function of formulating grand purposes and providing for their redefinition is one which needs sensitive systems of communication, experience in interpretation, imagination, and delegation of responsibility.

Perhaps there are none who could consider even so extremely condensed and general a description of the executive functions as has here been presented without perceiving that these functions are merely elements in an organic whole. It is their combination in a working system that makes an organization.

This combination involves two opposite incitements to action. First, the concrete interaction and mutual adjustment of the executive functions are partly to be determined by the factors of the environment of the organization—the specific cooperative system as a whole and its environment. This involves fundamentally the logical processes of analysis and the discrimination of the strategic factors. Second, the combination equally depends upon the maintenance of the vitality of action—the will to effort. This is the moral aspect, the element of morale, the ultimate reason for cooperation.

14. Marginal Men of Industry: The Foreman

Donald E. Wray

In the voluminous literature on first-line supervision in industry there are two major concepts which have been used repeatedly in sociological writing and in the technical literature of personnel and business administration. The first is that of the supervisor or foreman as the first point in a clear-cut "line of authority" extending from the worker to the highest executive, thus playing the part of the "key men of management," "the firing line in union-management relations," and "the most important link between management and the worker." This concept, variously expressed, rests on the assumption of a unitary system of control and two-way communication; it is at once an ideal and an assumed norm of industrial organization. It minimizes or ignores the impact of managerial specialization and worker unionization.

A second concept, arising from interest in deviations from the normative "line" concept, views the first-line supervisor as "the man in the middle." Emphasis is placed on the fact that first-level management is subject to two sets of demands which are frequently in conflict; the foreman must satisfy both top management and his work force, which is usually organized. The "man in the middle" interpretation is historical in that it stresses the progressive limitations placed on foremen through the growth of managerial specialization and the increasing pressure of worker unions. Supervision is considered as still within the traditional line organization but operating under severe restrictions.

It is the purpose of this paper to re-examine these interpretations and to suggest an alternative formulation of the position of industrial foremen. Neither concept seems to describe the functions and informal interpretations of supervision which the writer has observed in a number of factories. A few circumstances appear to be of major importance in understanding the role of first-line supervisors; the locus of the decision-making or managerial function; the focal points of union-management and employer-employee relations; the significance of size and complexity in management organization. The last-named has often been used to explain the decline in importance of the foreman in large-scale manufacturing enterprise. Many levels of supervision and the presence of many specialized staff departments restrict the power and authority of the foreman; they also tend to make relationships impersonal and indirect. The converse of this theory would be

Reprinted from the *American Journal of Sociology*, 54 (January, 1949), 298-301.

that foremen in smaller, less formal structures retain their broad powers over shop affairs and therefore are of considerable importance in managerial activity and in worker-management relations.

Unionization of the rank and file is commonly regarded as further limiting the supervisor's freedom of action and as setting up a type of relation between worker and management which parallels, and often conflicts with, the relationship established through the "line." Top management generally takes the position that, in the presence of a union, the foreman is still the primary representative of management, especially with reference to management policy and grievance procedure.

The role of foremen in managerial activity has been the subject of much discussion in recent years. Top management holds that the foreman plays an important part in decision-making, while the Foremen's Association of America states that foremen are mere "representatives of management" and have no power to make decisions. Restated, the question is whether foremen are active participants in managerial decision-making activity or are simply transmitters of these decisions. Here again the size of a given organization has been considered important, on the assumption that, with increased numbers of persons and a lengthened "line" organization, the share of foremen in decisions will be made smaller. Here, too, the converse would seem to be that, the smaller the organization, the greater the degree of integration of supervisors with active management.

Two cases are presented which afford comparison between a formalized plant with staff specialization and a small factory with a minimum of departmentalization. They are representative of many other factories and are not unusual in the degree of management specialization, efficiency, or disorganization, nor are they instances of exaggerated union-management cooperation or conflict. Both cases were observed in their day-to-day operations over several months to ascertain the actual patterns of behavior of supervisors, union officials, and top management.

The first is a plant which is part of a network of factories operated by a single company. While it had only six hundred employees, it was highly formalized, and staff functions were well developed, so that it possessed the organizational characteristics of larger factories. There were five levels of supervision: general manager, department manager, department superintendent, foreman, and assistant foreman. Operations were highly mechanized, and the flow of materials between departments required good coordination. Consequently the work schedules and techniques demanded planning and engineering.

The rank-and-file union had a company-wide contract with local supplementary agreements. Daily contact between union and management occurred through the grievance process and through a union-management committee which met every two weeks. Grievances supposedly started with the foreman and passed to higher levels. In practice the foreman usually sent a grievance directly to his department superintendent, since "there is no point in bothering with something you can't do anything about." The foremen did handle requests for information, requisitions for equipment, and some personal matters.

Grievances which required technical or policy statements were passed on by department superintendents to department managers and then to the union-management committee. This body included department managers, the personnel director and occasionally another staff head, and the union stewards and officials. In the committee grievances were settled and plant policies and plans were developed and interpreted. All union representatives had firsthand knowledge of committee decisions and were active participants; no foreman had ever attended, and department superintendents came only rarely.

The foremen entered into hiring and firing only through the reports they made of worker performance; the power lay in the department superintendent and the personnel department. The supervisors kept records on productions and worker assignment and had little other function.

The second example is a small factory of seventy-five employees, run by an owner-manager who personified the functions of management. Rudimentary staff activities were performed by a small clerical force which had no real specialized authority. Supervision below the manager was vested in a shop manager and first-line supervisors. Organization, policies, and communication were less formalized than in the first case, though the line concept was present. The concentration of management functions in one person not only eliminated staff departments but reduced the amount of authority delegated to the line.

The union-management relation was defined in an industry-wide contract written by the international union and a manufacturer's association, with local supplements. Grievances and policy discussions were taken up by stewards and officers of the union with the owner-manager and occasionally with the shop manager. The supervisors were not included in any negotiations and were considered unimportant by both parties. The workers and their representatives looked on supervisors as either well-meaning people who had no power or as trouble makers who could be "straightened out" by consultation with top management.

The supervisors were limited to training, checking on work flow, reporting operating procedures, and keeping the necessary records. Hiring and firing and disciplinary problems were handled by the shop manager.

Comparing these two cases, it seems that in neither instance did the first-line supervisors enter into decision-making. In the larger factory managerial activity was vested in the higher levels of supervision in combination with the heads of various staff units. In the small factory the concentration of authority in one person led naturally to the exclusion of the supervisors.

In both cases the foremen were reduced to the role of transmitter or interpreter to the rank and file. The significance of specialization as an element in reducing the power of supervisors has been fully recognized, but the concentrated authority of the owner-manager in small organizations has not been sufficiently emphasized. This tendency appears to counteract the relative absence of staff controls and is just as effective in relegating supervisors to a nonmanagerial position. The locus of decision-making lies either in the owner-manager (in the small enterprise) or in a group of higher-level supervisors in the large organizations.

In each case the contribution of the foreman to union-management relations appears to be a passive one. The real issues are settled between union representatives and higher management, and the foreman is expected simply to conform to the joint decisions of these representatives. In both cases, the foreman is subject to pressure from either union or management, but ultimately, when agreement is reached, he must follow the joint decision. Action by an individual foreman, which is rejected by workers is viewed, not as a threat to union-management relations, but as a problem to be settled by joint deliberation of union and management representatives—unless it is taken up to illustrate a general issue. The foreman must be viewed as the recipient of union-management agreement or conflict rather than as a positive contributor to union-management relations. This passivity differs sharply from the traditional assumption that the foreman is an active force in determining this relation.

In both these instances the workers were organized. It is likely that, in cases where the rank and file are not organized, the foreman can play a more important role in employer-employee affairs. In the absence of a union, the relation between worker and management resembles the personnel relation, and the foreman can implement personnel policies with considerable freedom. Under these circumstances first-line supervision can be of great importance in deciding employer-employee relations. Where unionization has occurred, however, the foreman cannot exert much influence on the bargaining relation, though he may implement some personnel policies. Here he is usually limited by the direct activity of the personnel department.

Since the general pattern of union-management relations, and in many cases the day-to-day differences, are settled by top management without the inclusion of first-line supervisors, it seems that it is entirely erroneous to view the foreman as the "key man" in this relation. He is rather a person who enters secondarily as the implementor of policies which have already been decided, and his success or failure depends on his ability to act on them, instead of on his own positive actions. Any deviation from union-management decisions will bring forth censure from one or both sides, but in no case can the supervisor himself enter into the formulation of the rules under which he works. This activity is vested in the union officials and higher management. The supervisor gets criticism from both management and union, but he is pushed aside when decisions are to be made.

It is also important to note that in larger organizations the decision-making function tends to reside, not in any line supervisor but in a group of persons representing the various specialized functions of management. In many cases this entire group meets when union-management negotiations are to take place. The simple unitary line breaks down and is replaced by a committee type of organization. This same tendency has been noted at the foreman level and was deliberately arranged by Fayol in his famous experiment with "functional foremen." First-level supervision still in most cases requires the co-ordination of several functions; this is more effectively and efficiently accomplished by one person than by several. However, it is questionable whether the functions which are so correlated are any more important than those which might be delegated to any minor staff employee. In many instances it seems that the lowest line supervisor is of no greater importance than many staff members; in other words, the first level of supervision is no longer a position of special importance.

This discussion suggests that neither the conception of the foreman which insists that he is an integral part of the "line," nor the suggestive phrase, "the man in the middle," indicates accurately the nature of the difficulties of his position. The foreman, as is shown in these two instances, is less than a full member of the management line; he shares with those higher up the responsibility for carrying out policies but does not share in the making of them. Furthermore, his position differs from theirs in that those higher up give orders to people who are indentified with management, while the essence of the foreman's job is that he must transmit them to people who are clearly not of management. In short, the position of foreman has some of the characteristics of management positions but lacks other crucial ones. Such marginal positions are common in society, and there is reason to believe that they are especially difficult to occupy effectively and with peace of mind. With respect to management, the foreman's position is peripheral rather than in the middle. The poor fellow is in the middle, of course, in the sense that a person may be the middle one of three in a bed; he gets it from both sides!

It is characteristic of such marginal positions that the people who occupy them consider that they are special victims of the disparity between social norms and social reality. Foremen express this in the phrase, "They say we are part of management, but they don't treat us that way." The implication is that they feel pressed to live up to the role of members of management, without being given the reward of full participation. This is a common feeling of people in "minority" or "marginal" positions. It presents them with a dilemma which results in a good deal of personal conflict. Sometimes they attempt to solve the conflict, individually or collectively, by defiantly adopting an alternative role; in the case of the foreman, that of the worker who may organize a union for bargaining with management. In at least one instance known to me the presentation to foremen of a training course was an important factor in precipitating the organization of a fore-men's union. The course emphasized their importance to and identification with management, thereby sharpening the foremen's consciousness of the cleavage between the expected norm held before them and the realities of their experience.

15. The New Office

C. Wright Mills

The modern office with its tens of thousands of square feet and its factory-like flow of work is not an informal, friendly place. The drag and beat of work, the "production unit" tempo, require that time consumed by anything but business at hand be explained and apologized for. Dictation was once a private meeting of executive and secretary. Now the executive phones a pool of dictaphone transcribers whom he never sees and who know him merely as a voice. Many old types of personnel have become machine operators, many new types began as machine operators.

I. The rise of the office manager, from a "chief clerk" to a responsible executive reporting directly to the company treasurer or vice president, is an obvious index to the enlargement of offices and to the rise of the office as a centralized service division of the entire enterprise. It is under him that the factory-like office has been developing. Specializing as he does in the rational and efficient design and service of office functions, the office manager can obviously do a better job than a detached minor supervisor.

The office manager had begun to appear in the larger companies by the late twenties. Many early office managers were "detail men" holding other positions, perhaps in the accounting department, but at the same time "handling" the office force. But as the office increased in importance and in costs, it grew into an autonomous unit and the office manager grew with it. He had to know the clerical work and the routing of all departments; he had to be able to design and to adapt to new administrative schemes and set-ups; he had to train new employees and retrain old ones. The all-company scope of his domain gave room for his knowledge and prestige to increase, or at least his claims for prestige *vis-à-vis* "other department heads." By 1929, about one-third of one large group of office managers came from non-office executive positions, whereas half worked up through the office, and some 17 per cent came up through other offices, so that one may assume the position already had a recognized status.

II. As office machinery is introduced, the number of routine jobs is increased, and consequently the proportion of "positions requiring initiative" is decreased. "Mechanization is resulting in a much clearer distinction between the managing staff and the operating staff," observed the War

From *White Collar: The American Middle Class* by C. Wright Mills. Copyright 1951 by Oxford University Press, Inc. Reprinted by permission.

Manpower Commission. "Finger dexterity is often more important than creative thinking. Promotions consequently become relatively rare. . . . Some large office managers actually prefer to hire girls who are content to remain simply clerks, who will attempt to rise no higher than their initial level."

As we compare the personnel of the new office with that of the old, it is the mass of clerical machine-operatives that immediately strikes us. They are the most factory-like operatives in the white-collar worlds. The period of time required to learn their skills seems steadily to decline; it must, in fact, if the expense of introducing machines and new standardized specializations is to be justified. For the key advantages of most mechanical and centralizing office devices are that, while they permit greater speed and accuracy, they also require cheaper labor per unit, less training, simpler specialization, and thus replaceable employees.

These interchangeable clerks often punch a time clock, are not allowed to talk during working hours, and have no tenure of employment beyond a week or sometimes a month. They typically have no contact with supervisors except in the course of being supervised. In large offices these people are the major links in the system, but in their minds and in those of their managers, there is rarely any serious thought of learning the whole system and rising within it. Even in the middle twenties 88 per cent of the office managers questioned in one survey indicated that they definitely needed people "who give little promise of rising to an executive status," and 60 per cent stated that there was "very little opportunity" in their office to learn, and hence rise, by apprenticeship.

The rationalization of the office, on the one hand, attracts and creates a new mass of clerks and machine operators, and their work increasingly approximates the factory operative in light manufacturing. On the other hand, this new office requires the office manager, a specialized manager who operates the human machinery.

III. The bookkeeper has been grievously affected by the last half century of office change: his old central position is usurped by the office manager, and even the most experienced bookkeeper with pen and ink cannot compete with a high-school girl trained in three or four months to use a machine. It is like a pick and shovel against a power scoop.

The bookkeeping or billing machine posts, enters, totals, and balances; from the accumulated postings control accounts are made up. And such a machine is a simple sort of apparatus, although it is still second only to the typewriter in offices today. Other new machines displace ten of the old, and their operatives, at one stroke. Just as the high-school girl with her machine has displaced the pen-and-ink bookkeeper, so the big new machines promise, in due course, to displace the high-school girl. At the top of the new "bookkeeping" world are the professional accountants and electronic technicians. But their predominance on any practical scale is still largely to come. In the meantime, the stratum of older bookkeepers is demoted to the level of the clerical mass.

"When recruiting new employees for this operation," says the manager of a bookkeeping operation in a large company, "we seek girls about seventeen years minimum age, at least two years' high school or its equivalent, with no previous business experience and good personal qualifications. We prefer inexperienced girls and those who have some economic incentive to work as we have found they make the steadiest workers; so we select from our recruits what we classify as the semi-dependent or wholly dependent applicant. . . ."

IV. The secretary has been the model of aspiration for most office girls. The typewriter has, of course, been the woman's machine, and in itself it has not led to factory-like effects. In and out of the office world, it has been a highly respectable machine. Its operator, equipped with stenographer's pad, has managed to borrow prestige from her close and private contact with the executive.

The standard girl-hierarchy in offices has been formed around the typewriter in the following way: (1) The private secretary, as someone's confidential assistant, in many cases can actually act for him on many not always routine matters. She takes care of his appointments, his daily schedule, his check book—is, in short, justifiably called his office wife. If her boss's office warrants it, she may even have stenographers and typists working for her. (2) The stenographer is a typist who also takes dictation. (3) The typist works only with the machine; because her work is a straight copying matter, her most important traits are speed and accuracy at the keyboard. Unlike the secretary, and to a lesser extent the stenographer, she is usually closely supervised.

In the new, rationalized office, this hierarchy—graded in income, skill, degree of supervision, and access to important persons—has begun to break down. There is now a strong tendency to limit the number of secretaries; many $15,000-a-year executives do not have private secretaries and never see a shorthand stenographer. Instead they dictate to a machine, whose cylinders go to a pool of typists. Although this pooling of stenographic services took place in many big offices before dictaphone equipment was installed, usually the two went together. Systematic studies clearly revealed the wastefulness of individually assigned stenographers, the alternate periods of slack and of frenzy rather than a smooth and efficient flow.

Since its beginnings in the twenties, the centralization of the stenographic operation has spread continuously, being limited only by size of office and inertia. The trend is for only the senior executives to have private secretaries and for both stenographers and typists to become pooled as transcribing typists. In one large insurance company's home office less than 2 per cent of the employees are assigned as secretaries to persons above the rank of Division Manager. The junior executive has his stenographer on his desk in a metal box, or may even dictate directly to the transcribing pool via inter-office telephone.

The centralized transcribing pool has further advantages: for the "poor dictator," the machines allow adjustments in audibility; they eliminate over-time imposed by late afternoon dictation, and also the strain of reading hurriedly written notes. "They hear it automatically and have only to punch the keys to get the results," the managerial literature states. "Girls with speed and accuracy" are what are wanted in the new office.

The skill of shorthand becomes obsolete; the white-collar girl becomes almost immediately replaceable; work in offices becomes increasingly a blind-alley. The new white-collar girl cannot know intimately some segment of the office or business, and has lost the private contact that gave status to the secretary and even the stenographer. The work is regulated so that it can be speeded up and effectively supervised by non-executive personnel. In short, the prized white-collar spot for women is becoming more and more the job of a factory-like operative. By the early thirties, Amy Hewes was ob-serving, "The shadowy line between many . . . clerical tasks and *unskilled* factory occupations is becoming more and more imperceptible."

The new office is rationalized: machines are used, employees become machine attendants; the work, as in the factory, is collective, not individual-ized; it is standardized for interchangeable, quickly replaceable clerks; it is specialized to the point of automatization. The employee group is trans-formed into a uniform mass in a soundless place, and the day itself is regulated by an impersonal time schedule. Seeing the big stretch of office space, with rows of identical desks, one is reminded of Herman Melville's description of a nineteenth-century factory: "At rows of blank-looking counters sat rows of blank-looking girls, with blank, white folders in their blank hands, all blankly folding blank paper."

The new office at once raises a hierarchy and levels out personnel. The hierarchy is based upon the power and authority held by the managerial cadre, rather than upon the levels of skill. The individual employee is a unit in an administrative hierarchy of authority and discipline, but he is also equal before it with many other employees. Within this hierarchy and mass, he is classified by the function he performs, but sometimes there are also "artificial" distinctions of status, position, and above all title. These dis-tinctions, to which Carl Dreyfuss has called attention, arise on the one hand from the employee's need to personalize a little area for himself, and on the other, they may be encouraged by management to improve morale and to discourage employee "solidarity."

In the enormous file, smaller hierarchies fit into larger ones and are interlinked in a dozen ways. There is a formal line-up expressed by titles, and beneath these, further gradations in status and rank. Rank does not always correspond to skill or salary level; in general, it is expressed in the authority to give orders. The managerial cadre, infiltrating all divisions and units, is the backbone of the hierarchy. Where one stands depends, first upon the extent to which one participates in the cadre's authority, and second, the closeness of one's association with its members. The private secretary of the top manager of a division may thus be superior in rank and status to the assistant manager of a division further down. Educational level and experience naturally lend status, but only secondarily. It is from the managerial cadre that esteem is derived and status borrowed.

If the white-collar hierarchy were purely bureaucratic it would be based upon sheer formal authority, as in an army; but actually, nowhere are bureaucratic principles of organization strictly carried through. Within and between offices, there is usually a system of cliques, which often cut across the formal line of authority and work. Through them "the man in the know" can cut red tape, and secretaries of top men, "administrative assistants" as they are called in Washington, can call other secretaries to expedite matters that would take much longer through the regular channels.

Status inside the hierarchy is not always in line with formal participation in management; a fictitious closeness to authority may bring prestige. Private secretaries, as well as other confidential assistants to managers, thus often stand out. Only in rare cases do they actively show or have authority, but their position requires close contact with authority and they handle and even help to shape its secrets. By inner identification, they often have a strong illusion of authority and, by outward manner, impress it on others. This is by no means discouraged by the managers, for the gap between the confidential employee and "the girls" is a guarantee of loyalty, and moreover a reciprocal influence in the increased prestige of the managers themselves. The scale of available beauty, for instance, may influence the selection as well as class factors—the Anglo-Saxon, upper middle-class girl having a better chance.

Those in intimate contact with authority form a sort of screen around the persons who carry it, insuring its privacy and hence heightening its prestige. In a great many offices and stores today the rank and file never see "the higher ups," but only their immediate supervisors, who are known as "the boss." Grievances and resentments are aimed at "the boss"; the "higher-ups" come within psychological view, if at all, only in fantasy: "If I could only get in contact with them, I know I'd be given my chance."

Titles and appurtenances, which are related in intricate ways to formal authority, are outward and crucial signs of status. To have a telephone on one's desk, to use one lavatory or another, to have one's name on the door or even on a placard on a desk—all such items can and do form the content of the employee's conscious striving and hope. A great deal has been made of such distinctions. Carl Dreyfuss alleged that they form "an artificial hierarchy" which is encouraged and exploited by the employer who does not wish solidarity. When many small gradations in status exist, the employee can more often experience the illusion of "being somebody" and of ascending the scale. Often "there are more rank than salary gradations but even the latter exceed the number of groupings actually required from a technical point of view."

But such distinctions, in so far as they are not based on work performed, fall, in time, before the cost-reduction drives of management and the egalitarian push of trade unions, which strive to classify jobs more systematically. According to this view, the norm of the "genuine" hierarchy is technical and economic, that is, strictly bureaucratic; but actually status elements are no more "artificial" than technical and economic ones. Differentiations do, of course, develop on status factors alone, and they are often of crucial, even overpowering importance in white-collar hierarchies. But the over-all trend is against them. Even though employers may try to exploit them to discourage solidarity, once a union tries to break the job divisions down and then to fight for corresponding income gradations, employers are usually ready to level out status differences in order to lower costs.

Only a sophisticated employer strongly beleaguered by attempted unionization might see reasons to make conscious use of prestige gradations. It would not, however, seem the most rational choice he might make and, in fact, the employer has been the leader of job descriptions and personnel work that reduce the number of complex functions and break down the work and hence lower pay. Machines implement and prompt such strict technical and bureaucratic gradation. And certainly, even if the artificial hierarchy has been used as a manner of control, rationalization and mechnization are now well on their way to destroy such schemes.

Mechanized and standardized work, the decline of any chance for the employee to see and understand the whole operation, the loss of any chance, save for a very few, for private contact with those in authority—these form the model of the future. At present, status complications inside office and store are still often quite important in the psychology of the employee; but, in the main drift, technical and economic factors and the authoritative line-up will gain ascendency over such status factors as now interfere with the rationalization of the white-collar hierarchy.

16. The Man on the Assembly Line

Charles R. Walker
Robert H. Guest

There are a lot of good things about my job. The pay is good. I've got seniority. The working conditions are pretty good for my type of work. But that's not the whole story. . . . You can't beat the machine. They have you clocked to a fraction of a second. My job is engineered, and the jigs and fixtures are all set out according to specifications. The foreman is an all right guy, but he gets pushed, so he pushes us. The guy on the line has no one to push. You can't fight that iron horse.
Worker on an assembly line, interviewed by the authors.

Machines alone do not give us mass production. Mass production is achieved by both machines *and* men. And while we have gone a long way toward perfecting our mechanical operations, we have not successfully written into our equation whatever complex factors represent man, the human element.
Henry Ford II, in a talk before the American Society of Mechanical Engineers, shortly after he was made President of the Ford Motor Company.

The principal social and psychological problems connected with mass production and human nature have been stated many times and in many different forms. Their importance in an age of advancing technology is hardly in dispute. The question has become rather: What shall we do about them?

Here are a few of the common problems. Since individuals react very differently to industrial occupations, what are the personality characteristics of those who adjust quickly to—and appear to thrive on—mechanically paced and repetitive jobs? What, on the other hand, are the personality characteristics of those who suffer mentally and physically on such jobs—and who therefore tend to perform them badly? Can the adjustment problem, in other words, be solved by selection? Or is the modern work environment simply *wrong* for the normal human being?

Or to take an engineering and management approach: In the present state of the mechanical arts, what part of a worker's skill and power can the engineer build into a machine? What must he leave out? Precisely how and to what extent in the most mechanized sectors of our economy does the human equation still affect quantity and quality?

Or again, granted that the principles of mass production such as break-

Reprinted from *Harvard Business Review*, **30** (May-June, 1952), 71-83.

down of jobs into their simplest constituent parts are sound and vital to efficient manufacture, have we yet found how to combine these principles with equally well authenticated principles of human behavior?

Or taking still another approach, if a man spends a third of his life in direct contact with a mass-production environment, why should we not consider important (to him and to society) the hours of living time he spends inside the factory—as important and valuable, for example, as the product he produces which is consumed outside the factory? We talk of a high standard of living, but frequently we mean a high standard of consumption. Man consumes in his leisure, yet fulfills himself not only in his leisure but in his work. Is our mass-production work environment making such fulfillment more difficult?

A short way to sum up these and a great many more questions is: To what degree can—or should—men be "adjusted" to the new environment of machines, and to what degree is it possible to adjust or rebuild that environment to fit the needs and personalities of men?

Need For Systematic Study

Despite the tremendous contribution of mass-production methods to the productiveness of the economic system under which we live, and notwithstanding the fact that editors, philosophers, and propagandists have long speculated and written about the beneficent or injurious effects of highly mechanized jobs on human behavior, there has been singularly little systematic effort to discover "whatever complex factors represent man, the human element" in the mass-production method as such. The relatively small number of studies which have been made of assembly-line and other types of repetitive work have been mostly laboratory experiments, not explorations of experience in actual industrial plants.

A notable exception is the series of monographs which for some 25 years have been published from time to time under the auspices of the British Medical Council on the effects of mechanization and the repetitive job on productivity and *mental* fatigue. Even these, however, have only touched occasionally on the subject of assembly lines, and have never at all —to the best of our knowledge—dealt specifically with that advanced sector of a mass-production economy, the final assembly line of a plant making a large, complex product like automobiles.

Survey of automobile assembly plant

For these reasons the authors undertook two years ago an exploratory survey of a modern automobile assembly plant.[1] This is intended as the first of a

[1] The full details of this survey are being published in book form, *The Man on the Assembly Line*, by the Harvard University Press (June, 1952).

series of studies designed to define more clearly the several "human equations" involved in assembly work, to prepare and sharpen tools of research, and to look for proximate and empirical answers to the more acute practical problems posed for men and management.

In this article we shall emphasize how an assembly line looks and feels to the men who work on it, rather than its importance to the engineers who designed it, the executives who manage it, or the public who buys its product.

In order to preserve the anonymity of those who freely supplied information—managers, workers, and union leaders—the plant in question has been called Plant X. Over a period of months 180 workers were interviewed in their homes about all phases of their life on "the line." These workers constituted a substantial—and representative—sample of the total number of productive workers in the plant.

Nearly 90% of the men working at Plant X came from jobs where the pace of work was not machine-governed in a strict sense, and from jobs over 72% of which were not repetitive. In short, the area from which they were recruited had few mass-production factories. One might say, then, that these men were like the majority of workers who in the past 30 years have made the transition from occupations characteristic of the first industrial revolution to work environments characteristic of a mass-production era. Their attitudes should be all the more revealing.

Most people, in thinking about an assembly line and the workers on it, focus only on the effect of the line on what a man does hour by hour, even minute by minute, with his mind and his muscles. Any serious study of the human effects of the mass-production method, however, must extend its field of vision. For the method not only impinges directly on a man's immediate or intrinsic job but molds much of the character of the in-plant society of which he is a part, including both his relations with his fellow workers and his relations with management. Accordingly we shall discuss the impact of the mass-production method not only directly but indirectly on human nature.

Definition of mass-production method

But what is the "mass-production method?" We must have a definition if our discussion and our findings are to be understandable.

Although the methods of mass production or, more accurately and specifically for our purposes, the methods of *progressive manufacture* have been defined and discussed in different ways by different writers, it is agreed by nearly everyone that these methods derive from at least two fundamental and related ideas: (a) standardization and (b) interchangeability of parts.

Given these basic ideas, plus the accurate machining methods which make them applicable to manufacture, Ford was able to work out and apply the three following additional "principles" of progressive manufacture: (c) the orderly progression of the product through the shop in a series of planned operations arranged so that the right part always arrives at the right place at the right time; (d) the mechanical delivery of these parts and of the product as it is assembled to and from the operators; and (e) a breakdown of operations into their simple constituent motions.[2]

Let us look now at how these principles translate themselves into job characteristics from the standpoint not of the engineer but of the man on the assembly line. In the first place, most automobile assembly jobs are *mechanically paced* (especially those on the main line). In the second place, since the engineer has broken the jobs down into simple and separate elements and assigned only a few to each man, they are clearly *repetitive*. Among other characteristics of most jobs are these: they have a low skill requirement, permit work on only a fraction of the product, severely limit social interaction, and predetermine for nearly every worker any use he may make of tools and methods.

Taken together, automobile assembly-line jobs exemplify all these characteristics, but not every job exemplifies all of them. Put another way, in spite of many common characteristics, automobile assembly jobs are far from being equal—either as to the quantity or quality of job content or as to the satisfaction or dissatisfaction which workers derive from them. They differ both in the number of the several assembly-line characteristics they exemplify and in the degree of impact of any one characteristic. An understanding of this point must mark the beginning of any serious inquiry into the relation of human behavior to assembly-line work.

Attitude Toward Jobs

But that is enough of making distinctions. Now let the men on the assembly line tell us themselves about their jobs, and tell us also what they like and what they do not like about them. Here are six jobs by way of illustration: two on the main moving line, one off the main line but on a moving conveyer, one off the main line and not on a moving conveyer, one repair job on the line, and one utility job on the line. These six will illustrate at least the principal differences in human impact of mass-production assembly-line jobs. (It should be remembered, however, that these six are not representative of the distribution of jobs in the whole plant, where one-half the jobs are on the *main moving assembly line*. Specifically the distribution of jobs in our sample was as follows: main assembly line, 86; subassembly on moving belt, 28; subassembly not on moving belt, 38; repairmen, 14; utility men, 11; and other, 3.)

2 This is a rephrased and slightly more explicit statement of the three principles of mass production as set down in "Mass Production" by Henry Ford in the *Encyclopaedia Britannica*, Vol. 15, 14th ed., pp. 38-39.

On the main moving line

Here is the way the assembler of the baffle windbreaker in the trim department describes his job:

As the body shell moves along the line, I start putting on a baffle windbreaker (two fenders fit on it) by putting in four screws. Then I put nine clips at the bottom which hold the chrome molding strip to the body. On another type of car there is a piece of rubber which fits on the hood latch on the side and keeps the hood from rattling. I drill the holes in the rubber and metal and fit two screws in. Also I put four clips on the rubber in the rear fender. On another type of body, I put the clips on the bottom molding, and in the trunk space I put two bolts which hold the spare tire clamp. I repeat these things all the time on the same types of car.

How does this man's job measure up in terms of some of the characteristics we have mentioned, particularly pace and repetitiveness?

To begin with, the job is on the main line and the worker rides along on the conveyer, completing his cycle of operations in less than two minutes while the conveyer is moving over a distance of about 30 feet. He then walks to his starting point and begins over again. In short, his pace is directly determined by the moving belt. On the other hand, he is sometimes able to work back up the line and so secure a breather for himself.

The job is clearly repetitive, but there is some element of variety since between five and ten operations are required to complete the job cycle. There are also different models to be worked on. Comparing the repetitiveness of this job with that of other assembly jobs, it is somewhere in the middle range—far less repetitive than a single-operation job and far more repetitive than the job of a repairman.

Similarly, in the matter of skill it is in the middle as assembly-line jobs go. Because of the number of parts handled, learning time is slightly longer than that for many assembly jobs. The worker reported that it took him a month to do the job properly. As for the expenditure of physical energy, it is a light job.

Also on the main moving line

Or consider the job of the worker who installs toe plates and who performs operations typical of short-cycle, on-the-main-line jobs:

I put in the two different toe plates. They cover the holes where the brake and clutch pedals are. I am inside the car and have to be down on the seat to do my work. On one kind of car I put in the shift lever while another man puts in the toe plates.

While doing his job this man rides along in the car and must complete the job before he is carried too far. After finishing his work cycle he returns to his station, climbs into another car, and begins another installation. Thus his pace is strictly governed by the moving line. This particular worker told the interviewer that he did not mind the pace.

Such a job which demands but two operations in a two-minute cycle is highly repetitive. Only slight variety is introduced when the man installs a shift lever instead of a toe plate on certain cars.

The job demands very little skill and has a learning period of just two days. Although the worker gets in and out of cars 20 or 30 times an hour, his expenditure of physical energy on the actual assembly operation is slight.

Off the main line but on a moving conveyer

The job of a seat-spring builder is typical of those off the main line but on a moving belt:

I work on a small conveyer which goes around in a circle. We call it a merry-go-round. I make up zig-zag springs for front seats. Every couple of feet on the conveyer there is a form for the pieces that make up the seat springs. As that form goes by me, I clip several pieces together, using a clip gun. I then put the pieces on the form, and it goes on around to where other men clip more pieces together. By the time the form has gone around the whole line, the pieces are ready to be set in a frame, where they are made into a complete seat spring. That's further down the main seat cushion line. The only operation I do is work the clip gun. It takes just a couple of seconds to shoot six or eight clips onto the spring, and I do it as I walk a few steps. Then I start right over again.

This job is clearly paced by a moving conveyer quite as much as if it were on the main line. A comment by the worker regarding his previous job emphasized the point: "I liked the piecework system on my old job. If I wanted to stop for a few minutes, I could. You can't do that here."

As for variety, there is none. The job is highly repetitive, consisting of one set of operations repeated every few seconds on a part which is standard for all models.

The skill requirement is minimum. This worker gave two days as his learning time, with a few days more "in order to do it like I do it now."

As for physical energy, the job would probably be rated as light since the worker guides an automatic hand gun. But there is considerable fatigue because the worker performs the operation standing up.

The workers' over-all estimate of the job is typical. As to what he liked about the job, he mentioned good pay, steady work, and good working hours —in that order of priority. As to what he disliked, he said that he could not set his own pace, that he did not have interesting work, and that his job was physically tiring.

Off the main line but not on a moving conveyer

We turn to a blower-defroster assembler who works off the main line and not on a moving belt:

I work at a bench on blower defrosters. The blowers come in two parts. I take one part and attach the blower motor to it. I then connect the fan to the motor shaft. Then I take the other half on the air pipe and put two parts together with fourteen screws. I test the motor to see if it works, and if it does, I put in a fifteenth screw which grounds it to the pipe. The materials are brought to me and put in a pile by a stock-chaser. After I finish, I put each assembled blower on one of six shelves.

Here is an example of a job where pace is only indirectly determined by the main line. The worker must keep his shelves stocked with a supply of blower defrosters, but he has some choice of pace in doing so. He may work fast and "build up a bank," then slow down and take a breather. Or he may choose to work quite steadily. The demands of the stock-chaser who brings him materials and takes away the finished assembly are the determinants of his work pace, rather than the moving conveyer.

There is not much variety since there are only three operations. However, a slight variation is introduced through differences in models. The worker called his job completely repetitive but said he did not mind it.

His job operations require a minimum of skill: "I learned it in a couple of hours, though it took me about a week to get up speed." He does not move around, and the materials he handles are light, so very little physical energy is demanded.

Summing up his job, this worker gave good bosses, good pay, and good working conditions as his first three reasons for liking the job. He mentioned only one thing he disliked: "I cannot do different things."

Repairman

Here is a job description by a repairman in the car-conditioning section of the chassis department:

I work in a pit underneath the final line. The cars move along over the pit. On the previous assembly operations, the inspectors for the under parts of the car have indicated where parts were missing or damaged or not properly attached. There are any number of things which can be wrong, and they are usually different for each car. Sometimes we have a run of the same thing which we have to work on until they get at the bug earlier in assembly operations. The shock absorbers may be bad, gas line in wrong, brake lines or spring attachments off. I fix whatever I see checked by the inspector. The others in the pit do the same thing. I just work down the line until I get it cleared up. Sometimes I have to work down a long way on one thing. Other times it's just a simple problem on a number of different things.

This worker is on the main line, but his pace is not strictly governed by the moving conveyer. "We don't feel the pressure of the line since we don't have to do just one thing in a given area and length of time."

The variety the job offers is derived from the nature of the work. "There are any number of things which can be wrong, and they are usually different for each car. . . . There is something different all the time."

As for skill, the job as repairman requires manual skill and mechanical experience. A garage repairman's job would be a good preparation. (The man whose job description is given here had, in fact, worked as a repairman in a garage before coming to Plant X.)

The job varies between light and medium-heavy work, with the expenditure of physical energy called for changing appreciably from job to job and from day to day.

The worker's personal satisfaction with his job was clear. He gave as three reasons for liking the job: "I can set my own pace, I have good working conditions, and I have steady work." He also commented favorably on being able to "use my brains," "do different things," and "choose how the job is to be done."

Utility man

A utility man in the chassis department describes his job as follows:

I work on the whole length of that part of the chassis line beginning with motor drop up to where the wheels are mounted. My job is to fill in wherever I am needed. A man might be absent or away from the job or may need help on the job.

We start where the motor is lowered onto the frame (motor mount). The clutch assembly is installed and hooked up. Then the exhaust system is attached and the bolts tightened. The clutch assembly bolts and the motor mount bolts are also tightened. In the next area on the line the brake chambers are filled and bled.

Off to the side, the subassembly men put the steering column together. The steering post and the Pittman arm assembly are put in. Further down the line, men put in air cleaners and inject hydraulic fluid for the transmission.

Next, the brakes are tested and the clutch linkage hooked up. The bumper brackets are put on; a serial number is attached next; and then the bumper brackets are tightened up. Finally, the chassis is sprayed, mounted on wheels, and moved on toward body drop. All in all, about 28 men work on these jobs, each man with his own special operation. I go on each of these jobs, depending on where I am needed most. It is different each day. Some of the jobs are hard to learn, so when I take over one on which I haven't had much experience, it's hard to keep up. I have been learning how to do the work ever since I've been in the plant. I can never learn everything because new changes are always being made.

The pace of this utility man's work, since it is on the main line, is as strictly governed as that of any assembly worker. In certain ways he may feel the pressure more acutely than some of those for whom he substitutes, since he has less practice on any single job than its regular holder.

To compensate him, however, there is plenty of variety, for, as he points out, he shifts about among 28 different jobs. Notice how in describing his many tasks this utility man gives a very clear account of a whole segment of assembly operations in the chassis department.

Notice, too, the character of a utility man's skill. It is the sum of many little skills of many repetitive jobs. The learning time is six months to a year. The worker said: "Sometimes I walk up and down checking the line. I ask questions of the different men. I rarely stay on the same job more than a couple of days." That his job is not easy is suggested by an additional comment: "Some days you feel like learning, other days you don't. On jobs that take time to learn, you get disgusted because it's hard to keep up. A utility man, when on a job, has more trouble keeping up than the regular man."

This man mentioned good pay, steady work, and good bosses as the three main reasons for liking his job, in that order. Other items bearing on the immediate job which he liked were "having interesting work, having to use my brains, doing many different things," as in the case of the repairman, and also "talking with others." He had only one complaint about the job: that it was "physically tiring."

Summary of attitudes toward jobs

In all of this classification of the automobile assembly workers' jobs, we have clearly been concerned not with an engineering analysis but with factors which have an effect on satisfaction or dissatisfaction with the immediate job. Mechanical pace, repetitiveness, minimum skill requirement, and the other factors were all found reflected in attitudes and feelings.

These examples underline some of the commonest facts and feelings which are part of the daily experience of the productive worker in an assembly plant. To recall a few:

1. Contrary to popular belief, all jobs on an assembly line are not alike, either in skill, variety, learning time, or the degree of satisfaction or dissatisfaction which they offer the average wage earner.

2. There are definite ways on certain jobs to get a break or a breather, such as "working back up the line," or "bank building."

3. There is a general, though not a unanimous, desire to move from highly paced to jobs which are less highly paced, and "off the line."

4. It is evident from the statements of the six workers—which for illustrative purposes we have selected from 180—that other factors such as good pay, a good foreman, and a secure job must be considered in appraising the total index of a worker's satisfaction or dissatisfaction.

Major Reactions of Workers

Looking over the range of factors connected with their immediate jobs by all the men interviewed, we see that the two which were given greatest prominence were (a) mechanical pacing and (b) repetitiveness.

To mechanical pacing

We asked no direct attitude questions on the first and central characteristic of any automobile assembly plant—the moving conveyer—but nearly every worker expressed his opinions about it when describing his job, when talking about the company, or at some other point in the interview. These free-association comments on pace as governed by the moving conveyer showed that: (1) A large majority of the workers regarded the moving line or belt as an undesirable feature of the job. (2) A small minority expressed themselves as enjoying the excitement of the moving line.

Following are typical comments of workers who were highly critical of the line:

The bad thing about assembly lines is that the line keeps moving. If you have a little trouble with a job, you can't take the time to do it right.

On the line you're geared to the line. You don't dare stop. If you get behind, you have a hard time catching up.

The line speed is too great. More men wouldn't help much. They'd just expect more work out of an individual. There's an awful lot of tension.

I don't like rushing all the time. . . . I don't mind doing a good day's work, but I don't like to run through it.

The work isn't hard; it's the never-ending pace. . . . The guys yell "hurrah" whenever the line breaks down. . . . You can hear it all over the plant.

In contrast, a minority liked the challenge and excitement of keeping up with the line:

I do my job well. I get some satisfaction from keeping up with a rapid-fire job. On days when the cars come off slowly, I sometimes get bored.

I get satisfaction from doing my job right and keeping up with the line.

It makes you feel good. . . . when the line is going like hell and you step in and catch up with it.

To repetitiveness

Turning now to the job characteristic, repetitiveness, our findings are that: (1) A majority of the workers were critical of the repetitive character of their jobs. (2) A minority preferred the repetitive character of their work or were indifferent to it. (3) A large number of workers compared on-the-line jobs unfavorably with off-the-line jobs, because off-the-line jobs offered more variety.

We found we were able to correlate the number of operations a man performed (which can serve as a rough measure of repetitiveness) with expressions of interest or lack of interest in his job. The number of operations performed on any given job was determined not by direct questioning but by analysis of the job descriptions. The workers, however, were asked directly: "Would you say your job was very interesting, fairly interesting, not at all interesting?" The correlation with number of operations was as follows:

OPERATIONS PERFORMED	VERY OR FAIRLY INTERESTING	NOT VERY OR NOT AT ALL INTERESTING
1	19	38
2-5	28	36
5 or more	41	18

In the column of workers giving a positive rating to "interest," the number of workers increases as the number of operations increases. In other words, there is a tendency for interest in work to vary directly with the number of operations performed.

Following are typical comments of those men who were critical of the repetitive nature of their jobs:

I dislike repetition. One of the main things wrong with this job is that there is no figuring for yourself, no chance to use your brain. It's a grind doing the same thing over and over. There is no skill necessary.

I'd rather work for a small company any day. They're interested in doing good work, and they are willing to allot enough time for it. The assembly line is no place to work, I can tell you. There is nothing more discouraging than having a barrel beside you with 10,000 bolts in it and using them all up. Then you get a barrel with another 10,000 bolts, and you know every one of those 10,000 bolts has to be picked up and put in exactly the same place as the last 10,000 bolts.

I'd like to do different things on this job. I get bored. It's the same thing all the time. Cars always coming down the line endlessly every time I look up.

I would like to perform different operations, but I do the same thing all the time. I always know what I'm going to do when I come in. There's nothing to look forward to like there was on my old job.

The monotony is what I don't like. It's pretty noisy, but you get used to that. I'd never get used to the monotony. I dislike the plant for this reason.

It's not a matter of pace. It's the monotony. It's not good for you to get so bored. I do the same thing day after day; just an everlasting grind.

The job gets so sickening—day in and day out plugging in ignition wires. I get through with one motor, turn around, and there's another motor staring me in the face.

A minority of workers who declared that they were indifferent to or preferred doing the same thing over and over again commented as follows:

I keep doing the same thing all the time, but it doesn't make any difference to me.

Repeating the same thing you can catch up and keep ahead of yourself. I like the routine. You can get in the swing of it.

We do the same thing all the time, but I don't mind it really.

I like doing the same thing all the time. I'd rather stay right where I am. When I come in in the morning, I like to know exactly what I'll be doing.

I like to repeat the same thing, and every car is different anyway. So my job is interesting enough.

Explanation of why this minority group either preferred or was indifferent to the factor of repetitiveness in contrast to the majority of workers in our sample would appear to lie in the pattern of their individual personalities. An investigation of the psychological characteristics of men who react this way is clearly suggested. We sought but found no other unique characteristics in the group as regards education, age, or any of the other categories of information we used.

Effect of Human Equation

In the introductory paragraphs of this article we reviewed some of the typical questions on which it was hoped research into the human equation of assembly-line work might throw light, including some of special interest to both the production manager and the engineer: What part of a worker's skill and power can the engineer build into a machine? What must he leave out? Precisely how and to what extent in the most mechanized sectors of our economy does the human equation still affect quantity and quality?

Influence of workers on quality

So far as assembly lines go, there is still a widespread belief on the part of *outsiders* that the machine has completely taken over and that on mechanized conveyer-line jobs the individual has no influence on quality. There is also a belief widely held by *insiders* (employers and production managers) that, even though the quality of individual performance on a mechanized job may still be important for the final product, the average worker no longer cares or gets satisfaction from doing a good job.

In Plant X, both beliefs were shown to be unfounded.

As many as 79 men in the sample of 180 felt that it was difficult to sustain the kind of quality performance which was expected of them or which they themselves wanted to sustain. To most of the 79, *this was a discouraging and negative feature of the job.*

About half the workers felt it was possible to do the kind of quality job expected of them. Few of these workers, however, had jobs which were strictly line-paced. Rather they included mostly repairmen, utility men, workers on off-line jobs, or men on the line who had longer time cycles or greater freedom to move up and down the line. Typical comments among this group were:

No time limit is set on my job, so I can do it right. I get satisfaction out of really fixing a job. I can usually get this, but sometimes the company doesn't want the cars fixed as well as I'd like to.

I get satisfaction and quality because I have time to complete my job right.

I never let a car go by with my number on it unless it is done right. Maybe some of the men on the line don't get quality.

You can take time to get quality. It's not like on the line when you have to rush so much. And I get satisfaction. It makes me feel good when I put out a good day's work and get no kickbacks.

The effects of poor-quality work on job satisfaction were reflected in many of the comments of men on conveyer-paced jobs:

The cars come too fast for quality. It's quantity instead of quality. I'm doing the best I can, but could do a neater job slower.

On an assembly line you just do it once; if it's wrong, you have no time to fix it. I get no satisfaction from my work. All I do is think about all the things that went through wrong that should have been fixed. My old job was nothing like this.

I try to do quality work, but I'm too rushed. This keeps me from getting pleasure from the work. They say "haste makes waste," and they're getting plenty of both.

I'd rather do less work and do it right. How can you get quality when they don't give you time? The "quality" signs they have mean nothing.

These comments tend to show that the characteristics or components of the assembly man's immediate job do have a significant bearing upon the quality of the product, and that mass production restricts rather than eliminates the "human factor" as a determinant of quality for any given part or for the total product. Most workers were conscious of this fact. For a substantial number, inability to put out quality was a source of irritation while putting out quality was a source of job satisfaction.

Constructive Measures by Management

Are there any measures that management can take to modify on-the-job conditions of work in the interest of greater efficiency and of increased satisfaction for the individual operator? One answer to this question may be sought in the elements of satisfaction or of compensation which some workers already found in their jobs. To begin with, it should be remembered that there was a minority of workers who preferred or were indifferent to repetitiveness and mechanical pacing. Presumably by improved methods of recruiting and selection this minority could be increased. Then there were a number of men who found their immediate jobs on and off the line satisfying—actually all the repairmen and utility men interviewed with one exception. The only measures needed here are protective—to make sure that the content of these jobs is not diluted.

This still leaves the majority of the production workers. Here the clue to constructive action lies in the fact that many of them reacted favorably to particular features of their jobs:

1. Social interaction breaking the monotony
2. Enough operations on their particular jobs to give variety
3. Opportunity to work back up the line and get a breather
4. Opportunity to build up a bank and get a breather
5. Opportunity to alternate one set of operations with another set of a substantially different character
6. Opportunity to alternate jobs with other workers within the same section
7. A long time cycle encompassing a larger number of operations than usual and of a more interesting character

A practical directive for management would appear to be exploration of the possibility of extending these and other desirable features, so that more assembly men could share in them. The degree of that extension would necessarily vary with the special circumstances—physical and organizational—of individual plants, and with the ingenuity of management; but there would be few plants where something could not be done in this direction.

Detailed discussion of such measures is beyond the scope of this article, but the tenor of our thinking may be indicated by reference to two of the seven features to which Plant X workers reacted favorably.

Job rotation

Take Number 6—alternation of jobs between workers, a technique often called "rotation." At Plant X we were struck with the unusually high degree of job satisfaction expressed by the members of one work group under a particular foreman. With the permission and encouragement of their foreman, the men were working under a system of job rotation. It was to this system that the members of the group ascribed their relatively high job satisfaction. And to the same system the section foreman owed in part a smoothly running and efficient work unit. Top plant management is now encouraging a more widespread application of this practice.

In connection with any system of job rotation the question immediately comes to mind: Since it requires some effort to learn several jobs instead of one, will not the worker—unless he is exceptional—object? Many managers seem to find it difficult to get workers to change jobs frequently.

The best answer to this question about worker resistance is the pragmatic one. In certain sectors on the line at Plant X rotation *is* working. Moreover, in other industries and on other types of assembly lines the practice of rotation is steadily gaining ground. For most people learning to do something new is hard work, and it is only undertaken when an adequate reward is held out. For a considerable number of assembly-line workers the rewards of variety and of possessing a repertory of skills will be sufficient.

Of course, some resistance to an experiment in rotation is to be expected. The key to the situation lies, we suggest, in the word "experiment." Where rotation has been successfully installed on other types of assembly lines, it has usually been started as an experiment, with management guaranteeing to the work group or to any single individual a return to stationary assignments if desired—and rarely have the workers wished to return.

Another question is: Will the work be done as well or as fast under job rotation? The answer for the Plant X section which practices it is an affirmative. For other work groups in other industries with which the authors are familiar, the answer has also been "yes." Of course there are work situations where job rotation appears either altogether impractical or less efficient. But always the real test is in the over-all and long-term performance of the group. Gains in quality and a drop in turnover or absenteeism may balance some decrease in output, if it occurs.

Job enlargement

Or consider Number 7—a long-time cycle encompassing a larger number of operations than usual and of a more interesting character, sometimes called "job enlargement." Here is a concept and a practice that has proved successful in decreasing monotony without impairing efficiency in certain sectors of other industries. We here suggest that it be introduced experimentally into automobile assembly work.

Job enlargement is simply the recombining of two or more separate jobs into one. Certain plant managers in other industries have been finding that a law of diminishing returns applies to the subdivision of jobs and that a recombination of certain fractured parts has increased efficiency. This points toward a lengthening of time cycles. Job enlargement in the sense in which we suggest it does not mean turning automobile assembly back into the hands of master mechanics with one worker assigned to the assembly of one car. It does mean paying greater attention to psychological and social variables in the determination of time cycles and, by the same token, paying more attention to the *content* of individual jobs.

To one unfamiliar with assembly-line work experience, the difference between a job with five operations and a job with ten, or between a job taking two minutes to perform and a job taking four minutes, might seem a matter far too trivial to concern anyone. Our data have shown that this is not true. Management has a vital interest in such matters; the proper assignment of time cycles throughout an assembly plant will make an important difference in the efficiency of the plant. As for the worker, one of the most striking findings of this study is the psychological importance of even minute changes in his immediate job experience.

At the risk of oversimplification, the point may be summarized this way: Other things being equal, the difference between a satisfied and a dissatisfied worker may rest on whether he has a ten-operation or a five-operation job.

Relationship Among Workers

Another place to look for possibilities of improvement is in the area of indirect influences—the impact of mass-production methods on the plant's social structure. Ever since the early studies of Elton Mayo, it has been widely accepted that the character of the "work group" frequently exercises a decisive influence on a worker's efficiency—not to mention on his satisfaction on the job. How did the technology of the automobile assembly line affect the grouping of men at Plant X?

Most workers are located along the "main line" according to the particular manpower requirements of each segment of the assembly process. Each operator works in a limited area completing his own operations independently of others as the car is carried by the conveyer down the line. A particular individual may talk with the men immediately around him, but these men cannot be said to comprise a bona fide work group in the usual sense of the term. Take as an illustration the polishing line. Figure 3-1 shows in diagrammatic form an actual interaction pattern of a left-front-door polisher, Worker E.

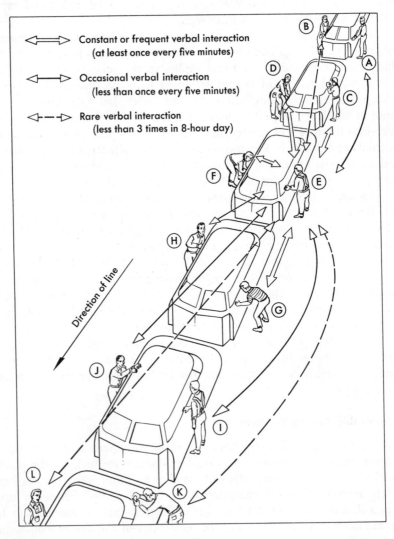

Figure 3-1.   Social Interaction Pattern of Typical Main Assembly Line Worker—Polisher Paint Department.

The ten men from A to J comprise a work group of which Worker E is a part, and he has some social contact with all the other nine. His really close contacts, however, are only with C, D, F and G. Note that these four workers comprise a group—*but only from E's point of view*. As to the social relationship pattern of G, his immediate group would consist of E, F, H and I; it would not include C and D, who were clearly members of E's group. Further variations occur, for example, when a line makes a bend or loop and brings men in different sections closer together. Thus each man, because of the nature of conveyer operations, has a slightly different circle of associates from that of the man next to him. So it goes along the entire stretch of a line, a line well over two miles long.

In our interviews these men exhibited little of what the sociologist would call "in-group awareness." Rarely, for example, did they talk about "our team" or "our group" or "the men in our outfit." Instead, the following remark was typical: "I've been here over a year, and I hardly know the first names of the men in the section where I work."

In sharp contrast, however, to the majority of line workers, a minority —principally off-line operators—worked on bona fide teams or crews; that is, they were members of a close working group, were functionally interdependent, and frequently assisted their fellows or exchanged operations with them. On charting the interaction pattern of such groups it was found that the frequency of conversational exchange was high and constant for nearly all members of the group. Of greater significance, the group exhibited a marked *esprit-de-corps* not found among the bulk of line operators.

It is clear that the present technology of an automobile assembly line limits social interaction and does not lend itself to the arrangement of men in bona fide teams or crews. It is suggested, however, that in the design of *new* plants, and at periods of retooling or of layout revisions, an effort be made to maximize the opportunities for social interaction and for team relationships.

Relations with Management

Still another area of social relationships—that of worker to supervisor—is crucial to an intelligent understanding of social organization.

The formal organizational structure of the various production departments in Plant X was similar to that found in many plants. In interviews with workers we came to know the quality of relationship between workers and supervisors.

Foremen

Qualitative comments by the men about their foremen suggested a relatively informal and friendly relationship on the part of the majority. The average foreman had from 15 to 25 men under him, and talking between worker and foremen was generally frequent, friendly, and informal. The sort of remarks one hears about any good foreman were also heard here, as for example: "Our foreman is a real good guy. We're lucky. If he got into trouble, the whole department would back him right up."

There were criticisms of foremen, but usually these were not directed at the individual. Rather they were aimed at the "line" and the role the foreman had to play with reference to the line. As one man said: "After all, the foreman has to be a pusher, and nobody likes to be pushed. He's got to hold his job. If he doesn't push, somebody else will get his job."

Often men exonerated foremen for "pushing" since they recognized that the compulsion of line production was not the fault of the foremen. One man put it this way: "I guess you'd say the foreman gets along with the men. But they don't need a foreman. *The line is the foreman.* You have to keep up with the line."

Higher supervisors

An interesting finding which came out of the study was the relationship, or lack of it, between workers and management above the foreman level. The 180 men in our sample were asked to indicate contacts with supervisors in their department at the general foreman and department-head levels. Only 59 reported that they talked with their general foreman as often as once a week; 15 put it at one to three times a month; and 88 said less than once a month. Contact between workers and upper departmental supervisors was even less, with 70% saying they spoke with their department heads less than once a month. (Departments ranged in size from 200 to 400.)

It is significant in this connection that in a steel fabricating plant which we recently studied the workers talked far more frequently with supervisors above the foreman level. There the nature of the process and the high degree of worker skills made for a closer relationship. It was an everyday experience to find a superintendent in charge of 400 men talking with an individual worker or group of workers. He did this because the technical and skilled judgment of the individual worker was important in the production process.

On the automobile assembly line, on the other hand, because of the high degree of mechanization and fractional assembly there appears to be less need for supervisors to discuss production matters with individual workers. Management relies on the judgment of the engineer, not the worker. Thus the basic factor which determines the rate and quality of worker-supervisor interaction is the technology of mass production.

Impact on Wage Structure

Not the least important secondary effect of the mass-production method has been its impact on the wage structure. A leveling of workers' skills has inevitably resulted in a narrowing of differentials between wage grades, in contrast to industries where the latest mass-production methods have not been applied. For example, in the steel fabricating plant which we investigated—a seamless tube mill—the differential between the rates of the lowest and of the highest paid workers was over a dollar an hour. At Plant X, however, the differential between the lowest paid and the highest paid was around 10 cents for the major categories of production workers, and over half the workers in the production departments received exactly the same hourly wage.

It is obvious that changes in skill levels and in wage categories affect what the wage administrator calls the "system of job progression." Before the application of mass-production methods most industries had many well-defined steps in their ladders of promotion. Mass-production methods, while often raising the general level of wages and bringing other benefits, have knocked out a good many rungs in these promotion ladders. To turn again to the steel mill for contrast: there were as many as seven or eight steps from laborer to roller, each one associated with progressively higher wages, skills, and prestige.

This system of promotion, with its connotations of growth, incentive, and progress, has been weakened or virtually eliminated on the assembly line. Almost any assembly worker can—and some do—say: "There are hundreds of jobs like mine, not much better, not much worse. The differences are so slight—or seem so slight to management—that I am interchangeable." Consequently, to escape a resulting sense of anonymity as much, perhaps, as to escape monotony, the average worker at Plant X does not aspire to climb into another slightly better production job, but rather into a utility man's job or a repairman's job or out of production altogether, where he can be recognized, and where also he can recognize himself, as an individual.

Most of the benefits of the mass-production method are obvious and have often been celebrated. If we are to continue to enjoy them and to expand and refine the method, we should understand more fully its impact on the traditional organization of industry. Surely the problems as well as the promises of mass production are worthy of study.

Conclusion

It is obviously impossible in a single article to do more than sketch some of the problem areas in the broad field of relations between mass production and human nature. Concerning the direct impact of the method on the individual we made a few empirical suggestions and tried to point out at least one direction in which management might seek practical solutions.

But what can be said about the *indirect* impact of mass production on human nature through the character of work groups, the wage structure, and the promotion system? In a negative sense, at least, all these phenomena appear to be related: At Plant X they tended to increase the workers' sense of anonymity within the production enterprise of which they were functional parts. In fact, one way to express the net result of these several influences might be to say that little sense of membership in a common work community existed. (Our evidence showed that to some extent membership in the union gave the worker the feeling of personal identity and "belonging" which neither the shop nor relations with management supplied.)

It seems to us significant that the average worker appeared to be oppressed by this sense of anonymity *in spite of the fact that he declared himself well satisfied with his rate of pay and the security of his job.* The answer to this problem in the most general terms would appear to be a program designed to re-create the sense *and also* the reality of a bona fide work community. And for such a program to be successful we believe that both union and management would have to agree on the measures to be taken.

A comment by a man on the line will suggest the nature of the problem more clearly than many paragraphs of exposition:

There is a different feeling in this plant. It's much bigger than the people around here have ever seen. It's just like the kid who goes up to a grownup man and starts talking to him. There doesn't seem to be a friendly feeling. At the plant I used to work in there was a different feeling. Everyone spoke to everyone else. . . . Nobody goes to other departments in this plant. The understanding could be better—happier and much easier. Here a man is just so much horsepower.

Perhaps the human needs in Plant X are merely an expression in more explicit terms of the needs of our industrial civilization. The problem of reintegrating the several faculties of man into a significant unity presents itself in many fields—in industry, science, and government, to name but three—in an age of overspecialization.

It is striking that throughout the survey of Plant X both union and management agreed with the authors that the more basic problems to be explored were not those connected with a particular plant, industry, or corporation. Rather they were problems related to technological and organizational trends common to modern industry. Both agreed that modern American civilization as we know it rests upon mass-production principles quite as much as upon the natural resources of the United States. The attitude of both, therefore, was a simple and heartening one: *Since these problems exist, let us get all the facts we can. In time we shall be able to solve them.*

As Saint-Exupéry, the French aviator and author wrote:

The Machine is not an end. . . . It is a tool . . . like the plough.

If we believe that it degrades Man, it is possibly because we lack the perspective for judging the end results of transformations as rapid as those to which we have been subjected. What are two hundred years in the history of the Machine when compared with two hundred thousand years in the history of Man? We have scarcely established ourselves in this country of mines and of central electricity. It is as if we had hardly begun to live in the new house that we have not yet finished building. Everything has changed so rapidly around us: human relations, conditions of work, customs. . . . Every step in our progress has driven us a little further from our acquired habits, and we are in truth pioneers who have not yet established the foundations of our new country.[3]

[3] Antoine de Saint-Exupéry, *Terre des Hommes* (Paris: Gallimard, 1939), p. 58.

17. Scientists in Industry

William Kornhauser

As a professional, an individual acquires stature from his colleagues in the profession. As an employee, he acquires status from his superiors in the organization. A series of accomplishments and rewards in the professions constitutes a "successful" professional career. A series of progressively higher positions in the organization constitutes a "successful" bureaucratic career. The contingencies of a professional career are not the same as those of a bureaucratic career, and may conflict with them.[1] Therefore, career lines of professionals in large organizations influence their motivation for professional work. The capacity of the work establishment to define the status and career of its professional employees is at the same time a way of motivating them toward the organization's objectives. The capacity of the profession to get its standards of performance incorporated into the organization's set of rewards and incentives is a major way of sustaining these standards. Organizational and professional incentives may be in part incompatible, so that a problem of integration of incentive systems arises.

We shall first specify the distinction between professional and organizational orientations and incentives, and then consider their variations in different kinds of organizations and professions.

Work Orientations, Functions, and Incentives

A professional employee may be strongly oriented toward the profession in which he has been trained, the organization for which he works, both the profession and the organization, or neither of them. These types of orientation have been distinguished in several organizational contexts. Reissman distinguished all four types in his study of civil service specialists in a state agency:

Functional Bureaucrat—One who is oriented towards and seeks his recognition from a given professional group outside of rather than within the bureaucracy. . . . He is active in his professional societies and seeks appreciation and recognition on the basis of his professional specialities.

Reprinted from William Kornhauser (with the assistance of Warren O. Hagstrom), *Scientists in Industry: Conflict and Accommodation* (Berkeley and Los Angeles, University of California Press, 1962), pp. 117-130; 155-157.

[1] In the words of the president of Bell Laboratories, "Organizational position must not be confused with scientific stature." James B. Fisk, "Basic Research in Industrial Laboratories," in Dael Wolfle, ed., *Symposium on Basic Research* (Washington, D.C.: American Association for the Advancement of Science, 1959), p. 165.

Job Bureaucrat—He is immersed entirely within the structure. Professional skills only provide the necessary entrance qualifications and determine the nature of the work to be done. He seeks recognition along departmental rather than professional lines.

Specialist Bureaucrat—Though he resembles the first type in his professional orientations, he exhibits a greater awareness of and identification with the bureaucracy. He seeks his recognition from the department and the people with whom he works rather than from like-professionals who are privately employed.

Service Bureaucrat—He entered civil service primarily to realize certain personally-held goals which center about rendering service to a certain [nonprofessional] group. The bureaucracy offers a framework through which he can best function and his task is one of utilizing that mechanism to achive his goals.[2]

Blau also distinguished between a professional and nonprofessional orientation among specialists in a state agency.[3]

Marvick distinguished three of the four types of orientation in his study of a military research agency:

Specialist orientation is one in which professional expertise is given primacy. Stress is placed on furthering a career in the profession, avoiding executive posts, and not being overly concerned whether professional employment is found in public or private organizations. Preoccupied with matters of skill gratification, this type tends to be indifferent and detached in respect to the material benefits and social life of the work establishment.

Institutional orientation is "place-bound"; gratifications are sought in the personal benefits available in the work establishment. Stress is placed on a career within the work establishment. This type tends to be indifferent to benefits that are derived from the application of skills to a task.

Hybrid orientation is neither "skill-bound" nor "place-bound." Rather, stress is placed on acquiring immediate personal advantages, such as power, prestige, and income. It is "opportunistic," in contradistinction to professional or organizational loyalty.[4]

In a study of scientists in a federal research agency, Marvick's distinction between "specialist" and "institutionalist" is related to scientific performance.[5]

---

[2] Leonard Reissman, "A Study of Role Conceptions in Bureaucracy," *Social Forces*, **27** (1949), 305-310.

[3] Peter Blau, *The Dynamics of Bureaucracy* (Chicago: University of Chicago Press, 1955).

[4] Adapted from Dwaine Marvick, "Career Perspectives in a Bureaucratic Setting," *Michigan Governmental Studies*, No. 27 (Ann Arbor: Bureau of Government, Institute of Public Administration, University of Michigan, 1954), *passim*.

[5] Donald C. Pelz, "Some Social Factors Related to Performance in a Research Organization," *Administrative Science Quarterly*, **1** (1965), 312.

Wilensky distinguished four types of staff specialists in trade unions:

[The Professional Service type is oriented toward the profession.] His main job problems and frustrations can be interpreted in terms of a conflict between the requirements of the job (and/or the values of union officials), on the one hand; and a professional ethos—expressed in a desire to render competent, efficient, objective, technical service of which professional colleagues outside the union would approve—on the other.

[The Careerist type is] highly identified with the hierarchy of his union and is oriented towards a career within it. He has . . . very little if any professional identification. His job satisfactions center around the chance for social mobility via the union career. What is unique in [the Politico's] role orientation is a basic preoccupation with the political process. . . . The Politico strives for influence and power as ends in themselves.

The Missionary is oriented in his job towards some more abstract concept of the labor movement; he is highly identified with an outside political or religious-political group. [He is not closely identified with either the organization or his field of specialization.][6]

Gouldner,[7] Caplow and McGee,[8] and Lazarsfeld and Thielens[9] have distinguished between professional and organizational orientations among academic men. Borrowing Merton's terms, Gouldner refers to these two types as "cosmopolitans" and "locals:"

Cosmopolitans: those low on loyalty to the employing organization, high on commitment to specialized role skills, and likely to use an out [professional] reference group orientation.

Locals: those high on loyalty to the employing organization, low on commitment to specialized role skills, and likely to use an inner [organizational] reference group orientation.[10]

Evidence collected on the faculty members of a small liberal arts college shows that the criteria (organizational loyalty, reference group, commitment to skill) for differentiating the two types are related in the predicted direction.[11]

These several typologies may be summarized according to the dis-

[6] Harold L. Wilensky, Intellectuals in Labor Unions (New York: Free Press, 1965), pp. 114, 129, 145, 153.

[7] Alvin W. Gouldner, "Cosmopolitans and Locals: Toward an Analysis of Latent Social Roles," Administrative Science Quarterly, 2 (1957-1958), 281-306, 444-480.

[8] Theodore Caplow and Reece McGee, The Academic Marketplace (New York: Basic Books, 1958).

[9] Paul F. Lazarsfeld and Wagner Thielens, Jr., The Academic Mind (New York: Free Press, 1958).

[10] Gouldner, op. cit., p. 290.

[11] Ibid., p. 294.

tinctions they make between the professional orientation (P) and the organizational orientation (O).

Table 3-1.

	TYPE I P O + −	TYPE II P O − +	TYPE III P O + +	TYPE IV* P O − −
Reissman	Functional bureaucrat	Job bureaucrat	Specialist bureaucrat	Service bureaucrat
Marvick	Specialist	Institution- alist		Hybrid
Wilensky	Professional service expert	Careerist		Missionary, politico
Gouldner	Cosmopolitan	Local		

*Type IV has two subtypes: those who identify with a third group, such as a social movement (e.g., the "missionary" and the "service bureaucrat"); and those who, for opportunistic reasons, avoid close ties to any group (e.g., the "politico" and the "hybrid").

This typology of orientations can be used to analyze two kinds of problems. One concerns the individual: how he comes to adopt one orientation rather than another, how he changes his orientation, and the consequences of his orientation for his personal career and other aspects of his life. The other treats these orientations in their significance for work establishment and profession. This interest leads to analysis of the *distribution* of orientations within work establishment and profession.

There is a strong tendency in the literature on personal orientations and social structure to argue for the differential significance of only one type of orientation for a given social structure. For example, it is postulated that a "democratic type" is required for a "democratic polity." This approach is useful mainly in its power to show the dominant psychological aspect of a social system. It is weak, however, in ignoring two obvious facts: (1) there are multiple types of orientation in any complex social system; and (2) there are multiple functions in any complex social system. In order to take account of these facts, we shall assume that *a complex system depends for its effectiveness on a certain distribution of types of orientation*, rather than on only one type. Specifically, we shall argue that three of the types of orientation designated above make *distinct* contributions to a work establishment, each by facilitating the contributions of the others. Our premise is that the division of labor in an organization calls for a diversity of work orientations.

There are at least three major functions to be performed if a professional specialty is to make a satisfactory contribution to the larger enterprise of which it is a part: (1) *production* of technical results (e.g., scientific research); (2) *administration* of the conditions under which technical results are produced; (3) *application and communication* of technical results. Correlatively, it may be hypothesized that those who have a predominantly professional orientation tend to be strong producers of technical results; those who have a predominantly organizational orientation tend to assume administrative responsibilities; and those who seek to combine orientations to both organization and profession are especially capable of facilitating the utilization of technical results. The rest of this section presents evidence for this proposition. Numerous studies are cited because the agreement among them makes it possible to place considerable confidence in the results in spite of the qualifications that must be attached to each.

In a liberal arts college, Gouldner found that faculty members who were strongly oriented to their profession but not to the college were more likely to be researchers than teachers or administrators; those who were strongly committed to the college but not to their profession were more likely to be administrators than teachers or researchers; and those who were committed to their profession but also to the college were as likely to be teachers as researchers, less likely to be administrators.[12] Differences between the three types of orientation are also associated with differences in the following factors: (a) academic productivity, as measured by college degree, publications, and interest in doing research; (b) college influence, as measured by number of policy decisions participated in; (c) bureaucratic sentiments, as measured by positive attitudes toward administration by formal rules and regulations. It will be noted (Table 3-2) that the professionally oriented excel in academic accomplishments, the organizationally oriented are more likely to favor bureaucratic controls, and the mixed type is more influential than both the other types.

In a government medical research organization, Davis found that scientific performance was closely related to a professional orientation, but not to an organizational orientation or to a mixed orientation.[13] In a military research agency, Marvick found that the professionally oriented wanted the agency to emphasize basic research, whereas the organizationally oriented favored research administration as "the main thing the agency should be doing." Those who were "hybrids" favored application (military research) as the major function.[14]

In industrial research organizations, we find a similar pattern of career orientations among scientists and engineers, corresponding to their primary functions of production of new research, administration of research, and

[12] *Ibid.*, pp. 454-455.
[13] Reported in Pelz, *op. cit.*, p. 312.
[14] Marvick, *op. cit.*, p. 95.

application of research through development and technical service. One of the firms we studied has formalized these career orientations by establishing three ladders of promotion in the research organization: one for researchers, another for supervisors, and a third for technical service people. Interviews with several members of each ladder show that those on the research ladder are strongly oriented toward advancement in their fields of specialization, those on the administrative ladder are primarily identified with the company, and those on the technical service ladder are likely to have a more mixed orientation.

Table 3-2.

Selected Correlates of Orientations of College Faculty

	CAREER ORIENTATION					
	Professional	N	Mixed	N	Organizational	N
Percent who are high on						
productivity	58%	(52)	*		37%	(73)
influence	55%	(29)	66%	(53)	53%	(43)
bureaucratism	32%	(29)	50%	(53)	56%	(43)

*The mixed orientation does not appear in the first row because a dichotomous indicator was used to classify subjects.

Source: Adapted from Alvin W. Gouldner, "Cosmopolitans and Locals," *Administrative Science Quarterly*, 2 (1957-1958), 294, 297, 299.

Riegel's inquiry into the relative importance of different kinds of rewards to technical professionals in industry yielded results closely parallel to our own. Two hundred seventy-six nonsupervisory engineers and scientists in ten companies were asked to indicate the relative importance of different sources of rewards. Respondents were divided into three groups: "research personnel, engineers engaged in application and development, and engineers whose work is closely related to production."[15] Since this sample included only nonsupervisory scientists and engineers, the function of research administration was not represented. However, production engineers, along with administrators, might be expected to have a strong organizational orientation, since their tasks are closely geared to the central operations of industry. The findings of this study conformed to our expectations. The professional orientation of the research personnel was indicated by the fact that they ranked professional sources of rewards higher than did the development and production engineers. They gave

[15] John W. Riegel, *Intangible Rewards for Engineers and Scientists* (Ann Arbor: Bureau of Industrial Relations, University of Michigan, 1953), p. 26.

comparatively high ratings to "opportunity to contribute to scientific knowledge," "respect of fellow professionals because of my achievements," and "association with other professionals of recognized ability." The researchers also gave the lowest rank to "membership in a company producing reputable goods and essential services"—an item that would indicate identification with the company. The organizational orientation of production engineers was indicated by their low ranking of the three "professional" items, and their high ranking of the "organizational" item. The mixed orientation of development engineers was indicated by the fact that they ranked two of the three professional items higher than the production engineers but lower than the researchers, and the organizational item higher than the researchers but lower than the production engineers.[16] Corresponding to the difference in orientation of researchers and production engineers was a difference in the kinds of incentives that management stressed for each group: executives in charge of these two groups gave different weights to monetary as against intangible rewards (such as professional recognition, and challenge and variety of assignments) for men under them. When 44 executives in the same ten companies were asked what they did to motivate their engineers and scientists to do their best work and to enhance their job satisfaction, "executives who were in charge of research activities placed more emphasis on nonfinancial rewards than did the executives in charge of engineering work which was closely related to production."[17]

In another study, engineers were given tests to measure the extent of their interest in ideas, in things, in people, and in manipulating people for a purpose. Engineers in administrative positions scored highest on "interest in people" and "interest in manipulating people for a purpose"—interests which are among the main requisites in sustaining managerial functions; and they scored lowest on "interest in ideas." In contrast, research engineers scored highest on "interest in ideas"—indicating their strong orientation toward science, and lowest on "interest in people" and on "interest in manipulating people for a purpose." Engineers in development and technical service (research application) fell neatly between the researchers and the administrators on both sets of interests. The orientation of the development and technical service engineers toward research utilization was indicated by the fact that they scored highest on "interest in things."[18]

The remaining data permit comparisons of only two orientations at a time. In two studies, professionals in research production can be compared with those in research application. In the first, 250 engineers in 21 indus-

---

[16] *Ibid.*, p. 34.

[17] John W. Riegel, *Administration of Salaries for Engineers and Scientists* (Ann Arbor: Bureau of Industrial Relations, University of Michigan, 1958), p. 3.

[18] Hollis Peter, "Human Factors in Research Administration," in Rensis Likert and Samuel P. Hayes, eds., *Some Applications of Behavioral Research*, Science and Society Series (Paris: UNESCO, 1957), p. 139.

trial research units were divided into two groups: those in research laboratories and those in development laboratories. Questionnaire responses showed that the research engineers were substantially more interested in scientific or technical achievement, while the development engineers showed much greater interest in "promotion within the organization (up and out of the laboratory)": 80 per cent of the researchers but only 20 per cent of the development group stressed "scientific and technical achievement," while only 20 per cent of the researchers but 80 per cent of the development group stressed "promotion out of the laboratory."[19] It was also found that research engineers tended to be task-oriented, and development engineers authority-oriented. These differences are in part due to the different degree of autonomy that is congruent with each type of function:

> The greater autonomy of the worker in the basic research laboratory presumably means that he works only on problems whose technical importance he appreciates. The worker in the development laboratory, however, depends more upon the authority of his superior.[20]

Technical service employees, like development engineers, are less committed to their professions than are laboratory workers. In choosing reasons that would be most important in deciding to take a job in another company, technical service personnel in an oil company were more likely than laboratory workers to mention advancement opportunities, whereas laboratory workers more frequently mentioned opportunity to obtain professional recognition outside the company.[21] The laboratory workers also showed much greater concern for securing professional working conditions, for protecting professional status, and for increasing professional skills. When asked how the company should improve its treatment of professionals, laboratory personnel more frequently mentioned greater freedom and responsibility in work, less regimentation, less supervision, more respect for professional men, and more opportunity for professional development. They also were more likely to feel that their present job did not fully use their professional training and that they had insufficient opportunity to discuss their work outside the company. The laboratory workers were more likely to think that frequent attendance at national meetings of professional societies was desirable, and they reported more frequent attendance at local society meetings.

While technical service workers are less professionally oriented, they are more closely identified with the company than are the laboratory workers. Thus, 90 per cent of the technical service workers but only 59 per cent of the laboratory workers said they would advise a friend to take a proffered

[19] Cited in *ibid.*, p. 137.

[20] *Ibid.*, p. 147.

[21] Elmo Roper, "A Survey of Baytown Refinery Employee Opinions" (1946). (Mimeographed.) The sample included 39 in the laboratory and 21 in technical service.

job with the company. Yet the difference in organizational commitment between the two groups cannot be due either to differential assessments of advancement opportunities or of company careers as interesting or profitable, for both groups replied similarly to these items. The two groups do differ, however, in the extent to which they believe they are being given opportunities to gain experience for positions of greater responsibility; here more technical service workers replied affirmatively. In sum, the stronger organizational commitment of technical service employees is indicated by their greater desire to move into management; and their weaker professional commitment is shown by less discontent with organizational requirements that hamper professional work.

Finally, a study of 622 scientists and engineers and 105 top managers in six large, scientific-minded companies permits comparison of the orientation of researchers and administrators.[22] The scientists and engineers, most of them located in the central research laboratory of their respective firms, were asked: "What things, other than salary, do you look for in your job to make it really worthwhile?" The managers were asked: "What things, other than salary, do you feel scientists and engineers desire to make their jobs really worthwhile?" Forty-five per cent of the scientists and engineers mentioned "opportunity to do sound scientific work" compared to only 19 per cent of the managers; on the other hand, 75 per cent of management but only 40 per cent of the scientists and engineers mentioned "chance to gain personal prestige." The large discrepancies in these figures indicate that managers, even when queried about the motivations of scientists and engineers rather than the motivations of managers, fail to recognize the importance of professional commitment. These discrepancies cannot be explained by management's "ignorance" of professionalism, for many of the top managers were themselves scientists and engineers who came up through the ranks; and in addition even more of them have Ph.D's (40 per cent) than do the scientists and engineers (30 per cent).[23]

This same study further subdivided the 622 scientists and engineers, none of whom occupied positions in *higher* management, into two groups on the basis of their job assignments: those engaged primarily in scientific and engineering work, and those in supervisory or administrative work. It will be shown later* that despite considerable variation, depending upon the importance of research to a firm, the balance of incentives in industry as a whole is generally heavily weighted on the organizational rather than the professional side. Normally the highest rewards go to those who assume administrative responsibility. In consequence, because of the increasingly large numbers of technical professionals in industry, many are doomed to

[22] *The Conflict between the Scientific Mind and the Management Mind* (Princeton: Opinion Research Corporation, 1959).

[23] *Ibid.*, p. A-16.

* *Editor's Note:* This reference is to pp. 130-149 of the book from which this selection was edited.

disappointment even when they lean toward an organizational orientation, given the limited number of managerial positions. Those who have a strong professional orientation are subject to a different kind of frustration, for their opportunities to gain high rewards *without* undertaking administrative tasks are even more limited. Here lies a clue to the relatively high level of job dissatisfaction expressed by industrial scientists and engineers. In the total sample of 622 scientists and engineers, only one-third stated that they were "very well satisfied" with their present jobs.[24] Other studies show that this figure is low compared to other nonmanual groups in industry, including office employees, office supervisors, sales personnel, and foremen (see Table 3-3).

Table 3-3.
Occupational Differences in Job Satisfaction

	Express Highest Satisfaction with Their Job
Study 1	
office supervisors	61%
sales	60
engineers and scientists	52
Study 2	
sales	53%
foremen	48
technical professionals	25
Study 3	
sales	46%
office employees	35
engineers and scientists	30

Source: *The Conflict Between the Management Mind and the Scientific Mind* (Princeton: Opinion Research Corporation, 1959), p. 3.

Compared with research scientists and engineers who do not have administrative duties, scientists and engineers in administrative positions are somewhat less dissatisfied with their jobs, more satisfied with their pay, more optimistic about their chances for advancement, and have more favorable attitudes toward their company. The higher morale of the administrators is solidly based in reality, for many more of them earn high salaries, have had a recent promotion, and participate in decisions affecting their work assignments. That their greater success is not necessarily related to superior professional competence may be inferred from the fact that

[24] *Ibid.,* p. 3.

fewer supervisors than nonsupervisors have Ph.D.'s. The organizational commitment of the administrators and the professional commitment of the practitioners is reflected in the higher proportion of administrators who deny there is any conflict between scientific or engineering goals and organizational goals, and by the lower proportions of administrators who would choose to be scientists or engineers again, or who believe that advancement in industry should be based principally on technical competence. The research and development administrators also are less critical of management and of the treatment accorded industrial scientists and engineers. Thus they are *less* likely than nonadministrative scientists and engineers to believe that (a) "engineers' and scientists' talents are channeled too closely to what *is* proven and profitable"; (b) "people in top company management often don't listen enough to understand engineers' and scientists' good ideas"; (c) "company practice often forces engineers and scientists to overspecialize"; and (d) "scientists and engineers ten years out of college are generally underpaid compared to others with similar training and responsibility. . . ."[25]

Conclusion

Professions and organizations are effective in achieving their goals only insofar as they can induce and sustain satisfactory levels of participation. However, they differ in the kind of participation each needs to realize its objectives. The need for participation, and for appropriate incentives, depends on the kind of work to be done and on the nature of the standards to be upheld.

An important aspect of this problem is the potential incompatibility of requirements for participation. For example, business firms seek to increase the commitment of their participants, so that the individual's main orientation, including his hopes for advancement, lies within the establishment. If, however, these participants are scientists or engineers, they also face demands for loyalty from their professions, which need member commitment in order to protect their own values and standards. As a result, interaction between professions and organizations produces competing orientations, career lines, and incentive systems.

Unless scientists are primarily concerned with their professional allegiance, they will be less likely to uphold scientific standards or to aspire to scientific excellence. Where scientific standards and aspirations are weak, the quality of scientific performance will not be high. Hence, where

[25] *Ibid.*, pp. A-40, A-42, A-45, A-48; cf. *Career Satisfaction of Professional Engineers in Industry*, in cooperation with the National Society of Professional Engineers (Washington, D.C.: Professional Engineers Conference Board for Industry, 1959), pp. 40-43, 53, 55, 61-62.

industry dampens the motivation of scientists to participate in outside professional activities, industrial research suffers.

At the same time, specialized organizations have their own needs, which cannot be served by professional competence alone. Industry, for example, requires coordination and utilization of a given expertise with other aspects of the firm. Hence, it needs other kinds of participation by scientists in addition to research excellence. Some scientists (and engineers) must be capable of lending administrative direction to research consistent with the firm's goals, while other technical specialists are needed to help bring research results to operational fruition. But insofar as research administration and utilization are stressed, research creativity and the professional commitment upon which it depends are weakened. Thus the tension between profession and organization becomes a tension within the organization itself.

One major area of conflict and accommodation lies in the relation between professional and organizational incentive systems. The scientific profession seeks contributions to knowledge by soliciting research papers for professional meetings and journals, and by rewarding intellectual excellence with honors and esteem. The industrial firm seeks contributions to production and sales by soliciting new or improved devices, and by rewarding commercial success with promotions in a hierarchy of status, income, and authority. The strain between these incentive systems may be counteracted in various ways, depending on the importance of excellence in research for the commercial achievements of the particular firm, and on the technical competence of the particular professional group. Where research is of great significance to the firm, it generally acquires a high-quality technical staff, which in turn exerts pressure on the company to provide opportunities for professional achievement. Thus we find in the first-rate industrial research organizations increasing use of professional incentives in combination with established organizational incentives. These adaptations of industrial firms to professional demands include time off for attendance at professional meetings sponsored by professional associations, as well as at additional meetings provided by the company itself; payment of professional dues; tuition refunds for further professional training; more liberal publication policies; professional ladders of advancement, which grant greater freedom in research rather than greater administrative responsibility; and so on. Professional people in turn have adapted to organizational demands by conforming to industrial routines; accepting responsibility for seeking commercially feasible devices; frequently assuming administrative positions; working closely with operations; and so on.

By means of these and other accommodations on both sides, the strain between professional and organizational requirements for participation is mitigated. The underlying conflict remains, of course, and is a continuing source of frustration on both sides. However, the relative absence of this tension holds its own dangers. For where the professional orientation gives way to organizational demands, as it tends to in the poorer research organizations, professional creativity suffers. Or where the organizational orientation gives way to professional demands, as occasionally happens in some of the best research organizations, professional utilization suffers.

Bibliography

Ahmad, J., *The Expert and the Administrator* (Pittsburgh: University of Pittsburgh Press, 1959).

Allen, R., "The Professional in Unions and His Educational Preparation," *Industrial and Labor Relations Review*, 16 (October, 1962), 16-29.

Argyris, C., *Executive Leadership: An Appraisal of a Manager in Action* (New York: Harper & Row, 1953).

Argyris, C., "Some Characteristics of Successful Executives," *Personnel Journal*, 32 (June, 1953), 50-55.

Bakke, E. W., *Citizens without Work* (New Haven, Conn.: Institute of Human Relations, Yale University Press, 1940).

Bakke, E. W., *The Unemployed Worker* (New Haven, Conn.: Yale University Press, 1940).

Barnard, C. I., *The Functions of the Executive* (Cambridge, Mass.: Harvard University Press, 1945).

Bellows, R., Gilson, T., and Odiorne, G., *Executive Skills: Their Dynamics and Development* (Englewood Cliffs, N.J.: Prentice-Hall, 1962).

Blauner, R., *Alienation and Freedom: The Factory Worker and His Industry* (Chicago, Ill.: The University of Chicago Press, 1964).

Blum, F. H., *Toward a Democratic Work Process: The Hormel-Packinghouse Workers' Experiment* (New York: Harper & Row, 1953).

Boggs, S. T., "The Values of Laboratory Workers," *Human Organization*, 22 (Fall, 1963), 207-215.

Chalmers, D., "From Robber Barons to Industrial Statesmen: Standard Oil and the Business Historians," *American Journal of Economics and Sociology*, 20 (October, 1960), 47-58.

Chinoy, E., *Automobile Workers and the American Dream* (Garden City, N.Y.: Doubleday, 1955).

Coates, C. H., and Pellegrin, R. J., "Executives and Supervisors: Contrasting Self Conceptions and Conceptions of Each Other," *American Sociological Review*, 22 (April, 1957), 217-220.

Dale, J. R., *The Clerk in Industry* (Liverpool, England: Liverpool University Press, 1962).

Dalton, M., "Managing the Managers," *Human Organizations*, 14 (Fall, 1955), 4-10.

Dalton, M., *Men Who Manage* (New York: Wiley, 1959).

Dalton, M., "The Role of Supervision," in A. Kornhauser, *et al.*, eds., *Industrial Conflict* (New York: McGraw-Hill, 1954), 176-185.

Danielson, L. E., "Management Relations with Engineers and Scientists," *Proceedings of the Industrial Relations Research Association*, December, 1957, 315-321.

Dearborn, D. C., and Simon, H., "Selective Perception: A Note on the Departmental Identifications of Executives," *Sociometry*, **21** (June, 1958), 140-144.

Denise, M., "The Personnel Manager and His Educational Preparation," *Industrial and Labor Relations Review*, **16** (October, 1962), 5-15.

Dick, H., "The Office Worker: Attitudes toward Self, Labor, and Management," *The Sociological Quarterly*, **3** (January, 1962), 45-56.

Drucker, P. F., *The Practice of Management* (New York: Harper & Row, 1954).

Dubin, R., "Industrial Workers' Worlds: A Study of the 'Central Life Interests' of Industrial Workers," *Social Problems*, **3** (January, 1956), 131-142.

Etzioni, A., "Lower Levels of Industrial Leadership," *Sociology and Social Research*, **43** (January-February, 1958), 209-212.

Foote, N. N., "The Professionalization of Labor in Detroit," *American Journal of Sociology*, **58** (January, 1953), 371-380.

Frank, A. G., "Administrative Role Definition and Social Change," *Human Organization*, **22** (Winter, 1963-1964), 238-242.

Friedmann, E. A., and Havighurst, R. J., *The Meaning of Work and Retirement* (Chicago: University of Chicago Press, 1954).

Friedmann, G., "Outline for a Psycho-Sociology of Assembly Line Work," *Human Organization*, **12** (Winter, 1954), 15-20.

Gardner, B. B., and Whyte, W. F., "The Man in the Middle: Position and Problems of the Foreman," *Applied Anthropology*, **4** (Spring, 1945), 1-28.

Gaudet, F. J., and Carli, A. R., "Why Executives Fail," *Personnel Psychology*, **10** (Spring, 1957), 7-21.

Ginzberg, E., ed., *What Makes an Executive* (New York: Columbia University Press, 1955).

Ginzberg, E., and Berman, H., *The American Worker in the Twentieth Century: A History through Autobiographies* (New York: Free Press, 1963).

Gordon, R. A., *Business Leadership in the Large Corporation* (Berkeley: University of California Press, 1961).

Granick, D., *The Red Executive: A Study of the Organization Man in Russian Industry* (Garden City, N.Y.: Doubleday, 1960).

Guest, R. H., "Foreman at Work—An Interim Report on Method," *Human Organization*, **14** (Summer, 1955), 21-24.

Guest, R. H., "Work Careers and Aspirations of Automobile Workers," *American Sociological Review*, **19** (April, 1954), 155-163.

Haire, M., Ghiselli, E. E., and Porter, L. W., "Cultural Patterns in the Role of the Manager," *Industrial Relations*, **2** (February, 1963), 95-118.

Henry, W. E., "The Business Executive: The Psychodynamics of a Social Role," *American Journal of Sociology*, **54** (January, 1949), 286-291.

Homans, G. C., "The Cash Posters: A Study of a Group of Working Girls," *American Sociological Review*, **19** (December, 1954), 724-733.

Homans, G. C., "Status Among Clerical Workers," *Human Organization*, **12** (Spring, 1953), 5-10.

Hubbard, H. G., and McDonagh, E. C., "The Business Executive as a Career Type," *Sociology and Social Research*, **47** (January, 1963), 138-146.

Humblet, J. E., "A Comparative Study of Management in Three European Countries: Preliminary Findings," *Sociological Review*, **9** (Winter, 1961), 351-360.

Jennings, E. E., *The Executive: Autocrat, Bureaucrat, Democrat* (New York: Harper & Row, 1962).

Kornhauser, W., *Scientists in Industry: Conflict and Accommodation* (Berkeley: University of California Press, 1962).

Langenderfer, H., "The Egyptian Executive: A Study in Conflict," *Human Organization*, **24** (Spring, 1965), 89-95.

Lauterbach, A., "Executive Training and Productivity: Managerial Views in Latin America," *Industrial and Labor Relations Review*, **17** (April, 1964), 357-379.

Mahoney, T. A., Jerdee, T. H., and Carroll, S. J., "The Job(s) of Management," *Industrial Relations*, **4** (February, 1965), 97-110.

Mann, F., and Dent, J., "The Supervisor: Member of Two Organization Families," *Harvard Business Review*, **32** (December, 1954), 103-112.

Marcson, S., *The Scientist in American Industry: Some Organizational Detriments in Manpower Utilization* (New York: Harper & Row, 1960).

Mills, C. W., "The American Business Elite: A Collective Portrait," *The Journal of Economic History*, **5** (December, 1945), 20-44.

Mills, C. W., *White Collar* (New York: Oxford University Press, 1951).

Moonman, E., *The Manager and the Organization* (London: Tavistock, 1961).

Moore, D. G., and Renck, R., "The Professional Employee in Industry," *Journal of Business*, **28** (January, 1955), 58-66.

Moore, W. E., *The Conduct of the Corporation* (New York: Random House, 1962).

Morse, N., *Satifactions in the White Collar Job* (Ann Arbor: Survey Research Center, Institute for Social Research, University of Michigan Press, 1953).

Parsons, T., "The Professions and Social Structure," *Social Forces*, **17** (May, 1939), 457-467.

Pfiffner, J. M., and Wilson, R. C., "Management Mindedness in the Supervisory Ranks," *Personnel*, **30** (September, 1953), 122-125.

Purcell, T. V., *Blue Collar Man: Patterns of Dual Allegiance in Industry* (Cambridge, Mass.: Harvard University Press, 1960).

Reiss, A. J., "Occupational Mobility of Professional Workers," *American Sociological Review*, **20** (December, 1955), 693-700.

Roethlisberger, F. J., "The Foreman: Master and Victim of Double Talk," *Harvard Business Review*, **23** (Spring, 1945), 283-298.

Roethlisberger, F. J., "The Territory and Skill of the Administrator," *Michigan Business Review*, **6** (November, 1954), 1-9.

Roethlisberger, F. J., and Dickson, W. J., *Management and the Worker* (Cambridge, Mass.: Harvard University Press, 1939).

Selznik, P., *Leadership in Administration* (New York: Harper & Row, 1957).

Seward, R. T., "Arbitration and the Functions of Management," *Industrial and Labor Relations Review*, **16** (January, 1963), 235-239.

Shartle, C., *Executive Performance and Leadership* (Englewood Cliffs, N.J.: Prentice-Hall, 1956).

Shostak, A. B., and Gomberg, W., *Blue Collar World—Studies of the American Worker* (Englewood, Cliffs, N.J.: Prentice-Hall, 1964).

Stepanek, J. E., *Managers for Small Industry: An International Study* (New York: Free Press, 1960).

Strauss, G., "The Changing Role of the Working Supervisor," *Journal of Business*, **30** (July, 1957), 202-211.

Strauss, G., "The Set-Up Men: A Case Study of Organizational Change," *Human Organization*, **13** (Summer, 1954), 17-25.

Tannenbaum, R., Wechsler, I. R., and Massarik, F., *Leadership and Organization: A Behavioral Science Approach* (New York: McGraw-Hill, 1961).

Tarkowski, Z. M., and Turnbull, A. V., "Scientists Versus Administrators: An Approach towards Achieving Greater Understanding," *Public Administration*, **37** (Autumn, 1959), 213-256.

Turner, A. N., "Foreman, Job and Company," *Human Relations*, **10** (April-June, 1957), 99-112.

Veblen, T., *The Engineers and the Price System* (New York: Viking, 1933).

Wald, R. M., and Doty, R. A., "The Top Executive—A Firsthand Profile," *Harvard Business Review*, **32** (July-August, 1954), 45-54.

Walker, C. R., and Guest, R. H., *The Man on the Assembly Line* (Cambridge, Mass.: Harvard University Press, 1953).

Walker, C. R., Guest, R. H., and Turner, A. N., *The Foreman on the Assembly Line* (Cambridge, Mass.: Harvard University Press, 1956).

Warner, W. L., and Abegglen, J. C., *Big Business Leaders in America* (New York: Harper & Row, 1955).

Wilensky, H. L., *Intellectuals in Labor Unions* (New York: Free Press, 1956).

Wray, D. E., "Marginal Men of Industry: The Foreman," *The American Journal of Sociology*, **54** (January, 1949), 298-301.

Zweig, F., *The Workers in an Affluent Society* (New York: Free Press, 1961).

THE INDUSTRIAL WORK GROUP AND INFORMAL ORGANIZATION

Introduction

This chapter deals with what has been called "bureaucracy's other face."[1] This expression refers to the fact that behavior in industrial organizations is regulated not only by formal rules and rationalized production technology but also by norms that develop spontaneously out of the interaction of people at work. One of the major early contributions of industrial sociology was an extensive documentation of this fact. There have been a large number of studies by industrial sociologists demonstrating the importance of taking informal work groups into account in understanding the functioning of industrial organizations. One of the purposes of this chapter is to present some examples of studies which illustrate major themes in the sociological concern with work groups. A second purpose is to provide the reader with a picture of the actual behavior of people in industry and some sense of how life in the factory is experienced by the people who work there.

.The traditional distinction between formal and informal social organization is between patterns of behavior resulting from the planned allocation of tasks and authority and patterns of behavior that simply emerge as the standardized ways of doing things in particular work groups. These unplanned work group norms may have direct relevance to the job, as in the case of a work group definition of what constitutes a fair day's work, but they also regulate actions having little or nothing to do with the work being performed. As Fred Katz points out in the first selection in this chapter, the formal rules and regulations regarding performance of work tasks leave a "sphere of autonomy" regarding nonwork related activities on the job. There are almost no jobs in industry that require constant attention or occupy all of the hours in a work day. Many of the studies of infor-

[1] Charles H. Page, "Bureaucracy's Other Face," *Social Forces*, **25** (October, 1946), 88-94.

mal social organization have focused upon the ways in which work groups regulate or establish expected patterns of behavior with regard to topics of conversation, horseplay, or other leisure activities during working hours. The distinction between formal and informal organization in these studies then is mainly a matter of differences in the regulation of work and non-work related activities on the job.

The fact that work group norms also affect the performance of work tasks and that these norms are frequently at variance with the norms formally established by management has been the subject of another large segment of studies of informal social organization. Particularly in earlier studies, the emphasis has been upon the restriction of output by work groups which establish and enforce a level of output regarded as an appropriate day's work. This research has dealt, for the most part, with piecework jobs where workers have control of the pace at which they work. There are possibilities, however, for output restriction even on more technologically advanced, machine-paced jobs although they are, of course, much more limited. The comparison of formal and informal organization in these studies has been largely a contrast between what people are *expected* to do on the job and what they *actually* do.

The two conceptions of informal social organization described above each have some deficiencies as guides to research on behavior in industrial bureaucracies. The view of informal organization as patterns in nonwork related behavior on the job does not pay sufficient attention to the fact that performance of the job is also regulated by informal group norms. The view that informal organization is what people actually do as opposed to what they are expected by management to do overemphasizes the dysfunctional consequences of informal work groups for organizational goals and underemphasizes the extent to which behavior on the job is controlled by technological and formal organizational factors. Also, neither of these approaches has been very consistently framed in terms that are relevant to sociological theory.

The conception of informal social organization used in this chapter begins with the distinction made by Katz between relatively controlled and relatively autonomous spheres of organizational structure. The emphasis, however, is upon the extent to which organizationally controlled activities are planned with reference to organizational goals, regulated through the formal authority structure of the organization, and subject to review and revision. The formal organizational structure represents, in other words, an attempt at "the methodical attainment of a definitely given and practical end by means of an increasingly precise calculation of adequate means": it is a *rationalized* structure in the sense that this term was used in the Introduction to this book.

It is impossible, however, to *devise* a set of relationships among people and a prescribed pattern of activities for them to engage in which is adequate for all contingencies in organizations as complex and subject to change as the modern industrial firm. The rationalized organizational structure does not precisely specify everything that is to be done even in regard to the work to be performed, and provides little or no regulation of nonwork related activities on the job.

In recurring social situations, such as the day-to-day contact of people at work, patterned or standardized ways of doing things almost universally develop. These patterns make it possible to predict and anticipate the behavior of others which is important both for psychological security and for reducing conflict in social relationships. Within the spheres of autonomy left unstructured by rationalized prescriptions and proscriptions or (and this is an important addition) where the formal specifications are not acceptable to particular segments of the organization, standardized definitions of situations develop out of the interaction of people in work groups. The important attribute of these work group norms for our purpose here is that group members seldom evaluate the adequacy of norms as means to specified ends and these norms are, in fact, more often valued, and tend to persist, as ends in themselves.[2] Informal organization in industry can be seen then as an example of the traditional mode of social organization described in the Introduction of this book.

The view of formal and informal social organization as involving a distinction between rational and traditional modes of organization represents a common element in most of the varied uses of these concepts in industrial sociology. It also places the analysis of informal organization in the context of the theory from which the general theme of this book is derived. The increasing rationalization of organizational structure and especially of technology has progressively reduced the sphere of autonomy in industry and, consequently, has diminished the impact of informal organization upon behavior at work. For blue-collar workers and lower level clerical workers this process has taken the form of an increase in the extent to which technology determines the nature of the job. For middle and upper level managers the change has involved an increase in the range of activities defined as work related and consequently subject to formal organizational control. At all organizational levels, however, work group traditions regulate some portion of behavior on the job.

Most sociological studies of informal organization have focused upon industrial workers and there have been relatively few studies of work groups at the managerial level. There is relatively less autonomy at this level and also a greater consistency between individual and organizational goals. Various studies, however, including some of those reported in Chapters

---

[2] Sociologists often speak of informal organization as though it were a means to specified ends as, for example, in the statement that participation in informal work groups is a means to relieve boredom. Workers themselves, however, rarely think in these terms.

II and III, leave little doubt that the informal or traditional mode of organization affects the behavior of industrial managers.[3] The study of work groups at this level represents a relatively neglected area of research in industrial sociology.

Another neglected area has been the analysis of differences among work groups and of the factors producing these differences. There is a tendency for studies of informal organization to speak of *the* work group as though it were a unitary phenomenon in spite of all the accumulated evidence regarding differences in work group norms. The one major study in this area is Leonard Sayles, *Behavior of Industrial Work Groups*.[4] Sayles, in a study of 300 groups in 30 plants, derived four basic types of work group: the "apathetic," the "erratic," the "strategic," and the "conservative." The differences among these four types are summarized in Figure 4-1.

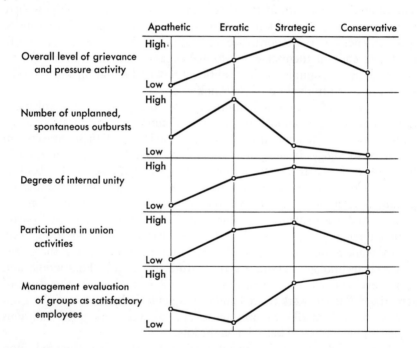

Figure 4-1.   Summary of Work Group Differences.

Source: Leonard R. Sayles, *Behavior of Industrial Work Groups* (New York: W 1958), p. 39. Reproduced by permission of the publisher.

[3] In addition to the readings by Dalton, Blau, Barnard and others in Chapters II and III of this book, see Michel Crozier, "Human Relations at the Management Level," *Human Organization*, **20** (Summer, 1961), 51-64.

[4] Leonard R. Sayles, *Behavior of Industrial Work Groups* (New York: Wiley, 1958).

Sayles' book contains extensive case descriptions of the four work group types and an explanation for the differences among them: ". . . the conclusions of this study indicate that the technology of the plant—the way jobs are distributed and flow into one another and the nature of the division of labor—molds the types of work groups that evolve within the plant."[5]

While this chapter is concerned mostly with the ways in which informal work groups regulate the behavior of their members, it should be kept in mind while reading it that the nature of the work group is determined to a considerable degree by the level and type of industrial technology.

The effects of technological change upon social relationships on the job represents, especially in recent years, one of the major themes in the industrial sociological study of work groups. These studies have dealt with the spacing between work stations, the functional interdependence of jobs, and the extent to which work is machine paced among other technological factors that affect work group formation. A disproportionate number of these studies have been done on assembly line and heavy machining operations, however, and there is a need for comparative studies of a broader range of industries.[6]

A second general theme, and the one which grows most directly out of the Mayo-human relations in industry tradition, is the study of the effect of work groups upon output. Group cohesiveness is one of the major variables used in these studies and there is ample evidence that a cohesive work group is a more effective social system in terms of ability to control its members through the informal or traditional mode of organization. Because work group control of the behavior of its members may be effective either in achieving or in subverting organizational goals, a major share of the research in this area has focused upon conflict between managerial and work group goals and upon ways to deal with this issue where it exists. It was particularly this "what to do about it" orientation of many early studies which produced the charge that industrial sociology was a "managerial sociology" in the sense of being biased toward management's goals.[7]

While these studies were concerned with the possible dysfunctions of cohesive work groups for the organization, another series of studies were being conducted demonstrating that informal social organization was *necessary* for the successful operation of the industrial firm. Many of the sociologists doing these studies were critics of classical bureaucratic theory and were concerned with documenting the fact that informal organization supplemented and complemented the rational organizational structure.

[5] Sayles, *op. cit.*, p. 4.

[6] Exceptions to this observation are Sayles, *op. cit.*, and Robert Blauner, *Alienation and Freedom* (Chicago: The University of Chicago Press, 1964).

[7] Cf. Harold Sheppard, "Managerial Sociology," Ph.D. dissertation, University of Wisconsin, 1948; and "Approaches to Conflict in American Industrial Sociology," *The British Journal of Sociology*, 5 (December, 1954), pp. 324-341.

Blau and Gouldner, samples of whose work appeared in Chapter II, are examples of sociologists who fall in this category. One of the principal ways in which informal organization assists in achieving organizational goals is by providing a communication channel among friends on the job that makes it possible to circumvent information bottlenecks in the formal communication network. There is also considerable evidence that membership in a cohesive work group improves the morale of people in functionally specialized jobs. Studies of this sort dealing with the functional consequences of work groups for the industrial firm may be regarded as a third major theme in the sociological study of informal organization.

A fourth theme has to do with effects of various styles of leadership upon work groups. The influence of Kurt Lewin and the field of group dynamics generally has been strong in this area. The hypothesis that has most often been tested is that a permissive or democratic style of supervision improves morale, increases output, decreases conflict between organizational and work group goals and has other generally favorable consequences. A considerable amount of evidence has been accumulated in support of this hypothesis. There is, however, conflicting evidence as well and it is clear that leadership style is only one of a number of variables determining the character and consequences of informal social organization.[8] The circumstances under which various supervisory styles are most effective is an important and, as yet, unresolved issue in industrial sociology.

In the preceding discussion we have identified four major themes in the study of informal organization in industry and three sociological traditions from which they derive: the Mayo-human relations approach, criticism of traditional theories of bureaucracy, and the Lewin-group dynamics orientation. During the early stages in the development of industrial sociology, studies of informal organization from these three perspectives represented a substantial proportion of the research being done by industrial sociologists. In recent years there has been a relative decline in interest in the industrial work group. To some extent, this may be due to the fact that sociologists in each of the major traditions have, in effect, made their point—the Mayoites have demonstrated that informal work groups affect output, the critics of older bureaucratic theories have demonstrated the importance of taking informal organization into account, and the Lewinians have, to some extent, demonstrated the efficacy of permissive supervision. There are, of course, still sociologists working in these areas and a more important reason for the *relative* decline in interest in field studies of industrial work groups has been a rapid growth in related areas such as the

[8] Cf. Harold L. Wilensky, "Human Relations in the Workplace: An Appraisal of Some Recent Research," in Conrad M. Arensberg, *et. al.*, *Research in Industrial Human Relations* (New York: Harper & Row, 1957), pp. 25-50.

study of formal organization and experimental laboratory studies of group processes.

Research dealing with the industrial work group represents a limited segment of a broader sociological concern with small, face-to-face groups. Published accounts of research in this area accumulated at a rate of about 10 per year prior to 1940 but at a rate of over 200 per year more recently.[9] Experimental studies conducted in small group laboratories account for much of this increase. The traditional industrial sociological concern with the work group—the linkage between the informal and formal organization —is, however, difficult to study in the laboratory. Field studies of actual work groups in industry are required for this purpose and research of this sort has been relatively less frequent in recent years. One additional reason for this decline in interest may be that some of the earlier studies had an applied or policy-oriented focus and there has been, as was noted in the Introduction to this book, a general shift in sociology away from a social problems orientation and toward a social scientific one. For whatever reasons, most of the major studies of informal organization in industry were conducted prior to 1960 and most of the selections included in this chapter were originally published prior to that time.

The first selection in this chapter is Katz' reformulation of the formal-informal dichotomy in terms of the concept of autonomous and controlled spheres of activity. The emphasis in this reading is upon the extent to which the autonomy permitted the industrial worker allows a continuity of the working class style of life between on the job and off the job activities. Katz states that the "white-collar worker takes his work role *outside* the organization; the blue-collar worker brings his nonwork role *into* the organization."

The next selection is a description of the important phases of Mayo's Hawthorne plant studies which have been identified as the starting point for industrial sociology as a separate field. This article details the gradual recognition by the researchers that physiological and individual psychological explanations were inadequate to account for their findings. One of the criticisms directed at these studies was that it took the researchers so many years to "discover" the importance of a sociological analysis of work group processes. Frederick W. Taylor had noted as early as 1911 that work group norms may have the effect of restricting output.[10] By all accounts, however, the Hawthorne studies were one of the important events in the history of industrial sociology.

The next selection, by Donald Roy, is based upon his experience as a radial drill operator in a machine shop. As a participant observer in this

[9] Robert T. Golembiewski, "Small Groups and Large Organizations," in James G. March, ed., *Handbook of Organizations* (Chicago: Rand McNally, 1965), p. 87.
[10] Cited in Golembiewski, *op. cit.*, pp. 105-106.

situation, he accumulated considerable evidence regarding the ways in which informal group processes serve to limit production to a level defined as appropriate by the work group. He makes a distinction between "gold bricking" and "quota restriction" and notes that the nature of the job determines which of these types of limitation of output are likely to occur. This reading, along with several others in this chapter, was selected in part because it contains many direct quotes from workers and may provide the reader with some sense of the nature of work in an industrial organization.

The major point in the next reading, by Edward Gross, is that informal group relations and norms supplement formally specified relations and norms and help to make them more effective. With data collected in a small manufacturing plant and a U.S. Air Force radar site, he examines the ways in which the informal organization helps to resolve problems occasioned by extreme functional specialization of jobs, formally prescribed channels of communication, and official personnel assignment procedures.

"Group Cohesiveness in the Industrial Work Group" by Stanley Seashore, the next reading in this chapter, is the concluding section of a book reporting one of the most extensive studies of work groups conducted so far in industrial sociology. Seashore studied 228 work groups having a total of 5,871 members in an attempt to discover the factors which produce group cohesiveness and the consequences of this work group attribute. This study demonstrates the importance of cohesiveness in order for groups to function as groups in the sense of facilitating communication, improving morale, establishing production norms, and, in general, controlling the behavior of group members.

The Coch and French reading which follows reports one of the most frequently cited studies of work group participation in decision-making. The experiment was a dramatic example of the effectiveness of involving members of work groups in a decision to change the nature of their jobs. Groups that were given this opportunity had higher levels of output and a faster learning time on the new jobs than groups which did not participate in the decision to change. One reason for the success of this experiment and for permissive leadership in general may be that it incorporates the informal organizational structure into the formal decision-making process and tends to place formally designated leaders within informal status and authority hierarchies. It should be noted, however, that a replication of the Coch and French experiment in Norway achieved only partially the same results and that, while other studies have shown the effectiveness of group participation in decision-making, there are also some with contradictory findings.[11]

The next selection, the one by Raymond Mack, presents another way

[11] Cf. J. R. P. French, Jr., J. Israel, and D. As, "An Experiment on Participation in a Norwegian Factory: Interpersonal Dimensions of Decision-making," *Human Relations*, 13 (February, 1961), 3-19; and Wilensky, *op. cit.*

in which informal organizational patterns may be shaped: elements of the structure of the community may intrude upon division of labor or other formal processes in the work place. The study reported here is of a railroad car repair shop in a community in which there are two residentially segregated ethnic groups—Swedes and Italians. This pattern of segregation within the community is carried over into the repair shop where the two ethnic groups work at different kinds of jobs, are spatially separated at work, and have different sets of tables in the company lunch room. Even formal seniority agreements are violated in order to preserve ethnic homogeneity in particular work areas. Segregation on the job serves to reduce conflict in this instance and is an example of the substitution of informal traditional patterns for formal rational ones.

The final selection in this chapter is from Charles Walker's book, *Toward the Automatic Factory*. It demonstrates the importance of technology as a determinant of the organization of social relationships on the job. As a result of the introduction of more automated machinery for making steel pipe, the size of the work group was reduced, opportunities for talking to coworkers were decreased, more contact between workers and higher supervisory levels occurred, and some informal status differences among jobs were eliminated. Various problems in adjustment of workers to the new technology were also reported, most of which were overcome later as machine breakdowns became less frequent and workers became accustomed to their new jobs. (This process is reported in more detail in a later section of the book from which this selection was edited.) While the plant Walker studied was, at the time, one of the most technologically advanced in the steel industry, it should be kept in mind while reading this selection that in industries like oil refining and chemical processing there are plants which come much closer to being "automatic factories." A different pattern of effects of technology upon informal social organization has been observed in these industries.[12]

[12] Cf. Blauner, *op. cit.*; William A. Faunce, "Automation and the Division of Labor," *Social Problems*, 13 (Fall, 1965), 149-160.

18. Explaining Informal Work Groups in Complex Organizations: The Case for Autonomy in Structure

Fred E. Katz

A generation after the Hawthorne studies, no one questions the existence of informal groups in complex organizations. Numerous studies have documented their existence, especially among employees in the lowest ranks. But the task remains of developing an adequate *conceptual* explanation of how persons in the lowest ranks, with their limited career prospects in their work and slight opportunity for advancement, are incorporated into work organizations on a relatively permanent basis. Stated differently, how can one account for the integration of organizations that include a large number of persons who are largely disenfranchised from the organization's reward system? How can one account for the apparent collaboration, if not loyalty, of persons who, since the time of Marx, have been described as being alienated from their work?[1] A brief, though oversimplified answer is that workers need work and factories need workers. One can hardly argue with this statement. Yet, the economic interdependence of workers and factories does not clarify the nature of the structural arrangement under which the interdependence is worked out.

The proposed answer to the question of how workers are incorporated into complex organizations has two aspects: (1) Workers have considerable autonomy within the confines of the organization. Even when their work is prescribed in exact detail, the work role tends to be defined narrowly. This leaves a considerable portion of the worker's life within the work organization *undefined*. (2) Workers tend to use this autonomy to bring their working-class culture into the organization, even though this is alien to the bureaucratic ethos of the higher echelons of the organization. This produces continuity between the workman's outside life and his participation in the work setting—a setting to which he has very limited alle-

Reprinted from *Administrative Science Quarterly*, **10** (September, 1965), pp. 204-223.

[1] For a survey and research application of the theme of worker alienation, see Robert Blauner, *Alienation and Freedom: The Factory Worker and His Industry* (Chicago: University of Chicago, 1964).

giance.[2] This continuity in turn promotes workers' integration into work organizations. After a general presentation of this perspective, it is illustrated through a detailed review of one of Donald Roy's case studies of factory workers. No attempt will be made to assess the degree of fit of this perspective to particular types of industries.

The guiding perspective is that the culture of informal work groups is a manifestation of autonomy within the confines of the organization, and that autonomy is an aspect of organizational structure that needs systematic study. Autonomy is defined as independence from external control. Here, it means that the activities of workers within the organization are not fully controlled by the organization. This leaves room for development of informal patterns of various sorts—those that lessen boredom of workers, those that help get work done, as well as those that are alienative to the organization. I shall attempt to view autonomy as an aspect of the very structure of organizations, as spheres of independence which are delegated by the organization. Direct and indirect delegation of autonomy suggest themselves. The first refers to specific rules that delimit an area of autonomy. For example, a rule specifying that the foreman can decide who will work the night shift indicates a sphere in which the foreman has autonomy, one in which he exercises discretion. By contrast indirect delegation of autonomy results from the absence of rules; in a sphere where no clear rules exist, autonomy exists by default. Both direct and indirect delegation of autonomy promotes spheres of activity that are not closely controlled by the organization. The present thesis is that the resulting autonomous behavior needs to be considered as an aspect of organizational structure, not merely as deviance. This paper will mainly examine autonomy based on indirect delegation, since this seems to characterize informal patterns among workers.

Worker autonomy can be regarded as part of the barter arrangement between workers and the organization, where limited affiliation with the organization is exchanged for a degree of autonomy. The arrangement has important adaptive functions for both parties. For the organization it is a way of promoting the affiliation of some of its employees with the organization, while at the same time excluding them from certain vital spheres of

---

[2] For a summary of the literature on the limited commitment of workers to the complex organizations in which they work, as well as to work itself, see Chris Argyris, *Integrating the Individual and the Organization* (New York: Wiley, 1964). In Part IV the author provides a summary of the debate as to whether the worker is alienated. Argyris' book is addressed to the same general issue as the present paper, but his approach differs in that it focuses on the issue—a very important one—of developing organizational patterns so that there is congruence between the psychological needs of members and the administrative requirements of the organization. The present paper, in contrast, attempts to remain entirely on the level of social structure. See, also, R. Dubin, "Industrial Workers' World: A Study of the 'Central Life Interest' of Industrial Workers," in Erwin O. Smigel, ed., *Work and Leisure* (New Haven, Conn.: College and University Press, 1963), pp. 53-72.

organizational activity. For workers it permits continuation of the working-class style of life and provides ties of sociability in a context that in many ways is alien to the workman's culture. In short, the autonomy appears to have adaptive and pattern-maintenance functions for the workers, and adaptive and goal-attainment functions for the organization. It must be noted that worker autonomy, although enacted *in* the work organization is essentially *external* to his work role. This contrasts with the autonomy pattern for white-collar workers, that is, all those who—from the lowliest clerk to the president—make up the administrative hierarchy. They have greater autonomy *within* their work role, but their role is more broadly defined than that of the worker.[3] In a sense the white-collar worker takes his work role *outside* the organization; the blue-collar worker brings his nonwork role *into* the organization.

This use of the term "autonomy" covers part of the same ground that is now covered by the term "informal organization;" but I hope it will eliminate some of the difficulties that exist in the way informal organization is now distinguished from formal organization. Simon and his colleagues summarize the existing distinction.[4] Formal organization is defined as "a planned system of cooperative effort in which each participant has a recognized role to play and duties or tasks to perform."[5] Informal organization is defined as "the whole pattern of actual behavior—the way members of the organization really do behave—insofar as these actual behaviors do not coincide with the formal plans."[6] One reason for questioning this distinction is that it has led to research strategies that appear to have produced a self-fulfilling prophecy by inadvertently reiterating the contention that informal patterns deviate from the planned system, without subjecting this contention to critical analysis. It comes about somewhat as follows: The official rules do not prescribe informal behavior patterns; therefore, informal behavior must be discovered through direct, detailed investigation —usually by direct observation of ongoing behavior. Direct observation is very likely to emphasize actual behavior rather than abstract rules, collaboration on the local level rather than collaboration with the total organization, innovation and departure from rules rather than compliance. All these artifacts of the research process are conducive to perpetuating the initial contention that informal patterns deviate from the planned system. As a result, despite evidence that informal patterns may be very firmly established within an organization,[7] the view persists that informal patterns lack

---

[3] This viewpoint is more fully developed in Fred E. Katz, "The School As a Complex Organization," *Harvard Educational Review*, **34** (Summer, 1964).

[4] Herbert A. Simon, Donald W. Smithburg, and Victor Thompson, *Public Administration* (New York: Knopf, 1962).

[5] *Ibid.*, p. 5.

[6] *Ibid.*, p. 87.

[7] Fritz J. Roethlisberger and William J. Dickson, *Management and the Worker* (Cambridge: Harvard University Press, 1939). This classic report is still one of the most

legitimacy and permanence. If the behavior patterns that are relevant to formal structure were subjected to detailed observational scrutiny, one might well discover a picture far closer to so-called informal patterns than we now have.[8]

The definition of formal organization focuses on a planned system, and the definition of informal organization on actual behavior. This is a weak distinction, theoretically. Actual behavior is undoubtedly relevant to planned systems; and system characteristics, even planned ones, are relevant to actual behavior. The distinction seems to need refocusing to enable orderly analysis of structure and ongoing behavior. I would suggest the following perspective: Organizational structure includes relatively controlled and relatively autonomous spheres. The controlled sphere is based on direct specification of behavior; the autonomous sphere is based on both direct and indirect specification of behavior. Direct specification of behavior approximates the formal organization concept; but it allows spheres of autonomy as well as spheres of controlled activity. The indirect specification of behavior approximates the traditional informal organization, but under comparable conceptual footing with the planned formal system.

The writings of Chester Barnard illustrate that autonomous and controlled behavior coexist within organizations and that the executive must fuse them together.[9] He notes that autonomy among personnel is not necessarily a disaster to executive control but may, in fact, be an asset to administrative processes. He suggests that the executive must rely on the "willingness to serve"[10] of those under his command; he must recognize that there is a "zone of indifference"[11] in which persons are prepared to accept orders, and beyond which they are prone to oppose orders. Informal patterns, in Barnard's view of the executive, are not divisive forces, but instead are "expansion of the means of communication with reduction in the necessity for formal decisions, the minimizing of undesirable influences, and the promotion of desirable influences concordant with the scheme of formal responsibilities."[12] From Barnard's perspective both formal and informal patterns can be harnessed in the service of a "co-operating system." But it seems that the real point is not the blending of formally and informally organized behavior, but the blending of controlled and autonomous behaviors that exist within organizations. Barnard's model of the

---

complete studies of informal groups. See also Peter M. Blau, "Structural Effects," *American Sociological Review,* **25** (1960), 178-193; also his *The Dynamics of Bureaucracy* (Chicago: University of Chicago, 1955).

[8] Indeed, Blau's work comes close to providing just such a picture; see Blau, "The Dynamics of Bureaucracy," *op. cit.*

[9] Chester I. Barnard, *The Functions of the Executive* (Cambridge: Harvard University, 1938).

[10] *Ibid.,* p. 83 ff.

[11] *Ibid.,* p. 167 ff.

[12] *Ibid.,* p. 227.

organization is suffused with autonomy patterns that can serve the whole organization; some of these patterns proceed from direct official specification of behavior and some come from indirect specification.

The Worker's Place in the Organization

Workers are here viewed as being permitted to develop relatively autonomous subcultures and subsystems of social interaction in their day-to-day routines. The autonomous patterns diverge from the officially prescribed patterns, but are very much in line with the workman's style of life and culture outside the organization. The culture of the working-class man is in many ways alien to the decorum and demeanor expected of white-collar members of the organization. In the routinized work of the white-collar worker there is no room for the sudden display of anger of the working-class male; in the face-the-public white-collar worker there is little scope for the pervasive sexual allusions of the working-class male. Yet within the working clique inside the organization the workman can enact the culture patterns of his life outside the organization. He can, for example, indulge freely in what is perhaps the workman's major form of creative mental activity: verbal play, imaginative exploits, and the romanticism on the theme of sex.[13] Indeed, the workman has a large sphere of verbal freedom, since much of what he says "doesn't count," so far as his work is concerned. Unlike the white-collar worker, whose work consists of a world of words, written and spoken, the worker is basically measured by the contributions of his hands. Therefore, his verbal jostlings, such as the razzing of the lowest person on the prestige totem pole, are not considered part of his job. There is every indication (as is shown in the review of the study by Donald Roy), that the content of the verbal banter contains reference to the workman's niche in the social order and the conditions of his social existence.[14] These are also reflected in patterns of practical jokes and prankish physical contact, which are characteristic of the workman's culture, but taboo in the culture of the white-collar worker.[15]

By contrast, the white-collar workers, whether senior executive or junior administrators, have a broad affinity for the organizational style of

[13] I am not suggesting that middle and upper class males do not engage in this form of mental sport, but I do suggest that for the working-class male it is a *major* creative outlet, and much less so for the middle and upper classes.

[14] S. M. Miller and Frank Riessman suggest that the "factory 'horseplay,' the ritualistic kidding" are partly an expression of the working-class theme of person centeredness; see their "The Working-Class Subculture," in A. B. Shostak and W. Gomberg, eds., *Blue Collar World* (Englewood Cliffs, N.J.: Prentice-Hall, 1964), pp. 24-35.

[15] Participating in physical contact—be it fighting, prankish shoving, or contact sports—are chiefly characteristic of male preadult culture. Presumably it is only at the low socioeconomic levels that this pattern continues into adulthood. It is not clear whether similar continuities exist between *preadult* and adult female culture among working-class women.

behavior. They are likely to be members of the middle or upper class, where they have learned the demeanor and proprieties of manner they will be expected to exercise in their position in the organization.[16] There is little abrupt discontinuity, for instance, between the style of dress and speech of their social class and that associated with the bureaucratic style of behavior. Stated differently, they can carry over elements of their external life into the organization and apply them to their job without having to make fundamental adjustments in their general style of behavior; although this does not mean that they have nothing to learn in their work. The organization-man thesis makes the same point in converse terms: The work habits and interests of the white-collar worker spill over into his family and community life. For the white-collar worker, the organization is less clearly differentiated from the culture of his private world than it is from the private world of the worker; the organization is not the enemy camp. The blue-collar worker, on the other hand, is eager to leave his work behind him as he leaves the gates of the factory.[17]

How does autonomy in the role of white-collar worker differ from that of the worker? Briefly stated, white-collar workers have greater autonomy *in their task-related activities* than does the blue-collar worker: the time clock; the regimentation involved in feeding a machine and gearing one's work to the pace of a machine, of doing one's work exclusively at the location of a particular machine—these apply to the blue-collar worker to a far larger extent than to the white-collar worker. For the latter, work is defined more broadly than it is for the blue-collar worker, requiring a more diffuse commitment. This means that for the white-collar worker a broad range of activities and personal attributes are defined as relevant to work, from personal grooming to getting along with others. Organizing a Little League baseball team, the fate of the local community chest drive, and participation in college alumni affairs—a good organization man's allegiance to the organization and his style of work include taking part in these activities after working hours and communicating these interests to his work peers. It is difficult to assess which activities are regarded as clearly *external* to his work role. On the other hand, the worker's tasks are defined more narrowly, leaving scope for activity that is defined as *external* to his work, but enacted while he is at his place of work.

The limited bases for the worker's *allegiance* to the work organization are given tacit recognition not only in the worker being excluded from administrative decision making, but also in his being allowed to bring into the work setting working-class culture patterns and to fashion them into relatively autonomous subcultures. In short, the worker's external affiliations;

---

[16] It makes little difference whether they are members of the middle or upper class or use these classes as a reference group to guide their behavior.

[17] Robert Blauner, "Occupational Differences in Work Satisfaction," in R. L. Simpson and I. H. Simpson, eds., *Social Organization and Behavior* (New York: Wiley, 1964), pp. 287-292.

i.e., with the working-class style of life, are permitted to intrude into the organization that employs him. This can be viewed as part of the exchange (in addition to monetary pay) for limited forms of reward and participation that the worker is allowed by the employing organization. In view of the differentiation between worker subculture and bureaucratic culture the worker's immersion in working-class patterns may serve to perpetuate his disenfranchisement from the administrative sphere, resulting in a vicious cycle.

The pattern pictured thus far of workers in relation to factory is chiefly characteristic of the modern western world. A contrasting example exists in the Japanese pattern, where the worker is expected to make a lifetime commitment to one firm.[18] The worker does not expect to leave his initial place of employment—the idea of moving to a better job seems highly incongruous. The firm does not intend to dismiss employees, no matter how uneconomical this may prove to be. In this arrangement the worker's affiliation with the firm is a relatively complete one, and there appears to be little external autonomy.

Enactment of Worker Autonomy: An Example

The empirical study of workers in factories has been a favorite of sociologists and social psychologists. The focus of many of these studies is on what actually goes on in work settings. Among the most eloquently descriptive studies of the culture and interaction patterns of workers are those by Donald F. Roy. One of his studies, his "Banana Time," will therefore be examined at some length.[19] Roy describes a small work group of men engaged in exceedingly simple manual work—operating a punch press—it took about fifteen minutes to learn the job. Roy himself participated, and his description bears the mark of intimate immersion in the field situation while, at the same time, bringing to it keen observational skills. He describes how he attempted, during the early days of work, to meet the problems of great boredom by inventing little games. He partly succeeded. After a while he noticed that the banterings and "kidding" by the workers around him were not purely haphazard, but actually served a similar function as his games; they, too, reduced boredom. Following this insight he made systematic studies and discovered *patterns* among the bantering and joking.

What I saw at first, before I began to observe, was occasional flurries of horse play so simple and unvarying in pattern and so childish in quality that they

---

[18] James C. Abegglen, *The Japanese Factory: Aspects of Its Social Organization* (New York: Free Press, 1960). Opinion differs as to whether Abegglen's formulation about life-long commitment applies to blue-collar workers in large factories. (I am indebted to the editors for this insight.)

[19] Donald F. Roy, "'Banana Time': Job Satisfaction and Informal Interaction," *Human Organization*, 18 (1960), 158-168.

made no strong bid for attention. For example, Ike would regularly switch off the power at Sammy's machine whenever Sammy made a trip to the lavatory or the drinking fountain. Correlatively, Sammy invariably fell victim to the plot by making an attempt to operate his clicking hammer after returning to the shop. And, as the simple pattern went, this blind stumbling into the trap was always followed by indignation and reproach from Sammy, smirking satisfaction from Ike, and mild paternal scolding from George. My interest in this procedure was first confined to wondering when Ike would weary of his tedious joke or when Sammy would learn to check his power switch before trying the hammer.

But, as I began to pay closer attention, as I began to develop familiarity with the communication system, the disconnected became connected, the nonsense made sense, the obscure became clear, and the silly actually funny. And, as the content of the interaction took on more and more meaning, the interaction began to reveal structure.[20]

Roy discovered that the day's routine was broken by activities other than those formally instituted (by the company) or "idiosyncratically developed disjunctions," but were an "ordered series of informal interactions." He describes many forms of interruption that took place and the patterning involved in them. One of these was "peach time," when one worker, Sammy, provided a peach and shared it. His beneficiaries greeted his contribution with disgruntlement and complaints about the quality of the peach. "Banana time" followed.

Banana time followed peach time by approximately an hour. Sammy again provided the refreshments, namely, one banana. There was, however, no four-way sharing of Sammy's banana. Ike would gulp it down by himself after surreptitiously extracting it from Sammy's lunch box, kept on a shelf behind Sammy's work station. Each morning, after making the snatch, Ike would call out, "Banana time!" and proceed to down his prize, while Sammy made futile protests and denunciations. George would join in with mild remonstrances, sometimes scolding Sammy for making so much fuss. The banana was one which Sammy brought for his own consumption at lunch time; he never did get to eat his banana, but kept bringing one for his lunch. At first this daily theft startled and amazed me. Then I grew to look forward to the daily seizure and the verbal interaction that followed.[21]

In addition to peach time and banana time there was coffee time, fish time, coke time, lunch time, and window-opening time. Each of them was marked by a distinctive pattern of interaction. In addition to these patterned times, Roy notes themes in verbal interplay.

The themes had become standardized in their repetition . . . topics of conversation ranged in quality from an extreme of nonsensical chatter to another ex-

[20] *Ibid.*, p. 161.
[21] *Ibid.*, p. 162.

treme of serious discourse. Unlike the times, these themes flowed one into the other in no particular sequence of predictability. Serious conversation could suddenly melt into horse play, and vice versa. In the middle of a serious discussion on the high cost of living, Ike might drop a weight behind the easily startled Sammy, or hit him over the head with a dusty paper sack. Interactions would immediately drop to a low comedy exchange of slaps, threats, guffaws, and disapprobations. . . .[22]

In this verbal interplay exaggeration was a common feature. For instance, one of the men had received one hundred dollars from his son; from that day he was seen as a man with a sizable, steady income—a man ready to retire. Roy, after having admitted that he owned two acres of land, became a large landowner, and his farm became populated with horses, cows, pigs, and chickens. Sexuality also came in for a large share of regular and inventive verbal play.

Roy's article is perhaps a culmination in a series of research findings that, since the days of the Hawthorne studies, have pointed to the demise of the economic man without, however, completing the task of making social organization the focus of analysis. The early studies, in their opposition to the economic-man thesis, pointed out that the individual was not guided only by his own monetary self-interest. Indeed, he could be guided against his own self-interest by his worker peer group; the individual worker might actually lose income by following the output control patterns of his peers. It was emphasized that there was a "group factor" in work situations; but an individualistic, social psychological focus was retained for this group factor. In the Hawthorne studies there was much concern with changes in attitude toward work; the meaning of work was considered a basic factor in individuals' performance; and work groups were considered in molding the meaning and attitudes for members of the group.[23] Roy's interpretation of his findings is similarly social psychological. It is that the informal patterns serve primarily to provide job satisfaction by relieving *boredom*. Along with many students of industrial relations in the last thirty years, he notes the existence of relatively distinct subgroups that have relatively distinct culture and interaction patterns, and that are separate from the formal structure in the factory. Yet, the basic interpretation is in individualistic, psychological terminology: it relieves boredom. Even if one accepts the psychological perspective, one must question whether routine, repetitive work is necessarily conducive to boredom. For example, Chinoy's study of automobile assembly-line workers suggests that workers' response to routine, repetitive work is perhaps better characterized by irritation over lack of control over one's work than by boredom.[24] To realize that routine,

[22] *Ibid.*, p. 163.

[23] Fritz J. Roethlisberger and William J. Dickson, *op. cit.*, and Edward Gross, *Work and Society* (New York: Crowell, 1958), Ch. XIV.

[24] Ely Chinoy, *Automobile Workers and the American Dream* (Garden City, N.Y.: Doubleday, 1955).

repetitive activity does not necessarily lead to boredom, one should allow for the influence of culture. The researcher may be exaggerating the activistic theme of Western societies. The Jicarilla Apache, for example, "have an infinite capacity for not being bored. They can sit for hours on end and apparently do nothing; they certainly don't intellectualize about doing nothing."[25]

The focus of the present paper suggests attention to what seems to be a basic feature in the social organization of the work situation, the autonomy enjoyed by the work group.[26] It does this on Roy's evidence that *considerable structuring of the work situation is done by the workers themselves.* What, then, is the content of the autonomous group culture? As Roy describes it, the work situation includes a great variety of behaviors that are not directly connected with *work.* Many of these fit Simmel's description of play forms of social reality.[27] Subjects that are of serious concern, such as economic security, sexual virility, health and death, submission to the authority of other men, family loyalty, and status aspirations are examined in a context where they are stripped of their serious content. But the manner in which attention is paid to these subjects is particularly important. Flitting from one topic to another—from the deeply serious to the comic, from the immediately practical to the remotely romantic—indicates the decided irrelevance of the practical, concrete reality in which each of the subjects is embedded. Perhaps it is because members are simultaneously engaged in serious work that they feel free to treat other concerns so detachedly. Roy's group appears to be a veritable haven for the enactment of play forms. Elements of life that are largely beyond the control of the individual are exposed and, in a fashion, are dealt with. All this is most clearly evident in the verbal themes. In addition to play forms, it may well be that the various social interaction patterns—the "razzing" of Sammy, the paternalism of George—are reiterations of serious realities in the larger social context in which the men find themselves. It is noteworthy that it is Sammy, the newest immigrant (all three men are immigrants) who is the scapegoat; it is George, the only Gentile, who quietly occupies the superior status; it is the Negro handy-man who is the object of stereotypical banter about uncontrolled sexuality.

These elements, whether they are fairly explicit reiterations or play forms of the workman's life outside the factory, are continuities between life outside the factory and life inside the factory and therefore are important for understanding the nature of the bond between the worker and the organization in which he is employed. Work peers participate in a

[25] Personal communication from H. Clyde Wilson.
[26] Focus on autonomy structure does not altogether avoid the pitfall of potentially overemphasizing one set of structures and one set of functions, just as social-psychological studies have done. But it should serve to broaden the existing basis of analysis.
[27] K. H. Wolff, ed. and trans., *The Sociology of George Simmel* (New York: Free Press, 1950).

common culture, which relies heavily on their common fate both within and *outside* the organization. In their commonality they retain a fundamental alienation from the white-collar ranks in the organization. This appears to be demonstrated in Chinoy's findings of workers' widespread lack of interest in becoming foremen or white-collar workers.[28] It is also supported by Walker and Guest's study of assembly-line workers. They found largely favorable reaction by workers to their immediate job, but intense dissatisfaction with the factory as a whole.[29] Although there is a lack of affiliation with the white-collar ranks of the organization, the worker *does* form bonds within the organization—with his own work peers.[30] For the organization, this dual relationship provides an uneasy truce without lessening the fundamental internal antithesis, and manifests itself in problems of morale and communications. At the same time the structure of the situation—the existence of two cultures—assures the continuity of the basic antithesis.

Roy points out that the group had developed a "full-blown sociocultural system." The group was to a considerable extent a separate and distinct system, one in which the members had active, at times even creative, participation—in sharp contrast to their minimal participation in the larger organization. But it does not seem that *work* was at all a major focus of this sociocultural system! If one accepts this point, one gains a tool for reconciling the dilemma as to whether factory workers are strongly alienated from their work.[31] It appears that work is *one of a variety* of topics around which Roy's group had developed behavioral patterns, but work was by no means the central point of attention of this "full-blown sociocultural system."

The contention that work is not a central feature of Roy's work group differs considerably from traditional explanations of informal groups. Although no claim is made about the representativeness of the Roy group, it must be understood that the sort of data he presented has traditionally

[28] Chinoy, *op. cit.*; see especially, Ch. V. See also, E. W. Bakke, *The Unemployed Worker* (New Haven: Yale University, 1940); and poll conducted by *Fortune* (May, 1947), both cited by Chinoy. Chinoy's explanation of the lack of desire for promotion is that workers have become so discouraged in the course of their work careers that they have given up. He notes that workers are reacting to "the limited opportunities available, to the uncertainties stemming from the informal procedures by which foremen were chosen, and to the nature of the foreman's job itself . . ." (p. 49). This explanation is not irreconcilable with the one offered here. The young factory worker, who does have visions of advancement, is presumably not sufficiently knowledgeable about the culture wall between himself and the administrative bureaucrat.

[29] Charles R. Walker and Robert H. Guest, *The Man on the Assembly Line* (Cambridge, Mass.: Harvard University, 1952), see, for example, pp. 139-140.

[30] Dubin's studies suggest, however, that workers' friendship bonds with work peers are less important than bonds with peers outside the work setting; see Robert Dubin, *op. cit.*

[31] Argyris, *op. cit.*, believes that workers are strongly alienated; Walker and Guest, *op. cit.*, note that workers they studied were relatively contented doing simple, repetitive work.

been interpreted largely in terms of its relevance to *work*. Statements to the effect that informal activities give meaning to dull, routine factory work[32] and that "work output is a function of the degree of work satisfaction, which in turn depends upon the informal social patterns of the work group"[33] are typical examples. These statements provide a social-psychological explanation of the group's mediating effect between the individual and his work, but they are hardly adequate in providing a structural explanation of the place of informal groups in a complex organization.

In addition to the social-psychological interpretations, there are well-documented studies—by Roy and others—which show production control and worker collusion against management by informal groups of workers.[34] Here there can be no doubt that informal patterns are relevant to work. But it is not certain, even here, that informal groups exist primarily for the worker's control over work or whether the explanation should not be reversed: that control over work exists because of the presence of informal groups which in turn exist because of the worker's relative autonomy.

In summary, it is suggested that Roy's work group exhibits a rich sociocultural system that is made possible by substantial worker autonomy. The autonomy exists by default; worker's roles are narrowly defined, leaving a considerable sphere of undefined action within the confines of the organization. The content of worker's sociocultural system is made up of a variety of elements from the culture and social context of workers outside the factory. These elements manifest themselves as direct reiterations as well as play forms of the reality. They provide continuity between the workman's life outside the factory and his participation within the factory.

In using the Roy study to illustrate autonomy patterns among informal groups, certain cautionary statements must be made. The group Roy studied may be atypical in the small amount of managerial supervision and in the degree of isolation from the rest of the factory, which might allow a disproportionately high degree of autonomy, as compared with other work groups. One can only answer that this requires investigation; it has not been demonstrated at this time. Also, worker autonomy structure is evident in other studies, as implied, for example, in Gouldner's conception of the managerial "indulgency pattern" toward workers,[35] and Bensman and Gerver's study of "deviancy in maintaining the social system" in a

[32] Gross, *op. cit.*, p. 526.

[33] Reinhard Bendix and Lloyd H. Fisher, "The Perspectives of Elton Mayo," in Amitai Etzioni, ed., *Complex Organizations: A Sociological Reader* (New York: Holt, Rinehart and Winston, 1961), p. 119.

[34] See, Donald Roy "Efficiency and 'The Fix': Informal Intergroup Relations in a Piecework Machine Shop," in S. M. Lipset and N. J. Smelser, eds., *Sociology: The Progress of a Decade* (Englewood Cliffs, N.J.: Prentice-Hall, 1961), pp. 378-390; also his "Quota Restriction and Goldbricking in a Machine Shop," *American Journal of Sociology*, **57** (March, 1952), pp. 427-442.

[35] Alvin W. Gouldner, *Wildcat Strike* (Yellow Springs, Ohio: Antioch Press, 1954).

factory.[36] In addition, autonomy patterns among employees who are operating on higher echelons than laborers have been explored by Chester Barnard[37] and in the various writings of Peter Blau;[38] but these are outside the scope of the present paper.[39]

Note on the Theory of Integration of Complex Organizations

Complex organizations must have ways of procuring and integrating the services of a variety of participants. On a commonsense level one can see the process of procurement and integration accomplished most readily in organizations that have coercive means at their disposal. Prisons can force inmates to peel potatoes. But organizations that do not have coercion at their disposal provide a problem for the analyst. There can be little doubt that most complex organizations do, in fact, solve the problem. How is it accomplished?

The concern of this paper has been the integration of a particular segment of the membership of complex organizations, namely blue-collar workers in factories. The particular issue, here, is how these persons are recruited and integrated into the organization, which offers them few of the rewards that it can bestow. The answer is that a federalistic type of solution exists: Workers are permitted ample separation from the total organization and, to a considerable extent, their integration into the larger system is left to them. Informal work group cultures are the concrete structures that make up the solution.

The separation of workers from the employing organization provides workers with flexibility and options as to the degree of alienation from the whole organization. At the same time, the separation gives the organization freedom to adopt means and goals that are disparate, if not alien, to those of the workers. The federalistic balance of autonomy for the blue-collar workers as against the white-collar staff allows flexibility to both sides; but it is also a potential source of divergence and conflict, which finds nurture in the separate subcultures.

In contrast to the form of integration suggested here, other writings have shown much concern with models of organization that dwell on lessening internal differentiation. Workers and the white-collar staff are seen as diverging in interest and this divergence can *and needs to be* lessened if the organization is to operate effectively.[40] These writings differ from the

[36] Joseph Bensman and Israel Gerver, "Crime and Punishment in the Factory: The Function of Deviancy in Maintaining the Social System," *American Sociological Review*, 28 (August, 1963), 588-598.

[37] Barnard, *op. cit.*

[38] Blau, "Structural Effects," *op. cit.*, and *The Dynamics of Bureaucracy, op. cit.*

[39] A broader formulation of autonomy structure has been attempted in Katz, *op. cit.*

[40] Argyris, *op. cit.*, and other writings by the same author. See also the writings of W. F. Whyte; for example, *Patterns of Industrial Peace* (New York: Harper & Row, 1951) and *Money and Motivation* (New York: Harper & Row, 1955).

present essay both in theoretical and practical focus. On the theoretical side, the present exposition is based strongly on the view that autonomy can be viewed as a structural principle of organizations, which can have positive or negative consequences for the operation of organizations. Structured autonomy manifests itself in internal divergencies, but these are not necessarily disruptive and maladaptive for the whole organization or any part of it. As to practical goals, many writers, notably Whyte and Argyris,[41] are concerned with the problem of improving human relations in industrial concerns. The practical focus here is not on improving social relationships in complex organizations; it is on the problem of improving the analytic theory of complex organizations. I do not claim that this is a more worthy or pressing problem than that of improving human relationships in complex organizations, merely that it *is* a problem.

Note on the Concept of Autonomy

The idea that autonomy may be conceived as a structural element of organizations owes a debt to the writings of Selznick[42] and Gouldner.[43] Both writers have recognized weaknesses in the Weberian model of bureaucracy, with its focus on the career official and assumption of bureaucracies as smooth-running machines. Selznick has pointed out that organizations must adapt to the concrete setting in which they find themselves. Adaptation affects not only the organization's dealings with its external environment, but its internal processes are continually influenced by pressures to which it must adapt. One of these is the fact that participants in the organization are whole men—affiliations, and needs, and interests outside the work organization—merely abstract role-enactors. This "recalcitrance of the tools of action"[44] lays the foundation for the development of various patterns of informal behavior. In the adaptive process Selznick emphasizes the persistence of tension, rival commitments, and constraint. The present perspective, that informal patterns are facilitated by the existence of structurally guaranteed autonomy, make the persistence of tension and strain questionable. To be sure informal patterns *may* give rise to hostile coalitions toward the organization, such as restriction of output; but they may also give rise to workers' developing, on their own, forms of integration with the organization that are acceptable to that organization as well as to the workers themselves. In short, many adaptive functions are delegated to the individual members of the organization by not being officially pro-

[41] *Ibid.*

[42] Philip Selznick, "Foundations of the Theory of Organization," in Amitai Etzioni, *op. cit.*, pp. 18-32.

[43] Alvin W. Gouldner, "Reciprocity and Autonomy in Functional Theory," in Llewellyn Gross, ed., *Symposium in Social Theory* (New York: Harper & Row, 1959), pp. 241-270.

[44] Selznick, *op. cit.*, pp. 30-31.

mulgated in a set of rules. The delegation has its origin in the possibilities for autonomy present in the organization's structure.

In contrast to Selznick's acceptance of informal patterns as part of the integral structure of organizations, Gouldner deals with the divisive aspect of these patterns.[45] He points out that even on a theoretical level, the interdependence of parts of a system should be regarded as problematical. In this connection he introduces the concept "autonomy." His use of the concept points to tendencies toward self-sufficiency of parts of a system; that is, parts of a system develop tendencies toward a separate existence. In the present formulation it is claimed that autonomy of parts of a system is not necessarily divisive; indeed, it may actually have unifying functions for a system. Furthermore, autonomy is regarded as neither all-pervasive nor totally absent. Instead, it is likely to be extensive in some *areas of behavior* while very limited in other areas. For instance, the worker who operates a lathe may have very limited autonomy in regard to physical movement while he operates the machine. But he may have a great deal of autonomy of speech during the same time. And the manner in which he utilizes this autonomy may be of fundamental importance for the organization.

[45] Gouldner, *op. cit.*

19. The Fruitful Errors of Elton Mayo

John McDonald

Hawthorne: The First Phase

In Chicago, Mayo saw the baffling results of a simple experiment in the effect of illumination on the productivity of workers. A group of first-rate engineers at [the Hawthorne plant of the Western Electric Company] had set up the experiment to find out why the administrative organization could not determine human cooperation as exactly as engineers determined technical and operational matters. Mayo found the conditions of scientific method apparently fulfilled: an experimental room with variable conditions, a control room with constant conditions; changes brought in one at a time while other conditions were held steady. Yet the results made no sense. With improved lighting in the experimental room, for example, production went up; but it went up in the control room too. With lighting diminished in the experimental room, production again rose, while in the control room, with lighting constant, production also rose. Although the engineers kept a logbook of physiological, social, and anthropological conditions as well as industrial and engineering changes during the experiment, the true determinant of rising production had escaped detection. Production held up, in fact, until illumination was reduced to moonlight.

Mayo and his group then went into the momentous project, from which it took them and W.E.'s engineers several years to recover. As Mayo's oldest colleague, Fritz Roethlisberger, describes it, the plan was to submit a segregated group of workers to different kinds of working conditions. "A group of five girls were placed in a separate room where their conditions of work could be carefully controlled, where their output could be measured, and where they could be closely observed. It was decided to introduce at specified intervals different changes in working conditions and to see what effect these innovations had on output. Also, records were kept, such as the temperature and humidity of the room, the number of hours each girl slept at night, the kind and amount of food she ate for breakfast, lunch, and dinner. Output was carefully measured, the time it took each girl to assemble a telephone relay of approximately forty parts (roughly a minute) being automatically recorded each time; quality records were kept; each girl had a physical examination at regular intervals. Under these con-

Reprinted from the November 1946 issue of Fortune Magazine by special permission; © 1946 Time, Inc.

ditions of close observation the girls were studied for a period of five years. Literally tons of material were collected. Probably nowhere in the world has so much material been collected about a small group of workers for such a long period of time.

But what about the results? . . . When all is said and done, they amount roughly to this: A skillful statistician spent several years trying to relate variations in output with variations in the physical circumstances of these five operators. For example, he correlated the hours that each girl spent in bed the night before with variations in output the following day. Inasmuch as some people said that the effect of being out late one night was not felt the following day but the day after that, he correlated variations in output with the amount of rest the operators had had two nights before. I mention this just to point out the fact that he missed no obvious tricks and that he did a careful job and a thorough one, and it took him many years to do it. The attempt to relate changes in physical circumstances to variations in output resulted in not a single correlation of enough statistical significance to be recognized by any competent statistician as having any meaning.

Now, of course, it would be misleading to say that this negative result was the only conclusion reached. There were positive conclusions, and it did not take the experimenters more than two years to find out that they had missed the boat. After two years of work, certain things happened which made them sit up and take notice. Different experimental conditions of work, in the nature of changes in the number and duration of rest pauses and differences in the length of the working day and week, had been introduced in this Relay Assembly Test Room. For example, the investigators first introduced two five-minute rests, one in the morning and one in the afternoon. Then they increased the length of these rests, and after that they introduced the rests at different times of the day. During one experimental period they served the operators a specially prepared lunch during the rest. In the later periods, they decreased the length of the working day by one-half hour and then by one hour. They gave the operators Saturday morning off for a while. Altogether, thirteen such periods of different working conditions were introduced in the first two years.

During the first year and a half of the experiment, everybody was happy, both the investigators and the operators. The investigators were happy because as conditions of work improved the output rate rose steadily. Here, it appeared, was strong evidence in favor of their preconceived hypothesis that fatigue was the major factor limiting output. The operators were happy because their conditions of work were being improved, they were earning more money, and they were objects of considerable attention from top management. But then one investigator—one of those tough-minded fellows—suggested that they restore the original conditions of work, that is, go back to a full forty-eight-hour week without rests, lunches, and what not. This was Period XII. . . . Output, instead of taking the expected nose dive, maintained its high level.

That was a poser. Mayo concluded logically that there could not have been in Period XII an actual return to original conditions. Years later Roethlisberger ruefully commented,

What all the experiments had dramatically and conclusively demonstrated was the importance of employee attitudes and sentiments. It was clear that the responses of workers to what was happening about them were dependent upon the significance these events had for them. In most work situations the meaning of a change is likely to be as important, if not more so, than the change itself. This was the great *éclaircissement*, the new illumination, that came from the research. . . . Curiously enough, this discovery is nothing very new or startling. It is something which anyone who has had some concrete experience in handling other people intuitively recognizes and practices. Whether or not a person is going to give his services wholeheartedly to a group depends, in good part, on the way he feels about his job, his fellow workers, and supervisors—the meaning for him of what is happening about him.

In other words, the experiment itself was the missing link, the unknown determinant. The workers were cooperating with the experiment—and they continued to do so even when the apparent "original conditions" of work were restored.

What was the meaning the experiment had for these workers? That was not an easy question, but the experimenters, led by Mayo, pulled themselves together and decided to go into the problem of meaning, "the twilight zone where things are never quite what they seem." In the second phase of the experiment, then, they dropped the purely quantitative earlier methods of measurement and went at the herculean task of interviewing more than 20,000 willing workers, under the seal of professional confidence. And thus began, unprecedented, a kind of mass psychoanalysis or confessional proceeding among industrial workers, which today is the core of Mayo's contribution to personnel relations and perhaps to industrial society as a whole. This, says Mayo, was "a new method of human control."

Hawthorne: The Second Phase

Interviewing became a program with a methodology, and required a trained skill in giving attention to the worker; in listening without talking, in the avoidance of argument and advice; in the ability to distinguish what the worker wanted to say, did not want to say, and could not say without help; in getting the real drift of what was said and restating it for comment; and in keeping a personal confidence. At first the experimenters assumed that "the meanings which people assign to their experience are essentially logical." But when the removal of objects of complaint sometimes did not alter the mental complexion of the complainant, and when other complainants ceased to complain even when the object was not removed, they got deeper into the nonlogical questions of attitudes, personal histories, and the social situation at work. They found that behavior of workers could not be divorced from their sentiments, that sentiments "are easily disguised and hence are difficult to recognize and to study," and that their manifestations "could not be understood as things in and by themselves, but only in terms of the total situation of the person."

At first the interviewing process worked such miracles of individual therapy that the project went off on a tangent of doing good works. A woman worker, for example, discovered during an interview that she disliked a supervisor because he reminded her of a detested stepfather; having found this out for herself, she and the supervisor had less difficulty.

But gradually the program went away from preoccupation with a variety of such individual obsessions to the study of normal groups. Since productivity was Mayo's most convenient index of well-being, the experimenters studied the results for clues in this direction, and after some time developed the hypothesis that "the working group as a whole actually determined the output of individual workers by reference to a standard, predetermined but never clearly stated, that represented the group conception of a fair day's work. This standard," they noted, "was rarely, if ever, in accord with the standards of the efficiency engineers." The hypothesis then led to the final experiment, known as the "Bank Wiring Observation Room," which was set up to study the behavior of groups.

By sticking to their code of scientific method instead of their presuppositions—for Mayo, as we shall see, it meant the undoing of his entire previous position in psychology—the experimenters here were struck by the verification of this hypothesis. As Roethlisberger describes it, "this room contained fourteen workmen representing three occupational groups—wiremen, soldermen, and inspectors." These men were on group piecework where the more they turned out the more they earned. In such a situation one might have expected that they would have been interested in maintaining total output and that the faster workers would have put pressure on the slower workers to improve their efficiency. But this was not the case. Operating within this group were four basic sentiments: (1) You should not turn out too much work; if you do, you are a "rate buster." (2) You should not turn out too little work; if you do, you are a "chiseler." (3) You should not say anything to a supervisor which would react to the detriment of one of your associates; if you do, you are a "squealer." (4) You should not be too officious; that is, if you are an inspector you should not act like one.

To be an accepted member of the group a man had to act in accordance with these social standards. . . . The best-liked person in the group was the one who kept his output exactly where the group agreed it should be. Inasmuch as the operators were agreed as to what constituted a day's work, one might have expected the rate of output to be about the same for each member of the group. This was by no means the case; there were marked differences. At first the experimenters thought that the differences in individual performance were related to differences in ability, so they compared each worker's relative rank in output with his relative rank in intelligence and dexterity as measured by certain tests. The results were interesting: the lowest producer in the room ranked first in intelligence and third in dexterity; the highest producer in the room was seventh in dexterity and lowest in intelligence. Here surely was a situation in which the native capacities of the men were not finding expression. From the viewpoint of logical, economic behavior, this room did not make sense. Only in terms of powerful sentiments could these individual differences in output level be explained. Each worker's level of output reflected his position in the informal organization of the group.

Here the experimenters, probing the informal group life of industrial workers, made their greatest discoveries: for example, that the wage incentive was weaker than the sentiment concerned with social recognition and group security. Mayo says,

. . . the important fact . . . was that the ordinary conception of management-worker relation as existing between company officials, on the one hand, and an unspecified number of individuals, on the other, is utterly mistaken. Management, in any continuously successful plant, is not related to single workers but always to working groups. In every department that continues to operate, the workers have—whether aware of it or not—formed themselves into a group with appropriate customs, duties, routines, even rituals; and management succeeds (or fails) in proportion as it is accepted without reservation by the group as authority and leader.

Roethlisberger wonders,

If this is true—and all evidence of the Western Electric research points in this direction—have we not a clue as to the possible basis for labor unrest and disputes? Granted that these disputes are often stated in terms of wages, hours of work, and physical conditions of work, is it not possible that these demands are disguising, or in part are the symptomatic expression of, much more deeply rooted human situations which we have not as yet learned to recognize, to understand, or to control?

The matters of importance to workers, which the Hawthorne researches disclosed, are not settled primarily by negotiating contracts. If industry today is filled with people living in a social void and without social function, a labor contract can do little to make cooperation possible.

The point is strategic, for Clinton Golden, of the Steelworkers union, remarks something the Mayo group passes by: "For all practical purposes," Golden says, "the findings resulting from these researches and the motives for union membership among workers are the same. These researches, therefore, constitute a study of the origin of labor unions." For Golden, in other words, the informal groupings of workers were incipient trade unions, and the unions have improved industrial relationships by formalizing them.

For Mayo and his colleagues, Hawthorne opened up a new world and a new point of view, which they confirmed to their satisfaction in numerous subsequent studies. Their recent research has extended into such memorable problems as absenteeism and labor turnover during the war, each with substantially the same conclusion. They tore the word "absenteeism" to pieces by breaking the concept down into several parts in accordance with various causes and conditions of absence. Their first, now familiar conclusion was that "the administrator is dealing with well-knit human groups and not with a horde of individuals. Wherever it is characteristic, as in the California of 1943, that by reason of external circumstance these groups have little opportunity to form, the immediate symptom is labor turnover, absenteeism, and the like.

20. Quota Restriction and Goldbricking in a Machine Shop

Donald Roy

Even those sociologists who nurse a distaste for studies of industrial administration, either because the problems involved are "practical" or because they fear managerial bias, will recognize that study of restriction of industrial output may yield knowledge free of both taints.[1] Systematic "soldiering" is group activity. One may learn about the "human group" by studying behavior on a production line as well as in an interracial discussion group. And, if someone should find the knowledge useful, even for making a little money, perhaps its scientific value will not be completely vitiated.

I here report and analyze observations of restriction made during eleven months of work as a radial-drill operator in the machine shop of a steel-processing plant in 1944 and 1945. For ten months I kept a daily record of my feelings, thoughts, experiences, and observations and of conversations with my fellow-workers. I noted down the data from memory at the end of each workday, only occasionally making surreptitious notes on the job. I recorded my own production openly in the shop. I did not reveal my research interests to either management or workers. I remained "one of the boys on the line," sharing the practices and confidences of my fellows and joining them in their ceaseless war with management, rather indifferently at first, but later wholeheartedly.

As a member of the work group, I had access to inside talk and activity. As a machine operator, I could put various operations under the microscope. These were great advantages, for *restrictus vulgaris* is a wary little thing. He does not like to be studied. Where groups are so sensitive and so skilled in eluding observation, participant observation can be a sensitive detector of relevant facts and relations (although the participant observer can spoil it all by overworking this method or by claiming that it is the sole means of scientific observation). I will limit this paper to the presentation

Reprinted from *The American Journal of Sociology*, 57 (March, 1952), 427-442.

[1] In my doctoral dissertation recently accepted by the University of Chicago I analyze the literature on this problem as well as other cases which I studied in the role of known research man. Cf. also Daniel Bell, "Exploring Factory Life," *Commentary* (January, 1947); Herbert Blumer, "Sociological Theory: Industrial Relations," *American Sociological Review*, 12 (June 1947), 271-278; Wilbert Moore, "Current Issues in Industrial Sociology," *American Sociological Review*, 12 (December, 1947), 651-657.

of a few discriminations which break up the blanket term "restriction" into several kinds and to a rough measuring of these restrictions in the shop where I worked.

From November 9, 1944, to August 30, 1945, I worked 1,850.5 hours. 1,350.9 (73 per cent) were "production-piecework" hours.[2] The remaining 499.6 hours were taken up with time study, rework, and set-up. In 669.4 (49.6 per cent) of the production-piecework hours, I "made out." That is, I produced enough pieces of work to "earn," at the piece rates for the kinds of work done, the 85-cent-per-hour "base rate" which we received for every hour spent on the job. I thus "earned" my 85 cents in about half the hours when there was opportunity—through completing more pieces—to earn more than that. Obversely, about half the time my "turn in" (work done and turned in) fell below the base-rate standard.

The Bimodal Pattern of Output

My hourly earnings on production piecework varied from $0.09 to $1.66, a range of $1.57. Table 4-1 shows that the spread of hourly earnings for the various jobs, or "operations" performed, was bimodal; this distribution suggests two major types of output behavior.

About one-half of my hours of piecework "earnings" fell on either side of the 85-cent-an-hour "day-rate" and "make-out" point, indicating 85 cents as an approximate median. However, this distribution by no means forms a bell-shaped curve, with 85 cents as a modal point. "Make-out" and "non-make-out"— piecework hours form two almost separate distributions with 74.1 per cent of the 669.4 "make-out" hours concentrated in the $1.25-$1.34 interval, and 43.2 per cent of the 681.5 "non-make-out" hours clustered in two adjacent intervals, $0.35-$0.54. Concentration of "make-out" hours is even more marked. For 82.8 per cent fall within three 5-cent intervals, $1.20-$1.34, and 64.1 per cent fall within the one 5-cent interval, $1.25-$1.29.

That this bimodal pattern of hourly earnings for the ten-month period does not represent the joining of the "tails" of two temporal distributions— i.e., one for an initial learning period and the other showing completely different production behavior with the acquisition of skill—is indicated by a comparison of earning distributions for two periods of four and six months, respectively. In this comparison (Table 4-2) the period from November through February represents one level of skill; that from March through August, a higher level. Although the proportion of make-out hours for the second period was more than double that of the first and although concentration of make-out hours in modal earning intervals increased, the pattern was clearly bimodal in both periods. Both "levels of skill" show the

[2] I have omitted some days worked in September, 1945, because of irregularities occasioned by reorganization of the shop at that time.

Table 4-1.

Production Piecework Hours Worked, by Ten-Cent Earning Intervals

Earnings per Hour (in Cents)	Hours Worked	Per Cent
Unknown*	103.9	7.7
5-14	3.0	0.2
15-24	51.0	3.8
25-34	49.8	3.7
35-44	150.1	11.1
45-54	144.5	10.7
55-64	57.7	4.3
65-74	63.8	4.7
75-84	57.7	4.3
Total under 85 cents	681.5	50.5
85-94	51.2	3.8
95-104	19.5	1.5
105-114	17.9	1.3
115-124	83.0	6.1
125-134	496.3	36.7
165-174	1.5	0.1
Total 85 cents or more	669.4	49.5
Total 1,350.9		100.0

*All "unknown" hourly earnings fell below the base-rate level of 85 cents per hour.

same modal earning interval of $1.25-$1.34 for make-out hours. The modal earning interval for non-make-out hours advanced but one notch, from $0.35-$0.44 to $0.45 to $0.54.

While I did not keep a complete record of the hourly earnings of my "day man" on the radial drill (I worked a "second" shift), I frequently jotted down his day's run. His figures were roughly correlative with my own. References to the diary will be made to show that I was not out of line with other operators in the shop.

The bimodal pattern was the rule of the shop. An outsider might believe that it reflects the struggle of workers with two kinds of jobs, hard and easy. He might then posit any number of reasons why the jobs fall into two piles rather than into one bell-shaped heap: some peculiarity of time-study men or some change of company policy. It would indeed be difficult so to set piece rates that it would be equally easy to "make out" on all kinds of work. But one sophisticated in shop ways and aware of all the devices of time-study men would hardly credit them with either the ability or the will to turn up "tight" and "loose" piece rates in other than a single

Table 4-2.

Production-Piecework Hours Worked, by Ten-Cent Earning Intervals,

per Two Diary Periods

EARNINGS PER HOUR (IN CENTS)	PERIOD I (NOVEMBER THROUGH FEBRUARY)		PERIOD II (MARCH THROUGH AUGUST)	
	Hours Worked	Per Cent	Hours Worked	Per Cent
Unknown*	66.4	11.4	37.5	4.9
5-14	3.0	0.5	—	—
15-24	13.5	2.3	37.5	4.9
25-34	37.8	6.5	12.0	1.6
35-44	93.0	16.0	57.1	7.4
45-54	74.0	12.8	70.5	9.1
55-64	43.1	7.4	14.6	1.9
65-74	36.8	6.3	27.0	3.5
75-84	49.0	8.5	8.7	1.1
Total under 85 cents	416.6	71.7	264.9	34.4
85-94	39.1	6.7	12.1	1.6
95-104	9.7	1.7	9.8	1.3
105-114	3.8	0.7	14.1	1.8
115-124	18.0	3.1	65.0	8.4
125-134	93.2	16.1	403.1	52.3
165-174	—	—	1.5	0.2
Total 85 cents or over	163.8	28.3	505.6	65.6
Total	580.4	100.0	770.5	100.0

*All "unknown" hourly earnings fell below the base-rate level of 85 cents per hour.

bell-shaped distribution. He would not attribute the bimodal distortion of hourly earnings to anything so improbable as bimodal distribution of hard and easy jobs. It could be that the operators, ignoring finer distinctions in job timing, sort jobs into two bins, one for "gravy" jobs, the other for "stinkers."

Let us assume that the average of worker effort will be constant from job to job. Job A might be rated as 5 cents an hour "harder" than Job B. But Job A turns out to yield 75 cents an hour less than Job B instead of the expected 5 cents an hour less. One suspects that effort has not been constant. When an operator discovers that he can earn $1.00 an hour on Job B, he will then put forth extra effort and ingenuity to make it $1.25. When, however, he finds that he can earn only 95 cents an hour on Job A, he rejects that amount and drops to a level of effort that earns only 50 cents an hour and relies upon his 85-cent base-pay rate for "take home." Job B has therefore become the "gravy" job, and Job A the "stinker." Into the "stinker" bin goes A, along with 90-cent jobs, 85-cent jobs, and 60-cent jobs.

The pronounced dichotomy in the production behavior of the machine operator suggests that restriction might be classified into two major types, "quota restriction" and "goldbricking." The heavy concentration of hours at the $1.25-$1.34 level with no spilling-over to the next level makes "quota restriction" appear as a limitation of effort on "gravy" jobs in order not to exceed set maximums. It could also be inferred that "goldbricking" appears as a "holding-back," or failure to release effort, when a close approach to the quota seems unattainable.

Quota Restriction

It is "quota restriction" which has received the most attention. The Mayo researchers observed that the bank-wiring group at Western Electric limited output to a "quota" or "bogey."[3] Mayo inferred that this chopping-off of production was due to lack of understanding of the economic logics of management, using the following chain of reasoning: Insistence by management on purely economic logics, plus frequent changes in such logics in adaptation to technological change, result in lack of understanding on the part of the workers. Since the latter cannot understand the situation, they are unable to develop a nonlogical social code of a type that brought social cohesion to work groups prior to the Industrial Revolution. This inability to develop a Grade-A social code brings feelings of frustration. And, finally, frustration results in the development of a "lower social code" among the workers in opposition to the economic logics of management. And one of the symptoms of this "lower social code" is restriction of output.[4]

Mayo thus joins those who consider the economic man a fallacious conception. Now the operators in my shop made noises like economic men. Their talk indicated that they were canny calculators and that the dollar sign fluttered at the masthead of every machine. Their actions were not always consistent with their words; and such inconsistency calls for further probing. But it could be precisely because they were alert to their economic interests—at least to their immediate economic interests—that the operators did not exceed their quotas. It might be inferred from their talk that they did not turn in excess earnings because they felt that to do so would result in piecework price cuts; hence the consequences would be either reduced earnings from the same amount of effort expended or increased effort to maintain the take-home level.

[3] Fritz Roethlisberger and J. Dickson, *Management and the Worker* (Cambridge, Mass.: Harvard University Press, 1939).

[4] Elton Mayo, *Human Problems of an Industrial Civilization* (New York: Macmillan, 1938), pp. 119-121.

When I was hired, a personnel department clerk assured me that the radial-drill operators were averaging $1.25 an hour on piecework. He was using a liberal definition of the term "averaging." Since I had had no previous machine-shop experience and since a machine would not be available for a few days, I was advised to spend some time watching Jack Starkey, a radial-drill man of high rank in seniority and skill.

One of Starkey's first questions was, "What have you been doing?" When I said I had worked in a Pacific Coast shipyard at a rate of pay over $1.00 an hour, Starkey exclaimed, "Then what are you doing in this place?" When I replied that averaging $1.25 an hour wasn't bad, he exploded:

"Averaging, you say! Averaging?"

"Yeah, on the average. I'm an average guy; so I ought to make my buck and a quarter. That is, after I get onto it."

"Don't you know," cried Starkey angrily, "that $1.25 an hour is the *most* we can make, even when we *can* make more! And most of the time we can't even make that! Have you ever worked on piecework before?"

"No."

"I can see that! Well, what do you suppose would happen if I turned in $1.25 an hour on these pump bodies?"

"Turned in? You mean if you actually did the work?"

"I mean if I actually did the work and turned it in!"

"They'd have to pay you, wouldn't they? Isn't that the agreement?"

"Yes! They'd pay me—once! Don't you know that if I turned in $1.50 an hour on these pump bodies tonight, the whole God-damned Methods Department would be down here tomorrow? And they'd retime this job so quick it would make your head swim! And when they retimed it, they'd cut the price in half! And I'd be working for 85 cents an hour instead of $1.25!"

From this initial exposition of Starkey's to my last day at the plant I was subject to warnings and predictions concerning price cuts. Pressure was the heaviest from Joe Mucha, day man on my machine, who shared my job repertoire and kept a close eye on my production. On November 14, the day after my first attained quota, Mucha advised:

"Don't let it go over $1.25 an hour, or the time-study man will be right down here! And they don't waste time, either! They watch the records like a hawk! I got ahead, so I took it easy for a couple of hours."

Joe told me that I had made $10.01 yesterday and warned me not to go over $1.25 an hour. He told me to figure the set-ups and the time on each operation very carefully so that I would not total over $10.25 in any one day.

Jack Starkey defined the quota carefully but forcefully when I turned in $10.50 for one day, or $1.31 an hour.

Jack Starkey spoke to me after Joe left. "What's the matter? Are you trying to upset the apple cart?"

Jack explained in a friendly manner that $10.50 was too much to turn in, even on an old job. "The turret-lathe men can turn in $1.35," said Jack, "but their rate is 90 cents, and ours 85 cents."

Jack warned me that the Methods Department could lower their prices on any job, old or new, by changing the fixture slightly, or changing the size of drill. According to Jack, a couple of operators (first and second shift on the same drill) got to competing with each other to see how much they could turn in. They got up to $1.65 an hour, and the price was cut in half. And from then on they had to run that job themselves, as none of the other operators would accept the job.

According to Jack, it would be all right for us to turn in $1.28 or $1.29 an hour, when it figured out that way, but it was not all right to turn in $1.30 an hour.

Well, now I know where the maximum is—$1.29 an hour.

Starkey's beliefs concerning techniques of price-cutting were those of the shop. Leonard Bricker, an old-timer in the shop, and Willie, the stock-chaser, both affirmed that management, once bent on slashing a piecework price, would stop at nothing.

"Take these $1.25 jobs. One guy will turn in $1.30 an hour one day. Then another fellow will turn in, say $1.31 or $1.32. Then the first fellow will go up to $1.35. First thing you know they'll be up to $1.50, and bang! They'll tear a machine to pieces to change something to cut a price!"

In the washroom, before I started work, Willie commented on my gravy job, the pedestals. "The Methods Department is going to lower the price," he said. "There was some talk today about it."

"I hope they don't cut it too much," I said. "I suppose they'll make some changes in the jigs?"

"They'll change the tooling in some way. Don't worry, when they make up their minds to lower a price, they'll find a way to do it!"[5]

The association of quota behavior with such expressions about price-cutting does not prove a causal connection. Such a connection could be

[5] John Mills, onetime research engineer in telephony and for five years engaged in personnel work for the Bell Telephone Company, has recently indicated the possibility that there were factors in the bank-wiring room situation that the Mayo group failed to detect: "Reward is supposed to be in direct proportion to production. Well, I remember the first time I ever got behind that fiction. I was visiting the Western Electric Company, which had a reputation of never cutting a piece rate. It never did; if some manufacturing process was found to pay more than seemed right for the class of labor employed on it— if, in other words, the rate-setters had misjudged—that particular part was referred to the engineers for redesign, and then a new rate was set on the new part. Workers, in other words, were paid as a class, supposed to make about so much a week with their best efforts and, of course, less for less competent efforts." *The Engineer in Society* (New York: Van Nostrand, 1946), p. 93.

determined only by instituting changes in the work situation that would effect a substantial reduction of "price-cut fear" and by observing the results of such changes.

Even if it should be thus indicated that there is a causal relationship, testing of alternative hypotheses would still be necessary. It may be, but it is not yet known, that "economic determinism" may account for quota restriction in the shop investigated. It may also be, but it is not known, that factors such as Mayo's "failure to understand the economic logics of management" are influential.

"Waste Time" on Quota Restriction

Whatever its causes, such restriction resulted in appreciable losses of time in the shop. I have evidence of it from observation of the work behavior and talk of fellow-operators and from my own work behavior. Since ability to "make out" early was related to skill and experience, it was some time before I found enough time wasted on quota restriction to record. But I discovered early that other operators had time to burn.

One evening Ed Sokolsky, onetime second-shift operator on Jack Starkey's drill, commented on a job that Jack was running:

"That's gravy! I worked on those, and I could turn out nine an hour. I timed myself at six minutes."

I was surprised. "At 35 cents apiece, that's over $3.00 an hour!"

"And I got ten hours," said Ed. "I used to make out in four hours and fool around the rest of the night."

If Sokolsky reported accurately, he was "wasting" six hours per day.

Ed claimed that he could make over "$3.00 an hour on the two machines he was running, but he could turn in only $1.40 an hour or, occasionally, $1.45 or $1.50 for the two machines together. Ed said that he always makes out for ten hours by eleven o'clock, that he has nothing to do from 11:00 to 3:00, and has even left early, getting someone to punch his timecard for him.

"That's the advantage of working nights," said Ed. "You can make out in a hurry and sit around, and nobody says anything. But you can't get away with it on day shift with all the big shots around. Jack has to take it easy on these housings to make them last eight hours, and that must be tough."

"Old Pete," another "old-timer" confided in me: "Another time when they timed me on some connecting rods, I could have made $20.00 a day, easy. I had to run them at the lowest speed on the machine to keep from making too much. I had a lot of trouble once when I was being timed, and they gave me $35.00 a hundred. Later they cut it to $19.50 a hundred, and I still made $9.50 a day."

If Old Pete could have made $20.00 a day, he was "wasting" four hours a day.

My own first "spare time" came on November 18.

Today I made out with such ease on the pedestals that I had an hour to spare. To cover the hour I had to poke along on the last operation, taking twice as much time to do 43 pieces as I ordinarily would.

But it wasn't until March, when I experienced a sudden increase in skill, that I was capable of making out early on any job but the pedestals. With this increase in skill I found the pedestals quickly fading as the supreme distributors of "gravy." One and one-half hours of loafing recorded on March 22 was a portent of things to come.

I stalled along tonight, turning out only 89 pieces, adding in my kitty of 40 pieces for a turn-in of 129. Joe had a kitty of 13, and I figured that the 116 pieces left would just do him tomorrow. I finished my last piece about 9:30 and started cleaning up the machine about ten o'clock. I noticed that Tony was also through early, standing around his machine.

"This is the earliest you've made out, isn't it?" he asked.

Dick Smith remarked to me, "That's the kind of a job I like. Then I can go at it and enjoy it."

On April 7 I was able to enjoy four hours of "free time."

I turned out 43 pieces in the four hours from three to seven, averaging nearly 11 an hour (or $2.085 per hour). At seven o'clock there were only 23 pieces left in the lot, and I knew there would be no point in building up a kitty for Monday if Joe punched off the job before I got to work. I could not go ahead with the next order (also a load of connecting rods) because the new ruling made presentation of a work order to the stock-chaser necessary before material could be brought up. So I was stymied and could do nothing the rest of the day. I had 43 pieces plus 11 from yesterday's kitty to turn in for a total 54.

I sat around the rest of the evening, and none of the bosses seemed to mind.

By August I was more sophisticated in the art of loafing, and complaints of being "stymied" were not recorded.

I had good luck with the reamers and had my needed 26 pieces by six o'clock. I did 10 more for a kitty for Monday and wound up the evening's work at seven o'clock. The last four hours I sat around and talked to various operators.

I reached my peak in quota restriction on June 27, with but three and a half hours of productive work out of the eight.

An Estimate of the Degree of Quota Restriction Practiced

The amount of quota restriction practiced by operators on the drill line may be estimated from my own production behavior.

During the ten-month diary period I received approximately 75 different piecework jobs, some of which were assigned from two to six times, but the majority of which were assigned only once. On only 31 of the jobs did I ever make out.

Of the 31 make-out jobs, only 20 afforded quota earnings of $1.25 an hour or more; 5 afforded maximum earnings of from $1.20 to $1.24 an hour; 1, maximum earnings of $1.09 an hour; and 5 of the 31 yielded maximum of less than $1.00 an hour (85-99 cents). Total quota hours were 497.8, or slightly over a third of the total piecework hours.

By extending effort past quota limits to find the earning possibilities of the jobs, I discovered that on 16 of the 20 quota jobs I could have earned more than $1.30 an hour; on 4 of the 20 I was unable to exceed $1.30 per hour.

For example, on the "NT bases," I turned out pieces at the rate of $2.55 for a test hour, and I turned them out at the rate of $2.04 for a full eight-hour shift. On the "G sockets," I was able to earn $2.53 an hour; this job was touted by experienced operators to yield $3.00 an hour.

I ran 4 other jobs at a rate in excess of $2.00 an hour. Maximums on another 4 jobs came to $1.96 or better. All but 3 of the 16 "excess-quota" jobs yielded possible earnings of over $1.75 an hour.

Besides the 16 excess-quota jobs, I found 4 "nonquota-make-out" jobs (maximum earnings less than $1.25) that showed potentialities in excess of quota limits. That I did not actually achieve quota on these 4 jobs was due to slow starts; since the 4 were not assigned to me again, I could not cash in on my discoveries. If these 4 are included, the number of jobs with excess-quota potentials total 20.

Given a quota of $1.25 an hour, or $10.00 an eight-hour day, and a job that will yield $1.25 an hour but not appreciably over that rate, the operator will have to expend a full eight hours of effort to achieve the quota. But, if the job will yield earnings at the rate of $2.50 an hour, it will take the operator only four hours to earn his $10.00. A $2.50-an-hour job is thus a four-hour job, and the remaining four hours of the workday may be considered wasted time. If the operator were to extend himself for the full eight hours on a $2.50-an-hour job and were permitted to turn in the results of his effort, his earnings would be $20.00 instead of his quota of $10.00. Thus there is incurred a financial loss to the operator as well as a loss of production time to the company when the quota is observed.

Table 4-3 lists the twenty jobs which showed potentialities of yielding hourly earnings in excess of $1.30. Waste time and loss in earnings is computed for each job according to maximum earnings indicated in each case by actual test and according to the number of hours devoted to each job. For instance, operation "pawls," which leads the list with 157.9 total hours worked, showed, by test, possibilities of earnings of $1.96 per hour. At potentialities of $1.96 per hour, over 36 per cent of each hour is wasted when the operator holds his turn-in to $1.25 an hour. Total waste time in the

157.9 hours expended on the pawls could then be computed at 57.2 hours, or over a third of the time actually put in. Earnings might have been, at $1.96 per hour, $309.48; whereas, at the quota level of $1.25, they would have been but $197.38—a loss of $112.10.

Total waste time for the 20 jobs is seen to be 286 hours, or 36.4 per cent of a total 786.5 hours actually put in on them. This represents a wastage of 2.9 hours on each 8-hour day put in, or a total loss of 35.75 days out of 98.3 actually worked. With potential earnings of $1,584.43 for the 98 days and with quota earnings at $983.18, the wage loss to the worker would be $601.25, or $6.12 per day, or 76½ cents per hour.

By this logic, if the worker could "cut loose" on the 20 jobs listed, he would average $2.01 an hour instead of $1.25. And since the 786.5 hours actually put in on the 20 jobs represented 58.2 per cent of the 1,350.9 total piecework hours for the period, and 42.5 per cent of a grand total of 1,850.5 hours that included all nonpiecework activity as well, it is evident that losses resulting from quota restriction alone could represent wastage of considerable magnitude—an over-all hourly income loss for 1,850.5 hours of 32½ cents an hour!

In order to generalize for the drill line from observation of my own behavior, I would have to establish (1) that I was an "average" performer and (2) that my job repertoire was representative of those of other operators.

Of the men on the same shift doing my kind of work, four (McCann, Starkey, Koszyk, and Sokolsky) could turn out greater volume than I and were my betters in all-around skills. Seven were below me in these respects, of them only three (Smith, Rinky, and Dooley) worked long enough to be in the core of the group. I was about average in skill and in the work assigned me.

The maximums on which the losses are figured represent only potentialities discovered in tests of relatively short duration. Yet it is likely that had I remained in the shop long enough to allow the 20 jobs another time around, I could have routinized many of the maximums and could have raised some of them. It is also likely that if organizational changes were instituted to induce operators to abolish quota limits and "open up" production, the writer's discovered maximums would be quickly raised to higher levels by the efforts of the group. Under adequate motivation the better operators would employ their superior skills and the results of their application would be disseminated to others. In my opinion, the production potentialities are underestimates of the output possibilities inherent in the situation. This hypothesis can be tested, of course, only through observation of experimental changes.

As a check of the foregoing appraisals, an estimate of the *actual* amount of time wasted by the writer through quota restriction may be made by reference to Table 4-4.

Table 4-3.

Time and Earnings Losses on Operations with Potentialities of Yielding Hourly Earnings in Excess of $1.30 per Hour

Operation Tested	Total Hours Worked	Maximum (per Hour)	Waste Time (per Hour)	Total Waste Time (in Hours)	Potential Earnings	Earnings at $1.25	Loss in Earnings
Pawls	157.9	$1.96	0.3625	57.2	$309.48	$197.38	$112.10
Pedestals	120.5	1.71	0.2625	31.6	206.08	150.63	55.43
NT bases	111.0	2.55	0.5125	56.9	283.05	138.75	144.30
Con rods	94.4	2.33	0.4625	43.7	219.95	118.00	101.95
Sockets	75.8	1.76	0.2875	21.8	133.41	94.75	38.66
B. housings	46.0	1.96	0.3625	16.7	90.16	57.50	32.66
Pineholes	37.7	1.87	0.3250	12.3	70.50	47.13	23.37
Casings	28.5	2.03	0.3750	10.7	57.86	35.63	22.23
Gear parts	24.0	1.83	0.3000	7.2	43.92	30.00	13.92
Replacers	19.3	2.20	0.4375	8.4	42.46	24.13	18.33
Spyglasses	18.0	1.57	0.1875	3.4	28.26	22.50	5.76
R. sockets	14.9	1.48	0.1375	2.0	22.05	18.63	3.42
Move. jaw	9.6	1.99	0.3625	3.5	19.10	12.00	7.10
Ped. $8.90	7.0	2.12	0.4000	2.8	14.84	8.75	6.09
Spot J1728	6.7	1.91	0.3375	2.3	12.80	8.38	4.42
G sockets	4.5	2.53	0.5000	2.3	11.39	5.63	5.76
Ped. $5	4.3	1.85	0.3250	1.4	7.96	5.38	2.58
CB hubs	4.1	1.65	0.2375	1.0	6.77	5.13	1.64
SD cups	1.5	1.89	0.3250	0.5	2.84	1.88	0.96
Bolts	0.8	1.96	0.3625	0.3	1.57	1.00	0.57
Total	786.5 (98.3 days)			286.0 (35.75 days)	$1,584.43	$983.18	$601.25

Table 4-4.

Quota Hours Loafed, by Percentages of Total Quota Hours and Average
Hours per Quota Day of Loafing, by Months, March through August, 1945

Month	Total Quota Hours	Quota Hours Loafed	Per Cent Hours Loafed	Hours Loafed per Quota Day
March	69.3	7.6	11.0	0.88
April	76.3	10.35	13.6	1.09
May	69.8	5.15	7.4	0.59
June	83.5	15.2	18.2	1.46
July	84.8	21.4	25.2	2.02
August	85.9	22.2	25.8	2.06
Total	469.6	81.9	17.4	1.39

The 469.6 quota hours represented 60.9 per cent of 770.5 total piece-work hours for the period, and 41.8 per cent of 1,123.2 total hours worked.

With an average of 1.39 hours "wasted" per day of "quota piecework," the average hours worked were 6.61; so, at quota limits of $1.25 an hour, or $10.00 per day, earnings while I was actually working on "quota piece-work" would be $1.51 per hour for the six-month period. If I had turned in 8 hours' production per day at $1.51, my daily earnings on "quota piece-work" would have been $12.08. I therefore lost $2.08 per day, or 26 cents per hour on quota piecework. Since quota piecework represented 41.8 per cent of total hours worked, the over-all loss per day due to quota restriction alone would be $0.87, approximately 11 cents an hour.

During the last two-month period, July and August, I was "wasting" on the average over 2 hours a day while on "quota piecework." If my pro-duction during August may be considered indicative of my developed skill, and portentous of things to come had I stayed, then estimates of future wastages become greater. With 2.06 hours per quota-piecework day loafed, the length of the "actual" average quota workday becomes 5.94 hours and the average earnings for "actual" work time put in becomes $1.68 per hour. At $1.68 per hour for a full 8-hour day, the writer would earn $13.44; the daily loss would then be $3.44 and the hourly loss 43 cents. And since quota piecework for August represented 71.5 per cent of total piecework for the month, the loss per day on piecework was $2.46. And, since quota piecework represented 46 per cent of total hours worked, the over-all loss per day was $1.58 and the over-all hourly loss nearly 20 cents.

This daily loss for August would be slightly reduced if the actual quota turn-in is considered in place of the assumed $1.25 per hour. The writer actually averaged $1.27 per hour on quota piecework, raising the assumed average by 2 cents per hour, or 16 cents per day. The computed average daily and hourly losses on quota piecework would then be $3.28 and $0.41, and the over-all losses would be $1.51 and $0.19.

Piecework Goldbricking

On "gravy jobs" the operators earned a quota, then knocked off. On "stinkers" they put forth only minimal effort; either they did not try to achieve a turn-in equal to the base wage rate or they deliberately slowed down. Jobs were defined as "good" and "bad" jobs, not in terms of the effort or skill necessary to making out at a bare base-rate level, but of the felt attainability of a substantial premium, i.e., 15 cents an hour or more. Earnings of $1.00 an hour in relation to a $1.25 quota and an 85-cent base rate were considered worth the effort, while earnings of 95 cents an hour were not.

The attitude basic to the goldbricking type of restriction was expressed succinctly thus: "They're not going to get much work out of me for this pay!"

Complaints about low piecework prices were chronic and universal in the shop.

The turret-lathe men discussed the matter of making out, one man stating that only half the time could a man make 84 cents day rate on a machine. It was agreed: "What's the use of pushing when it's hard even to make day rate?"

His 50-50 estimate was almost equal to my own experience of 49.6-50.4. Pessimistic though it was, it was less so than usual statements on the subject:

I asked Jackson if he was making out, and he gave me the usual answer, "No!"

"They ask me how I'm making out, and I always say, 'O.K.' As far as I'm concerned, I'm making out O.K. If they start asking me further, I'll tell them that this place stinks."

"The day man isn't making out either. We get a lot of little jobs, small lots. It's impossible to make out when you're getting small jobs all the time."

Joe was working on a new job, time study on some small pieces tonight. I asked him, "Something good?" and he replied, "Nothing is good any more!"

There seemed to be no relation between a man's ability to earn and his behavior on a "stinker." That the men who most frequently earned the quota goldbricked like the rest on poor jobs appears in the following extracts:

Al McCann (the man who made quota most often) said that he gives a job a trial, and if it is no good he takes his time. He didn't try to make out on the chucks tonight.

Joe Mucha, my day man, said of a certain job: "I did just one more than you did. If they don't like it they can do them themselves. To hell with them. I'm not going to bust my ass on stuff like this."

Old Peter, the multiple drill man, said "I ran some pieces for 25 minutes to see how many I could turn out. I turned out 20 at 1½ cents apiece (72 cents an hour). So I smoke and take it easy. I can't make out; so ———— it."

I noticed that when Ed Sokolsky, one of the better operators on the line, is working on an operation he cannot make out on, he does not go at his task with vigor. He either pokes around or leaves his machine for long periods of time; and Paul (set-up man) seems always to be looking for him. Steve (supt.) is always bellowing, "Where in hell is Ed?" or "Come on, Ed, let's have some production around here!" Tonight I heard him admonishing Ed again, "Now I want you to work at that machine 'til three o'clock, do you understand?"

Mike Koszyk, regarded as a crack operator: The price was a poor one (a few cents a hundred) and the job tough. Mike had turned out only 9 pieces in 3 hours. When Mike takes his time, he really takes his time!

According to Al, Jack Starkey turned in 40 cents an hour today on his chuck parts. Al laughed, saying, "I guess Jack didn't like this job."

Gus Schmidt, regarded as the best speed-drill operator on the second shift, was timed early in the evening on a job, and given a price of $1.00 per 100 for reaming one hole, chamfering both sides of three holes, and filing burrs on one end of one hole. All that for one cent!

"To hell with them," said Gus.

He did not try to make out.

The possibility of covering "day rate" was ordinarily no spur to the machine operator to bestir himself on a job. A remark of Mucha's was characteristic: "I could have made out," he said, "but why kill yourself for day rate?"

Average hourly earnings of less or even a little more than $1.00 an hour were usually thrown into the "day-rate" category.

Joe Mucha drilled 36 of the bases (at $8.80 per 100) today. "The most I'll ever do until they retime this job is 40," he said. "Do you know, they expect us to do 100? Why, I wouldn't bust my ass to do 50, for $8.00, when day rate is almost that!"

McCann was put to drilling some pieces at $6.50 per 100. I noticed him working furiously and walked over to see what he was doing. He asked me to figure out how many pieces at 6½ cents he had to turn out per hour to make $1.20. When I told him 18 or 19 he said, "I give up," and immediately slowed down.

A few minutes later I met him in the washroom, and he said, "I wouldn't work that hard for eight or ten hours even if I could make out. I thought I'd try it for an hour or so and see what I could do."

He figures that he was making 95 cents an hour. At lunch time he said that he had averaged $1.00 an hour for the two hours and thought maybe he would try to make out.

The Slowdown

Resentment against piecework prices that were considered too low to offer possibilities of quota earnings often resulted in deliberate attempts to produce at lower rates than mere "dogging it along" would bring. This kind of goldbricking was particularly noticeable on jobs that came relatively often and in large lots. Toward a short order of poor price that was assigned to his machine but once or twice a year, the operator's attitude was likely to be one of "I don't give a damn," and the result would be production below "standard." But toward a low-priced order assigned every month or two and in amounts that would take several shifts to a week to process, i.e., jobs that played a major part in the operator's repertoire, the attitude was likely to be, "Just for that, you'll get as little as I can turn out and still be operating this machine!"

The hinge-base fight is an example of deliberate restriction on a major job that was regarded as poorly priced. This fight went on for at least nine months at the machine operated by Jack Starkey. During this period three men worked second shift on Jack's machine in the following sequence: Ed Sokolsky, Dooley, and Al McCann.

December 19—Ed Sokolsky and Jack Starkey have not been doing well. Ed cusses intermittently and leaves his machine for long periods of time. The foreman finds the machine idle, and Steve bellows about it. Ed calls the piece he is working on a "stinker." I know it is, because Ed is free with his advertising on the "gravy" he finds.

Ed seems to have constant trouble with his jig, a revolving piece attached to the side of the table. Two disks seem to stick together, and Ed is constantly (every day or so) using the crane to dismantle the jig (a very heavy one). He sands the disks and oils them, taking several hours for the cleaning operation. Steve saw the dismantled jig again tonight and bellowed, "Again?" Steve does not like it.

Paul, the set-up man, gets concerned, too, when he finds the jig torn down and Ed away somewhere. He says, "Where the hell's Ed?" in a provoked manner.

February—I noticed that Ed was poking along and asked him if he had a good job. He shook his head, saying he was making but 46 cents an hour, turning out 2 pieces an hour that paid 23 cents each.

February 26—Jack Starkey told me tonight that although his job on the hinge bases was retimed, there was no raise in price. The price is still 23 cents.

I said, "All you've got to turn out is 5 an hour to make $1.15."

"I'd just like to see anybody turn out 5 of these an hour," said Jack, "with a tolerance of 0.0005!"

Later, Ed Sokolsky said that he and Jack were turning out about 24 pieces in a ten-hour period (2.4 an hour), that the job had been retimed several times, but no raise in price had been given.

Ed and Jack asked for a price of 38 cents. Ed said that they could turn out 3 an hour, but, until they got a decent price, they were turning out 2 an hour.

Toward the end of the evening I noticed that Ed's machine was idle, and Ed was sitting on a box, doing nothing.

"What's the matter, did they stop the job on you?" I asked.

"I stopped it," said Ed. "I don't feel like running it."

March—Dooley worked on the hinge bases again tonight. He admitted that he could barely make out on the job, but "Why bust my ass for day rate? We're doing 3 an hour or less until we get a better price!"

This 3-an-hour-or-less business has been going on several months. The price is 23 cents; so Dooley and Jack turn in 69 cents an hour (or less).

May—McCann said that Starkey was arguing all day over the price of the hinge bases. The methods men maintain that they can't raise the price "because the jacks that the parts go on sell for $14.00 apiece." They plan to retool the job and lower the price. According to McCann, Jack told them that if he didn't get a decent price he was going to make out on the job but scrap every one of the pieces.

"Jack fights it out with them," said McCann. "He'll stay right with the machine and argue. I get disgusted and walk away."

"Jack turned out 28 today," McCann went on. "That's too many, nearly 3 an hour. He'll have to watch himself if he expects to get a raise in price."

Starkey was running the hinge bases again tonight. I remarked, "I see you're in the gravy again."

His reply was, "Yeah! 69 cents an hour!"

McCann did not seem to enjoy the hinge bases either. He looked bored, tired, and disgusted all evening. His ten hours is a long stretch at day work. He cannot make out early and rest after 11 o'clock (for four hours), but has to keep on the machine until three.

August 14—Al McCann was working on the hinge bases tonight, one of the jobs that he and Jack are protesting as to price. Gil (the foreman) sat and stood behind Al for at least an hour, and I could see that Al did not like it. He worked steadily, but with deliberate slowness, and did not look at Gil or speak to him. Al and Jack have agreed to restrict production on the hinge bases until they get a better price, and Gil was probably there to see what Al could really do. I think that Al and Jack could make out on the job, but not at $1.25 an hour, and they cut production to less than 80 cents an hour.

August 16—Al told me that they had won a price raise on the hinge bases, from 23 to 28 cents, and another raise to 31 cents.

"But it's still not high enough. As it is now we can make exactly 94 cents an hour. We're trying to get 35 cents. We can turn out 1 in exactly 16 minutes. That's not 4 an hour. We've been giving them 3 an hour."

An Attempt to Estimate the Degree of Piecework Goldbricking

I failed to earn the base rate of 85 cents for slightly over half my piecework hours, but I cannot claim that I failed in spite of a maximum effort. There were only a few occasions when I tried to "make out," but could not, and did not let failure diminish my efforts. Normally, I behaved in the manner of my fellow-operators; I "tried out" a job for a short sampling period of an hour, more or less, and slowed my pace to a restrictive one if the job did not show "possibilities." There were numerous occasions when even "trial runs" were not attempted, when I was forewarned that the job was a "stinker." Since possible output was not determined, the amount of restriction cannot be computed.

There were times when the words of various operators indicated that they could have "covered" day rate if they had tried; the expression, "Why bust my ass for day rate?" was considered adequate explanation for failure to press on to maximum attainable. If claims of ability to achieve the scorned "day rate" could be accepted as indicative of the true possibilities inherent in a job, it is clear that the man who turned in 42.5 cents an hour for a day's average hourly earnings, and who says that he could have made 85 cents an hour, has accomplished but 4 hours' work in 8. A man who turned in 21.25 cents an hour, instead of a possible 85 cents, has done 2 hours' work in 8, and has "wasted" 6 hours. That an operator has turned in 42.5 cents an hour, or 21 cents, or 10 cents may be determined easily enough; the difficulty lies in inability to test his claims of what he could have done.

Recorded observations do allow some objective estimate of losses incurred by goldbricking in isolated cases. For instance, the four operators assigned to Jack Starkey's machine made it a practice to restrict production on the hinge bases to from 2 to 3 pieces an hour. To this restriction were attributed two price increases, from 25 cents to 28 cents to 31 cents per piece. Thus, at the 31-cent price in effect in August, and at the output rate of 3 pieces per hour, the men were turning in 93 cents per hour, or $7.44 per 8-hour day. Since their special base-rate, as experienced operators on a machine handling heavy fixtures, was $1.10 per hour, they were earning 17 cents an hour less than they were paid. One of the operators involved, Al McCann, claimed that by test they could turn out 1 piece in exactly 16 minutes. At this rate they could have turned in 3.75 pieces per hour for earnings of $1.16 per hour, or $9.28 per day. "Waste" time could be computed at 1.6 production-hours, and the loss in "earnings" at 23 cents per hour.

McCann's estimate of the job's possibilities proved to be low, however; for, a few weeks later, upon abandoning hope for a further increase in piecework price, he "made out easily in 6 hours."

Al said tonight that he was making out on the hinge bases, that he got disgusted Friday, speeded up the tools, and turned in 31 pieces for earnings of $9.60 (3 7/8 pieces per hour, or $1.20 per hour earnings).

"It was easy, just as easy as the frames. Now I'm kicking myself all over for not doing it before. All I did was to change the speed from 95 to 130. I was sick of stalling around all evening, and I got mad and decided to make out and let the tools burn up. But they made it all right, for 8 hours. What's the use of turning in 93 cents an hour when you can turn in $1.25 just as easy? They'd never raise a price you could make 93 cents on anyhow. Now maybe they'll cut it back."

Tonight Al made out easily in 6 hours, though he stretched the last few pieces to carry him until 10:30.

Since McCann reported a turn-in of 31 pieces for earnings of $9.60, or $1.20 an hour on the previous workday, his first day of "making out," it was likely that his "making out" at the 6 hours involved regular quota earnings of $1.25 an hour. A turn-in of 32 pieces would net $9.92 per day, or $1.24 an hour; accomplished in 6 hours, such output would mean that McCann earned $1.65 an hour while working and was now "wasting" 2 hours a shift on quota restriction. And the $1.65-per-hour earnings meant, when compared to previous earnings of 93 cents an hour while goldbricking, that McCann had been "wasting" 3.5 hours a day each time the hinge bases were assigned to his machine; his former earnings loss had been 72 cents an hour, or $5.76 per day. (Actually less than this if "earnings" be defined as "take-home" and not as "turn-in," for McCann's "day rate" had been raised to $1.10 an hour. His personal loss would thus have been 17 cents less per hour—55 cents an hour, or $4.40 per day.)

McCann, engaged in goldbricking, estimated that he could turn out a piece every 16 minutes; this means that he saw production possibilities to be 3.75 pieces per hour and earning possibilities to be $1.16 per hour. But under piecework incentive he actually turned out 5.33 pieces per hour and earned $1.65 per hour while working. If the difference between his estimated and his achieved production can be taken as indicative of such differences in general, then the man who claims that he could have covered his day rate of 85 cents an hour but did not try to do so could have boosted his earnings to $1.21 an hour. In other words, if an operator can see day-rate earnings in a job, he can make quota earnings. My experience would seem to bear this out. If I found that I could make out on a job at day rate, such a discovery motivated me to "wring the neck" of the particular operation for quota earnings. The bimodal pattern production would suggest this; my total quota-piecework hours were 75 per cent of my total make-out-piecework hours, and the latter included short runs of once-assigned jobs that did not receive adequate "test." Though the words of fellow-operators indicated the "pour-it-on" point to be $1.00 an hour, it is possible that energetic performance on 85-cent-an-hour jobs would yield the desired quota.

By the foregoing logic a worker who limits his output to 68 cents an hour, when he thinks he can make 85 cents an hour, is "potentially" limiting output by 44 per cent instead of by the assumed 20 per cent.

Daywork Goldbricking

Operators on "nonpiecework," or "daywork" jobs followed almost uniformly a pattern of restriction of the goldbricking type. They kept in mind rough estimates of output that they felt would fall appreciably below "day-rate" standards if and when the "nonpiecework" jobs were timed and priced.

Nonpiecework jobs in the shop were of two kinds: "time study" and "rework." "Time-study" operations were those that either were so newly established that they were not yet timed and priced or were jobs whose price had been "removed." In either case, timing procedures and a piecework price were expected in the immediate future.

"Rework" was the reprocessing of defective pieces that were considered salvageable. Rework carried no premium pay and no expectations of it, but rough standards of output limitation were applied.

I worked 300 hours at time study and 53 hours at rework, 16 per cent and 3 per cent of total hours put in. Thus, roughly, one-fifth of my time was employed at nonpiecework production, and for this one-fifth the operator could be counted upon, without fail, to be goldbricking. A concise bit of advice, offered by McCann, then set-up man and wise in the ways of production lines, stated the common attitude:

It was a time-study operation, drilling and tapping a set-screw hole in some sprockets.

"Take it easy," advised McCann.

This advice I, already of five months' shop experience, considered unnecessary. By no stretch of the imagination could my accustomed pace on time study be regarded as other than "easy." But, under McCann's expert tutelage, I discovered that there were degrees of goldbricking, and that for time study, a mere "punking along" exceeded worker standards.

McCann started me out at 95 speed on the drill and spot-facer, and 70 on the chamfer and taps.

"Isn't that too slow for the drill?" I asked.

"It's fast enough on this tough stuff for time study. Run it that way 'til they speed you up. If you go too fast today, you won't get a good price when it's timed."

Even this slow pace looked too fast for Gus Schmidt, who watched from the next machine.

Later in the evening Schmidt said to me, "Aren't you going too fast with that time study?"

I did not think I was going very fast and told him so.

"Well, maybe it just looks fast because you're going so steady at it. You've got to slow down on time study or you won't get a good price. They look at the record of what you do today and compare it with the timing speed when it's timed. Those time-study men are sharp!"

Toward the end of the evening I raised the speeds of the taps and chamfer to 95. It was going too slow for me and actually tired me out standing around and waiting for the taps to go through. My legs were tired at the end of the day; yet I had not worked hard.

Goldbricking on time study may be indistinguishable, even to a fellow-operator, from "quota restriction." On one occasion I noticed that Tony, the speed-drill man, was "fooling around," and asked him if he had made out already. Only through information supplied by Tony did I become aware that my neighbor was goldbricking on a time-study job and not relaxing his efforts after achieving quota. In order to classify operator behavior when an operator is "doing nothing," one must have access to additional facts not provided by casual observation. There are times when an operator may be mistaken in classification of his own restriction of output. He may think he is loafing on time study when he is in reality loafing on piecework.

I discovered, when I came to work, that yesterday's job on the pedestals had been timed.

Joe said, "I see you didn't make out yesterday."

I had turned in 60 pieces priced $4.90, for a day's earnings of less than $3.00. I was glad I didn't know the job was timed, with a price like that.

Rework Restriction

I received advice on "rework" that led to the same productive results on time-study operation.

Joe finished the gears, and I spent a slow evening on time study and rework. The first job was 15 gear brackets, a time-study job. The next was the reworking of 1 jack shell.

Said Al, when I told him I was on rework, "Well, you've got all night to turn it out. When they give you a rework job, that's a sign they've got nothing for you to do."

"You mean they expect me to take all night at it?"

McCann was hesitant. "No, I don't mean that. But you can take your time."

About ten o'clock Paul (set-up man) suggested that we "take it easy."

"We're doing too much as it is, on this rework," he said.

When Ed Sokolsky heard that we had done 4, he was surprised. "I wouldn't have done that many," he said.

An Attempt to Estimate the Degree of Nonpiecework Restriction

An indication of the amount of restriction practiced on nonpiecework operations can be obtained in a comparison of the writer's output on a job before it was timed and priced, and his output on the same job after a piecework price was set.

One day some gear parts were assigned as time study. I accepted the advice to take it easy proffered by the set-up man, McCann, and by a fellow-operator, Schmidt, and turned in a total of 64 pieces for the day's work. The next day I came to work to discover that the job had been timed at $7.95 a hundred. Joe Mucha reported the job a good one, but I was dubious.

"It's a good job," he said. "They timed me for $1.20 an hour, and it worked out just that. You can do 16 an hour. But watch yourself, now, and don't turn in too many!"

"Don't worry, I probably won't get 100," I assured him.

Yesterday's 64 had given me the feeling that I would have to push very hard to turn out 100 ($1.00 per hour).

I had underestimated the job. My effort reached a peak of $1.83 per hour, or 23 pieces per hour, and I completed 150 pieces in 7.5 hours for average earning of $1.59 an hour for the time worked.

After lunch I decided to try to see how many I could turn out. I did manage to complete 12 in half an hour but never got higher than 23 for the whole hour. The speeds were set at 225 for drilling and 95 for the other tools, just as I finished yesterday. At 10:30 I had completed 150 pieces.

At a price of $7.95 per 100, the 64 pieces turned out on time study would have represented average earnings of about 64 cents an hour. Since I expected to turn out no more than 100 pieces with full effort on piecework, my assumed restriction on time study was 36 per cent, with a "loss" of 36 cents an hour, or $2.86 a day, and with a time "waste" of 2.9 hours.

But with an actual subsequent output of 20 per hour for 7.5 hours, a rate of 160 per day, restriction the first day turned out to be 60 per cent, with a loss of 95 cents an hour, or $7.63 per day, and a time "waste" of 4.8 hours a day. And with a "potential" output of 23 per hour, a rate of 184 per day, restriction the first day turned out to be 65 per cent, with a "loss" of $9.55 a day, or $1.19 an hour, and a time "waste" of 5.2 hours a day.

Summary and Conclusion

These appraisals of output limitation can be accepted only as suggestive of the amount of time wasted by operatives in piecework machine shops. Certainly, the "waste" is great.

I have indicated that the time "wasted" on my own quota restriction for a six-month period was 1.39 hours out of every 8. I was 83 per cent "efficient" for the 469.6 quota piecework-hours put in, by my own standards of performance, and thus could have increased production by 21 per cent by abandoning quota limitations. If my wastage of 2 hours a day on quota restriction during the last two months of employment is accepted as characteristic of the behavior of more seasoned operators, efficiency would be 75 per cent, with immediate possibilities for a 33.3 per cent increase in production on quota jobs.

Also, by experimenting with twenty jobs which represented 58 per cent of the total piecework hours put in during a ten-month period, and which offered earning possibilities beyond quota limits, I derived an estimate of "potential quota restriction" of 2.9 hours a day. This restriction represented an efficiency of 64 per cent, with possibilities for a 57 per cent increase in production.

Furthermore, from observations of the work behavior of fellow-operators, I was able to speculate with some objective evidence on the degree of slow-down goldbricking practiced on non-make-out piecework. It was pointed out that four drill operators had been restricting production at a rate of 3.5 "waste" hours out of 8, as indicated by the output achieved by one of the four men when he ceased goldbricking. Efficiency had been 56 per cent, with immediate possibilities for a 78 per cent production increase. Renunciation of goldbricking did not, in this particular case, mean fulfillment of possibilities, however; for the conversion was to quota restriction with stabilization at 75 per cent efficiency.

In addition, I essayed an estimate on daywork goldbricking, first cousin to piecework goldbricking and easily mistaken for the latter. This estimate was obtained by comparing output on a job before and after it was timed. The "before" efficiency was determined to be at least as low as 40 per cent, possibly 35 per cent, with 150 per cent improvement in production a "cinch" and 186 per cent improvement an immediate possibility. But like the case of piecework goldbricking just cited, the switch was to quota restriction; so possibilities were never realized.

Since these appraisals were confined to the behavior of machine operators, the loss of time accountable to the sometimes remarkable restraint exercised by the "service" employees, such as stock-chasers, toolcrib attendants, and inspectors, was not considered. Likewise unmentioned were the various defections of shop supervisors. A more complete record might also include the "work" of members of management at higher levels, whose series of new rules, regulations, orders, and pronunciamentos designed for purposes of expediting production processes actually operated to reduce the effectiveness of the work force.

Confining scrutiny to the behavior of machine operators, the observer sees output restriction of such magnitude that the "phenomenal" results of the organizational innovations tried in the steel industry under the guiding genius of Joe Scanlon[6] do not seem at all surprising. The concept of "cultural drag" might be more descriptive than "cultural lag" in depicting the trailing of some of our industrial practices behind technological advance. Our organization of people for work is in general so primitive that anthropologists need not attempt to justify their interest in the "modern" industrial scene.

[6] John Chamberlain, "Every Man a Capitalist," *Life Magazine* (December 23, 1946), pp. 93-100; Russell W. Davenport, "Enterprise for Everyman," *Fortune* (January, 1950), pp. 55-59, 152-159.

21. Some Functional Consequences of Primary Controls in Formal Work Organizations

Edward Gross

The present paper concerns the proposition that primary controls may be functional within instituted social organizations. For this purpose, evidence will be submitted which suggests that such primary controls may make their appearance precisely when formal or institutional controls prove inadequate. As such, these primary controls enable the organization to accomplish its formal purpose.

The study uses two sources of data—one, a manufacturing concern in Chicago, with approximately 1500 workers, which produces plastic raincoats, belts, jewelry and other items; and second, a radar air site in the Air Defense Command, United States Air Force.[1] The two cases are utilized first in order partially to avoid the dangers of the unique case, and second, in order to provide a comparison between a small, independent civilian factory on the one hand, and a huge interlocking military organization on the other. The data in both cases were gathered by means of interview and participant observation techniques.[2] It is necessary to emphasize that the writer is still very much in the midst of the Air Force study, so that findings with reference to it are highly tentative.

Work organizations are characterized by purposiveness. Each has one

Reprinted from *American Sociological Review*, 18 (August, 1953), 368-373.

[1] The writer is on the professional staff of Air Site Project, a research organization within the Department of Sociology at the University of Washington. The project is under the direction of D. C. Miller. The research reported here was supported in part by the United States Air Force under Contract Number AF 33(038)26823, monitored by the Human Resources Research Institute, Air University, Maxwell Air Force Base, Alabama. Permission is granted for reproduction, translation, publication and disposal in whole and in part by or for the U.S. Government. (*Editor's Note:* The foregoing sentence presumably constitutes the permission for the *Review* to publish this material. Since the *Review* articles are copyrighted, permission to quote should be requested of the editor.)

[2] For a full description of method in the factory study, see Edward Gross, "Informal Relations and the Social Organization of Work in an Industrial Office," unpublished Ph.D. dissertation, University of Chicago, 1949, Ch. 1. The research the writer did there was concentrated in the office among the white-collar workers, though he also did some work with the factory personnel. There were approximately 100 workers in the office at the time of the study, and a total of 319 interviews (nondirective) were gathered. It is difficult to specify the nature of the Air Force population because of security regulations. However, it may be said that the writer has been with the project on a full-time basis for one and a half years, of which approximately one half has been spent at air sites. The writer is concentrating the major part of his efforts at one air site.

or more specified goals or objectives which it seeks to achieve. In the case of the factory, these are, mainly, the manufacture, sale, and distribution of certain physical goods, while in the case of the air site, there is the one objective or "mission" of maintaining radar surveillance against hostile aircraft. The fact of purpose creates the need for institutional or segmented controls on behavior so that this purpose or mission may be realized. To this end, it is necessary only that a segment of the personality be controlled; namely, the role as worker, but it is essential that *that* one role be controlled. This control is provided in the following manner in the two organizations under examination.

Formal control is instituted through a division of labor which serves to relate specialisms and specialists to one another, through an authority system which serves to coordinate specialists and to evaluate their contributions to the objective, and finally, through a selection system which serves to recruit personnel who, it is felt, can assume the work roles required.

We proceed next to discuss each of these instituted controls and the manner in which they may break down or prove inadequate, and how, in each case, primary controls then make their appearance. The paramount problem which any division of labor system must solve, as stated above, is that of relating the specialisms and specialists it creates to one another. Observation revealed that the following instituted means were used to attempt to solve this problem: (1) Minute specialization, and (2) Provision for formal horizontal communication. In general, specialization became more minute as operations increased in complexity. Each predictable act was planned for in advance and assigned to one or more persons. These acts were related to one another in flow charts, with the underlying conception that, if each person did what was expected of him, then specialisms would mesh and the goal be reached. It was felt that the more minute the division of labor, the easier it is to train persons and replace them. Further, the more carefully specialisms were defined, it was felt, the less likely would it be that specialists would overlap and conflict with one another. Formal horizontal communication between specialists, in turn, was expected to take place through a common supervisor, so that appropriate permission was secured and relevant persons informed of the action.[3]

But in actual practice, at both the factory and the air site, these instituted procedures gave rise to problems. The provision for formal communication through a common supervisor was found to be cumbersome and time-consuming. The required person was often busy, or, at the air site, which is on 24-hour shift duty, he was off-shift, and thus action came to a standstill. Yet some persons were loath to take action by simply going directly to the specialist concerned, while others did so, but in interviews, expressed anxiety about possible reprimand.

[3] See B. B. Gardner, *Human Relations in Industry* (Homewood, Ill.: Irwin, 1945), Ch. 2, for a discussion of this point.

The minuteness of the division of labor had two effects in both organizations.

1. While *specialties* were related to one another, the very minuteness of the division of labor and restriction of persons to their specialties operated effectively to isolate *specialists* from one another. Thus, when pressure was imposed for each person to do his job, persons sometimes refused to help others in difficulties. Most interesting was the expression in interviews of what might be called a "sphere of concern." One office worker in the Credit Department at the factory stated: "I check ledger cards to see what a man's past credit record with the Company is. All I want from the Accounting Department is clear, up-to-date postings on the cards. I don't know where they get their information and I don't care. I'm paid to do a job here, and how they do theirs is none of my affair."

On a later occasion, when mailing lists for the company catalogue were being drawn up, extensive checking of accounting records was necessary to determine who were to receive catalogues. The company experienced difficulty in getting persons from other departments in the office to assist in this emergency work, which required meeting a publication deadline. Persons stated that they were unfamiliar with accounting records, and, more important, could see no point in leaving their own work to assist the accounting personnel. The formal division of labor provided no way for rewarding such effort, unless a supervisor saw fit to recommend a raise or promotion, because such extra effort came to his personal attention. It is noteworthy that such a reward is only possible in an organization small enough for higher supervisors to be in close touch with lower employees.

At the radar site, a similar problem occurred in connection with specialty classification. Men are originally classified at induction depots by AFSC[4] and given commensurate training. In order to justify the time and money spent on a man, it is required that he spend at least one year in his AFSC before he is eligible for a change. Further, promotions in rank for airmen depend to a considerable extent on time spent in the AFSC. The job of radar operator was reported in interviews to be a highly tedious one for which it is apparently difficult to recruit volunteers in large numbers; therefore, some men are given that AFSC even though their primary wishes lie elsewhere. Now, some commanding officers have adopted the procedure of shifting men temporarily to other specialties wherein there are personnel shortages, and where those specialties are more in accord with the men's interests and wishes. This informal practice might actually assist the air site in accomplishing its mission more effectively. However, the restriction on promotion interferes, and men discover they are not accumulating time in their official AFSC's. Thus, they find themselves caught in the midst of a dilemma for which the formal system provides no solution. One consequence is considerable anxiety, "griping," and requests for

[4] An abbreviation for Air Force Specialty Code, a system of classifying specialties.

return to the official AFSC. Thus, as in the industrial office, specialization made it difficult for men to cross specialty lines when such action was necessary to the mission of the organization, and the promotions system is tied up inextricably with the specialization system.

2. The restriction of persons to their specialisms had the further effect of tending to strip work of meaning. Indeed, it seemed that the greater the restriction, the more meaningless the work. This was found to be the case in the small civilian organization but it seemed to be much more the case in the Air Force organization. Radar surveillance is but a minuscule segment of Air Force activities, and, in spite of movies and the Information and Education program, men in interviews expressed difficulty in being able to see where their particular activity fitted into the whole. This led, in some cases, to a loss of faith in the mission, with consequent depression and feelings of uselessness. The phenomena of payday sprees and debauches may be, in part, a function of this problem.

However, further examination revealed that a second set of controls was operative, which lessened the severity of these problems and even prevented their occurrence in some cases. These controls were primary in nature, and took the form of the clique or informal group, wherein workers met one another as more than segmented personalities. In the case of the office, it was discovered that the 11 cliques that were found in the office tended to cut across work sections, and thus brought together, on an informal basis, persons from various segments of the structure. Within these groups, horizontal communication was easy, persons volunteered assistance to one another, and, by being able to compare their specialisms with one another, gained some conception of the relation of their work to the whole. At the same time, isolates proved to be peculiarly vulnerable to the inadequacies of the institutional controls.[5]

In the case of the Air Force organization, a special situation prevailed by virtue of the fact of 24-hour-a-day shift operations. It is the practice to change men continually from one shift to another, so that, in a short period of time, in certain sections, a man has worked every shift. The writer, with two graduate student associates, L. W. Wager and H. J. Loether, became aware of what we have since called "work leisure cycles." The concept of work leisure refers to the amount of opportunity afforded by a specialty for informal recreational contacts while on the job. Some shifts coincide, but others run at different rates around the clock. Preliminary findings suggest that cliques tend to develop between work sections when their work leisure opportunities coincide. This, in turn, makes possible inter-specialty informal communication.

By contrast, one work section operates a special piece of equipment,

[5] For a fuller discussion, see Edward Gross, "Characteristics of Cliques in Office Organizations," *Research Studies of the State College of Washington*, **19** (June, 1951), 131-136.

while another work section does this section's maintenance work for it. Their shifts coincide, but here we have a case where work leisure periods do not coincide. When the operators of the equipment are working, maintenance personnel merely stand by. When the equipment requires repairs, or is given periodic maintenance checks, operators have leisure, but it is just then that maintenance personnel are busiest. Observation has revealed an almost complete absence of cliquing between these two work sections. Instead, there is considerable conflict between them, refusals to make allowance for each other's problems, and actual lack of knowledge, in some cases, of how interdependent they in fact are and must be. Solution of these conflicts required intervention by the commanding officer. These data, while only suggestive, imply that cliques which cross specialty lines act to reduce conflicts between work sections, by virtue of the intimacy provided by clique interaction. But if cliques are prevented from forming by a lack of coincidence of leisure periods, then conflict may and does occur. The writer has not had the opportunity to observe this work leisure phenomenon in civilian industries, but it is noteworthy that cliques in the civilian office tended to be composed of persons who had coffee "breaks" at the same time of day, and who ate lunch at the same hour. The times for the latter were different for different departments.

We turn next to the formal authority system. A work organization requires some means for coordinating and evaluating the work done in order that it shall be consistent with the purposes of the organization. In organizations of any size, this is usually accomplished by establishing a set of supervisors of graded rank who are held responsible for segments of the organization.[6] Institutional requirements in both organizations under examination provide that supervisors shall perform their work by reporting on their sections to the next higher supervisor, and so on. In the case of the factory, by virtue of its small size, much of this reporting was done personally, but in the case of the air force organization, a large amount of paper work is created by this requirement and the specter of SOP[7] is everywhere in evidence. Two consequences tend to occur: first, a fairly elaborate "covering-up" process, whereby higher supervisors were sometimes almost isolated from their work sections and were thus only partially aware of their degree of success in reaching organizational goals, and second, a tendency for persons to get buried in paper-work to such an extent that they were able to spend only a little time actually coordinating their departments.

At the air site, the informal organization related itself to these institutional concomitants as follows. Preliminary findings suggest that in addition to cliquing between specialties, there is also a considerable tendency

[6] See W. L. Warner, M. Meeker, and E. Eells, *Social Class in America* (Chicago: Science Research, Associates), Ch. 1, for a discussion of the functions of supervision.

[7] Abbreviation for Standard Operating Procedure.

for cliques to be confined to a given specialty. We are working now on the hypothesis that this phenomenon is related to the work section's ability to accomplish its mission without formal direction or in spite of ineffective direction. There is some evidence that the work section may be operated informally. The paper work problem is in part solved by informal sessions —one commanding officer sees to it that officers report to the club daily for coffee—where experiences are traded and higher-ranking officers gain knowledge of what is taking place in their work sections. This serves also to protect them should paper reveal inadequacies; they have at least been forewarned. It seems to serve the further function of providing opportunities for supervisors to evaluate one another's capabilities and thus develop confidence in one another.

This leads us to the third institutional control; namely, the selection system. At the factory, this is handled in the usual manner by a personnel office. Here, the individual's qualifications are examined and a decision reached concerning whether he can perform the work role for which there is a vacancy. In the Air Force, as in military organizations generally, entrance is facilitated, but the individual is then given a set of tests to determine aptitude and interests. Persons are then sent to a school (if necessary) in large numbers to equip them for jobs to which they are later assigned. Theoretically, if persons have been well-trained and have appropriate interests and aptitudes, the organization should succeed in filling its vacancies in this manner.

What is noteworthy about the approach in both instances is that it focuses attention completely on the individual and his abilities, and ignores completely the cooperative nature of the organization in which he must play a role. The individual may have the requisite skills, but before he can play the role successfully, other workers must be willing to accept him in that role. At the factory, it was discovered that employees engaged in a continuous process of mutual evaluation in terms of the following criteria: personal characteristics, marital ties, religion, education, race, ethnicity and language, experience, and union membership.[8] There were sentiments expressed that these characteristics made a difference in terms of the amount of respect or confidence one should have in fellow workers, and that the formal organization did not sufficiently reward possessors of what were considered desirable characteristics. Said the secretary to the office manager:

You know, there are quite a few refugees from Nazi Germany here. They don't seem to get along so well in the office. They seem to be set in their ways. I don't know what it is, but they just form a group apart. Fred (her husband) says it's because of their background. Most of them have never worked before in their life. They don't fit into our industrial system at all. They just don't seem to have the knack. Many times, Mr. Hanson (her supervisor) and I are going

[8] For a full discussion, see Ch. 3 of the reference cited in footnote 2.

over a form and I see immediately what the trouble is, but he has to go slowly and ploddingly around, taking small steps, until he eventually comes to the same conclusion that I do. But he has to do it in the roundabout slow, methodical way.

Another worker, commenting on the problem of trying to work with Mr. Hanson said, "Talking to Hanson is like talking to yourself."

Cliques, by their very nature tend to be made up of persons who feel at ease in one another's presence and feel confidence in one another. Indeed, it is through clique experience that such confidence may be highly developed. As the secretary to a vice-president explained:

A private secretary is the top of the heap. You need something else besides the ability to type and take shorthand. You've got to feel you're working for the company and not just for yourself. Now Mildred and Emma (other private secretaries)—we see eye to eye on that. Louise—she's a good little stenographer, but she'll never be a secretary. She doesn't fit into our crowd. When we go out for coffee, she tags along. Then she'll usually complain about her boss. She can't accept the idea that you don't work for a boss, you work for the company.

In the Air Force organization, the following situation prevailed. The air site, like all military organizations, is required to make the best use of the men assigned to it, whether they have what are regarded as desirable qualities or not. Since a large proportion of the personnel are either draftees or involuntary recalls,[9] one of the most important criteria for success in a work role is likely to be an identification with the Air Force and the mission of the squadron. The implicit question arises: Where do you feel you belong? Are you one of us, or do you still regard yourself as a civilian? The problem is complicated in surveillance work for two reasons. First, there exists a split between personnel with and without wings. Ability to fly is not related to the mission of the site; yet those with wings exhibit a tendency to identify with the flying air force outside the site. Second, not all radar personnel desire to remain in that work after their one year AFSC requirement has been met.

There is some evidence that the informal organization is used to discover primary identifications and also to change those identifications. Thus, the commanding officer at one site organized a duty night, which, after two hours of work, turned into a stag party till 3:00 A.M. There were later objections from the wives of officers present, about which the commanding officer said in an interview:

I called that a duty night because that's exactly what it was. There's too much of this dashing for the gate right after a man's shift is over to get home, or to get in flying time. I wanted to take this means of informing my men that radar

9 A considerable proportion qualify as "volunteers," but on questionnaires gave overwhelmingly as their reason for volunteering: "To avoid getting drafted into the Army."

comes first, family and flying second. If I, as their CO, want them to stay till 3 in the morning to work, they'll do it. If I want them to play poker till 3, they'll do it, because I said so. Let the wives gripe. It's time they found out their husbands are in the Air Force.

It was significant that the commanding officer employed an informal means of driving the point home, for the formal regulations are quite clear on this point. The point here is that the selection system does not insure a supply, either in the office or the Air Force, of persons who have what are regarded as "desirable" characteristics by persons within the organization. In the case of both the office and the air site, primary control devices are employed both to discover these characteristics and to try to develop them if they are absent.

Evidence has been submitted which suggests that primary controls on behavior are far from being inconsistent with institutional controls. There is an unfortunate tendency in the literature on the sociology of work to regard cliques as innocuous play groups, or else as being antithetical to the purposes of the organization, as exemplified in restriction of output.[10] While this is unquestionably the case in some situations, it is suggested here that cliques may have quite another purpose—they may actually be essential to the very functioning of instituted organizations.

The data presented here, based as they are on only two work organizations, are inconclusive. But they do suggest that the relation between primary and institutional controls is by no means a simple one, and that further research on this relation may prove fruitful in the examination of behavior in formal work organizations.[11]

[10] Cf. F. J. Roethlisberger and W. J. Dickson, *Management and the Worker* (Cambridge, Mass.: Harvard University Press, 1947), Chs. 22 and 23, and W. E. Moore, *Industrial Relations and the Social Order* (New York: Macmillan, 1947), Ch. 15. An exception to this emphasis is provided in D. C. Miller and W. H. Form, *Industrial Sociology* (New York: Harper & Row, 1951), Ch. 9.

[11] See also W. F. Whyte, *Street Corner Society* (Chicago: University of Chicago Press, 1943), for a discussion of the significance of informal organization in the slum, which deals with roughly the same theme as that discussed here, though in a different social situation.

22. Group Cohesiveness in the Industrial Work Group

Stanley E. Seashore

Prior research on the characteristics of groups has suggested that the variable group cohesiveness is of considerable consequence in relation to the functioning of the group and the behavior of the individual members. The variable has been explored principally in laboratory experiments with groups of small size, although there is a rich literature of anecdote and careful observation with respect to the cohesiveness of "natural" groups in industry and in other kinds of social settings.

For the present investigation, group cohesiveness was conceptualized as attraction of members to the group in terms of the strength of forces on the individual member to remain in the group and to resist leaving the group.

The objective of this study has been to explore in an industrial situation some of the facilitating conditions and consequences of group cohesiveness. The research hypotheses were as follows:

1. Members of high cohesive groups will exhibit less anxiety than members of low cohesive groups with respect to matters relevant to group activities or the group setting.

2. The degree of cohesiveness within a group determines the power of the group to create forces towards uniformity of behavior among members (group standards).

3. In the case of a cohesive group subjected to forces toward an uncertain or unobtainable goal imposed by an external agent, the point of equilibrium of forces toward and away from the goal (group standard) will be a function of the perceived supportiveness of the external agent.

4. The degree of cohesiveness developed in a group will be a function of the attractiveness of the members of the group as determined by the prestige of the members.

5. The degree of cohesiveness developed in a group will be a function of the attractiveness of the members of the group as determined by the degree of similarity among members of the group.

6. The degree of cohesiveness developed in a group will be a function of opportunities for interaction among members of the group.

Reprinted from Stanley E. Seashore, *Group Cohesiveness in the Industrial Work Group* (Ann Arbor: Survey Research Center, University of Michigan, 1954), pp. 97-102.

The study design uses the correlational technique with group cohesiveness treated as the independent variable, and measures of anxiety, productivity standards, member similarity, member prestige, and opportunity for interaction as dependent variables. The data are drawn from a population of 228 groups (formally designated work sections in a machinery factory) ranging in size from 5 to over 50 members. The data were obtained through a questionnaire completed by all members of these groups, 5,871 in number.

The major findings relevant to the hypotheses outlined above were as follows:

1. Members of high cohesive groups exhibit less anxiety than members of low cohesive groups, using as measures of anxiety: (a) feeling "jumpy or nervous," (b) feeling under pressure to achieve higher productivity (actual productivity held constant), and (c) feeling of lack of support from the company. The hypothesis was not clearly supported in the case of a fourth measure of anxiety, namely, report of frequent worry about certain work-related matters such as earnings, lay-off, etc., although a majority of these findings were in the predicted direction and one (out of eight) was statistically significant.

2. High cohesive goups have less variation in productivity among members than do the low cohesiveness groups. This is regarded as confirmation of the existence of a more effective group standard in the high cohesive condition.

3. High cohesive groups differ more frequently and in greater amount than low cohesive groups from the plant norm of productivity. These deviations are towards both high and lower productivity.

4. The direction of deviation of group productivity (i.e., towards higher or lower productivity) is a function of the degree to which the larger organization (the company) is perceived by group members to provide a supportive setting for the group.

5. The prediction regarding degree of group cohesiveness and similarity among members was not confirmed, using as measures similarity in age and similarity in educational level.

6. Group cohesiveness is positively related to the degree of prestige attributed by the group members to their own jobs.

7. Group cohesiveness is positively related to opportunity for interaction as measured by (a) size of group, and (b) duration of shared membership on the job.

8. The findings with respect to group standards (2, 3, and 4, above) using actual productivity as the measure, were not confirmed when an alternative measure of group productivity standard (perceived level of reasonable productivity) was used.

In addition to these findings, which relate directly to the research hypotheses, there were several theoretical and methodological by-products which seem worth a passing note. These are summarized below with suggestions for their interpretation.

1. Homans[1] makes the distinction between group norms (actual behavior) and group standards (ideal behavior). He further holds that there is likely to be a discrepancy between the two and that within a group there will be greater uniformity with respect to the verbalized standard of behavior than with respect to the behavioral norm. Our data do not support this conception; actual productivity is found to have about the same variability within groups as is perceived reasonable productivity. Both differ from the formal company standard of 100 per cent, which very few employees appear to accept even as an ideal level of productivity. It seems more useful to conceptualize group standards in terms of group-induced uniformities of behavior regardless of whether the behavior in question is overt physical behavior, verbal behavior, or private attitudinal response. This does not deny the utility of Homans' conception in a context of societal norms and the precedence of behavior change over ideal change.

2. Schachter, et al.,[2] in an experiment on group cohesiveness and productivity found differential group cohesiveness to be related to differential degrees of change in group productivity when the group induction was in a negative direction, i.e., towards lower productivity, and when there were external forces towards higher productivity. On the other hand, the differences in degree of cohesiveness of the group had no apparent effect when the group induction was in a direction consistent with external forces towards higher productivity. He gives a rationale leading to the hypothesis that positive group induction would have been accepted by the members, differentially in high and low cohesive groups, if the restraining forces against higher productivity had been of greater magnitude than his experimental conditions provided. Our findings are that the hypothesized relationship between cohesiveness and productivity holds for both positive and negative directions of group induction. This offers some confirmation for his formulation of the matter.

3. We have encountered the finding, not statistically significant but consistent for four sets of data, that under conditions of relatively low group cohesiveness, perception of a high degree of support from the company is coincident with low productivity standards while low support is coincident with high production. This result is paralleled by findings from other studies: for example, several studies relating productivity to employee attitudes toward the company suggest that high-producing employees may tend to be more critical of the company and its policies.[3] We are inclined to interpret this finding with reference to primary group processes, and hypothesize that in the absence of the security provided by a primary group,

[1] G. C. Homans, The Human Group (New York: Harcourt, Brace & World, 1950).

[2] S. Schachter, N. Ellertson, D. McBride and D. Gregory, "An Experimental Study of Cohesiveness and Productivity," Human Relations, 4 (1951), 229-238.

[3] D. Katz, N. Maccoby and N. C. Morse, Productivity, Supervision and Morale in an Office Situation (Ann Arbor: Survey Research Center, 1950); D. Katz, N. Maccoby, G. Gurin and L. G. Floor, Productivity, Supervision and Morale Among Railroad Workers (Ann Arbor: Survey Research Center, 1951).

the insecure employee will experience greater anxiety regarding his fulfillment of company demands and will tend to adopt productivity standards
which are relatively high in order to minimize this anxiety; in the opposite
case—an employee feeling relatively secure in relation to the company—
this additional force towards higher productivity will be minimized.

4. We assumed in designing this study that formally-designated section-shift groups, so designated for accounting purposes, would in fact
function to some degree as primary social groups. This seemed a rather
large assumption considering the fact that the "groups," for the most part,
are of a size greater than is ordinarily considered to be optimum or "natural" for primary groups, and in view of the fact that there is no assurance
that conditions of physical proximity and subgroup formation would permit
the section-shift units to function as groups. The assumption, however, appears to be supported by the fact of significant findings which stem from
group-related influences. To a significant degree, the formal units of organization in this factory—and presumably in other factories—function as
effective social units. This enlarges considerably the convenience and potential scope of future research on group processes in industrial settings.

We opened this report with the general assertion that the behavior of
people in large formal organizational settings cannot be understood unless
we take into account the forces generated by their association in primary
groups. We specifically set out to determine whether these group associations were relevant factors in the mental health and adjustment of the individual with reference to his work, and in the determination of standards
of productivity.

The formulation of our research hypotheses stemmed in part from
prior research focussing upon the problems of organization management
and the problems of the individual seeking a satisfactory way of life in a
society characterized by the association of people in large organizations.
Our manner of thinking about the problem—the choice of concepts, and
the development of relationships to be tested—was drawn largely from the
field theoretical approach which views the individual's behavior in terms
of a dynamic field of forces exerting influence upon the individual, with
the direction and magnitude of these forces determined in part by social
interaction and specifically by interaction within the primary group.

We emerge from this study with some new ideas, but mainly with
considerably increased respect for some old ones. We see demonstrated in
a typical social setting the dependence of the individual upon his primary
associations for feelings of security and the reduction of his anxieties. We
see the pimary group as a source of potent influences which may or may
not be marshalled in support of the goals of the larger organization. We
come to a conception of group cohesiveness—the attraction of the group
for the members—as a facilitating factor which determines the amount of
influence a group has, but not necessarily the direction or the goal toward

which the group influences operate. We see the variable, group cohesiveness, as being of sufficient importance so that its effects are measurable; they are measurable even in a complex setting in which the formal social structure is designed to ignore or even suppress group effects and in which there are strong factors, such as individual mobility, multiple group membership, out-plant associations, problems of reliable measurement, and others, which tend to obscure primary group effects.

Finally, we observe that some, at least, of the factors determining the degree to which group cohesiveness is developed, are external to and prior to group formation. The work group is more likely to become cohesive if administrative actions are designed with these ends: (1) to lend prestige to the group members, (2) to structure the organization so that there is provision for groups of relatively small size, and (3) to maintain a continuity in group membership over a period of time.

The administrator of an organization may draw from these findings some hints regarding policy and action. It is clear that the association of employees in cohesive groups may generate influences that are or may be of considerable consequence to the success of an organization. With respect to employee morale—in the context of anxieties at work—the cohesive work group appears to have a favorable influence. But with respect to productivity the positive value of cohesiveness in the work group appears to be contingent upon the administrator's success in developing among the employees a feeling of confidence and security in the management of the organization. The popular admonition to supervisors that they should develop a cohesive team, if carried out indiscriminately, may merely lend force to the divisive influences within the larger organization. To assure a positive benefit to the organization from group cohesiveness the administrator might well take steps first to provide the basic conditions of equity and supportiveness which warrant employee confidence in management. A policy of "divide and conquer," as expressed in an emphasis on man-to-man relationships and suppression of group processes, may be partially effective; but the greater gains appear to lie in a policy to "unite in common cause," as expressed in the positive emphasis upon the formation of cohesive work teams.

23. Overcoming Resistance to Change

Lester Coch
John R. P. French, Jr.

The Experiment

On the basis of the preliminary theory that resistance to change is a combination of an individual reaction to frustration with strong group-induced forces it seemed that the most appropriate methods for overcoming the resistance to change would be group methods. Consequently an experiment was designed employing two variations of democratic procedure in handling groups to be transferred. The first variation involved participation though representation of the workers in designing the changes to be made in the jobs. The second variation consisted of total participation by all members of the group in designing the changes. A third, control group was also used. Two experimental groups received the total participation treatment. The three experimental groups and the control group were roughly matched with respect to: (1) the efficiency ratings of the groups before transfer; (2) the degree of change involved in the transfer; (3) the amount of we-feeling observed in the groups.

In no case was more than a minor change in the work routines and time allowances made. The control group, the eighteen hand pressers, had formerly stacked their work in one-half dozen lots on a flat piece of cardboard the size of the finished product. The new job called for stacking their work in one-half dozen lots in a box the size of the finished product. The box was located in the same place the cardboard had been. An additional two minutes per dozen was allowed (by the time study) for this new part of the job. This represented a total job change of 8.8 per cent.

Experimental group 1, the thirteen pajama folders, had formerly folded coats with pre-folded pants. The new job called for the folding of coats with unfolded pants. An additional 1.8 minutes per dozen was allowed (by time study) for this new part of the job. This represented a total job change of 9.4 per cent.

Experimental groups 2 and 3, consisting of eight and seven pajama examiners respectively, had formerly clipped threads from the entire garment and examined every seam. The new job called for pulling only certain threads off and examining every seam. An average of 1.2 minutes per dozen

"Overcoming Resistance to Change" by Lester Coch and John R. P. French. *Human Relations*, Vol. 1, 520-524, 531-532. London: Tavistock Publications.

was subtracted (by time study) from the total time on these two jobs. This represented a total job change of 8 per cent.

The control group of hand pressers went through the usual factory routine when they were changed. The production department modified the job, and a new piece rate was set. A group meeting was then held in which the control group was told that the change was necessary because of competitive conditions, and that a new piece rate had been set. The new piece rate was thoroughly explained by the time study man, questions were answered, and the meeting dismissed.

Experimental group 1 was changed in a different manner. Before any changes took place, a group meeting was held with all the operators to be changed. The need for the change was presented as dramatically as possible, showing two identical garments produced in the factory; one was produced in 1946 and had sold for 100 per cent more than its fellow in 1947. The group was asked to identify the cheaper one and could not do it. This demonstration effectively shared with the group the entire problem of the necessity of cost reduction. A general agreement was reached that a savings could be effected by removing the "frills" and "fancy" work from the garment without affecting the folders' opportunity to achieve a high efficiency rating. Management then presented a plan to set the new job and piece rate:

1. Make a check study of the job as it was being done.
2. Eliminate all unnecessary work.
3. Train several operators in the correct methods.
4. Set the piece rate by time studies on these specially trained operators.
5. Explain the new job and rate to all the operators.
6. Train all operators in the new method so they can reach a high rate of production within a short time.

The group approved this plan (though no formal group decision was reached), and chose the operators to be specially trained. A sub-meeting with the "special" operators was held immediately following the meeting with the entire group. They displayed a cooperative and interested attitude and immediately presented many good suggestions. This attitude carried over into the working out of the details of the new job; and when the new job and piece rates were set, the "special" operators referred to the resultants as "our job," "our rate," etc. The new job and piece rates were presented at a second group meeting to all the operators involved. The "special" operators served to train the other operators on the new job.

Experimental groups 2 and 3 went through much the same kind of change meetings. The groups were smaller than experimental group 1, and a more intimate atmosphere was established. The need for a change was once again made dramatically clear; the same general plan was presented by management. However, since the groups were small, all operators were chosen as "special" operators; that is, all operators were to participate directly in the designing of the new jobs, and all operators would be studied by the time study man. It is interesting to note that in the meetings with these two groups, suggestions were immediately made in such quantity that the stenographer had great difficulty in recording them. The group approved of the plans, but again no formal group decision was reached.

Results

The results of the experiment are summarized in graphic form in Figure 4-2. The gaps in the production curves occur because these groups were paid on a time-work basis for a day or two. The control group improved

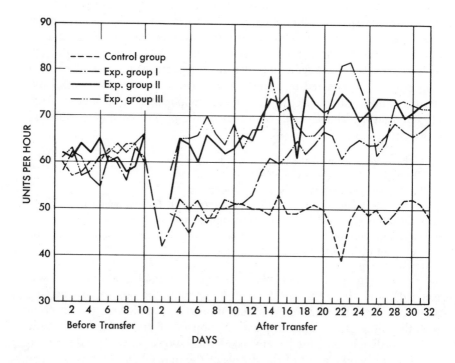

Figure 4-2.   The Effects of Participation Through Representation (group I) and of Total Participation (groups II and III) on Recovery after an Easy Transfer.

little beyond their early efficiency ratings. Resistance developed almost immediately after the change occurred. Marked expressions of aggression against management occurred, such as conflict with the methods engineer, expression of hostility against the supervisor, deliberate restriction of production, and lack of cooperation with the supervisor. There were 17 per cent quits in the first forty days. Grievances were filed about the piece rate, but when the rate was checked it was found to be a little "loose."

Experimental group 1 showed an unusually good relearning curve. At the end of fourteen days, the group averaged 61 units per hour. During the fourteen days, the attitude was cooperative and permissive. They worked well with the methods engineer, the training staff, and the supervisor. (The supervisor was the same person in the cases of the control group and experimental group 1.) There were no quits in this group in the first forty days. This group might have presented a better learning record if work had not been scarce during the first seven days. There was one act of aggression against the supervisor recorded in the first forty days. It is interesting to note that the three special representative operators in experimental group 1 recovered at about the same rate as the rest of their group.

Experimental groups 2 and 3 recovered faster than experimental group 1. After a slight drop on the first day of change, the efficiency ratings returned to a pre-change level and showed sustained progress thereafter to a level about 14 per cent higher than the pre-change level. No additional training was provided them after the second day. They worked well with their supervisors and no indications of aggression were observed from these groups. There were no quits in either of these groups in the first forty days.

A fourth experimental group, composed of only two sewing operators, was transferred by the total participation technique. Their new job was one of the most difficult jobs in the factory, in contrast to the easy jobs for the control group and the other three experimental groups. As expected, the total participation technique again resulted in an unusually fast recovery rate and a final level of production well above the level before transfer. Because of the difficulty of the new job, however, the rate of recovery was slower than for experimental groups 2 and 3, but faster than for experimental group 1.

In the first experiment, the control groups made no progress after transfer for a period of 32 days. At the end of this period the group was broken up and the individuals were reassigned to new jobs scattered throughout the factory. Two and a half months after their dispersal, the thirteen remaining members of the original control group were again brought together as a group for a second experiment.

This second experiment consisted of transferring the control group to a new job, using the total participation technique in meetings which were similar to those held with experimental groups 2 and 3. The new job was a pressing job of comparable difficulty to the new job in the first experiment. On the average it involved about the same degree of change. In the meetings no reference was made to the previous behavior of the group on being transferred. The results of the second experiment were in sharp contrast to the first (see Figure 4-3). With the total participation technique, the same control group now recovered rapidly to their previous efficiency rating, and, like the other groups under this treatment, continued on beyond it to a new high level of production. There was no aggression or turnover in the group for 19 days after change, a marked modification of their previous behavior after transfer.

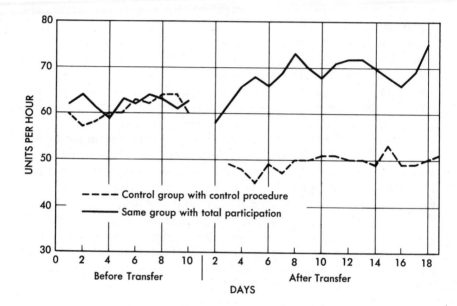

Figure 4-3.   A Comparison of the Effect of the Control Procedure with the Total Participation Procedure on the Same Group.

Some anxiety concerning their seniority status was expressed, but this was resolved in a meeting of their elected delegate, the union business agent, and a management representative. It should be noted in Figure 2 that the pre-change level on the second experiment is just about 60 units per hour; thus the individual transfers had progressed to just above standard during the two and a half months between the two experiments. . . .

Conclusions

It is possible for management to modify greatly or to remove completely group resistance to changes in methods of work and the ensuing piece rates. This change can be accomplished by the use of group meetings in which management effectively communicates the need for change and stimulates group participation in planning the changes.

For Harwood's management, and presumably for managements of other industries using an incentive system, this experiment has important implications in the field of labor relations. A majority of all grievances presented at Harwood have always stemmed from a change situation. By peventing or greatly modifying group resistance to change, this concomitant to change may well be greatly reduced. The reduction of such costly phenomena as turnover and slow relearning rates presents another distinct advantage.

Harwood's management has long felt that action research such as the present experiment is the only key to better labor-management relations. It is only by discovering the basic principles and applying them to the true causes of conflict that an intelligent, effective effort can be made to correct the undesirable effects of the conflict.

24. Ecological Patterns in an Industrial Shop

Raymond W. Mack

People who write about methodology often forget that it is a matter of strategy, not of morals. There are neither good nor bad methods but only methods that are more or less effective under particular circumstances in reaching objectives on the way to a distant goal. For this reason a general, in science as in warfare, is lost if his thinking is rigid. He must be a master of timing; what has served him well in the past may get in his way now.[1]

One of the most promising young specialisms in social science is industrial sociology. As yet, it is not completely formulated. One major factor in the success of the labor relations movement has been the ability and willingness of its founders to draw upon areas in economics and psychology which they found applicable to their field. Industrial sociology has been primarily concerned with social structure; industrial sociologists have concentrated upon formal and informal organization, status expectations, and role conflicts.[2] If industrial sociology is to mature beyond the state where it offers structural case studies of the economic institution, it must bring into play the whole armamentarium possessed by sociologists. One conceptual tool which has been largely ignored by industrial sociologists is that of human ecology.[3] This case study applies ecological analysis to an industrial situation.

Research in ecology has often been concerned with the spatial location of members of social categories, such as Negroes or alcoholics, rather than of social groups. When the variables are actually social groups, ecological

Reprinted from Raymond W. Mack, "Ecological Patterns in an Industrial Shop," *Social Forces*, **32** (May, 1954), 351-356, published by the University of North Carolina Press.

[1] George C. Homans, "The Strategy of Industrial Sociology," *American Journal of Sociology*, **54** (January, 1949), 330.

[2] See, for example, F. J. Roethlisberger and William J. Dickson, *Management and the Worker* (Cambridge: Harvard University Press, 1939), especially pp. 525-569; William Foote Whyte, *Human Relations in the Restaurant Industry* (New York: Mc-Graw-Hill, 1948), especially pp. 10-16, 152-170; B. B. Gardner and W. F. Whyte, "The Man in the Middle: Position and Problems of the Foreman," *Applied Anthropology*, **4** (Spring, 1945); Donald E. Wray, "Marginal Men of Industry: The Foremen," *American Journal of Sociology*, **54** (January, 1949), 298-302.

[3] The first textbook labelled *Industrial Sociology* devotes about four of its 860-odd pages to the significance of ecological location as a structural datum, but has little to say concerning the potentialities of human ecology as an analytical tool in the sociological study of industry. See Delbert C. Miller and William H. Form, *Industrial Sociology* (New York: Harper & Row, 1951), pp. 165-166, 284-285, and 353-354.

studies of segregation usually focus upon a consideration of residential segregation. Sociologists are aware, however, that the institutional agencies of a segregated population are customarily confined to the delimited area in physical space in which their clients dwell.

The writer was a participant observer for six months in an area where segregation as an accommodation mechanism had been informally extended from residential space to the social systems of work groups, and had thus projected upon the physical space used by the industry certain patterns of social space. By social space is meant that location within certain physical boundaries is taken as a status symbol and becomes a datum in defining social relations.[4] Although the town in which the situations discussed here were observed contains several ethnic groups, this analysis is concerned primarily with the social processes resultant from the contacts between the two largest ethnic minorities. The present state of human ecology makes it advisable to state early in a discussion one's school or theoretical position. The writer posits no mysterious ecological "forces" as causal factors in societal relationships. Rather, he assumes that ecological processes such as invasion and succession are the results of more general social processes such as competition, conflict, and assimilation. One theoretical example may suffice to clarify this position. Dominance is conceived of as a result of specific social and economic factors; social and economic relationships are not conceived of as resulting from a mysterious nonsocial force called dominance.

We shall deal first with the contacts between the residential communities of the two ethnic groups, and then with the contacts between the two work communities. This usage of the term community is consistent with Hiller's definition of the community as a social group with a locus. He says that the generic elements of all social groups are members, tests of admittance, roles of members, and norms of social relations.[5] The community is differentiated from the group in that it adds to this list of elements locality as a datum in group composition.

The residential and industrial communities mentioned above are located in an iron-ore receiving port on the shore of Lake Erie. Most of the town's pre-Civil War settlers came from Connecticut. During the greater part of the nineteenth century, it was a trading village serving the farmers of the surrounding area. The rise of the young iron and steel industry, however, coupled with its fine natural harbor, transformed the village into a major break in transportation between the ore fields of the northwestern Great Lakes region and the steel mills within a 150-mile radius.

Due to the sudden expansion of the docks and railroad yards about

---

[4] This definition, and the theoretical framework of this paper, are from E. T. Hiller's excellent theoretical construct of "The Community as a Social Group," *American Sociological Review*, 6 (April, 1941), 189-202.

[5] *Ibid.*, p. 193.

1880, there began an influx of immigrants from northern Europe sufficient to double the size of the town within a decade. Although the immigrants came in roughly equal numbers from Sweden and Finland, a few Swedes were the first to arrive, with the result that this whole population aggregate became known to the old residents as "the Swedes." Even today, although the Uptown people know that the descendants of these immigrants recognize divisions between the groups, such as the Swedish Lutheran Church and the Finnish Lutheran Church, an occasional nose is bloodied because an Uptown youth, having heard his parents refer to "those Swedes at the Harbor," calls a Finn a Swede and is coerced into a recognition of the Finn's pride in his national origin. Since the Uptown people consider both the Finns and the Swedes as one minority group and since, as an in-group which regards the rest of the town as an out-group, they consider themselves so, the remainder of this discussion will lump the two groups under the heading of Swedes.

Although some Irish immigrants settled there around the turn of the century, the town does not consider them to be foreigners, so they are not a major factor here. This analysis is concerned with relations between the Swedes and the other group considered by the residents of the town to be foreigners, the Italians.

The Italians came later than the Swedes; most of them arrived between 1890 and 1910. The population of the town has been relatively stable since the end of World War I, but during the forty years between its sudden boom as a shipping and railroad center and 1920, its population expanded from less than 2,000 to over 22,000.

The town is bisected by a railroad which runs east and west parallel with the lake front. The half of the town north of the east-west railroad tracks is bisected by another set of tracks connecting the docks and the railroad repair yards with the main railroad lines.

The portion of the city north of the main lines is inhabited almost entirely by the Swedes and the Italians, while the older section of the city south of the tracks is inhabited by the Uptown people, which means virtually everyone who is not of Swedish or Italian descent. In the northern section of the city, the Italians live on the east side of the dock-line tracks, the Swedes on the west side. To the Uptown people, any residence north of the east-west tracks is on the wrong side of the tracks, since it is inhabited by foreigners. To the Swedes, any residence east of the dock-line tracks is looked down on as being a "Dago" or "Wop." The Italians, on the other hand, define residences on the west side of the same dividing line as being undesirable, since they are not "in the community" but among the "dumb-Swedes," a popular compound on the Italian side of the line.

Before attempting to analyze segregation as an accommodation mechanism in the work situation, it seems advisable to trace the processes which have led to the existence of three residential communities within the city.

The Residential Communities

The Swedes, since they came to work on the docks and in the railroad repair yards close by the docks, settled in the northeast portion of the town. This resulted in that section's being known as "Swedetown." Only a few years later, the Italians began to arrive in large numbers. They too, were employed by the docks or the railroads and therefore wanted housing in the lake-front area. There followed what any student of ecological processes would expect: the Italians invaded the area of cheapest housing—"Swedetown." The Swedes had already begun to prosper due to the magnitude and expansion of the ore trade. Feeling that their section of the town was being devaluated by the Italian invasion, they began to build in the previously undeveloped area west of the dock-line tracks, an area known simply as The Harbor. The Italians accomplished a process of complete succession in "Swedetown," which has not since been challenged. The old names of the areas have never been changed to describe their new occupants, a phenomenon which the city's summer tourists find highly confusing, although the natives accept it without question. Civic leaders from "Swedetown" have recently attempted to get rid of the old name by having the area officially designated in the newspaper and on store fronts and club name prefaces as East Side, perhaps with the hope that some of the Uptowners' feeling about the foreigners would vanish with the name. As yet, however, the movement has met with little success on the informal level; Italians as well as other townspeople still refer to the area as "Swedetown." The reader must bear in mind, then, that "Swedetown" refers to the Italian section, while The Harbor is the name of the area inhabited by the Swedes.

Despite the fact that they are incorporated within the same city limits as Uptown, both The Harbor and "Swedetown" constitute separate sociological communities. Their members, almost without exception, are all inhabitants of the physical space occupied by the communities. The reason that this is true is linked with the principal test for admittance: ethnic origin. A person who is not of Swedish or Finnish descent finds it quite impossible to join in community life at The Harbor, nor is anyone not of Italian ancestry ever really a member of the group in "Swedetown." Both the roles of members and the norms of social relations may be traced to these singular combinations of the locality datum with the ethnic origin test of admittance. At The Harbor one finds two Finnish Lutheran Churches, two Swedish Lutheran churches, the Harbor school, the Suomi Athletic Club, several filling stations, grocery stores, *saunas* (steam baths), confectioneries, cafes, and a Swedish bakery, all operated by Swedes. On the other side of the dock-line tracks are found Our Mother of Sorrows Catholic Church, its affiliated parochial school, the Columbus Street school, the East Side Young Men's Athletic and Social Club, the Sons of Italy Lodge, and several filling stations, grocery stores, confectioneries, spaghetti and ravioli houses, and cafes, all operated by Italians. Despite the opportunity of several decades for assimilation into a small American town, these two cultural minorities still have distinctive patterns of behavior different from those of Uptown or of each other. A stroll through The Harbor on a summer evening reveals large, relatively new houses, neatly trimmed hedges, families seated on front porch swings or on lawn chairs in their large, well-cared-for yards. At the confectioneries, groceries, and filling stations one see customers make purchases quietly and leave. At the bath houses, men sit silently in the steam rooms or, having finished their "steam," lie on benches in the outer parlor and discuss work, women, or politics. After one crosses the bridge over the river and railroad tracks into "Swedetown," he is immediately struck by the fact that the people he had seen moments before were light-complexioned. Coloring is not exceedingly noticeable among the Italians or Swedes so long as the observer is with only one group or the other, but the contrast is striking. Here, too, one is struck by the difference in life's tempo and volume. Women are seated on the front steps of older houses, calling to friends passing on the walk or seated on the porch steps next door. Groups of men are clustered on the corners, by the filling stations, in the stores and bars—not always buying, but always talking. Even the children playing in the smaller, less tidy yards seem quicker and noisier.

In the above description, perhaps, lies the key to understanding the stereotypes, firmly grounded in ethnocentrism, which each group has of the other. To the Italians, the Swedes are slow, dumb, drab, or at best, dull and uninteresting. To the Swedes, the Italians are crude, immoral, gaudy, or at best, boisterous and ill-mannered. Although both groups take real pride in their Americanism, they also feel strong ties to their ethnic heritage. Hence, each ethnic minority thinks of itself as a hyphenated-American community, with the accent on the American, while each perceives the other as a community of foreigners. There are two ways, therefore, to live on the wrong side of the tracks. Residence in either portion of the lakefront area causes one to be defined as an out-group member by the Uptown people; residence on either side of the dock-line tracks causes one to be looked down upon by the population on the opposite side of the tracks.

In addition to meeting the four criteria for a social group, and the additional one of locality, which allows us to define them as communities, both areas have their separateness both from each other and from the Uptown community, further reinforced by two other differentiating data: language and religion. Language as a variant datum, of course, becomes increasingly less important with the passage of time. It is well to remember, however, that in 1930 over 17 per cent of the total population of the town was still foreign-born, and that as late as 1940 the percentage of foreign-born residents was still nearly 14. Religion as a differentiating item shows less sign of weakening so far. The Italian population is even further divorced from Uptown than the Swedish in this respect. The Lutherans are on reasonably amicable terms with the Uptown Protestants, but a minimum of effort is expended in friendly relations between the Uptown Irish Catholic Church and the Swedetown Italian Catholics.

The writer knows of no indication that the conflict between the Swedes and the Italians—which arose out of differences in language, religion, general cultural background, and out of early competition for jobs and living space—has been or is being replaced by cooperation. It is merely latent; it has been accommodated through the rather efficient medium of segregation. Segregation as an accommodation mechanism between these two groups seems partially self-perpetuating; it is continually "pulling itself up by its own bootstraps." When a man has gained the necessary money, occupational prestige, and education to give him a fair chance of being accepted by the Uptown community, his advantageous status nearly always depends upon his staying in his own community. A second generation Italian who becomes a lawyer or a doctor may have an Uptown office to satisfy the yearnings of both himself and his clients for prestige; but if he is to become and remain a successful professional man, he had best keep his residence, club membership, and church membership in "Swedetown" and send his children to the Columbus Street school. The Swedish alderman can be re-elected only so long as he lives at The Harbor and participates in its community life; the successful grocer or cafe operator must keep his social ties as well as his business establishment within his ethnic group.

With this description of the history and patterning of residential segregation, we should be prepared to analyze segregation as an accommodation mechanism in an industrial social system.

The Work Communities

Adjacent to the docks is the Railroad Car Repair Shop, which consists of a large factory building and an open area about 1,000 feet wide and 3,000 feet long, containing 20 spur tracks where gondolas, or coal cars, are sidetracked for wheel and body repairs. The shop normally employs about 400 men, of whom approximately 175 are Italian and 150 are either Swedish or Finnish. About 300 of the men are directly engaged in car repair—inspection, cutting metal patches, burning, drilling, riveting, blacksmithing, painting, driving cranes, oiling wheels, or supplying rivet gangs. The remainder of the shop's personnel are administrative workers or work in the yards as flagmen, switchmen, engineers, firemen, or brakemen. The car repair work is of two types: "light" repairs such as burning out rusted places in the side of a car and replacing them with riveted patches, and "heavy" repairs which involve tearing down the whole car and putting in new support posts or end gates. This work is done outdoors so that there is no wall or other physical barrier separating the two kinds of work. Nevertheless, the two types of repairs are done in different sections of the yard; the men work on the "lights" on the easternmost 10 tracks and on the "heavies" on the westernmost 10 tracks. The men working on the "lights" and those working on the "heavies" are two distinct social groups having different members, tests of admittance, roles for members, and norms of social relations. If the separate work areas are considered a locality datum, the two groups may be considered as analytical communities.

All of the workers on the "heavies" are Swedes; all of the workers on the "lights" are Italians. The only exceptions are a few part-time summer workers, such as the writer. If such part-time workers are members of one of the ethnic minorities, they are assigned to the appropriate side of the repair yard. If they are from Uptown, they may be assigned to either side of the yard. However, there are seldom more than 10 or 12 Uptowners employed there, since it is not considered a desirable place for employment by Uptown people. The supply shop which dispenses new parts to repairmen is located at the northern end of the yard, and its personnel are also divided along ethnic lines. The western end of the supply room which supplies the "heavies" employs only Swedes; the eastern end which supplies the "lights" is staffed with Italians. It should be emphasized that all persons connected with the "lights"—inspectors, foremen, rivet gangs, oilers, supplymen, crane operators—are Italians. The same situation exists with regard to Swedes on the "heavies."

In analyzing the two groups, then, it may be said that all persons employed in one of the work areas are the members of that group. As in the residential communities, the primary test of admittance is ethnic origin, although demonstration of on-the-job allegiance to the ethnic group with whom he works may suffice as a criterion of temporary admittance for an outsider, such as the writer. The roles of group members and norms of social relations demand a segregation as strict, or stricter, than that found in the residential communities. If, as occasionally happens, a "light" rivet gang gets ahead of the yard schedule and runs out of work, the members check in their equipment and go home. Even during the war, when the car shortage was acute and men were working overtime some days, the idea of a "light" rivet gang working on the "heavies" was unthinkable. When a crane is needed on the "heavies," which is more often than on the "lights" by the nature of the work, piece-work gangs are sometimes delayed until a "heavy" crane is available, even though a crane might at the same time be idle on the "lights." Even so, no Swede would suggest that a crane from the "lights" drive across the invisible barrier between track 10 and track 11. If two cranes from the "heavies" are laid up for repairs simultaneously, it becomes necessary to transfer one of the cranes from the "lights." The Italian driver, however, is not transferred in such a case; his crane is loaned to one of the Swedish drivers until the broken ones are repaired. The segregation system is extended even to the lunchroom. Here again, there is no visible dividing line; there are just some tables and benches which are for the Swedes and some which are for the Italians.[6]

This remarkable system of relations is, of course, informal. No railroad regulations prohibit an Italian's working on "heavy" car repairs, much less his eating at a "Swedish" lunch table. Local management, however, which is composed almost entirely of Uptown people, recognizes the situation by assigning new employees within the framework of the existing system. To a person familiar with the railroad unions and the railroad seniority system, the most astounding manifestation of this segregation pattern is the custom of ignoring seniority when it is in conflict with the segregated work situation. That is, if there is an opening for a supplyman to be advanced to the position of riveter on the "lights" and the next supplyman in line for a promotion is a Swede, he is passed over, and the next Italian in line for promotion from supplyman to riveter is given the job. This practise is accepted by both local railroad management and the local union.

The writer saw no cases of attempted invasion on either side during his work experiences in the shop. Such attempts have occurred, according to informants. However, the cooperation of his fellow workers is imperative if a man is to perform his duties in an occupation such as riveting, and past experience with the effectiveness of informal sanctions usually keeps both management and individual dissidents from attempting to break the segregation pattern.

A fascinating question, of course, is how this system of organizing social space originated. We are faced with the problem, then, of tracing the ecological distribution of the groups back to the social processes which brought about that distribution and, so far as possible, inferring the conditions which caused these processes to operate. The writer was unable to contact anyone in the shop with a definite answer. A large number of informants indicated that the present system arose out of the difficulties which language differences caused in communication between the two groups. Language, however, appears to be only one of the factors making cooperation between the two groups unlikely. The most popular theory among the workers seems to be a sort of culture-and-personality school approach which, when compared with the descriptions of the roles of members and the norms of social relations in the two residential communities, is challenging. The Italians say that the Swedes are "naturally suited" to the type of work found on the "heavies": they are dull, stupid, stolid workhorses—"born rate-busters." The work on the "lights," the Italians will tell you, involves finer craftsmanship, more intelligence. The Swedes, on the

---

[6] A similar case of "irrationality," where economic use of land rather than distribution of workers is the variable, is cited in Walter Firey, "Sentiment and Symbolism as Ecological Variables," *American Sociological Review*, 10 (April, 1945), 140-148.

other hand, claim that the work on the "lights" is a shreds and patches affair of minor importance which can be done by flighty, erratic workers, whereas the "heavies" require "real men," steady, capable workers. It seems reasonable to believe that these answers may indicate the process out of which the existing system has grown: the conflict between cultures with variant norms of conduct and of social relations. Such conflict would make it extremely difficult for a member from one of the groups to fit into the role expectations of the other group, even in a work situation. The obvious way to accommodate this conflict in the work area is to adopt the process utilized in the residential area: segregation.

Conclusions

The manifest functions of this division of labor along ethnic lines are two. Its first *raison d'être*, the avoidance of language confusions, is rapidly being outgrown. Were this the only justification for this unique system of social relations, we would be justified in labelling that system a survival, an illustration of cultural lag. The second explanation of the system, however, and the favorite of the men working in it, is that the two kinds of work call for two different national types. Both the language barrier and the "natural kind of work for that type of man" idea seem to the writer to be not causes but symptoms of the reason for work segregation. Segregation into two separate work communities along ethnic lines serves as a means for accommodating the conflicts caused by extended contacts between members of two variant cultures.

A latent dysfunction of the work segregation system as an accommodation mechanism is to shut off communication and any opportunity for even limited cooperation between the two work communities.

Since both the industrial and the residential segregation systems are based primarily upon the factor of cultural differences, the industrial situation will probably be relatively static so long as the present residential communities remain unchanged. When the inter-community situation alters from one of accommodation to one where the two ethnic residential communities are being assimilated into the Uptown community, then it seems probable that the industrial segregation system will gradually disappear.

This study illustrates for one case at least the value of human ecology as a frame of reference for the industrial sociologist. Ecological analysis offers not a substitute for structural analysis but a complement to it for industrial sociology. The informal organization of this railroad repair shop is more easily discovered and better understood through the conceptual eyeglasses of the ecologist, in terms of social space and segregation. Since a broadening of the industrial sociologist's viewpoint has proved helpful in this case, it is reasonable to believe that such an approach might frequently be useful.

25. Towards the Automatic Factory: Characteristics of Work Groups and Their Importance

Charles R. Walker

The work group on which this inquiry is focused consists of the thirty-three men (later reduced to twenty-seven) who made up the three hot mill crews of Number 4 Seamless Mill in Lorain, Ohio. There were certain differences in the crews, but as we shall see their similarities were far more striking. In particular they were more like than unlike one another in their attitudes and their actions with respect to the general elements of their job experience. The three crews are therefore treated as a single work group unless otherwise specified.

To understand this group of men and to review their history, which is a fairly adventurous one, over time as we now propose to do, we should know first *what kind* of a human group, and more particularly what kind of a work group, we have got. What characteristics give it real meaning and explain, for example, its considerable effect on its own members, and the powerful influence it was able to exert at times upon other groups, upon the group, for example, known then as the National Tube Company, the group known as the Steelworkers Union, and so on?

We shall start with an elementary question: How did the group come into being in the first place? What was its origin?

It happened because management found out how to make steel tubing in a new and revolutionary way. The men on their part joined the group among other reasons to protect their job security, and later had a good deal to do with making it the kind of group they wanted. In the beginning, however, management were the group's father and mother. Management decided on its general characteristics and the laws, so to speak, that would govern it. In some ways management were creating something entirely new when they manned the first continuous seamless pipe mill with a *group* of steelworkers. They were to produce something unique, and to do so the rules of their new social organization and their norms of behavior were to be *different*. But in other ways in setting up the hot mill crews for Number 4 members of management leaned heavily on tradition. They thought in terms of the crews on the old or conventional mills, Numbers 1, 2, and 3; they called for "bids" for jobs in the new group, according to well-established contract rules; they followed an established procedure in

Reprinted from *Toward the Automatic Factory* (New Haven, Conn.: Yale University Press, 1957), pp. 113-124.

developing job descriptions and job classifications for each member of the new group. They set time and motion study men to work to determine work loads, and they studied the question of incentive rates. So, to sum up how the group happened: management created it for their own and society's purposes, to make seamless pipe by a new and revolutionary process.

Behind this particular act of initiative by a particular management in a particular industry lay the broader social, political, and economic influences that gave the group its form and dynamic. Work groups in medieval times, for example, differed in important ways from the group we are studying. The physical environment might be the land of a feudal lord to which the worker was bound as a serf. Or it might be a small workshop where nearly everything about a man's life was minutely governed by guild rules. Or compare our group with a modern work group in a *non*capitalist country. In the Soviet Union crews of men make pipe in steel mills and are paid wages, but their organizational environment contains a quite different set of rewards and penalties. Productivity is encouraged by bonuses as in a capitalistic work group, but also by speeches and rallies about "socialist competition." Failure to meet standards may be punished by a severe docking of pay, or by sending a man to a concentration camp, where he joins still another kind of work group. Thus our work group is seen to be a particular species among many. As we describe and follow its history, we shall be able to see that many of its features derive from influences and behavior patterns some—though not all—of which can be summed up in the words "capitalism" and "Western culture." For example:

Members of the group joined it voluntarily and were free to leave it when they wished. This voluntarism and this freedom obviously had limits, such as the availability of other jobs, the individual's own skills, and so forth. Nevertheless, a measure of such freedom existed.

Payment by management at a certain rate and under a certain kind of group incentive plan was a particular characteristic of the segment of American capitalism in which the group functioned.

The existence of a labor union having a certain historical development associated with the American steel industry and able to bargain collectively and aggressively with management was another important feature of our group's environment.

Thus we are studying one species of work group among many, but a species, it may be added, which is thoroughly typical of our time and our culture.

Homans, in studying human groups in general, follows sound scientific precedent and starts out with the concept of "environment."[1] We shall do

[1] "This definition of the group implies, and is meant to imply, that the group has a boundary and that outside the boundary lies the group's environment. . . . Whitehead says that the idea of an organized whole, or system, existing in an environment is 'a fundamental concept which is essential to scientific theory.'" George C. Homans, *The Human Group* (New York: Harcourt, Brace & World, 1950), p. 86.

the same, looking at both the physical and the social or organizational environment of the thirty-three men. The immediate physical environment of the group was the building formed of structural iron parts and cement, together with the massive contours of heavy machinery which it contained. With this physical environment the members of the group were in daily contact, and they were limited by it in their daily activities. The social or organizational environment of the group was, of course, National Tube; that is, all of it not comprised in the group itself. But the immediate organizational and social environment of the three crews, which they themselves felt constituted a sharp *boundary*, was the supervisory force of the seamless tube mill, together with all other hourly wage earners who were *not* members of the three hot mill crews.[2]

In a broad sense, therefore, we are considering the Lorain Works and the National Tube Company as part of the environment of the work group we are studying. But does this environment as a whole, and do its parts, remain unchanged? They remain stable enough so that we can at least regard them as something *within* which and *against* which our group functions. But they do of course change; and it is obvious that if our arbitrarily chosen social or physical environment does change *radically* during the life history of our group we ought to take account of it. If an earthquake, for example, shook to pieces the Lorain Works, or if the Soviet Union captured this country and the state operated the United States Steel Corporation, we would most emphatically have to rewrite our story.

Nothing as drastic as either of these imagined events occurred during the period of our study to affect either the physical or the social environment of the group. Certain things of importance *did* happen, however, to the whole complex known as the Lorain Works of National Tube. They stemmed from changes initiated by plant management.

A program of modernizing certain plant facilities was undertaken during the years of our study, which in management's opinion had a positive effect on morale. This included new cafeterias for all employees, new washrooms, toilets, and so on for everybody, and better parking facilities. At the same time the program for safety and for "good housekeeping" throughout the plant was enlarged and intensified. The general literature on industrial safety suggests that correlations may often, though not always, be discovered between morale indices and safety. In certain instances a reciprocal relationship seems indicated. As morale rises—for whatever reason—the work force tends to maintain both a cleaner and a safer workshop. Conversely, if morale for any reason goes down, the same individuals become lax in both housekeeping and safety.

[2] For example, Number 4 Seamless Mill is divided organizationally between the hot end and the finishing end. Members of the hot mill crews were distinguished, here as in all other seamless mills, from the hourly wage earners who operated the cut-off machines, testing, etc., in the finishing end. The finishing workers, in other words, constituted another *boundary*.

Beginning in 1947 the general superintendent, who had recently been appointed, and the manager of industrial relations initiated a series of meetings at the department level which were attended by every supervisor in the plant. Out of these meetings came many suggestions for the improvement of human relations, including what came to be called the "management discussion program." Local plant management also introduced an extensive training program to include courses not only on technical subjects but on economics, the labor contract, the history of National Tube, and "human relations." It also introduced courses for hourly wage earners wishing to qualify for promotion to supervisor.

The above measures may be regarded as modifying to a degree both the plant-wide organizational and the physical environment in which the workers in Number 4 Mill carried on their working lives. In the absence of suitable indices the author can only guess at the degree to which during the years 1949 to 1952 they affected the morale of the plant as a whole and the morale of the crews on Number 4 Mill in particular. It seems reasonable to suppose, however, that such changes added impetus to the other forces which served gradually to lift the morale of our group in the latter part of 1951 and throughout 1952.

Of course, in a general way the environment of the group that worked on the new equipment in Number 4 Mill was similar to that of the men who worked on mills 1, 2, and 3 from which these men had come. We are primarily interested, however, in the *immediate* environment, which differed in important ways from the immediate environment of the workers in the old mills. The new mill was larger, the machinery more massive and more scattered. These and other differences we have noticed from time to time. Let us look at them more particularly as they have molded the characteristics of our group.

To begin with, the new technology of Number 4 radically reduced the size of the work group from what was traditional in the old mills. It was common for an old mill to have sixty-five to seventy-five men (three crews), as against the new mill's thirty-three (later twenty-seven). [A typical complaint was]: "With half as many men, we produce four times as much pipe."

Second, the new technological environment altered the interaction pattern among members of the group because the spatial relationship between machine units and their operators had been changed radically.

On the old mills the media of interaction or communication among crew members were the pipe itself and hand signals.[3] In Number 4 distances are far too great for this, and besides, some operators now work inside enclosed cubicles. Communication, when the mill is in operation, is through the public address system. On the old mills *some* verbal interaction, by way either of technical exchange of infomation or of social conversation, was still possible. But this type of interaction has now largely

[3] Charles R. Walker, *Steeltown* (New York: Harper & Row, 1950), p. 82.

disappeared because of the high speed at which the new machinery operates. Here, of course, is another influence with a technological origin. Thus, the new technological environment has changed the interaction pattern of the group in a variety of ways.

Significantly, that change applied to interaction not only between operator and operator but between operator and supervisor. In the old mills the number of levels between worker and department superintendent was four; in our new mill it is three.[4] Thus the new social structure permits a closer and more personal relationship between work groups and management.

So far we have noticed the effects of the changed technological environment on the size of the work group and on its internal pattern of interaction as well as on its pattern of interaction with supervisors. The new technology has also quite sharply changed the interior status relationships of group members. Such changes flow inevitably from changes in job classification, as pay or skills are increased or diminished. Take as an example what has happened on the heating units. As a result of the designers of the new mill substituting a rotary furnace for the old-fashioned roll-down type, not only are the billets or rounds heated more uniformly but much physical drudgery has been removed. Along with that removal, however, the new mill completely eliminates the jobs of heater and between eight and ten heater helpers. The heater, whose job called for overseeing his several helpers, had acquired a certain prestige and status from that fact. He has no true successor in the new mill. The furnace discharger performs a semi-automatic job, manipulating levers on a table within an enclosed cubicle. Considerable responsibility for equipment and for product still rests on his shoulders but it is of quite a different order.[5]

Comparison of the organizational structure of the old crews with the new ones will also show striking differences. As we pointed out earlier, the old crews were differentiated into subgroups, each corresponding to a machine unit, and for each subgroup there was a key man or leader. Thus, on the average mill, there were five operational subdivisions: heating, piercing, hi-mill rolling, reeling, and sizing. Under each key man were one to three helpers (in the case of the heater, as we have seen, eight to ten). As in the case of the heater and his gang, these subdivisions and their key men have disappeared. Thus, technology has, so to speak, leveled out status differences between members of the work group. The one exception is perhaps the nine-stand operator, who has maintained a level of skill and prestige

---

[4] In Number 4 Mill the levels are superintendent, general foreman, foreman. In the old mills an extra level existed between superintendent and general foreman. This level consisted of a separate hot end superintendent and a finishing end superintendent.

[5] Many of the earlier skills of the heater for checking and maintaining proper temperature have now been absorbed by automatic equipment, and by a newly created job of fuel man. The fuel man is no longer organizationally connected with the mill crew, but is considered "nonproduction labor" and is listed with the fuel and power department.

different from but probably equal to that of the roller in the old mills. A simple way to sum up quantitatively these changes in the internal structure of the work group, as between the old and the new mills, is to say that there are fewer jobs on the crew and that many of these jobs are in a lower job class than the jobs on the old mill. However, this review of changes is in some ways misleading. Although job classes have in several cases been lowered, the prestige of the work group *as a whole* has probably risen. One reason is the simple fact that there are fewer in the group. Certainly, in the broader area of plant society, the prestige of the group is as high or higher than that of the crews in the old mills. The reasons are obvious. All three of Number 4's crews are working in the newest mill in the seamless tube industry and are earning as much or more than seamless crews anywhere. Also they work with and are responsible for more costly and complex equipment.

Apart from relationships to one another, and corresponding ways of behaving, that stem from the internal structure of the group, there are other influences that determine the way a work group behaves. The job calls for a certain performance, which will result in this case in the output of pipe. Apart from all the rules and orders which supervision gives, any work group develops its own standard of work behavior and usually its own ideas about what constitutes a day's work. The men who make up the work group we are studying were no exception. Homans, in discussing this phenomenon in a variety of human groups, uses the term "norms" and we shall do the same. We shall find that the norms of working behavior in our work group changed over time, and shall indicate the genesis and dynamics of that change.

Many, though not all, of the men who joined the work group had inherited a relatively low norm for a "fair day's work." One foreman described the crew's attitudes and behavior toward production, toward the product, and toward most elements in their work experience quite simply: "The men don't give a damn." More specifically: "Most of the operators don't care about costs, or quality, or even their own earnings, provided they can earn a minimum and make it tough for management. Some don't even give a damn about their union."

The following quotations and examples illustrate the quality of this attitude and how it was for a time translated into habits and norms of daily work behavior. Here is the comment by an operator who came to Number 4 from another steel mill. He is referring to the early months of operation: "When something goes wrong on this mill everybody has the idea that the thing to do is shut the *whole* mill down. It may be possible for a maintenance crew to work while the mill is running, but *no*—the whole crew yells: Shut her down!"

For several months supervision reported, and the writer verified the fact, that there was little or no concern among members of the group for the quality of the product. Carelessness on the part of a crew member or of the crane man would occasionally destroy hundreds of dollars' worth of product in a few seconds. The writer was struck in the first period of operating at the contrast between the pride in product he had observed in crews in another plant and the indifference of the work group on Number 4. (This attitude was transformed at a later period.)

As to worker attitudes toward supervision, a foreman said to the writer early in 1949: "There seem to be two attitudes toward the foremen here. Neither in my opinion is good. Either a man tells his foreman to go to hell; or else a man is so scared that he never speaks to his foreman, even to ask necessary questions about production on his job."

Or consider the following contrasting attitudes toward tools and machines. In a previous study which the author made of a conventional seamless tube mill, in another plant of the National Tube Division, the work groups were careful to maintain tools and equipment in good working order. The average crew member regularly reported at the end of each work week all tools or equipment requiring repair over the week end by the mill's maintenance crews. In doing this each man would submit his own individual list of items to the foreman. Individual crew members took this practice for granted; several explained that it was to their pecuniary advantage. When the mill broke down, production ceased, so total bonus earnings were reduced. On Number 4 a whole different set of work habits, and corresponding motivations, was operative with a majority of the work group for a time. For some months breakdowns, instead of being feared, were welcomed as giving the men a rest and in other cases as exposing the inefficiency of their supervisors.

As to production, when change-overs were being made in the setup of the mills for handling a new order or during periods of mechanical breakdown, the men worked slowly and left as much of the job as possible to maintenance. In this way delays were prolonged and the amount of production time materially reduced.

Such practices as these we have seen to be "inherited."[6] The men

---

[6] Robert Guest comments on the probable influence of certain structural features of the community itself upon this "inherited climate":

"Some of the inherited worker-management antagonisms can perhaps be explained by an earlier treatment of certain groups by certain other groups as 'inferior' economically or ethnically. The community was for some years highly structured demographically, with workers living in certain sections of the town according to ethnic differences, and with the upper and managerial classes in another part. As in so many industrial towns, both political and economic powers were closely associated with the managerial group.

"In our earlier study of the Ellwood City Works of the National Tube Division (Walker, *Steeltown*) it appeared that one of the causes of in-plant harmony both between racial groups and between management and labor was the demographic structure of the town. There were few geographic allocations on the basis of either economic status or ethnic difference.

"Similarly I suggest that by the time the Lorain study was made the residential separation had begun to break down, and workers through higher wages were becoming more middle class. It might well be, therefore, that the breakdown you mention of previous 'bad work habits' was in part due to the lessening of the old class and ethnic antagonism, which in an earlier period had been reinforced by life outside the mill."

brought them with them to the new mill. Once the new mill opened, however, certain forces were released which acted to change or abolish old habits and set up new ones. For one thing a closer and more friendly relationship with supervision prevailed than most of the men had experienced on their old jobs. Hence the essentially negative attitude toward production, the product, and the supervisor which we have been describing began to be modified. It is important to emphasize, however, that in the first and formative period of the group's history these inherited norms of working behavior enhanced the frustrating effects of mechanical breakdowns and accentuated the normal irritations which flow from new jobs in a new mill.

Bibliography

Adams, S., "Status Congruency as a Variable in Small Group Performance," *Social Forces*, 32 (October, 1953), 16-22.

Albert, R. S., "Comments on the Scientific Function of the Concept of Cohesiveness," *American Journal of Sociology*, 59 (November, 1953), 231-234.

Arensberg, C. M., *et al.*, eds., *Research in Industrial Human Relations* (New York: Harper & Row, 1957).

Argyle, M., Godfrey, G., and Croffi, F., "Supervisory Methods Related to Productivity, Absenteeism, and Labour Turnover," *Human Relations*, 11 (February, 1958), 23-40.

Argyris, C., *Interpersonal Competence and Organizational Effectiveness* (Homewood, Ill.: Irwin, 1962).

Babchuk, N. N., and Goode, W. J., "Work Incentives in a Self-Determined Group," *American Sociological Review*, 16 (October, 1951), 679-687.

Bales, R. F., "In Conference," *Harvard Business Review*, 32 (March-April, 1954), 44-50.

Bales, R. F., *Interaction Process Analysis* (Cambridge, Mass.: Addison-Wesley, 1950).

Barkin, S., "A Pattern for the Study of Human Relations in Industry," *Industrial Labor Relations Review*, 9 (October, 1955), 95-99.

Barnes, L. B., *Organizational Systems and Engineering Groups: A Comparative Study of Two Technical Groups in Industry* (Boston: Division of Research, Harvard Business School, 1960).

Berkowitz, L., "Group Standards, Cohesiveness, and Productivity," *Human Relations*, 7 (November, 1954), 509-519.

Berrier, F. K., and Bash, H., *Human Relations: Comments and Cases* (New York: Harper & Row, 1957).

Blau, P. M., "Patterns of Deviation of Work Groups," *Sociometry*, 23 (September, 1960), 245-261.

Blau, P. M., "A Theory of Social Integration," *American Journal of Sociology*, 65 (May, 1960), 545-556.

Blum, F. H., *Toward a Democratic Work Process: The Hormel-Packinghouse Workers' Experiment* (New York: Harper & Row, 1953).

Boek, W. E., "Human Relations in Industry—Two Case Studies," *Human Organization* 15 (Spring, 1956), 25-28.

Burns, T., "The Directions of Activity and Communication in a Departmental Executive Group: A Quantitative Study in a British Engineering Factory with a Self-Recorder Technique," *Human Relations*, 7 (February, 1954), 73-79.

Burns, T., "The Reference of Conduct in Small Groups: Cliques and Cabals in Occupational Milieux," *Human Relations*, 8 (November, 1955), 467-486.

Cartwright, D., and Zander, A., eds., *Group Dynamics: Research and Theory* (New York: Harper & Row, 1953).

Chadwick-Jones, J. K., "The Acceptance and Socialization of Immigrant Workers in the Steel Industry," *The Sociological Review*, 12 (July, 1964), 169-184.

Coch, L., and French, J. R. P., Jr., "Overcoming Resistance to Change," *Human Relations*, 1 (June, 1948), 512-532.

Cook, P. H., and Wyndham, A. J., "Patterns of Eating Behavior: A Study of Industrial Workers," *Human Relations*, 6 (May, 1953), 141-160.

Cooper, H. C., "Perception of Subgroup Power and Intensity of Affiliation with a Large Organization," *American Sociological Review*, 26 (April, 1961), 272-274.

Coser, L. A., "The Functions of Small Group Research," *Social Problems*, 3 (July, 1955), 1-6.

Crozier, M., "Human Relations at the Management Level," *Human Organization*, 20 (Summer, 1961), 51-64.

Dalton, M., "Industrial Controls and Personal Relations," *Social Forces*, 33 (March, 1955), 244-249.

Dalton, M., "The Industrial 'Rate-Buster': A Characterization," *Applied Anthropology*, 7 (Winter, 1948), 5-18.

Davis, K., *Human Relations in Business* (New York: McGraw-Hill, 1957).

Davis, K., "Management Communication and the Grapevine," *Harvard Business Review*, 31 (September-October, 1953), 43-49.

Day, R. C., and Hamblin, R. L., "Some Effects of Close and Punitive Styles of Supervision," *American Journal of Sociology*, 69 (March, 1964), 499-510.

Demerath, N. J., and Thibaut, J. W., "Small Groups and Administrative Organization," *Administrative Science Quarterly*, 1 (September, 1956), 139-154.

Deutsch, M., "Some Factors Affecting Membership Motivation and Achievement Motivation in a Group," *Human Relations*, 12 (February, 1959), 81-95.

Dornbusch, S. M., "A Test of the Additional Worker Hypothesis," *Research Studies of the State College of Washington*, 22 (June, 1954), 103-109.

Dubin, R., "Human Relations in Formal Organization," *Review of Educational Research*, 29 (October, 1959), 357-366.

Etzioni, A., "Human Relations and the Foreman," *Pacific Sociological Review*, 1 (Spring, 1958), 33-38.

Evan, W. M., "Peer-Group Interaction and Organizational Socialization: A Study of Employee Turnover," *American Sociological Review*, 28 (June, 1963), 436-439.

Faunce, W. A., "Automation in the Automobile Industry: Some Consequences for in-Plant Social Structure," *American Sociological Review*, 23 (August, 1958), 401-407.

Faunce, W. A., "Social Stratification and Attitude Toward Change in Job Content," *Social Forces*, 39 (December, 1960), pp. 140-148.

Finley, W. W., *et al.*, *Human Behavior in Industry* (New York: McGraw-Hill, 1954).

Fleishman, E. A., "Leadership Climate, Human Relations Training and Supervisory Behavior," *Personnel Psychology*, 6 (Summer, 1953), 205-222.

Fleishman, E. A., Harris, E. F., and Burtt, H. E., *Leadership and Supervision in Industry* (Columbus: Bureau of Education Research Monograph No. 33, Ohio State University, 1955).

Foa, U. G., "The Foreman-Worker Interaction: A Research Design," *Sociometry*, 18 (August, 1955), 226-244.

Foa, U. G., "A Test of the Foreman-Worker Relationship," *Personnel Psychology*, 9 (Winter, 1956), 469-486.

Fogarty, M. P., *Personality and Group Relations in Industry* (London: Longmans, 1956).

French, J. R. P., Jr., Israel, J., and As, D., "An Experiment on Participation in a Norwegian Factory," *Human Relations*, 13 (February, 1961), 3-19.

Gardner, B. B., and Moore, D. G., *Human Relations in Industry* (Homewood, Ill.: Irwin, 1955).

Ghiselli, E. E., and Lodahl, T. M., "Patterns of Managerial Traits and Group Effectiveness," *Journal of Abnormal and Social Psychology*, 57 (July, 1958), 61-66.

Gilman, G., *Human Relations in the Industrial Southeast: A Study of the Textile Industry* (Chapel Hill: University of North Carolina Press, 1956).

Goldman, M., and Fraas, L. A., "The Effects of Leader Selection on Group Performance," *Sociometry*, 28 (March, 1965), 82-88.

Goldthrope, J. H., "Technical Organization as a Factor in Supervisor-Worker Conflict: Some Preliminary Observations on a Study Made in the Mining Industry," *British Journal of Sociology*, 10 (September, 1959), 213-230.

Goode, W. F., and Fowler, I., "Incentive Factors in a Low Morale Plant," *American Sociological Review*, 14 (October, 1949), 618-624.

Gross, E., "Characteristics of Cliques in Office Organizations," *Research Studies, College of Washington*, 19 (June, 1951), 131-136.

Gross, E., "Primary Functions of the Small Group," *American Journal of Sociology*, 60 (July, 1954), 24-29.

Gross, E., "Some Functional Consequences of Primary Controls in Formal Work Organizations," *American Sociological Review*, 18 (August, 1953), 368-373.

Gross, E., "Symbiosis and Consensus as Integrative Factors in Small Groups," *American Sociological Review*, 21 (April, 1956), 174-179.

Guetzkow, H., and Gyr, J., "An Analysis of Conflict in Decision Making Groups," *Human Relations*, 7 (August, 1954), 367-381.

Guetzkow, H., and Simon, H. A., "The Impact of Certain Communication Nets upon Organization and Performance in Task-Oriented Groups," *Management Science*, 1 (April-July, 1955), 233-250.

Haire, M., "Industrial Social Psychology," in G. Lindsey, ed., *Handbook of Social Psychology* (Reading, Mass.: Addison-Wesley, 1954), 1104-1123.

Hamblin, R., Miller, K., and Wiggins, J., "Group Morale and Competence of the Leader," *Sociometry*, 24 (September, 1961), 295-311.

Hare, A. P., *Handbook of Small Group Research* (New York: Free Press, 1962).

Hare, A. P., Borgatta, E. F., and Bales, R. F., *Small Groups* (New York: Knopf, 1955).

Hewitt, D., and Parfit, J., "A Note on Working Morale and Size of Group," *Occupational Psychology*, **27** (January, 1953), 38-42.

Hickman, C. A., and Kuhn, M. H., *Individuals, Groups and Economic Behavior* (New York: Holt, Rinehart and Winston, 1956).

Homans, G. C., "The Cash Posters: A Study of a Group of Working Girls," *American Sociological Review*, **19** (December, 1954), 724-733.

Homans, G. C., *The Human Group* (New York: Harcourt, Brace & World, 1950).

Homans, G. C., *Social Behavior: Its Elementary Forms* (New York: Harcourt, Brace & World, 1961).

Hughes, E. C., "Disorganization and Reorganization," *Human Organization*, **21** (Summer, 1962), 154-161.

Jacobs, J. H., "The Application of Sociometry to Industry," *Sociometry*, **8** (May, 1945), 181-198.

James, J., "Clique Organization in a Small Industrial Plant," *Research Studies, State College of Washington*, **19** (June, 1951), 125-130.

Jasinski, F. J., "Technological Delimitation of Reciprocal Relationships: A Study of Interaction Patterns in Industry," *Human Organization*, **15** (Summer, 1956), 24-28.

Kahn, R., and Katz, D., "Leadership Practices in Relation to Productivity and Morale," D. Cartwright and A. Zander, eds., *Group Dynamics: Research and Theory* (New York: Harper & Row, 1953).

Kahn, R., Mann, F. C., and Seashore, S., "Human Relations Research in Large Organizations, Introduction," *Journal of Social Issues*, **12** (April, 1956), 1-5.

Katz, D., "Satisfactions and Deprivations in Industrial Life," in A. Kornhauser, R. Dubin, and A. Ross, eds., *Industrial Conflict* (New York: McGraw-Hill, 1954), pp. 86-106.

Landsberger, H. A., *Hawthorne Revisited: Management and the Worker, its Critics and Developments in Human Relations in Industry* (Ithaca, New York: New York State School of Industrial and Labor Relations, 1958).

Lanzetta, J. T., and Roby, T. B., "Effects of Work-Group Structure and Certain Task Variables on Group Performance," *Journal of Abnormal and Social Psychology*, **53** (November, 1956), 307-314.

Lawrence, L. C., and Smith, P. C., "Group Decision and Employee Participation," *Journal of Applied Psychology*, **39** (October, 1955), 334-337.

Leavitt, H. J., "Small Groups in Large Organizations," *Journal of Business* (January, 1955), pp. 8-17.

Likert, R., and Seashore, S., "Employee Attitudes and Output," *Monthly Labor Review*, **77** (June, 1954), 641-648.

Lupton, T., *On the Shop Floor: Two Studies of Workshop Organization and Output* (New York: Macmillan, 1963).

Mack, R. W., "Ecological Patterns in an Industrial Shop," *Social Forces*, **32** (May, 1954), 351-356.

Magistretti, F., "Sociological Factors in the Structuring of Industrial Workers' Teams," *The American Journal of Sociology*, **60** (May, 1955), 536-540.

Marcus, P., "Supervision and Group Process," *Human Organization*, **20** (Spring, 1961), 15-19.

Mayo, E., *The Human Problems of an Industrial Civilization*, 2nd ed. (New York: Viking, 1960).

Mayo, E., *The Social Problems of an Industrial Civilization* (London: Routledge, 1949).

Morse, N. C., *Employee Satisfaction, Supervision and Morale in an Office Situation* (Ann Arbor, Mich.: Survey Research Center, 1953).

Mumford, E. M., "Social Behavior in Small Work Groups," *The Sociological Review*, **7** (July, 1959), 137-157.

Pope, H., "Economic Deprivation and Social Participation in a Group of Middle-class Factory Workers," *Social Problems*, **11** (Winter, 1964), 290-300.

Potvin, R. H., "Human Relations and Industrial Peace," *American Catholic Sociological Review*, **20** (Spring, 1959), 15-24.

Pryer, M. W., Flint, A., and Bass, B., "Group Effectiveness and Consistency of Leadership," *Sociometry*, **25** (December, 1962), 391-397.

Recknagel, K. H., "Teamwork in Industry," *Journal of Educational Sociology*, **26** (February, 1953), 223-230.

Roby, T. B., and Lanzetta, J. T., "Work Group Structure, Communication, and Group Structure," *Sociometry*, **19** (February, 1956), 105-113.

Roethlisberger, F. J., *Management and Morale* (Cambridge, Mass.: Harvard University Press, 1941).

Roethlisberger, F. J., *Training for Human Relations: An Interim Report* (Boston: Harvard University Graduate School of Business Administration, 1954).

Roethlisberger, F. J., and Dickson, W. J., *Management and the Worker* (Cambridge, Mass.: Harvard University Press, 1940).

Rogers, M., "Problems of Human Relations in Industry," *Sociometry*, **9** (November, 1946), 350-371.

Roy, D., "Efficiency and the 'Fix': Informal Intergroup Relations in a Piecework Machine Shop," *The American Journal of Sociology*, **60** (November, 1954), 255-266.

Roy, D., "Work Satisfaction and Social Reward in Quota Achievement: An Analysis of Piecework Incentives," *American Sociological Review*, **18** (October, 1953), 507-514.

Sayles, L. R., *Behavior of Industrial Work Groups* (New York: Wiley, 1958).

Sayles, L. R., *Technology and Work Group Behavior* (Ann Arbor, Mich.: Bureau of Industrial Relations, University of Michigan, 1956).

Schutz, W. C., "What Makes Groups Productive?" *Human Relations*, **8** (November, 1955), 429-466.

Seashore, S. E., *Group Cohesiveness in the Industrial Work Group* (Ann Arbor, Mich.: Survey Research Center, Institute for Social Research, University of Michigan, 1954).

Seeman, M., and Evans, J. W., "Apprenticeship and Attitude Change," *American Journal of Sociology*, **67** (January, 1962), 365-378.

Shure, G., Rogers, M., Larsen, I., and Tassone, J., "Group Planning and Task Effectiveness," *Sociometry*, **25** (September, 1962), 263-282.

Simon, H. A., "The Impact of Certain Communication Nets upon Organization and Performance in Task-Oriented Groups," *Management Science*, **1** (April-July, 1955), 233-250.

Spaulding, C. B., "Human Relations in Context," *Research Studies of the State College of Washington*, **25** (June, 1957), 178-185.

Speroff, B. J., "Job Satisfaction and Interpersonal Desirability Values," *Sociometry*, **18** (February, 1955), 69-72.

Speroff, B. J., "The Use of Sociometric Data in Industrial Counseling," *Sociometry*, **18** (November, 1955), 548-552.

Strauss, G., "Work-Flow, Interfunctional Rivalry, and Professionalism," *Human Organization*, **23** (Summer, 1964), 137-149.

Strodtbeck, F. L., and Hare, A. P., "Bibliography of Small Group Research 1900-1953," *Sociometry*, **17** (May, 1954), 107-178.

Sykes, A. F. M., "Unity and Restrictive Practices in the British Printing Industry," *The Sociological Review*, **8** (December, 1960), 239-254.

Tannenbaum, A. S., and Allport, F. H., "Personality Structure and Group Structure: An Interpretive Study of the Relationship Through an Event-Structure Hypothesis," *Journal of Abnormal and Social Psychology*, **53** (November, 1956), 272-280.

Tannenbaum, A. S., and Georgopoulos, B. S., "The Distribution of Control in Formal Organizations," *Social Forces*, **36** (October, 1957), 44-50.

Thompson, J. D., and McEwen, W. J., "Organizational Goals and Environment: Goal Setting as an Interaction Process," *American Sociological Review*, **23** (February, 1958), 23-31.

Trow, D. B., "Autonomy and Job Satisfaction in Task Oriented Groups," *Journal of Abnormal and Social Psychology*, **54** (April, 1957), 204-207.

Turner, A. N., "Interaction and Sentiment in the Foreman-Worker Relationship," *Human Organization*, **14** (Spring, 1955), 10-16.

Viteles, M. S., *Motivation and Morale in Industry* (New York: Norton, 1953).

White, H., "Management Conflict and Sociometric Structure," *American Journal of Sociology*, **67** (September, 1961), 185-199.

Whyte, W. F., "Engineers and Workers: A Case Study," *Human Organization*, **14** (Winter, 1956), 3-12.

Whyte, W. F., "Human Relations Theory—a Progress Report," *Harvard Business Review*, **34** (September-October, 1956), 125-132.

Whyte, W. F., *Man and Organization: Three Problems in Human Relations in Industry* (Homewood, Ill.: Irwin, 1959).

Whyte, W. F., *Money and Motivation* (New York: Harper & Row, 1955).

Wilensky, H., "Human Relations in the Work Place: An Appraisal of Some Recent Research," in C. M. Arensberg, *et al.*, eds., *Research in Industrial Human Relations* (New York: Harper & Row, 1957).

Yanouzas, J., "A Study of Work Organization and Supervisory Behavior," *Human Organization*, **23** (Fall, 1964), 245-253.

Zaleznik, A., *Worker Satisfaction and Development* (Boston: Graduate School of Administration, Harvard University, 1956).

Zaleznik, A., Christensen, C. R., Roethlisberger, F. J., and Homans, G. C., *The Motivation, Productivity and Satisfaction of Workers: A Prediction Study* (Cambridge, Mass.: Harvard University Press, 1958), 442.

Zeleny, L. D., "Sociometry of Morale," *American Sociological Review*, **4** (December, 1939), 799-808.

READINGS in
INDUSTRIAL
SOCIOLOGY

V

TRADE UNION STRUCTURE AND ADMINISTRATION

Introduction

Trade unions today are, for the most part, large scale bureaucracies. For this reason, much of what has been written in the preceding chapters would apply to unions as well as to the industrial firm. There are some ways, however, in which unions are different from most other formal organizations and it is these unique characteristics that have most often been studied by social scientists.

The history of trade unions has been the subject of an extensive amount of writing. The early, often violent struggles for recognition, the rise and fall of earlier national unions, the changing attitudes of government and of management toward unionism, and the emergence of the present patterns of collective bargaining represent a fascinating part of American economic history. It is the relatively rapid transformation in recent years of unions from a mass protest movement into a generally accepted and stable institution that has been of most interest to sociologists. The development of unions is a particularly good example of one pattern of social change; the successful social movement. While there have been sociological and social psychological studies of this process, most of the research on the history of trade unions has been done by labor economists and labor historians.[1]

The major interest of industrial sociologists in unions has been in their internal control structure or, more specifically, in the extent to which there is participation in and control of unions by the membership. Trade unions

[1] The student interested in union history might begin with the following references: Henry Pelling, *American Labor* (Chicago: University of Chicago Press, 1960); Joseph G. Rayback, *A History of American Labor* (New York: Macmillan, 1966); Foster Rhea Dulles, *Labor in America* (New York: Crowell, 1966); Philip Taft, *Organized Labor in American History* (New York: Harper & Row, 1964), and Thomas R. Brooks, *Toil and Trouble: A History of American Labor* (New York: Delacorte, 1964).

represent a type of organization which Blau and Scott have called the "mutual benefit association."[2] The distinguishing characteristic of this type of organization is that the membership is the prime beneficiary of organizational activities. Blau and Scott indicate that the crucial problem in such organizations is maintaining internal democratic processes in the face of a largely apathetic membership and a set of circumstances that encourage oligarchic control.[3]

Robert Michels, in a well-known study of unions and political parties in Germany, observed that even in organizations characterized by an egalitarian, democratic ideology there is a tendency to develop centralized bureaucratic controls, sacrificing democratic processes in the interest of efficiency of operation.[4] This general tendency he labelled the "iron law of oligarchy." Subsequent research on the governing of unions has made it clear that there are exceptions to this iron law, but it nevertheless describes a common pattern in the internal control structure of many unions.

Most American unions are committed to a democratic ideology and all unions are expected by the American public to operate in the best interest of their members. Almost all unions maintain the outward forms of democratic control including a constitution ratified by the membership, the election of leaders, and periodic conventions at which elected representatives vote on questions of union policy. With some notable exceptions, however, the national officers of unions maintain a considerable degree of control over union affairs and are able to keep themselves in office for long periods of time.

One of the explanations for the existence of centralized, hierarchical control in unions is that the rank-and-file members are generally apathetic with regard to union affairs. Many studies have documented the fact that only a small proportion of union members are active participants in the sense of attending meetings, voting in elections, or serving in leadership positions at any level.[5] During the early, mass movement stage of unionism, while the struggle for union recognition as the bargaining agent for workers was going on, there was a much higher rate of participation by rank-and-file members. There was at this stage, however, also strong centralized control and in some cases a quasimilitary form of organization. The amount of control exercised in an organization is usually conceptualized as a fixed quantity so that if leaders exercise more control, members necessarily exercise less. Tannenbaum, in a reading included in this chapter, notes that variations are possible in the total amount of control within

    [2] Peter M. Blau and W. Richard Scott, *Formal Organizations* (San Francisco: Chandler Publishing Company, 1962).

    [3] Blau and Scott, *op. cit.*, pp. 45-49.

    [4] Robert Michels, *Political Parties* (New York: Free Press, 1949). (First published in 1915.)

    [5] Cf. William Spinrad, "Correlates of Trade Union Participation," *American Sociological Review*, 25 (1960), 237-244.

organizations depending upon the presence of issues requiring a higher or lower level of control. During the organizing stage of most unions, more control of organizational behavior appears to have been exercised by *both* leaders and members.

Once unions have achieved their initial objectives and there is no longer any serious threat to their existence, a different pattern of member attitudes toward the union develops. In the early stage, the members feel that they collectively *are* the union; in the later stage the union is regarded as a representative of or as an agent for the members acting in their behalf. The relationship between the organization and its members becomes in some ways similar to that between a lawyer and his client. But in response to any external threat or important issue as, for example, in the case of a strike, the degree of rank-and-file involvement and participation in union affairs increases dramatically. An understanding of the relationship between external issues and internal controls in organizations represents one contribution of industrial sociological studies of unions.

One of the major themes in research dealing with unions has been the factors producing member apathy or participation. The findings suggest that it is generally those workers who have most to gain or lose, that is those who have a higher pay rate, more skill, more seniority, and higher job status, who are the most active participants. The last two readings in this chapter deal with the attitudes of leaders and rank-and-file members toward the union. A second major theme has been the circumstances tending to produce oligarchic control of unions. One of these factors is the absence, in most cases, of any desirable alternative to more highly paid and prestigeful leadership roles in unions. If the alternative to being a union leader is to go back to work in a semiskilled factory job, this represents a powerful incentive to avoid being voted out of office. In most unions the incumbent officers have a virtual monopoly of communication channels to the membership and of opportunities to gain leadership experience which are distinct advantages in elections. External threats to unions also serve to legitimize strong, centralized control. The first three readings in this chapter deal with issues of this sort.

The observation that many unions are oligarchically controlled should be qualified in terms of the particular meaning of union democracy used in most studies. A distinction can be made between procedures designed to achieve democratic objectives and the objectives themselves. An organization may be regarded as democratic to the extent that it acts in accord with the wishes of the majority while guaranteeing the right of those with minority views to seek majority status. A high rate of membership participation, frequent turnover of officers, a two-party political system, and frequent constitutional conventions are examples of *procedures* and *conditions* that tend to produce a democratic organization in this sense. The absence of these conditions, which is the case in most trade unions, does *not necessarily* mean that leaders are unresponsive or not accountable to the majority of members or that they are necessarily abusing the rights of those who differ from the majority view. Most studies of the control structure of unions, however, have used conditions like rate of participation in elections as measures of union democracy. There is a need for research designed to discover the extent to which democratic objectives can be attained in the absence of formal procedural supports.

The conflict between bureaucratic organizational forms and democratic values, which is the major concern of Chapter V, is linked in an important way to the general theme of this book. Complex, highly differentiated organizations pose problems of integration which call for a rationalized control structure. Rationalized control structures almost invariably take a hierarchical or "chain of command" form. This pressure toward a bureaucratic system of authority runs counter to the democratic tradition in mutual benefit associations like trade unions. It is impossible to maximize both the bureaucratic value upon efficiency and the democratic value upon member participation in decision-making. This dilemma, freedom versus control, is a very widespread problem in industrial societies. In order for complex, formal organizations to respond to a rapidly changing social environment, centralized controls are introduced at the expense of individual freedom of action. Some nations, such as the U.S.S.R. and most countries in the early stages of industrializing, have elected to sacrifice individual freedom of action thereby achieving sufficient control to institute rapid changes. Other nations, notably the United States and Great Britain where industrialization occurred over a much longer period of time, have been able to operate at a lower level of control permitting greater individual freedom. Although the type of resolution of the issue may differ, the dilemma exists for all industrial societies because it is an inevitable consequence of the differentiation-rationalization processes.[6] The internal control structure of trade unions provides a particularly good example of the conflict between freedom and control.

The first selection in this chapter is based upon one of the classic studies in sociology. The full report of the study can be found in a book entitled, *Union Democracy*, by Seymour Martin Lipset, Martin Trow, and James Coleman.[7] The subject of the study was the internal politics of the International Typographical Union. This union has maintained a considerable measure of internal democratic control largely as a result of having a stable and vigorous two-party political system. This selection focuses upon the reasons for a two-party system in the I.T.U. which include unique historical circumstances, social structural attributes of the union, and par-

---

[6] Cf. William A. Faunce, *Problems of an Industrial Society* (New York: McGraw-Hill, forthcoming).

[7] Seymour Martin Lipset, Martin Trow, and James Coleman, *Union Democracy* (New York: Free Press, 1956).

ticular characteristics of printers, such as their higher educational and occupational status levels.

The next reading is based upon a study of delegates to the 1959 Constitutional Convention of the United Automobile Workers. It is primarily concerned with the way in which size of local unions affects the nature of internal political processes at both the local and national union level. The data indicate that large locals may contribute more to democratic processes in the national union. The study also suggests that large locals may be more democratic internally and raises some questions regarding the applicability of formal procedural indexes of democracy to small local unions. Analysis of informal social processes in these locals may contribute more to understanding the extent to which democratic objectives are achieved.

Arnold Tannenbaum's, "Control Structure and Union Functions," introduces the distinction referred to above between the *distribution* of control in a union and the *total amount* of control exercised. He demonstrates variation in each of these attributes of control in a study of four small, local unions. Differences along both control dimensions were found to be related to level of member participation, ideology of members, and degree of conflict with management. The total amount of control exercised by all segments of an organization is an important but seldom studied organizational variable. Its relationship to the efficiency versus control dilemma is also noted by Tannenbaum.[8]

The next reading, by Seidman, London, and Karsh, reports a study of leadership in a large, United Steelworkers of America local. Because it focuses upon a major role in American industry, it might appropriately have been included in Chapter III of this book. It is a good example, however, of one of the dominant themes in industrial sociological studies of unions: the attitudes of leaders and other active participants in union affairs toward the union. Data were collected regarding the reasons why these local union leaders joined the union, why they became active in it, what they thought were major accomplishments of the union, and how important the union was to them. The findings indicate a particularly strong prounion and antimanagement set of attitudes.

The final selection, that by Form and Dansereau, is concerned with the attitudes of a sample of rank-and-file union members. The following types of orientation toward the union were identified: political, economic, social, hostile, and apathetic. The likelihood that a worker will have one or another of these orientations was found to be related to several variables including the level of participation in the union and the degree of social integration into the plant, neighborhood, and community. Three dominant life styles—the working class, the individualistic, and the isolated—appear to underlie differences in both union orientation and patterns of social in-

---

[8] For an additional report of this study, see A. S. Tannenbaum and R. L. Kahn, "Organizational Control Structure," *Human Relations*, 10 (1957), pp. 127-140.

tegration. This social heterogeneity of union members undoubtedly contributes to problems of coordination within the union and encourages the development of the type of rationalized control structure that is the major concern of this chapter.

26. Democracy in Private Government: A Case Study of the International Typographical Union

Seymour M. Lipset

Social Science has as one of its objectives the prediction of the behavior of classes of individuals or institutions under specific structural conditions. One of the few macroscopic sets of generalizations which appears to fit the scientific criterion of predictability is the theory of organization encompassed in Robert Michels' "iron law of oligarchy."[1] The skimpy data available on the behavior of nominally "democratic" large-scale organizations such as political parties, business corporations, trade unions and co-operatives would seem to confirm Michels' prediction that structural forces endemic in large-scale organization make control by the self-co-opting leaders of a bureaucratic hierarchy inevitable.[2]

There is, among American large-scale organizations, a clear-cut exception to Michels' generalization that oligarchic domination is inherent in the very nature of large-scale social organization. The International Typographical Union (A.F. of L.), the organization of the compositors, linotype operators and mailers in the printing industry, the oldest union in the United States, possesses an internal structure which cannot be fitted easily into a Michelsian oligarchic pattern.[3]

The democratic structure and process in the I.T.U. can be seen in the following facts. Since 1898, when the Union established the referendum system of electing international officers biennially, there have been seven changes in the Presidency in which incumbent officers were defeated, five of these occurring since 1920. During that same period the administration party failed to elect its complete slate for the four- to six-man executive board in eight elections out of the twenty-five which occurred. In no election since 1916 has any international official run without organized opposition. Defeated Presidential candidates have never failed to secure less than 23 per cent of the vote and have secured 35 per cent, or more, in 14

Reprinted from *British Journal of Sociology*, 3 (March, 1952), 47-63.

[1] Robert Michels, *Political Parties* (New York: Free Press, 1949).

[2] See Philip Selznick, "An Approach to the Theory of Bureaucracy," *American Sociological Review*, 8 (1943), 47-59; Sylvia Kopald, *Rebellion in Labor Unions* (New York: Boni and Liveright, 1924).

[3] While this paper deals mainly with the International Typographical Union, I do not intend to suggest that it is the only "deviant case" to Michels' "law" among American trade unions or other voluntary organizations.

of the 16 elections since 1918. The union membership has voted in over 500 referenda since 1889 to approve or disapprove suggested union policies which have been proposed by the International Board, an annual convention, or a number of local unions. Out of the 24 referenda to increase the salary of international officials since 1900, the increase has been defeated 17 times. In this period local unions have independently put forward 27 referenda and 18 of these have passed.[4] The constitution of the union provides that any candidate for international office shall have the right to write an uncensored article presenting his views in two pre-election issues of *The Typographical Journal,* the monthly organ of the union which goes to all members.[5] Union members have the right to organize permanent or temporary union political parties, and to publish literature attacking the administration of the union.[6] This right has been exercised by groups and individuals in almost every election since 1898.

The principal continual arena of significant membership participation in the I.T.U. is found in the frequent elections and referenda which are conducted in the union. The union members do take part in choosing among the candidates running for office and the policies submitted to union referendum. The number of members voting in these elections and referenda is proportionately considerably higher than the vote in national elections in the United States: in the last five elections an average of 73 per cent of the members voted.[7] Delegates to the annual convention are also elected by secret ballot in every union print shop. Many of the larger local unions conduct their elections in a similar manner, with the overwhelming majority of the membership voting. These elections and referenda present the membership with the possibility of choosing between alternative union policies.

The question must obviously be raised as to the factors related to the continued vitality of democratic institutions in the I.T.U. Here the most

---

[4] The data summarized above were secured from various issues of *The Typographical Journal,* the monthly organ of the I.T.U., which has been in existence since 1892.

[5] "Candidates who have received the requisite number of endorsements and who have filed their acceptance of the nomination for office sought shall be entitled to space in the April and May issues of *The Typographical Journal* for the publication of reasons and arguments in support of their candidacy, such matter to be personally prepared by the candidates, and no candidate shall issue, or sanction the issuance of, any other literature or printed matter in his behalf, unless signed by the candidate or three members in good standing . . ." *Book of Laws of the International Typographical Union* (Indianapolis, 1948), p. 46. This clause was first adopted in 1913.

[6] Various union political groups have made use of this right for the last fifty years or more. Regular and irregular newspapers, pamphlets, and leaflets have been and are still being published attacking and supporting the incumbent administration. The official history of the union used for educating new members discusses and praises the existence of opposition groups as a normal phenomenon. See I.T.U. Bureau of Education, *Lessons in Printing,* Lesson 5 (Indianapolis, 1939), p. 4.

[7] Calculated from election returns and membership statistics published in the *Typographical Journal.*

significant difference between the I.T.U. and other more oligarchical unions is the existence in the Typographical Union, alone among the older trade unions in North America, of two permanent rival trade union parties. These two parties, now known as the Progressives and the Independents, constitute the source of the effective checks in the union against usurpation of power by any group of leaders. The parties, or their predecessors under other names, together with occasional third parties, have contested almost every election in the union's history with virtually complete slates for every office. Since the turn of the century the two major parties have maintained permanent political organizations with their own press. At all times this institutionalized party system ensures a powerful, vocal, intelligent opposition. Regardless of which party temporarily controls the International administration, the opposition has always had a large nucleus of trained leaders—former officials of the International or incumbent officers of local unions still under opposition control—who comprise a potential alternative administration. The tendencies towards "bureaucratic conservatism" that arise within the leadership of most organizations have been checked by the existence of this permanent opposition group, which stands ready to capitalize on any fault of the administration and play up every demand which seems to have support among the members. Each party, when in opposition, has been too strong to be crushed or denied its opposition rights without destroying the union.

These parties arose out of a set of critical conditions in the early history of the union. As early as 1857, seven years after the foundation of the union, a group of members of the New York local met in Albany and formed a secret society of loyal union members to help preserve the larger organization in a period of crisis. 1857 was a year of large-scale unemployment among printers. The young union was consequently highly vulnerable to attack. Known and active unionists were fired; betrayal of a fellow worker as a member of the union often gained a man preference and a steady job.[8]

This early secret group, about which little is known, either developed into or was followed by a more formal secret organization known as the "Brotherhood of the Union of North America." Though there was a great deal of opposition to the secret societies, they continued through the latter part of the nineteenth century. Their members and leaders believed that they were serving the cause of unionism by preventing employers' spies and lukewarm union men from influencing union policy. The name of the principal secret lodge changed at different times, presumably to preserve se-

---

[8] See pamphlet, *Administration Party Was Founded in 1857* (New York: 1927). It is doubtful that the secret societies had continuity from 1857. The skimpy evidence available suggests that there was a succession of secret organizations between 1857 and the '90's when the last important one, the Wahnetas, was founded.

crecy. The final name under which they came to be known was the Wah-netas.[9]

These secret groups fulfilled certain definite functional needs of a weak labor union in a period in which unions were almost extra-legal. They served to protect the active union members from discrimination by employers, and kept policy control of the union in the hands of men who were willing to sacrifice to further the cause of the union. In order to carry out their objectives, the secret societies attempted to secure political control of the union and its locals, and endeavored to place their members in jobs in important plants. They also tried to recruit foremen, who had the power to hire and fire, into the union and the secret lodges.

The Wahneta organization continued to exist after the union had become a strong, stable organization. Its members, who included the leaders of many of the locals of the International as well as of the International itself, found that a secret group served as an efficient political machine to keep control of union posts. I.T.U. members who were not members of the Wahnetas organized their own group in the seventies and the union began to be torn apart by bitter internal conflicts. Gradually, the opposing groups developed into open factions competing for union office, the Wah-netas being known as the Administration Party, and their opponents as the Progressive Party. The Administration Party retained complete control of the International organization until the 1920's, when the Progressives finally won the major elective positions. Following a major defeat in 1928, the Administration Party broke up into conflicting factions, and the Wah-neta secret organization appears to have dissolved. The individuals who belonged to the Administration Party, plus a number of dissident Progressives, however, reformed an opposition party in 1932, known as the Independent Party. Since 1932, the two parties Progressive and Independent, have contested each international election, as well as many local elections.

The ideological differences among the various parties of the I.T.U. will be discussed in more detail elsewhere. In general, however, the split has been between greater and less militancy concerning internal trade union tactics. The Independents and, before them, the Administration Party and the Wahnetas, have advocated conciliatory tactics in dealing with the employer or the government as the best way to advance the economic position of the membership. The Progressives, on the other hand, have been more prone to favor militant action such as strikes. Internationally, the parties took a different position to the A.F. of L.–C.I.O. controversy when it first

---

[9] Woodruff Randolph, "Historiography: Bits of History of the I.T.U.," *The Typographical Journal*, June, 1941, pp. 817-821; July, 1941, pp. 6-8. See also Philip Taft, "Opposition to Union Officials in Elections," *Quarterly Journal of Economics*, **58** (February, 1944), 253-258.

developed in the mid-thirties. The Independents favored supporting the A.F. of L. in its fight against the C.I.O., while the Progressives, though not favoring secession from the A.F. of L., objected to paying a special war tax to the A.F. of L. to fight the C.I.O. The Progressive President of the I.T.U., at the time, served for a while as the first secretary of the C.I.O. Towards the end of World War II, the Progressives opposed the policy of the Independent administration in giving a no-strike pledge. Since the passage of the Taft-Hartley Act in 1947, the Progressive administration has led a number of major strikes designed to retain union gains which the Act challenges or makes illegal, and have refused to sign the non-Communist affidavits required by this law. The Independents, while also opposed to the law, have favored a policy of trying to live within the law, and urge that union officers sign the non-Communist affidavits.

While there is probably some correlation between I.T.U. party support and external political affiliations and beliefs, there is no connection between the I.T.U. parties and non-union political groups. The Old Wahneta-Administration Party, although the conservative party in the union, had a number of active Socialists in its leadership including Max Hayes, one of the leaders of the Socialists in the A.F. of L. On the other hand, Charles Howard, the Progressive leader from 1922 to 1938, was a life-long Republican.

The parties, originally organized by men bitterly hostile to one another as a result of the early secret society fight, have become securely institutionalized in the course of the last 50 years. Since 1918 neither group has been able to win enough strength to destroy the "out" party's hopes of success in the next election. Each party continues to work between elections to present its case and win recruits both in the locals and at national conventions. The leaders on each side attempt to bring into their party any union member who seems to have leadership ability and has won a personal following. At the local level, the party leaders look for individuals who have proven themselves in their shop unit, the chapel, while at the International level, party leaders attempt to win over convention delegates from smaller locals where the party system is not strong.

Joining a party has become the accepted means of rising in the union hierarchy. Discussion with union leaders suggests that the union politicians are persons with a strong mobility drive, or with intense interest in politics in general. Printing requires a six-year apprenticeship after leaving school. Once a man has become a union printer, there are few more lucrative or secure positions open to him, and it is extremely unlikely that he will ever change his occupation. The principal means through which a typographer can rise either in income or social status is by becoming a union official. A former International Vice-President stated, "Once you are a printer, there's no other job you can get except that of a union official. . . . I had once intended to go into business for myself, but once I realized that I would always be a printer, I became interested in the possibilities of working for the union."

There is also a second group of party activists who do not seem to be motivated by the hope of gaining political office. They are individuals who have little oratorical ability or special personality characteristics which would make them good candidates. These people take part in party discussions, help spread party propaganda either by word of mouth or through literature. This group seems to be composed of people concerned with politics in general, like some of the leaders, or by a desire to be near the center of power, to be "in on things." A knowledge of union gossip, and the sense of helping to determine party nominations and policies are among the rewards of party activity for this group.

The actual internal membership of the two parties is unknown to any but the leaders of the parties. In New York, where the union has over 10,000 members, informants estimated that both parties together have a total of about 1,000 dues-paying members, but only about 100 active ones. In crisis situations, such as during the depression, hundreds have attended party meetings in the hope of getting the party to adopt policies which they favored. Each party, also, has a large group of sympathizers who support it because of personal ties, tradition, sympathy with its program, or out of an antagonism which they may have developed against one party while it was in power. The party members and sympathizers serve to keep all union members aware of important issues. The party apparatus serves also to communicate to the top leaders of the party and union the attitudes of the union members toward any union issue, and enables the leaders to adjust their policies in the direction of the prevailing opinion in the shops —a continual process dictated by the sensitivity of the party leadership to the dangers of losing the next election.

The referendum and the biennial secret election of national officers constitutes in the last analysis the basic foundation of I.T.U. democracy, *when they are combined with a vigorous opposition party system.* It is through these institutions that the members have the last word on the policies of the officialdom. An examination of the election return suggests that this right is exercised, and that no set of leaders can afford to ignore rank and file sentiment and remain in office.

The election results cited in Table 5-1 suggest that neither party has the permanent loyalty of a large section of the union.

In addition to the regular and frequent turnovers in office already cited, lack of official control over the union is clearly indicated by the votes in referenda on salary increases. Since 1900 salary increases for officers have been defeated eighteen times out of twenty-six. There does not appear to be any close relationship between the electoral strength of an administration and its ability to secure a salary increase for itself. In 1916, the Wahneta

Election Returns in I.T.U. from 1918 to 1950 with Proportion of Members Voting

Year	Percentage President			Percentage 1st Vice-President			Percentage 2nd Vice-President			Percentage Secretary Treasurer			Percentage Members Voting for President
	P	W-I	O	P	W-I	O	P	W-I	O	P	W-I	O	
1918	35.9	64.1		36.9	63.1					35.7	64.3		67.0
1920	51.3	48.7		48.0	52.0		46.7	53.3		45.4	54.6		77.8*
1922	54.3	45.7		52.0	48.0		50.1	49.9		47.6	52.4		77.1*
1924	47.7	52.3		48.5	51.5		46.8	53.2		44.7	55.3		81.4
1926	51.7	48.3		47.4	49.1	3.9	50.0	50.0*		48.3	51.7		80.5*
1928	63.9	36.1		63.4	36.6		61.4	38.6		56.5	43.5		76.6
1930	59.1	23.1	18.8	58.9	25.7	15.4	62.9	21.0	16.1	61.9	38.1		74.7
1931				49.4	50.6								64.1*†
1932	54.6	45.4		58.7	25.7	8.8	51.2	40.0	8.8	63.5	36.5		72.0
1934	57.0	43.0		64.1	35.9		59.2	25.5	15.3	65.5	34.5		69.1
1936	58.8	41.2		63.7	36.3		57.4	31.1	11.5	66.5	33.5		69.1
1938	36.8	61.2		51.2	48.8		47.2	52.8		51.8	48.2		71.5*
1940	47.8	52.2		50.9	49.1		43.3	43.8	12.8	50.2	49.8		74.8*
1942	48.2	51.8		46.3	53.7		45.3	54.7		51.0	49.0		71.4*
1944	51.7	32.6	15.7	57.0	43.0		50.3	39.3	10.5	48.5	34.7	16.8	62.1*
1946										63.1	36.9		69.2†
1946	71.7	28.9		69.0	30.6		69.0	31.0		66.3	34.7		76.0
1948	57.5	42.5		61.4	38.6		59.2	40.8		62.1	37.9		74.4
1950	55.4	44.6		53.7	46.3		58.2	41.8		57.5	47.5		79.6

*Indicates that no party had complete control of the Executive Council   †Special Election. Incumbent died in office

P = Progressive   W-I = Wahneta-Independent   O = Other

Source: Calculated from election returns in *Typographical Journal*.

administration was elected without opposition, yet in the same year the membership voted down a proposal to increase the salaries of the President and Secretary-Treasurer from $3,500 to $5,000 by almost two and one-half to one. In 1948, a year in which the Progressive slate received about 60 per cent of the vote, the members voted 33,408 to 28,631 against a salary increase. (In 1949, a proposal to pension union officers was defeated by over two to one in referendum, though the convention which proposed it was overwhelmingly Progressive.) Attempts by union leaders to receive a wage increase resemble in many ways a collective bargaining session conducted by referendum between the members and the officials. The members, in general, refuse to give their officers a raise except during periods of great prosperity. The most recent increases took place in 1919, 1929-30, 1947 and 1950, and the increases which the officers secured were proportionately less than had been received by the membership in these periods.

It is significant to note that since 1912, every salary increase that was proposed by an International convention, except that of 1950, was defeated. The 1919, 1930 and 1946-7 increases which passed were first initiated by locals. The 1950 increase came from the floor of the convention, and was publicly opposed by the incumbent officers. Apparently the members resent a proposal for salary increases which comes from the union politicians in control of the convention.

The concern of the members to keep control over their officers can be seen in the fact that two proposals to increase the term of office from two to four years were both defeated. This proposal was defeated in 1918 by 18,649 votes to 14,611, and in 1929 by 29,400 votes to 19,967.[10] The first proposal was made by a convention while the Wahnetas controlled the administration, and the second during a period of Progressive supremacy. In 1924, the membership voted 24,371 to 18,005 to fill vacancies among the officers by direct special election rather than by Executive Council co-optation.[11]

The record of referenda on the most fundamental right of a self-governing body, the right to vote funds, is probably the most interesting example of the intention of the members to keep ultimate control in their own hands. The members, on a number of occasions, have refused to vote for a permanent dues increase, though there has been, of course, a secular increase in union dues. One might compare the voting record of the I.T.U. on dues increases with the historic struggles between the King and the English Parliament on the passage of appropriations. The I.T.U. members, like Parliament, will usually vote for temporary dues assessments of one year or less for a specific purpose such as a strike fund. Since 1920 four referenda to secure funds for one year or less have passed and two have been defeated. On the other hand, eight referenda proposing permanent

10 *The Typographical Journal*, **53** (1918), 16-33; *ibid.*, **76** (1929).
11 *Ibid.*, **65** (1924), 830-838.

dues increases have been defeated since 1920, while five have passed. Of these five, two were for ten cents a month increases for the maintenance of the Union Printers' Home. These votes do not reflect an unwillingness on the part of the membership to support the union, for the two most heavily supported assessments were for a 10 per cent and a 4½ per cent tax on wages to support striking members. The 10 per cent assessment was passed in 1921 by a vote of 40,703 to 11, 499, to support the 44 hour week strike, while the second large tax was passed, 44,829 to 21,477, in 1948 to support the many Taft-Hartley strikes of the union. The generosity of the members in supporting their fellow unionists, rather than their officers or union apparatus, can be seen from the above votes and from the fact that in 1946, the union voted by 44,539 to 11,203 to increase strike benefits from 40 to 60 per cent of the regular wage for all married men, and from 25 to 40 per cent for all single men.[12]

Since 1900 the union has held over 250 referenda. Most of these referenda have been on constitutional changes or on assessments. There have been many votes on changing the pension system; defining the jurisdiction of the union; the question of affiliation with the A.F. of L.; adjusting the constitution to war needs; changing the date of the convention or the period of inauguration of officers; the number of days and hours which a union member may work; unemployment relief; and many other subjects which are covered in the constitution, or which a convention, Executive Council, or local find it advisable to submit to the membership.

The extent of membership control over the officialdom can be seen in the fact that the members have defeated 29 per cent of the 83 proposals submitted by International Conventions for their approval since 1920. This figure would be much higher if the non-controversial technical changes were omitted from consideration. In most organizations, union or non-union, it is assumed that the national convention of delegates, elected by the members, therefore represents the wishes of the members. It is clear from the record of contentions and referenda in the case of the I.T.U. that this assumption need not be true. A convention, in fact, usually represents the local formal leadership structure, and the leaders, even those of the small I.T.U. locals, may and frequently do have values and interests which are different from those of the members whom they represent. This gap is generally obscured by the absence of any means for the direct expression of the desires of the membership. Referenda provide such a means of expression, but only when they operate in the context of an institutionalized party system. Otherwise, as in plebiscitarian democracies, they serve to legitimize the power and decisions of a ruling group. The relation between the referenda voting and the two-party system can be seen in the fact that from 1900 to 1919, before the present system was completely institutionalized, only 16.2 per cent of the convention proposals were turned down.

[12] *The Typographical Journal*, **109** (1946), 297-311.

The results of referenda initiated by the International Executive Council present an even more dramatic picture of membership control. Nine out of the twenty-two, or 40.9 per cent of proposals by the officials, were defeated between 1920 and 1948, compared with one out of nine, or 11.1 per cent proposed between 1900 and 1919. The defeated Executive Council proposals have included dues increases, proposals to rejoin the A.F. of L., and to postpone the annual convention.[13]

The above data suggest that a large percentage of the members of the I.T.U., though supporters at election time of one or another party, do not necessarily accept the policies of the leaders whom they support. The defeats of proposals to increase officers' salaries or to extend their term of office indicate that a certain suspiciousness of or at least lack of complete enthusiasm for officials exists even among the supporters of a given administration. This suspicion has made it difficult if not impossible for an incumbent administration to so amend the constitution as to perpetuate its hold on office.

Preliminary interviews with members of the union suggest the existence of two seemingly contradictory sentiments as a consequence of the two-party system. The members are critical of the motives of union "politicians," but at the same time are extremely loyal to the union—the most critical oppositionists boast that the I.T.U. is the best and most democratic union in the country. The distrust of the leaders and the loyalty to the institution appear to be related to the intense political life of the organization. Every union politician is exposed to vigorous attack at all times from the opposition. The effect of such attacks may be reflected in the fact that even supporters of a given party are suspicious of the power or income aspirations of their own leaders. On the other hand, the fact that any given administration may be defeated within two years, and that the union cannot be identified with a permanent leader or group of leaders, appears to result in the members focusing their dissatisfactions on the temporary incumbent leaders rather than on the union. The prevailing sentiment among critics of a given administration seems to be: the officials are bad but the union is good. Such sentiments once developed in a democratic society or organization, are an important part of the cluster of factors which help maintain democratic practices.

The question obviously arises, what are the significant differences between the Typographical Union and other trade unions which are related to the perpetuation of the two-party system. The officials and members of the union with whom I have discussed this problem suggest two hypotheses— one which points to the historic traditions of chapel and union democracy,

---

[13] The above data on referenda were gathered from *The Typographical Journal* from 1900 to 1948. It is possible that I overlooked some referenda or misinterpreted the meaning of some, but the possible errors are small and would not change the general direction of the statistics.

going back in some cases to the seventeenth century or earlier, and another which cites the high educational level of printers compared to other crafts. Fortunately there exists a control with which to test these hypotheses—the International Pressmen's Union, an organization which was part of the Typographical Union until the start of the century. The Pressmen have the same historical traditions and institutional framework, such as chapels, as the Typographers. They work side by side in the printshops of the continent with the members of the I.T.U., and earn roughly the same wages. There is no reason to believe that the pressmen are significantly different from the compositors and linotype operators in their personal characteristics. If the above hypotheses were true, one should expect to find the same mechanisms of democratic control operative in the Pressmen's Union.

Actually, the International Pressmen's Union is one of the most dictatorial unions in America. One administration held power in the union for over thirty years until its leaders died. Various locals of the union have been suspended for opposing the policies of the International leaders. Until the death of President George Berry in 1948, the administration was repeatedly elected without opposition, and many locals were denied the right to choose their own officers.[14] These facts suggest that the above hypotheses do not explain the uniqueness of the I.T.U. Other hypotheses have been grouped in the following table.

Conclusions

While it has not been possible to filter out a single factor which alone would account for the democratic organization of the I.T.U., preliminary research suggests that there is a unique cluster of variables making for a competition of alternative governments in the union. These factors would include: the peculiar events which initiated the two rival factions; the existence within the larger locals of a large number of private social and athletic clubs which provide independent sources of power and influence, and opportunities for the training of new leadership; the fact that the union is stabilized but at the same time is subject to enough challenges to its security by the vicissitudes of the economic system and government legislation to require it to make important policy decisions upon which men may differ; the fact that it contains the large nucleus of aspiring union officials mentioned above; the smallness of the union so that there is a direct and visible link between the bottom and summits of the organization; the lack of division within the union between a sophisticated educated "élite" and an uneducated mass membership; the anti-bureaucratic values and juridical checks which developed out of the attempt to eliminate "secret society"

[14] Selig Perlman and Philip Taft, *History of Labor in the United States* (New York: Macmillan, 1935), pp. 449-451; and Joel Seidman, *Union Rights and Union Duties* (New York: Harcourt, Brace & World, 1943), p. 25.

Table 5-2.

Hypotheses Adduced to Explain Party Democracy in the I.T.U.	Evidence for Not Accepting or for Rejecting Hypotheses
1. Conflict of different socio-economic groups within union accounts for democracy in the I.T.U.	The majority of the members are typesetters, except a minority of mailers and machinists. All typographers in the same location receive the same scale, yet the large and many small locals are internally divided in support of the major parties.
2. Allegiance to extra-union groups such as splits between communists and their opponents, or conflicts along ethnic and religious lines.	Majority of members are of north European or native white origin. Only a small percentage belong to ethnic minority groups. External political parties have little influence in the union.
3. Homogeneity of membership and lack of an educated native elite as against a large mass of uneducated politically inexperienced immigrants or lower class natives.	This cannot be rejected *but* it is also true of the Pressmen and some Railroad Brotherhoods which have not developed internal political democracy.
4. The comparatively small size of the union (87,000 members) and the large number of small locals permit direct contact with the administration. More than 4,000 local officials. This means one member of 20 has direct contacts with officials.	See 3.
5. Defeated officials and personally ambitious members tend to remain in the union and form a reservoir, larger than positions available, of persons capable and desirious of union leadership jobs.	Other skilled crafts have a low turnover because of high economic status of craft. They may not possess many former union officials but this is more a consequence of a vital political system than a determinant.
6. The stability of the union removes it from pressure towards internal unity. Thus dictatorial measures cannot be justified by leaders on the basis that the union is like an army at war.	Partially challenged by fact that many dictatorial trade unions also have stable employer relations and good conditions of work but no union democracy.
7. The great personal antagonism existing when printers were divided in secret societies is institutionalized, as a kind of permanent Civil War in the party system.	Election results show that locals voting overwhelmingly Wahneta in one election shifted to the opposition in the next and vice versa.

Table 5-2.(continued)

8. Perhaps the antagonism of small groups of union politicians is too great to permit merger of opposing groups.

Leaders in one party have shifted to the opposition and have been elected on the opposition slate.

9. Democratic mores are so ingrained that leaders abstain from using union apparatus to perpetuate themselves in power.

This is true but more likely an outcome of a democratic political life. Yet I.T.U. leaders of both sides have used the Journal for partisan purposes, and given patronage. In one instance a constitutional technicality was used by the incumbent to bar the opposition candidate from the ballot. Their desire to stay in power does not seem to differ from that of other union leaders.

Professor Philip Taft, in a Study of the I.T.U., Has Suggested Additional Hypotheses:

Evidence for Not Accepting or for Rejecting Hypotheses

---

10. "In contrast to many labor unions, the I.T.U. has never experienced an influx of thousands of new members. Membership increases have been slow and steady. As a result new members are assimilated by the organization; they become aware of the Union's practices and learn its ideals."* (Taft compares the I.T.U. to the United Mine Workers who had an influx of hundreds of thousands of new members in 1933. He suggests that this influx was a large determining element in enabling Lewis to eliminate opposition.)

The comparison of I.T.U. with the United Mine Workers begs the question as there are other unions more comparable to the I.T.U. than the U.M.W. By 1930, long before the great mass influx into the U.M.W., only ten out of twenty-nine districts still had the right to elect their own officers. Moreover, Pressmen similar to the I.T.U. in having gradual increase in membership, do not have political democracy.

11. Bargaining is conducted primarily by the local. The international officers or representatives merely assist but do not play the dominant role as when negotiations are conducted on a regional basis.†

Again, the Pressmen and the Carpenters are composed of local bargaining units. The I.T.U., in fact, has a high degree of control through the Executive Council which approves all contracts and authorizes all strikes. Locals sometimes turn against incumbent administrations because they feel the International does not permit them to bargain as they desire.

Table 5-2. (continued)

12. "The great interest manifested by the membership in the affairs of the Union (as demonstrated by the large proportion voting in the International elections) further encourages the vitality of the democratic process."‡

It may be questioned again whether a result is not taken as a cause. The elections of 1906 and 1914, in which the major posts of President and Secretary-Treasurer were uncontested, brought 54.3 and 57.9 per cent of the members to the polls while the contested elections of 1904 and 1912 resulted in participation of 72.4 and 80.2 per cent of the membership respectively.§ Interest in the members seems to be related to the two-party system, with the vote turnout being secured by the two-party machines competing for power.

---

*Philip Taft, "Opposition to Union Officials in Elections," *Quarterly Journal of Economics,* 58 (February, 1944), 262.

†*Ibid.,* pp. 262-263.

‡*Ibid.,* p. 263.

§*Ibid.,* p. 261.

control; and the educational and status level of printers which places them among those groups who tend to exhibit more political interest in the country as a whole.[15]

The perpetuation of the party system in the I.T.U. may be explained functionally, not in terms of the union as the reference unit, but in terms of the parties themselves. Once established, they give status, privilege and power to the leaders, as well as other satisfactions to less important party activists. The parties established and perpetuated juridical protections for themselves.

Ever since 1920, "out" parties have always had a real possibility of returning to power within two years. Only twice in this period did the "out" party vote fall below 40 per cent. The opportunities of a return to power were considerably greater than those which could have been offered by the "in" party as inducement to end opposition. In fact, the most prominent defections have not been from the "outs" to the "ins", but rather from the "ins" to the "outs."[16] Perhaps the men who deserted could not hope to secure higher positions from their own party since it was standard practice

---

[15] The article referred to earlier, "Trade Unionism in the Printing Trades," presents in some detail the analysis of a number of structural factors which appear to be related to the high level of political democracy in the I.T.U.

[16] In 1931 Leon Rouse, former Progressive President of New York Local 6, ran as an independent after failing to obtain the vice-presidential nomination from his party. In 1936 Claude Baker, having been elected to the first vice-presidency as a Progressive, switched to the Independents while in office and headed the opposition ticket in 1938.

to renominate incumbents. An ambitious leader of the "ins" can often only secure a nomination to a higher post from the "out" group.

The existence of the political system within the I.T.U. suggests that the "iron law of oligarchy" as Michels presented it is not a "law." His generalizations may be qualified to include recognition of the fact that oligarchy is endemic in large-scale organization only when there is no permanent base for an opposition party system which gives the masses the opportunity to choose between alternative programs and forces competing sets of aspiring rulers to yield to the desires of the rank and file in order to secure or maintain voting strength. Moreover, Michels only discussed those aspects of organization which in and of themselves are functional to the power position of incumbents and ignored the possibility that office has dysfunctions if an opposition exists. Decision makers create enemies as well as friends when they decide a conflict of interest. In the case of the I.T.U., as in society at large, the administration not only is negatively affected by the immediate small decisions which it must make but it may bear the brunt of the resentment against uncontrollable external situations which adversely affect the members. The three significant periods of party shift, 1920, 1938 and 1944, were times of either depression or inflation. Power in a democratic organization is not only self-perpetuating but also self-destroying, *if there is an institutional framework for mobilization of critical sentiments.*

The I.T.U. is also a deviant case to the rule that organization necessarily breeds conservatism. The "law" of organization is not conservatism but survival. Conservatism, the maintenance of an existing equilibrium, will be found, as it is frequently, when it seems to be an adequate method of keeping power. There are, however, conditions under which the problem of retaining power prescribes militancy and radicalism on the part of the power-holder. In the I.T.U. the conciliatory reaction of the Independents to restrictions of the War Labor Board during the last war was followed by their defeat. The Progressives, faced since 1947 with a similar restrictive situation as a result of the Taft-Hartley Act, have reacted by increased militancy.

Before exploring the generalizations that the unique pattern of the I.T.U. permits about the labor movement in the United States and its political structures, it is well to examine an idea which is basic in the consideration of organization. Emil Lederer in *The State of the Masses* has raised questions regarding the relationship between the varied organizations of a political society and the stability of that society.[17] What he characterizes as the state of the masses is one in which the numerous organizations that we regard as normal and generally irrelevant to political organization have disappeared, have been destroyed or are otherwise non-existent or incorporated into the state. It is his suggestion that these organizations—labor, religious, agricultural—all have a definite function in the preservation of democracy.

[17] Emil Lederer, *The State of the Masses* (New York: Norton, 1940).

It is the amorphous mass, the state of the masses, the state without a multitude of internal organizations, that has high explosive potential. This concept of the state of the masses is one which deserves far more detailed examination than it has been given.

In large part, the principal source of continued power of a union administration flows from the possession of the union machinery itself. In many unions, the incumbent administration is the only legal and, in almost all unions, the only existing national organization concerned with getting and maintaining power. The formal right of free speech or secret ballot means little as an effective check on administrative power, if the union leaders have complete possession of the union administrative and field staff, union newspaper and expense account. Lazarsfeld and Merton have noted that monopolization of the channels of communication and the consequent absence of counter-propaganda is one of the basic conditions for effectiveness of propaganda in shaping attitudes and behavior.[18] This condition, as they note, is indigenous to the structure of totalitarian states; it is also characteristic of the one-party political structure of most labor unions. Without a continuously functioning and comparatively well-financed organization to develop issues, print and disseminate literature, and provide a rostrum for potential leaders, dissident members are at a considerable disadvantage in provoking significant opposition even under circumstances which might be expected to create membership discontent. In effect, therefore, the union which does not have any source of internal organization, except for the administration itself, is similar to the state of the masses.[19]

These ideas should be considered in terms of the central problem of this paper, political life in private governments, especially in trade unions. An oligarchic structure which is in effect a one-party system is so common in the trade union government in America that a defender of the Soviet Union within the American labor movement has pointed to the internal structure of the trade union here as justification for the one-party system in that country.[20]

[18] R. K. Merton and P. F. Lazarsfeld, "Mass Communications, Popular Taste, and Organized Social Action," Lyman Bryson, ed., *Communication of Ideas* (New York: Institute for Religious and Social Studies, 1948), pp. 95-118.

[19] In the larger locals of the I.T.U. large numbers of leisure-time organizations exist which have created the equivalent of an "occupational community." The factors inherent in the occupation which have led to the breakup of the "state of the masses" are discussed in Lipset and Trow, *op. cit.*

[20] Harry Bridges, President of the International Longshoreman's and Warehousemen's Union, presented this argument at the 1947 convention of his union: "What is totalitarianism? *A country that has a totalitarian government operates like our union operates.* There are no political parties. People are elected to govern the country based upon their records. . . . That is, totalitarianism . . . if we started to divide up and run a Republican set of officers, a Democratic set, a Communist set and something else. We would have one hell of a time. . . ." (Quoted in *Proceedings of the Seventh Biennial Convention*, I.L.W.U., April 7-11, 1947 (San Francisco, 1947), p. 178.) Bridge's statement is, of course, concealing the fact that in the U.S.S.R. and in the Longshoremen's

The significance of the two-party system of the International Typographical Union lies at least in part in the fact that this system is almost unique in American private associations. There are abundant examples of temporary factionalism within trade unions and other private organizations. Long standing institutionalized opposition *parties*, however, are very largely a phenomenon of the political organization known as the state. The existence of the two-party system in the I.T.U. suggests, however, that even in the labor movement there may be sources for institutionalized opposition permitting a direct membership influence on organization policy through their power to overturn a union government. Such two-party systems existed loosely in the A.F. of L. before World War I. Also the Histadrut, or Jewish Confederation of Labor, in the new state of Israel has had continuous internal political struggles since 1920.[21]

These examples should indicate that one-party government is not inherent in the labor movement. Nevertheless, the divisions in the above examples were and are related to outside political forces—the Socialist Party in the case of the A.F. of L., and the two leading Socialist political groups in Palestine, i.e., the Mapai and the Mapam. Political divisions within the I.T.U., however, are not related to external political groups.[22] This suggests the hypothesis that the structural basis for the division of political opinion does exist within the trade union movement, but that the repressive powers inherent in the bureaucratic structure of a union are usually stronger than the factors that might sustain organized opposition.

Political divisions such as those in the A.F. of L. before 1920, and the contemporary struggles in the labor movements of other countries, may reflect as well as determine basic divisions in political outlook within unions. We know little of the structural sources of political differences *within* social classes, especially among workers. The fact remains, however, that unless restrained by totalitarian or oligarchic political machines which prevent workers from choosing between alternative union governments, men seem to divide themselves within the labor movement, as in other areas of life, be-

---

Union political machines do exist. He is in effect saying that "we would have one hell of a time" if we had an an organized opposition. Bridges believes that there is no class base for opposing political groups within the "one-class" trade union.

[21] For a more extensive discussion of this problem, see S. M. Lipset, "The Two Party System in the I.T.U.," *Labor and Nation* (Fall, 1950), pp. 33-35; Lipset and Trow, *op. cit.*

[22] The fact that most dissident factions in the labor movement are tied to external radical political groups is not solely related to the proletarian orientation or composition of such parties. In most unions, opposition can only exist if organized and financed, and socialist and communist groups are, in effect, the only existing organizational rivals of union administrative bureaucracies. The fact that in the United States, communist trade union factions are able to win considerable support from obviously non- and anti-communist workers, is evidence of the fact that organization rather than ideological appeal is often the key to Communist success in the labor movement. That is, workers who are discontented with their union officials often have no institutional alternative except the opposition communist faction.

tween Conservatives and Liberals, between Gomperites and Socialists, between Independents and Progressives.

These differences which appear to be present within the trade union structure, and probably within other large-scale private governments as well, must be institutionalized as political parties if the members of an organization are to be able to bring their influence to bear on the summits of the structure. The incumbent leaders of a private government will usually deny that the basis for internal difference exists within their organization. Recognition that the basis for a "loyal opposition" exists within the framework of the association may mean that in the course of normal political life the incumbents, whether of the left or right, will go out of office. Convinced that they are serving the best interests of the organization and desiring to retain the only source of their power and status, leaders of labor unions use the union political apparatus to eliminate and suppress organized opposition. It may be suggested that the power of bureaucratic organization, rather than the absence of significant sources of political difference, accounts for the apparent unanimity of opinion which exists in most American unions.

The "normal" life of many American trade unions is similar to Lederer's "classless" state of the masses. The union, without any source of power for leadership outside of the administration apparatus, is easily controlled from the top. Challenges to the incumbent administration in such monolithic organizations usually take the form of revolution, which develops into life or death struggles resembling civil wars. If one faction wins, it usually suppresses the other by force. If neither group has the strength to eliminate the other, secession may occur, with two or more unions competing as separate structures. Revolutions, however, do not occur often, and are a result of serious problems of long duration; when they do occur, they are most frequently unsuccessful. The organization, therefore, like the one-party state, may appear to be in a state of political quiescence for long intervals. If the leadership is capable and is actually satisfying the needs of large sections of the membership, it may hold power indefinitely. In such a situation, however, the problem of sources of new leadership develop.

The International Typographical Union has established and maintained a functioning party system. It suffers from the reverse malady, if it be a malady, of too many aspirants for union office. The two parties in the union are engaged in a constant search, within the locals and at international conventions, to find and recruit to their party individuals who have political leadership ability. In their struggle to win and maintain office they are also on the lookout for issues which may be popular with the rank and file. This competition for office has made the officials of the union much more militant than any other corresponding group of A.F. of L. craft union leaders.

It should be realized that there is a basic strain between the democratic values of the trade union movement and the system of internal stratification that is inherent in the structure of a large organization. Union officials have moved up in the social structure by leaving the bench. Union office necessarily involves superior income, status, and power as compared with those of ordinary members. Parsons has suggested that no system of stratification can be linked completely to an achievement pattern. That is, a certain degree of ascriptive status is unavoidable in any social system. The status system of the trade union movement necessarily cannot develop a pattern of ascriptive status. A system of stratification which is based on achievement criteria alone will subject its high status members to the need at least to legitimate or make permanent their new high position during their lifetime. The assumptions implicit in democratic trade unionism, however, require the return of union leaders to their trade upon being defeated in elections. This would be equivalent to a system of stratification in which members of the upper classes customarily moved to the bottom after a few years at the top. It is fairly obvious that such a social structure could not exist for any length of time. An elite faced with the possibility of loss of position will, therefore, make strenuous efforts to preserve its status.

The last decade has witnessed a renewed interest in the problems of bureaucratic structure, or, synonomously, large-scale organization. The emergence of the bureaucratic pattern as the dominant organizational form of a large centralized industrial society has made many people despair of the possibility of democratic control of the bureaucrats. The current interest in the work of Robert Michels, as evidenced by the fact that two of his books were republished in the last year, appears to be related to the feeling among many persons that Michels was right, that large-scale social organization is inherently non-democratic.[23] In evaluating the potentialities of large-scale social organization, the unique structure is as important as the nine hundred and ninety-nine which take another form. In a world in which large-scale social organization is becoming synonymous with control from the top, it is important to know that in at least one large trade union, a significant measure of democracy has existed for fifty years.[24]

[23] Michels, op. cit.; Introductory Lecture in Political Sociology (Minneapolis: University of Minneapolis Press, 1950).

[24] I would like to acknowledge with thanks the financial assistance of the Institute of Industrial Relations of the University of California and the Social Science Research Council. The data contained in this article and in a subsequent article, "Trade Unionism in the Printing Trades" to be published elsewhere, was gathered while I was a Research Associate of the Institute of Industrial Relations or using a grant from the Social Science Research Council. Further, at the present time a survey research study of the Typographical Union is being conducted under the auspices of the Bureau of Applied Social Research of Columbia University. This latter study is being supported by a grant from the Rockefeller Foundation and from the Columbia University Council on Research in the Social Sciences. I am especially indebted for aid to Robert Raschen and Grant McConnell, Research Assistants in the Institute of Industrial Relations, University of California.

27. Size of Locals and Union Democracy[1]

William A. Faunce

Introduction

The size of an organization has an important bearing upon the nature of its control structure. Both the necessity for formal mechanisms of control and the character of authority relations within an organization are affected by its size. This paper is concerned with the relationship between local union size and the internal political structure of a trade union. Because local unions are in some measure autonomous political units, union government may be studied at either the local or the national union level. Data regarding political processes at both levels were collected in this study. The data permit analysis of the contribution of larger and smaller locals to democratic control of the national union as well as analysis of the extent of democracy within locals of varying size.

There is some agreement among students of union government that small locals tend to be more democratic internally than large locals but contribute less to democratic processes at the national union level. Large locals are seen as a force for democracy in the national union primarily because they are less dependent upon the national office and therefore in a better position to express opposition to it. Organized party conflict, which is more likely to occur in large than in small locals, may produce pressures that also result in more active opposition to policies of the national officers. It has also been suggested that members of small locals are less likely to be exposed to, and are less well informed about, opposing views on political issues at the national union level.[2]

The proposition that large locals are less democratic internally than small locals is based primarily upon their lower rate of rank-and-file participation in union politics and lower rate of turnover of officers.[3] According

Reprinted from *American Journal of Sociology*, **68** (November, 1962), 291-298.

[1] I am indebted to Professors Jack Stieber and William H. Form, Michigan State University, and to Professor George Y. M. Won, University of Hawaii, who worked with me on this project.

[2] Cf. Joel Seidman, *Democracy in the Labor Movement*, Bulletin 39, February, 1958 (Ithaca, N.Y.: New York State School of Industrial and Labor Relations, Cornell University, 1958), pp. 19-36; Seymour Martin Lipset, Martin Trow, and James Coleman, *Union Democracy* (New York: Free Press, 1956), pp. 364-390.

[3] Cf. Seidman, *op. cit.*; Lipset *et al.*, *op. cit.*, pp. 14, 78; George Strauss, "Control by the Membership in Building Trades Unions," *American Journal of Sociology*, **61** (1955-56), 527 ff.; Joel Seidman, Jack London, Bernard Karsh, and Daisy L. Tagliacozzo,

to this view, officers of large locals are more likely to use undemocratic means to stay in office because the rewards of office are much greater. Their success in subverting democratic procedures results from greater control of means of communication, a more complete monopoly of political skills, and less rank-and-file concern with union affairs. Seidman summarizes this point of view as follows:

Conditions are most favorable for the development of local union democracy in a small organization, of several hundred at the most, all of whose members are employed in a single plant. There the members are likely to be in daily contact with each other and also with their officers. Typically, they work side by side because the organization neither needs nor can it afford the services of a full-time official. In these circumstances the union officer can have no greater income, not much more prestige, and little more power than the rank-and-file membership. The factory worker is hired by management and, assuming proper conduct on his part, his job lasts for a relatively long period of time so he enjoys a reasonable degree of economic security. As a union member he has little reason to be fearful of his union official or dependent upon him. The officer, in turn, has little reason to seek to perpetuate his stay in office by undemocratic means and little opportunity to accomplish that objective should he have the desire. The rewards of offices of this type are meagre, the annoyances many, and relatively few wish to perpetuate themselves in office. Contests for this type of office are frequent and turnover is high.[4]

The results of the study reported in this paper support the view that large locals contribute more to democracy in the national union. They cast some doubt, however, upon the assertion that small locals are more democratic than large locals and raise some questions regarding the meaning of democracy under the conditions described above by Seidman.

Research Design

Data bearing on the relationship between local size and union democracy were collected from two sources. The first was a study conducted at the Seventeenth Constitutional Convention of the United Auto Workers in 1959. A questionnaire was distributed to all delegates in attendance on the second day of this convention. Although not all the delegates were present at these sessions, completed questionnaires were obtained from 1,815 delegates representing 753 UAW locals. Approximately three-fourths of all delegates who attended the convention are included in our sample. The various geographic regions of the UAW, locals of various sizes, and cities of

---

The Worker Views His Union (Chicago: University of Chicago Press, 1958), pp. 185-219; Leonard R. Sayles and George Strauss, The Local Union (New York: Harper & Row, 1953), pp. 238-258; Arnold S. Tannenbaum and Robert L. Kahn, Participation in Local Unions (New York: Harper & Row, 1958).

[4] Seidman, op. cit., p. 33.

various sizes are represented in almost exactly the same proportion among our respondents as in the total delegate population.

Questions dealing with delegate attitudes toward the convention, delegate election procedures, and general background characteristics of delegates were included in the questionnaire. The number of votes allotted each local at the convention was used as the basis for classifying locals according to size.

After the convention, an intensive followup study of delegates from locals in Lansing and Flint, Michigan, was conducted: 108 of the 112 delegates from these two cities were interviewed. The emphasis in this study was upon varying orientations to the delegate role. Information was also collected regarding the delegates' experience at the convention, their experience upon reporting back to their locals, the general level and nature of political activity within each local, and opinions regarding the extent of democratic control of the convention and of the policy-making process generally at the national and local union levels. While it cannot be assumed that the Lansing and Flint locals are representative of all locals within the UAW, there is no apparent reason to assume that differences observed between large and small locals in these two cities would not be found elsewhere. The limitations of the sample should be kept in mind, however, in interpreting findings from this study.[5]

Findings

The focus of these two studies upon a constitutional convention provided an opportunity to study the relationship between local size and local contributions to democratic policy-making processes at the national union level. In principle, at least, the convention has primary responsibility for determining UAW policies. The national officers and executive board are elected by the delegates and presumably operate within a broad policy framework established by the convention. Observation of the convention in operation and data collected from the delegates suggest that the 1959 UAW Convention functioned democratically in the sense that important issues were brought before it, were thoroughly debated with opposing views freely expressed, and were resolved in favor of the majority view. The extent to which delegates from larger and smaller locals participate in this process is one index of their respective contributions to democratic union government.

While there are many informal channels of communication between UAW locals and the national office, the convention is the only *formal*

---

[5] For reports of other findings from these studies see William A. Faunce, "Delegate Attitudes toward the Convention in the UAW," *Industrial and Labor Relations Review*, 15 (1962), 463-473; George Y. M. Won, "Democratic Sentiments in Unionism: A Case Study of the UAW Convention," unpublished doctoral dissertation, Michigan State University, 1962; and Jack Stieber, *Democracy in the UAW* (New York: Wiley, 1962).

structure in the UAW through which local views on general policy issues are expressed. One way in which these views may be presented is in the form of resolutions submitted to the convention. Resolutions are sent to the national office at least three weeks before the convention begins and may be considered by the convention whether or not the locals submitting them are represented at the convention. Table 5-3 indicates that resolutions are submitted almost exclusively by the larger UAW locals.

Table 5-3.

Percentage of Resolutions Submitted to 1959 UAW Convention and of Locals Not Sending Delegates to Convention, by Size of Locals*

Size of Local	Number (N=1,239)	Per Cent	Percentages of Resolutions Submitted (N=339)	Percentages of Locals not Sending Delegates
149 or fewer members	443	35.7	1.5	51.7
150-1,049	535	43.2	6.8	17.9
1,050-1,549	59	4.7	1.5	5.1
1,550-4,049	145	11.7	44.2	4.1
4,050 or more	57	4.8	46.0	0.0

*Because number of votes at the convention was used as the basis for classifying locals according to size, the intervals in this table and subsequent tables reflect the formula used in the UAW for distributing votes among locals. Locals are allotted one vote for the first one hundred or fewer members and an additional vote for each additional hundred members or major fraction thereof.

Whether or not they initiate policy issues, small locals may have their views represented at the convention if their delegates participate in debate on issues with which they are concerned. Data in Table 5-3 indicate, however, that smaller locals are less likely to even send a delegation to the convention.[6] If it can be assumed that small locals have some common interests that are different from those of large locals, at least these interests may be served to the extent that they are actively pursued by delegates from those small locals that are represented. Data from both the questionnaire and interview studies suggest, however, that the size of the local the delegate represents affects his views of the purpose for the convention, his definition of the delegate role, and, consequently, the nature of his participation in the convention proceedings.

The delegates at the convention were asked to rank various purposes for the convention in order of their importance. Table 5-4 indicates that delegates from large locals are significantly more likely to regard the primary

[6] Small locals are also underrepresented at conventions of the International Typographical Union (cf., Lipset et al., op. cit., p. 370).

function of the convention as the determination of UAW policy. Among the 125 delegates from the smallest locals in our sample, 27.7 percent indicated that the convention's primary purpose was "to make sure that members back home are informed about UAW policies." Only 18.6 per cent of the 501 delegates from the largest locals gave this response. The desire to simply keep the membership informed, or in fact any view of the convention that excludes policy-making as its most important function, is unlikely to serve as a motive for active participation in the business of the convention.

Table 5-4.

Function Attributed to Convention by Delegates from Large and Small Locals

LOCAL SIZE	FUNCTION OF CONVENTION*	
	Policy-Making	All Others
1,049 or fewer members	290	329
1,050 or more members	609	478

*$x^2 = 13.33$; P $<.001$.

Data from the Flint and Lansing interviews also suggest that there is a difference between delegates from large and small locals in their conception of the delegate role. The UAW constitution specifies that convention delegates are not bound by local instructions on any issue they may vote on at the convention. There are variations, however, in the extent to which delegates feel a personal commitment to act in accord with the wishes of their constituents. Delegates from small locals are, first of all, less likely to have even received any instructions regarding local preferences on issues to be considered by the convention. Of the twenty delegates from locals having 2,300 or fewer members, almost three-fourths indicated they had not received any instructions prior to the convention while only a little over one-third of the eighty-eight delegates from larger locals indicated that this was the case. Among delegates who were instructed how to vote on any issue, half of those from the smaller locals but over two-thirds from the larger locals indicated that they felt bound by these instructions when they went to the convention. Most of this difference is accounted for by the responses of the forty-seven delegates from the two largest locals in our sample, 81.5 per cent of whom felt that they should vote as instructed. When asked how they had actually voted at the convention, 66.7 per cent of delegates from the smaller locals and 87.2 per cent of those from larger locals answered that they had voted in accord with what a majority of the local membership wanted.

A much higher proportion of delegates from large locals indicated that important issues should be decided by a referendum rather than by the convention. This may be interpreted as another indication of greater concern on the part of these delegates with rank-and-file views. In this instance, however, it may also reflect a greater willingness to oppose the administration of the national union. Use of the referendum became an issue during debate on a proposed dues increase. The International Executive Board, which favored the dues increase, argued that the issue should be decided by the convention. Almost two-thirds of the forty-seven delegates from the largest locals in our sample indicated that "important issues like the dues increase should be decided by a referendum." A considerable majority of delegates from smaller locals supported the International Executive Board's position.

There is other evidence that delegates from large locals are more willing to oppose national officers. The Flint-Lansing delegates were asked which caucuses, if any, they attended at the convention. The few delegates who reported attending an antiadministration caucus were exclusively from large locals. They were also asked whether they felt that the national officers had a right to expect them to support proposals they favored. Well over half the delegates from the largest locals indicated that the officers had no right to expect delegates to vote the way they wanted them to while only a third of the delegates from the smallest locals reported this view. When asked about the legitimacy of rank-and-file expectations, half the small local delegates indicated that their constituents had "every right" to expect them to vote for proposals they favored. This view was reported by more than three-fourths of the delegates from the largest locals. Responses to questions dealing with the kinds of pressures the national officers might use during a convention to get support for resolutions they favored suggest that delegates from large locals are more aware of the existence of such pressures but less concerned with them. Their awareness of these pressures may result from greater political sophistication while their lack of concern may reflect the greater autonomy of large locals.[7]

Delegates from small locals who are less likely to regard policy-making as the purpose of the convention, who are less concerned with representing rank-and-file views in this process, and who are more willing to simply accept the International Executive Board's program could be expected to be less active at the convention. There is some evidence that this is the case. Of delegates from Flint and Lansing locals with 2,300 or fewer members, only 16.7 per cent reported having addressed a general session of the convention while 25.8 per cent of those from larger locals reported having done so. Delegates from small locals also appear to be less active in convention politics. Over half these delegates reported that they had not attended any caucuses at the convention while two-thirds of those from large locals indicated that they had attended at least one caucus.

The findings from these two studies appear to be consistent with the

---

[7] Difference in size of locals is likely to have a greater effect upon local autonomy in industrial unions like the UAW than in most craft unions where fewer decisions are made at the international level.

position that large locals contribute more to democratic processes at the national union level. We will turn now to analysis of political processes at the local level. If we rely solely upon the customary indexes of union democracy, rates of rank-and-file participation and turnover of leadership, our data would support the hypothesis that small locals are more democratic internally than large locals. The delegates at the convention were asked to estimate the percentage of the membership of their unit or local voting in the delegate elections for the 1959 convention. Table 5-5 shows a strong relationship between local size and rank-and-file participation in the elections with the greatest participation occurring in the smallest locals.[8] Data from the followup interviews indicate that small locals may have better attendance at local meetings as well as a higher proportion voting in elections. Almost two-thirds of the delegates from small locals reported attending all local meetings while less than one-third of those from large locals reported doing so. Both studies also suggest more frequent turnover of leadership at least in the delegate role in small locals. Data from the questionnaire study indicate that 57.4 per cent of the 125 delegates from the smallest locals and 40.2 per cent of the 501 from the largest locals were attending their first convention.

Table 5-5.
Percentage of Membership Voting in Delegate Elections in Locals of Varying Size*

Membership Voting (Per Cent)	PERCENTAGE OF LOCALS				
	149 or Fewer Members (N = 143)	150-1,049 (N = 320)	1,050-1,549 (N = 51)	1,550-4,049 (N = 132)	4,050 or More Members (N = 55)
0-25	19.6	23.5	29.4	32.6	41.8
26-50	23.1	30.0	31.4	31.8	27.3
51-75	26.6	24.4	13.7	25.8	23.6
76-100	30.8	22.2	25.5	9.8	7.3
Total	100.1	100.1	100.0	100.0	100.0

*Totals may not add to 100 due to rounding.

Rank-and-file participation in union politics and turnover of leaders are used as indexes of democracy under the assumption that they produce

[8] Because the questionnaires were completed independently, the extent of agreement among the estimates of delegates from the same local provides some indication of the accuracy of these estimates. The mean deviation among estimates in each local and the average mean deviation in all locals were computed. Since there is a limited range of possible estimates, the maximum possible mean deviation could also be computed. The average observed deviation for all locals was less than 9 per cent of this maximum.

leadership that is more responsive to the wishes of a majority of the members. For this assumption to hold, it is necessary that elections involve a choice of candidates. The data in Table 5-6 show that there is a much higher proportion of *uncontested* elections in small locals. In addition, if it is the election process that is responsible for turnover in the delegate position, we would expect that there would be delegates at the convention who had previously run for this position and lost. The relationship between this variable and local size is clearly shown by the data in Table 5-6.

Table 5-6.

Locals with Uncontested Elections and Delegates Who Had Run
for Election Previously and Lost, by Size of Local

SIZE OF LOCAL	LOCALS IN WHICH ELECTIONS WERE UNCONTESTED		DELEGATES HAVING PREVIOUSLY RUN AND LOST	
	Number	Percent	Number	Percent
149 or fewer members	143	35.0	154	9.1
150-1,049	311	21.2	484	18.6
1,050-1,549	52	3.8	139	21.7
1,550-4,049	131	3.8	495	27.1
4,050 or more	54	3.7	500	29.0

These findings plus the fact that delegates from small locals are less likely to regard the convention as having a policy-making function suggest that the delegate selection process in these locals may involve something other than a choice among candidates advocating differing positions on policy matters. While we do not have data bearing directly upon this interpretation of these findings, it is possible, that turnover in the delegate position in some small locals simply reflects the distribution of an honorific title (and a trip to Atlantic City) among a local elite. Turnover of leadership may have a different meaning and greater relevance to democratic decision-making processes in large UAW locals where there is more likely to be an active, internal political structure with an organized party system.[9]

Differences in the internal political climate of large and small locals are clearly in evidence in the Flint and Lansing locals. Political party systems exist in virtually all locals with 4,000 or more members but in only one-third

[9] The differences in internal political activity between large and small UAW locals are somewhat similar to those found between large and small shops in the ITU. See Lipset *et al.*, *op. cit.*, pp. 150-197, who also report a curvilinear relationship in which the highest level of political involvement occurs in medium-sized shops employing between one hundred and two hundred ITU members. Our data do not show a pattern of this sort although it is possible that it is obscured by the greater size of political units in the UAW and by differences in the measures of political activity used in the two studies.

of the locals with 750 or fewer members. Even where there is a party system in smaller locals there are less likely to be separate slates of candidates run at elections than in large locals. Delegates from small locals also report that the opposition party is less active between elections, that the same groups do not oppose each other at all elections, and that there are less likely to be recognized leaders of the opposition party. These findings suggest that whatever factionalism exists in small locals is less likely to be institutionalized. A much higher proportion of delegates from large locals report that there is some tie-in between their local parties and parties from other locals or factions in the national union. These relationships may be a source of strength for opposition parties within large locals and may also strengthen their position should they decide to oppose some policy of the national officers.

Rank-and-file participations in elections and turnover of elected leaders may have no relevance at all to union democracy if elections and other formal procedures are not important aspects of the control structure of the union. If policies are formulated and leaders selected as a result of informal social relationships on the job, the formal structure of control may serve only to legitimate these decisions.[10] The number of uncontested elections and the absence of a formal party system suggest that this may be the case in small UAW locals. There is some additional evidence that supports this position more directly. The Flint-Lansing delegates were asked whether or not they would be affected in any way if a majority of their constituents were dissatisfied with decisions made at the convention. Over three-fourths of the twenty delegates from locals with twenty-three hundred or fewer members reported that they would not be affected in any way. Less than half of the eighty-eight delegates from larger locals gave this response. Among those indicating that they would be affected, there is a difference by size of local in the type of anticipated response of the membership. The delegates were asked in what ways they would be affected by unfavorable reactions to convention decisions. Their responses were classified as either formal controls, like being voted out of office, or informal controls, such as those involved in interpersonal relationships in the plant. The delegates from small locals were concerned almost exclusively with informal controls while a majority of those from large locals were concerned with the possibility of not being re-elected. There is some related evidence from the responses to a question that asked for a definition of union democracy. Delegates from large locals were much more likely to include formal structural guarantees of democracy like free elections in their definitions while small local delegates were more concerned with certain individual rights like freedom of speech. One reason for the greater concern among delegates from large locals with the election process and with formal accountability to

[10] For an excellent discussion of this process see Joseph Kovner and Herbert J. Lahne, "Shop Society and the Union," *Industrial and Labor Relations Review*, **7** (1953), 3-14.

their constituents may be the fact that they are more interested in maintaining the positions that they occupy in their locals. Almost two-thirds of the delegates from large locals and less than half of those from small locals reported that keeping the office they hold in the local is very important to them. If the election process is to contribute toward making leaders more responsive to their constituents, it would appear that their responsiveness would have to be motivated by desire for re-election. The data reported above suggest that this motive is more likely to be found in large than in small UAW locals.

Summary and Conclusions

Data collected from delegates to the 1959 Constitutional Convention of the UAW suggest that small locals contribute less than large locals to democratic policy-making processes at the national union level. Small locals are less likely to be represented at the convention, they infrequently initiate proposals on policy matters, and their delegates are less actively involved in the convention proceedings. A possible explanation for these differences is that delegates from small locals are less likely to regard the convention as having a policy-making function, are less concerned with representing rank-and-file views at the convention, and appear to be more willing to simply accept the position of the UAW International Executive Board on policy issues.

The data regarding political processes within local unions suggest that rates of rank-and-file participation and leadership turnover may not be appropriate indexes of democracy in small political units. The small locals in our sample had a higher proportion of members voting in elections and more frequent turnover in the delegate position. These locals, however, also had fewer elections that were contested and were less likely to have an active opposition party to represent minority views on local issues. In addition delegates from small locals appeared to be less responsive to rank-and-file wishes and less concerned with accounting to their constituents for actions at the convention. In general, the data suggest that formal control structures have a different and perhaps less important function in small local unions.

These findings have a number of implications for studies of union democracy. First, definitions of democracy are often phrased in terms of formal structural characteristics. Lipset, Trow, and Coleman, for example, define union democracy as "the possibility that an official can be defeated for re-election."[11] There is a variety of structural forms that may contribute to achieving democratic objectives. Indexes of democracy that measure the existence of particular structural forms may or may not be measures of the achievement of these objectives. Further analysis is needed of the variables

[11] Lipset et al., op. cit., p. 404.

that determine the effectiveness of different structural arrangements in achieving and sustaining union democracy.

Our data suggest that organizational size is one of these variables. An understanding of democratic processes in large local and national unions requires analysis of formal policy-making and policy-implementing procedures. When indexes of democracy based upon these procedures are applied to small local unions, they generally indicate that small locals operate more democratically than large locals. High rates of participation in elections and at meetings in small locals may, however, be accounted for by the nature of interpersonal relations in these locals and may have little or no bearing upon the policy-making process. Turnover of elected officials may reflect only the desire of the local elite to distribute onerous duties or to share more rewarding ones like attendance at a convention. If, as Seidman and others have suggested, officials of small locals do not wish to perpetuate themselves in office, at least one motive for responsiveness to majority views is eliminated.

More frequent interaction between officers and rank-and-file members in small locals may help to keep local policies consistent with majority views. Frequent interaction is not in itself, however, a guaranty that this will be the case, and primary group relationships in small locals may generate coercive pressures that prevent those with minority views from voicing their opposition.

Among the primary objectives of a democratic form of government is an orderly resolution of conflict of interest in which majority views prevail but in which the right of the minority to oppose these views is protected. Analysis of the structure of informal, interpersonal relations may contribute more than formal structural analyses to our understanding of the way in which these objectives may be achieved in small local unions.

28. Control Structure and Union Functions[1]

Arnold S. Tannenbaum

Introduction

The importance of control in organizations has led to the development of a number of hypotheses relating it to other aspects of functioning. Relationships have been suggested, for example, between the goals of a union and the form which control will take within it. The "business union," devoted primarily to the enhancement of wages and other specific benefits from management, is predicted to develop strong leadership and an autocratic government.[2] A union's commitment to large social goals, on the other hand, is often considered to be associated with internal democratic procedures.[3] The relationship between union-management conflict and control has also been the subject of some thought and speculation. Militant conflict with management is said to contribute to membership interest and the maintenance of democracy within the union.[4] A related view suggests that unions may be led into undemocratic procedures in an effort to achieve a harmonious relationship with management. Autocratic control is seen as a correlate of "union responsibility."[5] These hypotheses are consistent with the general notion that the form or structure of a union is related to its functions or goals. Furthermore, they imply that the relationship goes one way; the functions determine the structure.

Social psychologists have been interested in control from another point of view: as an independent variable. Interest in the effects of control

Reprinted from *The American Journal of Sociology*, **61** (May, 1956), 536-545.

[1] The material presented here is adapted in part from a larger report written by the present author in collaboration with Robert L. Kahn and subsidized by the Rockefeller Foundation. The larger study of which this is a part is one of a continuing series on organizational functioning conducted by the staff of the Human Relations Program of the Survey Research Center. I would like to thank Erving Goffman and Joan Lohmann for their contributions to the design and execution of this study, as well as Elizabeth Douvan, Basil Georgopoulos, and Ernest Lilienstein for their helpful comments concerning this paper.
[2] R. F. Hoxie, *Trade Unionism in the United States*, 2nd. ed. (New York: Appleton-Century-Crofts, 1923), p. 46.
[3] Irving Howe and B. J. Widick, *The UAW and Walter Reuther* (New York: Random House, 1949), p. 244.
[4] *Ibid.*, p. 259.
[5] Seymour Martin Lipset, "The Political Process in Trade Unions: A Theoretical Statement" in *Freedom and Control in Modern Society*, Morroe Berger, Theodore Abel, and Charles H. Page, eds. (New York: Van Nostrand, 1954), pp. 82-124.

is reflected in a number of studies from the early research in laboratory groups to the more recent experimental studies in large organizations. Control has been shown to have implications for group cohesiveness, morale, and productivity;[6] it seems of importance as both a cause and an effect.

The study of control in unions is especially fruitful because of the great variety of practices encountered among the local and international unions in America. One can easily point to unions which exemplify democratic or, if one wishes, autocratic procedures. This great diversity of structural form offers a field for unlimited exploration and comparison. It also poses a serious problem, that of developing descriptive techniques which are capable of capturing some of the essential qualities of union organizations and which at the same time are amenable to standardization and replication.

We have attempted to meet this problem by developing a method of description which is both quantitative and conceptually meaningful. We have called it the "control graph." This scheme characterizes the control structure of an organization in terms of two axes.[7] The horizontal axis is based on a universal characteristic of formal organizations: the system of hierarchically defined ranks. This axis is designed to represent the various hierarchical levels, from low to high, in the organization. In many local unions, for example, the rank and file would be placed at the low end of this axis, and the president would be placed at the high end, with other officer groups (e.g., the executive board and the bargaining committee) at intervening levels. The vertical axis of the graph represents the amount of control over the organization's policies and actions that is exercised by each of the hierarchical levels. For example, a given level, conceivably, could have very little control in determining the policies and actions of the organization. This might be true of the rank and file in some locals or of the president in others. On the other hand, certain levels might be extremely influential in controlling the affairs of the organization. Again, this might be true of the rank and file, the president, *or* any combination of hierarchical levels. One can see that varying shapes of curve might be generated from these axes, depending on how much control is exercised by each of the hierarchical groups. Four simple prototypes will serve to illustrate the numerous possibilities. These are a few ideal types but by no means the most important

[6] See, e.g., Kurt Lewin, Ronald Lippitt, and Ralph K. White, "Patterns of Aggressive Behavior in Experimentally Created 'Social Climates,' " *Journal of Social Psychology,* 10 (May, 1939), 5-40; James C. Worthy, "Factors Influencing Employee Morale," *Harvard Business Review,* 28 (January, 1950), 61-73; and Nancy Morse and Everett Reimer, "The Experimental Change of a Major Organizational Variable," *Journal of Abnormal and Social Psychology,* 53 (January, 1956), 52, 120-129.

[7] A more detailed discussion of the control graph as a descriptive technique is presented in an article by Arnold S. Tannenbaum and Robert L. Kahn, "Organizational Control Structure: A General Descriptive Technique as Applied to Four Local Unions," *Human Relations,* 10 (May, 1957), 127-140.

theoretically. The graphs as a descriptive technique subsume them all while accounting at the same time for the many variations from these extremes.

1. *The democratic model*—This is a curve which rises (i.e., control increases) as one goes down the hierarchy. Groups at lower levels in the hierarchy (such as the rank and file) have more power than groups at higher levels (such as the executive board or the president).
2. *The autocratic or oligarchic model*—This is a curve which falls (i.e., control decreases) as one goes down the hierarchy.
3. *The laissez faire or anarchic model*—This is a curve which remains low (i.e., control is low) for all hierarchical levels. No one exercises much control.
4. *The polyarchic model*—This is a curve which remains high (i.e., control is high) for all hierarchical levels. All hierarchical groups have important influence in this type of organization.

The foregoing examples help illustrate the importance of two distinct aspects of control in organizations: *the distribution of control*, i.e., who or what hierarchically defined groups exercise control over the affairs of the organization, and the *total amount of control*, i.e., how much control is exercised within the organization, from all sources. The first is represented by the shape of the curve, the second by its average height. The one emphasizes the relative power of individuals and groups within the organization, while the other considers its absolute amount. Discussion of control in organizations has more often recognized the former. However, an understanding of control in unions requires an accounting not only of where control resides but of how much it all amounts to. Unions vary much more than do their industrial counterparts as to both these dimensions. Furthermore, locals which have the same distribution of control may differ markedly in the total amount of control. Similarly, in unions with the same total amount of control, the control may be distributed in quite different ways.

Several hypotheses are discussed later relating these dimensions of control to membership participation, to the ideology of the union, and to the extent to which the union engages in militant conflict with management. An organizational syndrome is suggested which relates control in the union to a larger pattern of variables, including organizational power, inter- and intra-organizational conflict, participation, loyalty, and conformity. While the limited sample of locals does not permit a definitive test of any of the hypotheses, the data are sufficiently suggestive to justify reporting.

Sample

This article is based on a study of four local unions, all of the industrial type. They are located in Michigan and include between 350 and 850 members. None of the officers is employed full time by the union. Since the study was initiated as an investigation of the factors affecting membership participation, locals were chosen which differ on this variable. Two locals, one high and one low in participation, are in each of two internationals. Differences in participation among the locals as judged by international officers were found to agree with our own measures, which include measures of meeting attendance (both regular and special), member activities at meetings (such as raising and seconding motions, asking questions, etc.), work on committees, and voting in union elections. The locals are assigned fictitious names and, in the order of their level of membership participation, are National, Sergeant, Ensign, and Walker. Sergeant is the largest of the locals, while Ensign is the smallest. The major findings reported here were obtained through paper-and-pencil questionnaires administered to a representative sample of about 150 members in each local. The rate of questionnaire returns averaged over 90 percent.

Control in the Four Locals

What picture do the control graphs present of the four locals? Four hierarchical levels were chosen to represent the possible loci of control within each of the locals. The horizontal axis was constructed by employing these hierarchical levels in the following order: (1) the president, (2) the executive board, (3) the plant bargaining committee, and (4) the rank-and-file membership. The amount of control exercised by each of these levels was ascertained through a series of parallel questions. In determining the amount of control exercised by the president, for example, the following question was employed: "In general, how much do you think the president has to say about how things are decided in this local?" Answers were checked on a five-point scale from 1, "He has no say at all," to 5, "He has a great deal of say." This question was repeated for the executive board, the plant bargaining committee, and the rank-and-file membership.[8]

Figure 5-1 presents the control curves based on the mean responses to these questions in each of the locals. Three of the curves approximate the prototypes discussed previously. National resembles the democratic model most closely, while Sergeant and Walker approach the polyarchic and laissez faire models, respectively. Ensign does not conform closely to any of the previously discussed prototypes, although the general slope of this curve is positive, with the membership having a relatively high level of control.[9]

---

[8] The ratings receive some support from observations of the locals as well as from statements of international officers. Further validation of the control graphs as a descriptive technique comes from their recent application in a study of industrial organizations. The curves found in these organizations differ markedly from those in the locals of the present study and, as expected, tend much more in the oligarchic direction.

[9] Statistical tests were performed to determine the significance of the differences in control between the various levels in each local. For example, in National, where the curve is steep, the membership has a significantly greater amount of control than each of the other groups; in Walker, where the curve is flat, none of the differences is significant (see Tannenbaum and Kahn, op. cit.).

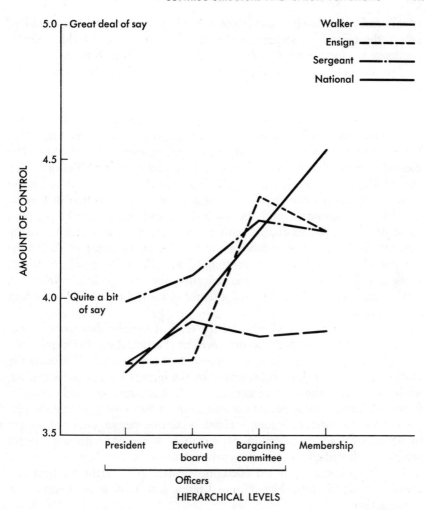

Figure 5-1.   Control Cures of Four Union Locals Based on Mean Scores of Rating on How Much Say Various Persons and Groups Have in How Things Are Decided in the Local. The Means Are Based on N's of About 150 in Each Local.

Walker and Sergeant, both characterized by relatively flat curves, represent locals differing sharply in their total amounts of control. As we shall see, this difference helps explain a number of other variations. On the other hand, while National and Sergeant are similar in total amount of control, the sources of power differ. In National the rank and file is the single, most powerful group. In Sergeant the bargaining committee ranks above the membership (although this difference is not statistically significant), and other levels follow close behind. When acting as a concerted group, the officers in Sergeant are extremely influential and can seriously challenge the members on many issues. This is unlikely in National.

In discussing some of the hypotheses suggested in the literature, we shall assume that the distribution of control, as represented in the control graph, provides an index of "democratic control." National is the most democratic local of the four, having a curve with the steepest average slope. The rank and file exercises more control in it than in any of the other locals. Ensign is second, having the next most positively sloped curve. The control exercised by its membership ranks second to that in National. Sergeant follows, having a less positively sloped curve. The amount of control exercised by the membership in this local is about equal to that in Ensign, but both the president and the executive board are relatively powerful there. Walker is ranked fourth, with a practically flat curve, and the members are the least powerful among the four locals. In terms of their total amount of control, the locals are ranked as follows: Sergeant, National, Ensign, and Walker. This index, reflecting the average height of curve, was obtained by simply adding the amount of control exercised by the four levels in each local.

Considering these rankings and the level of membership participation in the four locals, two facts become evident. Participation and democratic control, though not synonymous, appear to be correlated. National, the most democratic local, is characterized by the highest level of participation, while in Walker, the least democratic local, it is correspondingly low. Although this relationship seems obvious, another fact emerges which is perhaps of greater interest. Strong leadership control, per se, does not appear to be inimical to membership participation. Sergeant, with a powerful president (described by one international officer as an "autocrat") and with a strong executive board (described as part of a "tight political machine"), is significantly higher than Ensign and Walker in membership participation.

It would seem that the total amount of control as well as the distribution of control may be related in important ways to participation. Control reflects an active interest on the part of the controllers in the affairs of the local. Furthermore, control itself, if properly oriented, may be instrumental in mobilizing participation and conformity to union norms. In both National and Sergeant, the members are subject to greater pressures toward participation than are the members in either Ensign or Walker. If a member fails to attend a meeting, vote in a union election, or help out during a strike, he is more likely to hear about it in these relatively active locals. However, in Sergeant such pressures are more likely to originate with the leaders, while in National it is with the members themselves. In either event, whether administered by leaders or members, sanctions for failure to participate constitute a significant force in the direction of membership activity. The relationship of control to participation is illustrated by the relative rankings of the four locals in Table 5-7.

Table 5-7.
Rank Order of Locals on Participation and Control

	Membership Partici- pation	Democratic Control	Total Control	President	Officer Control Executive Board	Bargaining Committee
National	1	1	2	4	2	3
Sergeant	2	3	1	1	1	2
Ensign	3	2	3	3	4	1
Walker	4	4	4	2	3	4

Control and Ideology

Two hypotheses relating control to the goals or ideology of the union were suggested previously: (1) the greater the members' interest in broad and general social goals, the more democratic the union; and (2) the greater the members' interest in narrow and specific ("bread-and-butter") goals, the less democratic the union.

A number of questions were asked to determine the extent of member support for union goals of a relatively general social nature and those of a relatively narrow, bread-and-butter type. The former include a desire for the union to "work to improve the general welfare of all the people in the community," "increase its political action," and "support the international and other unions in organizing workers." The latter include a desire for the union to "try to get higher wages for the workers," "try to get better working conditions in the shop," and "work for better health, pension, and insurance benefits." In addition, two questions were asked concerning the extent to which the international union should spend time and money organizing non-union places and getting things for people already in the union. The former is included among the items representing an interest in relatively broad issues. The latter is treated with the bread-and-butter issues. Table 5-8 presents the rank order of the four locals as to democratic control and as to each of the items used to measure member support for "broad and general" goals.

National ranks first on all items, and, with one exception, Walker ranks fourth. The summary rank order appears to be correlated (though imperfectly) with the level of democratic control, thus lending tentative support to the hypothesis that democratic control will be related to member interest in broad social goals. It is of further interest to note that support for broad union goals corresponds perfectly in these locals with the level of membership participation. Although these data provide some support for

Table 5-8.

Rank Order of Locals As to Support by Members of Broad and
General Goals, and Level of Democratic Control

	Democratic Control	Union Should Work to Improve Welfare of Community	Union Should Increase Political Action	Union Should Support International in Unionizing	International Should Spend Money Unionizing Non-Union Places	Summ Rank All Br and Ge Item
National	1	1	1	1	1	1
Ensign	2	2	4	3	3	3
Sergeant	3	3	3	2	2	2
Walker	4	4	2	4	4	4

the hypothesis as stated, two qualifications appear in order. A general social orientation or ideology will be associated with strong internal democracy in a local union, provided that (1) the idealogy itself is not undemocratic (an ideology, however broad and general, however socially or politically oriented, will not be associated with democratic procedures if it emphasizes autocratic ideals); and (2) the ideology is not held as an absolute desideratum (absolute adherence to a set of ideas may be the basis for justifying undemocratic means; these ideals may conceivably become so important as to override all other considerations—including the maintenance of democratic procedures).[10]

Generally, however, if the ideology expresses a broad social responsibility and a general interest in the welfare of the larger society, it is very likely to exert an influence in the direction of increased membership control within the local. Such an ideological orientation may be particularly important for the officers. A philosophy or ideology may be necessary to sustain them, to enable them to sacrifice immediate goals for long-range ideas, to resist materialistic temptations, and to think in terms of altruistic purposes. Lack of social ideology on the part of persons in power may make them especially vulnerable to appeals to personal interests, to possible racketeering and corruption.

In contrast to the foregoing data, no relationship is evident between members' orientation toward immediate and specific goals for the union and democratic (or autocratic) control. Sergeant ranks first on a summary measure of these specific issues, while both Walker and National rank next. Ensign is last. These data suggest that while members of more democratic locals may tend to have a somewhat greater interest in broad and general union goals, they need not be less interested in bread-and-butter issues.

[10] See Merton's discussion of aberrant behavior as a function of overemphasis upon specific goals without a corresponding emphasis on institutional means (Robert K. Merton, *Social Theory and Social Structure* (New York: Free Press, 1949), Ch. IV).

Union-Management Conflict and Control

In addition to the ideology of the union, the extent of aggressive, union-management conflict is often considered a correlate of democratic control within the union. While we do not have a measure in the questionnaire of the unions' actual militancy toward management, personal observations of the four locals have been sufficiently intensive to permit a clear ranking of them in the following order: Sergeant, National, Ensign, and Walker. This ordering, however, does not correspond with the index of democratic control and does not support the original hypothesis. There is little indication in these data that militancy on the part of the union is related to the practice in that union of democratic control. However, another hypothesis is suggested: that connecting union-management conflict to the *total amount of control* exercised within the local. This relationship appears explicable in terms of two contrasting and perhaps contravening implications of union-management conflict. On the other hand, we have the suggestion that "continued . . . antagonism between corporations and unions prevents the latter from sinking into bureaucratic sloth. Merely to survive, the union must remain vital, democratic and militant."[11] Conflict will often activate an otherwise apathetic membership. On the other hand, conflict between social groups frequently leads to the restriction and not the expansion of internal freedom. In some instances the fact of external conflict is more rationalization than cause, and the abandonment of democratic procedures within an organization undergoing conflict may be justified "as a desperate measure to unify the union in time of economic distress and organizational disorder."[12] Nor is it completely unlikely that conflict may be manufactured by leaders as a means of consolidating power within an organization. Democratic control is sometimes seen as "inefficient" and as impeding the effectiveness of an organization in crisis, while control by the leaders is often explained as an expedient necessary to pull the union through periods of conflict and difficulty:

It is a question of whether you desire your organization to be the most effective instrumentality . . . or whether you prefer to sacrifice the efficiency of your organization in some respect for a little more academic freedom in the selection of some local representative . . . What do you want? Do you want an efficient organization or do you want merely a political instrumentality?[13]

Conformity within the union is considered a requirement of success in its struggle with management. The truth of this assertation might be

[11] Howe and Widick, *op. cit.*, p. 259.
[12] James A. Wechsler, *Labor Baron: A Portrait of John L. Lewis* (New York: Morrow, 1944), p. 80.
[13] John L. Lewis, quoted *ibid.*, p. 79.

questioned, but it is nevertheless believed by many; an international president observed: ". . . democracy does not come cheap: the price is a certain amount of confusion and disunity."[14] But "confusion and disunity" cannot always be tolerated during times of strife, and conflict with an outside enemy often has the effect of banishing them. Lines are drawn, a common purpose is accepted, and control is very likely to be increased. An organization under these conditions must be more highly regulated in order to survive. Common acceptance of this notion increases the amenability of members to the regulations of the organization.

However, viewing the issues in terms of the control graphs suggests that increased control need not be autocratic any more than it need be democratic. Interorganizational conflict may serve as an incentive for concentrating control in the hands of a few *or* for increasing the total amount of control in the organization in other ways. The important thing is that the organization be more tightly controlled. We are therefore led to the hypothesis that interorganizational strife will create an increase in total control—but not necessarily exerted at the top or at the bottom of the organization. The increased control may come primarily from the rank and file, it may come relatively more from the officers, or it may come from *both*. The distribution of this increased control is determined by other factors, among them, perhaps, the ideological orientation of the participants. We are suggesting, therefore, that while conflict may have a bearing on the shape of the control curve, its most predictable effect will be on the average height of this curve: conflict may be associated with a high degree of control either by members or by leaders, but it will almost invariably be associated with an increase in total control. The data of the present study, which reveal a direct correspondence between the extent of aggressiveness toward management and total control, provide support for this notion.

The Organizational Power Syndrome

The data discussed here have given tentative support to the hypotheses that the level of democratic control in a local is related to the members' interest in broad and general goals for the union and that the total amount of control is related to the extent of union-management conflict. We are led, however, to the further view that control in a union is part of a larger syndrome. A high level of control within the local and militant conflict with management is part of an organizational pattern characteristic of many strong and vital labor unions. Among the correlates of this syndrome we would expect the following variables: organizational power, total control, inter- and intra-organizational conflict, participation, loyalty, and conformity (see Table 5-9). The connections among these variables, of course,

---

[14] Paul L. Phillips, "Unions and Politics, Anglo-American Contrasts," *Nation*, **1529** (October 30, 1954), 382-384.

are not rigid and inexorable, but we would predict their association as a pattern. Furthermore, the effects of these variables may be reciprocal in some cases. This becomes evident when we consider further the union in conflict with its management. The union's success in achieving its goals is often contingent on its power—its ability to impose, or threaten the imposition of, sanctions. This power in turn depends partly on concerted member action and member readiness to "stand behind" their organization in the face of adversity, on conformity to union norms, and loyalty to its goals. The increased control created by conflict is an adjustment, instrumental to mobilization. It becomes directed partly toward co-ordinating member action and partly toward the internal administration of sanctions for breaches in union policy. It is an internal mechanism designed in part to bolster external power.

Table 5-9.

Rank Order of Locals on Variables in Organizational Power Syndrome

	Union Power	Total Control	Union-Management Conflict	Intra-local Conflict	Loyalty	Conformity	Partici-pation
Sergeant	1	1	1	1	1	1	2
National	2	2	2	2	2	2	1
Ensign	3	3	3	4	3	3	3
Walker	4	4	4	3	4	4	4

This increased control serves other functions for unions engaging in conflict with management: in a very real sense, there is *more to be controlled* during such periods. The repertory of union actions increases, committees become activated, decisions must be made concerning the dispensation of benefits anticipated or achieved from management. All this stimulates the interest and participation of the members—and they, too, may have to be controlled. Union policy becomes a day-to-day affair, changing with the tide of battle. New issues arise which require regulation; and, although the leaders are not likely to relinquish power during such periods, the members may increase theirs. They now want a say on issues which are of vital importance to them.

The loyalty of members is associated with this syndrome in a number of ways. Conflict creates, or at least arouses, the members' loyalty.[15] During times of conflict, danger to the union is more imminent and awareness of the union's importance to the members more apparent. Furthermore, a union "carrying on aggressive struggles" may be demonstrating its value to the members: it is attempting to derive benefits for them, and its

[15] See, e.g., William Becker, "Conflict as a Source of Solidarity," *Journal of Social Issues*, **9** (1953), 25-27.

success in this endeavor is likely to be a cause for satisfaction and loyalty. Thus the results of organizational power return ultimately to enhance this power. The adage that "nothing succeeds like success" is especially apparent in unions. To this extent, power can become its own mainstay.

Intra-organizational conflict is also expected as part of this syndrome.[16] The fact that there is greater involvement and activity and a correspondingly greater interest in control of the organization is likely to lead to some element of conflict within the local through which different interests and points of view are reconciled. In the extreme case of the "power centers," for example, "internal political rivalries between factional machines are likely to be intense because the stakes in the struggle over power are so large."[17] Furthermore, this internal conflict may contribute to the intensity of the conflict between the union and its management. Under these circumstances "each side may be committed before the bargaining starts to programs which stem from protracted discussions and expedient compromises of conflicting viewpoints within its own group. There is usually an absence of flexibility, therefore, in the joint union-management decision making process. This fact makes agreement much more difficult."[18]

Finally, we might consider the relation of member conformity to some of the other elements of the syndrome. The existence of conformity is contingent upon the (formal and informal) definitions of rules and policies around which uniformity is to take place. Control implies the formulation of such rules (legislative control) and the regulation of behavior in accord with these rules (administrative and sanctions control).[19] The possible receipt of criticism or punishment for failure to adhere to the rules of an organization is an effective force toward uniformity. A high level of total control, therefore, leads to a greater degree of order and uniformity in an organization. Control creates conformity. Second, external conflict develops an ostensible need for unity. Members are willing to sacrifice and conform in a crisis who otherwise might be less subject to the influence of the union. Conflict justifies uniformity. Third, loyalty motivates the member to support the rules, standards, and policies of the organization. The loyal member *wants* to adhere to organizational norms. He wants to do what is "right" for the organization. Loyalty fortifies uniformity. Finally, participation has a bearing on conformity. It is through participation that the member comes into contact with organizational norms, sees what is "right"

[16] Although factionalization of intra-organizational conflict may imply special subgroup loyalties within the union, these need not contravene the loyalty of the members to the union itself. On the contrary, such intra-union affiliations may serve to arouse greater loyalty among the participants to the larger organization. Lipset has observed this phenomenon in the ITU (personal communication).

[17] F. H. Harbison and R. Dubin, *Patterns of Union Management Relations* (New York: Science Research Associates, 1947), pp. 185-186.

[18] *Ibid.*, p. 186.

[19] Nancy C. Morse, Everett Reimer, and Arnold S. Tannenbaum, "Regulation and Control in Hierarchical Organizations," *Journal of Social Issues*, 7 (1951), 41-48.

and what is "wrong," and learns what is required of him. He himself may also help set the norms. Participation thus expedites uniformity.

In the preceding material are outlined briefly some of the interconnections among the variables in the organizational power syndrome. The dimension of total control is one aspect of this larger pattern. Table 5-9 presents the rank order of the four locals on each of the items discussed. Measures are available in the questionnaire for each, exclusive of union-management conflict and organizational power.[20] For measures of these, reliance is placed on personal observations of the locals, in addition to general comments of international and company officials as well as comments of members. For example, Sergeant which is ranked first in power, is widely recognized as "carrying a hell of a lot of weight," as one regional director of another international described it. The personnel manager at the Sergeant plant also recognized its power and militancy when he pointed out, philosophically, that the union "keeps management on its toes."

In contrast, the weakness of Walker, the least powerful among the four locals, is evident to all who know it; a field representative commented: "If the company wanted to take advantage, they could make the people live hard here." An old-timer expressed his disillusionment with the effectiveness of this local: "We feel that it's not what it used to be. . . . Nothing happens to grievances. You can't find out what happens to them —they get lost. . . . The (bargaining) committee doesn't fight any more."

Summary

The control graph illustrates the importance of two distinct aspects of control in organizations: the distribution of control and the total amount of control. Variations on these dimensions are hypothesized to relate to other aspects of union functioning, including membership participation, the expressed ideology of the members, and conflict with management. A

[20] Intra-organizational conflict was measured through an index of three questions: "Do these (groups within the local) disagree on most matters or only a few?" "Do these groups have leaders who speak up for them?" "When these groups disagree, how much do you find yourself taking sides?"

Loyalty, similarly, was measured by three items: "Suppose the union went through a strike which so weakened it that it was in real danger of folding up. How much would you be willing to do about it?" "Suppose that there was so much disagreement within the local that it was in real danger of folding up. How much would you be willing to do about it?" "If the local went out on strike, how willing would you be to do picket duty?"

Uniformity within the local was measured as the inverse of variance on a number of items chosen as a priori to reflect union norms. These items include perceived norms about voting, attending meetings, and helping out on strikes; the likelihood of sanctions against members for failure to perform these functions; the intensity of member involvement in the union; and the alacrity with which members utilize union channels for the expression of grievances.

A more detailed discussion of these measures is to appear in a forthcoming book by A. S. Tannenbaum and R. L. Kahn.

broader syndrome of variables is suggested, including a number of determinants and implications of control. These include union power, intra- as well as inter-organizational conflict, membership loyalty, particpation, and conformity.

29. Leadership in a Local Union

Joel Seidman
Jack London
Bernard Karsh

I. Introduction

The local union, with its group of leaders and active members, is the basic unit of the American labor movement. Although current academic and popular interest centers upon the national leadership of important national unions or federations, to the fifteen million organized workers of the country their national union is a distant source of power and the federation with which the national union is affiliated is little more than an abstraction. The union experiences of the member are in the local union, which is one of between sixty-five and seventy-five thousand locals in the country. The officers who mean most to him are those who manage the affairs of his local union, together with the grievance man or steward who represents the union in his department.

The leaders in these locals are often unknown beyond the ranks of their members and the companies with which they bargain, but they constitute the backbone of the labor movement, influence the attitudes of members and employers toward it, and shape its functions to a significant extent. Who are these leaders? How and why did they join the union and become active in it? What do they think they accomplish? What is their conception of the accomplishments of the union, and why, in their judgment, do some workers refuse to join? Would it matter to them if their union disappeared?

In an effort to find preliminary answers to these and related questions the authors undertook to study, as a pilot project, a local union of the United Steelworkers of America. This study, which is part of a larger project carried on by the authors at the Industrial Relations Center of the University of Chicago, is concerned with the orientation or attitudes of local union members at three levels of participation—leaders, active rank-and-file members, and inactive members. A comprehensive interview guide was constructed, with the aid of an interdisciplinary committee,[1] to include

Reprinted from *American Journal of Sociology*, **56** (November, 1950), 229-237.

[1] The interdisciplinary committee was composed of faculty members from sociology, economics, political science, human development, industrial relations, and the social science staff of the College of the University of Chicago.

questions on the union, the employer, the community, and family and organizational background.

The United Steelworkers of America local selected for study has a reputation for militancy. It has about fourteen thousand members, all employed in a midwestern integrated steel mill. The mill produces finished steel products, which are then fabricated by other companies. Between the local union and the steel company there is conflict and suspicion. The authors selected this local because the local was large enough to raise problems with regard to significant differences in orientation between the leaders and rank-and-file members; the union bargained with a company where policy was made locally—a bargaining relationship in which a high degree of autonomy was enjoyed by both parties; and a great deal of co-operation was offered by the officers of the local. Finally, the plant was readily accessible to university investigators.

The local union has thirteen officers and twenty-one grievance committeemen, or "grievers" (four of whom are also officers at present), elected biennially. To these thirty officials were added chairmen of key committees and past presidents, to form a group of thirty-six leaders. Thirty of these thirty-six have been interviewed,[2] and the material thus gathered has been supplemented by observation of virtually all types of local activities over eleven months. The authors also had the advantage of frequent conversations with the leaders and active rank-and-file members. This paper summarizes and analyzes the responses of the leaders in this one local to a few significant questions in the interview.

Out of the total of one hundred and nineteen questions, eight were selected for analysis in this paper. Taken as a whole, the responses to these eight questions reveal the concept of unionism held by a group of local leaders. Two of the questions relate to the circumstances under which the leader joined the union and to his judgment of the reasons why some workers refuse to join. Two other questions relate to union activity, one on how the leader happened to become active and the other on what keeps him active. Two questions deal with the achievements of the union as viewed by its leaders. Finally, two questions inquire into the leaders' opinions and feelings with regard to the disappearance of the union. These questions de-

---

[2] The union leaders were interviewed at the union hall or at any other place convenient to them. Some interviews were held at home, some in bars, some on picket lines. Inactive members, however, were interviewed at their homes, unless they suggested the union hall. An effort was made to interview each person in an environment to which he was accustomed, in the belief that rapport is more readily established there and that more honest and revealing answers are given. The interviewers were careful to avoid showing disapproval, by word or gesture, of any attitude expressed. Everyone interviewed was assured that all material would be kept confidential and that his identity would not be revealed to anyone. The interviews averaged from one to four hours in length, the most frequent length being between one and a half and two hours. Notes were taken during the interview and were written up as quickly afterward as was possible under the circumstances.

fine the role that the union plays in the lives of its leaders, the reasons given for joining and becoming active, the leaders' conception of the local's accomplishments, and the importance to them of the continued existence of the union.

II. Joining the Union

The circumstances under which a worker joins a union suggests his initial orientation toward unionism. Those interviewed were asked, "How did you happen to join local _____?" and, later in the interview, "Why do you think some refuse to join?" In response to the earlier question, an overwhelming majority of the leadership group reported themselves sympathetic to unions prior to the organization of the local at the plant.[3] Twenty-two out of twenty-eight[4] joined the union when the original organizing efforts were made at the mill, some because of family background, earlier work experience or union membership, or their experiences at the plant under nonunion conditions. These men had independently become union sympathizers. They were among the earliest to join, and many of them helped to organize the workers in their departments.

Sometimes conditions in general were responsible, sometimes a particular experience. Illustrative of the former was the statement, "After only two or three days I caught on to the setup, and I didn't like it. The men were being pushed around a lot. The only way to get some action was to join the union and start beefing about conditions." With others, union interest began with some unpleasant incident:

We were having trouble with oil in our furnace. I found out what was the matter and told them what do do. The superintendent walked up and started questioning me and told me that maybe I did it on purpose because I corrected the trouble at once. A helper helped me argue, and he asked me to join the union because I had guts enough to argue with a superintendent. They made me a steward as soon as I joined.

Another leader became a union member after he was discharged for what he considered a minor offense.[5]

Typically, then, the leader of this local joined the union when it was

[3] In evaluating these responses, the possibility must be borne in mind that a leader, with the best of intentions, may no longer be able to report accurately how he happened to join the union. The passage of from five to fifteen years may have blurred his memory or have led to a rationalization or idealization of his conduct consistent with his conception of himself as a union leader.

[4] The reason that a varying number of leaders answered the questions is that not all leaders gave usable answers. The authors added and revised questions during the initial stage of their study. Time did not permit re-interviewing of those who were not asked the questions subsequently added to our interview guide.

[5] At the time of this incident a worker discharged in one department could secure a job in another part of the mill under different supervision.

organized and was instrumental in getting other workers to join. He was sympathetic to unionism before entering the company's employ or became a union sympathizer because of his experiences there. Sympathetic persons such as these are to be found in virtually any unorganized plant in this country, and the success of an organizing effort largely depends upon the union's ability to discover them and to persuade them to accept union leadership.

Only six of the leaders held no pro-union convictions at the time the union started. One was convinced he should join the union by the argument that it was hopeless to expect improvement through individual effort: "I heard the fellows talk about it in the mill. They were all saying that you can't get any place by yourself, but you have to get the guys together, and then maybe you can do something."

A significant minority joined under pressure. Some did not believe in unions at the time, and still others were simply ignorant of them. "I didn't know anything about the union," one stated; "I suppose I joined in order to jump in line with the majority to say I was a union member. It didn't mean much to me at that time." Finally, there was a leader who joined, despite his opposition to the union, in response to a suggestion from his foreman, whose interest was in uninterrupted production:

Personally, I joined in one of the dues-inspection lines.[6] . . . I didn't think the union was very good. I felt that they were a bunch of radicals stirring up a lot of trouble. . . . To tell you the truth, one of the foremen convinced us to join because everybody else was joining. A couple of times I climbed over the fence to get into the mill. The foreman said that instead of holding men out of the plant, we might as well join and get our production going.

Later in the interview we asked the leaders, "Why do you think some refuse to join?" None of the union leaders pointed to defects in the union or to practices of its leaders in their explanations. The largest group of reasons related to the antiunion environment surrounding many and the antiunion propaganda to which the workers had been exposed. One leader explained: "I think some of them are sincere in their principles in thinking that the union is no good. Others don't belong because they just don't think it's right, without analyzing it. Some think we are a bunch of reds and not fit to associate with. Some may be management-oriented through family ties . . . I think they shy away from anything so radical, and they are conservative." A major reason was that some could not afford, or did not want to pay, dues. As one leader put it: "There are free-riders who don't want to pay $2.00. If membership were voluntarily available to members without dues, we would have 100 per cent. If it was voluntary but with dues, we

---

[6] The dues-inspection line is a device employed by this local to exert pressure upon nonunion workers to join the union. The local maintains pickets for three or four days, who demand that workers entering the mill show their union membership cards. Nonmembers must join in order to get into the mill. Many active members and leaders joined in this way, including a former president of the local.

would have only 6 per cent. With dues inspection and pressure, we have 98.7 per cent."[7]

Others agreed that some men were sympathetic to management and hoped to get better jobs by keeping out of the union.[8] Some workers expected to stay in the mill only a short time; some had belonged to unions elsewhere without receiving benefits and were therefore disillusioned; a few men were "rugged individualists"; and certain workers had religious objections to unionism.

Several of the leaders held very unflattering opinions of the present and future value to the union of nonunionists. One who believed that the union had no choice but to compel them to join stated: "Some don't join because they are too cheap; some are company stooges who think that they can get ahead faster by not joining the union. Those people aren't any damn good anyway, but we have to force them in the union because it makes us stronger with the company."

It is important to note that those who joined under pressure of the dues-inspection line or who signed cards without conviction when requested to do so have become as ardent unionists as those who joined because of prior conviction. The authors have been unable to find any relationship between the circumstances of joining, so far as those now in positions of leadership are concerned, and their subsequent behavior and activity as leaders. This suggests that the circumstances of joining a union become relatively unimportant where the union's method of operation, the status it achieves, or the pressure of events leads people to take an active part in its affairs.

III. Becoming Active

To understand why members become active in an organization is of crucial importance in the study of all types of formal and informal organizations and groups. It offers some insight into the selection process which determines leadership and affects, to some extent, the kind of policies pursued by the organization. Of course, in supplying information, the leaders may reinterpret circumstances and motives for becoming active in the light of their subsequent experience.

The local union leaders were asked, "How did you happen to become active?" The interview data, supplemented by observation of the local and its leaders, provides the following reasons:[9] (1) resentment against treat-

---

[7] Actually, the membership in 1949-50 was about 95 percent.

[8] However, other evidence shows that a large number of leaders believe that the company now gives preference to union members in selecting foremen.

[9] Repeated conversations with union leaders and active rank-and-file members which tended to validate the responses obtained in interviews formed the basis of the rationale for the list. This list with some changes might apply to other labor organizations and even to organizations outside the labor movement. The sixth and seventh points listed are based partly or entirely upon observation.

ment by managerial personnel; (2) dissatisfaction with working conditions or wages; (3) failure to receive desired or expected promotions; (4) lack of other available leaders; (5) prior union sympathy; (6) desire to obtain personal power, recognition, or financial gain; and (7) unsatisfactory marital or home experience.

Of those who said that company treatment had made them active, one explained that it was a denial, after he had participated in the 1937 strike, of promotions that he thought were due. Another leader stated that he was discharged for what he considered a very minor offense and that he thereupon decided to become active in the union, then being organized. Another stated that it was working conditions, and with another it was the frequency with which workers were short in their pay.

Treatment by the foreman was another of the reasons assigned: "I was always the kind of a guy who didn't want anyone to jump down my throat all the time. Before the union came in, they (the foremen) did that in the mill." Sometimes a belief that the foreman is discriminating against members of minority groups leads the latter to become active in the union: "I had a foreman who was discriminating, had prejudice against my religion. He refused to recognize my seniority, and I wanted to be part of the union to settle it; and I succeeded."

A group of seven became "unwilling" leaders. As one leader put it: "When I came here in '45, we had a griever that drank a lot and was never around when you needed him. He was always off the job drunk somewhere. We couldn't get anything done, and conditions were piling up. The guys in the department asked me if I would take the job, and I told them 'Yes.' So they elected me."

In other cases the initiative was taken by the present leader, but only after he and others had become thoroughly dissatisfied with the performance of the previous officer. In some instances the present officer sought originally to persuade someone else to accept responsibility: "I wasn't satisfied with the work the previous griever was doing, so I went around and tried to get someone else to run for the job. I didn't want it, but as I went around, everybody encouraged me to run, and I've been a griever since."

Those who stated that they were pushed into leadership probably were not unduly modest. In the early stages of organization, especially when no political machine has as yet taken form and few persons are well known throughout the plant, anyone who shows any capacity for leadership may find himself pushed into office. This may be true even after the local has achieved a recognized status, since the stratum of leadership or potential leadership available in the plant is very thin. This may be due partly to barriers of language or education, partly to the fact that a steel mill will probably attract proportionately fewer energetic and able persons than more desirable places of employment. Not all workers with leadership ability, obviously, are interested in union activity, whether because of lack of conviction, conflicting interests, or family responsibilities. Whatever the reason, the number of competent persons available for union office in this local is very limited, considering the size of the membership; consequently, a worker with the ability to lead who shows an interest in the union may rise quickly to a position of influence and may find that the union office seeks him rather than the reverse. The Steelworkers have a requirement that a candidate for local office must have attended half the meetings during the previous year, except when he is working or is engaged in other union business. This often results in only one or two persons being eligible to run for office in a department of some hundreds.

In addition to the somewhat larger groups who became active in the union because of the company's treatment of its employees or because of the inadequacy of the persons holding office, there were some who traced their activity to their beliefs in unionism acquired before entering the company's employ. The father of one of these leaders had been active in his union and also in the Socialist movement. Another, whose father had been active in the United Mine Workers, said, "I attended union meetings with my father before I was ever inside a church." Others referred to the interests of the working class, a sympathy for the underdog, or experience with union benefits in another plant as explanations.

The union leaders were asked, "What keeps you active—what do you get out of it?" More than half listed the desire to win improvements for their fellow-workers as a reason. "I get satisfaction in seeing that people get what they should," was a typical response. One of the Mexicans said, "It gives me a chance to do something for my people. As a griever, I can make sure that we continue to fight discrimination."

Seven of the leaders spoke of the feeling of power that their office gave them or of the pleasure of recognition. Often this feeling of power was associated with the opportunity to treat supervisors as they had once been treated by them. As one expressed it: "I get a chance to rub it into the supervision when they make a false step. I feel that it's up to the active people to keep the company on the ball. It gives me a feeling of satisfaction that they can't get away with what they did before the union came in."

Another referred to the sense of power he enjoyed in the internal politics of the union, and two others spoke of their recognition by the company or of their prestige with their fellow-workers.

None admitted that the desire to get pay for union services helped make him active, though one stated frankly that his supplementary income from the union helped keep him active. Some leaders, less charitable in describing the motives of others, pointed out to us persons who, they said, were primarily interested in getting on the union pay roll. Particularly was this likely to be true in the case of factional enemies. Likewise, we did not discover one person who entered the company's employ with the intent to become a union leader, though we suspect that this happens in some cases.

When a union achieves recognition and status, it attracts persons who seek the prestige and power of office. There may be such among the leaders of this local union who may by now really believe in a more idealistic motivation of their earlier views and activities. Similarly, we found no evidence or expressed belief that any of the leaders became active because some other organization to which they belonged—for example, a left-wing political group—sought through their activity to increase its influence in the union. We do know that certain of the leaders, now or in the past, have been identified with one or another such group, and we suspect that a desire to extend its influence or to influence union policy in the direction it desired may have been a factor in some cases. Such persons, obviously, would be very unlikely to admit this to others, especially to outsiders.

IV. Accomplishments of the Union

The authors sought to discover the leaders' conception of the accomplishments of the local union. In all cases we found a high degree of identification on the part of the leaders with the local and a belief that it had very substantial achievements to its credit. The main achievements of the local, as they saw them, are improvement in wages and working conditions, including the winning of job security through a seniority system and a voice in the determination of conditions of employment; increased respect for and better treatment of workers; and progress toward elimination of discrimination against minority groups.

Over half of the leaders mentioned wages. A number listed improved working conditions, either in general or in specific terms, such as safety, showers, toilet facilities, or lockers. Several stressed the increased respect won for workers or their loss of fear, and others listed the grievance machinery, the seniority system, and the greater equality of treatment now given workers.

Typical of those who emphasized the human aspects of union accomplishments was the leader who said: "The union knocked the fear out of the workers. They're no more afraid. They used to be like slaves, used to do everything the company wanted. You had to, or you got thrown out." Others stressed the respect that now had to be shown workers, one of them asserting that in the pre-union days "the worker wasn't even considered as a human being."

One who had been active in the affairs of the local since its formation summarized its achievements in this way:

One of the biggest and most fundamental things is that it has given the workingman a voice in the conditions of employment. Before the union came in, a man could get fired for little or nothing, as telling the boss that he was wrong on something. The atmosphere was if you don't do everything the boss said, out you go. Also, wages have been increased on various jobs, and now we have

seniority in promotions. Before the union came in, the company had no established seniority system; it moved men as it saw fit. The same was true in layoffs. The bosses gave some consideration to seniority, but there was no established policy. Now seniority governs for promotion, with a thirty-day tryout.

Another leader gave this picture of the local's gains:

Before the union, a man would be laid off by favoritism or how much the men
paid off in vegetables or in getting foremen drunk on payday. Working conditions changed 100 per cent. Men had to work in water or lose their jobs; now
the union would shut the mill down before allowing that to happen. . . . Now
the company has to negotiate with the union before changing (incentive) rates.
Formerly, if the mill didn't work nineteen turns in a row, the men's bonus
would be cut in half. Now they can't cut the men's bonus unless the union
agrees. You don't have to go out and kill yourself any more. The men don't
compete with each other like they used to.

To secure elaboration of the accomplishments of the local and further
understanding of why leaders remain active, persons interviewed were asked,
"Do you feel that the union has done anything for you personally?" All the
leaders answered in the affirmative. Some made such comments as "They
have done for me what they have done for everybody else" or "It's helped
every man. Regardless of whether he thinks so or not, he's been helped."

Members of minority groups, notably Negroes, Mexicans, and Jews,
proved very alert to instances of discrimination, whether these represented
company policy or the act of some prejudiced minor supervisor. Their reaction to the union was conditioned largely by the effect of unionism upon
their group. Negro and Mexican leaders were attracted to the union largely
because it promised greater security for them, because it forced supervisors
to treat them with more respect, and because they resented prejudiced
treatment of members of their group. Said one: "It (the union) moved me
up on the job I've got now. I got the job through the union. Before I became a _____, a Negro had to work here twenty years before he'd even
be considered for the job." Another, speaking of the improved working
conditions won for all, regardless of race, creed, or color, added: "I have
been able to be respected by supervision. They have had to come up to me
and respect me, which is a wonderful thing, since I'm a Mexican. In the
old days, they would say, 'Hey you!' Now they ask you civilly."

Only one of the leaders mentioned any disadvantages offsetting the
gains he had enjoyed because of the union:

Personally, the union did me a lot of harm. It took all my time—five years of
solid work and five more years of relaxed effort, all of this while my family was
growing up. All the same, the union has given me the personal satisfaction of
building an organization very necessary to our form of government—of, by,
and for the people. The union enabled me to get my just due in regard to jobs
I asked for. The union has created a condition where I could stand up and
have my say, without fear that I was endangering my job as in the past.

V. Importance of the Union

The leaders' opinion of the probable consequence of the disappearance of the union was investigated. The leaders' close identification with the union discussed in Section IV was affirmed, with a complete acceptance of the union as a way of life significantly illustrated. The authors asked, "Would it make any difference to you if local _____ disappeared? Why?" All the leaders replied that it would make a great difference. Over half stated that they would be discharged immediately, and others implied that they would leave voluntarily. A considerable number asserted that conditions of employment would deteriorate rapidly to the pre-union level.

The local leader believes that his own personal security depends on the continued existence of the union. All who felt that they would be discharged at once if the union disappeared believed that their union activity would be the cause. As one put it, "I would be the first to be kicked out. I have been behind the 8-ball since 1940. Too much activity." Another, who compared the disappearance of the union with the world coming to an end in the mill, stated: "They're trying every way they can to get rid of me now —even trying to make me a foreman, no less." Still another was afraid that he would be blacklisted; if the local disappeared, he said: "I would get fired tomorrow. To be truthful, I don't think I could get a job in any other steel mill. I know they keep a record of all the grievers and the trouble they cause. . . . They wanted to fire me in _____, but the men threatened to shut the mill down if I was fired, and they didn't."

Thus the officer protects his own job by building the power of the union and seeking to extend its control. Similarly, the union leader may refuse offers of promotion to foreman, since that would take him out of the bargaining unit, deny him union protection, and permit the company to discharge him for past union activity. The wife of one union leader, who was present during the interview, said of her husband, who had refused a promotion to be foreman: "He fights for the union too much and never could be a company man. The only reason they want to make him a foreman is so they could fire him a couple of weeks later. And I wouldn't stand for his being a foreman, anyhow. The union is his life—not the company."

Those who declared that conditions would quickly return to the pre-union standards listed wage cuts, speedups, arbitrary discharges, loss of security, favoritism instead of seniority, discrimination, and dictatorial rule by foremen among the evils that they foresaw. One compared the disappearance of the union to the imposition of slavery. Another said that it would be "like losing the war, losing the country." A typical response was that "union men would be discharged, working conditions would drop, guys would be pushed—more production, less wages. Bosses would rule with an iron hand like before, even more than before." One said, "I'd be lost.

I wouldn't know where to turn to." Said another, "With me, the organization (the union) is what would be a religion to other fellows."

Asked whether they thought the disappearance of the union would make any difference to others, all the leaders again answered in the affirmative, the majority stating explicitly or implicitly that the local's disappearance would matter to everybody and an additional large group stating that the majority would be concerned.

One leader felt that any threat to the union would create an upsurge of membership activity: "I think that if the men in the mill were led to believe that the union would disappear tomorrow, they would be up here in a body tonight, to try to keep it going." Another thought that, while it would matter to everyone if the union disappeared, the older union members would be affected first: "To the old-timers, it would be a terrible thing. To the younger people in the mill, they wouldn't realize it at first, but in a short time they would also be behind the 8-ball."

Other comments were: "We would go back to the conditions in the old days, and nobody would like that except the stooges"; "As little interested in the activity of the union as most members are, they still want a union"; "About 90 per cent of the rank-and-file feel the same way I do. I've talked to them and they know what would happen if the corporation destroyed the union. In fact, life wouldn't be worth living in the mill."

A Mexican said, "My people wouldn't have any good jobs like before," and another leader declared that ". . . the colored and the Mexican boys would be out in a short time if they didn't have a union. Why, right now there are eight hundred applications for jobs on file in the company office. And all from white boys with high-school education. The only reason they aren't getting jobs is because the union won't let the company fire the colored and Mexicans. They wouldn't last a minute here without the union."

Such viewpoints further reveal that the union has become a way of life, serving the needs of its members apart from, and in addition to, the reasons that initially brought it into existence. Convictions such as those reported by the leaders under scrutiny make it appear certain that the union is here to stay.

Concluding Note

In this article we have sought to discover the concept of unionism held by a group of leaders of a local union. To understand unionism in our modern urban, industrial society it is necessary to know why leaders join a union, why they become active, and what role the organization plays in their lives. The authors hope that their study, now under way, of the rank-and-file active and inactive members of this same local will yield significant points of comparison and of contrast with the leaders' concept of the union. The authors then plan to apply similar techniques of investigation to several other local unions, chosen because of variations in size or bargaining relationship, to see what similarities or differences will emerge. They hope, moreover, that the questions they raise will encourage other students to engage in like investigations so that a reliable and systematic body of knowledge about local labor organizations may be accumulated.

30. Union Member Orientations and Patterns of Social Integration

William H. Form

H. K. Dansereau

A persistent problem in the study of organizational behavior concerns the degree to which members assimilate the various goals of an organization. Although mere membership does not necessarily signify general endorsement of all organizational purposes, the degree of such endorsement is a valid indication of organizational vitality. The labor union is an association, ideally suited to the study of organizational involvement. Typically it has various manifest goals or functions: the improvement of economic status, protection from arbitrary management rule, provision of fraternal associations, the offering of a political program. The degree to which one of these functions is emphasized at the expense of others partially reflects the concerns of the membership. The social heterogeneity of the membership usually reduces the possibility of complete consensus on all organizational purposes. Thus the typical situation is one in which most members vary in their endorsements of the several organizational goals, while others are apathetic toward some goals, if not actually hostile toward the union itself.

While considerable research has been done on membership participation,[1] few studies have investigated differential involvement of members with alternative goals of unionism. The research reported here is premised on the assumption that various functions of labor unions have differential appeals to different types of members and that different orientations toward the union may be related to the social characteristics of a heterogeneous membership.

Scholars agree that trade unions have three or four main functions.[2]

William H. Form and H. Kirk Dansereau, "Union Members Orientations and Patterns of Social Integration," *Industrial and Labor Relations Review*, Vol. II, No. 1 (October, 1957), pp. 3-12.

[1] See especially Daisy L. Tagliacozzo, "Trade-Union Government, Its Nature and Its Problems, A Bibliographical Review, 1945-55," *American Journal of Sociology*, 61 (May, 1956), 554-581; Bernard Barber, "Participation and Mass Apathy in Associations," in Alvin W. Gouldner, ed., *Studies in Leadership* (New York: Harper & Row, 1950), pp. 477-504.

[2] Some of these studies are reviewed in Delbert C. Miller and William H. Form, *Industrial Sociology* (New York: Harper & Row, 1951). Studies specifically concerned with types of union officers and members include: Daisy L. Tagliacozzo and Joel Seidman, "A Typology of Rank and File Union Members," *American Journal of Sociology*,

Although classifications of functions differ in detail, three general functions are commonly listed: (a) improvement of wages and economic security, (b) protection from arbitrary management rule, and (c) the provision of fraternal and social contacts. These functions, abbreviated as economic, political, and social, may be internalized by members as *orientations* toward unions.[3]

Theoretically these functions may be internalized in different ways: (a) they may have equal salience for given types of members, (b) they may be arranged in different kinds of priority for different groups, (c) they may have no salience for some members, or (d) they may be rejected by some as not being legitimate organizational functions.[4] Further, the degree of involvement with a given organizational purpose or a number of such purposes may vary from low to high, and the translation of involvement into action may also vary. The research reported here is based on the assumption that local union members tend to have one dominant orientation toward union functions.

Hypotheses

Four main hypotheses guide the research. The first was that type of union orientation is related to the degree of union participation. Specifically, those socially oriented toward the union would be most active, followed by the political, economic, apathetic, and hostile orientational types. Theoretically, since the socially oriented have integrated the union into their way of life, they should be most active. The politically oriented, concerned with the struggle with management on various fronts, should also be highly involved with the union. The economic orientation is functionally more specific and may call for less participation. Since apathetic members, by definition, are not involved with union goals, they should be less active. Hostile members should be inactive since they see the union as interfering with their life patterns.

The second hypothesis is that the degree of union participation is positively related to the degree of integration of the member in such other areas as the plant, neighborhood, and community.

---

61 (May, 1956), 546-553; Eli Chinoy, "Local Union Leadership," in Gouldner, *op. cit.*, pp. 153-173; John W. Alexander and Morroe Berger, "Grass Roots Labor Leader," in Gouldner, *op. cit.*, pp. 174-186; Toimi E. Kyllonen, "Social Characteristics of Active Unionists," *American Journal of Sociology*, 56 (May, 1951), 528-533; Lois R. Dean, "Social Integration, Attitudes, and Union Activity," *Industrial and Labor Relations Review*, 8 (October, 1954), 48-58; George Strauss and Leonard R. Sayles, "Patterns of Participation in Local Unions," *Industrial and Labor Relations Review*, 6 (October, 1952), 31-43.

[3] For a discussion of value orientation, see Robert K. Merton, "Patterns of Influence," in Paul F. Lazarsfeld and Frank N. Stanton, *Communications Research; 1948-49* (New York: Harper & Row, 1949).

[4] The hostile member may perceive the union's functions as economic, political, and/or social, but he rejects the right of the union to assume these functions for him.

Third, type of union orientation is associated with the degree of integration of the member to plant, neighborhood, and the community.[5] The underlying proposition here is that wage workers are not homogeneous in their "social class" references.[6] It has been observed that some workers are identified with the "working class," others are identified with the "middle class," while still others appear to have no observable identifications. Those oriented toward the working class tend to have diffuse social interests which involve interpersonal relations which are most commonly found in *local* associations, such as the union, plant, and neighborhood. Workers identified with middle status groups are more specifically concerned with individual economic mobility. They prefer to cut their local and personal ties and become associated with broader community interests, commonly identified with middle status groups.[7]

In accord with this reasoning, those with a social orientation toward the union should be most integrated with plant and the neighborhood, but not with the wider community.[8] The politically oriented should follow the same pattern, but be somewhat more concerned with community associations. Those with an economic orientation, and especially those hostile toward the union, should be less involved with the plant and neighborhood and more involved in community-wide activities. Apathetics should display low involvement in all areas studied.

The fourth hypothesis is that differences in union orientations may be partly related to different community backgrounds and occupational career patterns of a socially heterogeneous membership.

Research Site

The field work for this study was done in 1953 and 1954 in Lansing, Michigan, a middle-sized city of almost a hundred thousand. Automobile manu-

---

[5] This research hypothesis grew out of a wider concern with problems of how urban dwellers become socially anchored in the allegedly impersonal and anonymous character of city life. See William H. Form, Joel Smith, Gregory P. Stone, and James D. Cowhig, "The Compatability of Alternative Approaches to the Delimitation of Urban Sub-Areas," *American Sociological Review*, **19** (August, 1954), 434-440; Joel Smith, William H. Form and Gregory P. Stone, "Local Intimacy in a Middle-sized City," *American Journal of Sociology*, **60** (November, 1954), 276-284.

[6] For earlier discussions of reference groups, see Herbert H. Hyman, "The Psychology of Status," *Archives of Psychology*, **269** (1942); and Alice S. Kitt, "Contribution to the Theory of Reference Groups Behavior," in Robert K. Merton and Paul F. Lazarsfeld, eds., *Studies in the Scope and Method of "The American Soldier"* (New York: Free Press, 1950).

[7] These observations are derived from the literature on social stratification. See, among others, Alfred Winslow Jones, *Life, Liberty and Property* (Philadelphia: Lippincott, 1941); Richard Centers, *The Psychology of Social Classes* (Princeton, N.J.: Princeton University Press, 1949); W. Lloyd Warner and Paul S. Lunt, *The Social Life of a Modern Community* (New Haven: Yale University Press, 1941); Bernard Barber, *Social Stratification* (New York: Harcourt, Brace & World, 1957), pp. 186-231.

[8] Cf., Dean, *loc. cit.*

facture, metal processing, state government, and trade comprise the main sources of employment. The union selected for study was an amalgamated industrial local of the United Automobile Workers of America, made up of sixteen participating units, with a membership of approximately thirty-two hundred. Over half of the members were employed in six foundries and forges; the remaining were employed in six metal-processing plants and three chemical concerns. Slightly over six tenths of the members were semi-skilled or unskilled, three tenths were skilled, and less than one tenth were office workers. Both southern and northern born Negroes, foreign born, migrants from nearby rural areas, and migrants from northern cities were represented in the local. The local was highly respected in union circles. After a difficult organizational period, it had achieved considerable maturity. It appeared to be democratically run; no single faction had dominated it for more than two years.

A random sample of two hundred members who had been in the union for at least sixty days was selected from the total membership. Of these, only those living in the city and in the immediately surrounding suburban and rural areas were interviewed.[9] This resulted in a significant underrepresentation of rural residents in the final sample of 142 and must be kept in mind in interpreting the subsequent findings.

Types of Union Orientations

Types of union orientation were based upon the members' responses to questions probing: (a) what they considered the main functions of the union to be, (b) their attitudes toward unionism, and (c) the nature of their involvement with union activities. From these the following orientational types were derived:

Political orientation. Thirty percent of the members felt "the most important jobs of the union" to be the protection of their welfare and the settling of disputes with management. They thought of the union primarily as an agency to restrict the abuse of managerial power. This group also included those who believed in unionism as an ideological movement dedicated to advance the welfare of the workers.

Economic orientation. Included in this category were members who saw the union's main jobs to be raising wages, guaranteeing economic security, and acquiring fringe benefits. Also included were those who felt that the power of the union should be used primarily to achieve economic goals. Altogether this group comprised one fifth of the sample.

Social orientation. Somewhat over 16 percent indicated by their attitudes and activities that for them the union's main function was to provide a social world.

Hostile orientation. These respondents were most easily identified be-

---

[9] Members residing beyond five miles of the city boundaries were omitted due to the high costs involved in obtaining interviews.

cause they indicated an unwillingness to join the union when hired and expressed a distaste for the organization as it was. They comprised 8.5 percent of the membership.

Apathetic orientation. Since attendance at union functions is restricted for many reasons, it was not used specifically to identify apathetic members. Respondents who had no clear image of union functions, who went to meetings only under facilitating circumstances, and who had no particular involvement with union programs were classified as apathetic. Also included were those who vaguely perceived union functions but indicated no interest in them. Altogether, the apathetics made up one quarter of the total membership.

The orientational types were theoretically derived and then empirically located. To locate the types two main questions were used as filters. The first question was, "What do you think should be the most important job of this union?" From the answers to this question, about five eighths of the respondents could be clearly classified and some others tentatively classified. The responses of most of these indicated primarily an economic or a political orientation. Those who gave multiple, ambiguous, or uncertain replies were then examined for their responses to the question, "What are the main things your local should work for now?" Answers here confirmed the typing of some of the cases, especially the socially oriented. Those surviving these filters turned out to be mostly the hostile or apathetic types. The hostile were easily classified because they indicated they were unwilling to join the union and were still unsympathetic to it. The apathetics, almost a residual category, responded vaguely to all the questions which separated the other groups. The interview as a whole was used to classify the very few remaining cases. This method of classification is admittedly subjective, for some arbitrary decisions were inevitable, but a sample check of decisions by the two researchers indicated a high reliability in their classifications.

Union Orientation and Union Participation

The first hypothesis was that those socially oriented toward the union would be more active, followed by the political, economic, apathetic, and hostile types in descending order. Members were considered "active" when they attended half or more of the union meetings *and* when they voted in half or more of the elections. "Inactive" members were those who attended less than half of the meetings *and* voted in less than half of the elections. The "moderately active" attended *or* voted more than half of the time. Data in Table 5-10 reveal a significant association between types of union orientation and degree of union activity (as measured by the chi-square test).[10] The ranking of orientation types for degree of activity was almost as hy-

[10] Margaret Jarman Hagood, *Statistics for Sociologists* (New York: Holt, Rinehart and Winston, 1941), pp. 447-448, 512. All findings reported in this paper are below the .05 probability level unless otherwise indicated.

pothesized. The social type was the most active, followed by the economic, political, apathetic, and hostile types in descending order. The fact that the economically oriented were slightly more active than the politically oriented was probably due to an arbitrary classification decision. Thus, those who perceived the union's function as fighting the employer for economic gain were classified on the basis of their objective (economic gain) rather than on the basis of the process involved (the application of power).

Table 5-10.
Degree of Union Activity for Orientational Types (Percent)

UNION ORIENTATION	DEGREE OF UNION ACTIVITY			NUMBER OF CASES
	Active	Moderately Active	Inactive	
Political	60%	21%	19%	42
Economic	67	20	13	30
Social	78	9	13	23
Apathetic	20	46	34	35
Hostile	—	58	42	12
Total	49	28	23	142

$x^2 = 37.206$; $P = .001$

Articulation of Related Systems

The United Auto Workers became established in many Lansing plants about twenty years ago. Although first regarded by many as a strange, extraneous, and perhaps a temporary organization, it now appears to be accepted as a genuine part of the community social structure. It is assumed that labor unions have become articulated to segments of the community life relevant to manual workers. Two research hypotheses were derived from this assumption: (a) that there is a positive association between degree of union *activity* and the degree of integration of its members to the plant, neighborhood, and community; (b) that type of union *orientation* is related to the degree of the worker's integration to the plant, neighborhood, and community. In order to test these hypotheses, it was necessary to construct indexes of integration as follows:

a. *Community integration:* a composite index made up of the number of organizations to which the respondent belonged, his rating of the city as a place to live and work, and the residential location of his best friends.
b. *Neighborhood integration:* a composite index including an evaluation of the neighborhood as place to live, residence of best friends inside or outside the neighborhood, and amount of participation in neighborhood functions.

c. *Plant integration:* an index reflecting the degree of satisfaction with the job
and the department as "a place to work."
d. *Union activity:* the degree of participation in union elections and the frequency of attendance at union meetings.

To test the first hypothesis, chi-square tests were run between degree
of union activity and degree of plant, neighborhood, and community integration. Table 5-11 indicates, as expected, a significant and highly positive
association between degree of union activity and degree of plant integration.[11] Positive associations between union activity and integration with
neighborhood and community were not found to be statistically supported.
On the contrary, there was a tendency for union participation to be negatively associated with degree of community integration. Thus, the hypothesis concerning the integration of the union to other community areas was
rejected in favor of evidence pointing to an apparent cleavage between
union and plant integration, on the one hand, and neighborhood and community integration on the other.

Table 5-11.
Plant Integration and Union Activity

UNION ACTIVITY	LEVEL OF PLANT INTEGRATION			
	High	*Medium*	*Low*	*Total*
High	32	3	—	35
Medium	38	37	16	91
Low	—	—	16	16
Total	70	40	32	142

$x^2 = 87.49$; $P = .001$

The second hypothesis concerns the relations between types of union
orientation of workers and their degree of integration to the plant, neighborhood, and community. Specifically, those socially and politically oriented
toward the union may be expected to be most highly integrated to the social
life of the plant and less integrated to the neighborhood and community.
The economically oriented may be expected to be moderately integrated in
all areas, while the hostile types should reveal low integration to the plant
and higher integration to the neighborhood and community. Those with
an apathetic orientation toward the union may be expected to have a low
degree of integration in all areas—plant, neighborhood, and community.[12]

[11] These results partially confirm the findings of Dean, *loc. cit.*
[12] These specific hypotheses were derived from a study of the literature on urban
social stratification, which point to a cleavage in the participation patterns of the working class, middle status groups, and socially anomic types.

Table 5-12.

Degree of Plant Integration for Orientational Types (Percent)

UNION ORIENTATION	DEGREE OF PLANT INTEGRATION			NUMBER OF CASES
	High	Medium	Low	
Political	26%	69%	5%	42
Economic	27	73	0	30
Social	52	39	9	23
Hostile	—	58	42	12
Apathetic	11	69	20	35
Total	25	64	11	142

$x^2 = 32.918$; $P = .001$

Data in Table 5-12 reveal a statistically significant association between type of union orientation and degree of integration in the plant. The ranking of orientation types generally was as hypothesized. Thus the socially oriented had highest plant integration scores, followed by the economically and politically oriented. Respondents apathetically oriented toward the union and especially those with a hostile orientation had moderate to low plant integration scores.

The association of orientational types to degree of neighborhood integration in Table 5-13 approaches statistical significance. Although the trends are not decisive, the hostile type seemed to display the highest degree of neighborhood integration, followed by those with political and economic union orientations. The apathetically oriented, and especially the socially oriented, seemed to be least involved in their neighborhoods. This ranking of orientational types is contrary to the hypothesis that the neighborhood is an area of *local* identification, as are the plant and the union. In this urban area at least, it appears that those highest involved in union and plant activities are least involved in the neighborhood.

Data in Table 5-14 indicate that seven tenths of the union members were concerned with the social life of the community to some degree. Like manual workers elsewhere,[13] only a small proportion (one sixth) showed a high degree of community participation and interest. Although the orientational types were not clearly distinguished, their ranking for community involvement was as hypothesized. Thus the hostile and the economically oriented had the highest representation among those highly integrated with the community. The politically oriented revealed a slightly lower degree of community integration, while the socially oriented and the apathetics had the lowest degree of community integration.

In summary, there is reason to qualify the finding that there is no sharp

[13] Mirra Komarovsky, "The Voluntary Associations of Urban Dwellers," *American Sociological Review*, 11 (December, 1946), 686-697.

Table 5-13.

Degree of Neighborhood Integration for Types of
Union Orientation (Percent)

UNION ORIENTATION	NEIGHBORHOOD INTEGRATION			NUMBER OF CASES
	High	Medium	Low	
Political	14%	74%	12%	42
Economic	17	70	13	30
Social	9	61	30	23
Hostile	—	100	—	12
Apathetic	17	60	23	35
Total	13	70	17	142

$x^2 = 11.150$; $P = .20-.10$

break between life on the job and life in the outside world.[14] Patterns of
participation for people with different union orientations differed in this
study. Apathetic union members displayed the most consistent pattern: a
low degree of integration in the plant, union, neighborhood, and community. An apparent cleavage was suggested for both hostile and social types
between plant and union, on the one hand, and neighborhood and com-

Table 5-14.

Degree of Community Integration for Types of
Union Orientation (Percent)

UNION ORIENTATION	COMMUNITY INTEGRATION			NUMBER OF CASES
	High	Medium	Low	
Political	19%	69%	12%	42
Economic	16	77	7	30
Social	13	70	17	23
Hostile	25	58	17	12
Apathetic	14	72	14	35
Total	17	70	13	142

munity, on the other hand. Whereas, as expected, those hostile toward the
union had low integration to the union and the plant, they tended to be
more highly involved in neighborhood and community life. The socially
oriented were characterized by an opposite pattern: lower involvement in
the neighborhood and community and higher integration in the plant and
the union. Workers exhibiting political and economic orientations displayed

[14] Dean, *loc. cit.*

almost identical patterns. They tended to be moderately integrated in all of the areas and exhibited less cleavage between plant and union, on the one hand, and neighborhood and community, on the other.

Community Origin and Union Orientations

Union orientations may be accounted for, in part, by the community backgrounds of the members, the types of job mobility they have experienced, and their stratification positions. While the literature is not conclusive, it does suggest that workers reared in rural areas tend to be most hostile toward unions,[15] and that assimilated urban manual workers tend to be socially and politically oriented.[16] Occupationally mobile workers have been thought to be economically oriented, while workers with middle-class references have been seen as apathetic or hostile toward unions.[17]

In the present study, birthplace and place of longest residence did not clearly differentiate the union orientations of the respondents.[18] The data in Table 5-15, however, suggest that workers born in rural Michigan were more heavily represented among those with a hostile orientation toward the union than those born in Michigan cities. Although both groups had equally high representations among apathetic members, the urban-born had higher representations among the economically oriented and lower representation among the politically oriented. Other urban-born were as hostile as the Michigan rural-born.

These patterns did not apply for workers born and reared in the rural South. Allegedly, Southerners have been reared in an individualistic tradition antithetical toward unions.[19] Yet the data show that they had relatively high proportions among the politically oriented and, more important, had relatively fewer members among the hostile and apathetic types compared to those born or reared elsewhere. It also appears that southern migrants used the union as a vehicle of social adjustment to the city more than other groups, for they had the highest proportion of socially oriented members. These trends were not affected by the racial distribution of the southern-born.

Although there were relatively few migrants from other areas, some trends characterized them as a group. The foreign-born, unlike the South-

[15] William F. Whyte, "Who Goes Union and Why," *Personnel Journal*, **23** (December, 1944), 215-230.

[16] C. W. M. Hart, "Industrial Relations Research and Social Theory," *Canadian Journal of Economic and Political Science*, **15** (February, 1949), 53-73.

[17] Centers, *op. cit.*

[18] Data on birthplace and place of longest residence showed the same general patterns. The relevance of these indexes for the distribution of labor in a community labor market is clearly examined by Sigmund Nosow, "Labor Distribution and the Normative System," *Social Forces*, **35** (October, 1956), 25-33.

[19] Glen Gilman, *Human Relations in the Industrial Southeast* (Chapel Hill: University of North Carolina Press, 1956), pp. 232-248.

Table 5-15.
Union Orientation by Birthplace (Percent)

UNION ORIENTATION	PLACE OF BIRTH					TOTAL
	Urban Michigan	Rural Michigan	South	Urban North	Foreign Born	
Political	15%	24%	35%	42%	25%	30
Economic	27	16	26	12	37	21
Social	18	12	26	9	13	16
Apathetic	36	32	13	18	25	25
Hostile	4	16	—	18	—	8
Number of cases	45	25	31	33	8	142

$x^2 = 23.886$; $P = .10-.05$
Note: Percentages do not add to 100 in all cases because of rounding errors.

erners, were more disposed to perceive the union's functions as economic than as political or social. Possibly the primary source of social integration for the foreign-born was the immigrant colony outside the plant. On the other hand, workers who had resided in other urban regions of the North before migrating to Lansing, primarily had political orientations toward the union. Coming from older and larger urban areas and probably better adjusted to urban life, they saw the union's social functions as relatively unimportant. Workers residing in the urban fringe tended to be more apathetic toward the union, while those living in the central city were more concerned with the economic functions of the organization.[20]

Occupational Stratification and Union Orientation

Social and economic attitudes are frequently associated with position in a stratification system and with mobility aspirations.[21] The most important index of stratification available was occupation. Although stratification differences within the sample were small, some internal variation was present. Among workers with economic, political, and social orientations, the ratio of semiskilled and unskilled workers to skilled workers was over three to one. Those apathetic and hostile toward the union, however, were relatively more skilled; the occupational ratio here was one to one. Moreover, the apathetic and hostile workers were more highly educated than the others. Significantly, Negroes were not represented among the hostile type and had the smallest representations among the apathetics.

[20] The probability of the chi-square between union and orientation and urban-fringe residence was .10-.05 with most of the variation concentrated in the apathetic orientation for fringe dwellers and economic orientation for central city residents. Southerners were more heavily concentrated in the central city, while those born in the urban North were more concentrated in the fringe.

[21] Centers, op. cit.

Workers may also be stratified according to their aspirations for higher jobs and the degree to which they accept their present status. In his study of a different local of the same union in Lansing, Chinoy found that over three quarters of his respondents wanted to escape the factory to obtain jobs with more skill and independence.[22] In this study workers were also asked whether they wanted a different job and whether they sought self-employment. Slightly over one half indicated they wanted a different job; slightly over one quarter wanted self-employment. The apathetic and hostile types revealed more job dissatisfaction; over two thirds of these workers wanted a different job while only one half of those with political, economic, and social orientations expressed this desire. When the two groups were compared for their desire for job independence, again a significantly larger proportion of the apathetic and hostile types desired job independence.

Can these differences in job satisfaction and aspiration be accounted for by different occupational career patterns? Data on job seniority and occupational mobility were examined. No great differences in job seniority were found by union orientation. Two tendencies, however, were noted: the socially oriented had the longest seniority, the hostile group had the least despite their longer work histories. Thus the hostile were occupationally more mobile and, despite their higher skill, had achieved little job security.[23]

All job histories were analyzed for amount of vertical mobility. It was found that those economically oriented toward the union had experienced the most upward occupational mobility, followed by those politically and apathetically oriented. The social and hostile types had experienced the least mobility. The socially oriented had experienced little mobility but seemed satisfied with their present circumstances, while the hostile type, despite their higher occupational level, appeared frustrated by a lack of upward occupational mobility. It may be concluded that the occupational reference groups of those hostile toward the union were outside their actual membership groups.

Conclusions

Two assumptions underlie much research on local labor unions: (a) that a greater degree of membership participation may attend union stability, and (b) that union stability elicits greater membership participation in the plant, neighborhood, and community. This study suggests that these assumptions need to be refined to take into account the different meanings which labor unions have for their members. Research in a union local of a middle-sized city revealed the existence of several distinguishable orientations toward union functions on the part of the members. These orienta-

[22] Eli Chinoy, *Automobile Workers and the American Dream* (Garden City, N.Y.: Doubleday, 1955), p. 82.
[23] See confirming evidence in Dean, *loc. cit.*; Strauss and Sayles, *loc. cit.*

tions were differentially related to the degree of membership integration within the union itself, the department in which the member worked, the neighborhood, and the community. A cleavage was found to exist for some union orientational types between integration with union and plant, on the one hand, and neighborhood and community, on the other. While such a cleavage could be accounted for, in part, by different community backgrounds and occupational career patterns of the members, three dominant life styles seemed to underlie both union orientations and broad patterns of integration. They are: (a) a working-class life style in which the union and plant play a dominant role, (b) an individualistic life style in which community associations are more vital, and (c) an "isolated" life style in which the family and possibly the neighborhood are primary sources of social integration of the person. These life styles may be expected to change gradually during a person's work career and over the generations.

Bibliography

Alexander, K. J. W., "Membership Participation in a Printing Trade Union," *Sociological Review*, 2 (December, 1954), 161-168.

Allen, V. L., "The Ethics of Trade Union Leaders," *British Journal of Sociology*, 7 (December, 1956), 314-336.

Allen, V. L., *Power in Trade Unions: A Study of the Organization in Great Britain* (New York: Longmans, 1954).

Barbash, J., *Labor's Grass Roots: A Study of the Local Union* (New York: Harper & Row, 1961).

Barbash, J., *The Practice of Unionism* (New York: Harper & Row, 1956).

Barbash, J., ed., *Unions and Union Leadership* (New York: Harper & Row, 1959).

Barber, B., "Participation and Mass Apathy in Associations," in Alvin W. Gouldner, ed., *Studies in Leadership* (New York: Harper & Row, 1950).

Becker, W., "Conflict as a Source of Solidarity: Some Notes on the California Farm Labor Scene," *Journal of Social Issues*, 9 (Fall, 1953), 25-27.

Bell, W., and Force, M. T., "Social Structure and Participation in Different Types of Formal Associations," *Social Forces*, 34 (May, 1956), 345-350.

Brody, D., *Steelworkers in America: The Nonunion Era* (Cambridge, Mass.: Harvard University Press, 1960).

Brooks, G. W., "Observations on the Changing Nature of American Unions," *Monthly Labor Review*, 80 (February, 1957), 151-154.

Brown, J. S., "Union Size as a Function of Intra-Union Conflict," *Human Relations*, 9 (February, 1956), 75-89.

Brown, L. C., "Unionization in Small Plants: I," *Social Order*, 6 (April, 1956), 163-167.

Claessen, A., *Understanding the Worker: Problems of Labor Organizations Analyzed in the Light of Social Psychology. Backgrounds in Trade Union History* (New York: Rand School Press, 1954).

Clegg, H. A., Killick, A. J., and Adams, R., *Trade Union Officers: A Study of Full-Time Officers, Branch Secretaries and Shop Stewards* (Cambridge, Mass.: Harvard University Press, 1961).

Cohany, H. P., "Membership of American Trade Unions, 1956," *Monthly Labor Review*, 80 (October, 1957), 1202-1210.

Cole, D. L., "Jurisdictional Issues and the Promise of Merger," *Industrial and Labor Relations Review*, 9 (April, 1956), 391-405.

Coleman, J. R., "The Compulsive Pressure of Democracy in Unionism," *American Journal of Sociology*, 61 (May, 1956), 519-528.

Cook, A., "Dual Government in Unions: A Tool for Analysis," *Industrial Relations Review*, 15 (April, 1962), 323-349.

Cook, A., *Union Democracy: Practice and Ideal* (Ithaca, New York: New York State School of Industrial and Labor Relations, Cornell University, 1963).

Curtis, R. F., "Occupational Mobility and Union Membership in Detroit: A Replication," *Social Forces*, 38 (October, 1959), 69-71.

Dean, L. R., "Interaction, Reported and Observed: The Case of One Local Union," *Human Organization*, 17 (Fall, 1958), 36-44.

Dean, L. R., "Social Integration, Attitudes and Union Activity," *Industrial and Labor Relations Review*, 8 (October, 1954), 48-58.

Dean, L. R., "Union Activity and Dual Loyalty," *Industrial and Labor Relations Review*, 7 (July, 1954), 526-536.

Dunlop, J. T., "Structural Changes in the American Labor Movement," *Monthly Labor Review*, 80 (February, 1957), 146-150.

Eby, K., "The 'Drip' Theory in Labor Unions," *Antioch Review*, 13 (Spring, 1953), 95-102.

Eby, K., "Organized Labor and American Ethics," *Annals of the American Academy of Political Science*, 297 (January, 1955), 83-89.

Edelstein, J. D., "Democracy in a National Union: The British A.E.U.," *Industrial Relations*, 4 (May, 1965), 105-125.

Epstein, M., *Jewish Labor in U.S.A., 1914-1952, an Industrial, Political and Cultural History of the Jewish Labor Movement* (New York: Trade Union Sponsoring Committee, 1953).

Estey, M. S., "The Strategic Alliance as a Factor in Union Growth," *Industrial and Labor Relations Review*, 9 (October, 1955), 41-53.

Faunce, W. A., "Delegate Attitudes toward the Convention in the U.A.W.," *Industrial and Labor Relations Review*, 15 (July, 1962), 463-473.

Faunce, W. A., "Size of Locals and Union Democracy," *American Journal of Sociology*, 68 (November, 1962), 291-298.

Form, W. H., "Organized Labor's Place in Community Power Structure," *Industrial and Labor Relations Review*, 12 (July, 1959), 526-539.

Form, W. H., and Dansereau, H. K., "Union Member Orientations and Patterns of Social Integration," *Industrial and Labor Relations Review*, 11 (October, 1957), 3-12.

France, R. R., *Union Decisions in Collective Bargaining*, Research Report No. 90 (Princeton: Industrial Relations Section, Princeton University, 1955).

Galenson, H., *Trade Union Democracy in Western Europe* (Berkeley: University of California Press, 1961).

Galenson, H., and Lipset, M. S., *Labor and Trade Unionism: An Interdisciplinary Reader* (New York: Wiley, 1960).

Goldberg, A. J., *AFL-CIO Labor United* (New York: McGraw-Hill, 1956).

Goldstein, B., "Some Aspects of the Nature of Unionism among Salaried Professionals in Industry," *American Sociological Review*, 20 (April, 1955), 199-205.

Goldstein, B., "Unions and the Professional Employee," *Journal of Business*, 27 (October, 1954), 276-284.

Goldstein, J., *The Government of a British Trade Union* (New York: Free Press, 1952).

Gulick, C. A., Ockert, R. A., and Wallace, R. J., *History and Theories of Working-Class Movements: A Selected Bibliography* (Berkeley: University of California Press, 1955).

Hardman, J. B. S., "Labor in Midpassage," *Harvard Business Review,* **31** (January-February, 1953), 39-48.

Harrington, M., *The Retail Clerks* (New York: Wiley, 1962).

Hart, P. E., and Phelps-Brown, E. H., "The Sizes of Trade Unions: A Study in the Laws of Aggregation," *Economic Journal,* **67** (March, 1957), 1-15.

Horowitz, M. A., *The Structure and Government of the Carpenters' Union* (New York: Wiley, 1962).

Howe, I., and Widick, B., *The UAW and Walter Reuther* (New York: Random House, 1949).

Hudson, R. A., and Rosen, H., "Union Political Action: The Members Speak," *Industrial and Labor Relations Review,* **7** (April, 1954), 404-418.

Jacobs, P., "Union Democracy and the Public Good," *Commentary,* **25** (January, 1958), 68-74.

James, R. L., "Unionization Attitudes in Three Small Retail Store Work Groups," *Research Studies of the State College of Washington,* **24** (June, 1956), 183 ff.

Kahn, R. L., and Tannenbaum, A. S., "Union Practices and Membership Participation," *Personnel Psychology,* **10** (Summer, 1957), 277-292.

Kannappan, S., "The Gandhian Model of Unionism in a Developing Economy: The TLA in India," *Industrial and Labor Relations Review,* **16** (October, 1962), 86-110.

Karsh, B., Seidman, J., and Lilienthal, D. M., "The Union Organizer and His Tactics: A Case Study," *American Journal of Sociology,* **59** (September, 1953), 113-122.

Kovner, J., and Lahne, H., "Shop Society and the Union," *Industrial and Labor Relations Review,* **7** (October, 1953), 3-14.

Kramer, L., *Labor's Paradox: The American Federation of State, County, and Municipal Employees, AFL-CIO* (New York: Wiley, 1962).

Krauss, W. R., and Kennedy, V. D., *The Business Agent and His Union* (Berkeley: Institute of Industrial Relations, University of California, 1955).

Lahne, H. J., and Kovner, J., "Local Union Structure: Formality and Reality," *Industrial and Labor Relations Review,* **9** (October, 1955), 24-31.

Landsberger, H. A., Barrera, M., and Toro, A., "The Chilean Labor Union Leader: A Preliminary Report on His Background and Attitudes," *Industrial and Labor Relations Review,* **17** (April, 1964), 399-420.

Landsberger, H. A., and Hulen, C. L., "A Problem for Union Democracy: Officers Attitudes toward Union Members," *Industrial and Labor Relations Review,* **14** (April, 1961), 419-431.

Leiserson, W. M., *American Trade Union Democracy* (New York: Columbia University Press, 1959).

Lipset, S. M., "Democracy in Private Government: A Case Study of the ITU," *British Journal of Sociology,* **3** (March, 1952), 47-63.

Lipset, S. M., "The Political Process in Trade Unions: A Theoretical Statement," in Monroe Berger *et al.*, eds., *Freedom and Control in Modern Society* (New York: Van Nostrand, 1954), 82-124.

Lipset, S. M., "Trade Unions and Social Structure: I," *Industrial Relations,* **1** (October, 1961), 75-90.

Lipset, S. M., "Trade Unions and Social Structure: II," *Industrial Relations*, 1 (February, 1962), 89-110.

Lipset, S. M., Trow, M. A., and Coleman, J. S., *Union Democracy* (New York: Free Press, 1956).

Marcus, P. M., "Organizational Change: The Case of American Trade Unions," in G. K. Zollschan and W. Hirsh, eds., *Explorations in Social Change* (Boston: Houghton Mifflin, 1964), pp. 749-777.

Marcus, P. M., "Union Conventions and Executive Boards: A Formal Analysis of Organizational Structure," *American Sociological Review*, 31 (February, 1966), 61-70.

McCoy, R. E., *History of Labor and Unionism in the United States: A Selected Bibliography* (Champaign: Institute of Labor and Industrial Relations, University of Illinois, 1953).

Meyers, F., *European Coal Mining Unions: Structure and Function* (Los Angeles: Institute of Industrial Relations, University of California, 1961).

Miller, G. W., and Young, J. E., "Member Participation in the Trade Union Local: A Study of Activity and Policy-Making in Columbus, Ohio," *American Journal of Economics and Sociology*, 15 (October, 1955), 31-47.

Neufeld, M., "Structure and Government of the AFL-CIO," *Industrial and Labor Relations Review*, 9 (April, 1956), 371-390.

Peck, S. M., *The Rank and File Leader* (New Haven, Conn.: College and University Press, 1963).

Perlman, M., *Democracy in the International Association of Machinists* (New York: Wiley, 1962).

Perlman, M., *The Machinists: A New Study in American Trade Unionism* (Cambridge, Mass.: Harvard University Press, 1961).

Popiel, G., "Bureaucracy in the Mass Industrial Union: A Theoretical Inquiry into the Limits of its Growth," *American Journal of Economics and Sociology*, 15 (October, 1955), 49-58.

Powell, F. D., "Origins and Perspectives of the International Representatives," *American Catholic Sociological Review*, 19 (October, 1958), 210-223.

Raffaele, J. A., *Labor Leadership in Italy and Denmark* (Madison: University of Wisconsin Press, 1962).

Romer, S., *The International Brotherhood of Teamsters: Its Government and Structure* (New York: Wiley, 1962).

Rose, A. M., *Union Solidarity* (Minneapolis: University of Minnesota Press, 1952).

Rosen, H., and Rosen, R. A. H., "Personality Variables and Role in a Union Business Agent Group," *Journal of Applied Psychology*, 41 (April, 1957), 131-136.

Rosen, H., and Rosen, R. A. H., *The Union Member Speaks* (Englewood Cliffs, N.J.: Prentice-Hall, 1955).

Rothbaum, M., *The Government of the Oil, Chemical, and Atomic Workers Union* (New York: Wiley, 1962).

Sayles, L. R., and Strauss, G., *The Local Union* (New York: Harper & Row, 1953).

Sayles, L. R., and Strauss, G., "What the Worker Really Thinks of His Union," *Harvard Business Review*, 31 (May-June, 1953), 94-102.

Seidman, J., *The Brotherhood of Railroad Trainmen: The Internal Political Life of a National Union* (New York: Wiley, 1962).

Seidman, J., *Democracy in the Labor Movement*, Bulletin 39, February, 1958 (Ithaca, N.Y.: New York State School of Industrial and Labor Relations, Cornell University, 1958).

Seidman, J., "Democracy in Labor Unions," *Journal of Political Economy*, **61** (June, 1953), 221-231.

Seidman, J., London, J., Karsh, B., and Tagliacozzo, D. L., *The Worker Views His Union* (Chicago: University of Chicago Press, 1958).

Sheppard, H. L., "The Union as a Political Influence: Ethnic and Generation Factors in Union Members Behavior," *Journal of Social Issues*, **9** (Fall, 1953), 44-48.

Sheppard, H. L., and Masters, N. A., "Union Political Action and Opinion Polls in a Democratic Society," *Social Problems*, **5** (July, 1957), 14-21.

Sheppard, H. L., and Masters, N. A., "The Political Attitudes and Preferences of Union Members: The Case of the Detroit Auto Workers," *American Political Science Review*, **53** (June, 1959), 437-447.

Skeels, J. W., "Early Carriage and Auto Unions: The Impact of Industrialization and Rival Unionism," *Industrial and Labor Relations Review*, **17** (July, 1964), 566-583.

Solomon, B., "Dimensions of Union Growth, 1900-1950," *Industrial and Labor Relations Review*, **9** (July, 1956), 544-561.

Spinrad, W., "Correlates of Trade Union Participation: A Summary of the Literature," *American Sociological Review*, **25** (April, 1960), 237-244.

Starr, M., "Freedom and Authority in Labor Unions," in Lyman Bryson, Louis Finkelstein, R. M. MacIver, and Richard McKeon, eds., *Freedom and Authority in our Time: 12th Symposium of the Conference on Science, Philosophy and Religion* (New York: Harper & Row, 1953), pp. 63-77.

Stephenson, T. E., "The Changing Role of Local Democracy: The Trade Union and its Members," *Sociological Review*, **51** (July, 1957), 27-42.

Stieber, J., *Governing the U.A.W.* (New York: Wiley, 1962).

Strauss, G., "Control by the Membership in Building Trades Unions," *American Journal of Sociology*, **61** (May, 1956), 527-535.

Strauss, G., *Streamlining the Union Meeting* (Ithaca, N.Y.: New York State School of Labor and Industrial Relations, Cornell University, 1955).

Strauss, G., "White-Collar Unions are Different," *Harvard Business Review*, **32** (September-October, 1954), 73-82.

Strauss, G., and Sayles, L. R., "Leadership Roles in Labor Unions," *Sociology and Social Research*, **38** (November, 1953), 96-102.

Strauss, G., and Sayles, L. R., "Occupation and the Selection of Local Union Officers," *The American Journal of Sociology*, **58** (May, 1953), 585-591.

Strauss, G., and Sayles, L. R., "The Local Union Meeting," *Industrial and Labor Relations Review*, **6** (January, 1953), 206-219.

Sturmthal, O., *Workers' Councils: A Study of Workplace Organizations on Both Sides of the Iron Curtain* (London: Oxford University Press, 1964).

Taft, P., "Independent Unions and the Merger," *Industrial and Labor Relations Review*, **9** (April, 1956), 433-446.

Taft, P., "Local Independent Unions and the American Labor Movement," *Industrial and Labor Relations Review,* **15** (October, 1961), 102-105.

Taft, P., *The Structure and Government of Labor Unions* (Cambridge, Mass.: Harvard University Press, 1954).

Tagliacozzo, D. L., "Trade-Union Government, Its Nature and Its Problems: A Bibliographical Review 1945-1955," *American Journal of Sociology,* **61** (May, 1956), 554-581.

Tagliacozzo, D. L., and Seidman, J., "Typology of Rank-and-File Members," *American Journal of Sociology,* **61** (May, 1956), 546-553.

Taira, K., "Japanese 'Enterprise Unionism' and Interfirm Wage Structure," *Industrial and Labor Relations Review,* **15** (October, 1961), 33-51.

Tannenbaum, A. S., "Control Structure and Union Functions," *American Journal of Sociology,* **61** (May, 1956), 536-545.

Tannenbaum, A. S., "Mechanisms of Control in Local Trade Unions," *British Journal of Sociology,* **7** (December, 1956), 306-313.

Tannenbaum, A. S., and Kahn, R. L., "Organizational Control Structure: A General Descriptive Technique as Applied to Four Local Unions," *Human Relations,* **10** (May, 1957), 127-140.

Tannenbaum, A. S., and Kahn, R. L., *Participation in Union Locals* (New York: Harper & Row, 1958).

Troy, L., *Local Independent Unionism: Two Case Studies* (New Brunswick, N.J.: Institute of Management and Labor Relations, Rutgers, 1961).

Turner, H. A., *Trade Union Growth, Structure and Policy: A Comparative Study of the Cotton Unions in England* (Toronto: University of Toronto Press, 1962).

Ulman, L., *The Government of the Steel Workers' Union* (New York: Wiley, 1962).

Ulman, L., *The Rise of the National Trade Union* (Cambridge, Mass.: Harvard University Press, 1955).

Weber, A., "The Craft-Industrial Issue Revisited: A Study of Union Government," *Industrial and Labor Relations Review,* **16** (April, 1963), 381-404.

Wilensky, H. L., *Intellectuals in Labor Unions* (New York: Free Press, 1956).

Wilensky, H. L., "The Labor Vote: A Local Union's Impact on the Political Conduct of its Members," *Social Forces,* **35** (December, 1956), 111-120.

UNION-MANAGEMENT RELATIONS

Introduction

The segmentalized or structurally differentiated character of contemporary industrial societies inevitably generates conflicts of interest. In contrast to less complex peasant societies, where conflict occurs predominantly on an interpersonal basis, industrial societies are made up of an enormous array of interest groups which necessarily come into conflict with each other as they pursue their differing objectives. This chapter is concerned with the conflicting interests of unions and management and with the ways in which industrial conflict is accommodated.

Unions and management, of course, have common as well as conflicting interests. The success of the enterprise is a necessary condition for both parties to achieve their objectives. The nature of union-management relations, however, is determined to a much greater degree by their conflicting than by their common interests. And conflict of interest is an inherent element of this relationship. There are two sets of mutually exclusive organizational goals that produce most industrial conflict. First, wages represent a cost to management and income to workers. So long as management seeks to reduce costs and unions seek to raise wages, an obvious conflict of interest exists. The second major area of conflict has to do with control over decisions regarding conditions of employment. Unions, in order to achieve their objectives, seek to gain control over these decisions; management regards this effort as an intrusion upon its prerogatives. Economic issues (level of wages and fringe benefits) and control issues ("who has the right to make which decisions") are the core areas around which conflicts of interest between unions and management develop.

We have been speaking so far of conflict of interest. A distinction should be made between this concept and overt or open conflict of the sort represented by the strike, slow-down, or lock-out. It is possible for interdependent organizations with conflicting goals to relate harmoniously to each other if there are institutionalized or standardized and agreed upon ways of settling their differences. Collective bargaining represents a social invention through which conflicting interests may be compromised. The peaceful settlement of most union-management differences attests to the success of collective bargaining as an accommodative device. The extensive news coverage given to strikes tends to obscure the fact that they are a relatively rare occurrence in union-management negotiations. When they do occur, it is important to recognize that they represent a part of rather than a break down of the bargaining process. The threat of a work stoppage is an important ingredient of collective bargaining and where it does not exist little genuine bargaining occurs.

The presence of threats and counter-threats in the bargaining process serves to illustrate the fact that union-management relations are *power* relations. Robert Dubin, in a selection included in this chapter, defines power as the "importance that consequences of actions have in a social relationship." To the extent that one or the other party in a relationship has exclusive control over the performance of some essential function it may be regarded as powerful. Herbert Blumer emphasizes the degree to which power relations are neither rigidly codified nor between parties sympathetic to each other's objectives. He states: "Where people in pursuit of goals are thrown into opposition to one another, with sanctioned or allowable leeway in the forging of actions to achieve success in the face of such opposition, and where the pursuit is not made subservient to considerations of each other's welfare, the stage is set for power action."[1]

Successful collective bargaining between powerful, contending interest groups can only take place under circumstances where the groups have approximately the same amount of power. Long or violent industrial disorders are most likely to occur when either unions or management have a distinct power advantage. This was the case, for example, in the early struggles by unions for recognition from management. Unless a relative balance of power is maintained, decisions are reached by dictation rather than negotiation and the weaker party has the choice of simply accepting the decision or resorting to extraordinary or extralegal means to achieve its ends. By and large, the industrial relations system that has evolved in the United States has functioned remarkably well in preventing industrial disorder.

The collective bargaining process and the resulting contract are particularly good examples of end products in the differentiation-rationalization sequence which has served as the theme of this book. Wage earners and managers are clearly differentiated from each other in the structure of modern industry. Because they perform mutually interdependent functions, the conflicting interests produced by their differing positions must be accommodated in order for the enterprise to operate successfully. The collectively bargained contract is a frequently evaluated and periodically revised means

---

[1] Herbert Blumer, "Social Structure and Power Conflict," in Arthur Kornhauser *et al.*, *Industrial Conflict* (New York: McGraw-Hill, 1954), p. 235.

to this end. In this sense it represents a rationalization of the relationship. The rationalized character of the relationship is further evidenced by the increasing involvement of experts and professionals of various sorts in the bargaining process.[2] In addition, the body of federal and state laws regarding collective bargaining provide a rational-legal framework within which union-management relations occur. These relationships today are in marked contrast with, for example, the *traditionally* based relations between employer and employee in the medieval manorial system or between the owner-manager and *his* workers in small, early industrial shops.

Most of the research on industrial relations has been done by economists rather than by sociologists. Dubin states that "most serious students of the field have their intellectual roots in economics, and their studies have been the backbone of knowledge about union-management relations."[3] Sociological concern with this field has been concentrated in two areas: (1) the study of power relations between contending interest groups and (2) the study of interpersonal relations between workers, union leaders, and management representatives at the plant level. Particularly in the early history of industrial sociology these two areas were seen not as complementary fields of study but as competing interpretations of the "true" nature of industrial relations. Some proponents of the interpersonal approach argued that industrial relations were, in the last analysis, relations among individuals and that industrial peace or conflict could be predicted by studying the quality of human relations in the plant. Proponents of the conflict of interest approach argued that individuals functioned in *institutionalized roles* as *representatives* of unions or of management and that industrial relations could only be understood as power relations between organizations. To some extent there was an ideological issue underlying these different perspectives. Following Elton Mayo, some human relations researchers saw conflictive relationships as necessarily bad, harmonious relationships as necessarily good, and sought ways to eliminate conflict by improving the quality of interpersonal relations between workers and managers. Other sociologists noted that conflict between unions and management served definite social functions under circumstances where it is accommodated through rational, institutionalized means as in collective bargaining.[4]

[2] Most standard texts on personnel relations contain some discussion of the professionalization of this function on the management side. See, for example, Cyris C. Ling, *The Management of Personnel Relations* (Homewood, Ill.: Irwin, 1965), pp. 338-402. For a discussion of the role of experts in trade unions see, Harold L. Wilensky, *Intellectuals in Labor Unions* (New York: Free Press, 1956).

[3] Robert Dubin, *Working Union-Management Relations* (Englewood Cliffs, N.J.: Prentice-Hall, 1958), p. vii.

[4] The classic statement of the value of industrial harmony is Elton Mayo, *The Social Problems of an Industrial Civilization* (London: Routledge, 1949). For discussion of the functions of conflict, see Robert Dubin, "Constructive Aspects of Industrial Conflict," in Kornhauser, *et al.*, *op. cit.*, pp. 37-47; L. Coser, *The Functions of Conflict* (New York: Free Press, 1956); H. L. Sheppard, "Approaches to Conflict in American Industrial Sociology," *British Journal of Sociology*, **5** (December, 1954), 324-342.

The heritage of these differing perspectives today are two sets of research interests, one in interpersonal relations and the other in interorganizational relations, that are generally regarded as complementary—an understanding of both being necessary for a complete picture of relations between unions and management. The distinction between the two is similar to that drawn in Chapter IV between studies of formal and informal organization. The rationalized, formal structure of industrial relations is designed to cope with conflict of organizational interests and provides a set of guidelines regulating the behavior of union and management representatives. These guidelines cannot cover all contingencies, however, and there are spheres of autonomy as well as spheres of control in the relationship. Actions not specified in the formal guidelines, to the extent that they are recurring and socially patterned, are likely to be seen as ends in themselves or, at least, as unlikely to be consciously evaluated as means to specified ends. The reciprocal expectations that develop between union stewards and foremen in the day-to-day operation of a plant, for example, are regulated only to a limited extent by the contract; the pattern in the relationship emerges and is perpetuated through the traditional rather than the rational mode of organization.[5] In the same sense that studies of both formal and informal organizations are necessary to understand the industrial firm, studies of both formal and informal regulation of interorganizational relationships are necessary for a complete understanding of union-management relations.

The contract between union and management is necessarily a flexible and changing document because of the rate at which change is occurring in the social and economic environment of American industrial relations. One major change has been a shift in the occupational composition of the labor force so that the wage workers traditionally represented by unions have become an increasingly smaller proportion of the total. Unions are recognizing that in order to maintain their power position they will need to organize salaried, white-collar workers. A second major change is in the nature of production technology. Automation is posing some new issues for union-management relations and forcing an adjustment in contract provisions regarding old issues. The last two readings in this chapter deal with adjustments in our industrial relations system growing out of these two types of changing conditions.

The first reading in this chapter is by one of the major contributors to the analysis of power relations, Robert Dubin. In this selection he is primarily concerned with the institutionalization of power relations between

---

[5] It should be noted that genuinely inter*personal* relations, where the individuals involved are not functioning as representatives of their organizations, do not constitute union-management relations. It is only where the content of the interaction has something to do with union or management affairs that the relationship between a foreman and a steward is relevant to the concerns of this chapter.

unions and management. He describes the evolution of disputes over ends, the shift from disputes over ends to disputes over means, the standardization of forms of conflict, the routinization of continuing relationships, latent or unintended functions of industrial power relations, and the ways in which unions and management justify their positions to the public. The important point in the reading is that conflict and power are permanent elements of union-management relations and that recent changes have not been a matter of a shift from change to stability or from conflict to cooperation but, instead, involve the *institutionalization* of relations between these powerful, contending interest groups.

"Wildcat Strikes," by Leonard Sayles analyzes the causes and consequences of unauthorized strikes. These strikes are described as primarily a rank-and-file weapon although they may on occasion be tacitly authorized by union leaders. Wildcat strikes are seen as resulting from national union policies which encourage but do not authorize such strikes, issues on which there is disagreement between the national and local unions, internal political issues in local unions, unique characteristics of particular industries, and grievances of groups or departments within a plant that are not adequately handled by the established grievance procedures. Problems posed by wildcat strikes for unions as well as management are discussed. Most types of unauthorized strikes are seen as likely to decline in number but spontaneous walkouts by small groups or single departments are likely to continue because there will continue to be issues and grievances that develop between contract negotiations that are not covered by the provisions of the existing contract. The existence of wildcat strikes is evidence of the inability of rationalized control systems to take account of all possible contingencies.[6]

The next reading, by Melville Dalton, makes a similar point but with regard to the ongoing, day-to-day relations of union and management representatives at the plant level. Through participant observation, Dalton discovered that many of these relations are outside of and, in some cases, at variance with the formal or contractually specified relations. Lower-level union leaders and supervisors often tacitly agree to ignore the contract, in some instances, because they are acting on a basis of expediency and personal interest rather than group loyalty and in others because the contract provisions are regarded as being too inflexible to handle differences that need to be settled quickly. It is apparent that there is a bargaining relationship at the lowest level of union-management relations as well as at the top where agreements between international unions and corporations are negotiated. Stewards and foremen each have things to give or take from the other and a continuous, informal process of exchange goes on at this level.

The basic issue in the reading by William F. Whyte which follows is how to produce more harmonious relations between unions and manage-

---

[6] For a general analysis of strikes, see K. G. Knowles, *Strikes—A Study in Industrial Conflict* (New York: Philosophical Library, 1952).

ment at all levels. The solution of the problem, according to Whyte, lies, at least in part, in a more balanced interrelationship in which actions are originated at each level of contact by *both* unions and management and not just by one or the other. A framework is presented for analyzing the frequency of origination of action at various organizational levels and information from case studies is presented in support of the contention that balanced origination of action reduces conflict. Whyte has been one of the leading contributors to the study of interpersonal or human relations between labor and management and his analysis is framed in these terms rather than in terms of power.

The next selection is a previously unpublished article by Seymour Martin Lipset concerned with the organization of white-collar and professional workers into unions. These workers have generally not been attracted to unions because many lower-level, white-collar employees are females and only marginally attached to the labor force; because they regard themselves as having higher status than blue-collar workers; and because of their closer association with higher levels of management. There are, however, white-collar and professional workers who are union members, for example, railroad clerks, retail clerks, teachers, airline pilots, actors, and musicians. An explanation why people in these particular occupations have joined unions is offered in the reading. One reason that most professionals have *not* joined unions is that they are already represented by organizations performing some of the same functions. Lipset concludes that unions will undoubtedly lose collective bargaining strength unless they can find some way of organizing the employed middle class.

The final reading in this chapter is Charles Killingsworth's analysis of the effects of automation upon industrial relations. The issues for collective bargaining that are most directly attributable to automation are the combination of old jobs or the shifting of tasks among jobs, the creation of new tasks such as monitoring panels of lights or gauges that can be performed by supervisors or other persons not represented by the union, and the changes in methods of wage determination required when rate of output is determined mechanically rather than by the skill or effort of the worker. Some possible indirect or long-run effects of automation are also considered. Strikes may become a less effective union weapon in highly automated industries such as telephone and gas and electrical utilities. Where workers are involved primarily in machine maintenance rather than machine operation, it is possible for a *supervisory* force to keep the plant in operation. Another indirect effect has been an increasing amount of bargaining over job security provisions. Whether or not automation will produce unemployment, the threat that it *may* do so has produced union concern with negotiating greater job security. According to Killingsworth, automation has not produced any great or unusual problems for collective bargaining, but it may do so as it spreads into a wider variety of industries.

31. Power and Union-Management Relations

Robert Dubin

Central to any analysis of union-management relations is the concept of social power. It is, therefore, pertinent to start this analysis with a definition and discussion of power. Bargaining power is a much-used and abused term in the study of union-management relations. The term is typically associated with the use of force or the exercise of authority. In this study we shall examine power as it relates to the performance of functions in a social relationship. As a consequence of this view of power we can understand how conflict can become institutionalized in a society.

Power Defined

We mean by function that an act has observable consequences in its environment. As the late Professor Louis Wirth was fond of observing, "If there is a difference, it makes a difference," a statement which puts very succinctly the meaning of function.[1] When an act has observable consequences in the environment we can say it is functional in that environment.

Power may be defined as the importance that consequences of actions have in a social relationship. If the consequences of an act are highly important for everyone involved in the act, then the actor is powerful.

Power relations result from the execution of functions that are necessary to a social relationship. Power relations bind the actors in a social relationship into a system of functional interdependence.[2] The action counterpart of functional interdependence is the power relationship between people or groups caught up in some system of interdependence. Typically, power relations involve contests over the performance of functions. It is for this reason that conflict is a characteristic feature of power relations.[3]

It should be pointed out, particularly for the analysis of collective bargaining, that power relations do not depend upon consensus between the groups interacting. It is the recognition of interdependence, rather than

Reprinted from *Administrative Science Quarterly*, 2 (June, 1957), 60-81.

[1] R. K. Merton, "Manifest and Latent Functions," *Social Theory and Social Structure* (New York: Free Press, 1949).

[2] Emile Durkheim, *On the Division of Labor in Society*, George Simpson, trans. (New York: Macmillan, 1933).

[3] Herbert Blumer, "Social Structure and Power Conflict," in A. Kornhauser, R. Dubin, and A. Ross, eds., *Industrial Conflict* (New York: McGraw-Hill, 1954), pp. 232-239.

agreement on its nature, that constitutes the bond establishing the mutual dependence. From this standpoint collective bargaining in modern American industry is a necessary rather than a voluntary relationship.[4] A particular union and management can deal only with each other in the industrial establishment over which they jointly exercise control. In this enforced relationship the control of the functions establishing interdependence is precisely the subject matter of the power contest. Who shall perform what functions and in what manner become the central issues of collective bargaining. It is lack of agreement on these issues that leads to the power struggles for their settlement.

A second important consequence of this view of power for union-management relations is that power relations become an organized and orderly set of integrated functions. As each power contest is resolved, the resultant agreement is a form of consensus between the parties. Thus lack of consensus leading to conflict is converted into specific consensus on given issues by the agreements reached through collective bargaining. These agreements specify the distribution of power between company and union. The agreements have a systematic character. As we shall show below, the consensus reached through collective agreements constitutes the basis upon which industrial power relations can be said to be institutionalized.

There are two aspects to the empirical measurement of power. Every function in a system of functional interdependence has some degree of essentiality to that interdependence. The degree of essentiality of a function to a system is one measure of the amount of power that surrounds the performance of that function.

A second measure of power is the specificity or diffuseness with which the function is executed. If the function may be performed by a variety of participants in the relationship, then the amount of power attaching to its performance will be relatively low. On the other hand, if a function is performed exclusively by a single party to the relationship, the power may be correspondingly increased.

Thus we measure power in terms of the *essentiality* of the function performed and in terms of the *exclusiveness* with which it is performed.

These twin empirical indices of power have particular pertinence to union-management relations. For example, the *determination* of wages, hours, and working conditions is a central function in the whole employment relationship between employer and employees. If this function is not fulfilled we do not have an employer-employee relationship. Consequently, this is a highly essential function, and its performance unilaterally by either the employer or the employees, or jointly by union and management, is an act of considerable power in their relations. If we look at the exclusive facet of power, we can see that the unilateral determination of wages, hours, and

---

[4] Robert Dubin, "Discussion of W. E. Moore, Industrial Sociology: Status and Prospects," *American Sociological Review*, 13 (1948), 392.

working conditions is an act of greater power than a bilateral determination. When through government regulation we have a third force entering into the determination of aspects of the employment contract, the power explicit in the execution of this function is thereby more diffuse. No single group has as much power regarding wages, hours, and working conditions as would be true in a bilateral or unilateral determination of them.

Collective Bargaining as Systems

Collective bargaining systematizes union-management relations. The nature of this system can be seen in the union contract. The union contract provides the framework establishing orderly relations between union and management. The union contract is a constitution specifying rights, duties, obligations, and privileges accorded the parties to the contract. The collective agreement, as a constitution, is an orderly, integrated, and systematic statement of the mutual expectations of all parties to the agreement.

The boundaries of the system established through collective bargaining can be seen by examining areas of behavior excluded from the scope of the contract. Management still has within its unilateral jurisdiction a whole range of business decisions having to do with pricing, production, purchasing, product determination, plant location, determining level of output, and staffing managerial ranks. The union, on its side, has decisions over internal structure, union-government procedures, relations with other unions or federations, programs of membership education or welfare (including medical services, recreation, and counseling services), and political activity. At the same time, certain aspects of the collective agreement must fulfill the legal requirements established through governmental action. These include safety standards, restrictions on the employment of women and children, features of the health-and-welfare programs (relating to the taxing system and the system of public assistance and unemployment compensation), acknowledgment of minimum wages, as well as the legal rules governing collective bargaining itself.

We can then see that the system of group relations established through collective bargaining has an internal consistency and structure. It also has a clearly defined, but often shifting, set of boundaries distinguishing this system of group relations from other systems of interaction to which the parties in collective bargaining are also a party.

Institutionalizing Power Relations

Institutionalization can be viewed as systematic social relations. The establishment of an orderly set of satisfactory relations is an important means of preventing power conflict from wreaking social havoc. When we can delineate the features of standardized behavior patterns that are characteristic of collective bargaining, we shall have established the institutionalized features of union-management relations.

There appear to be six basic features of institutionalized collective bargaining. These are: (a) the evolutionary character of the disputes over ends; (b) the transformation of disputes over ends into disputes over means; (c) the standardization of principal forms of overt conflict; (d) the routinization of continuing relations; (e) the growing self-consciousness about latent functions in industrial power relations; and (f) the self-conscious development of ideologies of public self-justification. We shall consider in order each of these features.

Evolution of disputes over ends

A historical examination of the evolution of collective-bargaining issues from epoch to epoch reveals a developmental process in two senses. First, the bargaining demands and claims of a given period represent a logical outgrowth of the demands and claims that were dealt with in prior periods. Second, a forward planning of demands looking toward their successful accomplishment at some point in the future is instituted once the primary demands are resolved.

It is characteristic that the goals of the parties to collective bargaining are not achieved uniformly throughout the entire economy. At given points in history particular unions or particular industries are the leaders in collective-bargaining developments. Leadership in introducing demands for American labor rested largely with certain craft unions through the period up to the 1930's. For example, the printing trades, the clothing trades, and to some extent the building trades had unions which made considerable advances in the settled issues of collective bargaining.[5] In more recent periods the initiative has shifted to the industrial unions and the industries they cover, including steel, automobiles, and the vast jurisdiction covered by the teamsters' union.

One of the obvious consequences of this uneven development is that somewhere in the economy there is always either a union pressing for new gains or one that has already won gains beyond those achieved by the bulk of the labor movement at the time. These landmark ends become in turn goals for other unions that have not been as successful.

At the same time individual managements, fearful of making concessions on new issues to unions, learn through the experience of other managements which have made the concessions that the predicted dire consequences are not always fulfilled. There is, accordingly, a preparation by resistant managements for future changes in the number and character of the concessions they will grant as they study the experience of managements already granting the concessions.

[5] S. H. Slichter, *Union Policies and Industrial Management* (Washington, D.C.: Brookings Institution, 1941).

The evolution of the disputes over the ends of collective bargaining can be seen in still another framework. As each issue is accepted as a proper subject for collective bargaining, new areas of enterprise open up for the union to pursue additional goals. Solomon Barkin, for example, has pointed out that there has been a general evolution from a concern with a right *in* a job to a concern with a right *to* a job.[6] This distinction suggests that once unions have won some protection for a worker on his particular job in his particular company (a protection guaranteed by seniority provisions and a grievance procedure), the broader issue of whether an individual has a right to continuing employment anywhere in the economy becomes a logical next step. Thus the guaranteed annual wage and the supplementation of unemployment compensation through additional company-supported payments, or through generous severance arrangements, represents a logical evolution of union concern.

A second major feature of the evolution of issues incorporated in collective bargaining is forward planning looking toward future gains. The automobile workers succeeded in securing from the automobile industry a scheme of company-supported payments supplementing unemployment compensation. Walter Reuther pointed to this not as a victory for the guaranteed annual wage but as a step in that direction.[7] This kind of forward planning can, in general, be observed in those demands which continually reappear but which are not resolved in current union-company negotiations.

Many union plans for broadening collective bargaining never succeed. These plans represent trial balloons which either fail to gain adequate support from memberships or which are vigorously and successfully resisted by companies. Similarly many company plans looking toward restricting the scope of collective bargaining to a narrower range of issues than those presently included also prove futile.

We have suggested that there is an evolution of the ends sought by union and management in collective bargaining. This evolution is revealed in the first instance in the developmental character of new demands growing out of gains already achieved. Each established goal of bargaining becomes embedded in the collective consciousness of union and management bargainers. The really new advance gradually diffuses through the economy as more and more contracts include these new ends in their provisions. The evolution of the ends of collective bargaining is also evident in the forward planning from established gains to future possibilities. Here the outcome is less certain. Nevertheless, the base from which the future projections are made is clearly established in the existing pattern of collective agreements.

It has been asserted that institutionalization is the standardization of

---

[6] Solomon Barkin, "Labor Unions and Workers' Rights in Jobs," in Kornhauser, Dubin, and Ross, *op. cit.*, pp. 121-131.

[7] Public statements at the time of the 1955 contract settlements in the automobile industry.

behavior. There seems to be clear evidence from American collective bargaining that behavior of the bargainers becomes standardized with respect to the ends for which they bargain. It is in this context that we can understand, for example, the hypothesis of "key bargains" and "pattern-setting union-management relations."[8] The "key bargain" is the innovating one. It is crucial in the structure of union-management relations as the point at which significant modifications of the issues of bargaining are hammered out and established.

Disputes over ends into disputes over means

The second aspect of the institutionalization of collective power relations is the shift away from disputes over ends toward disputes over means for achieving approved ends. Here we are concerned with procedural disputes and disagreements centering on structural aspects of the union-management relationship.

The essence of disputes over means is twofold. There is first the established base from which the bargaining proceeds. Both parties are agreed on a given goal or objective. There is an initial mutual commitment to the goal of the bargain. This mutual commitment obviously solves half the problem of reaching a bargain, since the end is already accepted. The second feature of disputes over means is the wide range of procedural or structural solutions that typically exist for resolving the conflict. Disputes over ends tend to be polarized, often into mutually incompatible alternatives. Disputes over means have alternate solutions lying much closer together, sometimes with only narrow differences to be distinguished among them.

Some illustrations of disputes over means will make their character clear. The first is a typical example of a *procedural* dispute over means. A union and a management may agree upon some objective measure to establish output standards. Having agreed to this, they find that their subsequent disputes center entirely upon the techniques for establishing the objective measure of output. The company may urge time study; the union may counter with a demand for joint time study with union representatives actually participating in the study of jobs. The union may make a more modest demand to have all time-study results submitted for consideration to the departmental union representative for his acceptance before becoming official. The union may simply agree to accept time study with recourse to the grievance procedure when individual output standards are disputed. These alternatives are grouped within a relatively narrow range.

A second example deals with a typical dispute over means centering

[8] F. H. Harbison, R. K. Burns, and R. Dubin, "Towards a Theory of Labor-Management Relations," in R. A. Lester and J. Shister, eds., *Insights into Labor Issues* (New York: Macmillan, 1948). See also F. H. Harbison and R. Dubin, *Patterns of Union-Management Relations* (Chicago: Science Research Associates, 1947).

upon the *structural* aspects of union-management relations. An agreement in principle may be reached to establish a health-and-welfare program. It then becomes exceedingly important for both sides to determine how to distribute control over the welfare program, its policies, and its finances. The function of controlling the welfare program may be an important source of power in the union-management relationship. The fight to settle such an issue may be long and bitter and may even entail a strike.

In actual bargaining, the road to final agreement may be relatively smooth on disputes over procedural means. These are the typical issues that get settled on a "You take one, I'll take one" basis. These issues are the pawns in the bargaining chess game, early removed from the game as each side bargains off its minor pieces for like concessions from the other side. The road to final agreement on disputes over structural features of the relationship, however, may be difficult and strewn with violent conflict. These disputes involve the power positions of parties to the bargain. Concessions are made only under pressure. Considerable conflict can therefore exist in disputes over means where power aspects of the union-management relationship are involved.

Standardizing forms of conflict

A third basic feature of institutionalized industrial power relations is the standardization of the forms of conflict. This can be observed in several areas of collective bargaining.

In the most overt form of conflict, the strike, there is a clearly established pattern in American collective bargaining. The strike threat enters as an important part of bargaining strategy. If any progress is being made in bargaining as the strike deadline approaches, considerable pressures develop both within and outside the union to set a new strike deadline. If it becomes apparent that a strike is almost inevitable, very systematic preparations are made to carry out the strike. In some industries where advance preparation of the plant is necessary, the union cooperates actively with management. Thus in the steel industry the banking of furnaces has become a ritualistic part of the strike preparation.

The actual cessation of work takes on a ceremonial aspect. Pickets are posted, of course. But increasingly their presence is to advertise the existence of the strike rather than to constitute a physical barrier to strikebreakers. Violence on picket lines has become very infrequent and is likely to continue to be notable by its absence.

In the fundamental process of collective bargaining the strike has become increasingly a ceremonial social crisis that signalizes the need for active government intervention in the labor dispute. Particularly since World War II the existence of a strike has become the public stimulus for government intervention looking toward settlement.

We can conclude that the strike as a mode of industrial conflict has become highly ritualistic in large segments of American industry. Even the so-called "wildcat" strike, which, by definition, occurs from a welling up of worker discontent, has come to be a union instrument for forcing management attention to local-plant problems.[9] The wildcat, or unauthorized, strike is viewed by union officials, with a considerable amount of concurrence by management, as a primitve form of democratic revolt by the workers. This image of the wildcat strike makes it an effective weapon to dramatize a crisis requiring immediate attention at the collective-bargaining table. The unauthorized strike as a mode of industrial conflict calls attention to local-plant issues requiring attention by local-plant management. In this sense the unauthorized strike parallels the large-scale strike as a mode for calling attention to unresolved conflict. The large-scale strike is the signal for government intervention; the unauthorized strike is the signal for local-management attention to issues in conflict.

The widespread use of the grievance procedure illustrates another area in which a mode of industrial conflict has become standardized. The grievance procedure is a quasi-judicial system for handling disputes under the contract. It has become widely accepted in American collective bargaining and has proved exceedingly effective in institutionalizing the handling of relatively minor and special problems under the collective agreement.[10]

In a number of industries the grievance procedure culminates in an appeal to an impartial umpire or arbitrator whose function is to act as a court of final appeal. Where such office is not incorporated in the collective agreement there may be resort to an *ad hoc* umpire or arbitrator to handle grievances on which the management decision is unacceptable to the union. The very existence of the office of umpire illustrates how a permanent social structure has been built up around the grievance procedure. It is not within the scope of this paper to examine the grievance procedure in detail. It is, however, clear that the widespread use of this procedure is an important aspect in the institutionalization of the modes of industrial conflict.

Finally, at still another level there is a characteristic institutionalization of conflict. In the nonofficial relations between company and union officers there is strong evidence that a great deal of minor conflict is handled through private deals between the officers.[11] The unofficial settlement of disputes is

[9] J. F. Scott and G. C. Homans, "Reflections on the Wildcat Strikes," *American Sociological Review*, **12** (1947), 278-287.

[10] Robert Dubin, "The Grievance Process: A Study of Union-Management Relations" (unpublished doctoral dissertation, University of Chicago, 1947); B. Karsh, "The Grievance Process in Union-Management Relations" (unpublished master's thesis, University of Chicago, 1950); Van D. Kennedy, "Grievance Negotiation," in Kornhauser, Dubin, and Ross, *op. cit.*, pp. 280-291.

[11] Melville Dalton, "Unofficial Union-Management Relations," *American Sociological Review*, **15** (1950), 611-619.

typically made within the broad framework of the collective agreement. The basis of agreement reached in unofficial collective bargaining, however, shifts from standardized principles of the union contract to private and personal higgling involving the mutual exchange of minor favors. Once the collective agreement is accepted, company and union officers at all levels are expected to conform to the standards of interaction established under the contract. But issues still arise for which the contract does not provide means for settlement and which lead to nonofficial bargaining in which the individual exchange of favors becomes the medium of exchange. Thus even issues requiring solutions outside the union agreement are settled in systematic ways through private bargaining.

In this brief survey of the forms of industrial conflict we have suggested that routinization of conflict methods is evident in American industrial relations. At four levels—authorized strikes, wildcat strikes, grievance settlement, and nonofficial bargaining in the plant—established patterns of conflict action seem to exist. It seems fair to conclude that the modes of industrial conflict have been institutionalized.

Routinization of continuing relations

The routinization of continuing relations is best revealed in the distribution of time spent in the collective relations between union and management. It is estimated that between 75 and 90 per cent of the total investment of time of union and management officials who are involved in union-management relations is devoted to the continuous relations between them. The routinization of continuing relations between management and union is signalized in part by the professionalization of official positions in the bargaining relationship. Management has developed industrial relations departments, and unions have developed characteristic offices for dealing with management at all levels.[12]

In addition to the specialization of personnel on both sides there has grown up the general acceptance of what is often designated as a system of industrial jurisprudence.[13] Much of the substance of continuing relations is centered on the maintenance of balance between previous decisions arrived at through bargaining or through grievance-settlement procedures and current decisions made in existing disputes. The common law of plant relations is a reality. It provides a sociological framework of norms, standards, and procedures into which most future developments can be fitted.

[12] See any standard text dealing with collective bargaining, such as Neil W. Chamberlain, Collective Bargaining (New York: McGraw-Hill, 1951). On the union side an excellent treatment will be found in J. B. S. Hardman and M. F. Neufeld, The House of Labor (New York: Prentice-Hall, 1951).

[13] Ordway Tead, "Perspective on Democratic Industrial Government," Annals of the American Academy of Political and Social Science, 224 (November, 1942), 46-53.

Latent functions in industrial power relations

Unions have become important as organized social groups in areas other than collective bargaining. Management has always been important in the economic and political systems of this country independently of its collective relations with unions. It is beyond the scope of this paper to make an extended analysis of union and management latent functions in power relations.[14] At best, we can illustrate the growing consciousness of the parties to collective relations in industry about such functions.

On the union side, one of the most significant latent power functions is that of providing, through collective bargaining, a mechanism for collective social mobility, that is, of using collective bargaining to enhance the standing of a union membership relative to other organized and unorganized groups in the labor market. In their policies individual unions have become increasingly self-conscious of their role in providing collective social mobility. To a considerable extent the old-fashioned union demand for "more, more, more" has been modified into a demand for more than the steelworkers, or more than the automobile workers, or more than the teamsters, or more than the coal miners. The invidious comparisons made by union officers and union members between their standing and the standing of other groups in the labor market is substantial evidence of the growing importance of unions as a mechanism for collective social mobility. Increasingly the economic demands of individual unions are cast in comparative terms. While it is true that the cost-of-living index is a standard base of comparison of economic status through time, the more cogent argument for advance by a single union is that some other union has secured for its membership a substantial economic advancement.

On the management side of the bargaining table, one illustration of the growing importance of the latent function of collective bargaining is perhaps outstanding. Management has become increasingly aware of the shift in its own functions in the management enterprise. Collective bargaining has been an important factor in this shift.

Management has a reawakened awareness of the growing limitations in its discretion to manage.[15] The power contests between management and unions have always centered upon who controls the activities of policy making in the employment contract and related areas. The "related areas" have taken on importance as bilateral determination of the employment contract has become largely institutionalized in the economy. The current concern for control of related areas is no doubt fostered by the rapid technological

[14] Cf. Merton, *op. cit.*, for a classic analysis of latent functions.

[15] A recent example is found in National Association of Manufacturers, Employee Relations Department, *Information Bulletin #24* (May, 1955). An earlier treatment is in L. Hill and C. R. Hook, *Management at the Bargaining Table* (New York: McGraw Hill, 1946), with a more analytical treatment to be found in Neil W. Chamberlain, *The Union Challenge to Management Control* (New York: Harper & Row, 1948).

advances being made through automation. Where does management stand in its ability to control the amount and rate of technological change? To what extent and on what issues will technological change become a matter for bilateral consideration and sharing of decision with unions? The National Association of Manufacturers is fostering a vigorous effort to convince management that it must stop making further concessions to unions in sharing decisions in related areas and must even attempt to recapture unilateral control in those areas where the union has already won the right to co-determination.

There is no logical or functional boundary line between the traditional areas of collective bargaining (wages, hours, and working conditions) and related areas like technological change and health-and-welfare services. The extent to which unions gain a voice in the related areas will be determined in the power struggle with management. It is now clear that management is being alerted by its own spokesmen to the indirect consequences of collective bargaining as they affect the full range of management functions.

A very significant point about the growing awareness of the latent functions of collective bargaining for both parties is that once power relations have become institutionalized for the standard areas of conflict the parties develop a growing awareness of the unanticipated consequences of their relationships. This is clearly happening in the collective-bargaining arena. We can suggest that the major arena for power relations is relatively well stabilized for both parties. They are now very much concerned with the issue of where the boundaries lie which establish the limits of their relations.

The problems of the shifting boundaries of collective bargaining are, of course, directly related to the evolution of disputes over the ends of union-management power relations. We are now suggesting, in amplifying the first section of this part of the paper, that the evolution of the ends or goals of collective power relations in industry is in the direction of making explicit the latent functions of union-management relations. Once these latent functions become explicit, the power struggle will shift to the determination of their control.

Ideologies of public self-justification

The analysis of the self-images of unions and management is the last aspect of institutionalized power relations that we shall examine. The moral self-images and self-justifications of any organized group constitute critically important data for functional analysis. One of our major premises is that the analysis of social functions can be clarified rapidly by examining the kinds of functions that are the subject matter of moral self-images. In particular, we would assert that those functions most requiring public justification are the content matter of moral self-images.[16]

---

[16] The remainder of this section of the paper is taken from a part of Kornhauser, Dubin, and Ross, *op. cit.*, pp. 18-22, written by the author.

It is, of course, possible to characterize organized management and organized labor as special-interest groups in our society. It is possible to point to the private and selfish character of some of their collective goals. But more important from our standpoint is the fact that every organized group seeks to orient itself significantly toward the larger society within which it operates. Each group fits its collective action to the range of acceptable behavior of the society. Each group, furthermore, develops a program and a moral justification for its purposes and goals. In examining the self-defined moral positions of management and labor, we can find still another point of leverage for an analysis of the functions over whose control the power struggle in union-management relations is constituted.

The moral justification of the goals and policies of management in relation to industrial relations takes two courses. The first is the broad contention that the stability of our society is dependent upon management's stout defense of the principles of free enterprise in the collective-bargaining relationship. The second course is the assertion that supervisory and managerial techniques are designed to maximize the status of the individual worker, providing him with psychological as well as material security. Thus individual integrity and social stability are the twin moral pillars of management's position respecting collective bargaining.

American industrial management necessarily identifies itself as both the product and the protector of the free enterprise system. Many management pronouncements identify the basic welfare of our society with the strengthening of the free enterprise system. Bendix has clearly indicated how the manager's own view of his moral position has shifted from emphasis on individual opportunity and responsibility to one of social responsibility and industrial statesmanship. Bendix relates this shifting perspective to the bureaucratization of business organizations and to the complex interdependence they have with an industrial society.[17]

At the same time there has been an elaboration of countless supervisory and managerial techniques designed to provide for the material and psychological security of the employees of industry.[18] The moral position underlying these practices is the managerial concern for individual integrity. This concern is variously labeled "the new personnel philosophy," "the human-relations approach," or "scientific management," in terms much broader than Taylor implied in that phrase.

It is notable that this attitude represents a fundamental transformation of the Puritan ideology, in which the individual is viewed as duty bound to give to his job and to his employer the full measure of his efforts and dili-

---

[17] Reinhard Bendix, "Bureaucratization in Industry," in Kornhauser, Dubin, and Ross, op. cit., pp. 164-175.

[18] Charles A. Meyers, "Basic Employment Relations," and Mason Haire, "Group Dynamics in the Industrial Situation," in Kornhauser, Dubin, and Ross, op. cit., pp. 319-329, 373-385.

gence. Now the burden of duty is seen as falling upon the employer to provide the kind of environment in which the employee is able to reach the fullest self-realization and, thereby, the highest level of performance in the interests of the enterprise. The moral imperative has shifted from the shoulders of the worker to the hands of management.

On the union side there are also two moral positions that represent self-justification of union objectives. The one of largest scope is the contention that trade unions are instruments of social justice. The second moral justification is that the union protects the individual worker in his immediate work environment from exploitation and degradation. These self-justifications are inter-related, serving to give moral sanction to union policies at different levels of action.

As the social balance wheel to managerial power, unions are viewed by their officials and members as the most effective curb upon the societal dominance of management. The unions see themselves as the only effective force in the society capable of checking the growing social power of a managerial class. Government may respond to the direct or indirect blandishments of the managerial elite to serve its private or special interests. The industrial and commercial middle class is relatively unorganized and impotent as a social force. The farmers are organized largely in the pursuit of very narrow interests. Only labor unions are locked in direct battle with the managerial class and have the social power to checkmate or at least to balance the power of organized capital. Organized labor is fighting the battle for social justice at the only effective point in the social system, in the industrial arena itself. So goes the general tenor of one moral self-image of the union movement.

At the plant level and at the level of the individual worker-member, the union sees itself as the champion of the individual enmeshed in a bureaucratic structure over which he can exercise no control. But for the collective power of the union, the employer would have almost unrestricted opportunity to exploit his work force. Through all the instruments of collective bargaining the union seeks to minimize the exploitation of the individual worker at one of the most sensitive points of his contact with the social order, his job and means of livelihood.

In some of the classic interpretations of the American labor movement,[19] it was concluded that only radical unions perceived themselves as instruments of social justice, since they had an articulated program for social change. The labor union rooted in American industrialism was seen as amoral and materialistic, as job conscious and as striving toward the simple goal of "more, more, more." What was not so readily perceived was that, in order to achieve job control and gain more, organized labor had to enter into direct power contests with industrial management.

[19] Selig Perlman, A Theory of the Labor Movement (New York: Macmillan, 1949).

The conflict also required that each party seek the approbation of legitimacy for its goals from the larger society. In short, each side had to provide moral justifications for its immediate goals and tactics in order to secure, if not approval, at least the neutrality of public opinion and of the governmental instruments of social control. Thus, as one consequence of the restructuring of social power through collective bargaining, each side found it necessary to erect moral shoring for its goals and policies.

How do the self-justification of management and organized labor match up? Particularly, how do they relate to the issue of industrial conflict? Both groups look forward to the satisfaction of their goals within the structure of a free enterprise system. While management insists that the system has reached its mature and effective form, unions contend that further development still lies ahead. Management wants to consolidate the system and urges its course on the grounds that social stability will bring tranquillity and permanent order to the social system. The union movement wants additional steps as the fulfillment of social justice for workingmen and, therefore, seeks to shift the centers of social power in the direction of organized labor.

At the plant level, management finds at its disposal a wide range of managerial techniques for adjusting people to jobs, or jobs to people, in the interests, at least in part, of preserving the individual's psychological and material integrity. The union justifies much of its plant-level activities as being motivated by the same values. Here the difference between labor and management turns on means, in relation to the moral self-images that each has.

We have given a more extended treatment to the moral self-justifications of unions and management than to the other aspects of the institutionalization of industrial power relations. The reason is simple. These self-images are diagnostic, first, of the functions over whose control authority is uncertain and therefore requires legitimation. Attempts by the parties to collective bargaining to renew or establish the legitimacy of their functional roles in the society reveal the functions that are uncertainly established. Second, the analysis of self-images neatly summarizes the main features of the other five aspects of institutionalized power relations. Finally, these self-images have a strong moral component making for ideological conviction and commitment. The self-images structure the moral values of groups and give to them their main drift in the social system.

In summary, we can now suggest that the institutionalization of power relations does not change their character. The social expression of power can be routinized; power relations can become systematic in character; yet the nature of the social relationship does not change. Once this simple yet fundamental notion is firmly established, we shall be able to analyze industrial relations in realistic terms.

Change and Stability

Students of union-management relations have tended to tailor their analytical frameworks to the developments of the current industrial scene. During the late '30s and early '40s, when trade unionism was making rapid strides, the analysts were concerned with problems of change. The industrial scene was undergoing marked transformation. Unions were growing in size very rapidly, with positive government support. The major industrial firms established collective relations with their employees, often after long years of bitter and repressive hostility to unionism. Also, the content of collective agreements included an ever-increasing number of issues. The challenge for the analyst was to determine what forces and factors were causes for the rapid changes. A secondary problem was to determine the probable directions in which future changes would occur. The classic study of change is the collection of case studies edited by Harry A. Millis.[20]

In the more recent period analysts of union-management relations have turned their attention to the phenomenon of stability in these relations. It is notable that the National Planning Association studies were unsuccessful in producing generalizations relevant to stability.[21] The cause is not hard to find. The analysts were still working primarily with an analytical framework designed to make sense out of change. In large measure they saw stability as the opposite of change. Those factors leading to change were, therefore, seen as the opposite of those factors leading to stability. For example, in the concluding analysis of these studies, lists were drawn up in which paired opposites were listed in two columns, one headed "causes of industrial strife" and the other headed "causes of industrial peace."

One of the most obvious implications of carrying an analytical framework for studying change over into the analysis of stability was that these two polar types of union-management relations were seen as points on a continuum. There was the inevitable temptation to conclude that every union-management relationship was ultimately moving toward stability and that it had not yet reached this state of affairs only because of its immaturity.[22] There was an additional implicit assumption that in moving toward stability the union-management relationship was in the process of transformation from a power relation to some other kind of social relation.[23]

It is our general contention that both a rapidly changing union-management relationship and one that is stable are still power relations. We

[20] Harry A. Millis, ed., *How Collective Bargaining Works* (New York: Twentieth Century Fund, 1945).
[21] Clinton S. Golden and Virginia D. Parker, *Causes of Industrial Peace under Collective Bargaining* (New York: Harper & Row, 1955).
[22] See various of the individual case studies in *ibid*.
[23] W. F. Whyte, *Pattern for Industrial Peace* (New York: Harper & Row, 1951).

have tried above to set forth in some detail the general point that stable union-management relations are so because the power interaction has become institutionalized. There is no modification of power into some other form of interaction. When power does become institutionalized, however, the social structure in which it is expressed and the social relationships through which it is expressed become stabilized.

We now recast the problem of stability versus change in the following terms. The social relationship that is changing rapidly is one that is characterized by a minimum of institutional imperatives. The relationship is in a state of flux precisely because it lacks standardized and repeatable features. When the relationship becomes stable, it can be said to be institutionalized without changing its forms or modes of interaction. It thus turns out that stability and change in union-management relationships are, indeed, part of a continuum. The continuum, however, is that of degree of institutionalization. On a scale of institutionalization we have at the low end highly unstable or changing union-management relationships and at the high end stable or relatively slow-changing relationships.

Conflict and Cooperation

The problem of conflict and cooperation in union-management relations has had a parallel history to the problem of change and stability. There has been general belief that conflict is characteristic of the period of rapid change and that as a union-management relationship matures it tends to take on many more elements of cooperation. For some analysts of union-management relations this idea has reached almost the level of a law of historical evolution. This view suggests that conflict lies at one end of a continuum with cooperation at the other.[24] Individual union-management relationships tend to move between these poles in either direction. For the economy as a whole it would appear that the trend is from the conflict pole toward the cooperation pole.

In terms of our analysis we would characterize the conflict-cooperation problem in the following terms. Institutionalization of power relations means that increasing areas of the relationship come to be standardized and mutually defined by the parties to the relationship. This is the real meaning of cooperation in union-management relations. This kind of cooperation may be developed to a considerable degree through such measures as joint time studies and jointly administered health and welfare programs. At the same time that institutionalization is taking place, however, new areas of conflict are opening up over the ends of collective bargaining, or the means of collective bargaining, or the latent functions of collective bargaining. From this standpoint it then becomes clear that

[24] George C. Homans, "Industrial Harmony as a Goal," in Kornhauser, Dubin, and Ross, *op. cit.*, pp. 48-58.

every union-management relationship is always characterized by the simultaneous presence of elements of conflict and of cooperation. Where emphasis is placed upon the institutionalization of the relationship, cooperation tends to overbalance the elements of conflict. When new issues are opening up in collective bargaining, the elements of conflict predominate.

Permanence of Power Relations

This is the central thesis of this paper: union-management relations are systems of institutionalized power relations. So long as collective bargaining is the central way that unions and managements order their relations, power will always be the dominant social process relating management and unions.

Power relations are permanent: they involve a contest over the performance of functions. In union-management relations the functions in question are the policy-making opportunities affecting the employer-employee relationship. Unions are clearly pressing for an ever-expanding voice in the determination of the employer-employee relationship. Furthermore, the relationship itself is undergoing a marked transformation, so that the areas of collective bargaining do not remain stable and clearly defined. Nevertheless, significant areas of collective relations do become institutionalized. Short of complete destruction of unions or stringent governmental regulation of their activities and particularly of the scope of collective bargaining, union-management relations will continue to be power relations.

32. Wildcat Strikes

Leonard R. Sayles

The growing emphasis on industrial peace, both in the writings on industrial relations and in the thinking of union and management leaders, may give the impression that most of the problems of industrial unrest have been solved. Granted that there are still some unorganized firms "to conquer" and some real differences of opinion concerning federal labor policy "to reconcile," most observers seem to agree that the number of open conflicts between union and management is rapidly diminishing.

With this growing maturity we might well expect that the most unrestrained and least disciplined weapon in an industrial power struggle—the wildcat strike—would completely disappear. In recent years we have grown accustomed to the businesslike way in which both sides in a strike cooperate for an orderly shutting down of the industrial processes, respect all the "rules of the game," and thus insure a highly rational test of strength. Given such an environment, the wildcat strike, with its lack of discipline and primitive disregard for the rules incorporated in the labor-management contract, seems almost like some relic of the past; it might occur in unusual circumstances, but certainly it no longer serves the functions for which it was originated.

Yet the wildcat strike has not disappeared, nor is there any evidence that it will in the foreseeable future. Indeed, as we shall see, there may be some reason for expecting the number of such unauthorized work stoppages to increase. (The fact that both management and union, embarrassed by such situations, are reluctant to provide the necessary data, and in many instances are hesitant even to discuss the question, simply means that it is difficult to assess the incidence of wildcat strikes with any degree of precision.)

What are the factors responsible for this vestige of open conflict, and what special problems are posed for management and union officials who must cope with a wildcat?

Types of Wildcats

The wildcat can take many forms besides the well-known walkout: a group "sits down" at the work place refusing to perform the work, or a number of men call up to report ill, or some of them report in but "forget" the keys

Reprinted from *Harvard Business Review*, **32** (November-December, 1954), 42-52.

to their tool boxes—almost anything short of a situation involving picket lines.

While strictly speaking the wildcat is a work stoppage called by a local union without the authorization of (or even in direct opposition to) the national union, *any* cessation of work during a contract period is essentially the same kind of phenomenon. Furthermore, the matter of authorization not only is difficult to determine in many cases, but it may actually be misleading since many "quickies" gain recognition *ex post facto* when the national leadership sees no alternative. (Note, also, that under the Taft-Hartley law, the union is probably responsible in most cases for the acts of its membership regardless of the question of authorization.)

Perhaps the most useful way to see the wildcat strike is as the result of several quite distinct types of collective bargaining situations. On occasion they may be a selected instrument of national union policy or a weapon in the struggle for power over the contract between the national union and its locals; more often they reflect instabilities within the local union itself. Let us examine each of these in some detail.

National union policy

In some circumstances (presumably less frequent than in the past) the national union itself finds that some type of concerted action is necessary but the traditional strike weapon is not available. Perhaps the industry is being operated by the government, or a government-sponsored board has rendered an unpalatable decision, or public opinion militates against a formal strike. In such circumstances the union may resort to wildcats.[1]

There are times when the membership would not support a potentially lengthy and expensive struggle, or the cost to the employer in comparison with the cost to the union would not warrant such drastic action. So, lacking other leverage, the union may engage in what are expected to be short-lived work stoppages in critical locations in order to pressure management to make some specific concession. These strikes generally involve minimum costs to the workers since the duration is limited and the numbers concerned are relatively small, while the cost to management is proportionately greater.

The explanation usually given for such stoppages is inability to "hold the men in." Actually these work stoppages are not unauthorized, even in terms of the formalities of the situation. The union is openly using economic pressure to achieve a collective bargaining objective. (A recent decision of the National Labor Relations Board may make such action relatively more expensive for unions. The NLRB has declared that where

---

[1] Cf. Richard A. Lester's description of the Trainmen's strikes in 1950 and 1951 in his *Labor and Industrial Relations* (New York: Macmillan, 1953), pp. 233-234.

"hit-and-run tactics" are designed merely to disrupt the enterprise, they are not deemed to be "protected" activities under the Taft-Hartley law. As a result management may "discriminate against" workers so involved without fear of unfair-labor-practices charges.)

In some cases the union may utilize specific provisions of the contract that are not arbitrable as the basis for a wildcat strike during the life of the contract. For example, in the automobile industry it is quite common to have production standards, health and safety matters, and rates on new jobs exempted from the arbitration procedure of the contract. One of these matters may be made an issue, even though the real target is an arbitrable matter which has not been settled to the union's satisfaction.

The fact remains—as I think most observers would agree—that the wildcat as an instrument of national union policy never played a really significant role, and it is likely to have an even less important place in future labor relations. With the exception of a few situations where the union lacks real bargaining strength and institutional security, most labor leaders assume that the negative effects of such disruptive activities on their relationship with management outweigh any possible gain. The attitude of trying to cause trouble for the sake of trouble—an occasional characteristic of the early organizational phase when labor leaders were first "feeling their oats"—is rare today.

National-local struggle

We are witnessing a continuing shift in power from the local unit to the national union, particularly in unions where multiunit and over-all industry considerations are of prime economic importance. As a result of this shift, policies and agreements become more inflexible for the local union that may desire to adjust a specific problem with a specific management.

The writing of any contract covering many units is likely to involve a realistic "trading off" of individual local demands, and this can be a source of rank-and-file unrest. Under the umpire system as it has developed, many national unions take the responsibility of "screening out" local grievances that they feel are unjustified under the contract or that are unlikely to receive favorable consideration by the arbitrator.

The result may be a rebellious demonstration, one form of which is the wildcat. Here, although the basic issue may involve management, the strike is against the top union hierarchy. The question being decided is who really has the power, local or top union officials.

Undoubtedly this problem is much greater in countries like Great Britain where the unions not only have had to make commitments on an industry basis, but also have had to negotiate with the government more frequently. For example, a noted British authority, K. G. J. C. Knowles, comments:

Tightening trade union discipline has tended to restrict the size and length of strikes. But this restriction of the scale of strikes has been achieved at the cost, so far, of a greater number of separate strikes. The wider scope of agreements, with their inevitable anomalies, has probably helped to increase the number of strikes occurring as well as having affected their formal causes. Unofficial strikes (occasionally "strikes against the union") have become more frequent.[2]

So far this kind of national-local union struggle has become severe in this country only in war time when the national officers were committed to a no-strike policy and enforcement of other government-imposed regulations. However, the increasing emphasis on standard contract terms may accentuate conflicts of interest between a local and its national (or between locals of the same union).

Within the local

It is likely that the great majority of wildcat strikes originate at the local union level as a result of circumstances in the individual plant.

Struggle for power. Just as some wildcat strikes involve struggles for power between local leaders and national union officials, they are also used as tactical weapons within the local.

The "outs" have often sought to embarrass the incumbents by a well-timed walkout, recognizing that the situation will be a difficult one for the leadership to handle. Typically the office seekers will find problems that affect a strategically placed rank-and-file group which to date have defied settlement through negotiation, stimulate them to walk out, and thus present the existing leadership with a critical dilemma. Supporting the strikers may seriously hamper further negotiations; failure to support them will pave the way for the charge of siding with the company. In the resulting confusion the existing leadership may be overthrown.

Radical elements in the local, particularly Communists and similar groups, may use such tactics. They may not be seeking office directly, and certainly they are not seeking a settlement of the issue; they are simply trying to bring about chaotic conditions to make their own behind-the-scenes program more effective. In fact, local as well as national union leaders always try to blame the Communists for unauthorized work stoppages if they can. But there is some possibility that the number of such radically led disturbances is exaggerated since, as Knowles points out in discussing the British experience: ". . . the power of political agitators to play on grievances is largely a function of the reality of the grievance and the time elapsing before it is dealt with . . . ; one cannot agitate in a vacuum."[3]

---

[2] K. G. J. C. Knowles, *Strikes—A Study in Industrial Conflict* (Oxford: Blackwell, 1952), p. xi; see also the excellent work by W. W. Haynes, *Nationalization in Practice: The British Coal Industry* (Boston: Division of Research, Harvard Business School, 1953).

[3] Knowles, *op. cit.*, p. 39.

Demonstration over local issues. In a number of instances, undoubtedly, the local leadership itself sponsors the strike for reasons that are obvious to both management and the membership. Usually there are a number of unsettled issues in the plant, grievances on which the union feels management may be stalling. The means of getting management to "move" on some of these is one or more walkouts. In this connection, one close observer, Jack Barbash, points out:

In the garment industries, strikes have been called to strengthen the enforcement of an agreement previously concluded when it appears that certain employers are attempting to "chisel" on the agreement. The strikes are frequently called "stoppages" in order not to fall under the ban on strikes which the agreement specifies. . . . Many workers were convinced that management was taking advantage of labor's no-strike pledge [during the war] to stall on the handling of day-to-day grievances.[4]

Under some circumstances, the local union leaders may feel it important to prove to management that they have the power to demand action on their grievances and to strike the plant when necessary. Very often the membership itself feels that a strike is essential to show management that unilateral decision making is at an end. In some newly unionized situations, the attitude Scott and Homans describe as prevailing during the war is still prevalent: "For the first time in many years, the labor force was not large enough. There is no doubt that many working men felt that this condition, which they never enjoyed before, enabled them to insist that their demands be listened to."[5]

As one union leader told me, "The men seem to think they've got to show the company their power."

Occasionally, too, there are instances when management does the unpardonable in changing an accepted and expected practice, hints at some drastic change in method or schedule, or disciplines the workforce in a manner interpreted as arbitrary or discriminatory. The issue becomes plantwide, and the union is placed in the position of supporting plant sentiment or losing prestige.

A recent National Planning Association study in the *Causes of Industrial Peace* series records such a case:

Management had decided to start up a grinding and polishing line which had been idle since before the war. The bonus rate on this line was the subject of an unsettled grievance when the line was shut down in 1941, and union officials warned the company that the men would not start work on the line again until the bonus was changed. . . .

At the time all the local and International officers of the union and the officials of the company were in Chicago trying to negotiate a new agreement. . . .

    [4] Jack Barbash *Labor Unions in Action* (New York: Harper & Row, 1948), p. 126.
    [5] Jerome F. Scott and George C. Homans, "Reflections on the Wildcat Strikes," *American Sociological Review*, 12 (June, 1947), 279.

When the top union officers were finally confronted with the issue they seemed to agree that the company might have been technically correct in its position [that it had the right to start the line again without agreement on a new bonus plan], but by this time the Ottawa local had shut down the plant and the company's "right" had become an academic matter. The local and International officers tried but were unable to get the men back to work. . . . [Management declared it would negotiate no further because the issue now was union irresponsibility.] The union countered by calling an authorized strike in all plants. . . .[6]

Knowles describes the situation very well:

If these [serious grievances] were allowed to pass without immediate protest or were unable to be dealt with save by complex and lengthy procedures, the men's sense of solidarity—and hence the strength of their Trade Union in negotiation—might be severely weakened. Thus, even though many agreements contain provisions against striking before the procedural conditions have been fulfilled, quick strikes in breach of agreement may strengthen the union's possessive hand even though its officials are bound to repudiate them.[7]

Indeed, though there often may be formal repudiation, both the membership and management are aware that the walkout has union sanction.

Characteristics of the industry. In some cases the incidence of wildcat strikes is not attributable to specific plant problems, at least not to problems that are unique to a particular company. Rather, the strike becomes the accepted means for employees to deal with work pressures that are industrywide, thus taking the place of the usual grievance procedures.

Longshoremen and miners, for example, feel an unusual degree of common involvement in the problems of work; theirs is a social solidarity almost unequaled in other work environments. Resistance or barriers to wildcat walkouts are almost nonexistent. Uncertainties and insecurity are so commonplace on the docks and in the mines that the men who work there, feeling that they are isolated from the rest of society (if not despised by society), are not reluctant to express displeasure by concerted action. Moreover, the hazardous nature of the work causes them to be dependent to an unusual degree on one another. This may explain not only why strikes are accepted as a part of the daily routine but also why the pressures to conform to the norm of group action are almost irresistible.[8] The men live and work, play and strike as a single group. There are no competing allegiances.

[6] Frederick H. Harbison and King Carr, *Causes of Industrial Peace Under Collective Bargaining: The Libbey-Owens-Ford Glass Company and the Federation of Glass, Ceramic & Silica Sand Workers of America* (Washington, D.C.: National Planning Association, 1948), pp. 28-29.

[7] Knowles, *op. cit.*, p. 33.

[8] Cf. R. P. Lynton and S. C. M. King, *The London Docks, A Framework for Study* (London: British Institute of Management, mimeographed); Wayne Hield, "What Keeps Harry Bridges Going?" *Labor and Nation* (January-March, 1952), pp. 34 ff.; Haynes, *op. cit.*, p. 96.

Dr. Gerald Somers of the Department of Economics of the University of West Virginia, researching on labor relations in the bituminous mine fields, has called my attention to the absence of any pressures or barriers against striking in the mines. The strike is the accepted means of dealing with grievances. It may be that the safety problem is a partial explanation of the traditional reluctance to follow the more time-consuming channels of grievance processing.

A study of the 1951 wildcat dock strike in New York confirms the "industry" basis for some wildcat strikes. The leaders of the International Longshoremen's Association (now independent) in policy opposed strikes, particularly wildcats, and made efforts to quell their occurrence, but the structure of their industry precluded their success.[9]

Department or group grievances. So far we have been considering the wildcat strike at the local level as a product of internal political problems, a desire to assert power on the part of local leaders, or the membership's need to express itself violently and definitively toward management. All wildcats do not stem from these sources, and perhaps the most important ones do not.

Many problems that arise in the day-to-day life of an industrial plant affect only a small group within the union—for example, an unsatisfactory incentive rate, a poor line of promotion, or an unfair job classification. Some of the men involved may decide to take matters into their own hands. It becomes important to be able to answer the question: When is such a dispute likely to be processed through the grievance procedure, and when is it likely to take the form of drastic action such as a wildcat?

In most circumstances union leaders are anxious to restrain individual groups from expressing themselves by concerted action. As many union leaders have told me, "It hinders you in your bargaining with the company when they see that you can't control your own men and that you are not a responsible union." However, some problems do not automatically rise through the steps of the grievance procedure; in fact, some problems may not even be suitable for the grievance procedure since they are matters for direct bargaining during the life of the agreement.

Experienced negotiators on each side recognize that both management and the union are likely to act with greater dispatch on matters where there is some urgency, whether in relation to production needs or workers' needs. Accordingly, if after some period of unsuccessful negotiation the union leader indicates that he "may not be able to control the men much longer," results may develop more speedily. Most union leaders feel that during some crucial part of the negotiations it will be to their advantage to show the company that "the men are behind us." The task of the union

[9] Robert Lamson, "The 1951 New York Wildcat Dock Strike: Some Consequences of Union Structure for Management Labor Relations," *The Southwestern Social Science Quarterly* (March, 1954), p. 28.

leader is to control the pressure exerted so that management will expedite the settlement and yet the men do not take direct action, which might jeopardize the chances of settlement.[10]

Also as Riesman and others have observed, the union's bargaining position (power) is, in a sense, strengthened at times because it *cannot* control the rank and file.[11] While the membership, if dissatisfied with the settlement reached by their leaders, can "wildcat," local plant management or the first-line supervisors are unlikely to take matters into their own hands. This difference in the ability of these two institutions to demand conformity gives a very real advantage to the union. Perhaps a periodic display of uncontrolled passions will enable the union negotiator to bargain even more effectively at some future time. The union's internal public relations problems are thus useful as a counter in bargaining.

Actually, not all work groups or departments within a particular plant will be able to respond to the needs of the situation. Union leaders recognize that some groups are unable to act in concert even in the event of a rather serious group problem. The groups I have been referring to are those that *can* engage in premeditated concerted action. At times, indeed, they will be ahead of their leaders in demanding an immediate solution to some problem and threatening to walk off the job. When their demands are not met or when the tactics of collective bargaining require a demonstration, these groups have the internal cohesion required for a walkout.

It may seem surprising that a substantial amount of group solidarity is required for a wildcat. But from any plant survey, it is evident that most workers have never contemplated direct action and that they are incapable of demonstrating as a group.

Why is a strong informal organization necessary to a wildcat? While many managements would doubt it, the rank and file take a strike very seriously. Most companies have made it clear that such a breach of industrial discipline is a "capital" crime. The risks of punishment are great, and there is always the chance that neither the other work groups nor the union will support the wildcatting worker with sufficient vigor to protect his right to return to his job. One rank-and-file leader described graphically his feelings about initiating a wildcat:

The men are all afraid something is going to happen to them, something is going to go wrong and they will suffer. When you walk off the job, you feel the world's against you then; you're scared, awfully scared. You wonder what those supervisors are thinking when they're looking at you. The minute you stop work you think you should be back at work.

[10] For a more complete discussion of this problem of "controlling pressures on management," see Leonard R. Sayles and George Strauss, *The Local Union* (New York: Harper & Row, 1953), pp. 72-74.

[11] Quoted in R. Bendix and S. Lipset, *Class Status and Power* (New York: Free Press, 1953), p. 157.

It's like schoolboys going off to do something they shouldn't. They've learned to take orders for so long that they're afraid not to. They're afraid of being hurt for doing wrong, and they think they're doing wrong.

Aside from the barriers of having to break plant discipline, of having to ignore every established rule and probably the contract as well, there is another hurdle in the way of any group intending to stage a strike. Within the group itself people may be divided on the importance of the issue. It may not affect all of them equally; they may distrust their leaders; there may be other issues that some think more important; there is always the worry that they will not share equally in any gains. When wildcats do take place, they frequently involve less than half the number of workers presumably affected by the grievance in question.

Research is just beginning to tell us what it is that makes for divided and unified work groups. For our purposes it is important to recognize that unity is not always present. It is known that strong subgroups—with special interests and problems—vitiate over-all group strength. It follows that homogeneous work groups would be more prone to take direct action.

At the same time, there are work groups that engage in wildcat strikes without the premeditation and planning typical of the well-organized, cohesive department. These groups are at the opposite end of the scale from those described above. Lacking crucial unity of purpose and organization, they have often been unable to achieve even elementary objectives in the plant economy. Their grievances have gone unanswered; their scale of benefits may have declined relative to the rest of the plant. Frustrations gradually mount and tensions increase with the number of unsettled problems and the inability of the group to demonstrate concertedly their needs to union or management officials. Then some spark, perhaps minor in comparison to the backlog of grievances, ignites the conflagration. The ensuing walkout shocks both management and the union.

These strikes are the hardest to settle because the issue which causes the wildcat usually is not the basic problem. Often the group members are unable to agree among themselves on the basic problem or to express it to their leaders. These groups demonstrate an erratic and contagious type of concerted activity, as Barbash describes:

These kinds of strikes were started typically by what appeared to be trivial incidents. A foreman struck a worker and immediately the entire department stalked out. Or the management fired an active union steward for smoking in the toilet during working hours, or the infinite number of grievances which an incentive system can provoke. They were likely to be the culmination of a mounting number of disagreeable incidents, and what seemed to them management's arbitrary ban, say, on taking a "two-second drag" on a cigarette was the straw that broke the camel's back.[12]

[12] Barbash, *op. cit.*, p. 26.

While to management, and even to some union officials, there may be no apparent differences between walkouts that are a deliberate tactic of a well-organized pressure group and those that are the result of a spontaneous explosion in a relatively disorganized, typically ineffectual work group, the solution to the problems posed are totally different. It is therefore most important to be able to make these distinctions. To do so requires an intimate knowledge of the balance of power within the local and within the plant community itself as among various departments, occupations, and worker groups—a picture management rarely has or believes important to obtain.

Cost of wildcats

What is the extent of the wildcat strike problem in industry?

During the war a study of the strike problem in Detroit indicated that there were 118 work stoppages in a two-month period (December 1944 and January 1945).[13] It should be remembered that this was during a period in which management had guaranteed there would be no lockouts and unions had signed a no-strike pledge.

As far as the current period is concerned, from a firsthand study of the Detroit area I have only been able to glean isolated statistics like the following:

One company reported more than two dozen such walkouts during a one-month period in a single division that employs approximately 5,000 hourly paid workers.

In a division twice that size in another corporation, less than a half-dozen wildcat strikes were recorded during an entire year.

In a third company, companywide records indicate one strike per year for each thousand employees, causing an average loss of 17,000 man-hours each—in all, 0.7% of the man-hours worked.

There is no means of assuring the comparability or accuracy of these statistics. However, as far as I can tell from my own field work, they are illustrative of the scope of the problem.

It is difficult to draw any systematic conclusions from such scattered data, beyond the fact that wildcats are not disappearing. These figures very likely understate the problem since some companies do not even record a dispute in which no employee loses an entire shift. I think this much is clear: wildcat strikes may actually involve a greater loss of working time than formal strikes called over contract demands.

It would be interesting to know the average number of employees in-

---

[13] 79th Congress, 2nd Session, "Wartime Record of Strikes and Lockouts, 1940 to 1945," Senate Document No. 136, submitted by Senator Ball, as quoted in Scott and Homans, *op cit.*, p. 280.

volved in each strike. One informant told me that the average wildcat in his company involves 25 to 100 workers, roughly one-half the workers in the departments concerned. Of course in some circumstances the striking group is so strategically placed as to shut down the entire operation. This tends to be particularly true in the automobile industry where closely timed operations and the absence of raw material "banks" lead to vulnerability of the manufacturing process, although a strike of powerhouse workers, such as the one which recently shut down a large Canadian automobile plant, would affect any kind of manufacturing.

Sometimes, also, the walkout of one group of workers causes a sympathetic demonstration on the part of their fellow employees. Further research may clarify what determines a group's "influence" in the plant community and the extent to which a walkout tends to spread. In the meantime it is clear that the seriousness of the strike cannot be measured just by the numbers engaged in the initial walkout.

It is unfair to measure the cost to management of concerted worker resistance solely in terms of man-hours not worked. Wildcat strikes are only one form of concerted group activity designed to pressure management and/or the union. Well-planned slowdowns may last for a year or two and cost the company 15% to 50% of its normal production in a given department. Similarly, high rates of absenteeism, excessive turnover, or poor workmanship are often results of unsettled grievances. While the wildcat strike may provide the most dramatic, most easily measured loss, it is itself generally of relatively brief duration.

As managements well know, there is another loss involved in the wildcat—perhaps a more serious loss—in terms of plant discipline. A clear-cut victory for a group of wildcat strikers may well be demoralizing for the rest of the employees in the plant.

Problems of the Wildcat

Having seen that the wildcat strike is an important factor in production, in management-worker relations, in internal union operations, as well as being an indication of rank-and-file feeling, let us go on to consider in some detail the problems that the phenomenon raises for management and for the union.

For management

Management has a very tight wire to walk. The grievances that have reached the walkout stage are obviously of vital importance to the workers involved. Except in erratic groups the wildcat strike is a sharp signal that management has neglected an important area of worker interest which is magnified with the passing of time—particularly in its capacity to cause trouble. Yet acceding to such measures may be seen as more damaging than the cause of the resistance.

It is significant that the average worker does not contemplate a walk-out lightly, being aware that this is a serious breach of plant discipline and that a stiff penalty—perhaps discharge—may be the result. This means that real problems *must* exist before there is a walkout. It also means that fellow workers may support the walkout of one small group because they recognize that to fail to do so may subject the few who do leave the plant to "capital" punishment, while if they all go out together, management cannot easily discharge the entire department or plant.

Because major pressures are involved in any walkout, the task of getting people to go back requires the greatest skills. Once the men are out of the gate, the big risk has been taken; they have little more to lose; the worst is behind them. The feeling is stronger than ever that "we have to win!"

Yet management cannot afford to condone or reward the wildcat striker. Knowles draws the moral very cogently: "There is one thing which can be more damaging to the orderly conduct of industrial relations than an unofficial strike; it is a successful unofficial strike."[14]

In off-the-record remarks union leaders have been highly critical of companies that have been unable to withstand deftly applied worker pressure. They imply that management is neglecting its responsibility to manage when it consistently concedes the issue to the wildcat striker. Yet the fact is that the position many companies find themselves caught in can be most difficult. For example:

A supplier company in the automobile industry manufacturing a part not stock-piled by the assembly plant was under tremendous pressure from the buyer to settle a wildcat strike with dispatch and thus to avoid the enormously costly process of shutting down a major plant.

As the personnel director for the supplier noted: "The assembly plant doesn't want to hear about the issues involved or how it's going to hurt your discipline problem if you give in to them [the wildcat strikers]. They want those parts every hour on schedule, and if they don't get them they will look for another supplier."

Contract clauses. As a solution to management's problem, contract clauses penalizing participants in wildcat strikes have not been notably successful. Where an attempt is made to discover the leaders, some form of espionage may be required. Penalizing the entire group through a layoff or other disciplinary measure, even if it is carried out over a long period of time, may still upset production. In any event, the heritage of recriminations and ill feeling that results is not conducive to a resumption of normal plant relationships.

[14] Knowles, *op. cit.*, p. 35.

Further, in many instances management's agreement not to press for severe discipline is a condition for "getting the men to go back." There have been cases where the discipline question precipitated a new walkout, often involving the whole plant. Other workers realize that they may be in a similar position some day and that failure to support fellow members now may leave them "to sink" later.

It is still an open question whether penalties for strikers should be negotiated with the union. (Of course, penalties may always be protested through the grievance procedure *after* they have been imposed.) Union leaders argue that this is an excellent means of preventing a wildcat walk-out over the penalties for a wildcat walkout—a most vicious circle; but many managements are reluctant to adopt a policy which denies them an important prerogative. In practice such negotiations do take place quite often. Most companies assume the position that they will not bargain over the merits of the issue raised by the strikers during the illegal walkout, but they do negotiate over the discipline to be imposed.

Some managements concentrate their efforts on finding the ringleader or organizer of the wildcat. If he is discovered and is proved the leader, discharge may likely result—if the company is willing to fight the issue through. One company prepared the following checklist for its supervisors as an aid to identifying the leaders:

Someone in the group will lead the stoppage. The most common examples of directing or encouraging a strike or work stoppage are:

1. Orally spreading information on a contemplated strike or stoppage.
2. Leaving department to obtain information on strike or stoppage in another area of the plant.
3. Waving or calling others off the job or shouting such phrases as "Come on, boys"—"Let's go"—"We're through here"—"O.K., men," etc.
4. Shutting down machines or equipment.
5. Spreading feeling of antagonism among employees over management's position on issue in question.
6. Making obvious moves:
   a. First to quit work.
   b. In front of group.
   c. Giving signals.
   d. Giving directions to others.
   e. Encouraging others directly or indirectly to leave.
   f. Giving guidance to others on how to leave building or not to return.
   g. Demonstrating, i.e., whistling, calling, etc., during the stoppage.
7. Acting as spokesmen—if in sympathy with strike and trying to use the strike as a bargaining weapon.
8. Picketing or directing pickets.
9. Negative leadership—union representatives standing idly by.

Some managements probably blind themselves to the realities of the situation by their belief: *find the leader and you eliminate the problem.*

They assume there is no such thing as a *real* wildcat, that in fact such concerted activity is always carefully premeditated by formal or informal leaders within the plant. This theory argues that such organization and coordination are required that it is inconceivable that a spontaneous decision could be reached within a group to cease working.

A recent British study, among others, presents excellent evidence contrary to this belief. Here a trained team of observers was actually present when a group of workers did decide, as a group, to "walk out." Leadership became important only after the decision had been made.[15]

The conclusion to be drawn is that those individuals of influence who would favor such outbursts can be effective only when there is a predisposition, if not an actual decision, to take concerted action. More attention to the actual groups involved rather than to the leadership is thus required.

For the union

If management's problem is difficult, the union leader's situation is sometimes impossible under the circumstances of a wildcat strike. The problem in simple terms is whether or not the leadership should support the actions of a small group of union members. Increasingly, this burden is being shifted to the national union which is in a more protected position *vis à vis* the rank and file. But no matter who bears it, the burden of siding with management and getting the men back to work is a heavy one. Even the national union cannot accept the appellation "company stooge" without trepidation. Barbash sums this up:

At the same time, a union in which the leadership is highly responsive to local sentiment cannot be too harsh in meting out penalties to outlaw strikers. First, because the strikers may feel there is ample justification for their actions since effective and speedy adjustment of a grievance was not possible any other way. Second, because in the eyes of the local membership the union leadership is taking the side of management as against the workers.[16]

At the same time the wildcat strike puts the union in a very difficult position with management. Except where the union itself has threatened such "uncontrollable outbursts," it is a clear sign to the company that the union is not in control of its own members. In addition, the strike hurts union discipline, which is often just as vital to the union as plant discipline is to management. Groups striking at will destroy union strategy and responsibility and weaken the ability of the organization to withstand concerted management pressure at some future time. And the economic losses to the company can be reflected in the union's inability to demand satisfactory wage increases at contract termination points.

[15] T. T. Paterson and F. J. Willett, "Unofficial Strike," *The Sociological Review*, **43** (1951), 57.
[16] Barbash, *op. cit.*, p. 127.

In most cases the national union takes the position that the men must go back to work before the union can negotiate their grievances. As one national representative put it, "We get them together and read the riot act to them—to get them back somehow!"

Another national official summed up his experiences this way:

The easiest cases to handle are those where the men don't actually leave the plant. Then you can often get them back to work without too much trouble. But once they're out, you may have to leave them out for one, two, or three days, until the time is right. The trouble is management doesn't realize this; they expect you to be able to get them back to work almost immediately.

However, you have just got to learn from experience that there is a time when no appeal or threat will work. And when the union calls a meeting and is unsuccessful in getting the men to go back, then we're really in trouble.

In effect he was saying that if the company will leave it to union leaders, they can handle it, but it may take time. When the union does get the strikers together at a meeting, the staff representative must be a forceful advocate of his position; the men are not receptive to having their own union tell them to go back without a settlement assured or without knowing what discipline may be imposed by the company. In the face of a potential or actual mob, the union representative argues in terms of their violation of the union's constitution and contract, and often points out that they are depriving other, uninvolved workers of jobs (because of parts shortages and the like).

Union leaders may try to shift the blame for wildcats to management, alleging failure to correct grievances more rapidly, breaking of promises or contract provisions, or even actual *instigation* of walkouts. Some unions believe that a management will purposely encourage a walkout in order to harrass the union leadership and justify repressive measures. Even worse, there have been intimations that such action has been taken to reduce the company's liabilities under a merit-rated unemployment insurance program when layoffs are imminent.

The Future of Wildcats

What can we conclude concerning our original question: Will the number of wildcat strikes decrease in the future? Certainly it would be fair to say that those attributable to union organizing attempts will gradually become fewer. We have noted that the national union has rarely used the wildcat as a bargaining tool and has often taken the position that local walkouts will not be countenanced. National presidents in both the Rubber Workers (CIO) and the Auto Workers (CIO) among others have made strong, unambiguous statements at conventions and during actual wildcats that everything would be done to get the men back to work and to see that the problem did not recur. Thus, former president Sherman H. Dalrymple of the Rubber Workers has been quoted as saying: "If you want officers with responsibility but no powers—if you want a union that permits stoppages and slowdowns then get those kind of officers—but I'm not one of them!"[17]

These strong words of condemnation have been supported by union penalties assessed against ringleaders. Dalrymple himself quit as president of the Rubber Workers in July 1945 as a protest against strikes in Akron, Ohio. Undoubtedly there still are instances of the unauthorized work stoppage as a deliberate tactic of union leaders. Certainly at the local level encouragement is sometimes given to slowdowns and walkouts as the means of pressuring management. However, these occasions are definitely in the minority and represent a diminishing problem.

Those wildcats that have been the result of internal union factionalism and politics will also decline with the growing institutional security and stability of unions. Just as they have learned that collective bargaining brings responsibilities as well as privileges, unions have also learned that the existing plant relationship can be seriously damaged by the settlement of internal political matters in management's front parlor.

I cannot be so optimistic about wildcats resulting from concerted action by small groups in their own interest. The development of serious issues and crises is not restricted to contract negotiation periods. Problems can become acute at any time and there are times when the delays involved in the grievance procedure apparently are unendurable.

There is the myth that these blowups are entirely attributable to young, inexperienced, relatively unskilled employees. Scott and Homans note with surprise that "several of the most paralyzing strikes were set off by the discharge of men who had been with their companies for a long time."[18] My own data confirm the implication that many wildcat strikes take place in departments where skill levels and seniority are relatively high and where the men are experienced in the ways of the industrial community.

Management has much to gain if it can identify those groups which are likely to take such concerted action, either as a premeditated stratagem or as the result of unavoidable, contagious spontaneity. Particularly where management raises a high discipline barrier—usually the threat to punish severely any employee leading or participating in a walkout violating the contract—it should be clear that any group overcoming this barrier must have some serious reason for doing so.

But discipline alone is not enough. In one plant, for example, year after year a single group was responsible for all the wildcats that occurred; yet management discipline, even when accompanied by the threat of union discipline, did not deter them.

The wildcat is one of the few remaining "sure" methods by which

[17] *Labor Relations Reporter* (October 4, 1943), p. 162, as quoted in Barbash, *op. cit.*, p. 127.

[18] Scott and Homans, *op. cit.*, p. 281.

a rank-and-file group can initiate action aimed at either management or its own leaders. Mature collective bargaining means increased screening of grievances and increased union responsibility which militates against rank-and-file initiative. Whether this is "good" or "bad" is a judgment I shall leave to the reader.

Conclusion

While the wildcat strike has been used as a deliberate tactic of union policy, it is primarily a rank-and-file weapon. To deal effectively with the problem of the wildcat, it is necessary to acknowledge that its source *is* likely to be rank-and-file dissatisfaction, not leadership demagoguery and deceit as generally assumed.

Another position to be avoided is the one that *all* wildcats are the product of poor management and inattention to specific group grievances or inequities. In some instances the phenomenon, which is indeed a complex one, may be related more correctly to internal union structure, the technology of the plant, or the nature of the industry. More responsible, mature administrative unionism has its cost in terms of its inability to respond to the countless and often conflicting self-interest demands of members.

Continuously frustrating work in some industries, particularly where there is a socially isolated community of workers, as in longshoring and mining, makes fertile ground for concerted action that is unrestrained by paper contracts.

Within the industrial plant there are also groups that are prone to exercise this form of protest when individual discontent is magnified by the "resonance effect" of consensus. In one instance it may be the mark of the politically powerful work group that is sure of itself and its ability to obtain concessions without undue cost. Or, in the opposite instance, an internally divided group which has been unsuccessful in obtaining hearings for its problems, or even in vocalizing them so that management and union can "hear" them, may reach the flash point when enough unresolved issues accumulate.

Thus, paradoxically, in some circumstances the groups that are most capable of concerted action have the least need for it, while those typically considered incapable of united self-help measures may, in fact, be "forced" to take them.

I can offer no solution to the problem of wildcat strikes except to point to a trained group of "firefighters"—the experienced union representatives who are willing to "stick their necks out" to get the men back to work. More thorough answers will require further research in an almost unexplored relationship: that between technology, industrial organization, and work-group behavior.

33. Unofficial Union-Management Relations

Melville Dalton

The purpose of this paper is to discuss some phases of informal behavior occurring between union and management at the plant level in some of the larger industrial organizations working under national labor agreements. At this level, contrary to expectations of top union and management, there are frequent departures from provisions of the negotiated contract.[1] It is this area of activity that will be examined: the unofficial and often formally unacceptable behavior, evading and manipulating the formal labor agreement, but nevertheless constituting a great part of the actual functioning relations between management and union at the plant level.

Data for this report are drawn from participant experiences in three factories.[2]

Methodologically, there are obvious limitations to the activities of the industrial participant observer. Regardless of the number and variety of positions such an observer may hold, or the number of years he may spend in industry, or the aid given him by participating intimates, he cannot hope to cover all behavior important for his purposes in large organizations. He

Reprinted from American Sociological Review, 15 (October, 1950), 611-619.

[1] Though there is practically nothing in the sociological literature treating the difficulties that top union and management have in enforcing strict conformity down the line to provisions of the contract, there has been considerable published research and theory pointing to the gap between "management logics" and actual behavior among industrial personnel (chiefly production workers) and stressing management's need to recognize the necessity of personal group relations. Among others, see F. J. Roethlisberger and W. J. Dickson, Management and the Worker (Cambridge, Mass.: Harvard University Press, 1939); W. F. Whyte, ed., Industry and Society (New York: McGraw-Hill, 1946); W. Lloyd Warner and J. O. Low, The Social System of the Modern Factory (New Haven, Conn.: Yale University Press, 1947); B. M. Selekman, Labor Relations and Human Relations (New York: McGraw-Hill, 1947); B. B. Gardner, Human Relations in Industry (Homewood, Ill.: Irwin, 1945).

[2] The writer spent several years in various departments of these factories, both as a worker and a member of management. Some aspects of experiences at the work level were reported earlier as "Wage Incentive and Social Behavior" (Unpublished M.A. thesis, Department of Sociology, University of Chicago, 1946); "Worker Response and Social Background," Journal of Political Economy, 55 (August, 1947), 323-332; "The Industrial 'Rate-Buster': A Characterization," Applied Anthropology, 7 (Winter, 1948), 5-18, an intensive study of the personality characteristics of workers likely to respond most strongly to the appeal of money incentive.

Research among managers was reported as "Conflicts Between Staff and Line Managerial Officers," American Sociological Review, 15 (June, 1950), 342-351.

A report of several areas of managerial behavior in one plant only was given in "A Study of Informal Organization Among the Managers of an Industrial Plant," (Unpublished Ph.D. thesis, Department of Sociology, University of Chicago, 1949).

is further handicapped when, as in the present case, the behavior in which he is interested is carefully guarded. Hence the discussion here does not presume to cover all the informal behavior that occurred in these plants[3] in the category of union-management relations.

But despite such limitations, there were discernible axes along which behavior moved. From a study of these, informal union-management relations appeared in the main to stem from (1) a tacit agreement by members of both union and management to work outside the contract when "necessary," (2) lack of union-consciousness among workers, (3) managerial incohesiveness, and from (4) the effects of economic and production pressures. These four conditions will be used as analytical categories.

Tacit Evasion of the Contract

The plants to be discussed were all under contract with national unions, but both labor and management in the local plants winked at the agreements. This attitude was not the result of intentional neglect by top officials, for the national unions and corporation headquarters periodically sent questionnaires to both groups requesting statements of their problems. These requests were treated lightly. There was much cynicism about the ability of top officials to care for local problems. Local groups believed the contracts were too general and inflexible to cover the problems of many widely-scattered plants functioning under different conditions.[4]

In one of the plants a departmental superintendent declared: "[The plant manager and his assistant] have both said they don't give a damn what kind of arrangements are made with the union as long as things run smoothly and it's kept out of writing."

Grievance committeemen made similar statements. Two of those

---

[3] Names and locations are confidential, but these are the same plants—ranging in size from 4,500 to 20,000 employees—that were discussed in the earlier paper on staff-line conflict. As noted in that paper, there were at least three additional areas of conflict: (1) the union-management relations of the present paper; (2) inter-departmental power struggles to keep operational costs down and win favor with top management; and (3) the disturbing influence of numerous managerial officers seeking to increase their status in the hierarchy. These areas were interrelated and often reciprocally compromising. Because of this a separate discussion of union-management relations will be admittedly somewhat unrealistic. Areas number two and three are probably also characteristic of many other organizations, industrial and otherwise.

[4] It is likely that some element of rationalization existed in these beliefs, for, as will be shown, behavior in the plants was so expedient and variable that probably the most detailed local contract would have been evaded to some degree. Slichter stresses the remoteness of professional officers of the national union from the rank and file: Sumner H. Slichter, *The Challenge of Industrial Relations* (Ithaca, N.Y.: Cornell University Press, 1947), p. 15. This may have been a factor in the complaints and behavior of workmen in the two larger plants discussed here. In a sense they were rebelling against the restrictive effects of this distance on their control of policy. Simultaneously the white collar workers were competing with the production workers for favors from the national union and felt that their numerical inferiority was a handicap "because we can't make as much noise as they can."

whom I knew intimately were quite specific. One stated: "The top people [policy makers] lay down too many hard and fast rules to follow. But we get around the contract by doing a lot of things that we can work out and keep off the record." The other said: "Top union and management are always bothering the local plant. We can work out our own arrangements if they'll leave us alone. [The plant superintendent and assistant] told us they don't care what arrangements we make but if we get in trouble the contract will have to be followed to the letter right down the line."

This was the only case in which a union officer admitted direct informal communication from management approving evasion of the contract, but actual behavior was similar in all the plants, and had a character that could hardly have existed if local managerial and union officers had been opposed to evasion.

Lack of Union Consciousness

Ninety per cent or more of the production workers of the three plants were union members. They responded to strikes called by the national union. They showed considerable solidarity in holding production to agreed levels. However, there was a general lack of union-consciousness among them.

On matters that could be handled secretly, even enthusiastic supporters of the union engaged in private dealing that was advantageous to them in terms of income, a better work position, desirable days off during the work week, preferred weeks of the year for vacation, and so on. This covert bargaining usually involved a grievance committeeman and a departmental superintendent. These officers would trade favors that often led to the development of an exchange structure. For example, there were cases (occurring too often to be exceptional) of workmen being reclassified from lower to higher pay categories without actually proving the skill formally required by tests.[5] For such considerations the grievance committeemen would accept "frozen schedules" (easy to prepare but less flexible than workmen liked), refrain from forcing "tough" or "rotten" grievances on the superintendent, and so on.

The behavior of successful (see below) grievance committeemen was revealing with respect to informal union-management relations. They were skilled in manipulating both workers and managers. Some of them confi-

[5] E.g., A machinist wished to move from "B" to "A" rating. By arrangement between his grievance committeeman and departmental superintendent, he won his reclassification by giving only the appearance of passing the test. Formally the test required setting up and operating the machine for one hour unaided. In this case the candidate found the job already setup. The cutting heads were adjusted, the tool bits were properly ground and inserted to the correct depth and at the proper angle. The feeds, and timing were adjusted so that the machine could have run unattended beyond the required hour. The candidate had but to press the starting button, stand by the machine one hour, and press the stopping button.

dentially stated that a measure of political artifice was necessary for success in that office.[6]

Quite often expediency drew grievance officer and superintendent together in alliance against similar cliques. Though leaks of these practices sometimes occurred, the uncertainty among all participants as to what behavior future situations might require of them served to check formal protests. Two brief cases will indicate the strength to which some union-management cliques could grow.

In the largest of the three plants, the superintendent of a division of 3,500 workers was demoted to a foremanship which he had earlier held. The committeeman with whom he had dealt as superintendent volunteered to call a "wildcat" strike (which the foreman opposed) for the purpose of returning him to his former position.

In the plant[7] of 4,500 employees such a strike *was* initiated by a grievance committeeman and nearly a hundred workers because their foreman failed to get the vacated office of assistant superintendent. Though the strike lasted but four days and failed of its purpose, its significance is apparent.

Relationships of the successful grievance committeeman with his constituents are instructive. Grievance officers who succeeded in being re-elected were those showing political astuteness rather than fiery opposition to management. For instance, in each shop there were informal leaders whom the area grievance man employed as political whips. They defended his behavior to workmen and campaigned for his re-election. In

---

[6] Explaining his third re-election, one officer said: "Industrial relations is all based on good relations. You've got to be friends to some extent. You can't have industrial relations without giving and taking on both sides. You'll always win more cases by getting along with supervision than by being tough. You've got to swap for swap and make trades. . . . A griever [committeeman] has the problem of holding the union together and keeping peace in it while he tries to please both the union and management. Some of the big shots don't like me—they want to win all the time. But I figure that some of the best friends I have are big shots here in the plant. Sometimes I have to talk like hell to explain some of the deals I make with them—and sometimes I keep what I'm doing to myself if I see a chance to get something good later on. The thing some grievers never get through their heads is that a lot of the bosses are on the spot theirselves. If you go a little easy on them when they're on the pan, by G— you make friends—they'll stand by you sometime when you're back of the eight ball. Sometimes when I have a rotten grievance, I'll take the case up to the soop [supt.] and let him know I won't push it hard."

[7] In this same plant informal bargaining involved the president of the union local. Management wished to drop a wage incentive system that had got out of hand, and was prepared in the future to pay workmen "average earnings," i.e., the average of bonus pay (above guaranteed hourly pay) that had been earned over a specific period. The president of the local, whose average earnings were 9.5 cents an hour, opposed management. Shortly thereafter the records of his past performances were "lost," and his average earnings were found to have been "in error." After re-calculation his average earnings were 34.5 cents an hour. He agreed to withdrawal of the incentive plan. At the same time he did not oppose reduction from 2.5 cents to 1.5 cents in the average earnings of several aging, unaggressive workmen.

return he rewarded them with favors growing out of his unofficial dealings with management, as in the case of reclassification noted above which was given to an informal leader. As a rule, the belligerent committeeman served only one term. Instead of such an officer, the rank and file preferred a griever who could win them individual and group gains—even though he might "play ball" with management to some extent. Admittedly the behavior of committeemen and their informal leaders was somewhat oligarchical, but the fact that such officers were re-elected indicated that a majority of the workmen, consciously or not, accepted this as the best practical working arrangement.

Available data suggest that the successful griever quickly learned to settle grievances informally and to use formal procedure only as a last resort. Data on nine of the seventeen (of a total of 46) committeemen who had served more than one term showed that each officer's annual total of formally processed grievances (those in the first three steps[8]) declined with each succeeding year in office. The total in each of these steps also declined annually.[9] Decline in number of grievances among these committeemen did not necessarily mean a decrease in union-management tensions, but rather that friction was more and more being resolved informally.

At least up through the divisional level,[10] grievance officers found managers who, because of the contradictory situations in which they were caught, were quite willing to settle their differences informally, as will now be shown.

Managerial Incohesiveness

Industrial organizations are usually regarded as bureaucracies in the technical sense of having hierarchies of officials, with specific authority and status, functioning inside a set of guiding rules.[11] Contrary to the assumption that such structures are integrated and function impersonally, the

---

[8] Steps in the formal grievance procedure were as follows: First step, the foreman; second step, the departmental superintendent; third step, the plant manager or assistants; fourth step, between representatives of the national union and management; fifth step, arbitration.

[9] E.g., the total first step grievances during their first year in office for each of the nine committeemen ranged from 149 to 194; total second step grievances ranged from 65 to 91, while those settled in the third step varied from 15 to 31. By the fourth year, formal grievances in the same steps for the same men varied respectively from 30 to 98, 10 to 44, and 2 to 9.

[10] Strata of the managerial hierarchy from the worker level up were, in order, first-line foremen, general foremen, departmental superintendents, divisional superintendents, and plant manager. In the two larger plants there were usually additional strata consisting of "assistants" at most of the levels indicated.

[11] See Max Weber, *The Theory of Social and Economic Organization*, Talcott Parsons and A. M. Henderson, trans. (New York: Oxford University Press, 1947), pp. 329-340; *From Max Weber: Essays in Sociology*, H. H. Gerth and C. Wright Mills, trans. (New York: Oxford University Press, 1946), pp. 196-244.

plants discussed here[12] showed much rule-evasion, disorganization, and conflict.

First-line foremen, for instance, often considered themselves as abandoned by higher management to the union.[13] Many of their earlier functions, such as hiring, firing, and influencing the pay of workmen, had been assumed by various staff organizations. Entertaining ambivalent sentiments toward higher management, first-line foremen defended themselves and salvaged what they could from the situation. Having been reversed many times by their superiors because of decisions they had made that led to the filing of grievances, these foremen in most cases refused to process grievances and instead passed them on to the general foremen, thus working contrary to expectations of the managerial organization. On the other hand, first-line foremen sought to control, or at least bargain with, the union in officially unacceptable ways.

One control device was to delay giving reclassification tests to workmen after the latter had received official approval to take the tests. During the interim the foreman derived satisfaction from indicating to the candidate that he had better be a "good guy" or expect to receive a "tough" test.[14]

An extreme case will make clear the process of informal bargaining at the work level. A first-line foreman had an arrangement with the grievance committeeman of the division which allowed the foreman to give his brother,[15] a workman, higher-paying jobs than other members of that work group (numbering 18) received. In return the foreman was to approve by signature the use of certain bonus-increasing factors (when questioned by management's incentive-appliers as to whether use of the factors was warranted by "good shop practice") applicable to the operations of another group of 95 workers also under his authority. The larger group was content with the arrangement, but the other 18 men were not. They made threats, but filed no grievances, for occasionally they did receive "good" jobs. Formal action would have precluded their ever getting such jobs or winning a "legitimate" grievance.

Informal bargaining of this kind occurred also among departmental and divisional heads. The case above of worker reclassification without meeting formal requirements was fairly common and, as earlier mentioned,

---

12 For one aspect of these tensions see "Conflicts Between Staff and Line Managerial Officers," *op. cit.*

13 Depression of the first-line foreman seems to be nearly universal. See Selekman, *op. cit.*, pp. 53-54; Donald E. Wray, "Marginal Men of Industry: The Foremen," *American Journal of Sociology*, **54** (January, 1949), 298-301.

14 Standardization of tests, in terms of skill or knowledge required, was usually next to impossible.

15 Plant rules forbade individuals related by blood or marriage to a member of management to work directly or indirectly under his supervision.

was usually effected with the aid of the departmental chief.[16] In another case, however, a departmental superintendent refused to cooperate. He gave the tests strictly according to rules to three candidates sponsored by the committeeman. All three failed. The griever then carried the case to the divisional head and claimed that the tests had been "too tough." The division chief himself had two employees whom he considered to have uncommon ability, that he wished to promote, but they lacked seniority and he knew the union would block their promotion. So he now brought the case of his two protégés to the attention of the committeeman. The latter agreed to their promotion if his three men were given tests they could pass and if he were allowed to witness the testing of the superintendent's two candidates.

In another case bargaining between a division head and a grievance man evolved a method for inducing the less enthusiastic members of the union—under certain conditions—to sign the check-off ticket.[17] In those parts of two of the plants where workmen were reclassified on the basis of proven skill, they petitioned for a test. When the division chief received this request he indicated his approval by signing it and passing it back to the petitioner's foreman. However, in the present case the griever succeeded in having the division chief return such petitions to him rather than the foreman. If the candidate had not signed the check-off, the griever then told him that he could not take the test until he did sign. Once he signed, the grievance man notified the division head that the petition was ready for final approval.[18]

In another case a departmental superintendent made an informal pact with his committeeman which allowed the bonus hours for certain jobs to be increased. However, the bonus system had been developed by the industrial engineering staff which restudied the jobs and cut the time to its original figure. The aggressive committeeman then coerced the superintend-

---

[16] It was not always possible to conceal these relations, as shown by the sequel to one case. When two workmen learned of a manipulated reclassification, they asked their committeeman for a similar favor. The superintendent (who had aided others in this way before) feared that he was going too far and refused to cooperate. In seeking a way out of his dilemma, the griever and his informal shop leaders utilized the safety rules to win the superintendent's cooperation. They contended that a safety hazard existed when a candidate was placed before a strange machine to prove his skill without benefit of communication with others, and that certain other workmen should be allowed to caution him if and when they saw him about to endanger himself or others. The superintendent agreed, thus allowing, as he knew, manipulation of the safety rule so that a candidate, who might not be ready for the test, could receive helpful hints from his friends.

[17] As the reader will recall, the Labor Management Relations Act of 1947 forbids the employer to check off union dues unless the employee authorizes it in writing.

[18] Top union officials not only were ignorant of this arrangement (according to the committeeman) but had issued specific orders, when the Labor Management Relations Act became law, that unwilling workers were not to be forced into signing the check-off.

ent (who was too deeply involved in unacceptable activities to risk exposure) into bargaining with the staff organization for a compromise. This was a case of one managerial group bargaining with another in the same plant for the benefit of the union.

Unofficial behavior of management toward the union as an organization also showed a marked absence of the usually presumed antipathy. For example, many of the managers (1) revealed sentiments of indebtedness toward the union for salary increases, (2) insisted that workmen sign the check-off, and (3) bought raffle tickets from the union knowing that the proceeds would be used to strengthen the union as an organization.

Concerning point one, all members of management in all three plants received unannounced salary increases soon after every general wage increase won by production workers. At least in some cases the percentage of increase was greater than that received by workmen. Numerous managerial officers, from first-line foremen through department heads, confidentially declared that they "might never" get a salary increase "if it wasn't for the union." One high officer regarded by some workmen as "reactionary," said:

After all these years of just existing, now for the first time my wife and me are able to get our noses up for a breath of air. And by G— we owe it all to the union! If the union hadn't come in we'd stayed in the same damn old rut. In the last few years I've put four kids through high school and three of them through college. They're all on their own now, but they'd never have had a chance if my income hadn't shot up. I still believe in the law of supply and demand, but by G— I know which side my bread's buttered on, too.

A case was cited above of a divisional superintendent cooperating covertly with a union officer to force workmen to sign the check-off. But in a number of other cases in that plant and others, general foremen and department heads personally urged reluctant workers to authorize the check-off, and (according to workmen) in some cases threatened them with discharge. Workmen were told that they should sign for their "own good," and because failure to sign "makes the other men sore and causes trouble."

In a similar vein was management's purchase of raffle tickets from the union. Television sets, automobiles, and other articles were raffled off by the union. Especially from 1946 on, presidents of the locals, grievance men, and shop stewards went about the plants freely selling chances to everyone, with the managers buying more per person than the workers. Management was aware that the proceeds were being used for political action, because a receipt of membership in the union's political organization was offered with each minimum purchase of three chances.[19]

Possibly the most objective indication of management's lack of an-

---

[19] Remarks after these purchases gave an insight into managerial fantasies. Though all the managers smilingly declined receipts of membership, some of them later expressed a fear concerning "what might happen" to them if the signatures they had given for the tickets should "turn up in some . . . spy-investigating committee."

tipathy towards the union as such was the fact that individuals were often members of both management and the workers' union. Data are incomplete, but in over thirty cases in these plants first-line foremen were also dues-paying members of the union and many of them were known to be members at the time they were selected as foremen.[20] And in one of the plants the president of the local was called on each summer to substitute for vacationing foremen.

These cases indicate that management, like the union, was guided in its behavior less by sentiments of group loyalty than by the demands of expediency and friendship, and the fear of exposure for rule-evasion.

Economic and Production Pressures

Pressures by top management for greater production caught the first-line foreman between the union and his superiors. (Some of his escapes were noted earlier.) Since the union prevented application of any large-scale productive coercion, the foreman discreetly sought to reward those workers who "put out" with such favors as giving them (1) the higher-paying jobs,[21] (2) more desirable jobs in terms of the ease with which they could be done, and/or their freedom from dirt, heat, hazard, unpleasant odors and drafts, and (3) available overtime in his own and other departments in which he knew such time was to be had. The characteristic willingness of workmen to accept confidential favors made such exchanges relatively easy, and sometimes grievance committeemen collaborated by (1) denying to suspicious workmen that such conditions were deliberate, and (2) refusing to process grievances filed on such issues.

Cost to the union of carrying grievances to the fourth step was a compulsion toward settlement at some lower step. The fourth step in disputes was argued in the "area office" of the plants. This office was sufficiently

[20] These cases of workmen entering management suggest that American workers have not yet resigned themselves to remaining in that category.

Though policy was contradictory on the point of whether individuals could be members of both the workers' union and management, when such aspirants did become managers and were able covertly to strengthen the unofficial exchange structure, union officers usually gave informal approval. E.g., one such officer stated: "We don't try to keep our men from entering supervision. We've got a number of men in supervision who are in the union. . . . We're glad to see them get up. It helps us as long as they remember who helps them out and keeps things running smooth for them. We help them by seeing that their seniority runs unbroken. If they go on salary and become officially part of management, they can still pay their dues and keep their seniority. . . . In case they get bumped, we'll stand back of them. When cases like this come up, we argue that we only *lent* the men to the company and that they never ceased being part of the union. So far we've got away with it. It's a good policy for us to follow. You know, the company *could* dislike a man and put him on salary so they could can [discharge] him. But they can't do that the way we work it."

[21] See the paper, "The Industrial 'Rate-Buster': A Characterization," *op. cit.*, p. 16, for specific data on the shifting of a job to reward high producers though the change increased the cost of the job more than five times.

distant that the unions regarded the cost of travel and maintenance of personnel as a strain on their resources. Depending on the number of men involved and the number of conferences required, each grievance taken to the fourth step cost the union from two hundred to four hundred dollars. Hence it carried to the fourth step only those grievances it felt sure of winning. These economic limitations reduced the union's aggressiveness at the third step for fear that management might throw the grievance into the fourth step. (Union officials confidentially admitted that bluffing was a major element in their tactics at the third step.) This constraint to settle grievances preferably below the third step and certainly below the fourth, thus intensified informal bargaining.

According to some of the divisional superintendents, management, too, had its fear of the fourth step because the central offices "preferred" that grievances be settled in the local plant. And in the local plant, from the divisional level down, managerial officers feared[22] the wrath of top local management which, as mentioned earlier, had indicated its approval of any informal arrangements that could be contained, and had implied its dislike of being drawn into grievances by vague threats of strict interpretation of the contract if such involvement occurred. The fear which middle and lower level officers had of top officers has already been indicated by their use of nonpecuniary bribes, favors, and exchange devices in connection with union-management relations.

Summary and Implications

Study of three factories showed that despite the existence of labor agreements to guide union-management relations, the formal contracts were often evaded. These unofficial relations were analyzed as due largely to (1) the belief by union and management that the agreements were, paradoxically, both too general and inflexible; (2) the lack of group consciousness among both workers and managers and a willingness among members of each group to bargain privately with members of the other; (3) the intricate conflict system in which other processes, such as staff-line friction and inter-departmental struggles occurred and colored union-management relations, and in which dynamic situations called for quick, compromise decisions that fully satisfied no one and were, hence, subject to ceaseless pressures by individuals and groups for further changes to bring conditions more in line with demands; (4) the wish among managerial and union officers to realize personal goals, deal with enemies, reward friends, protect themselves, increase their status, and the readiness to use expedients for these ends; (5) the economic restrictions on the union and production pressures on management, with the expectation by top officials that differ-

---

[22] Career ambitions were of course important in this fear, but that problem will be discussed in a separate paper.

ences between the two be settled below a certain level of argumentation.

The conditions in these plants probably have importance for union-management relations in most large corporations. Instead of the clear-cut behavioral distinctions in which this phase of industrial life is usually presumed to operate, relations become a shifting intermixed matter of conflict, cooperation, and accommodation carried on largely through the media of personal relations between members of management and of the union. In the area of these immediate relations there is little of the strict adherence and loyalty of members to the presumed interests respectively of management and the union.

Implications for communication and control of members in giant organizations are important. American managerial theory,[23] in terms of an efficient and impersonally functioning hierarchy, is in most cases similar to that presented by Max Weber as the ideal-type bureaucracy, but the actual relations in industry are seldom covered by such theory.[24] Our changing society, our lack of an administrative tradition, and our emphasis on individual success combine to prevent impersonal relations in this area. Exhortations for union-management cooperation sometimes appear only to aggravate disapproved informal relations. Often union and managerial officers are forced to make decisions when they are not prepared to act and when alternative courses of action cannot be brought into the open because of prior informal commitments and possible damage to their own status and/or the status of individuals who have claims on them and on whom they in turn are dependent for favors. In such cases formal rules and communication channels are likely to be side-stepped.

There was little indication that the workers in these plants were inclined to regard themselves as members of the "lower class," or as permanent members of labor unions. The latter condition would seem to be essential for continued strong union-consciousness. The relative absence of such feeling may be in part related to (1) forgetfulness with increasing distance from the critical union-fomenting period of the early thirties, (2) over a decade of high employment and income, and (3) the growing number of workers who never experienced responsibilities during the recent depression.

Some social scientists contend that friction between union and management would disappear if industrial "bureaucracy" could be eliminated and if "inflexible executives" could be "educated to their responsibilities." If bureaucracy as here used refers to impersonal relations and blind adherence to rules as a cause of industrial friction, it is clear that such thinking

[23] See R. C. Davis, *Industrial Organization and Management* (New York: Harper & Row, 1940), and A. G. Anderson, *Industrial Engineering and Factory Management* (New York: Ronald, 1928).

[24] Those who wish to hear a successful, practicing industrialist on this point may read H. Frederick Willkie, *A Rebel Yells* (New York: Van Nostrand, 1946), especially pp. 186-192.

does not explain what occurred in the plants reported here, where relations were informal and personal, yet not without conflict. Furthermore, in most corporations executives themselves are employees (rather than owners) subject to orders and with little power to initiate formal changes. In such cases it may be extreme to put the onus of blame on management when many of its members, like the worker, are caught in a scheme that limits mobility, causes anxiety and frustration, and stimulates evasion.

There is no wish here to present informal union-management relations as a type of behavior unique in our society. We all know the dynamic and experimental nature of our institutional life, especially in the areas of political and sexual behavior. There is probably much similar conduct in our theoretically rigid and impersonal bureaucracies. Ralph Turner has indicated the need of personal, rule-evasive behavior to survive in at least one area of a military bureaucracy[25] (which, unlike industrial bureaucracies, has the power of life and death to enforce its rules).

The extreme positions, that destructive union-management conflict is unavoidable or that perfect cooperation is possible, may need modification. In practice, the sharing of a common human nature stimulates members of both union and management to work under an appearance of conformity and cooperation while manipulating top-level contractual expectations to ease multiple pressures and win personal aims.

This condition[26] is likely to continue as long as (1) workers (a) hope to rise socio-economically, (b) crave personal distinctions, (c) elect ambitious union officers on the strength of their political skills, and (d) aspire to enter the ranks of management; and as long as (2) union and managerial officers find that evasion is of more aid than adherence to rules in protecting themselves against the resentments, aggressions, and expectations of others as all persons involved behave expediently in a social order holding personal success as a major value.

[25] Ralph H. Turner, "The Navy Disbursing Officer as a Bureaucrat," *American Sociological Review*, 11 (October, 1946), 501-505.

[26] It is possible that behavior in these plants was exceptional, but according to a lawyer who has been intimate for several years with union-management relations at the plant level in Northeastern United States, the conditions depicted in this paper are common. However, this informant insisted during a conversation on the subject that I have "misinterpreted the meaning" of informal relations. He declared with feeling that behavior of the kind described here is not evasion of the contract but "democracy at work," and that a "semantic approach" would clarify the seeming difficulty.

34. Patterns of Interaction in Union-Management Relations

William Foote Whyte

At the present time research in the field of industrial relations is being carried on much more actively than in the past. But while the completed studies yield interesting insights, in few cases can we add the conclusions of one study to the conclusions of others. This necessary step in the building of a scientific discipline is generally impossible because the studies are carried out with many different frames of reference.

It is the aim of this article to set forth a frame of reference which will make it possible to organize the data of industrial relations on a more fruitful basis, although I do not claim that the scheme to be elaborated can cope with every pertinent problem in the field. My intention is to set up some objective, if rough, measures that will differentiate various types of union-management relations, that will enable us to locate certain special problems, and that will point out where changes must be introduced into the social systems in order to achieve certain definable results.

The following scheme of analysis consists of four basic terms: interaction, actions, sentiments and symbols. Under interaction fall the contacts among people with special reference to their frequency, duration and origination.[1] Under actions, reference is made to the things people do apart from or along with the interaction process. Many kinds of actions may be noticed, but I prefer to pay closest attention to those most readily observable and even quantifiable in the industrial plant: for example, such rough categories as whether men are at work at their machines, or absent, or out on strike. Such information is available since the majority of plants keep detailed reports as to the quantity of production, absenteeism and so on.

By sentiments is meant the way people feel about each other and the institutions to which they belong, and the moral standards in which they believe.

Symbols include the phrases used by people when conversing, the physical objects that define their social world for them, and so on.[2]

Reprinted from William Foote Whyte, Society for Applied Research, *Human Organization*, 8 (Fall, 1949), 13-19.

[1] See Eliot D. Chapple (with the collaboration of Conrad M. Arensberg), "Measuring Human Relations," *Genetic Psychology Monographs*, no. 22 (1940).

[2] See Eliot D. Chapple and Carleton S. Coon, *Principles of Anthropology* (New York: Holt, Rinehart and Winston, 1942), p. 465 ff.

In this article, particular attention is focussed upon interaction because it seems to provide the best framework in which to explain people's actions, the sentiments they feel and the symbols used by them. This is a study, then, of the relationship between interaction and actions, sentiments and symbols, in union-management relations.

I regard unions and managements as two social systems made up of highly interdependent parts. Since the two systems closely interlock at several points, it follows that one is mutually dependent upon the other. This means that if, in one system, there is a change in the pattern of interaction, it will have repercussions throughout both that system and the interlocked system. Our problem is to observe the varying patterns of interaction we commonly see and to determine the sentiments, actions and symbols that go with them.

What are the factors that contribute to a situation where there are sentiments of harmony or conflict between union and management? What conditions of interaction lead union and management people to discuss the other party with expressions of hostility, and under what conditions do they speak of each other with respect? As research proceeds it will be necessary to define the sentiments much more narrowly, but for the present such marked contrasts are observed that it is possible to draw some preliminary conclusions about the organization of interaction to fit each pattern of sentiments.

Before getting down to cases, certain limitations should be stated. In the first place, I am referring only to industrial unions, and not to craft unions, and to situations where bargaining is done on a plant-to-plant basis, rather than to those where a master contract is worked out for a large company or an entire industry. However, this does not mean that the conclusions drawn here are limited to small business. There are many large industrial organizations operating on a basis where the local plants have a considerable degree of autonomy and where the union-management relationship is worked out at that level.

Whether this scheme will work in analyzing relationships in the coal industry or in the building trades is unknown as no attempt has been made to apply it. In the development of scientific work in this field it is not necessary, in my opinion, to elaborate a scheme that will encompass all possible variations of phenomena. In fact, I feel that one thing holding back progress has been the effort to arrive at universal solutions. I shall be entirely satisfied if the tentative formulation set forth here operates effectively in the field for which it has been designed.

The diagrams used are very much over-simplified. They describe only four levels of organization, leaving out staff organizations in order to concentrate upon the relations between the line organization of management and the union—except for one diagram in which it has been necessary to include staff. In studying any particular case it will, of course, be necessary for the researcher to draw his diagrams in terms of the actual number of levels of organization and to tie in staff with line.

These diagrams are not intended to cover all possibilities of union-management relationships, even within the limitations already stated. They represent merely an outline of a few of the common types to be observed. If the scheme proves to be of value, other researchers may introduce other observed patterns.

The analysis begins with the period before the union enters the plant, Figure 6-1, concentrating here as in the other diagrams upon the frequency of interaction and the origination of that interaction.

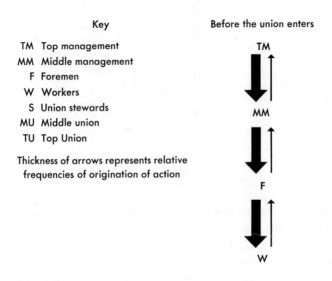

Key

TM Top management
MM Middle management
 F Foremen
 W Workers
 S Union stewards
MU Middle union
TU Top Union

Thickness of arrows represents relative
frequencies of origination of action

Before the union enters

TM

MM

F

W

Figure 6-1.

In a non-union plant there are many varieties of interaction patterns, but emphasis here is placed on one very common type. In studies such as this, we found that origination of action proceeded with a very high frequency down the line from top management to the worker, with very little action being originated up the line. As indicated in the key, the thickness of the arrows indicates a rough estimate of the relative frequency of interaction.

Figure 6-1a, representing the situation when the union enters, shows what a drastic change is introduced into the social system of management when this occurs. New and unfamiliar people enter the picture to originate action for management at various levels. Furthermore, one of the chief effects of the union organization is to place limitations upon the frequency with which the foremen can originate action for the workers. The foreman thus finds himself in a position whose difficulty will be elaborated upon later.

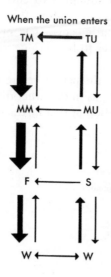

Figure 6-1a.

Various studies have shown that such a drastic change in the pattern of interaction presents a difficult adjustment problem to those concerned. The top management, accustomed to unilateral control, finds it difficult to respond to the origination of a new group of people. Management's efforts to cope with this situation will be described in terms of two common patterns of interaction.

Figure 6-1b, depicts management's "soft policy." By following this policy, management adheres to the theory that it can win peace and a harmonious adjustment with the union through satisfying the demands of the union leadership as often as possible. They look fondly toward the day when their generosity will be rewarded—the day the union leaders will cease pushing their demands. Unfortunately for management that day never dawns, and if we regard the problem in terms of the pattern of interaction, we recognize that such an outcome is impossible. The union leaders, accustomed to originating action for management at a relatively high frequency, will not adjust easily to a situation calling for a cessation of their origination. Also, we should note in this diagram the strong control exercised upon the rank and file by the union leadership. As their demands are granted by management, the union leaders are able to offer constant rewards to the rank and file, thus strengthening their efforts to originate action down the line in the union.

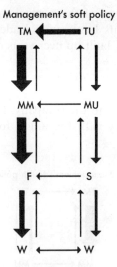

Figure 6-1*b*.

As long as management continues to give in, trouble may be avoided, but such behavior on management's part is not unlimited. For example, we may take the case of the Blank Manufacturing Company which operated a chemical plant employing about 350 workers. The president of the company had given in to the union leaders so often and so readily that wages in his plant had become the highest in the industry, approximately 25 percent above the level of his competitors. The men also had the finest working conditions in the industry. At the same time, however, costs were high and productivity within the plant compared unfavorably with competitive plants. Consequently, the Blank Company was losing money. The president reluctantly decided that the time had come to say "No" to union demands. Since he did not feel able to take this step himself, he hired an industrial relations man to act for him. The first time the new executive put his foot down, the union went out on strike. The strike was unauthorized, in violation of the contract, and the international officers of the union exercised all their influence to persuade the men to return to work, but the control of the local leadership over the rank and file was so tight that the strike continued with solid ranks for many weeks.

At the end of the fifth week, the international officers ruled the strike a clear violation of contract, and wrote to all employes telling them that unless they returned to work within 10 days they would lose their jobs. Even under this pressure, only 10 percent of the 350 workers returned to the plant. The international union then began to recruit new workers to break the strike, and three months later the plant was back in operation, but with a highly inexperienced and unskilled working force. Throughout this entire period, only 10 percent of the original work force showed a willingness to break away from its local union leadership, thus illustrating the strength of that leadership, built up over years of gaining concessions from management.

This strike was, of course, disastrous for the local union leaders and for the nine-tenths of the workers who lost their jobs in the plant. It was also a terrible financial blow to the company. Furthermore, it indicated to management that its policy with the union for so many years had been basically misconceived.

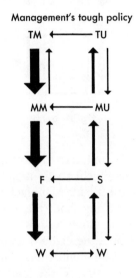

Figure 6-1c.

If a soft policy is impracticable, let us observe the results of a "tough policy." In Figure 6-1c, we see such a situation. To maintain union-management relations, the management must respond to origination of action from the union at certain times. But each time the union demands some action, it seems to the management people that they are giving away some of their powers and prerogatives. Therefore, it becomes highly important in management thinking to draw the line between those powers and prerogatives that can be safely yielded or shared with the union and those that must remain sacred to management. The tough policy management then seeks to draw this line in order to protect its prerogatives and takes a strong defensive position behind it, defending its privileges in an elaborate, legalistic manner. As a result, there is much pressure up the union structure toward management, the union feeling compelled to originate action upon management, but with only limited success because of the narrowly defined areas in which management is willing to give ground. In a situation of this kind we find that management is generally a stern disciplinarian who takes firm steps on questions of discipline. Within the union this attitude may generate much antagonism toward management, but if the punishments are followed through fairly consistently there are not likely to be many undisciplined outbreaks. Wildcat strikes may be more a product of confusion and inconsistency than of a tough management. However, the management that pursues a tough policy builds up strong hostilities toward itself within the union, and those strikes that are authorized may be long and bitter. In such situations it may be found that the workers are not particularly interested in stepping up productivity for management, the latter achieving production through its technology and the various controls it exercises over the job.

Many management people have surveyed the results of both a soft policy and a tough policy and recognize the drawbacks in each approach. In making their decision to be neither tough nor soft, they resolve to be "firm but fair." For the analysis of interaction, this policy has one basic difficulty: it is meaningless. One may announce that one is being firm, but to others one's attitude may appear stubborn and unyielding. One may believe one is being fair, but the reaction of others may be that they are being badly cheated. The terms "firm" and "fair" are so vague and are subject to so many different interpretations that no particular pattern of interaction is defined. They are simply a set of symbols which may be described as a management ideal.

There is, nevertheless, an alternative to the tough and soft policies. This can be seen from examining the figures alone. As we compare b and c, we note one striking similarity: management rarely originates action directly for the union. Management has only one channel through which to originate action: through its own structure. Whether they are acting tough or soft, the managerial people in these situations feel themselves in a defensive position, and regard any move on the part of the union as an attempt to take away ground from management. For them it is a highly unrewarding position and does not augur well for harmonious relations with the union. A way out of this problem is shown in the figure called "Union-Management Reciprocity."

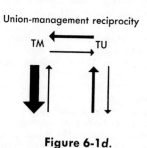

Union-management reciprocity

Figure 6-1d.

While most of the observations in this article are rather tentative and based upon a small number of cases, one generalization can be made with considerable confidence: wherever union and management in industry get along well together and express favorable sentiments toward each other we find management originating action directly for the union to some degree, as well as originating down its own management structure. What arises may be termed a reciprocity in the origination of action,[3] and when this develops we also find what is generally described as a sharing of responsibilities between union and management. Tough managements constantly talk about union irresponsibility and demand that the union leaders become more responsible. But what do they mean by responsibility? We find that according to their conception, management has the responsibility of organizing production, effecting technological changes, setting up the marketing and advertising facilities, and so on, through a wide range of vital and interesting activities. On the other hand, the union leaders are responsible for preventing their members from going on strike or participating in slowdowns, and encouraging them to follow the plant rules in general. The union leaders are supposed to make their position felt only in the grievance procedure. Their responsibilities, therefore, are entirely of a negative character, that is, the union leaders in exercising their "responsibilities" have a punishing effect upon the members. This is hardly the foundation upon which to build a harmonious union-management relationship. If the leaders are to hold their positions, they cannot follow through on this negative conception of responsibility, as desired by management.

A sharing of responsibilities does not necessarily mean that the management must have the full concurrence of the union before acting upon every problem. There are varieties of adjustments in this area, but it is certain that in some of the major problems affecting the union, no new action should be taken by management without a thorough discussion with the key union people.

With the development of reciprocity between union and management at the top levels we find the people concerned expressing favorable sentiments toward each other and speaking with some pride about the way they get along together. However, the fact that an adjustment has been reached at top levels does not necessarily mean that relations will flow harmoniously at the lower levels. Since the social systems are made up of interde-

[3] Those who have read our article on the Buchsbaum Case, ("From Conflict to Cooperation: A Study in Union-Management Relations,") Introduction and Analysis by Andrew H. Whiteford, William Foote Whyte and Burleigh B. Gardner, members of the Committee on Human Relations in Industry, The University of Chicago: *Applied Anthropology,* 5 (Fall, 1946) may remember that we did not diagram this point. The only diagram we used described a situation in which only the union originated action for management. However, the discussion of that case itself clearly shows that one important aspect of the harmonious relations that developed was President Buchsbaum's willingness and ability to originate action for the union on many occasions. We simply did not see the relevance of this point at the time the case was written up.

pendent parts, changes in one part will affect other parts; but a change that leads to more harmonious relations at one point will not in itself necessarily have the same impact at other points. Further compensatory changes at many points in each system are essential.

To illustrate this observation, let us look at the situation in Figure 6-1e, "Foremen Under Pressure." Here we see that it is possible to work

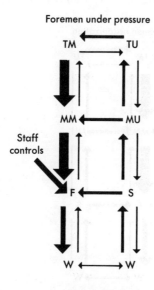

Figure 6-1e.

out a harmonious relationship at top levels in such a manner that the foremen feel themselves under increasing pressure from above as well as from the union. For a complete understanding of this situation, we should consider the pressure of staff organizations, for in recent years the foreman's freedom of action has been seriously curtailed by the development of staff activities in engineering departments, in industrial relations staffs, and so on. The foreman's situation today often means that while the union is originating action for him, the very presence of the union limits his freedom to originate action for his subordinates. Moreover, the presence of the union may also lead to increasing pressures on the foreman from the top down. We often find top management regarding the foreman as something of a scapegoat. As union-management frictions chiefly crop up at this point, some top management people regard the whole problem as one of foreman-training and, therefore, they seek to devise more elaborate methods of telling the foreman what to do.[4] With all these pressures converg-

---

[4] This kind of situation is not confined to union-management systems where cooperative relations have developed at the top. Rather, it seems a general problem in

ing upon him, the foreman finds himself limited in his opportunities to compensate for them, consequently it is not unusual to find him complaining that he has become a bumping-post between labor and management, and expressing in many ways the feeling that he is what we have described as "The Man in the Middle."[5]

How is the foreman to reestablish his own personal equilibrium in the face of these pressures? One answer is shown in Figure 6-1*f*, "Foreman

Foremen organization

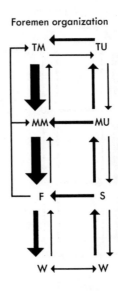

Figure 6-1f.

Organization." Here we find foremen joining organizations such as The Foreman's Association of America, which enables them to originate action up the line of management as far as the highest levels, if necessary. The Foreman's Association of America has declined in strength considerably in post-war years for reasons beyond the scope of this study. However, we still find foremen expressing the desire for a representative to convey their wants to the higher levels of management.

It is not suggested that an organization of foremen is the only method

modern industrial organization. The problem of the role of the foreman was very acute during the war in the Ford Motor Company and in the Packard Motor Company. Conflict with the union was common within Packard, and while the Ford top management expressed the desire to get along, there were many difficult unresolved problems even at top levels between union and management.

[5] Burleigh Gardner and William Foote Whyte, "The Man in the Middle: Position and Problems of the Foreman," *Applied Anthropology*, 4 (Spring, 1945). Also F. J. Roethlisberger, "The Foreman: Master and Victim of Double Talk," *Harvard Business Review* (Spring, 1945).

by which they can reestablish their equilibrium in management's system of relationships. Figure 6-1g shows the possibilities of adjustment in three

Foremen adjustment within management

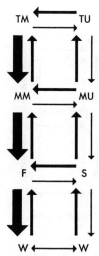

Figure 6-1g.

directions: Foremen may be encouraged to increase the frequency with which they originate action upon their superiors. The origination of action from superiors to foremen may be decreased. The foreman may be encouraged to originate action for the union steward. To put this statement of possibilities into subjective language, high levels of management should encourage foremen to make their needs felt, and should allow them more freedom to organize and operate their departments. The foremen should also consult with union stewards before taking action on discipline and other problems involving the union within their department. In general, we find that where a situation giving scope to these adjustments prevails, the foremen have high morale and express favorable sentiments toward both management and the union.

Cooperation between top union and top management presents hazards for union organization also, as is shown by the situation in Figure 6-1h. In this diagram we find management originating action for top union with a relatively high frequency and top union originating action down the line inside the union, with identical frequency. Here, also, originations of action up the union line and from top union to top management have been relatively curtailed. This situation has certain definite characteristics in terms of symbols and sentiments. We find that after a certain number of

The split within the union

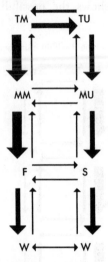

Figure 6-1*h*.

encounters, both top union and top management people establish personal ties and a feeling of mutual trust. Union leaders become aware of and interested in management's problems, such as costs and productivity, and realize that the management people are not the ogres they expected to have to deal with. There is awakened in the union leaders a sympathetic attitude toward management's point of view. Furthermore, they begin to use the same symbols used by management to describe union-management problems. As these symbols fail to win a response from the rank and file, the union leaders come to feel that the former don't understand sufficiently what is going on and need to have "the true picture" described to them. We sometimes hear top union leaders speak in the same disparaging terms management people tend to of the intelligence and lack of understanding of the rank and file. The management man who hears such talk should not regard it as a healthy sign of organization, but rather as a danger signal pointing to a possible future split within the union. In several cases a situation of this kind has led to a rank and file uprising where the top union officers were voted out of office; in other cases we find top union leaders making commitments for the rank and file which they are then unable to carry out.

The union-management men who see this danger approaching may find a possible solution by referring back to Figure 6-1g in which relatively high frequency of origination of action prevails within the union from the bottom up. Interaction within the union in these two directions (up and down) are closely related. When top union and top management get together to increase the frequency with which top union originates down the line of its structure, they should not ignore the necessity to build up activity up the line of the union. If this is not done, the equilibrium of the system will be destroyed.

Beginning with the Chapple-Arensberg interaction scheme, this system of analysis has been developed on the basis of observation of a number of cases. We have tested it out on studies now in progress and find it highly useful for pointing out areas of stress and strain in the social system and for indicating possible ways of relieving such stresses.

For example, a study by Orvis Collins of union-management relations in the Tennessee Valley Authority showed that foremen and union steward relations were remarkably good, both sides speaking favorably of those they dealt with in the opposite structure. According to this framework of analysis, we would then expect to find the foremen originating action for the stewards on matters of discipline, and in other areas, in addition to their normal activity of responding to the stewards. When we interviewed on the topic, that was precisely what was found. On the other hand, although Collins found that over-all union-management relations in TVA were remarkably harmonious, he did find one area where some minor tension between members of middle management and the union existed. In TVA, indeed, the middle management people alone seemed to feel themselves in a defensive position and to fear that the union was depriving them of some power. On their part, the union men spoke highly of most members of management but were critical of many middle management people. According to our conceptual scheme, we should expect to find that members of middle management did not originate for the union to any appreciable extent, while their opposite numbers in the union originated action for them with a relatively high frequency. When we interviewed to test this hypothesis, we found it amply substantiated by the data. Applying the scheme in this manner points out tension areas and gives some explanation of how these tensions are related to the social system, as well as indicating possible changes that would relieve the tensions.

The scheme of analysis has practical utility and also certain limitations. It can show a union or management man what pattern of interaction to aim at in order to get certain results in actions and sentiments from this structure of interaction. For example, in the foregoing TVA example, if we were to relieve the pressure upon middle management people ways would have to be devised to decrease the frequency of origination of action upon them from above, and perhaps to increase their frequency of origination up the line and to enable them to originate action for the union.

This states what must be done in interaction terms, but it does not explain how it is possible to move from one pattern of interaction to another. Obviously, we cannot accomplish change simply by telling an executive, "What you need is to originate action more frequently upon the union." The problem of effecting transitions in the patterns of interaction in union-management relations is a vital one that now absorbs a large part of our research interest. For this purpose it is especially useful to study cases where there has been a marked shift from conflict to cooperation, such as the study of S. Buchsbaum and Company and the International Chemical Workers Union, which was the first case of this nature analyzed on a human relations basis. I am now at work on a detailed study of a comparable change in the relationship between Inland Steel Container Company and the United Steelworkers.

Observations made so far point to the importance of the contract negotiating process itself in affecting transitions in union-management relations. Work is also underway in this field and we hope to be able to show how day to day relations between union and management affect the negotiations process, and how that process itself may stimulate the development of a new pattern of interaction.

35. White Collar Workers and Professionals — Their Attitudes and Behavior Towards Unions

Seymour Martin Lipset

Introduction

Since the turn of the century, those concerned with estimating the potential strength of labor-based organizations, whether political parties or trade unions, have recognized that the growth of the white-collar workers, or, as some writers have termed them, the "new middle class," has constituted the largest single obstacle to socialist and labor parties winning the safe majority that Marx anticipated for them, and to trade unions securing overwhelming membership strength among the employed classes. The literature written by socialists, labor experts, and sociologists on this question has been extensive, and almost every conceivable factor that might affect white-collar behavior has been dealt with in some detail.

Out of this plethora of writing and analysis, two concrete facts stand out. First, inherent in the various technological and business practices of modern industry has been the rapid growth of the non-manual labor force. In the United States, the occupations called "white-collar" have grown from 17.6 per cent of the labor force in 1900 to 42.4 per cent in 1959. There are now more white-collar workers than manual ones, and the trend is to widen this discrepancy in favor of the non-manual.

Second, almost everywhere the majority of the white-collar workers have rejected efforts to place them in the same political or trade-union camp with manual workers. Thus, studies of the electoral support of political parties in the various democracies indicate that about two thirds of the white-collar workers vote for the nonlabor-based or "bourgeois" parties. In most countries, the majority of non-manual employees do not belong to labor unions, and usually where they do belong, these unions are separate from those of the manual workers. Thus in Sweden, where over 60 per cent of the employed nonagricultural labor force is organized, white-collar unions have their own union federation. In France the more left-wing, Communist-dominated federation, the CGT, is primarily composed of manual workers, the strength of the Socialist-influenced *Force Ouvrier* is found among government employees, and the Catholic CFTC appeals to the

Reprinted from *Research Developments in Personnel Management* (mimeographed), Institute of Industrial Relations, University of California, Los Angeles, 1962, pp. 31-54.

privately employed white-collar workers. In Great Britain white-collar workers are weakly organized, and the white-collar unions, though affiliated with the national Trades Union Congress, differ from the manual-worker unions in rejecting affiliation with the Labor Party. In the United States less than 15 per cent of the white-collar workers are members of trade unions. As a recent ILO report puts it, "whatever the degree to which collective bargaining exists in a given country, it will be found to apply to non-manual workers significantly less than manual workers."[1]

What are some of the reasons for this apathy on the part of the white-collar sector toward organizations that have revolutionized the position of workers? When faced with such a startling success story, why does the white-collar worker refuse to act in his "own best interest?" In order to understand this phenomenon, perhaps we should inquire into what the white-collar worker does see as his "best interest." What are some of the factors that reduce the attractiveness of unions to them? Since there are a few unions among white-collar workers, we will then examine them in order to ascertain the variables associated with their unionism. After looking at unionism among office workers in several industries, we will turn to the rapidly growing group of professionals and technicians and investigate some of the obstacles to unionization, as well as some of the occupational strains that appear to promote organization among them. The last section will examine some of the functions of the already existing organizations and unions in the white-collar and professional sectors.

Differentiation Within the White-Collar Stratum

Any effort to analyze the potential of the white-collar stratum for trade unionism or leftist politics must begin by differentiating within this sector. For, basically, the most important correlation between support of the left or of trade unionism and any other variable is position in the stratification structure. That is, the more privileged a group is in terms of income or status, the more likely it is to be conservative in its politics. The same pattern would appear to hold up for the appeal of trade unions as well. Professionals, who as a group receive the highest income and prestige of any occupational stratum, are the least prone to belong to trade unions, although, as I will discuss later, there are certain significant exceptions to this pattern.

In recent years, the most rapidly expanding groups in the labor force have been the technical and managerial sectors, most of which now require a university education. In the second large non-manual stratum, the white-collar employees are mainly in subordinate positions requiring little skill and only a high school education. Although it is well known that during the past decade the proportion of white-collar positions surpassed the man-

---

[1] ILO Advisory Committee on Salaried Employees, *Non-Manual Workers and Collective Bargaining* (Geneva: International Labour Office, 1956), p. 31.

ual, few have noted that within the ranks of the white-collar the number of people employed in professional, technical, and managerial tasks is now greater than the number in clerical and sales work and the rate of growth of the former remains higher. In the 1950's, the number of manual workers grew at a rate of only 4 per cent, clerical and sales jobs increased by 32 and 14 per cent respectively, while professional and technical categories increased by 55 per cent. Within the manufacturing industries, the professional and technical category increased between 1952 and 1960 by 65 per cent, while clerical occupations increased by only 13 per cent, and manual occupations declined slightly.[2]

Table 6-1.

Per Cent Distribution by Major Occupation Group for the Economically Active Civilian Population, 1900-1960

Major Occupation Group	1960	1950	1940	1930	1920	1910	1900
White-collar workers	42.0	36.6	31.1	29.4	24.9	21.3	17.6
professional, technical, & kindred	10.8	8.6	7.5	6.8	5.4	4.7	4.3
managers, officials, & proprietors exc. farm	10.2	8.7	7.3	7.4	6.6	6.6	5.8
clerical & kindred	14.5	12.3	9.6	8.9	8.0	5.3	3.0
sales workers	6.5	7.0	6.7	6.3	4.9	4.7	4.5
Manual workers	37.5	41.1	39.8	39.6	40.2	38.2	35.8
craftsmen, foremen, & kindred	12.9	14.1	12.0	12.8	13.0	11.6	10.5
operatives & kindred workers	18.6	20.4	18.4	15.8	15.6	14.6	12.8
laborers, exc. farm & mine	6.0	6.6	9.4	11.0	11.6	12.0	12.5
Service workers	12.6	10.5	11.7	9.8	7.8	9.6	9.0
private household workers	3.3	2.6	4.7	4.1	3.3	5.0	5.4
service, exc. private household	9.3	7.9	7.1	5.7	4.5	4.6	3.6
Farm workers	7.9	11.8	17.4	21.2	27.0	30.9	37.5
farmers & farm managers	4.0	7.4	10.4	12.4	15.3	16.5	19.9
farm laborers & foremen	3.9	4.4	7.0	8.8	11.7	14.4	17.7
Total	100.0	100.0	100.0	100.0	100.0	100.0	100.0

Source: Industrial Union Department, AFL-CIO, Research Department, *Selected Tables Depicting the Changing Character of U. S. Labor Force* (mimeographed, June, 1961), Table 2.

[2] Everett Kassalow, *Occupational Frontiers of Trade Unionism in the U.S.* (mimeographed), Table I, Table III.

Stratification and Sex Roles

It is difficult to relate the objective stratification position of white-collar workers to political or union behavior without examining the interrelationship of stratification and sex within the stratum. For there is one predominant fact often ignored by those who cite total statistics of white-collar employment—that, on the whole, males are privileged and women underprivileged. Thus, in the United States in 1950, females held 62 per cent of all clerical positions. Conversely, men held 84 per cent of all managerial jobs, and 64 per cent of professional and technical positions.[3] The one-third of the professional and technical positions which are held by women are predominantly concentrated in the lower paid and lesser statused portion of this sector. The 1950 census data indicate a female majority among the more than one million teachers and the half million nurses, as well as among the smaller categories of medical and dental technicians, dieticians and nutritionists, librarians, and social workers.

A detailed survey of hiring practices in two American cities, Charlotte and New Haven, indicates that employers' attitudes sustain these differences. In both cities routine clerical jobs are predominantly "women's work." Conversely, the ranks of middle management in these cities were dominated by men at the time of the survey and there was "no indication of a desire of employers for a change. Only about 8 per cent of the people in this category now employed in the two cities were women, and they are chiefly in jobs like a president's secretary who has some quasi-executive duties, or assistant in the personnel department with particular relations with women workers."[4]

The "proletarianization" of white-collar work is a tendency concentrated among women. One might expect to find behavior and attitudes among female employees akin to those which have emerged among manual workers. There are, however, several factors mitigating against such developments.[5] First, for many women, employment is not a major source of self-identification. Young women look forward to leaving their jobs after marriage or on the birth of their first child. They are, consequently, not much concerned about opportunities for advancement. Second, the frustration of low status may also be reduced by the fact that a woman's class position is defined largely by her husband's status, and to a certain extent by total family income, rather than by her job. Thus one would anticipate that among women who are supplementary earners there should be less concern about opportunities for promotion. Furthermore, the subordinate

[3] Lawrence Thomas, *The Occupational Structure and Education* (New York: Prentice-Hall, 1956), pp. 116-136.

[4] E. William Noland and E. Wight Bakke, *Workers Wanted* (New York: Harper & Row, 1949), p. 79.

[5] See Waino Suojanen and G. C. Hoyt, "Differences in Motivation Among White-Collar Workers," *Personnel*, 34 (1957), 26-31.

status of women in the social structure seems to contribute to their acceptance of an inferior position in industry. As the Myrdals, among others,
have pointed out, the general value system of most contemporary societies
still supports the norm of a paternalistic relationship between men and
women; the man is expected to lead and protect the weaker woman, for
a woman to play a man's role in any sphere of life is "unnatural."[6] Women
supervisors violate social expectations about the sex relationship, and both
men and women find such changes objectionable. Evidence of the continued strength of these norms is found in a survey of white-collar workers
which asked both men and women whether they preferred a male or female supervisor, or did not care one way or the other. Almost all of the
men (85 per cent) and most of the women (65 per cent) said that they
would prefer a male supervisor.

That male white-collar workers are more ambitious than women is indicated by another survey. When asked, "Is it your ambition to hold the
same position as your supervisor in your company or isn't that important
to you?", 48 per cent of the men as against 27 per cent of the women replied that they were eager to obtain the supervisory position.[7] Thus, the
division of labor and the status among the sexes serves to eliminate possible sources of discontent.

The greater opportunities for promotion into higher positions for male
white-collar workers not only occurs because of the discrimination against
women, but also results from the way in which white-collar bureaucracies
are internally differentiated into many hierarchical gradations. The larger
the bureaucracy the more likely it is to contain a long ladder of positions.
Where there is a number of such gradations, there is more opportunity for
advancement as the sub-divisions prevent a sense of "consciousness of
kind" from developing. Carl Dreyfuss has pointed out that many white-
collar workers

. . . welcome the artificial differentiation and complication of the business
gradation and grasp the chance of exercising even the smallest power of command, despite the fact that the authority bestowed on them may be only fictitious. Some promotions—to manager of a sub-department, to a semi-independent post, or to representative of the firm—afford the employee deep satisfaction
and flatter his pride to an extent not justified by the importance of such events
from an organizational and economic standpoint. . . . Jealousy and envy
among employees of the same rank or among those just one step higher or
lower in rank are incited and inflamed by the continuous struggle for promotion. . . .[8]

[6] See Gunnar Myrdal, *An American Dilemma* (New York: Harper & Row, 1944),
p. 1077, and Alba Myrdal, *Nation and Family* (New York: Harper & Row, 1941).
[7] Opinion Research Corporation, "Wartime Implications of White-Collar Thinking" (Princeton: Princeton University Press, 1950), p. A-36.
[8] Carl Dreyfuss, "Prestige Grading: A Mechanism of Control," in R. K. Merton
et al., Reader in Bureaucracy (New York: Free Press, 1952), p. 261.

Obstacles to White-Collar Union Membership

Perhaps the chief obstacles to union growth among white-collar workers which are cited by those writing on the subject have been their sense of high status, as contrasted to manual workers or to others with whom they might compare themselves, and various aspects inherent in their work milieu. These factors are to some extent interrelated but it seems worth while to treat them separately.

Sense of Higher Status

There seems little doubt that in various countries those engaged in different forms of non-manual work see themselves in a higher status category. Thus, in his famous study of class identification, Richard Centers found that only 10 per cent of American professionals placed themselves in the "working class," as an alternative to describing their status as "middle" or "upper" class, as contrasted with 24 per cent among small businessmen, 34 per cent among white-collar workers, and 71 per cent among skilled workers.[9] In France, a similar study indicated that no professionals saw themselves as part of the working class, as compared with 11 per cent among shopkeepers, 35 per cent among those in clerical and sales occupations, and 53 per cent among artisans and skilled workers.[10]

In two American national samples, when white-collar workers below the rank of supervisor were questioned as to whether they regarded themselves as belonging more with management or more with production workers, about three quarters responded "more with management," while about one eighth identified more with production workers.[11]

But if the sense of high status among professionals and the self-employed, particularly the more well-to-do among them, may be justified by higher incomes (as total groups they are the two best-paid occupational categories) and by the general public's conception of occupational status, a favorable self-image is not justified by the objective position of American lower level white-collar groups when measured by income or community status. The most comprehensive analysis of the prestige accorded to occupations by a national sample of Americans reveals that the average pres-

[9] Richard Centers, *The Psychology of Social Classes* (Princeton: Princeton University Press, 1949), p. 86. Centers also presented the alternative of "lower class," which few chose at any level.

[10] Natalie Rogoff, "Social Stratification in France and the United States," in R. Bendix and S. M. Lipset, eds., *Class, Status and Power* (New York: Free Press, 1953), p. 585.

[11] See *Strengthening Relations With White-Collar Workers* (Princeton: Opinion Research Corporation, 1952), p. A-16, and *Can Management Hold White-Collar Loyalty* (Princeton: Opinion Research Corporation, 1957), p. A-8.

tige rating of various clerical and sales jobs is identical with that accorded to skilled manual work.[12]

The factors underlying the upward class identification of the white-collar workers inhere in the very nature of a stratified society. Stratification is a ranking of positions as higher or lower on a variety of values, that is, basically, as better or worse. Every individual necessarily seeks to magnify his sense of importance in the eyes of others. Consequently, basic to the structure of stratification is the effort by individuals to upgrade their self-image, to identify with whatever in their position gives them a claim to higher status. Or to put it another way, when faced with a choice of identifying down or up, almost everyone will identify up. The ambiguous position of the white-collar worker in the stratification hierarchy based on the historic linkage of the occupational with the entrepreneurial role, combined with the continuation of such objective distinctions as higher education, cleaner work, social definition as being part of the staff side of industry, all operate to give white-collar workers more of a "choice" as to where to identify.[13]

Identification with the middle classes obviously has clear-cut consequences for unionism. Studies have shown that those who identify with the middle class are more likely to be conservative in their general political orientation, to vote Republican, and to abstain from joining unions than those who identify with the working class.

Work Milieu

Both in the past and present much white-collar work has been carried on in a setting different from manual work. Office employees, in particular, work closely with managers and executives. In small concerns, they often work side by side with the owner. Needless to say, this contributes to their sense of apartness from, and even superiority to, blue-collar workers.

The importance of the size of the work unit was noted by Karl Marx when he pointed out that workers in small shops were markedly less class-conscious and less involved in working-class organizations than those in

[12] See National Opinion Research Center, "Jobs and Occupations: A Popular Evaluation," in R. Bendix and S. M. Lipset, eds., *Class Status and Power* (New York: Free Press, 1953), p. 414. It may be noted that professional and semi-professional positions ranked much higher than clerical and skilled work, while unskilled and semi-skilled labor were lower.

[13] White-collar work has a long association with the administrative and management end of business. When businesses were small, the duties of the white-collar workers were performed by the employer or his relatives. This distinction between manual and non-manual became established as a worker-employer difference. This difference is still reflected today in that regardless of how simple the work of technicians or the office staff may be, it is always salaried employment because it is part of the work previously done by executives. See Fritz Croner, "The Salaried Employees in Modern Society," *International Labour Review*, 49 (1954), 105-108. Thus from the very outset, white-collar workers had a different and higher social status than manual workers.

larger plants. He accounted for this difference by the fact that the former were much more likely than the latter to associate informally with their employers and to develop personal ties to them.[14] The larger the size of the plant, the more impersonal the relationship between the supervisors or owners and the workers. Workers and supervisors tend to see each other in terms of conflicting roles, one seeking to earn as much as possible for as little work, and the other having the opposite goal. The rigidities of bureaucratic structure promote unresolved conflicts and hence hostility between workers and management. Studies of factories have revealed some of these consequences. Evidence supporting the proposition that the size of the plant is inversely related to personal communications between supervisors and subordinates is contained in a 1953 German study, as shown in Table 6-2.

Table 6-2.
Relationship of Size of Factory to Interpersonal Communication in German Companies*

EMPLOYER OR	SIZE OF FACTORY			
SUPERVISOR BEHAVIOR	Under 10 Workers	10-49	50-299	300 Plus
Does chat	79%	79%	73%	65%
N	(120)	(113)	(161)	(255)

*Responses to the question: "What does your boss (or section manager) generally do: does he chat sometimes with you or does he only give directives?"
Source: Calculated from IBM cards of Study of German Public conducted by the UNESCO Institute of Cologne, Germany.

Even in large firms, the specialization of office work allocated white-collar workers to small groups in close contact with supervisors and executives.[15] Secretaries, probably the most extreme example of such employees, are more loyal to management and more hostile to unionism than any other occupational group of white-collar workers.

Management has given office workers many marks of consideration and distinction, such as pleasant working conditions, a good deal of control over pace of work, regular working hours during the day, and little supervision, as well as many traditional privileges derived from being associated with the managerial role, such as weekly wages, sick leave, greater job security during business declines, time off for personal errands, and

[14] "Germany: Revolution and Counter Revolution," in Selected Works of Karl Marx, Vol. 1 (New York: International Publishers, n.d.), p. 470.
[15] David Lockwood, The Black-Coated Worker (London: Allen & Unwin, 1958), pp. 77-78.

paid vacations. (It should be noted that the nature and tempo of office work make these things possible without too much cost to management.) Their situation is distinguished not only from that of manual workers but from clericals involved in "production" type activities. Thus, physical proximity plus privileges enable office workers *to identify with* their superiors.

The separation of office workers from each other may make them more fearful of joining unions because they do not have

. . . a work group that affords the comfort of numbers; that is, a physical association with fellow employees of comparable work status . . . The mutual aid and comfort and the courage of numbers, which keeps union sentiment alive in an industrial situation, is relatively lacking in the physical arrangement of the modern office. The legal right to join a union is probably more than offset in these situations by the insecurity which stems from the close working proximity to executive and supervisory personnel.[16]

Summary

These are some of the reasons for apathy on the part of the white-collar worker toward unionism. The white-collar employee is an individual who sees himself as quite different from the manual worker. His view of his employment as having higher status is promoted by the situation in which he works. Often working in small groups, close to management and away from his own peers, he tends to feel closer to management than to manual workers. And the objectively most deprived sector of the white-collar stratum is disproportionately composed of women, who do not have as much reason for ego identification with an occupation which is often only a temporary or supplementary source of family income. Hence they are less likely to develop the negative attitudes to their work or to management that might support unionism. Conversely, the very role of women as the underdog in the occupational structure gives male white-collar workers an opportunity for advancement into management ranks, a prospect which should inhibit pro-union attitudes among them as well. The fact remains, however, that a significant minority of white-collar workers do belong to trade unions. An analysis of the factors related to such strength should supply more clues to the prospects for increased white-collar unionism.

Where Is White-Collar Unionism Found?

If there are strong anti-union feelings in white-collar jobs where the worker has close association with management and works in isolated or small groups, we can expect to find pro-union sentiments in industries where the employee is with many others of his own kind, and where white-collar

[16] Jack Barbash, *The Practice of Unionism* (New York: Harper & Row, 1956), pp. 14-15.

work is closely associated with manual work both in conditions and/or physical proximity. From the available evidence this seems to be so.

Work Conditions

Among low-level white-collar workers, strong trade unionism is generally found in situations where the work conditions are similar to those of the manual worker, often also involving the employment of a significant number of males.

The older strong white-collar unions are all in such industries. The two clerical unions in the highly organized railroad industry have unionized nearly all of the employees. Between 50 and 70 per cent of the white-collar employees in the telephone industry belong to unions. The Communication Workers of America, the major union in this field, was organized by the highly skilled male workers, linemen, maintenance, and installation men. The Commercial Telegraphers Union, an organization once predominantly male though now primarily female, has organized most of its jurisdiction. Within government service, the one group of workers who are almost totally organized are the postal employees, most of whom are men. Over 300,000 of them belong to trade unions, many more than belong to all other white-collar federal government unions.

Currently one of the few growing large unions is a white-collar organization, the Retail Clerks International Union. It now has close to 400,000 members. An analysis of the forces underlying its success suggests processes similar to those which are related to the strength of the older powerful non-manual unions. As a recent study of this union by Michael Harrington points out: "The employees in the jurisdiction of the RCIA have become less and less white-collar, their conditions of work have tended toward those of the factory."[17]

Proximity to Manual Workers

The closer contact both in physical proximity and socially that clerical workers have with manual workers, the more likely they are to be unionized. In manufacturing, clerks who work close to organized manual workers are more likely to be unionized than office workers, and office workers in offices attached to production plants are easier to organize than those in the downtown, main offices of the same companies. Strauss has observed in a study of white-collar union locals: "In most factories there is a fairly sharp distinction between the shop and the office. But in the shop there is also a group of white-collar men—timekeepers, production schedulers, expediters, time-study men, and so on. In the situations studied, these

[17] Michael Harrington, *The Retail Clerks* (New York: John Wiley & Sons, Inc., 1962), p. 1.

shop clericals were the easiest to organize and, once organized, they showed the highest participation in union affairs."[18]

The Steelworkers Union, for one, has organized half of the clericals in offices physically located next to steel production plants, but not the main offices of the same companies.

Thus it appears that closeness to manual workers both of a physical and interpersonal kind promotes positive feelings on the part of the white-collar workers toward them as well as a propensity to organize, especially if the manual unions are both prestigeful and successful. Such a situation can be described as a "learning experience" in that it provides models of union organization, leadership, and probably most important of all, an opportunity to learn about unionism directly through personal friends.

Alienation

Except in a few industries, white-collar unionism is not institutionalized. That is, unionism is not the "legitimate" or customary way for such employees to act in relation to their employers.[19] It also violates some of the traditional conceptions white-collar workers have of their place in society. Consequently, one would anticipate that those employees who favored unionism would be deviants within their stratum in that they would exhibit attitudes not congruent with the majority of their group. Evidence drawn from surveys sustains this anticipation. A comparison of the class identification of unionists and non-unionists among non-manual and manual workers indicates there is no difference in this respect among manual workers but considerable variation among white-collar workers.

Among white-collar union members as compared with white-collar non-union members, a much larger proportion (63 to 32) say they are members of the working class (see Table 6-3). Election studies indicate that trade-union members are more likely to vote Democratic than non-unionists among both manual and white-collar workers. However, union membership made a greater difference among white-collar employees than it did among manual workers (see Table 6-4).

It can be tentatively stated that white-collar unionism draws considerable support from people who feel resentful about their jobs, who do not identify with the middle class, and who tend to be liberal politically. Since

[18] George Strauss, "White-Collar Unions are Different," *Harvard Business Review*, 32 (1954), 77-78.

[19] In a recent analysis of traits related to membership in trade unions among manual workers, Ruth Kornhauser reports that manual worker unions "have become institutionalized to the extent that the membership is no longer based principally on selection of workers with a singularly favorable orientation towards unions but instead tends more or less indiscriminately to include large numbers of individuals who are subject to the same working conditions (males in manual work) in a milieu shaped by the predominance of those conditions of work (the urban-industrial North)." "Some Social Determinants and Consequences of Union Membership," *Labor History*, 2 (1961), 58.

Table 6-3.
Relation of Union Membership to Class Identification
Among Males, by Occupation (1952 Sample)

CLASS	NON-MANUAL		MANUAL	
IDENTIFICATION	Union Member	Non-Union Member	Union Member	Non-Union Member
Upper	—	2%	1%	1%
Middle	37%	60	15	14
Working	63	32	80	79
Lower	—	2	2	4
Refused, DK, NA	—	4	2	2
Total	100%	100%	100%	100%
Total Number	35	215	204	160

Source: Tables computed from data supplied by the University of Michigan Survey Research Center from its study of the 1952 elections.

this evidence comes from different studies, there is no way of telling whether or not these characteristics belong to the same group of people.

The majority of white-collar workers do not share these attitudes. They are on the whole satisfied with their jobs, have favorable attitudes toward management, see themselves in a relatively high status position, middle class rather than working class, and are relatively conservative in their political values and voting preferences. All of these attitudes are negatively related to support for unionism, and seemingly to some extent account for the weakness of unions among American white-collar workers.

Given the paucity of research, it is not yet possible to know to what extent these attitudinal differences among non-manual employees are associated with the objective variations in work environment that correlate

Table 6-4.
Relation of Union Membership to Voting Choices,
1952 Presidential Vote (Males Only)

VOTED	CLERICAL AND SALES			MANUAL		
	Union Member	Non-Member	Total	Union Member	Non-Member	Total
Democratic	54%	30%	37%	54%	41%	49%
Republican	46	70	63	46	59	51
Number	50	136	186	399	305	703

Source: Calculated from data collected by Samuel Stouffer for his study, *Communism, Conformity, and Civil Liberties* (New York: Doubleday, 1955).

with support for unions. Thus, to what degree do attitudes toward class position and general view of the occupational, social, and political structures result from factors such as the size of the work unit, the size of the company, nearness to manual workers, and so forth?

Professionals and Trade Unionism

If factors basically inherent in the stratification system account for the relative weakness of unions among lower-level white-collar workers, this would lead us to anticipate much less support for unions among more privileged occupational groups, particularly among the rapidly growing stratum of professional and highly trained technical personnel. And viewed as total groups, this expectation turns out to be valid. Only 10 per cent of persons classified as professionals belong to unions, as contrasted to 17 per cent among clerical and sales personnel. Yet the fact remains, there are a number of unions, some fairly strong, among these groups. Actors, musicians, and others in the entertainment field, air pilots and flight engineers, ship captains, marine engineers, teachers, and social service employees are among those who have long bargained collectively. Engineering unions, while always weak, have been able to secure some support in various countries. And in some countries, such as England, Sweden, Australia, and Japan, unionization of significant sections of professionals has occured.[20]

An examination of the factors associated with unionization in the upper echelons of the occupational structure seems called for in any effort to anticipate the potential strength of unionism as the composition of the labor force changes drastically in response to technological and organizational innovations.

Professional Ethics and the Business System

One of the major differences between professional occupations and others is that the former are assumed to be governed by norms of service, different from those of money-making. As Talcott Parsons has pointed out:

The dominant keynote of the modern economic system is almost universally held to be the high degree of free play it gives pursuit of self-interest. . . . But by contrast with business in this interpretation the professions are marked by "disinterestedness." The professional man is not thought of as engaged in the pursuit of his personal profit, but in performing services to his patients or clients, or to impersonal values like the advancement of science.[21]

[20] "Unionization of Professional Engineers and Chemists," *Industrial Relations Memos*, no. 84 (July 25, 1946), p. 3.

[21] Talcott Parsons, *Essays in Sociological Theory Pure and Applied* (New York: Free Press, 1949), p. 186.

The professional schools, whose faculties stand apart from the business sector and the practical activities of the working professionals, are in large measure the citadels of the professional codes of ethics. It is there aspiring professionals learn an occupational ethos which stresses service and support of the intellectual standards. On the other hand, once out of school the professional is faced with adjustment to the requirements of the everyday work situation. For instance, the physician finds that economic rather than service motives sometimes intrude into decision-making, the lawyer discovers that reputations are built in other ways than holding fast to the tenets of justice, and the teacher learns that parochial rather than more universal interests fashion the curricula.

This strain between maintaining occupational integrity or compromising with the system is probably maximized for the professional in a bureaucratic system of authority. Though the popular conception is that of the independent professional such as the physician, lawyer, or dentist, such a group composes only a small minority within the professions.

The Engineers

Thorstein Veblen in his famous discussion of engineers argues that a basic cleavage exists between the pecuniary norms of modern capitalism and standards of engineering excellence. (He even felt this conflict was so deep that engineers might, in time, become a revolutionary group.) In writing of this problem he said:

It is an open secret that with a reasonably free hand the production experts would today readily increase the ordinary output of industry by several fold. . . . And what stands in the way of so increasing the ordinary output of goods and services is business as usual.

Right lately these technologists have begun to become uneasily "class conscious." . . . Their class consciousness has taken the immediate form of a growing sense of waste and confusion in the management of industry by the financial agents of the absentee owners . . .

. . . Indeed, they are beginning to understand that commercial expediency has nothing better to contribute to the engineer's work than so much lag, leak, and friction . . . So also, to these men who are trained in the stubborn logic of technology, nothing is quite real that cannot be stated in terms of tangible performance; and they are accordingly coming to understand that the whole fabric of credit and corporation finance is a tissue of make-believe.[22]

Ironically, he was speaking about the very group that today of all the professionals appears to be the most satisfied, if we use as an index of dissatisfaction the tendency to unionize or to vote for leftist parties.

[22] Thorstein Veblen, *The Engineers and the Price System* (New York: B. W. Huebsch, 1921), pp. 70-75.

There is some evidence, however, that Veblen's thesis does apply to a segment of engineers, especially those in large companies. A study of unionism among engineers suggests that one of the main reasons for organizing was the need for an organization that would defend engineers' professional interests, such as the opportunity for research and the right to publish.[23] A national survey of scientists and engineers asked: "How much conflict do you feel there is between a man's personal goals as a scientist or engineer and the goals of the organization he works for?" Of the 622 respondents, only 25 per cent said there was no conflict, 26 per cent thought there was serious conflict, and about half, 49 per cent, reported some conflict, but not serious.[24] When asked what are the primary goals of management, most respondents indicated they saw these as mainly pecuniary. For example, "improve profits and sales" (74 per cent), "improve competitive position" (36 per cent), "promote company growth" (30 per cent). Those who checked off service objectives were much fewer: "promote product development" (30 per cent), "provide superior employment" (16 per cent), "service to nation and community" (3 per cent), "betterment of society and mankind in general" (2 per cent). Less than half of these men (41 per cent), when asked whether they thought scientists and engineers were interested in the same goals as management, replied that they were. The majority felt that as a group scientists and engineers were less interested in money than management, and more concerned with helping mankind, or developing research ideas.[25] When asked "From what you know, would you say top management in your company gives adequate support to the new ideas scientists and engineers develop?", only 21 per cent said management gave continuous sustained support, 72 per cent felt that some ideas were adequately supported but others were not, and 6 per cent felt that management simply did not give adequate support for new ideas.[26] In general, a variety of items from this comprehensive survey indicate that many engineers see themselves as having somewhat different goals and concerns from those of top management.

Although modern industry has moved in the direction Veblen anticipated, becoming more and more controlled by absentee owners, these changes have not sharply reduced the engineer's commitment to the political and economic status quo. Many still work for small companies, or in small work units where they have close contact with management and absorb its viewpoint. Too, the growth of large corporations has presented many engineers with the opportunity of advancing to the top of the economic hierarchy. The boards of directors of companies like Standard Oil

[23] Bernard Goldstein, "Unions and the Professional," *The Journal of Business* (1954), pp. 268-275.

[24] Opinion Research Corporation, *The Conflict Between the Scientific Mind and the Management Mind* (Princeton: Princeton University Press, 1959), p. 39.

[25] *Ibid.*, pp. 8-9.

[26] *Ibid.*, p. A-12.

of New Jersey and the American Telephone Company are largely filled by engineers who rose through the company. As the largest single source of recruitment for top management, engineers are perhaps more upwardly mobile than any other group. The Opinion Research 1959 study indicates that 48 per cent have had at least one promotion to a position involving "a higher level of authority and responsibility" in the last five years, and this figure does not include those already in administrative work, the large majority of whom have had such promotions.[27] Thus forces making for discontent and protest are counterbalanced by others making for identification with management and support of the status quo.

Table 6-5.
Support for Need for Unions As Means of Keeping Abreast of Gains Made by Other Employee Groups

	Engineer Total	Pro-Union	Anti-Union	Undecided
	(409)	18%	71%	11%
Under 30	(99)	19	70	11
30-44	(234)	18	72	10
45+	(76)	14	74	12
Under $6,000	(68)	22	66	12
$6,000-8,000	(170)	24	67	9
$8,000-10,000	(81)	17	69	14
$10,000+	(76)	4	88	8
Mostly creative work	(101)	15	80	5
Middle group	(92)	14	71	15
Mostly detail work	(205)	20	69	11
25 Engineers or less	(105)	13	79	8
26-100	(140)	17	70	18
100+	(153)	22	68	10
Senior engineers	(126)	15	76	9
Lower level	(265)	20	70	10
Highest job morale	(155)	16	78	6
Middle group	(150)	13	74	13
Lowest morale	(104)	27	60	13
Excellent mgt. relations	(73)	11	82	7
Good mgt. relations	(219)	14	76	10
Fair or poor	(108)	31	55	14

Source: Opinion Research Corporation, *What Is Troubling Industry's Engineers?* (Princeton: 1956), p. A-39.

[27] *Ibid.*, p. A-55.

There is, however, a small minority who, like the "deviant" white-collar group belong to unions, vote Democratic, and even identify with the working class. There is no evidence that this minority is growing, and there is little information concerning other traits related to such "deviant" behavior. One survey suggests certain factors similar to those found among other left-opinion or pro-union groups. Those engineers favorable to unions are more likely than the anti-unionists to work in larger companies, receive lower pay, carry out routine work, hold lower-level positions, and be younger. They also differ from anti-unionists in that they are less satisfied with their jobs and have poorer relations with management. The data are presented in Table 6-5.

Ideal of Craftsmanship and the Business System

Although it is difficult to demonstrate that conflict between occupational norms and institutional requirements produces leftist sentiments or trade-union members among engineers, evidence supports this thesis among the more intellectual professionals such as journalists, actors, musicians, and writers. Members of these occupations hold standards of creative accomplishment clearly at odds with market demand.

Since in modern capitalist society, rewards for cultural products increasingly depend on a market organized around business norms, the views of the employer are bound to diverge from those of the creative artist. This diversity produces hostility in the artist toward the businessman when, in rejecting business norms, he also rejects a comfortable livelihood, or when, in adapting to the market, he feels he has surrendered his personal integrity. As Bertrand de Jouvenal has pointed out, business is institutionally committed to giving the public what it wants, for the customer is always right.[28] In contrast, the creative artist views his products' value apart from their market utility.

Journalism, though not in the category of creative arts, supplies interesting evidence concerning the nature of this conflict. Professional norms define good craftsmanship as accurate reporting of significant news. Often, however, publishers want stories written to reflect the views of the owner, which are those of a well-to-do businessman. The journalist finds that "slanting" rather than objective reporting is required. He may even have to dróp stories which are likely to offend important advertisers or other powerful groups. More commonly, reporters must work for papers that cater to a mass circulation, writing about crime, scandal, and other local items, and neglecting news of international significance because it does not interest their readers. The ideal of many journalists is *The New York*

---

[28] Bertrand de Jouvenal, "The Treatment of Capitalism by Continental Historians," in F. A. Hayek, ed., *Capitalism and the Historian* (Chicago: University of Chicago Press, 1954), pp. 118-120.

Times, but they must work for the *Podunk Cronicle.* Some evidence that journalists are consciously aware of such pressures on them is presented by Leo Rosten in his study *The Washington Correspondents,*[29] in which a majority of those he questioned indicated that they were forced to "slant" stories or were prevented from publishing the truth as they saw it.

One result of this conflict between occupational norms and working reality is that many journalists become extremely cynical about social values. An incompleted study of this profession by Maurice Stein, based on depth interviews, points to the deep frustration occasioned by their inability to publish what they feel to be true. Their cynicism is probably reinforced because they are exposed to the seamy side of life, and see many examples of discrepancies between public and private morality. Such resentments and experiences may account for the fact that journalists are on the left in their national voting preferences. Interviews with a well-paid elite group of journalists, the Washington correspondents, in the 1930's showed that only 30 per cent had voted Republican in 1936, 6 per cent had supported the Socialists, and the rest were for Roosevelt. Although the average salary of this group of 104 men was over $6,000 in the midst of the depression, a considerable income for this period, 38 per cent favored government ownership of mines, public utilities, and railroads, and the majority (56 per cent) supported the organization of a newspapermen's union "to improve salaries and bargain collectively."[30] In recent years, straw ballots conducted among reporters covering Republican campaign trains indicate that most of them favored the Democratic candidate in 1952, 1956, and 1960. A study of American foreign correspondents stationed in western Europe reported that as of 1953-54 58 per cent were for Stevenson, and only 35.5 per cent favored the reelection of Eisenhower.[31]

Leo Rosten has also pointed up many of the frustrations felt by creative people in the motion picture industry. When sent a questionnaire asking them to comment on American movies today, the 141 Hollywood writers who responded supplied entirely unfavorable responses in 74 per cent of the cases.

The writers . . . feel most frustrated by the constricting demands of producers, the public and censorship. The writers . . . want to create stories different from those being told on the screen today—stories with deeper motivation and wider purpose, stories with relevance to our times, stories with characters freed from the vacuum of stereotypes, stories with dramatic situations rooted in a reality which is largely ignored in the contemporary film. But whether such stories would be popular with the public is dubious. . . .

[29] Leo Rosten, *The Washington Correspondents* (New York: Harcourt, Brace & World, 1937).

[30] *Ibid.,* pp. 348, 353-355.

[31] Theodore E. Kruglak, *The Foreign Correspondents, A Study of the Men and Women Reporting for the American Information Media in Western Europe* (Geneva: Librairie E. Croz, 1955), pp. 87-89.

The movie industry, which operates with high costs, and the multitudinous customers, who are not distinguished by esthetic sophistication, impose limitations which Hollywood's creative talents will forever dislike and against which they will forever discharge the antagonism born of frustration.[32]

Musicians tend to react the same way. Within this occupational group, great stress is placed upon preserving the integrity of their art. Economic success, unfortunately, depends on pleasing popular taste, and since popular taste is low, economic success is at cross purpose with artistic success. Contempt for popular taste extends to a dislike of non-musicians as well. To the jazz musician, reports Becker, non-musicians are outsiders, "squares" who are held in utmost distrust. "The square is thought of as an ignorant, intolerant person who is to be feared, since he produces the pressures forcing the musician to play inartistically."[33] The musicians feel that they are "completely different from and better than other kinds of people."

This hostility toward business and the public seems to be reflected in the propensity of creative artists to support left or liberal politics and trade unions. In voting statistics, these groups tend to support the Democrats and minority groups. A poll conducted in Hollywood in 1936 found all professional groups at least 5-1 for Roosevelt. This propensity of artistic professions to back more leftist politics does not simply flow from their antagonism to existing institutions, but may also reflect self-interest. In many countries the left parties are more likely to back state support for artistic activities than are the conservative parties and business groups.

Other Groups

Another factor involved in professional unionism, suggested by the behavior of social workers, is the influence of the clientele upon the outlook of the practitioner. Social workers are engaged in performing services to the less privileged section of the community. Their day-to-day activities make them well aware of the dire need of large sections of the population. Analogous to the engineer, who through his contact with management comes to see the world through management's eyes, the social worker develops a sympathy for the underdog and an outlook that supports the implementation of egalitarian values, especially in the economic sphere.

There is still another group of professionals who are highly organized, those who run the ships and airplanes. At first hand, these would appear to be a curious stratum for union organization. Air line pilots and engineers are among the highest paid groups in the country. The same is true, though to a lesser extent, for ship officers. Both groups can be considered

[32] Lee Rosten, *Hollywood: The Movie Colony, The Movie Makers* (New York: Harcourt, Brace & World, 1941), pp. 326-327.

[33] Howard S. Becker, "The Professional Dance Musician and His Audience," *American Journal of Sociology*, 57 (1951), 138-139.

as executives. They manage the particular "plant" that they work in. Without entering into a detailed analysis of these occupations, it may be suggested that to some degree the factors related to unionization among them are similar to those affecting certain lower white-collar groups discussed earlier. In large measure, these occupations have close links with certain manual occupations which are strongly organized. Thus, they are among the elite of the highly organized transportation industry, which includes railroads and trucking as well as planes and ships. All of these share in common the ability to seriously affect the economic life of the nation, and hence have strong bargaining power. The conditions of their work—irregular hours, week-end work, frequent travel away from home—help create strong occupational community ties among them, ties which often produce a sense of "industrial solidarity" against outsiders and those who profit from their work. The manual sectors of these industries have created strong unions, often in advance of the more privileged groups, and the latter have found this example an attractive one to follow. To a considerable degree, those going into these more professional occupations, in earlier periods particularly, seem to have come from lower strata, often working-class groups.

The Future of "Middle-Class" Unionism

The analysis of the factors which affect the reactions of white-collar and professional workers toward unions does not suggest that such organizations are likely to become a powerful element on the American scene. White-collar work is likely to continue to be predominantly a female occupation, and while increasing numbers of women are committed to permanent careers, it would seem true that most of them will continue to secure their primary sense of self-identification away from the job.

If it is true that the majority of white-collar workers are not hostile to unionism, and that at least as many are in favor of joining unions as now belong, the question must be faced as to why such organizations are not more successful. At least part of the answer lies with the unions themselves. Objective factors which predispose individuals to act in one way rather than another do not by themselves result in such actions. *Predispositions must be activated.* In the context of competition between organizations for the loyalty or support of individuals, those groups which are active in a situation may secure support or at least passive acquiescence from people who are basically disposed to oppose them. Thus, in a one-party society or organization, many may vote for the party simply because they know of no other alternative. This situation obviously applies to the problem of union membership. Few workers, manual or non-manual, take active steps to join unions which are not actively trying to organize the company in which they work.

To some degree the weakness of white-collar unionism may be explained by the failure of the union movement to reach the vast majority of the unorganized employees. This is clearly shown by the data from the Opinion Research Corporation studies. Over the years from 1945 to 1957, between 66 per cent and 71 per cent of those interviewed indicated that they did not know of any union efforts at the place in which they worked. (See Table 6-6).

Table 6-6.

Awareness of White-Collar Unionism Among Employees in Private Employment

	1945	1950	1953	1957
As far as you know, do any people where you work belong to a white-collar union? Yes.	23%	25%	24%	23%
Among those who say there is no union for their place of work — has there been talk of organizing a white-collar union where you work? Yes.	8	9	9	6
Total aware of union, or efforts to organize a union where they work.	31	34	33	29
N	(1347)	(1300)	(1519)	(1003)

Source: *Can Management Hold White Collar Loyalty,* Princeton: Opinion Research Corporation, 1957, pp. A-10, A-12.

These findings suggest that a large part of the answer to the issue of the organizability of the white-collar strata may lie with an analysis of the decision-making process within the labor movement. For there is reason to believe that much of the American labor movement has been unreceptive to the need to organize white-collar workers, that it has simply not devoted extensive organizational resources to this objective. The reasons for this are obviously complex, but on the most general level it would appear to be related to a kind of trained incapacity to deal with non-manual people. Both the craft and industrial unions have developed habits of work and behavior which reflect working-class culture. To specify this problem in detail would require another elaborate discussion.

The problem of the potential of professional unionism is a somewhat different matter. It may be argued that the most decisive fact in this context about professionals is that *they are already organized* into vocational organizations, many of which undertake economic and status representation functions. A picture of the extent to which employed Americans belong to vocational interest groups may be seen in Table 6-7.

Table 6-7.

Membership in Unions or Professional Organizations Among Different Occupational Groups

	Unions	Professional Associations	N
Professionals and semi-professionals	3%	42%	(33)
Clerical and sales	15	4	(52)
Skilled, semi-skilled, and protective services	52	2	(113)
Unskilled, service, and farm labor	37	0	(54)

Source: From data supplied by the Survey Research Center of the University of Michigan from a question asked of one third of the respondents to its 1954 election study.

Although the number of cases in the sample are too small to permit any claim of reliability, data from other sources suggest that the estimates in this table are relatively accurate. A survey of engineers, who constitute one of the largest professional groups, indicates that 53 per cent of them belong to professional societies. Similarly, the National Education Association, the largest teachers' professional group in the United States, reported a membership in 1956 equaling 53 per cent of all elementary and secondary school teachers. If we look at the claims of various professional organizations in the fields of education and engineering, the only professions in which over one million persons are engaged, we find that the professional organizations covering these fields claim a total membership about equaling the number of practitioners.

Numerically, the nearly half million student and professional nurses constitute the third largest group of professionals after the teachers and engineers. They clearly are different from most professions since they have relatively low status (the lowest status of the professions associated with medicine) and tend to be lowly paid. Their work situation is more similar to that of factory workers than it is to that of more high statused professionals. On the other hand, the existence of a formal training program and their association with the medical profession have facilitated their efforts to create a sense of professional identity.

There has never been a formal nurses' union, but the American Nurses' Association, the occupation's professional organization, has increasingly acted as a collective bargaining agency. Its 1946 national convention unanimously passed a program recommending that its local affiliates engage in collective bargaining, and many state organizations have done so. Their agreements are like those of unions. They set forth wages and working conditions in detail and provide for a grievance machinery terminating in arbitration.

While the American Nurses' Association resembles a union more than does any other professional association, its behavior points up the general statement that professionals in the United States are on the whole an "organized group." Unions, of course, object that such associations violate all the canons for good defense organization, particularly since many if not most of them include management officials and even employers among their membership, and few of them engage in formal collective bargaining. Nevertheless, it may be argued that the very fact that professional employees already belong to organizations which carry on economic and status enhancement activities, and which are formally democratic and representative, stands in the way of all efforts by "dual organization," in this case unions, to gain members from among such groups. Commitment to a going institution, whether political party, church, union, or professional organization, usually serves to so structure the social interactions and sentiments of members as to prevent shifts to another group purporting to serve the same functions better. People do change from one religion to another, from one party to another, from one union to another, but such changes on a massive scale are relatively rare. They occur only under conditions of great stress which clearly upset existing social relations, and call into question the legitimacy of given institutions.

The same point may be made with regard to another large section of the non-manual labor force not previously discussed here in any detail, government workers. Many of these, particularly those employed by state and local government agencies, belong to civil service associations. Such associations have many hundreds of thousands of members, and many of them have considerable political power. The California State Employees' Association, with close to 90,000 members among state employees, is generally recognized to be one of the most effective political lobbies in the state. It not only presses for higher wages and better working conditions through legislative action, but it acts to service the grievances and local complaints of its members much as does a trade union. Efforts to recruit government employees already organized in strong associations into unions run up against obstacles similar to those involved in recruiting organized professionals.

As yet, there is no reliable estimate of the extent to which the American labor force is organized. Clearly any estimate of economic organization which only counts trade unions is remiss. Perhaps it may be said that the least organized major sector is lower-level white-collar clerical and sales workers in private employment. A majority of manual workers, and of professionals, and a large but unknown proportion of government employees and technicians belong to organizations which *they* view as best for them. In a real sense, therefore, it may be argued that the United States is a highly organized country. The greater economic conservatism of its values as compared with Europe, and the slightly illegitimate connotation given to unionism as a class organization in a society that formally eschews class, may explain why American middle-class vocational organizations are more moderate or conservative in their social, political, and economic outlook than some comparable groups in Europe and Asia. But as was noted at the beginning, in these countries as well, middle-class organizations, even when formally identified as unions, tend to be much more conservative than those comprised primarily of manual workers.

The strategy suggested by these comments for trade unions in this country is two fold. First, concentration on new organization should be largely limited to the clerical and sales force of private industry. Here there is some reason to believe that many more can be organized. Second, in dealing with groups which already belong to vocational interest associations, it may be better to seek to win their cooperation with the union movement, and a modification of their tactics so they come more to resemble the American Nurses' Association, than to engage in the relatively unrewarding effort to take away their members. Manual-workers unions should approach existing professional groups in their industries with offers to support their efforts to gain better conditions without requesting that they join unions. The minority of unionists within such professions might better use their efforts to change the methods pursued by their professional associations than to engage in dual organization. Local and statewide union federations could propose working alliances with civil service and teachers' associations. In some cases, particularly in the case of government employee groups, such tactics could and have resulted in these associations deciding to affiliate as a group with an existing union.

The search for new approaches to deal with the diverse groups of non-manual employees should be a major objective of American unions. Structural trends, the decline of manual work, will inevitably weaken the collective bargaining strength of American unions as a whole unless a *modus vivendi* can be found between unions and the employed middle class.

36. Industrial Relations and Automation

Charles C. Killingsworth

A widely noted collective-bargaining agreement of 1959 was that between Armour and Company and the two meat-packing unions which represent most Armour employees. The portion of the agreement which attracted attention was a provision for an "Automation Fund" of $500,000 to be provided by the company and for an Automation Committee to be composed of labor, management, and neutral representatives. The committee was empowered to study employee displacement problems, to experiment with certain remedial measures, and to formulate recommendations for consideration by the parties in collective bargaining. One rather anomalous aspect of this development which has escaped general attention is that automation has as yet scarcely made an appearance in the production operations of the meat-packing industry. Armour had a substantial employee displacement problem in 1959, but it resulted from a management program of closing obsolete plants to reduce excess capacity and to centralize production. This program had resulted in the permanent closing of six plants and the termination of about 5,000 employees immediately prior to the negotiation of the 1959 agreement.

The Armour development is illustrative of the fact that, in a great many collective-bargaining situations, "automation" has become a synonym for "any development that may cause employee displacement." However convenient it may be to have a word—or a catchword—for referring to the problems of employee displacement, this usage tends to obscure some of the present and prospective effects of automation, more precisely defined, on collective bargaining.

Any discussion of the effects of automation on collective bargaining must recognize that one outstanding characteristic of collective bargaining in the United States is diversity. This diversity, broadly speaking, is largely the result of the decentralization of bargaining and the consequent shaping of bargaining systems and working rules to the circumstances of particular industries, particular plants, even particular departments and shops. Automation, too, takes many forms. The diversity both of bargaining systems and of automation limits the possibility of broad generalization.

Sometimes automation completely wipes out particular jobs. More frequently, automation reduces the content of a number of jobs, creating the technical possibility of combining these fractional remainders into

Reprinted from *The Annals*, **340** (March, 1962), 69-80.

new jobs. Automation often changes skill requirements, the degree of responsibility, and the working conditions of particular jobs, and it frequently reduces the extent to which the worker can control the speed of production. These changes obviously affect the relative value of jobs for wage-payment purposes and the appropriate method of payment. Automation sometimes blurs the distinction between production work and supervisory or office work. These are some of the direct and immediate effects of automation, strictly defined. These are effects that have been dealt with in a variety of collective bargaining relationships in the past decade. The main emphasis in this discussion will be on reactions to these direct and immediate effects of automation. Speculation concerning assumed long-run and indirect effects of automation may titillate the imagination more than analysis of this kind. But the understanding gained from a study of actual experience is likely to be more reliable than speculation, however inspired.

Job Combination

Let us consider first the matter of job combination resulting from automation and the important differences between industries in the collective-bargaining rules on this matter. Two specific examples will illustrate the differences. The rubber industry is in the process of installing highly automatic curing presses for tires. The positioning of green tires in the presses, the timing of the cure, the removal of cured tires, and, in some instances, some post-cure shaping and loading on conveyor belts are all performed automatically. Only one employee is needed to place tires on loading conveyors. Older, less automatic press lines require a number of employees to perform a variety of operations. Hence, the automatic features of the presses, plus the one employee who brings tires to them have in effect replaced a dozen or more employees in perhaps four or five occupational groupings. In a few plants, some questions have arisen concerning rates of pay on the new presses, but I know of no instance in which the union has seriously challenged the elimination of the old occupational groupings, or the substantial reduction in force on the new press lines as compared with the older ones.

Compare the case of the flight engineers in the airline industry. The introduction of pure-jet aircraft substantially changed the nature of the work load in the cockpit. Many of the control functions which the flight engineer performed on certain types of piston-powered airplanes are performed automatically or not at all on the jets. The duties of the pilots on the jets, especially during take-offs and landings, are substantially more demanding than on the piston-powered craft. Furthermore, the much greater speed and carrying capacity of the jets make it possible to fly many more passenger miles in the same time with the same number of cockpit employees. Since passenger traffic has not increased at the same rate as passenger-mile capacity per airplane, the employment opportunities for cockpit crews have sharply decreased. Hence, the pilots have insisted that the crew member who performs the residual flight-engineer duties should have the full skills of a pilot and take over some pilot duties; this would probably mean that the third seat in the jet cockpits would go to the displaced pilot of a piston-engine craft. The flight engineers have insisted that the third seat should go to a man with intensive mechanical training—which is the basic qualification of the present flight engineers.

The public bodies that have considered this controversy have generally found considerably more merit in the position of the pilots than in that of the flight engineers. However, when the first jets were placed in service, a number of airliners tried to satisfy both the pilots and the flight engineers by adding a fourth man (with pilot qualifications) to the cockpit crew. Neither group was entirely satisfied by this device, however, and the controversy broke out anew in 1961 when a strike by flight engineers shut down most of the major airlines of the country. As this is written (November, 1961) a presidential board is attempting to resolve the controversy by mediation.

The Nature of a Job

With some exceptions which will be noted shortly, neither job elimination nor job combination which is related to technological change creates formidable collective-bargaining problems in most large-scale, mass-production industries such as rubber. Why not? Largely because the typical "job" in such industries has long been an impermanent, shifting bundle of duties. In automobiles, rubber, and many other industries producing durable goods, seasonal and cyclical fluctuations are strong, and, as production expands and contracts, many jobs are necessarily changed by the addition of duties or the assignment of some of the former duties to other jobs. A large proportion of the jobs in such industries do not require very much specialized training; a few hours or days of training is usually sufficient. The seniority agreements in such industries generally provide relatively broad transfer rights to other jobs in the bargaining unit. Typically, one union represents the great bulk of production and maintenance employees, and virtually all agreements contain no-strike clauses which are applicable to all occupational groups.

The cockpit of an airliner exemplifies a setting in which quite different working rules have developed. While the business of the airliners is subject to some seasonal and cyclical fluctuations, the amount of service offered is adjusted by adding or deleting flights. If an airplane flies, it is manned by the standard cockpit crew. The standard duties of each crew member are prescribed in great detail, not only by company rules and in some respects by governmental regulations, but to a considerable degree by the terms of collective bargaining agreements. The pilots belong to one union, the flight engineers to another. On most overseas flights, a navigator has also been necessary, and he has belonged to still another union. The unions have separate agreements with the employers. All of the cockpit jobs require many months or years of training, and the typical pilot cannot perform the flight-engineer job without additional training, and vice versa. In any event, neither has any seniority rights on the other job.[1] Each union has the right to strike to secure new contract terms without consulting any other union, and such a strike usually grounds the company's planes.

The airliner cockpit typifies many segments of industry in which job lines are firmly drawn, with the result that reassignment of work—even those dictated by technological change—are often resisted by the employees and the unions involved. This situation is prevalent in such fields as the maritime trades, the construction industry, the railroads (especially train operation), most entertainment fields, many smaller establishments in the metal trades, and the printing trades, among others. Automation, strictly defined, has made little progress as yet in most of these fields.[2]

Until quite recently, the most extensive applications of automation techniques were in the large-scale mass-production industries like automobiles, in process industries like petroleum refining and chemicals, in communications, in electrical utilities, and in data processing in many industries. Here, generally speaking, the employees have been organized in general (or industrial) unions rather than craft (or occupation-based) unions, or else unions have been weak or non-existent, as in most data-processing operations. Hence, up to now, the kind of conflict that has developed in the airliner cockpit has not been a common result of the application of automation techniques. If automation spreads to areas of rigid job lines, then the reassignment of duties within work groups which automation frequently compels may generate the kind of stubborn collective-bargaining problems that we have observed in the airliner cockpit.[3] For example, the introduction of tape-controlled machine tools in small metal-working shops may create some difficult problems of work jurisdiction.

[1] The collective-bargaining agreements covering cockpit personnel vary from one airline to another, and their terms are frequently renegotiated. Hence, the generalizations in the text are not equally applicable to all airlines at all times.

[2] There has been a great deal of discussion of "automation" (very loosely defined) in a great many of these fields. For example, "automation" has been an issue in collective bargaining in East Coast longshoring, but there "automation" means principally the use of large containers which are packed and unpacked away from the waterfront.

[3] The kind of automation applications represented by space craft have indirectly contributed to some jurisdictional problems at missile-launching sites, partly because some new kinds of work are involved and also because familiar kinds of work are performed in strange contexts and for strange purposes.

Skilled Trades Jobs

We must now return to the mass-production industries to note one rather important exception to the generalization that job lines there are impermanent and shifting. Most large factories employ substantial numbers of skilled tradesmen for maintenance, setup, tool and die work, and similar activities which are auxiliary to production. Even where these tradesmen are represented by industrial unions, the job lines are far more stable and change in them is resisted more stubbornly than is the case in direct production work. The United Auto Workers, for example, has repeatedly adopted resolutions pledging to protect "the integrity of the skilled trades," which means, among other things, to resist any reassignment of tasks or any job combinations in the skilled trades. Many, perhaps most, employers in the mass-production industries observe at least to some degree the established jurisdictional lines between the skilled trades in making work assignments. In one of the large automobile companies, for example, a long line of arbitration decisions requires that such "lines of demarcation" be observed. In a number of rubber plants, to cite another example, contract provisions give enforceable status to such lines under most circumstances.

The fabrication and installation of many kinds of automation equipment require unusual combinations of skills and some new skills, and such requirements have come into conflict with the established lines of demarcation in some instances. In several of its plants, Ford has attempted to establish a new skilled-trades classification identified as "Automation Equipment Maker and Maintenance," which combines some of the duties of seven different skilled trades. In one new plant, this classification was established before the union organized the plant, and the company succeeded in retaining the classification after union recognition despite efforts of the international representatives of the union to eliminate it. In another new plant in which the company had established the classification, the union succeeded in getting an agreement to eliminate it, but the *quid pro quo* was a concession from the union that the company could assign the tradesmen across traditional lines of demarcation on automation equipment. In still another Ford plant, a long-established one, the company attempted to induce the union to agree to the establishment of the combination classification, but the union refused—with the strong support of the skilled tradesmen of the plant. In a rubber plant, the company attempted to establish a new skilled classification of "Instrument Repair," combining elements of several existing skilled trades, in order to provide for the servicing of the complex instrumentation of many kinds of automatic equipment. The union protested and carried the matter to arbitration, where the ruling was that the plant contract as interpreted by the parties themselves for a number of years barred the company from unilaterally establishing the proposed new classification under the circumstances of the case.

The point is that even the industrial unions tend to behave like craft unions with regard to jurisdictional lines in the skilled trades. This fact suggests that the basic source of resistance to this kind of change is not merely union policy but also the nature of the jobs involved and the attitudes engendered in the occupants. The skilled tradesman in the industrial plant, like the pilot or the flight engineer in the cockpit, has invested years of his life in training for his occupation, and his capability and contractual right to transfer to another occupation of comparable pay and status are usually severely limited. Hence, management's efforts to realign job duties to conform to the new requirements established by automation usually encounter stiff and sometimes bitter resistance. But the collective-bargaining problems are generally less difficult in the mass-production industries than in the industries where separate unions represent each skilled group. The industrial union rarely attempts to get detailed statements of job duties written into contracts (and thereby frozen at least for the life of the contract), and the factors of interunion rivalry and independent strike power in the hands of several different groups are rarely present in industrial-union bargaining.

Thus far, the discussion has been concerned mainly with job combination or other realignment of those duties that survive automation. The collective-bargaining problems are often less difficult where specific jobs are completely eliminated by automation and no residual duties remain to be allocated. This has happened to a great many production-line jobs in manufacturing industry. Occasionally it happens to a skilled group represented by its own union. We find another example in the cockpits of certain airliners. Until recently, navigators have been required on most overseas airline flights. Small electronic computers have been installed in some cockpits, and, with the aid of certain other electronic gear, the computers are able to perform all of the functions formerly assigned to the navigators. The navigators' union threatened to strike when its contract with the airline involved expired, but the obvious and the only real issue was the amount of severance pay, if any, that the navigators should be granted. The settlement was generous, and there was no strike.

Border Disputes

The application of automation techniques often changes basically the nature of the human contribution to the production process. Engineering, designing, programing, and similar work gain in relative importance as manual machine operation by workers diminishes. Much of the engineering, designing, and programing work indisputably falls outside the conventional production and maintenance bargaining unit. But the increase in office and supervisory forces in most industries, accompanied by decline in the number of bargaining-unit employees, has stimulated a number of "border disputes"—cases where the union claims that new work related to the use of automation equipment should be assigned to bargaining-unit employees rather than to employees who are excluded from it. Most present-day collective-bargaining agreements in large-scale industry define the border lines between these two groups only in quite general language, and this fact has helped to make the resolution of some of these disputes difficult.

The nature of the problems involved can be illustrated by two of the many relevant arbitration cases. A rubber plant converted a mixing machine (known as a Banbury) to completely automatic operation. Formerly, an operator, and sometimes one or more helpers, had been required to weigh and add materials, to operate control levers, and to push, start, and stop buttons throughout the production cycle. The installation of automatic controls made it possible for the machine to operate for hours without human assistance after a punched card had been inserted in the control equipment, dials had been set, and a button had been pushed. The only attention that the operation required was periodic monitoring of the control panel for signals of unexpected trouble. The company assigned the monitoring function, the card handling, the dial setting, and the button-pushing to a supervisor, who performed them in a control booth several hundred feet away from the automatic machine. He spent virtually all of his time on unquestionably supervisory duties such as the preparation of reports. The union claimed that the monitoring and button-pushing functions should be assigned to a bargaining-unit employee rather than to a supervisor.

The arbitrator ruled that the protested assignment was proper. He based his decision primarily on the fact that closely similar monitoring and button-pushing duties on semiautomatic systems had long been assigned to supervisors in the plant involved without protest from the union and no comparable work had been assigned to production employees. This plant assignment practice helped to establish the borders of the bargaining unit, he held. In the 1961 contract negotiations in the rubber industry, the Rubber Workers Union obtained from two of the major companies a contract provision to the effect that automation would not be used as a basis for removing jobs from the bargaining unit.

An automobile-industry case involved the programing of a newly installed, tape-controlled machine tool. The company had assigned the preparation of tapes for this machine to a production engineer, an employee not in the bargaining unit. The union claimed that this work should have been assigned to tool-makers who are bargaining-unit members. The arbitrator held the programing of such a machine is essentially the determination of its operational sequence and involves the computation of distances, locations, and angles; this type of work had always been part of the toolmaker's job, he said, and he concluded that it was a violation of the union-recognition clause of the contract to exclude the toolmaker entirely from the programing work.[4]

The increase in the number of these border disputes and the vagueness of most collective-bargaining agreements concerning the precise boundaries of the bargaining unit may prompt efforts in some contract negotiations to lay down additional guidelines, as in certain rubber-industry contracts in 1961. If the guidelines are to be really helpful in disposing of particular cases, they will necessarily be rather detailed and they will not be easily negotiated. Most companies and unions, therefore, may prefer to take their chances with their present indefinite language and to leave to arbitrators the task of deciding the difficult borderline cases.

Wage Determination

Labor economists generally agree that one result of collective bargaining over the past several decades has been the development of a far more systematic approach to wage structures and wage-payment systems than was common in an earlier era. By considerably altering job content and by changing man-machine relationships in many industrial operations, automation is creating a need for reconsideration of some of the wage determination and wage-payment systems now in use.

When the output per man is sharply increased, as frequently happens in automation applications, the employees and their union may insist that this higher productivity justifies a higher wage rate even though the automated job may require far less physical effort and less skill than the predecessor job. In companies where wage-rate determination is not on a systematic basis, the productivity argument has sometimes been accepted. The fact that unit labor cost may be greatly reduced by automation and the desire to "buy" employee and union acceptance of new technology have also been persuasive factors in the decision to grant higher wage rates. A series of such decisions, taken without regard to the emerging pattern, may result in an illogical wage structure and, perhaps ultimately, a crisis in bargaining.

A great many larger companies set wages on the basis of job-evaluation plans which assign rates on the basis of varying degrees of factors such as training, skill, responsibility, and working conditions. Such plans vary considerably in the relative weights which they assign to different factors. The prevalent plan in the steel industry, for example, gives much greater emphasis to responsibility factors than to skill factors; the most widely used

---

[4] A union official later commented that this decision would probably affect 100,000 jobs within the jurisdiction of the union in the country as a whole. To my mind, there is some question whether the decision will be as universally accepted and whether the ultimate number of programmers for machine tools will be as large as this comment seems to assume.

plan in the metalworking trades and electrical manufacturing gives greater emphasis to skill than to responsibility factors. In the steel industry, changes in operating jobs resulting from automation have frequently been interpreted to increase the responsibility factors sufficiently to offset decreases in other factors such as working conditions and skill, so that wage rates have often remained unchanged or have increased. In some maintenance fields in steel, however, the companies and the union have found it necessary to negotiate what might be regarded as a modification of the usual application of the plan; an example is the new job of "electronics repairman."

Little information is available concerning the application of the evaluation plans emphasizing skill to jobs affected by automation. It seems reasonable to deduce, from the nature of automation, that skill requirements on production jobs would generally tend to decrease as higher levels of automation are achieved, and there are some case-study findings which lend support to this deductive conclusion. Hence, straightforward application of skill-oriented evaluation plans to production jobs affected by automation might be expected to reduce wage rates in a number of cases. Such a result could hardly be expected to create enthusiasm for the new technology or for the job evaluation plan. In one aircraft company which uses a large number of tape-controlled machine tools, the job evaluation plan has simply been ignored. Skilled tradesmen are assigned to monitor the operation of the machines and they are paid their established rates although many executives are positive that the skill of the tradesman is not needed for the work. Such a policy may lead ultimately to a substantial revision of the job evaluation plan rather than outright abandonment of it. Since job evaluation is usually a rather technical matter, it seems reasonable to anticipate that bargaining over the revision of a job-evaluation plan will frequently prove to be difficult.

Incentive Systems

Various kinds of incentive-payment systems are widely used in American industry. In general, these systems provide for extra pay for extra production above a prescribed minimum. The general assumption, of course, is that extra effort results in extra production which justifies the extra pay. Broadly speaking, automation tends to transfer control over the rate of production from the worker to the machine; hence, it tends to undermine the basic, rationale of incentive payment. This is a factor which has contributed to the increasing difficulties with incentive-payment plans experienced in many plants. Some time ago, the large automobile companies and the United Auto Workers recognized that incentive plans were poorly suited to most operations in the industry, largely because of the high degree of machine (or assembly line) control of the pace of work. Hence, incentive plans are rare in the larger automobile companies, and automation has not created for them the kind of problem under consideration here.

Some other companies in other industries have also moved away from incentive types of wage payment, sometimes with union assent and sometimes despite strong union resistance, sometimes in part because of the automation of operations and sometimes because of other considerations. Under some agreements, management has the right to make the decision whether an entirely new operation—for example, one performed on equipment that is substantially different from that used on the predecessor operation—is to be placed on incentive. It seems likely that some attrition of incentive plans will occur under such agreements as automation spreads.

A widespread practice under many incentive payment plans is limitation of output by workers.[5] The degree of limitation varies quite markedly from one plant to another and even from one operation to another in the same plant. Some automation applications reduce the possibility of such limitation. It is not easy to eliminate completely all employee control over output, however; in some cases, such control is achieved simply by limiting the number of hours that the employees actually work during the scheduled shift. Automation commonly increases the amount of capital investment per employee and tends to make underutilization of equipment a more serious problem for management than under older types of technology. To meet this problem, some companies have fundamentally revised their incentive plans to provide for payment on the basis of the percentage of time that the employee (or the group) actually utilizes the equipment rather than on the basis of output. Another approach has been to make the production quota under the incentive system a matter of explicit bargaining between union and management representatives instead of leaving the matter to *sub rosa* unilateral determination by the employees involved.

General Effects

The discussion to this point has considered primarily the direct and immediate effects of automation, carefully defined, on collective bargaining. This emphasis is not intended to imply that there are no indirect, long-run effects. They are much harder to assess, however. One reason is that, as one moves away from immediate and direct effects, it becomes increasingly difficult to determine the extent to which the observed developments are the result of automation (carefully defined) rather than other forces which are also at work. Moreover, since automation and collective bargaining are both relative newcomers in most industries in which both are found, most

---

[5] The reasons for such limitation are diverse. Probably the most common are the fear of rate-cutting, the desire to spread the available work among as many employees as possible, and the desire to protect the average or below-average workman from unfavorable comparisons with high producers.

discussion of long-run effects rests far more on speculation than on experience. Some points of a general nature deserve attention, however.

In a few situations, automation appears to be the principal factor in a substantial decline in the effectiveness of strikes. In the telephone and gas and electric utilities industries, which are the most notable examples, most operations have now been made so automatic that the little direct labor that is required to maintain essential services can be provided by supervisory employees in case of a strike. Most production employees are normally assigned to repair, installation, and maintenance work, much of which is simply postponed for the duration of a strike. It does not seem justifiable, however, to conclude that most unionized industries will soon reach the same level of automation and, therefore, that the strike will wither away.

In manufacturing as a whole, automation is one important factor in the decline over the past decade in the number of blue-collar workers and the rise in the number of white-collar workers. As has often been pointed out, this trend will result in declining union membership and perhaps declining union influence unless white-collar workers are organized in far greater numbers than at present.

Automation and Job Security

As was pointed out at the beginning of this discussion, automation has become a subject of debate in an increasing number of collective-bargaining negotiations during the past decade, but the term has been given an extremely broad definition. "Automation" has frequently been used to mean any development that causes displacement or unemployment in an industry or even in the economy generally. Obviously, many factors in addition to automation (carefully defined) cause displacement and unemployment. Among these additional factors are the decentralization of certain industries, the elimination of excess capacity in others, the growth of substitute materials, products, and services in many fields, the massive shift in emphasis in defense expenditures, and the lagging growth rate of the economy as a whole.

Other articles in this symposium discuss from various viewpoints the difficult question of how much of the recent increase in general unemployment is attributable to automation rather than to other factors.[*] I will not go into that question, important though it is. The pertinent point for this discussion is that there is a widespread belief that automation is a new force in the economy which is decreasing job security and that collective

* *Editors note:* The articles referred to are Walter Buckingham, "The Great Employment Controversy," *The Annals,* **340** (March, 1962), pp. 46-52; Malcolm L. Denise, "Automation and Employment: A Management Viewpoint," *op. cit.,* pp. 90-99; Walter P. Reuther, "Policies for Automation: A Labor Viewpoint," *op. cit.,* pp. 100-109; Arthur J. Goldberg, "The Role of Government," *op. cit.,* pp. 110-116.

bargaining in recent years has increasingly involved job-security measures. Thus, whatever its real economic impact, the psychological impact of automation has been an important factor in producing this new emphasis—or change in emphasis—in collective bargaining.

The result of this interest in job security has been an extensive repertoire of agreement provisions intended to prevent unemployment or to alleviate its effects.[6] Some companies and unions have tried to minimize unemployment by providing a number of aids to worker mobility—provisions for advance notice of major changes to permit joint planning, provisions for transfer to other operations or plants and to broadening of seniority units, provisions for payment or moving expenses under certain circumstances, and provisions for training or retraining programs to be provided by the employer. For those whose employment is interrupted either temporarily or permanently, cushions have been provided—supplementary unemployment benefits, short work-week benefits, and severance pay. Early retirement benefits have been provided to encourage some voluntary withdrawals from the labor force. Some unions have demanded, with increasing urgency, reductions in the work week or the work year in order to spread the available work among larger numbers of people; and, in a few instances, unions have proposed job "freezes" to avert unemployment. Thus far, neither the hours-reduction nor the job-freezing proposals have made much progress in collective bargaining.

Another approach to the quest for job security has been for labor and management or the government to set up study committees to formulate recommendations for consideration in collective bargaining. Kaiser Steel and the Steelworkers have set up a tripartite committee, and the union and the largest companies in basic steel have a joint committee at work. One assignment of both committees is to consider ways of adjusting to technological change. The tripartite Automation Committee established in 1959 by Armour and two meat-packing unions is continuing its work. Several public boards have been appointed to study job-security matters (among other subjects) on the airlines. A tripartite Presidential Railroad Commission was at work, as 1961 ended, on recommendations for handling displacement and other problems of train-operating employees. Other, less formalized studies were also under way in some other industries. By the end of 1962, we should know a great deal more about the efficacy of these varied approaches to a solution of the job-security problem under collective bargaining than we do at present. Even now, however, it seems safe to predict a considerable measure of agreement with the conclusion stated by the Armour Automation Committee in a progress report:

---

[6] I do not intend to imply that all collective-bargaining agreements now include all of the measures discussed in this section. However, provisions of the kinds described are becoming increasingly common.

Only through a coordinated approach in which public policy and private action mutually reinforce one another can the employment problems of technological change be met. Collective bargaining by itself cannot fully solve these problems.

Conclusion

Let us return briefly to the principal subject of this discussion, the direct and immediate impact of automation on industrial-relations systems. A superficial examination of the experience of the past decade might readily induce an optimistic view of the future. The spread of automation has created controversy and conflict over job rights, assignment of job duties, bases and methods of pay, and related matters. But with only a few exceptions, the controversy and conflict have been contained and resolved within the established institutions for negotiation and arbitration. We should not conclude too quickly, however, that the further spread of automation in the future will be accomplished with as little disruption of industrial-relations systems as in the past decade.

Up to now, the technical characteristics of automation have made it most adaptable to certain operations in mass production industries.[7] The environment in which most of these industries operate has compelled them to develop ways of adapting to rapid change. Most of them have also developed fairly efficient arbitration machinery. As automation becomes more versatile and more economical, it may have greater impact on collective-bargaining systems that have developed impediments to adjustment to change—rigid job lines, restrictive working rules, wage-payment systems that are hard to adjust—and that lack effective arbitration machinery. The limited experience of the past decade suggests that conflict over automation in these bargaining situations is not likely to be as effectively contained as it has been in the generally different environment of the mass-production industries.

[7] Or to data-processing operations in which collective bargaining is rather rare.

Bibliography

Abrams, M., and Rose, R., *Must Labour Lose?* (Baltimore: Penguin, 1961).

Allen, L. E., "Games Bargaining: A Proposed Application of the Theory of Games to Collective Bargaining," *The Yale Law Journal,* **65** (April, 1956), 679-693.

Baker, H., and Frances, R. R., *Centralization and Decentralization in Industrial Relations* (Princeton: Princeton University Press, 1954).

Banks, J. A., *Industrial Participation: Theory and Practice* (Liverpool, England: Liverpool University Press, 1963).

Baratz, M. S., *The Union and the Coal Industry* (New Haven, Conn.: Yale University Press, 1955).

Barbash, J., "Union Response to the 'Hard Line'," *Industrial Relations,* **1** (October, 1961), 25-38.

Beal, E. F., "Origins of Codetermination," *Industrial and Labor Relations Review,* **8** (July, 1955), 483-498.

Benewitz, M. C., "Social Cost and Collective Bargaining," *American Journal of Economics and Sociology,* **15** (January, 1956), 189-193.

Bloom, G. F., and Northrup, H. R., *Economics of Labor Relations* (Homewood, Ill.: Irwin, 1954).

Blum, A. A., "Collective Bargaining: Ritual or Reality?", *Harvard Business Review,* **39** (November-December, 1961), 63-69.

Boulding, K. E., *Conflict and Defense: A General Theory* (New York: Harper & Row, 1962).

Braun, K., *Labor Disputes and the Settlement* (Baltimore: Johns Hopkins Press, 1955).

Brown, D. V., and Myers, C. A., "The Changing Industrial Relations Philosophy," *Proceedings of the Industrial Relations Research Association* (December, 1956), 84-99.

Brown, L., "Labor Arbitration," *Social Order,* **7** (February, 1957), 62-69.

Carlton, F. T., "Collective Bargaining and Capitalism," *American Journal of Economics and Sociology,* **12** (July, 1953), 393-396.

Carlton, F. T., "Trends in Labor-Management Relation," *American Journal of Economics and Sociology,* **12** (April, 1953), 261-265.

Carpenter, W. H., Jr., and Handler, E., *Small Business and Pattern Bargaining* (Babson Park, Mass.: Babson Institute Press, 1961).

Cartwright, D., *Studies in Social Power* (Ann Arbor: University of Michigan Press, 1959).

Chalmers, W. E., Chandler, M. K., McQuitty, L. L., Stagner, R., Wray, D. E., and Derber, M., *Labor-Management Relations in Illini City* (Champaign: University of Illinois, Institute of Labor and Industrial Relations, 1954).

Chamberlain, N. W., *Social Responsibility and Strikes* (New York: Harper & Row, 1953).

Chamberlain, N. W., "The Structure of Bargaining Units in the United States," *Industrial and Labor Relations Review*, **10** (October, 1956), 3-25.

Chamberlain, N. W., "The Union Challenge to Management Control," *Industrial and Labor Relations Review*, **16** (January, 1963), 184-292.

Chamberlain, N. W., and Schilling, J. M., *The Impact of Strikes; the Social and Economic Costs* (New York: Harper & Row, 1954).

Child, J., "Quaker Employers and Industrial Relations," *The Sociological Review*, **12** (November, 1964), 293-316.

Ching, C. S., *Review and Reflection; a Half Century of Labor Relations* (New York: B. C. Forbes and Sons, Inc., 1953).

Clelland, S., *The Influence of Plant Size on Industrial Relations* (Princeton: Princeton University Press, 1955).

Clump, C. C., "Priest as Mediator," *Social Order*, **4** (September, 1954), 300-303.

Cole, D. L., "Government in the Bargaining Process: The Role of Mediation," *Annals of the American Academy of Political and Social Science*, **333** (January, 1961), 42-58.

Coser, L., *The Functions of Conflict* (New York: Free Press, 1956).

Crumb, J. A., "Dispute Settlement and Third Party Intervention: A Discussion," *Canadian Journal of Economics and Political Science*, **21** (November, 1955), 531-534.

Dalton, M., "Unofficial Union-Management Relations," *American Sociological Review*, **15** (October, 1950), 611-619.

Daugherty, C. R., "Import of the AFL-CIO Merger for Management," *Monthly Labor Review*, **79** (December, 1956), 1427-1444.

Davey, H. W., *Contemporary Collective Bargaining*, 2nd ed. (Englewood Cliffs, N.J.: Prentice-Hall, 1959).

Davey, H. W., "Labor Arbitration: A Current Appraisal," *Industrial and Labor Relations Review*, **8** (October, 1955), 85-94.

Derber, M., "Plant Labor Relations in Israel," *Industrial and Labor Relations Review*, **17** (October, 1963), 39-59.

Derber, M., Chalmers, W. E., and Edelman, M. T., "Local Union-Management Types," *Human Organization*, **21** (Winter, 1962-1963), 264-270.

Derber, M., Chalmers, W. E., and Edelman, M. T., "Union Participation in Plant Decision-Making," *Industrial and Labor Relations Review*, **15** (October, 1961), 83-101.

Derber, M., Chalmers, W. E., Stagner, R., and Edelman, M. T., *The Local Union-Management Relationship* (Urbana: Institute of Labor and Industrial Relations, University of Illinois, 1960).

Douty, H. M., "Labor Status and Collective Bargaining," *Monthly Labor Review*, **79** (June, 1956), 647-653.

Dubin, R., "Industrial Conflict and Social Welfare," *Journal of Conflict Resolution*, **1** (June, 1957), 179-199.

Dubin, R., "Constructive Aspects of Industrial Conflict," in A. Kornhauser, R. Dubin, and A. Ross, eds., *Industrial Conflict* (New York: McGraw-Hill, 1954), pp. 37-47.

Dubin R., "Decision-Making by Management in Industrial Relations," *American Journal of Sociology*, **54** (January, 1949), 292-297.

Dubin, R., *Human Relations in Administration* (Englewood Cliffs, N.J.: Prentice-Hall, 1961).

Dubin, R., "Power and Union-Management Relations," *Administrative Science Quarterly*, 2 (June, 1957), 60-81.

Dubin, R., "Union-Management Co-operation and Productivity," *Industrial and Labor Relations Review*, 2 (January, 1949), 195-209.

Dubin, R., *Working Union-Management Relations* (Englewood Cliffs, N.J.: Prentice-Hall, 1958).

Dunlop, J. T., and Myers, C. A., "The Industrial Relations Function in Management—Some Views on its Organizational Status," *Personnel*, 32 (March, 1955), 406-413.

Dunlop, J. T., and Healy, J. J., *Collective Bargaining: Principles and Cases* (Revised Edition) (Homewood, Ill.: Richard D. Irwin, Inc., 1953).

Estey, M. S., "The Impact of Labor Force Changes on Labor Relations," *Annals of the American Academy of Political and Social Science*, 333 (January, 1961), 1-4.

Fensen, V., "The Process of Collective Bargaining and the Question of its Obsolescence," *Industrial and Labor Relations Review*, 16 (July, 1963), 546-558.

Fisher, W. E., *Bases for Industrial Relations*, Bulletin No. 24 (Pasadena: California Institute of Technology, Industrial Relations Section, 1954).

Flanders, A., and Clegg, H. A., eds., *The System of Industrial Relations in Great Britain; its History, Law and Institutions* (Oxford: Blackwell, 1954).

Galbraith, J. K., *American Capitalism: The Concept of Countervailing Power* (Boston: Houghton Mifflin, 1952).

Garfield, S., and Whyte, W. F., "The Collective Bargaining Process: A Human Relations Analysis," *Human Organization*, 9 (Summer, 1950), 5-10; part II (Fall, 1950), 10-16; part III (Winter, 1950), 25-29; part IV (Spring, 1951), 28-32.

Gitlow, A. L., *Labor Economics and Industrial Relations* (Homewood, Ill.: Irwin, 1957).

Golden, C. S., and Parker, V. G., eds., *Causes of Industrial Peace under Collective Bargaining* (New York: Harper & Row, 1955).

Gouldner, A. W., *Wildcat Strike* (Yellow Springs, Ohio: Antioch Press, 1954).

Gray, R. D., *The Scope of Collective Bargaining* (Pasadena: Industrial Relations Section, California Institute of Technology, 1954).

Haire, M., "Role Perception in Labor-Management Relations," *Industrial and Labor Relations Review*, 8 (January, 1955), 204-216.

Harbison, F. H., and Dubin, R., *Patterns of Union-Management Relations* (Chicago: Science Research Associates, 1947).

Harsanyi, J. C., "Approaches to the Bargaining Problem before and after the Theory of Games: A Critical Discussion of Zeuthen's, Hicks', and Nash's Theories," *Econometrica*, 24 (April, 1956), 144-157.

Heron, A. R., *Reasonable Goals in Industrial Relations* (Stanford: Stanford University Press, 1954).

Hildebrand, G. H., "American Unionism, Social Stratification and Power," *American Journal of Sociology*, 58 (January, 1953), 381-390.

Janis, I. L., and Katz, D., "The Reduction of Intergroup Hostility: Research

Problems and Hypotheses," *Journal of Conflict Resolution*, 3 (March, 1959), 85-100.

Jaques, E., "Studies in the Social Development of an Industrial Community: Collaborative Group Methods in a Wage Negotiation Situation (The Glacier Project, I)," *Human Relations*, 3 (August, 1950), 223-249.

Jensen, V. H., "Notes on the Beginnings of Collective Bargaining," *Industrial and Labor Relations Review*, 9 (January, 1956), 225-234.

Jones, D., *Labor Arbitration: Principles, Practices, Issues* (New York: Simons-Boardman, 1961).

Karsh, B., *Diary of a Strike* (Urbana: University of Illinois Press, 1958).

Karsh, B., Seidman, J., and Lilienthal, D. M., "The Union Organizer and His Tactics: A Case Study," *American Journal of Sociology*, 59 (July, 1953), 113-122.

Kerr, C., "Industrial Conflict and Its Mediation," *American Journal of Sociology*, 60 (November, 1954), 230-245.

Kerr, C., and Siegel, A., "The Inter-Industry Propensity to Strike—An International Comparison," in A. Kornhauser, R. Dubin, and A. Ross, eds., *Industrial Conflict* (New York: McGraw-Hill, 1954).

Khalaf, S., "Industrial Conflict in Lebanon," *Human Organization*, 24 (Spring, 1965), 25-33.

Knowles, K. G., "Strike-Proneness and Its Determinants," *American Journal of Sociology*, 60 (November, 1954), 213-229.

Knowles, K. G., *Strikes—A Study in Industrial Conflict* (New York: Philosophical Library, 1952).

Knowles, W. H., "Industrial Conflict and Unions," in W. E. Moore and A. S. Feldman, *Labor Commitment and Social Change in Developing Areas* (New York: Social Science Research Council, 1960).

Kolaja, J., *A Polish Factory: A Case Study of Workers' Participation in Decision-Making* (Lexington: University of Kentucky Press, 1960).

Kornhauser, A. W., "Ideology and Interests: The Determinants of Union Actions," *Journal of Social Issues*, 9 (January, 1953), 49-60.

Kornhauser, A. W., et al., eds., *Industrial Conflict* (New York: McGraw-Hill, 1954).

Kuhn, H. W., "Game Theory and Models of Negotiations," *Journal of Conflict Resolution*, 6 (March, 1962), 1-4.

Lahne, H. J., "The Intermediate Union Body in Collective Bargaining," *Industrial and Labor Relations Review*, 6 (January, 1953), 163-179.

Lamson, R., "The 1951 New York Wildcat Dock Strike: Some Consequences of Union Structure for Management-Labor Relations," *Southwestern Social Science Quarterly*, 34 (March, 1954), 28-38.

Landsberger, H. A., "The Behavior and Personality of the Labor Mediator: The Parties' Perception of Mediator Behavior," *Personnel Psychology*, 13 (Autumn, 1960), 329-347.

Landsberger, H. A., "Interaction Process Analysis of the Mediation of Labor-Management Disputes," *Journal of Abnormal and Social Psychology*, 51 (November, 1955), 552-558.

Landsberger, H. A., "Interaction Process Analysis of Professional Behavior: A

Study of Labor Mediators in Twelve Labor-Management Disputes," *American Sociological Review*, **20** (October, 1955), 566-575.

MacDonald, R. M., *Collective Bargaining in the Automobile Industry* (New Haven, Conn.: Yale University Press, 1963).

Mack, R., and Snyder, R. C., "The Analysis of Social Conflict—Toward an Overview and Synthesis," *Journal of Conflict Resolution*, **1** (June, 1957), 212-248.

Magoun, F. A., *Cooperation and Conflict in Industry* (New York: Harper & Row, 1960).

Marciniak, E., "Some U.S. Approximations to the Industrial Council Idea," *American Catholic Sociological Review*, **17** (March, 1956), 24-29.

McPherson, W. H., "Codetermination in Practice," *Industrial and Labor Relations Review*, **8** (July, 1955), 499-519.

Myers, C. A., and Turnbull, J. G., "Line and Staff in Industrial Relations," *Harvard Business Review*, **34** (July-August, 1956), 113-124.

Northrup, H. R., "Management's 'New Look' in Labor Relations," *Industrial Relations*, **1** (October, 1961), 9-24.

Porter, A. R., Jr., *Job Property Rights: A Study of the Job Controls of the International Typographical Union* (New York: King's Crown, 1954).

Potvin, R. H., "Belgian Enterprise Councils: Attitude and Satisfaction of Management and Labor," *American Catholic Sociological Review*, **18** (December, 1957), 301-306.

Rogow, A. A., "Labor Relations Under the British Labor Government," *American Journal of Economics and Sociology*, **14** (July, 1955), 357-376.

Sayles, L. R., and Strauss, G., *The Local Union: Its Place in the Industrial Plant* (New York: Harper & Row, 1953).

Schneider, L., and Lysgaard, S., " 'Deficiency' and 'Conflict' in Industrial Sociology," *American Journal of Economics and Sociology*, **12** (October, 1952), 49-61.

Schnepp, G. J., "Codetermination," *American Catholic Sociological Review*, **14** (June, 1953), 66-83.

Scott, W. H., Mumford, E., McGivering, I. C., and Kirby, J. M., *Coal and Conflict: A Study of Industrial Relations at Collieries* (Liverpool: Liverpool University Press, 1963).

Sexton, B., "The Intervention of the Union in the Plant," *Journal of Social Issues*, **9** (January, 1953), 7-11.

Sheppard, H. L., "Approaches to Conflict in American Industrial Sociology," *British Journal of Sociology*, **5** (December, 1954), 324-342.

Sheppard, H. L., "The Treatment of Unionism in 'Managerial Sociology,' " *American Sociological Review*, **14** (February, 1949), 310-313.

Shultz, G. P., "Decision Making: A Case Study in Industrial Relations," *Harvard Business Review*, **30** (May-June, 1952), 105-113.

Spaulding, C. B., "The Psychosocial Dynamics of Union-Management Cooperation," *Sociology and Social Research*, **39** (March-April, 1955), 230-236.

Spielmans, J. V., "Measuring the Results of Organizational Union Representation Elections," *Industrial and Labor Relations Review*, **9** (January, 1956), 280-285.

Stagner, R., Parcell, T., Kerr, W., Hjalman, R., and Gruen, W., *Dual Allegiance* to *Union and Management—A Symposium* (Urbana: University of Illinois, Bulletin No. 79, 1954).

Stone, R. C., "Conflicting Approaches to the Study of Worker-Manager Relations," *Social Forces*, 31 (October, 1952), 117-124.

Strauss, G., "Factors in the Unionization of a Utility Company: A Case Study," *Human Organizations*, 12 (Fall, 1953), 17-25.

Strauss, G., "The Shifting Power Balance in the Plant," *Industrial Relations*, 1 (May, 1962), 65-96.

Sturmthal, A., *Worker Councils: A Study of Workplace Organization on Both Sides of the Iron Curtain* (Cambridge, Mass.: Harvard University Press, 1964).

Tannenbaum, A. S., "An Event-Structure Approach to Social Power and to the Problems of Power Comparability," *Behavioral Science*, 7 (July, 1962), 315-331.

Thompson, K. M., "Human Relations in Collective Bargaining," *Harvard Business Review*, 31 (March-April, 1953), 116-126.

Vollmer, H. M., *Employee Rights and the Employment Relationship* (Berkeley: University of California Press, 1960).

Wellisz, S., "Strikes in Coal-Mining," *British Journal of Sociology*, 4 (December, 1953), 346-366.

Whyte, W. F., "Culture, Industrial Relations, and Economic Development: The Case of Peru," *Industrial and Labor Relations Review*, 16 (July, 1963), 583-594.

Whyte, W. F., *Pattern for Industrial Peace* (New York: Harper & Row, 1951).

Whyte, W. F., "Union-Management Cooperation: Toronto Case; An Analysis of W. R. Dymond's Study," *Applied Anthropology*, 6 (Summer, 1947), 1-9.

READINGS in INDUSTRIAL SOCIOLOGY VII

EPILOGUE — THE FUTURE OF INDUSTRIAL SOCIETY

Introduction

The readings that have been included in this book represent a sample of the work done by industrial sociologists in their effort to understand the social structure of industrial society. Throughout the book an attempt has been made to show the way in which this work illuminates some central features of the industrial way of life. Industrial societies are inherently highly differentiated and rapidly changing. Because of these attributes, industrial societies and organizations are faced with problems of coordinating complex structures, accommodating conflicting interests, and controlling heterogeneous memberships. This is another way of saying that structural differentiation and social change tend to decrease the level of social integration of industrial societies and organizations. To counteract this tendency, increasingly rationalized social structures have been developed. At the most general level, this means that the search for better means to specified ends has been built into the structure of industrial societies and organizations. Social control in industry has become a matter of formal rules, regulations, laws, explicit division of authority among positions, and, most importantly with regard to the rationalization process, there are *standardized procedures for evaluating and revising these control mechanisms*. Division of labor in industry also involves sets of minutely specialized tasks that are created and frequently changed by personnel managers and industrial engineers. Industrial technology is a rapidly evolving product of the efforts of engineers and scientists. Relations between labor and management are regulated by a contract that is periodically revised through formally established procedures. Each of these examples of rationalization call for increasing numbers of professionals who apply their expertise to the search for better means to specified ends. It is particularly in this way that rationalization has become a built in response to complexity and change.[1]

The differentiation-rationalization sequence has been used as a general theme throughout this book. The purpose of such a theme is to provide at least some integration of the material that has been presented. To achieve a highly integrated collection of readings in industrial sociology, however, it would have been necessary to leave out some of the diverse areas that make up the field. Not all of the selections in this text have any direct relevance to its major theme; most were included because they are well-known studies and are frequently referred to in the writings of industrial sociologists. An attempt has been made, however, to relate the major concerns of each chapter of the book to the structurally differentiated and rationalized character of industrial societies. In the introductory chapter the differentiation-rationalization sequence was described in some detail. In Chapter I the relationship of this sequence to the process of industrialization was discussed. The focus of Chapters II and III was upon rationalized, bureaucratic authority and control. In Chapter IV the distinction between the formal-rational and informal-traditional modes of organization was made and some limitations of rationalized structures were noted. Chapter V was concerned with a dilemma faced by unions and many other organizations within industrial societies: rationalized, efficient operation in a complex, changing society can be achieved only through some sacrifice of individual freedom of action. The major point in Chapter VI was that *inter*organizational as well as *intra*organizational relations are affected by the processes of differentiation and rationalization.

This final chapter is concerned with the future of industrial societies. If the sequence of events we have selected as a theme describes some central features of the industrial way of life at the present, it may also suggest some possibilities regarding the future. Complexity, rapid change, and lack of social integration all increase the difficulty of making accurate predictions. Through analysis of the rationalization process, however, something of the future shape of industrial societies may be seen. Although the present state of knowledge in industrial sociology provides only hazy outlines in our crystal ball, we will suggest a few possible outcomes of continuing rationalization, particularly as it affects the division of labor.

The form of division of labor has a more profound impact upon the nature of a society than any other aspect of its structure. The dominant pattern of change in division of labor accompanying industrialization has been increasing functional specialization. Most jobs involve little training, produce only a limited emotional commitment of people to their work, and

[1] Weber states, for example, that "we can be most certain of the rationality of the choice of means to ends to the degree to which logical or scientific standards have been established permitting judgments of adequacy or appropriateness." Max Weber, *The Rational and Social Foundations of Music* (Carbondale, Ill.: Southern Illinois University Press, 1958), p. xviii.

require considerable supervision. This process has been going on for so long that it appeared to be an irreversible trend in industrial societies. There is some evidence today that this pattern is changing.[2] Technological and organizational developments are producing more integrated production systems and are combining previously separate job specialties into more broadly based occupations. Most repetitive manual operations at the blue-collar and lower white-collar levels will undoubtedly be mechanically performed sometime in the future. Even middle-management positions, where the job involves making decisions among a limited set of alternatives, may be eliminated by the increasing use of computers. Higher levels of income along with more leisure time in which to spend it will increase the proportion of the labor force in less specialized, service occupations. The major trends in labor force composition today are an increase in the proportion of professionals and technicians and an increase in the proportion of people in general service occupations. There will almost certainly be an acceleration of these trends in the future.

Whether or not the industrial economy and society can manage these changes without mass unemployment or other major disruptions is a moot point. Some writers believe we are at the "threshold of a golden tomorrow" while others have predicted the downfall of industrial civilization. The evidence to date would suggest that we will make a successful adjustment to the changing demands of the labor market although there are bound to be some crises along the way. Avoiding major problems will require a substantial effort by government, schools, management, and unions and there appears to be a disposition by all concerned to make this effort. The key may lie in our increasing ability to anticipate problems and develop solutions before they become major crises. Research in the social sciences has an important part to play in this process.

Assuming a successful transition, the postindustrial society may differ in some important ways from present industrial societies. A labor force composed primarily of professional, technical, skilled, and service workers requires a quite different organizational structure than that typical of industry today. The readings of Marcson and Kornhauser in Chapters II and III described the type of control structure appropriate for professionals in industry. Organizations made up primarily of skilled workers are similar in some respects to professional work organizations.[3] The specialized, hierarchical authority system in contemporary bureaucracies is designed to control and coordinate the behavior of people in narrowly defined jobs who are not socialized within or committed to norms of workmanship in their occupations. It is precisely these latter attributes, however, that distinguish

[2] Cf. William A. Faunce, "Automation and the Division of Labor," *Social Problems*, 13 (Fall, 1965), 149-160.

[3] Cf. Arthur L. Stinchcombe, "Bureaucratic and Craft Administration of Production: A Comparative Study," *Administrative Science Quarterly*, 4 (September, 1959), 168-187.

professionals and skilled workers from persons in other kinds of jobs. The long period of training required to become a doctor, an engineer, or a master plumber or carpenter involves not only the acquisition of skills but also the learning of a set of norms regarding behavior on the job. For this reason, professional and skilled workers require and receive less supervision than other workers. Behavior in future industrial work organizations should be regulated to a much greater degree by traditional occupational norms than by rationalized, organizational controls. These changes in the structure of industrial organization will result in a larger "sphere of autonomy" and greater individual freedom of action at work. The number of hours worked per day, days worked per week, and weeks worked per year will also continue to decrease so that the total amount of time during which people are subject to organizational controls will also decrease.

While individuals may have greater freedom of action in the future, organizations will undoubtedly have less. In order to regulate the relations between powerful interest groups, the amount of control exercised by the state will necessarily continue to grow. Political and economic power will be concentrated in fewer organizations as the number of separate, special interests declines and the representational base of organizations grows in a more integrated society. The number of corporations, unions, and occupational associations, for example, is likely to decrease. Technological advances will probably give an even greater competitive advantage to large corporations and the number of unions and other occupational associations will decline as a result of changes in the division of labor. With increasing concentration of power, it will become increasingly common for interorganizational relations to be governed by a rational-legal framework imposed by the state in the interest of the people.

This brief discussion of possible changes in the division of labor, in the structure of industrial organizations, and in interorganizational relations may be sufficient to illustrate the major point that is intended regarding the future of industrial societies. In direct contrast with its earlier effects, the continuing rationalization of industrial technology and social structure may result in a *decrease* in the extent to which industrial social systems are structurally differentiated. Less segmentalized industrial societies, communities, and organizations may achieve a higher level of social integration. Social change may continue to occur at a rapid rate but it is likely to be channeled and subject to rationalized controls to a much greater extent than at present. In short, the future of industrial society may include a reversal of the direction of change in those particular processes that have shaped its past.

The two readings that have been included in this chapter are very different from each other in their view of the future. In both readings industrialization is regarded as a relatively new, irreversible, and pervasive force. Both regard extensive differentiation as an important feature of industrial society. The selection from Meadows, *The Culture of Industrial Man*, however, is a poetic indictment of the quality of industrial culture. He points to the isolation of individuals, groups, and organizations, and to the paradoxes and conflicts in the industrial way of life. He sees these problems, moreover, as ineradicable and inherent in industrialism and he takes a very pessimistic view of the future of industrial society.

Kerr, Dunlop, Harbison, and Meyers, in the final chapter of their *Industrialism and Industrial Man*, view the future in a quite different light. Their greater optimism rests largely upon confidence in the ability of a more educated population, through rationalized processes, to *choose* their future: "chance may elude man, but choice need not; and the choice of men, within fairly broad limits, can shape history." The future industrial society is seen as characterized by a "pluralistic industrialism" in which a more limited set of power centers will be governed both internally and in their external relations by an effective "web of rules."

The contrast between the two readings in this chapter results largely from differing assessments of the ability of rationalized processes to cope with the problems created by industrialism. While the two readings are quite different, their positions are not mutually exclusive. Some of the problems noted by Meadows may continue undiminished in the pluralistic industrial society of the future. What is seen in either the present or the future of anything so complex as the industrial way of life is almost inevitably affected by the particular things valued by the viewer. The *quality* of the future, at least to some extent, is "in the eye of the beholder." The reader may find in this chapter, and in the preceding chapters of this book, ample support for whatever biases he holds about the probable future of industrial society.

37. Human Relations in Industrial Civilization

Paul Meadows

A Culture in Conflict

The crisis of our age—to use a familiar phrase—is nothing less than the crisis of industrialism as a culture. Industrial society is characterized by a tragic separation of its inner and outer structures and a like disjunction has developed within the outer structure itself, within the general pattern of human relationship.* Industrialism is beset by a deep and ineradicable conflict which is the mothering body of its crises. The real directive force of industrialism lies not in its machine technology but in its system of human relationships; here, however, are far-reaching and devastating oppositions.

What, then, are the conflicts which distress and besiege industrial man?

One way to describe them is by means of a contrast. It is fashionable in anthropological quarters to describe human relationships in an industrial civilization by comparing them with those of a pre-industrial people. For example, the city life of industrial "Middletown" may be compared with the village life of non-industrial Guatemala in some such terms as the following.

Guatemalan villagers are fairly immobile, family-centered, with developed and transmitted rituals for nearly every daily or unusual occasion. Their pattern of living is smooth, personal, simple, concrete, and homogeneous. The motives of their lives respond to the sanctions of the sacred and the customary, and piety intertwines with the secular occasion in their daily living.[1]

In glaring contrast is the life of Middletown Americans.[2] Middletown ways are secularized, mobile, heterogeneous, and dominated by pecuniary valuations and advantages. Personal life hardly centers around the family

Paul Meadows, *The Culture of Industrial Man* (Lincoln, Neb.: University of Nebraska Press, 1950), pp. 23-34.

* *Editors note:* The inner structure of industrialism is described by Meadows as "specialized machines and tools; a body of knowledge about machine processes, properties and tasks; and human beings disciplined for machine work." The outer structure refers to the factory, the industrial firm, and the industrial city.

[1] For example, see Robert Redfield, *Folk Culture of Yucatán* (Chicago: University of Chicago Press, 1941).

[2] Robert and Helen Lynd, *Middletown* and *Middletown in Transition* (New York: Harcourt, Brace and World, 1929, 1937); also L. Wirth, "Urbanism as a Way of Life," *American Journal of Sociology*, 44 (1938), 1-24.

but is qualified and conditioned by a network of formal institutions. The sacred is weak and ineffectual, sometimes even nonexistent, and the comfortable routines of religious ritual are things apart from daily interests. The culture, although resting upon the natural environment, is not of it. The continuity of existence with the historic past and the unquestioning dependability of a personalized society belong to other days, happy in retrospect. Opinion, frequently if not usually dogmatic, is charged with differences and hostilities, strangeness and hate; it is too seldom just and reserved.

Almost two generations ago a great religious leader sensed this mood and temper of human relations in industrial society and wrote about it in his famous *Rerum novarum*. Said Pope Leo XIII: "The elements of a conflict are unmistakable. We perceive them in the growth of industry and the marvelous discoveries of science; in the changed relations of employers and workingmen, in the enormous fortunes of individuals and the poverty of the masses; in the increased self-reliance and the closer mutual combination of the labor population; and, finally, in the general moral deterioration." Leo XIII was by no means the first to feel the leaderless drift of the twin forces of isolation and opposition within industrialism. David Ricardo had spoken of the conflicts of landlord and tenant, of agricultural and manufacturing. Karl Marx had systemized the oppositions in his terrific ideological onslaughts. The utopian socialists of the nineteenth century, the Owenses and the Rauschenbusches, as well as the humanitarians, had been sorely perplexed by them. Today, whatever else industrial culture may contain by way of promise of peace and human fulfillment, it rests uneasily upon the mobile foundations of isolated and opposed interests. Industrialism has both atomized and organized human relations, and this paradox makes it tragically unmanageable.

The Conflicts of Ownership

The oppositions show most markedly in the area of industrial operations. Here the stakes are high; they include control over men and machines, the direction of the amount and flow of income, compensatory leisure and differential sharing in the goods of life, the command of resources, and the right to determine policy. Common interests are few, if for no other reason than that human relationships *to* and *in* the system of massed mechanization are not uniform. As a matter of fact, so great has become the differential sharing in social life that the human being in industrialism is pushed first one way and then another on a gridiron of claims and counterclaims. The net consequence is shifting conflicts which weaken and exploit loyalties, confuse issues and create anxieties. These conflicts have a number of distinct patterns. The most important of them seem to grow out of the explosive questions of ownership and out of industrial relations.

Conflicts over ownership are ancient, but the form which they have taken under conditions of industrialism are historically novel. Absentee ownership, for example, was a central principle of the agricultural feudalism of medieval Europe. Great areas of land and people were often held in fief, subject to the fixed charges and decisions of distant masters represented by a graded series of subordinates. However, unlike its modern industrial counterpart, agricultural feudalism was built upon an intricate and respected set of reciprocal rights and duties which extended from the lowliest villein to the highest lord. On the other hand, industrial feudalism is a creation of the pecuniary complex; it is a one-sided structure of demands, expressed in expectations of continuing money-income with little or no concern over the cost to physical or social or human resources. Its philosophy is unadulterated colonialism in which wealth and talent are drawn off to its metropolitan centers of power and influence while its hinterlands are drained of initiative and enterprise. The same dramatic themes are enacted over and over. The concentration of authority, the debauching of politics, the fraudulent misrepresentation of values, the desiccation of integrity have become commonplace.

As if this scattering of cohesive social forces were not enough, industrial evolution has given aid and comfort to every agency which would, in the name of concentrated wealth, fragment the honored unity of ownership and control of property. The tools for this operation have consisted in the creation of classes who own without controlling, who control without owning, and who neither own nor control. Though hates abound in such a cultural situation, it is ironic that the system itself is neither hated nor hateful to its people.

The Conflicts over the Scale of Business Enterprise

Another conflict of industrialism which is bitter, widespread, and ominous arises over the relationship between small and large businesses. American industrial history, for example, has been filled with it from the 1860's on. The steady march toward increased size was made possible by conquests over nature and the small man. Combinations, conspiracies, cut-throat competition, and corruption have been significant and powerful tools of massed mechanization in the hands of the corporate revolution. The protection of small business is still the rallying cry of industrial peoples with democratic dreams. At the same time, trust-busting continues to be an alter of sacrifice on which an occasional corporate goat is laid to appease a wrathful public.[3] The language of small business employs the vocabulary of classic industrialism. Its phrases and word magic are picked up by the big and successful enemies of small business who delight in exploiting them as a

[3] This point was developed very tellingly in T. W. Arnold, *The Folklore of Capitalism* (New Haven, Conn.: Yale University Press, 1937).

cloak for their own iniquities and as a seamless garment for their diseases. For in our day the Fritz Thyssens have discovered that the omnipotent State is no respector of persons, and the large and small must bow before the mysterious providence of its manifest destiny. And even in those places where big business has not fallen on the evil days of Fascism, it reads with alarm the handwriting of successive social legislations which redefine the authority and curb the excesses of business enterprise. For this reason, then, big business seeks safety behind the protective coloration of the little man. "Freedom of enterprise" becomes a line of defense—for bigness!

The Conflict of Owners and Non-Owners

Less articulate, perhaps, and certainly more diffuse, but hardly less emotional, is that conflict which goes on between non-owners and owners of industrial enterprise. Marx wrote of it as a conflict between tool-less labor and tool-owning capital. Perhaps it is. But its backgrounds lie among the resentments felt by individualistic people who know that their prospects for private property in production technics are poor if not hopeless.

In any case, the ultimate remedy is not likely to be that proposed by the Marxists. On the face of it, public ownership of property is no less abstract than corporate ownership of property. Yet, ironically enough, collective ownership has been the goal of most left-wing political movements for a century in the industrial West. It has made moderate headway, and in one country it has been completely adopted; in several others it seems to be marching with seven-league boots. However, it ought to be, though it seldom is, clear that the difficulties and evils of an industrial culture change only their names when that culture moves from individual abstractness of property to collective abstractness. The razor-sharp dichotomy between a capitalist and a communist industrialism is a pathetic, if pleasurable, self-delusion!

Nevertheless, we should not lose sight of the fact that this underlying conflict, the one between owners and non-owners, has its origins in a moral assertion of the right to property. Property ownership is a human and social institution protected and promoted by even the most primitive peoples.[4] For this reason it is possible to hold that on this institutional rock alone can be built an enduring human personality and social structure. A society whose property aspirations are blocked is not secure. Its mood is dangerous, and its morale seeks the emotions of nationalism—or some other displaced aggression—in order to canalize its frustrations.

Marxian socialism sought to lift this social sensitivity on to the plane of depersonalized dialectics in order to win for it an irrefutable cogency

---

[4] See Melville J. Herskovits, *The Economic Life of Primitive Peoples* (New York: Knopf, 1940).

which it does not and probably cannot have. But while Marxists were busy spinning their web of a philosophy of history, social protest movements were whittling away at the industrial system with such reforms as would maintain, if not enlarge, the sphere of personal jurisdiction over production.[5] This is the story behind the social legislations of the past two generations. In the industrial West "have not" has been a fighter's phrase, not of a people seeking a cash dole but of those who hope to achieve a just and honorable property system which provides for all men a means to express their being.[6] The leaders of industrial peoples dare not tamper with the emotions which are aroused in those who picture themselves, with or without just cause, in the "have-not" camp.

The Conflict of Labor and Management

Without any doubt the storm center in industrial life has come to be in our day the conflict between labor and management. Here opposition in industrialism loses vagueness and lack of direction and becomes overt, organized, and engineered. Its vehicles are the labor union and the employers' association. Both have developed as a means of safeguarding and advancing special interests. At times, both have drawn a hard and fast line between their worlds, have declared war on each other, and have been forced by various circumstances to negotiate peace. Increasingly these circumstances are imposed by the State itself. Both labor and management make overtures to the general public—whatever that mythical reference may be!—and both have recourse to government; but unfortunately neither is fully prepared to confess a community of interest between them. Indeed, there is a strong case for the thesis that there may be under conditions of industrialism in the West no such community of interest anyway.

The labor movement has been a protest movement. Its objects of concern have grown out of the contractual wage status, the depersonalized and massed relationships of industry, and the propertyless and unprotected position of labor as a commodity sought and bought in a changing market. Violent when provoked, and occasionally revolutionary, organized labor has become primarily a business-like response to a businessman's civilization.[7] The union movement, an outgrowth of the mass phenomena of industrialization, is also an expression of the several technological interests and roles of the industrial worker. In many ways, unionization and its attendant activities represent the introduction of civil rights into industrial-

[5] For example, see F. W. Coker, *Recent Political Thought* (New York: Appleton-Century-Crofts, 1934) and H. F. Simon, *Revolution, Whither Bound?* (New York: Holt, Rinehart and Winston, 1935).

[6] Peter F. Drucker, *The End of Economic Man* (New York: John Day, 1939) and *The Future of Industrial Man* (New York: John Day, 1942).

[7] Perhaps this has been a major weakness; see A. Sturmthal, *The Tragedy of European Labor* (New York: Columbia University Press, 1943).

ism.[8] It aims to establish an industrial jurisprudence made imperative by failures in the bargaining procedures, by the black-listing, espionage, paternalism, and superior economic strength of employers' associations.[9] But though grown up, organized labor has still to mature. It cannot forever be on the receiving end of grants, making demands without also giving concessions. It is apparent to all observers that in terms of economic and social resources, organized labor is rapidly on its way to becoming a peer of corporate business. And as a result, the desire to control the dominant policy-making institution of industrialism, the State, has become a passion with both of them, adding immeasureably to the tensions between them.

From the standpoint of advanced management and possibly of an informed public, a strong labor movement need be no unmixed evil. Management is swinging—not wildly but cautiously to the view that the industrial worker is not a machine but a customer, not a commodity but a citizen, not an operative but a person. The business of management is agreement. The essential job of production is one of collaboration. Human beings, though not to be regarded as machines, must have a machinery of social adjustment. In order to operate effectively, the technical organization of production must rest upon a community organization which is free to operate efficiently. The values which the enlightened industrial statesmanship of a George Johnson or a Chester Barnard are realizing and promoting are in the last analysis precisely what an enlightened labor leadership has been urging upon industry for two or three generations.[10] One of the most heartening signs of our time is the gradual, even if limited, acceptance of labor-management councils, personnel departments, labor-management forums, worker education, and similar ideas, as the folkways and mores of industrial production. Nothing could be more effective in reducing the risks and incidence of industrial war.

The Conflicts of the Industrial Community

Many students of modern society are inclined to regard labor-management and other such conflicts of industrialism as the fruit of isolation rather than of innate differences of interest. They point to the mobility and the distance of human contacts which industrialism has stimulated. They emphasize particularly the specialization of the productive process and point out that division of labor induces bondlessness, except in the narrow, self-centered, horizontal economic groups. In no other society, it is con-

8 Cf. S. H. Slichter, *Union Policies and Industrial Management* (Washington, D.C.: The Brookings Institution, 1941).
9 For a full discussion, see Philip Taft, *Economics and Problems of Labor* (Harrisburg: The Stackpole Co., 1942).
10 Cf. C. I. Barnard, *The Functions of the Executive* (Cambridge, Mass.: Harvard University Press, 1938); W. Inglis, *George F. Johnson and His Industrial Democracy* (New York: Huntington Press, 1935).

tended, has the individual found it so difficult to become a significant human being, and in no other society is community of interest and purpose so improbable, if not impossible.

There is no single explanation of this situation, but one phase of the explanation seems to lie in the industrial community. Human relations are formed in and expressed through the community. Much of the impact of industrialism upon human relations has been delivered by way of this organization for living. While not inevitable perhaps, the transformation of community life by industrialism has been far-reaching, if not devastating. Indeed, the keen interest in community study of the last twenty-five years in the United States grew directly out of the concern over community disarrangement as a result of industrial misorganization.[11] The community life of today has pathologies which, although not unique historically, are certainly more common and aggravated than at any other period. Into the pattern of the community industrialism has built walls which isolate, highways which accelerate, and dead-end streets which frustrate human relations. The fast-moving stream of human contacts turns out to be a shallow volume of socialized life; forms must do the work of impulses, while mass gains the significance which rightfully belongs to individuality. In no place have human ends become so lost and subordinate to human means as in the crowded modern industrial city. It becomes the prototype of the industrial society: it is large, impersonal, mechanical, and unwieldy.

The urban system has been the twin of the factory system, and neither could have survived without the other. They are both the fruit of massed mechanization. Industrial society has nullified the small, face-to-face primary groups. It has seceded from the union of intimate and direct association, and it has set up a confederacy of loosely organized, autonomous interest groups. As a result, it has plunged human relations into a continuing civil war of incompatible, uncomprehending, and contending social forces. As in all warfare, it is the individual who pays the price of victory and defeat, and the subtle tactics of individual expression are submerged by the mass strategies demanded by commercialized culture. The individual becomes a partisan of mass organizations which deal in harshly-drawn and ill-understood issues.

The carrier of this culture has been industrial metropolitanism. Of course, there have been great cities before in history and, whenever they have appeared, life has revolved around them. But the modern metropolis is something new, and it is a place of strange and disturbing paradoxes.[12] The organization of its life is centralized and hierarchical, but its spatial

---

[11] Cf. J. F. Steiner, *Community Organization* (New York: Appleton-Century-Crofts, 1930), Chs. I-III.

[12] Cf. Lewis Mumford, *The Culture of Cities* (New York: Harcourt, Brace & World, 1943).

pattern sprawls without design. The metropolis concentrates huge, mixed segments of population, but it fosters social distances among its people. Though it has been both responsible for, and the product of, an incredible multiplicity of interests, it has made the life of the average individual citizen plain and unattractive. A remarkable level of material success has been made possible, but the physical structure of metropolitan existence is shabby, costly, monotonous and barren.

The industrial city has been built upon technological conquest of space, and yet its perennial problem is one of congestion. Its growth has been quickened by the economic calculations of profit and loss, but the city is an expensive investment with its assets frozen and its future bound by complicated credits and speculative ventures. There is a fantastic range of personal income and mass poverty amid scenes of tremendously rich operations. The city is the product of engineering, yet no engineering entered into its over-all expansion.

The paradoxes of the modern industrial city extend beyond its economic aspects and reach into the philosophic, cultural and human aspects of society as well. The metropolis is maintained by a diversely talented population whose individual members seldom achieve significant status and are content with narrow specialties and spectator enjoyments. Among its people there is little philosophic insight into the values of the new way of life which the city makes possible. The extent and variety of occasions for human contacts have been marvelously magnified, but there is no ritual or mediating service for those contacts except specialized interest or cash. Education for group life is scarce, academic, and narrow. "City people" become an "urban mass" in search of external activities as opiates for their inability to find substance within. The metropolis has evolved a new culture, urbanism; at the same time, it has failed to achieve an organic synthesis.[13] By scattering its appeals, it has failed to give them depth in time and experience. Like the machine on which it depends, its life organization is repetitive, detached and disinterested.

In brief, there is a sense, no longer weak but tragic, that the whole texture of modern man's means and meanings is in considerable jeopardy as long as the industrial city in the form and spirit of the past is maintained as the matrix of his multitudinous and differentiated relationships.

Above all, there is the brooding thought that the industrial city is only the industrial culture in microcosm. A dark and anxious conflict theme prevades the whole of contemporary technological culture. The inner structure of its industrial technology is at variance with the outer structure of its industrial society. A Greek-like tragedy of ownership hostilities unfolds relentlessly in every national culture. Industrialism, far from being an integral whole, is a congeries of disturbing paradoxes. Organization domi-

[13] Cf. Eliel Saarinen, *The City* (New York: Reinhold, 1943).

nates the social life of industrial man in an atmosphere of isolation. Matthew Arnold's "Dover Beach," haunting and perennially relevant, is a song of the lonely human being no more than of the isolated corporation or nation. The human being in an industrial society finds both his "being" and his "humanity" in life-ways far removed from the comfortable routines of his ancient traditions.

38. Pluralistic Industrialism

Clark Kerr
John Dunlop
Frederick Harbison
Charles A. Meyers

By the mid-twentieth century, at least a third of the population of the world, or close to one billion people, lived in countries well established in the process of industrialization, and most of the other two-thirds of the world's population was in countries in the throes of starting to industrialize. Relatively few remnants of mankind were as yet untouched by this new and vital force. By the middle of the twenty-first century, industrialization will have swept away most pre-industrial forms of society, except possibly for a few odd backwaters.

This is a great transformation in the long history of mankind on this planet—more basic, more rapid, and more nearly universal than any earlier transformation.

Modern industrial civilization, with its technical evolution and intellectual drive, is, as we know, the most aggressive form of civilization that mankind has ever known. Its twin impact of science and industry is one that involves a total transformation of all aspects of life—not only of organization and technique but of fundamental habits of thought and social behavior. You have only to consider the impact of this type of society upon people who have not yet moved beyond the simplest patterns of living and working to see that, without immense patience, understanding, and restraint, the incoming settlers will annihilate the whole social apparatus of the backward local peoples. Yet these qualities are not usually the qualities of conquerors or pioneers.[1]

Industrialization creates vast urban areas; makes possible a great explosion of population; yields a new standard of living and of leisure; draws on new skills both social and technical; requires a vast network of rules to guide and coerce men in the complex and interrelated tasks essential to its successful growth; spawns new centers of organized power and furthers the concentration of authority in old centers, particularly the state; forges new

Reprinted by permission of the publishers from Clark Kerr, John Dunlop, Frederick Harbison, and Charles A. Meyers, *Industrialism and Industrial Man*, Cambridge, Mass.: Harvard University Press, Copyright, 1960, by the President and Fellows of Harvard College.

[1] Barbara Ward, *Five Ideas that Change the World* (New York: Norton, 1959), p. 87.

methods of attaining and retaining this power; links men together in new chains of subordination and invites frictions at each of the links in these chains; and provides a new culture based on mass tastes and mass consumption which gradually overwhelms the many and varied pre-existing cultures. It is the great transformation—successful, all-embracing, irreversible.

Central to this transformation are the relations of managers and the managed. Much of the working lives of men is spent in constant contact with the reciprocal relations of manager to managed; and these relations set the occupational roles and working behavior of most members of the labor force. But manager and managed do not form any separate and clear-cut classes. Many of the managers are in turn managed from above, and many of the managed in turn manage someone below. Few are those who only manage, and many are those who are only managed; but there is a hierarchy of managerial relations far too complex to compress into simple class relations. Instead a society develops of the semi-managers and semi-managed.

Industrial man develops new patterns of relations different from those of tribal members and chieftain, serf and lord of the manor, craftsman and merchant prince, or even worker and capitalist. These relations are more varied and more complex than in pre-existing societies. Industrial man leads a new kind of life and, in the course of it, becomes a new kind of person. He views himself and others, society and the universe in new ways. The old ideologies and the old theories lose their meaning.

. . . Men attempt to peer ahead, to understand the structure of history, to alter the process of history, if possible, in accord with their preferences. The history of industrialization to date has not been a smoothly unilinear one; it has been uneven and multilinear. It is likely that in the future it will continue to be both somewhat uneven and multilinear; and there will continue to be some latitude for choice and for chance. Chance may elude man, but choice need not; and the choice of men, within fairly broad limits, can shape history. To predict the future with any accuracy, men must choose their future. The future they appear to be choosing and pressing for is what might be called "pluralistic industrialism."

This term is used to refer to an industrial society which is governed neither by one all-powerful elite (the monistic model) nor by the impersonal interaction of innumerable small groups with relatively equal and fractionalized power (the atomistic model in economic history). The complexity of the fully developed industrial society requires, in the name of efficiency and initiative, a degree of decentralization of control, particularly in the consumer goods and service trades industries; but it also requires a large measure of central control by the state and conduct of many operations by large-scale organizations.

As the skill level rises and jobs become more responsible, any regime

must be more interested in consent, in drawing forth relatively full cooperation. For the sake of real efficiency, this must be freely given. The discipline
of the labor gang no longer suffices. With skill and responsibility goes the
need for consent, and with consent goes influence and even authority. Occupational and professional groups, of necessity, achieve some prestige and
authority as against both the central organs of society and the individual
members of the occupation or profession.

Education brings in its wake a new economic equality and a new community of political outlook. This in turn, along with many other developments, helps bring consensus to society. The harsh use of power by the
state is no longer so necessary to hold society together at the seams. Education also opens the mind to curiosity and to inquiry, and the individual
seeks more freedom to think and to act. It brings a demand for liberty, and
can help create conditions in which liberty can safely be assumed. It leads
to comparisons among nations with respect to progress and participation.

Industrialism is so complex and subject to such contrary internal pressures that it never can assume a single uniform unchanging structure; but
it *can* vary around a general central theme, and that theme is pluralism.
While it will take generations before this theme will become universal in
societies around the world, the direction of the movement already seems
sufficiently clear.

The State That Does Not Wither Away

The state will be powerful. It will, at the minimum, have the responsibility
for the economic growth rate; the over-all distribution of income among
uses and among individuals; the basic security of individuals (the family
formerly was the basic security unit); the stability of the system; providing
the essential public services of education, transportation, recreational areas,
cultural facilities, and the like; and the responsibility of providing a favorable physical environment for urban man.

In addition, any pluralistic society is subject to three great potential
internal problems, and the state is responsible for handling each. One is
the conflict among the various power elements in a pluralistic society. The
state must set the rules of the game within which such conflict will occur,
enforce these rules, and act as mediator; conflicts between managers and
the managed are the most noticeable, but by no means the only ones. Another is the control of collusion by producers against consumers, by any
profession against its clients, and by labor and management against the
public. Undue aggrandizement of sectional interests is always endemic if
not epidemic in a pluralistic society; in fact, one of the arguments for mon-
ism and atomism alike is the avoidance of sectionalism. Additionally, the
state will come generally, under the pluralistic industrialism, to set the rules
relating members to their organizations—who may get in, who may stay

in, what rights and obligations the members have, what the boundaries are for the activities of the organization, and so on. It will, almost of necessity, be against too much conflict among, or collusion between, or domination of the members by the subsidiary organizations in society.

All these responsibilities mean the state will never "wither away;" that Marx was more utopian than the despised utopians. The state will be the dominant organization in any industrial society. But it may itself be less than fully unitary. It may itself be subject to checks and balances, including the check of public acceptance of its current leadership and its policies.

The Crucial Role of the Enterprise—The Middle Class and the Middle Bureaucracy

The productive enterprise, whether private or public, will be a dominant position under pluralistic industrialism. It will often be large and it must always have substantial authority in order to produce efficiently. This authority will not be complete, for it will be checked by the state, by the occupational association, by the individual employee; but it will be substantial.

The distinction between the private and the public manager will decrease just as the distinction between the private and the public enterprise will diminish; and the distinction among managers will be more according to the size, the product, and the nature of their enterprises. The controlled market and the controlled budget will bring more nearly the same pressures on them. The private enterprise, however, will usually have more freedom of action than the public enterprise; but the middle class and the middle bureaucracy will look much alike.

Associated Man

The occupational or professional association will range alongside the state and the enterprise as a locus of power in pluralistic industrialism; and there will be more occupations and particularly more professions seeking association. Group organizations around skill and position in the productive mechanism will be well-nigh universal. These organizations will affect output norms, comparative incomes, access to employment, and codes of ethics in nearly every occupational walk of life. Their containment within reasonable limits will be a continuing problem; and some of the groups will always seek to invade and infiltrate the government mechanisms which are intended to supervise them.

The Web of Rules

Uniting the state, the enterprise, and the association will be a great web of rules set by the efforts of all the elements, but particularly by the state.

This web of rules will also relate the individual to each of these elements. In the contest over who should make the web of rules, the end solution will be that they will be made or influenced by more than one element; they will not be set by the state alone or by the enterprise alone or by the association alone. The web of rules will not equally cover all aspects of life.

From Class War to Bureaucratic Gamesmanship

Conflict will take place in a system of pluralistic industrialism, but it will take less the form of the open strife or the revolt and more the form of the bureaucratic contest. Groups will jockey for positions over the placement of individuals, the setting of jurisdictions, the location of authority to make decisions, the forming of alliances, the establishment of formulas, the half-evident withdrawal of support and of effort, the use of precedents and arguments and statistics. Persuasion, pressure, and manipulation will take the place of the face-to-face combat of an earlier age. The battles will be in the corridors instead of the streets, and memos will flow instead of blood. The conflict also will be, by and large, over narrower issues than in earlier times when there was real disagreement over the nature of and the arrangements within industrial society. It will be less between the broad programs of capital and labor, and of agriculture and industry; and more over budgets, rates of compensation, work norms, job assignments. The great battles over conflicting manifestos will be replaced by a myriad of minor contests over comparative details.

From Class Movement to Special Interest Group

Labor-management relations will conform to this new context. Labor organizations will not be component parts of class movements urging programs of total reform, for the consensus of a pluralistic society will have settled over the scene. Nor may they be very heavily identified by industry, particularly with the increasing multiplication and fractionalization of industries. Rather, they may tend to take more the craft, or perhaps better, the occupational form. With skills more diverse, at a generally higher level, and obtained more through formal education, and with geographical mobility greatly increased, professional-type interests should mean more to workers than industry or class ties.

The purpose of these occupational and professional associations will be relatively narrow, mostly the improvement of the status of the occupation in terms of income, prestige, and specification of the rights and duties that accompany it. Generally these organizations will be a conservative force in society, opposed to new ways of doing things, resistant to increased efforts by members of the occupation. The enterprise managers will be the more progressive elements in the society, although they too may become heavily weighted down by checks and balances and rules.

The techniques of the professional associations for achieving their ends will be those of the bureaucratic organization everywhere; a far cry from the individual withdrawal, or the guerilla warfare, or the strike or the political reform movement of earlier times. They will constitute the quarrels between the semi-managed and the semi-managers.

Individuals will identify themselves more closely with their occupation, particularly if it involves a formal training period for entry, and mobility will follow more the lines of the occupation than the lines of the industry or the job possibilities of the immediate geographical area. In terms of identification, the orientation will be more nearly that of the member of a guild than of a class or of a plant community. Mayo will turn out to be as wrong as Marx. Just as the class will lose its meaning, so also will the plant community fail to become the modern counterpart of the primitive tribe. The occupational interest group will represent the employee in his occupational concerns and the occupation will draw his allegiance. Status in the tribe will not give way to status in the plant; nor will status have given way to the individual contract through the march of civilization; rather interest identification will take the place of both status and individual contract in ordering the productive arrangements of men.

Education, occupation, occupational organization will all be drawn together to structure the life-line and the economic interests of many if not most employees.

The New Bohemianism

The individual will be in a mixed situation far removed from that of the independent farmer organizing most aspects of his own life or from that of the Chinese peasant in the commune under total surveillance. In his working life he will be subject to great conformity imposed not only by the enterprise manager but also by the state and by his own occupational association. For most people, any complete scope for the independent spirit on the job will be missing. However, the skilled worker, while under rules, does get some control over his job, some chance to organize it as he sees fit, some possession of it. Within the narrow limits of this kind of "job control," the worker will have some freedom. But the productive process tends to regiment. People must perform as expected or it breaks down. This is now and will be increasingly accepted as an immutable fact. The state, the manager, the occupational association are all disciplinary agents. But discipline is often achieved by a measure of persuasion and incentive. The worker will be semi-independent with some choice among jobs, some control of the job, and some scope for the effects of morale; but he will also be confined by labor organizations, pensions, and seniority rules, and all sorts of rules governing the conduct of the job.

Outside his working life the individual may have more freedom under pluralistic industrialism than in most earlier forms of society. Politically he can have some influence. Society has achieved consensus and the state need not exercise rigid political control. Nor in this "Brave New World" need genetic and chemical means be employed to avoid revolt. There will not be any rebellion, anyway, except little bureaucratic revolts that can be settled piecemeal. An educated population will want political choice and can effectively use it. There will also be a reasonable amount of choice in the controlled labor market, subject to the confining limits of one's occupation, and in the controlled product market.

The great new freedom may come in the leisure-time life of individuals. Higher standards of living, more free time, and more education make this not only possible but almost inevitable. Leisure will be the happy hunting ground for the independent spirit. Along with the bureaucratic conservatism of economic and political life may well go a New Bohemianism in the other aspects of life—partly as a reaction to the confining nature of the productive side of society. There may well come a new search for individuality and a new meaning to liberty. The economic system may be highly ordered and the political system barren ideologically; but the social and recreational and cultural aspects of life should be quite diverse and quite changing.

The world will be for the first time a totally literate world. It will be an organization society, but it need not be peopled by "organization men" whose total lives are ruled by their occupational roles.

The areas closest to technology will be the most conformist; those farthest from the requirements of its service, the most free. The rule of technology need not, as Marx thought it would, reach into every corner of society. In fact, there may come a new emphasis on diversity, on the preservation of national and group traits that runs quite counter to the predictions of uniform mass consumption. The new slavery to technology may bring a new dedication to diversity and individuality. This is the two-sided face of pluralistic industrialism that makes it forever a split personality looking in two directions at the same time. The new slavery and the new freedom go hand in hand.

Utopia never arrives, but men may well settle for the benefits of a greater scope for freedom in their personal lives at the cost of considerable conformity in their working lives. If pluralistic industrialism can be said to have a split personality, then the individual in this society will lead a split life too; he will be a pluralistic individual with more than one pattern of behavior and one dominant allegiance.

Social systems will be reasonably uniform around the world as compared with today's situation; but there may be substantial diversity within geographical and cultural areas as men and groups seek to establish and maintain their identity. The differences will be between and among individuals and groups and subcultures rather than primarily between and among the major geographical areas of the world. Society at large may become more like the great metropolitan complexes of Paris or London or New York or Tokyo, urbanized and committed to the industrial way of life, but marked by infinite variety in its details.

Pluralistic industrialism will never reach a final equilibrium. The contest between the forces for uniformity and for diversity will give it life and movement and change. This is a contest which will never reach an ultimate solution. Manager and managed also will struggle all up and down the line of hierarchies all around the world; quiet but often desperate little battles will be fought all over the social landscape.

The uniformity that draws on technology, and the diversity that draws on individuality; the authority that stems from the managers, and the rebellion, however muted, that stems from the managed—these are destined to be the everlasting threads of the future. They will continue in force when class war, and the contest over private versus public initiative, and the battle between the monistic and atomistic ideologies all have been left far behind in the sedimentary layers of history.

Index of Names

Index of Subjects

B1023